THE WORLD UNITED BY THE POSTAL UNION

This monument by René Marceaux stands in Berne, Switzerland, the administrative center of a number of international unions. It shows the five continents girdling the world friendly-wise with a wreath of letters and symbolizes the world unity which comes by unofficial and nonpolitical means as well as by treaties and diplomacy. The many international unions already in successful operation are described in Paul S. Reinsch's *Public International Unions*

AMERICAN PROBLEMS

A TEXTBOOK IN SOCIAL PROGRESS

BY

FRANCES MOREHOUSE
OF THE UNIVERSITY OF MINNESOTA HIGH SCHOOL

AND

SYBIL FLEMING GRAHAM
INSTRUCTOR IN SOCIAL SCIENCE, EXTENSION DIVISION
UNIVERSITY OF MINNESOTA

GINN AND COMPANY
BOSTON · NEW YORK · CHICAGO · LONDON
ATLANTA · DALLAS · COLUMBUS · SAN FRANCISCO

COPYRIGHT, 1923, 1924, BY FRANCES MOREHOUSE AND
SYBIL FLEMING GRAHAM
ALL RIGHTS RESERVED

424.8

The Athenæum Press
GINN AND COMPANY · PRO-
PRIETORS · BOSTON · U.S.A.

TO THE TEACHER

The uniting of the essentials of the more important of the social sciences in one subject, to be given to high-school students in the final year of their course, is a new idea, and the exact content of the work has not been agreed upon. The present book is offered in the hope that it will provide a worthwhile basis for experiment and definition, as well as in answer to the insistent demand for a text. All are agreed that "the problems of democracy" are to be studied, but scarcely any two persons can agree as to just what those problems are or which of them require stressing in the high school. This book is based on several years' experience in teaching unified social science in the high school of the University of Minnesota. The authors hope that any teacher to whom there occur either criticisms or suggestions for inclusion, growing from the use of the text, will write them freely; for it is realized that wide experience must be brought to bear on the development of high-school unified social science.

The book is built upon the idea of a variable standard of work for schools of many kinds and for students of many degrees of ability. Several cumulative levels of work may be planned with this book as a basis, beginning with the text itself and working through the problems, easy and difficult, and the supplementary reading, according to circumstance. The essential facts to be learned are in the main text. These facts should be illustrated and fixed by further material, indicated in the search problems at the close of each chapter. The problem work varies much in difficulty and may be assigned either to groups or to individuals, always with regard to the ability of the assignees. It is not expected, of course, that teachers will use the problems in the book when pertinent practice in application can be had from local and contemporary situations. For instance, local taxation problems, local water-supply questions, local school-support conflicts, are far more valuable when thoughtfully and fairly considered than material imported from a distance either of time or of space.

For this purpose it is important that teachers should collect material on local conditions and on state, national, and international problems. Before the year's session begins a week can profitably be given to this work. The material should be properly filed and indexed as to subject, so as to be ready for use when needed and readily found. Large filing-cases with clearly marked index cards are an important part of the social-science teacher's equipment. As each subject is reached the illustrative material should be brought out and put where the students can go through it freely.

Descriptive civics, except where it ties up with other topics, has been omitted from this book because there already exist several good texts in that subject, which make it unnecessary to include such material in a book already crowded. Varying state laws and the differing convictions of teachers will provide interesting variety in the teaching of advanced civics; the result of experimentation in the combination of formal civics with unified social science will be awaited with much interest.

Of one function of this text the authors wish especially to speak. This book is intended to help develop a vocabulary—the vocabulary of social relationships. It uses many technical terms which might have been avoided by circumlocution or explanations, but which are used deliberately, in order that students may learn to talk easily and correctly of the things of which it treats. But students will not develop this vocabulary unless their teachers see to it that they do. No teacher, being asked for the loaf of immediate, varied-to-need, illustrated-from-environment definition, should give a student the stone of reference to a dictionary. And having explained a term clearly, it is the teacher's business to see that his students use it freely and correctly. Then the battle is half won.

TO THE TEACHER

Notebooks are a necessity in such a course, and should contain not only notes from supplementary reading but class notes, tables, references, and the results of problem work.

By far the most important part of a course in social science it lies with the teacher to give or withhold. This is the contagious spirit of brotherliness, of genuine interest in the welfare of all sorts of human beings, and the assumption that every man, whether of high or low degree, has a right to respect and consideration because of his humanity. It is the simple and fair-minded attitude of him who remembers that "none of Arthur's noblest dealt in scorn." This attitude cannot be taught didactically, but it will largely teach itself if it overflows conscious expression in a teacher who is himself a lover of mankind. A text supplies the basis of that practical knowledge of economic principles and sociological facts which enables citizens to act wisely, but only the infectious enthusiasm of a big heart can arouse the desire to help in the great tasks of social regeneration

This book subscribes quite frankly to the now generally accepted doctrine that social efficiency is the aim of education. It does not consider people to be truly educated who are selfish and self-centered. It believes in a propaganda of social service which is to be carried on in the social agency of the public schools It believes in a propaganda of friendly and sympathetic coöperation between the different social and economic classes of the world; it has no sympathy for a one-class program of any kind, knowing the elimination of any element in the closely knit and delicately poised social structure to be destructive to the whole. This propaganda of friendly constructiveness becomes a lifeless and impotent thing unless it be vitalized by a similar spirit on the part of the teacher, who may by example and interpretation convey more of the social spirit in an hour than any book can infuse into the work of a year.

It is, then, with a hope that every teacher will exalt scientific inquiry and friendly fair-mindedness that this text in a new subject is sent out. If it succeeds in guiding teachers and students into a more careful preparation for the duties of citizenship;

if it becomes the means of clarifying the content of this new course and of securing helpful criticism of the methods followed in its construction; if it contributes in any degree to the wider study of the problems of democracy, it will amply have repaid the labor of its production.

For permission to quote the lines from John Hay thanks are due Houghton Mifflin Company, publishers of the Complete Poetical Works of John Hay.

The authors are indebted to several friends and colleagues in the preparation of this work. They wish to make especial acknowledgments to President Lotus D. Coffman and to Professor Ross L. Finney for encouragement in undertaking the work, to Dr. N. S. B. Gras for many facts in economic history and for new points of view, and to Dr. S. A. Graham for aid in the preparation of the charts. With especial gratitude also the authors wish to acknowledge the very painstaking and helpful editorial coöperation of Mr. Roswell T. Pearl of Ginn and Company and the suggestions of Miss Mary Carney, who read the book in proof.

NOTE. The foreword To the Student is intended to be used as part of the initial lesson of the course.

CONTENTS

	PAGE
CHAPTER I THE ESTABLISHING OF CIVILIZATION	1

The age of invention Primitive economic relations. Primitive social institutions The changing bases of social organization The economy of Rome.

CHAPTER II. ECONOMIC CONTRIBUTIONS OF THE MIDDLE AGES 31

In agriculture In industry In commerce

CHAPTER III MEDIEVAL SOCIAL AND POLITICAL GAINS . 50

Social organization and ideals Social welfare Sharing the king's power The extension of self-government

CHAPTER IV AN ERA OF REVOLUTIONS . . . 69

Changes in agriculture The Industrial Revolution A revolution in commerce and transportation A revolution in social conditions Changes in politics and government.

CHAPTER V NINETEENTH-CENTURY PROGRESS 99

Social progress in England Social progress in America, 1780–1860. A second period of progress, 1860–1920 Political progress in England Political progress in America Elections

CHAPTER VI PRODUCTION 132

The material factors: land and capital The human factor of labor Labor organization. The labor supply Organization The processes of production. Security in production

CHAPTER VII PRICES, THE MIDDLEMAN, AND CONSUMPTION 164

Price Transportation and storage Marketing Consumption The standard of living

CHAPTER VIII. THE TRUST PROBLEM 192

The growth of big business The trust and the government. The solution of the problem

AMERICAN PROBLEMS

PAGE

CHAPTER IX. THE TOOLS OF BUSINESS 208

Money. The worth of money Credit, a substitute for money The use of credit. Banks and their functions Recent improvements in the banking system.

CHAPTER X CRISES AND HARD TIMES 242

Crises in the past The business cycle. Prevention of crises through better banking Prevention of crises through better business

CHAPTER XI DISTRIBUTION 268

General principles The present system—labor The present system—capital. The present system—land The present system—organization The apparent conflict of social and economic justice Improving the present system.

CHAPTER XII SOCIAL CONTROL 302

Modern development Limiting the right of contract The growth of a new idea. Federal control of railroads A war-time experiment Local control of natural monopolies Conservation

CHAPTER XIII. TAXATION 328

The justification of taxes The problems of taxation The tariff. Other Federal taxes State and local taxes

CHAPTER XIV. THE ELEMENTS OF POPULATION IN THE UNITED STATES 351

The old stock and its standards The old immigration The new immigration The immigration policy of the United States Americanizing our population

CHAPTER XV POVERTY 379

Hereditary causes Physical mishaps Disease, a potent cause Economic and social causes Remedies

CHAPTER XVI. CRIME 408

Kinds and extent of crime Crime and the home Crime and society. The treatment of crime in the past Criminal procedure of today The question of punishment

CHAPTER XVII TRAINING FOR CITIZENSHIP 442

The home. The press The church. The school Recreation

CONTENTS

CHAPTER XVIII PROBLEMS OF RURAL LIFE 466

Tenancy in America Dealing with the tenancy problem. Agricultural production under changing conditions Social problems of country life The community idea.

CHAPTER XIX PRESENT-DAY PROBLEMS OF DEMOCRACY 494

Executive organization Defects in Congressional legislation Legislative inaction Financial mismanagement Problems of state and municipal government Judicial issues of the day The evils of party government The need for election reform.

CHAPTER XX FOREIGN RELATIONSHIPS 538

Traditional policy and the Monroe Doctrine International commerce The merchant marine The consular and diplomatic services The goal of better international relations World peace and federation

A CLOSING WORD 565

BIBLIOGRAPHY i

THE CONSTITUTION OF THE UNITED STATES . . . v

INDEX xxiii

TO THE STUDENT

The "American problems" dealt with in this book have to do with the social life of our nation—problems considered in what are called the "social" sciences.

A social science is any science which deals with society (as the whole body of human beings is called), just as the natural sciences deal with the forces of nature. The social sciences include anthropology, or the study of man's development as a thinking and working being; sociology, or the study of man in his relations to other men, economics, or the study of wealth in its relations to human welfare, history, which is the story of man's achievements in many fields; and political science, which deals with his governments. History is the key and the introduction to all the other subjects, for in history we have an account of what has actually taken place; and although imaginative construction plays a great part in the progress of sciences, their basis must always be accepted facts.

The object of a course in social science is to make well-informed and valuable citizens of young men and women. This subject is placed at the end of the high-school course in order that all the knowledge gained by that time, and especially the knowledge of history, may be brought to bear upon this most important of all the parts of a liberal education. The time may come when every boy and girl in America will have a high-school education, but that time is not yet; and until then the boys and girls who do attend high schools, and especially those who are graduated from them, will largely comprise the future leaders of America. They are a selected group to whom society has given special advantages They have received from the past a rich heritage of the wisdom that men have gleaned from long experience and many sacrifices. Therefore they are under a great moral obligation to society to return that gift with interest by doing their part to shape a better future.

The method of study. Our modern world is made up of a multitude of great and small institutions. An institution is any custom or organization of forces which has become habitual and established among men. This book deals with the social institutions of the modern world, since it is concerning them and their work that our common problems arise. The method followed is, first, to ascertain the nature of our institutions by tracing their development, and especially by noting the trend of change—the direction in which institutions move in that development This study of the direction of change shows, in part at least, what is likely to occur in the future, although the power of foretelling is always limited by the limit of man's knowledge of the elements that enter into the process of growth.

After explaining the institutions which affect our lives, this book attempts to make clear the problems which face men and women for solution. It tells about the methods of dealing with them which have been at least partly successful, and about some of those which have failed. These successes and failures throw light on the way. Citizens who have studied former efforts at bettering things need not lend themselves to wasteful repetitions of past blunders.

There have been too many blunders in the past; they have come because men have not studied conditions scientifically and devised reasonable remedies for evils, but have slowly and painfully battled their way to better things by the trial-and-error method. They have lost time and frittered away their strength in experiments. There must always be more or less of trial and error, for no experience is ever a ready-made preparation for the next one But the amount of error and waste may be reduced constantly as intelligence grows; and it is the business of educated men and women to lead in the new type of conscious, intelligent, economical, businesslike solution of social and economic problems.

AMERICAN PROBLEMS

CHAPTER I

THE ESTABLISHING OF CIVILIZATION

History is inspiring only in so far as it gives some notion of the aims of mankind, and shows how the hopes and aspirations of one generation translate themselves into the welfare of the next.—A C BENSON

"Independence" is a favorite word with Americans, and there are some people who pride themselves greatly on possessing this quality. As a matter of fact, civilized people are rarely independent at all, and the more civilized they are the less independent they become. If one wants to test the actual degree of independence he possesses, he should go into the forests of Brazil or Africa or Alaska, and, leaving behind him the clothes, weapons, food supply, and trained animals that civilization has given him, there find out just how good a living he can make for himself

The man or boy who tried this plan would probably at first give way to despair, thinking it impossible to meet the dangers and privations of such a situation. But on taking stock he would find himself possessed of several good helpers that he had forgotten he had: a set of teeth, two hands and two feet, ears that soon grow sharp to hear significant sounds, eyes that learn to see signs of danger, and a keen sense of smell There is food to be had if one can distinguish the wholesome from the poisonous; clothing, if one can kill a beast and appropriate its skin; and a shelter, if one can find a cave or build a house in a tree.

Primitive man. The earliest men found themselves in the situation just sketched. They had problems to deal with that demanded keen intelligence and hard work; and when they had thought their problems through and worked until they were worn out, their reward was far less than ours would be for a like expenditure. For they enjoyed the fruits only of their own toil, whereas modern man receives not only the result of his

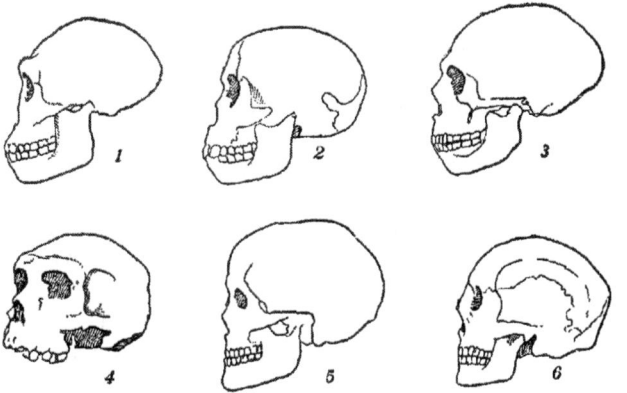

EARLY TYPES OF MEN

1, J. H. McGregor's restoration of Pithecanthropus erectus, the ape-man that once lived in Java. *2*, the Piltdown skull, restored by Smith Woodward. This man lived in England and was geologically older but more highly developed than *3*, the Neanderthal man of the Rhine valley (McGregor restoration). *4*, the skull recently found at Broken Hill, Rhodesia, showing the typical flat head, broad face, and retreating forehead of the earlier, lower species of men. *5*, the man of Crô-Magnon, France (after Verneau), represents a much higher type, an earlier Homo Sapiens, the present species of human being, shown in *6* (after Huxley). All the earlier species of men are undoubtedly human; no "missing link" has ever been found. Most if not all of the great advances of prehistory were made by the present species of man, which embraces all races now on the earth. Note that as man became more intelligent his head became more domed and his jaw more prominent. His feet and legs also became adapted to an erect posture and to walking rather than climbing

own industry, but interest on the age-long investment of effort made by countless generations of men that have preceded him in the long and varied epic of man's struggle to make himself better than he was.

Existence needs and the survival of the fittest. Men work for three things that are necessary to life itself: food must be had if life is to be kept, clothing will protect the body from cold and wet, and keep it fit for work, and a good shelter enables one to sleep in safety and comfort, and so renew one's strength for the next day's repeated hunt for food. For thousands of years, when men first began to lift themselves above the higher animals, the struggle for food, clothing, and shelter was so intense that they scarcely thought of anything else.

This hard, day-after-day struggle for mere existence was, however, a very good thing for the race. The men and women who lived through it were the most intelligent people of their day, for the stupid and lazy could not cope with the hard conditions they met. The competition for food was keen, not only human beings, but beasts as well, were seeking the berries, roots, and edible leaves that nature offered. Sometimes fresh, sweet water was hard to find, for men had not yet learned to dig wells or to store water in cisterns, and the worn paths to springs and brooks were beset with human and animal enemies And since only the shrewd, energetic, and patient could survive, the human breed gradually improved, and life grew easier as knowledge increased among the ranks of men.

The searching mind of man. For man, at first so much like the ape, had one advantage over all animals. he had a mind which was capable of unlimited development His skull was shaped differently from that of an anthropoid ape. Different species of men had skulls of different shapes; and when the earlier species of men, which have now entirely disappeared from the earth, had been conquered by our own species or had fallen in the too-difficult struggle for existence, it was the man with the high forehead and the strong chin who remained as the sole human inhabitant of the earth. This species spread, probably from Asia, its parts becoming very different as they encountered a variety of climates. But the species remained the same in its main characteristics and in the ability, distinguishing man from animals, to attain unlimited spiritual development.

The Age of Invention

The great basic inventions on which civilization is founded were all made before the time of formal written records. Writing, the last of these basic arts, crowned and completed the series, and made it possible for men to set down the stories of their lives and of their ideas for the guidance of the future. The inventions of modern times have not fundamentally changed the methods of production; they have only shortened the time required, multiplied the amount of the product, and lessened the effective distance between producer and consumer, through the use of new machinery and mechanical power. These changes in production, however, are bringing about new changes in the human race perhaps quite as important as those which came to early man through his basic inventions.

The fundamental inventions may be summarized thus:

1. Tools.
2. Fire-making.
3. Domestication of animals.
4. Domestication of plants.
5. Textile arts.
6. Ceramic arts.
7. Building arts.
8. The wheel, the lever, and other mechanical devices which furthered building and transportation.
9. Communication arts, especially writing systems.

These inventions came in no fixed order that applied to all early peoples, except that, probably in all cases, tool-making was the first art practiced, and writing the last. Monkeys pick up stones and throw them at their enemies; but man first showed his superiority over the anthropoid apes by choosing stones or sticks that fitted his hand and best answered his purpose, and then saving these natural tools to use again. From selection man passed to shaping, first by means of chipping and then by means of grinding, until he had produced tools which are practically the same as those used today. Men have never been able to invent better hammers, axes, or adzes than the stone-age men made, except that their mastery of metal arts and machine processes has improved material and finish.

The mastery of fire led to the mastery of metals; and the advance from stage to stage of stone and metal working is considered so important that scholars have named the various eras of man's advance from the materials used. The domestication of plants and animals made life surer and safer, and gave a controllable supply of clothing, baked clay made a plentiful supply of containers and material for dolls and religious images; and the tree top or cave that had at first sheltered our clever if slow-moving ancestors gave place to real houses, slowly evolved as one architectural principle after another was copied from birds or animals, or was thought out by primitive masons and carpenters. It was a great day for mankind when the first lintel stretched across its rude uprights, or the first massive wheel turned creakingly upon its axle, or the first woven sheet of grasses took form in its frame of tied sticks. Such crude beginnings were the great forward steps of the human race.

The need of transportation came with tribal migrations and with the production of a surplus of goods which must be taken to a distant market. The story of the development of land and water transportation, with its triumphant progress from sledges and drags to wheeled carts, and from dugout canoes to swift ships, is in itself an epic worthy of many books, but the story of this development belongs to books of history, and concerns us here only because it brought with it the establishing of fundamental economic and social institutions which have persisted to our own times and with which society today has to deal.

Primitive Economic Relations

Among animals, except when the young are helpless and must be cared for by the mother, male and female work alike for the necessities of life. At first human beings also made little if any difference between the work of men and of women;

all alike hunted for food, sought and found shelter, and scraped skins for coats. But very early among the Northern races there appeared a difference in the work of the sexes. As the mothers were kept at home with their babies much of the time, it was agreed that men, who were stronger and bolder and made better hunters, should make the long, hard trips after game. The women, left at home, dressed the skins, cooked the meat, and kept the precious fire from dying on the hearth. So women became the fireside creatures, the home-makers, very early in human history.

Division of labor. This difference in the work of the two sexes is the first example of the division of labor. Man, who had weapons for hunting, became also the warrior, fighting for the defense of his home and for the profit that came from killing other men and stealing their goods. The women became the first farmers, the first spinners and weavers, the makers of clay dishes and woven baskets; in short, the craftsmen of the primitive world.

By and by the home arts grew to be so many and paid so much better than the arts of hunting and fishing that men began to stay at home to help their wives. Sometimes, also, game grew too scarce to be depended on for food, especially as population increased. As plow-culture with oxen succeeded hoe-culture on the farms, men took over the farm work and freed women for household arts. So basket-weaving, cloth-making, dish-molding, and leather-dressing developed into regular trades, with the division of labor extended by that time to the men of the community. Age provided another division of labor, for old men could make weapons when their fighting days were over. Some wanted to pound out copper bowls; some liked to tend the herds; some could make fine cheeses; some were farmers. Each man produced what he could produce best, made more of it than he needed, and traded his own surplus product for his neighbor's. Intra-village trade developed first; then, since lake-village men had fish and hill-village men had salt, trade became inter-village. For a long time trade was confined to related clans; it was a great day for progress when some brave trader ventured outside his friendly home-country to trade with strangers.

Reaction of trade on production. As no one could trade who had not a surplus over his own needs, men worked hard to "get ahead." They learned to work more and more steadily, saving for a more needy time what was left over from a period of gain. Steadiness of production is one of the signs of civilization A thrifty family found itself a powerful family because of its possessions, and especially because of its tradable wealth.[1] At first people exchanged gifts with each other, but they soon learned to trade frankly. From "trading even," the simplest form of exchange, to a sharp judgment of relative values, the trader developed his art. Gradually there now was developed a trading class which did not produce goods, but handled them in exchange. The merchant had appeared among men.

The acquaintance with new products which trade brought to primitive peoples stimulated production. Men who before had been content to produce enough for existence only now exerted themselves to secure more wheat, more salt, more cloth or fish than they could themselves use, to trade for coveted possessions. So we see that trade tends to produce a surplus as surely as it disposes of it. The amount of trade will clearly depend upon both the amount and the variety of production.

When many people had discovered the generous rewards of surplus production, there sometimes arose a rivalry in the disposal of goods. Then the only trader who had fish to offer found himself at an advantage; he might choose, we may say, between several measures of wheat. Naturally he would take the best wheat first, and the second best next, and he would certainly leave the poorest wheat until the very last, if he took it at all. The marginal wheat—the wheat on the edge of

---

[1] Wealth is anything of material value, even if that value be very small In a wider sense unseen and immaterial things are wealth also—such things as education, a good reputation, or a love of the beautiful But the economist usually confines his meaning to things with a calculable market value

no-value—ran such a risk of not being exchanged at all that men began to take more pains in raising and harvesting their crop, and the result after a time was better wheat. So trade not only increased the amount and variety of products, but also improved their quality. Cloth that had before been woven and fulled[1] only was now dyed and embroidered. Baskets at first were made strictly utilitarian; later they were made of selected reeds and were painted or stained with dyes. Jugs and bowls were made in graceful shapes and were decorated. Trade was a stimulator of art and skill.

Capital. The merchant was one example of a new economic class which increased as wealth increased. The merchant must have a supply of grain or sheep or cloth to trade with. This stock of goods was a form of capital, and was the result of someone's saving. The saver either had more than he could use, or else, knowing that his wealth would be worth more at a future time than at the present, he chose to deny himself an immediate gratification for a future profit. People who produce only their existence needs, or have not enough imagination to picture to themselves this future pleasure, use up what they have at once. The man who saves his wealth and then uses it to produce more wealth is a capitalist. *Capital is saved wealth used in the production of more wealth.*

From the first, capital had many forms, and today its forms are practically infinite. It was gained in many ways, and these ways are still in use among men. It is always originally a surplus over existence needs, often saved with much self-sacrifice; but its owner may have inherited it, or won it as a dowry, or stolen it. There are countless ways of stealing capital: thieves and brigands, pirates and able-bodied beggars, take it by force or cajolery; powerful and clever people may cheat the rightful owners of what belongs to them.

[1] What is fulling? There is an interesting account of the ancient methods of what we should call dry-cleaning and laundering, under the word "fullo," in Harper's "Dictionary of Classical Literature and Antiquities." Trace the change in meanings.

THE ESTABLISHING OF CIVILIZATION

The capitalist had an advantage over other men. Because he had what many men needed, he could, in times of shortage and distress, demand a high price for his hoarded wealth. If other men had skins to trade for seed in the spring, when grain must be planted, the capitalist could demand more skins than seed grain was usually worth, and so gain a great capital of skins. These skins could then be saved and sold when cold weather brought keen demand for them. If the planters had no skins to trade, they might promise their next winter's catch of fur, and so come to be in the debt of the capitalist. This put them into his power in many ways, and made him a great man in the community. Perhaps the capitalist wanted work instead of material wealth in exchange for his food or seed; then poor men became practically his slaves, bound to do what he told them. They could be made to work his land for him, while he ate the fruit thereof. They could be made to carry his burdens and build his house. The man who produced and saved became the man of influence and authority; his wealth gave him a power not possessed by his less successful fellows.

The easiest way to wealth, for an adventurous man, was stealing. Stealing from one's clansmen was dangerous and forbidden, for primitive people had strong ideas of loyalty to those of their own blood. But their feeling of detachment from other peoples was as strong as their group loyalty, and so there was no prejudice against taking from an outside group. This meant war. It meant an expedition against people that one hoped to find weaker than oneself. If they could be beaten in the fight, their wealth was appropriated and their families were placed at the mercy of the conqueror. Among the lowest savages it was customary to eat the conquered enemy The more fastidious men, perhaps the less hungry men, and certainly the cleverer men, saw that to use man's labor paid better than to eat him. So they instituted slavery. The institution of slavery grew out of the institution of war. In time men became used to the idea of making other men work for them without paying them a fair share of what they produced.

Personal-service givers. Some slaves became members of the economic class of personal servitors. Such people were not direct producers, but received their living for the service of making life easier, surer, or pleasanter for others. Priests, the earliest personal-service givers, were free and influential men who spent more time in propitiating the gods than other men could spare from their work. Because the priest offered sacrifices for the whole tribe and was supposed to know just what would please the gods most, he was given food and other necessities and excused from ordinary work. As ideas of religion became gradually higher, the priest remained in the social order, changing his functions in accord with new ideas, and often, but not always, teaching the people better ideas of right and wrong. Personal servants, physicians, and teachers belonged to the same class, which was never a large one until civilization had been well advanced; for before that there was never enough surplus food to support many nonproducers of the existence essentials.

Money. By the time that society became differentiated into distinct economic classes, another important change had taken place. This was the change from barter to money economy. When primitive people had learned that things have different values, they began to use "eveners" in their trading. These eveners must be capable of measurement into various quantities, and they must have real and permanent value; otherwise they could not serve to bridge the gap between selling what one did not want and buying what one did. The material must be common enough to afford a convenient supply, and not so common as to be valueless.

To fill these needs money was invented. All sorts of things were used: cowrie shells, wampum, bars of metal, cattle, and furs. In the seventh century B.C. the kings of Lydia made the first-known coined money; and since that time gold and silver coins have been the usual medium of exchange among civilized peoples, for these metals when coined combine the requisites of good money as nothing else does.

Roads. Money always flows to the places where things are exchanged, that is, to markets. Between the markets the traders and adventurers, the first travelers, made the first roads. If one were to see the same road in Asia at intervals of a few centuries apart, from very ancient to quite modern times, he would see upon it a continuing pageant of traveling merchants, or peddlers. These peddlers have been important agents in the uniting of peoples and the furthering of civilization The first ones traveled afoot, bearing their packs upon their shoulders. A later trader, if he belonged to a powerful tribe, would probably follow a band of slaves, who packed his burden and did his bidding When animals came to supplant human pack-bearers, they varied much in different parts of the earth. The camel and the ass were always the most useful animals of burden, but llamas, reindeer, dogs, oxen, and ponies have been widely used. So slow is custom to change that today, to all appearances, the same caravans may be seen winding over the deserts of Asia that traversed the worn paths in the time of Abraham or Confucius.

Primitive Social Institutions

While the economic development outlined above was taking place, mankind was also working out many changes in social and political relations, and experimenting with different kinds of land tenure. Some of these experiments are of great interest to us, for from them society arrived at the kinds of institutions which now hold in the United States and other civilized countries. These institutions are now generally accepted; but frequently they are challenged by people who think them wrong, and who want either to go back to the institutions which have been tried and abandoned, or to try some new scheme. To laugh at such people and to dismiss their ideas by calling them cranks is the utmost foolishness, to suppress them by force or intimidation is as unjust as it is unwise. If they are right, they should be followed; if they are wrong, they should be shown their mistakes. But only those people who know something of the history of institutions are intelligent enough to discuss the subject at all. The purpose of this chapter is to introduce the student to the story of how and why our present basic institutions developed and of how closely they are interrelated. The student who follows this introduction with further study and observation will find himself in a position the more fairly to judge whether our institutions should be kept and improved, or be abandoned for something better.

The three great institutions which were established in ancient times were

1. The monogamous and permanent family.
2. Private property.
3. The geographical unit of social organization.

The family. There is today much complaint of the decay of family life. It may perhaps be true that in the United States family life is not so good as it was in our early history (although that thesis is open to argument, and in any case could be accounted for by the picked character of the early settlers in some parts of the country). But there is no doubt that in the world at large family life grows better and better as time passes.

The earliest men had no family life at all. Then a monogamous group tended to form through the influences of economic and social needs, but without any guaranty of permanence either from custom, law, or religion. And because there were no set standards, people changed their form of family life when it was affected by such changes as a scarcity of food, or war, or a migration bringing a new climatic environment.

At various times and places man has experimented with about every form of marriage and family life that could be devised. There were elaborately controlled intra-clan and inter-clan systems, with both polyandry and polygamy. These latter systems often came as a result of war, which leaves a surplus female population, or from a shortage of food. But among the Northern races the tendency is to return to monogamy as the normal custom. In the beginning this was not because of moral scruples, but because it was economically more practicable. Plural marriage seems to be a result of some kind of abnormal condition in the distribution of wealth or the supply of food or the balance of population; a removal of the abnormal condition brings back a prevalence of monogamous marriage.

The monogamous marriage tended to become a permanent marriage by custom as time passed, until under classic law and Christian influence in the Middle Ages it became the standard. It always characterized the healthy periods of social life among the people of Persia, Palestine, and Rome. The common interest of parents in their children was a strong factor in making marriage permanent, as was also the filial piety taught by religion Even the hope and expectation of support in old age tended to make marriage permanent. The standard is now so well understood that the prevalence of divorce is accepted generally as a sign of social decay.

Property and social organization. The right of private property is not the result of legislation, but of a gradually evolved social organization which could not exist without it, and of production and exchange systems now woven into the basic fabric of the world's life. Few if any primitive people seem to have had private ownership in land, although in very early times clothing and ornaments and weapons were considered to belong to individuals. The fact that the white men who came to America in the sixteenth and seventeenth centuries had practically the same ideas as we about private property, while the Indians were still in a state of group ownership of land, led to misunderstandings that brought on bloody Indian wars and shameful breaking of treaties.

Indian customs may serve to illustrate how early peoples held land in groups If an Indian woman wanted to raise maize and beans, she asked for a patch of land and received it for the season, and raised her crop. After that the land was supposed to pass back to the control of the group which owned it —a tribe or a clan. The woman might raise a crop on the same patch the next season, or try another. Land was not valued; only the usufruct counted. And this was because there was more than enough land, so that there was little if any competition for it; also because hunting, the main form of land-using, required large tracts of land and social effort to realize its product.

Private property in chattels probably began with man's history, but it extended as wealth and knowledge grew. Such things as weapons and ornaments had not their modern value in early times, partly because of the custom of burying them with the dead. If a man knew that his personal belongings would be buried with him, he did not care to accumulate a surplus of them; he was content with what he could personally use. But when men began to hand down their possessions to their children, they wanted customs and laws which would insure exclusive personal possession. So inheritance and private ownership are closely related.

The landholding groups varied greatly in different parts of the world. Sometimes a household, sometimes two partners, sometimes a clan or part of it, and sometimes a whole tribe owned the land in common. If the landowning group coincided with a village, then there was communal ownership; that is, a whole community held the land together and granted the use of it to individuals as the chiefs or the assembly saw fit. When population increased, the more clever and powerful men of the group attempted, usually with success, to secure their allotments for life, and even to hand them down to their children. The struggle for land among the Romans, where the patrician families secured the practically perpetual control of the nominally public pastures, is the best illustration of this struggle; while the present-day struggle of the Mexican peons to retain their ancient group rights of land tenure against modern legal private ownership shows how universally the process of transition brings suffering and bitterness with it. In countries where private ownership went with a reasonable distribution of the land in small tracts worked by the owners, as in the United

States quite generally, or in modern France, society has profited by the change; but where land barons held it in great stretches and kept the workers submerged in hopeless poverty and ignorance, society has probably lost in the ultimate measure of social weal—the condition of the majority of the people.

Private ownership of land seems always to have come with several other signs of changing conditions: money economy, increased population, improved agriculture, and the growth of towns. Therefore it is clearly involved in our modern economy as an intrinsic factor. Private ownership of movable wealth— money and machinery—did not trouble mankind much until the Industrial Revolution, when for the first time it existed in such quantities as to become a real problem. This wealth was owned by individuals, for it had multiplied rapidly from private hoards stolen from American Indian treasures, or gathered in legitimate trade, or saved from the high returns of war-time farming. Some people who do not question the private ownership of land doubt the wisdom of private ownership of capital; for although it is as old as human history, these people think it should not apply to the great amounts now in existence.

The Changing Bases of Social Organization

Before the change from early to modern political organization can be explained, it must be understood that mankind has had several bases for organization. Today citizens live in a town or in a city ward or in a county, and that unit forms a little nation in itself, which carries on its own affairs by the coöperation of the citizens. Some of those citizens may be "old stock" Americans, some may be Irish-Americans who came to America in the 40's, and some may be Italians who landed within the last decade. They are of many races, and the people of the same race may claim no blood relationship. They act together to manage their community affairs simply because they all live in the same territorial unit; that is, their basis of union is a geographic one.

But this was not always the case. In the childhood of the race the people who were descended from a common ancestor (usually in the maternal line) grouped themselves into clans, or gentes. The clans were usually united into phratries or tribes, or sometimes both. Among the more advanced peoples the tribes were sometimes united into confederacies, which might finally become, as among the Romans, real nations.[1]

Out of tribal government there developed, by a great many different steps and processes, the varying forms of civilized government now on the earth. Some tribes were little absolute monarchies from the first. But among the American Indians, the Romans, and the early Greeks tribal government was very democratic. In some tribes there was felt the need of a permanent war lord to lead the tribesmen in battle. This chief was elected, therefore, and in that office we find the germ of a later kingship. In the same way the tribal and clan assemblies by mutation sometimes became the councils which developed finally into parliaments and senates.

We may take the Greeks as an example of a people who changed from group to private ownership of property and shifted their social organization from a blood basis to a geographic one, through an intermediate stage in which property served as a basis. These people were first organized into tribes and clans, counting descent through the father. Much evidence goes to show that they held their property in a modified communism; that is, the patriarchal chief had control of it, but was understood to manage it in the interests of his family and dependents. In the earlier days the clan inherited all his

---

[1] The tribe was composed of all who spoke a common language and were at least traditionally descended from common ancestors. In America probably all tribes were descended from one original tribe which somehow had found its way across the Pacific from Asia; for the American Indians closely resemble the Mongolian tribes of eastern Asia. This tribe subdivided again and again in the course of several millenniums and furnished the wide land with its continually dividing, differentiating, and, finally, fighting tribes. Few of the tribes had advanced to the stage of forming confederacies by the time of Columbus; the Iroquois were an exception. In no case had a true nation been formed.

property; but, later, inheritance was narrowed to the dead man's agnates (that is, to his relatives in the male line, for the management of property was one of the duties of men). Then the nearest agnates were given precedence, and as the nearest agnates were usually a man's sons, in time the inheritance of property by children became the rule. By the sixth century B C. property was much greater in amount and more valuable than it had been in the earlier days. Athens and its citizens had beautiful stone temples, a city wall, flocks of sheep and herds of cattle on the neighboring hills, and granaries for holding the corn raised on the gentile lands of Attica. Men who owned so much wealth sometimes quarreled about it, and the Athenians appointed dicasts and archons to settle disputes. The complaints came usually from poor men who thought they had been mistreated by rich ones; for property then had the same troublesome tendency that it has now, of becoming concentrated in the hands of a few able men, leaving great numbers of poor men in actual distress. The lots of land which had once been common tribal property, and which had been distributed (perhaps, as their tradition said, equally) among the people, were too small to support a family now; for with more trade and more division of labor came new conditions of money economy and high prices. The farmer then mortgaged his land to a rich man, but being unable to pay the debt (the interest was usually at 18 per cent) he had to sell himself and perhaps his family also into slavery to the capitalist.

While this was happening in the country, the city was changing from a village of tradesmen to a manufacturing center. So many farmers' sons found that they could make good wages in the city making vases or harness, or working in the Piræus shipyards, that the city grew rapidly at the expense of the country Its varied manufactures were carried throughout the Mediterranean by the merchant ships built in the Piræus, and the new class of business men who made and sent out the rich cargoes grew wealthy. They were often cultured, too, and used much of their wealth to promote public welfare. But the older class of nobles, bred in gentile pride, considered all men who dealt in trades or in trade their inferiors. They despised them even more than they did the poor peasants whose land they took for debt.

A property basis. Under the archon Solon, about 600 B.C., class antagonism between the peasants and the landowning nobles, and between these and the prosperous tradesmen, became so bitter that a complete reorganization took place. Under the tribal organization the nobles had been able to concentrate all the political power in themselves. Abandoning the blood basis of social organization and government, therefore, Solon took property, the most prominent feature of the economic life of the day, as a basis for his new scheme. He divided all the citizens into classes according to the amount of wealth they had, and gave to each class duties corresponding to its possessions. All men, no matter how poor, belonged to the popular assembly, and immigrants, who had before been denied citizenship because they belonged to no gens, now received that privilege. The gens, as a basis for social organization, was passing away.

Solon made other reforms, scarcely less epochal, regarding property and government. He canceled the mortgages and debts of the peasants, which gave them a fresh start and a fairer chance. He limited the amount of land a man might own. But he refused to redivide the lands—a sign that landownership had reached a permanent status among the Athenians. New courts and new officers were created, in which both the old tribes and the new economic divisions were recognized. The whole set of laws shows how a wise, moderate man may keep part of an old system and introduce phases of a new one in the process of evolving a satisfactory solution to a difficult problem.

The laws of Solon worked well for a time, but eventually the wealthy classes succeeded to the power of the nobles, leaving the poor in almost as wretched a plight as before. Neither blood nor property, as a basis for social organization, gave the people the two things they wanted: a fair economic chance, and a fair share in the government. Pisistratus again redivided the land

THE ESTABLISHING OF CIVILIZATION 19

and gave the peasants money with which to restock their farms; but while this relieved the economic distress, it did not bring the government abreast of the economic situation, which had forged ahead of governmental forms. Finally Clisthenes, in 510 B C, struck at the root of the trouble by doing away with tribal organization altogether. He made territory the basis of the units instead of blood or property, and so secured a mixture of blood and a variation of economic status in each unit He divided Attica into a hundred townships called demes, each with clearly marked boundaries, and each with powers of local self-government like those of American townships. The demes were united into a county, which Clisthenes called a tribe—an interesting concession to old custom. But the new counties were geographical, not consanguine, and now neither nobles nor rich merchants could form a solid body to perpetuate their privileges.

Some features of this same process were experienced by the Romans and by the English in making the transition from the blood basis to the territorial basis for social organization. The details differed in each case, the result was the same. No advanced stage of production can exist without the institution of private property, and with private property it becomes necessary to have units of government in which people of various degrees of wealth are members. Otherwise it becomes easy for class rulership and class tyranny to exist, and the government is sure to be overthrown sooner or later by the classes which have been imposed upon. The evidence of history is unanimous upon this point: no government, of whatever kind, can be called a permanent government which allows one class of people to dominate and oppress another class. For that reason the geographical unit has proved so far the most successful of all units in managing the common affairs of men. It allows people of many degrees of wealth and of many sorts, with diverse interests, to unite in a corporate body. They must meet each other, learn from each other, concede to each other, compromise differences, and compare ideas It insures majority rule, but permits minority influence and demands toleration of all.

The Economy of Rome

"To understand medieval and modern history it is needful to understand that Roman Empire from the ruins of which so many modern nations have emerged," says Professor William Stearns Davis. The reason for this is that the Roman Empire, stretching at its greatest extent from Mesopotamia to the Atlantic and from Britain to the Sahara, gathered up in itself the sum of ancient civilizations and passed on to the nations that succeeded it such parts of them as could be used later on.

Not only has the modern world inherited much from Rome; the record of Rome's failures is perhaps the most useful thing left by the mighty empire. For there exist interesting parallels between many situations in the Rome that decayed and fell and the world of today. It is because of these likenesses that a review of some points in Roman history becomes useful to us in our search for facts helpful in solving the hard problems of the present.

Production. It is notable, in the first place, that from the days of Augustus to those of Marcus Aurelius, production in the Roman Empire had reached a remarkable degree of development. It was as great and varied as it could be in an age of handwork. A system of transportation quite as remarkable served to distribute these products throughout the empire, and especially to bring the offerings of all the provinces to the imperial city. Trade and manufacture were, however, mainly in the hands of Jews, Syrians, or Greeks, for the Romans despised trade and looked with contempt on the trader. Romans of good family sometimes engaged in trade secretly through a slave or agent, but the only honorable career for a Roman was that of public service, political or military. This snobbish attitude toward work was the cause of many blunders, for it divided the people into permanent economic classes irrespective of talent, and kept good thinkers and influential citizens from devoting themselves to the solution of economic problems. The business of the empire was in the hands of freedmen or of provincials, who were denied an honorable part in the conduct of the State. Naturally they were not patriotic; naturally they did not contribute the acumen that was needed to the organization of the social body, and naturally the social fabric, unsound in places where it might have been made strong and good, gave way under the strain of barbarian attacks.

But until the later empire Roman economic life seemed prosperous and well organized There was an immense output, a large part of which flowed in tribute to Rome This piling up of wealth in the capital gave to observers there a false appearance of ample resources, they could not see that in the provinces there were starving producers and decaying industries, because the returns had been diverted from those who had earned them to the all-devouring conqueror. The banking system was orderly and internationally organized. A few very rich men spent money lavishly, and the court lived in magnificent palaces in a degree of luxury hard to imagine even today.

A militaristic state. The Roman Empire is the most brilliant example the world has ever seen of an economy dominated by militarism. The Romans themselves were primarily soldiers, who, through the efficient organization of force, were able to compel the whole known world to support them by its productive activity. They levied tribute through

1 A civil government organized and administered more efficiently than any other to that time.

2. A system of roads, coinage, taxes, and military force.

3. A slave system which exploited the productive power of subject peoples.

These three forces kept the vicious circle of militarism in working order for centuries. The government was so well managed that people did not know how to rebel against it, even if they wanted to do so. The taxes supported the soldiers, who secured the continuance of the government. And the slaves were forced by the power of the State and of long tradition to do the producing which kept the whole artificial structure upright and apparently intact.

That Roman Empire, which seemed to itself to be the very pinnacle of the world's life, the sum and glory of its long development, fell finally with a ruin so entire and stupendous that it has been the figure of the vanity of human accomplishments ever since. Through the centuries many historians and philosophers have speculated and preached on the reasons for its fall. Even today it is impossible to name all the causes of that tragic failure. But there are four things on which scholars are pretty well united as the main causes of the fall of the Western Empire. These four things were

1. The moral degeneration of the people.

2. A land system which did not produce enough for the normal consumption of an increasing population.

3. A labor system which did not give men freedom and opportunity and which did not pay a fair return for toil.

4. A tax system which took from men an unfair share of their product and made no compensating return.

Of these causes the breakdown through moral decay was the most fundamental. The Romans did not develop elegant living through a normal process of increasing refinement of thought; they conquered more cultured peoples and appropriated their elegance and wealth without knowing how to appreciate them. A nation which develops elegant living through the slow process of increased and improved production may be able to live in luxury without losing its virtue at the same time; but a nation which captures luxury by sheer force, and which then lives luxuriously without having gained true refinement of character, becomes effeminate, indulgent, and weak.

Wine-drinking, spectacular shows, unwholesome social life, and parasitism undermined the Roman character, so that the later empire found the people devitalized and dependent. The remaining sound and virtuous citizens could not stem the tide of ruin that self-indulgence poured upon Roman civilization.

Added to this fundamental decay in character, which could not fail to bring ruin with it, were the three economic blunders named above. The land, used at first more or less equally by all the citizens, came to be held exclusively by the original tribesmen, or patricians. Immigrants and their descendants were not allowed its use except as a concession after stiff fights. Even with the redistributions which were forced from time to time, the land tended always to be concentrated in the hands of a few wealthy families, who worked it with slave labor. The long struggle for land as shown in the constant recurrence of Licinian legislation makes no small part of the history of Rome, and illustrates the obstinate blindness with which privileged classes in society cling to their traditional rights against every consideration of justice. A few men saw the danger, and tried to remedy the injustice before it was too late; but being opposed by the patricians, and given only fickle support by the proletariat[1] they sought to help, they failed of their purpose. Under the early empire there was a period of relief; but with the closing-in of forces induced by the economic blundering of centuries in the late empire the bad land-tenure system came to its logical result: the land lay idle and unproductive while men starved.

The labor system. Slavery was taken for granted in the ancient world. It came from debt and war, from slave piracy on the seas and child-stealing forays among barbarian folk. The Roman State itself dealt in and used slaves, and accepted the system without protest. The slaves used on the plantations fared worst, as they served in chain gangs and were miserably clad, fed, and housed. Their lives were embittered by disease, privation, monotony, and savage cruelty. A slave who killed his master was usually put to death by crucifixion, and every slave who was with him in the house at the time, whether an accomplice or not, shared his fate. In spite of this severity murders of masters were rather frequent.

Personal attendants were better treated. The town slaves dreaded most the punishment of being sent to the country to

[1] Look up the meaning of the word "proletariat." Is there a proletariat in America?

work on the master's estate. Handsome and clever slaves from Greece, Cyprus, and Egypt managed the house, cleaned and cooked and sewed, amused the master and the mistress, and corrupted the once simple Roman manners until, in the time of the empire, Rome was another Babylon.

A third class of slaves comprised the artisans, and a fourth was used by the government in offices and warehouses, thus supplanting that whole class of free labor known in modern nations as civil servants. The fire department of Rome used six hundred slaves as fire watchmen, and as many more in the public temples and the police department. Men who owned slaves skilled as carpenters, shoemakers, weavers, masons, or plumbers hired them out by the day, at wages that were less than would have supported the family of a free laborer.

Effects of slavery. The effect of servitude upon the slaves is degrading enough; but slave owners suffer a corruption of character far more tragic. Slavery reduces to absurdity the ancient maxim that he who does not work shall not eat. The owners live upon the work of others, and come to have a contempt for work and for workers, seeing work relegated to beings without freedom, and the workers the dupes of the strong. The attitude toward work is always an index to social conditions. Slaves in Rome corrupted their masters; for slaves must win their points by flattery, not having the legitimate means that free men have. They must win favor by appealing to some weakness or appetite of their masters. They may gain their freedom by using their knowledge of some secret crime or disgrace. The effect of slavery upon the economic condition of Rome was to put the free farmer, the free artisan, the free professional man largely out of work, but the effect upon the free will of the owners was far more disastrous. The most enslaved man under a slave system is the master, for he has lost the most essential of human freedoms—the freedom from dependence upon others.

Christianity, which taught that slave and master are alike before God, and that all men are brothers, brought a kinder treatment of slaves. One after another, beginning with the right of masters to condemn their slaves to fight wild beasts in the arena, the life-and-limb control of slaves was taken away by law. Antoninus Pius gave slaves the right to appear before the prefect of Rome or the procurator of a province and complain of their treatment, and if their statements were found to be true, they could be sold to another master. By Constantine's time the killing of a slave had become legal murder. The Christian emperors stopped the crucifixion of slaves. All these ameliorations, coming when the empire itself was weakening, and when free men were becoming worse and worse off, led to a gradual breaking down of the lines of demarcation that had once separated the conditions of slave and free. When the empire broke up, human slavery as such had largely come to an end. This did not mean that men lived freer lives or had more happiness and intelligence; it meant mainly that every property right broke down in a period of anarchy, and that the right of holding human chattels was lost with the rest.

Serfdom. Serfdom existed in medieval Europe, with a condition of at least partial freedom, which in the course of centuries became complete. In America slavery was revived in a curiously atavistic[1] economy, dependent upon conditions of almost unlimited land that can never occur again. It became a vested institution, and had to be done away with as a war measure. Although it still survives in the Mohammedan lands and in a few other backward and semicivilized places, it is an obsolescent institution, doomed to pass away before advancing civilization.

Taxes. Slavery and militarism in Rome alike worked toward an abnormal tax burden, as both produced large numbers of idle folk who must be supported at public expense. Slave labor, being paid a wage allowing only the lowest possible standard of living (that is, an existence level of clothes, food, and shelter), reduces the cost of production to a level at which free

---

[1] The word "atavistic" is borrowed from the study of heredity. What does it mean here? Does American society display any atavistic institutions today?

labor cannot compete. So working-people become idlers and must be supported at public expense. The consumer buys his goods cheaper, perhaps, than if they had been made by free labor, but he loses in the end because his taxes are raised. As to free labor, it suffers from a labor version of Gresham's law: *Cheap labor drives dear labor out of a job.*

The taxation system of early Rome was much like our own. There were two main sources of revenue: the *tributum*, or direct tax, and the *vectigalia*, which included many kinds of excise or indirect taxation. The provinces paid heavy taxes of two kinds: the *soli*, or ground tax, and the *capitis*, partly a poll tax and partly a tax on property and trade. The Romans used the inheritance tax freely. It was levied at first in Rome on inheritances of about $4000 (100,000 sesterces) when they fell to the next of kin; and all inheritances not falling to the next of kin were taxed. Caracalla extended the inheritance tax to the whole empire, and raised the rate to 10 per cent. The evil of tax-farming made taxes more of a burden than they would have been had a modern collection system been used.

Under Augustus the tax system was reformed, but these reforms did not last. Taxes then became part of another vicious circle of forces: they served to keep an idle and luxurious court in existence, which, in turn, kept the army officers in their places; and the army enabled the provincial governors to collect the revenue. The two sets of parasites throve in their coalition.

Under that coalition both agriculture and industry suffered and finally almost ceased. The State tried to remedy affairs by a program of drastic regulation, which only made things worse. Nothing that men did was free; government officials watched every move and regulated every sale. Whatever was produced beyond the existence needs of the producers went to keep the nonproducing soldiers; for unpaid soldiers are likely to make trouble, while an unarmed and ignorant citizenry is more docile. When the barbarians came, they found no force capable of withstanding them. Their relatives had been admitted already as *coloni*, or settlers, and the army was largely composed of Germans. In some places they destroyed ruthlessly, but for the most part the ruin of the empire was the ruin of uncertainty, purposelessness, and lack of leadership among the Romans themselves. It was the inevitable result of a civilization which had ignored the laws of economic and of moral justice.

During this period civilization almost ceased over large areas of what had been the empire. Roads, transportation, and production decayed, schools closed, and money was hoarded instead of being invested. Farms grew up to weeds, cities became villages, and villages disappeared. What used to be called the Dark Ages followed the superficial brilliancy of the Roman world.

Creating a new civilization. The so-called Dark Ages proved to be emerging ages for a new type of civilization, which, although far from perfect, has proved to be greatly in advance of that of Roman times. The three great forces of that remolding period seem to have been the idealized memory of the orderly Rome of the past, the fresh and vital Germanic races, and the liberalizing principles of Christianity. As often happens, when once Rome had become a memory its faults and shortcomings were lost to view, and only its good phases remained in men's minds. The new religion differed from the various cults taught in the empire, in that it emphasized the next world more than this, and the spirit more than the body. Out of this emphasis, which Hebrew prophets had preached and which Persian mystics had taught in the ancient East, but which had never before affected men as it did in medieval times, there developed a new spiritual consciousness that has been a mighty factor in human life ever since. Slowly the people subjected to this teaching of the all-importance of the soul, of the value of character over all material things, worked out a new set of ideas about social relations. They kept the best of what was already won, and added new features to their stock of ideas, which we shall study later. Our next chapter shows the contributions which medieval people, beginning again with new materials, brought to the upbuilding of the modern world.

SUPPLEMENTARY READINGS

CHAPIN, F. S. Introduction to the Study of Social Evolution, chap. vii, "A New Theory of Race Development."

DAVIS, W. S. A Day in Old Athens, chaps. xii and xiv. Industry.

ROBINSON, J. H., BREASTED, J. H., and SMITH, E. P. General History of Europe, pp. 1–9, 54–56, 62–69, 137–143, 171–179.

ROOSEVELT, THEODORE. "How Old is Man?" in the *National Geographic Magazine*, Vol. XXIV (February, 1916), pp. 111–127.

TACITUS. Germania (description of the Germans), extracts in Cheyney's "Readings in English History," pp. 41–43, or Tuell and Hatch's "Readings in English History," pp. 1–9.

TUFTS, J. H. The Real Business of Living, chap. ii, "Invention and Progress."

SEARCH QUESTIONS AND PROBLEMS

1. Are there any people in the world today whose attention is centered entirely on the three essentials of existence? What does the world expect or demand of such people? Do people more fortunately situated owe them anything? Why?

2. How does a modern apartment house compare with an Iroquois long-house? What does each indicate as to the socialization of its inmates?

3. Read the article on shipbuilding in the best encyclopedia available. See if you can make a diagram showing the successive elaborations for design, power, carrying room, and speed of early (that is, presteam) boats and ships.

4. Do you find primitive ideas of property rights among young children? Is there much difference of ideas as to individual ownership in different families? If so, what does this indicate? What is the effect of a great emotional crisis, or a great emergency, on our ideas and practice with regard to property? For instance, what would happen if a fire destroyed your town completely, or if our nation had to defend itself in a war that threatened our very existence?

5. Read Herodotus, Book IV, chap. 196, for an account of early trading operations. In what period must this have taken place?

6. For the laws of Hammurabi see Davis's "Readings in Ancient History," Vol. I, pp. 35–38; for the laws of Moses see Exodus xx, 1–17. How much progress in ethical ideas had been made by the Semites between the time of Hammurabi (2240 B. C.) and Moses (c. 1500 B. C.)?

7. We find that debt among ancient peoples sprang from the need of the essentials of existence, the need of bridging some crisis (such as the sudden death of a relative, which necessitated a funeral feast), improvidence and illness, and war. Have the causes of debt changed in modern times? To obtain a loan, the borrower sometimes offered a present in addition to repaying the loan What do we find here?

8 The Hebrew prophets taught that slaves held for debt should be set free every seventh year Why? What did "the law and the prophets" say on this subject? See Deuteronomy xv, 12, and Jeremiah xxxiv, 8–17.

9. Until Roman times the Persians were the only great road-builders. The most famous road of antiquity was the Royal Road from Susa to Sardis Find it in a map of ancient Persia How does it compare with the much-discussed "Berlin to Bagdad" railroad? What was the object of each?

10. What did early European traders give the Indians for their valuable beaver and otter skins? Was this "trading even"? Think twice.

11. What peoples in the world today are coming rapidly forward in their civilization? Which nation has made the most progress in the last fifty years? For an example of what can be done through the influence of one man, read the autobiography of John G. Paton.

12 The Athenian assembly, called the agora, gave its name to its meeting place, this was later used as a market place, which came to be the common meaning of the word What corresponds to the agora, or forum, in an American town? Why do Americans carry on their civic business under a roof?

13 Study the Roman roads of England from the map in Cheyney's "Short History of England," p. 24. Can you plan a motor trip through England that will take you to the leading places of interest today, using these old roads?

14 Was there ever such a state slavery system in America as Rome had?

15. Find the amount of taxes, in American money, raised by the vectigalian levies about the time of Pompey's earlier conquest (Plutarch's "Pompeius," 45) Compare this with the internal-revenue taxes of the United States for any one year

16 See the World Almanac for 1917, pp 161–180 and 310–316, for the revenue regulations of the United States and the several states at that time Compare with the taxes of Caracalla's day. See the article "Vectigalia" in Harper's "Dictionary of Classical Antiquities"

17. What characteristics of Roman life in its decay hold true of American life today? Are there any constructive forces in America now that the Romans did not have? Will these constructive forces be strong enough to combat the forces of decay?

18. Study the cross sections of different American roads as shown in N. S. Shaler's "American Highways," or find the information in an encyclopedia. From inquiries of local authorities prepare a cross-section drawing of the best road in your vicinity. Discuss comparative advantages.

19. L. W. Page, in "Roads, Paths, and Bridges," pp. 13-15, says that Roman road-law is the basis of modern road-law. Compare the Roman ideas (to be found in an encyclopedia article on the subject) with those shown in the road-law of your own state, and criticize the accuracy of Mr. Page's statement. If you have no copy of your state road-law, apply to your county or state commission or commissioner of roads.

20. What were the peculiar duties of a Roman tribune? See the article "Tribunus" in Harper's "Dictionary of Classical Literature and Antiquities."

21. Read a full account of the work of the Gracchi, whom their mother Cornelia called her jewels, in a Roman history. With their experience in mind, what effect do you say the pauperizing of a people has upon such virtues as justice, constancy, and gratitude?

22. The British Empire is the only modern government which can compare with the old Roman Empire. Do you know how much tribute this empire exacts of its provinces? See Ogg and Beard's "National Governments and the World War," p. 308.

CHAPTER II

ECONOMIC CONTRIBUTIONS OF THE MIDDLE AGES

> ... Who love to analyze great ideas and understand great causes, have found the Middle Ages a mine of wealth. And others, again, to whom all that is done by mortal man is dear, eagerly question the past to see how that incalculable being, ever the same, faced his dangers and grappled with his tasks.—F. M. POWICKE

IN AGRICULTURE

It was formerly the custom to think of the medieval period in history as the "dark ages." In reality any close study of the centuries between the fall of the Roman Empire and the beginning of the modern era reveals a wealth of bright spots which give the lie to the old epithet. In the economic fields of agriculture, industry, and commerce there were hundreds of practical experiments carried on; in most cases, to be sure, quite unconsciously by the experimenters, but none the less with the result that whatever proved to be unpractical and inefficient was gradually if slowly replaced by what was more advanced and more adequate in meeting the needs of a growing and changing world.

Ownership of land. In no field was there more progress toward modernity than in agriculture. The beginning of the Middle Ages found the farmers of northern and western Europe living in one-room cottages grouped together at crossroads in little hamlets, with their farm lands surrounding them. Individual farmers did not own or rent separate farms as at present. Instead, the villagers held the surrounding territory in common, dividing off the land into sections for meadow, pasture, and plowland. Each village had the right to use the meadow and pasture, and scattered strips through the plowland. Once a year in council the plowland was apportioned anew among its co-workers, according to tribal custom. From a stage of free occupation of land, man had now progressed to a stage of actual landownership, which some historians term communal ownership and others co-ownership. With the scanty evidence at our command for this early period it is difficult to say for certain whether it was the community of villagers as an entity which owned the surrounding fields or whether each man within the group possessed individual ownership of, say, thirty acres, but not of any definite thirty acres; just as a man who puts ten one-dollar bills into a savings bank has personal ownership of ten dollars of the funds of that bank, but he cannot be said to own any definite, specific ten one-dollar bills in its vaults. The weight of best historical research would seem to indicate at present that at the opening of the Middle Ages (with the exception of the house and garden plots, which were owned privately and personally) all the land which was owned was under this co-ownership system.

Agricultural methods. The agricultural methods of the early medieval era were very crude. In many parts of Europe the nomads were still collecting food without any real culture of the soil. In the settled areas around the hamlets the fields were planted year after year with the same crops. The pasture lands were kept distinct from the tillage, and no attempt was made to fertilize the soil. When the results of soil exhaustion began to be evident, the villagers either moved on to new territory or more wisely divided their lands into two huge fields, one of which lay fallow every year. By means of this rest for the land its fertility was kept longer.

The manor system. This system of land ownership and cultivation, known as Free Village Economy, was supplanted after a few centuries by the Manorial System. Russia returned to free village economy in 1861 after the imperial abolition of the manor, but western Europe worked out better schemes for both landownership and cultivation.

The change from free village economy to manorial, or unfree village, economy was not due to any conscious desire of the villagers to try out a different system. It came about naturally through the marauding expeditions of venturesome peoples, such as the Norsemen and the Saxons, who left their native villages, took ship, and, landing on foreign shores, conquered and subjugated the peaceful villagers.

To all outward appearance the villages remained nearly the same, but in reality a fundamental change had taken place, for the surrounding land was no longer the property of the villagers. It was held by the warrior lord, who let it out to the villagers (now known as villeins, or serfs) for cultivation on terms set solely by him. The very cottages in which they lived, with their diminutive gardens, were now no longer their personal property, but were considered as part of the lord's estate. Now although this was true, all historical evidence seems to indicate that so far at least as theory was concerned, it was not the manorial lord who owned the land but the king of the country. In reality very little was cared about who owned the land, the important question being who possessed it, and of this there is no doubt: the lands of each manor were in the possession of a conquering lord who subjugated the old owners into a status of "serfdom" which was superior only to actual, outright slavery.

Less change was made in the methods of land cultivation than in landownership. The old two-field system was supplanted by three fields, thus allowing only one third of the arable lands to lie idle each year. The fields were divided into acre and half-acre strips as of old, with each serf's holdings scattered afar. But now there must be raised enough crops from the land to support the lord and his retinue as well as the villagers and their families. The result was that output somewhat increased. This was made possible by the three-field division, by the custom of fertilizing the fields through the turning of the stock upon the stubble, and by the simple rotation of crops in the two cultivated fields. By planting wheat or rye for bread in a field one year, and barley the next, all the yield of the soil was higher than if the same crop had been raised for two successive years.

From an economic point of view the manorial system, although an improvement on the free village, was still exceedingly wasteful. Good land was still left idle in the balks of unplowed turf between the serf's strips, in the odd corners where the irregular "shots," or subfields, joined one another in a "crazy quilt" fashion, and in the fallow fields. Time was wasted as profusely as was land. The hours spent by a serf in going to and from his scattered strips would have been ample to have cultivated some fifteen acres if his original thirty to forty-eight had been concentrated in one place. Moreover, there were only a few clumsy plows and harrows owned by all the serfs on a manor; hence they often had to wait days before their turn came to use the common implements; and when their time came, they might be called away to work on the lord's special plots of land.

The system is not to be blamed for all these wastes. The early agriculturalist had to learn in the slow school of experience, and he might be prevented from applying his ideas by the iron-bound laws of custom. An enterprising serf could not venture out into fields of experimentation. He must do as his community did. He was bound by manorial custom.

There were two classes of people on the manor who might have worked out improvements in the agricultural system, the lords and the freemen. Neither of them embraced its opportunity. The lord's interests were not in agricultural pursuits; his manor was but a means of income whereby he could spend his time in hunting and fighting, the real business of his life. He did not even trouble to do the actual supervising of the manor, but left that to a "seneschal" if he held many estates, or to a bailiff if he held but one. Attached to practically every manor there were a few freeholders who were not a servile part of it. These non-noble freemen might perhaps have experimented, but their numbers were few, and they seem in all cases to have followed the same scheme of three-field crop rotation as was practiced by the serfs and their lords.

As we look back now on the manor system from almost a thousand years of subsequent progress, it is not the deficiencies so much as the remarkable self-sufficiency of this rural unit which surprises us Every great manor was practically a self-supporting unit. It produced all its own food with the exception of pepper and salt, the latter article being a necessity for preservation purposes in the absence of the use of ice. Ale and wine were made at home. The clothes were made of cloth woven from homespun wool Wooden and leather shoes were constructed by a village cobbler. Carpenters did all their tasks with wood from the neighboring forests, but the blacksmiths were called upon to secure iron from distant markets. The millers had often to secure millstones from a distance. When a disease known as scab attacked the sheep, tar from the northern pine forests was found to be the only remedy. With these few exceptions, the manor was a self-sufficing economic unit.

The passing of the old order. The passing of the manor system, except in Russia, occupied several centuries and resembled a slow decay. As with most great lasting changes many factors played a part in destroying the old and introducing the new. The crusades (1091–1272) contributed their part by bringing an influx of money and encouraging trade. This made it possible for an enterprising villein to sell his surplus produce and buy his freedom, with the right to rent land or even in many cases to purchase a farm outright.

The serf was assisted in this process of buying his freedom and a bit of property by a great plague called the Black Death, which swept from the Orient to the northern part of England during the Hundred Years' War The number swept away is variously estimated at from one tenth to one half of the population. Probably the total losses were smaller than is given by most accounts, but at any rate they were sufficient to reduce materially the force of laborers. Manors were left in a state of no cultivation, and famishing lords were led to give freedom and an accompanying piece of land to any serf who would remain and work for wages on the demesne. If selfish and obdurate lords refused to make these concessions, serfs could now run away to other, wiser landlords or else into the new and growing towns.

A series of peasant revolts throughout Europe, with their accompanying destruction of the records of serfdom, hastened the passing of villeinage. By the middle of the fifteenth century its end had come in England. France soon followed suit, but gave to its peasants a lot scarcely better than they had enjoyed as serfs. Ancient feudal obligations still burdened them until the French Revolution. In Germany the serf remained until the Napoleonic wars, and in Russia until the Imperial Ukase of 1861.

Private ownership and convertible husbandry. Except in Russia, the new order brought in the régime of the private ownership of land. At first most of the land was owned by the lords and their descendants. In England, because of the custom of primogeniture, this meant that no more than 10 per cent of the population owned all the soil, while the other 90 per cent became renters and farm laborers, or left the land to collect in the growing towns and cities. On the Continent the holding of land was more widely diffused, but it was still almost the monopoly of the nobility.

Agricultural methods underwent quite as radical a change. The fields were no longer divided and subdivided into shots and strips, but became of necessity consolidated. In the new "inclosures," as they were called, grain-growing was largely supplanted by sheep-raising. The cereal land which was left was converted into pasture after two years of tillage, and a bit of pasture was in turn converted for two years into tillage. From an agricultural point of view this system of "convertible husbandry" marked a step beyond the three-field system, for it eliminated waste land, encouraged private initiative, and produced larger returns with less exhaustion to the soil. This system was far from producing an agricultural Utopia, for it allowed weeds to grow rank, subsoil to go unused, human food to be insufficient in amount and variety, and the land to be depopulated; but with all its defects agriculture was on its way toward modern efficiency.

In Industry

The usufacture stage. When we speak of manufacturing we are prone to think of it as something of very modern development, something connected with noisy factories, crowded storehouses, and trusts; but when we come to analyze the word, we find it means simply "making by hand." When the farmer takes the wheat he has raised and turns it into flour, which the housewife makes up into bread, they have together been occupied in manufacturing. In this broad sense, as we have seen in Chapter I, primitive manufacture began in the dawn of history, and went through several marked stages of progress in ancient times and in the Middle Ages.

At first almost all manufacture was for home use (hence the word "usufacture," or "making for use"), with no thought of sale in the minds of the makers. Usually the work was all performed by members of the household, although occasionally an outside helper was hired, just as many families employ seamstresses today. With the advent of outside labor the wage question may be said to have originated, but in those days there was no labor problem. This was because most laborers owned homes and plots of land and hence were not dependent on wages.

As time advanced, the question of capital appeared. Certain equipment, such as a wine press, a gristmill, or a bake-oven aided manufacturing greatly, but was too expensive or elaborate for every family to possess. Raw materials were then brought to the owners of these machines, and a fee paid them for the use of their capital. Under the manor system the lord was in essence a petty capitalist, but for all this the processes of manufacturing were simple and within the reach of all.

Since there was little specialization there was little skill; products were crude; but there were no such things as high prices or business failures to worry one, and each man was free to put in his spare time at whatever task appealed to him.

The handicraft system. With the decline of the manor system and the growth of towns, manufacturing for sale came largely to take the place of usufacture, although manufacture for home consumption has continued to exist in every country of the world down to the present time. On the manors there had been some carpenters, cobblers, smiths, and other men who specialized in the production of articles, but in the town the crafts found an environment eminently fitted to their growth and development. Domesday Book (1086) contains an account of those who gathered around the monastery of Bury St. Edmunds: "bakers, ale-brewers, tailors, cooks, shoemakers, . . . and robemakers."

These workmen, having been freed from all manorial services, could now devote their whole time to one occupation. No longer did each family construct, with little or no outside help, all the necessary articles for its consumption. The new method of production came to be called the handicraft system. It produced the most skilled workmen the world has ever known, but it was also responsible for the faint beginnings of many of the real problems of capital, labor, and prices which today have become the burning issues of life.

In the first stages of this system practically no capital was needed, for the craftsman either went to the house of the man who wished a job done or else the man came to him. In both cases the consumer furnished the raw material, and the only capital needed by the craftsman was his tools. The next step came when the craftsman invested some of his earnings in raw materials. He still made articles only upon order and so received his returns from one job before he began another. This "custom order" practice is followed today by many tailors and milliners. The next step demanded an increase in capital, for the craftsman began to make a surplus in the hopes of a chance sale. Soon he came to make things up in quantities so that customers could take their choice from a variety of ready-made articles. This necessitated more capital still, to be tied up for indefinite periods in finished products for consumption It also meant the employing of assistants, who were not owners but merely hired workers. The profits remained in the hands of the master craftsman in return for his invested capital, his reputation as a tradesman, and his risk in foretelling demand So among the socially and economically equal inhabitants of the town there arose the first signs of a class division between those who employed men and received profits and those who worked for the employers at set wages.[1]

As time went on these first divisions were sharpened, and other new ones appeared in almost every craft. The head man possessing capital in the form of a shop, tools, raw materials, and surplus finished products was called the master After the masters became established as a separate class, it grew increasingly harder for a worker to enter that rank. Now he must needs spend from three to thirteen years as an apprentice, learning the craft, while living at the house of his master. After this he became a journeyman with the right to go out and work for wages by the day (*journée*), but not to set up a shop Finally, after some years in this capacity, he was allowed at last to enter the class of masters, provided he had saved the necessary capital.

Rules for apprenticeship and craftsmanship were made and rigidly enforced by the guilds. During the twelfth century all the merchants, traders, and craftsmen of one town were joined in the Guild Merchant. After the thirteenth century men of each craft were organized in their own craft guilds. Both kinds of guilds admitted mere journeymen to membership, but the power and authority became more and more concentrated in the hands of the masters.

[1] Note that all this development had previously taken place among several ancient peoples, but all memory of it having passed away in the Middle Ages, the whole process was gone through again

Thus, as the sixteenth century advanced, we find that the guilds made ever and ever stricter regulations to build up a protective wall around the masters. Economic conditions were such as to further this division in the manufacturing class. More complicated tools and machines became necessary, and further capital was needed to secure more raw materials and to provide the finished products awaiting sale. So the master and the workman in the same craft, once closely knit by common interest, now began to find their interests different and to disagree as to the terms of their coöperation. The employee thought he was being paid too little; and as he could no longer look forward to the happy days when he himself would be a master, he had a distinct grievance. Since journeymen no longer received the best benefits from the craft guild, they began to organize into journeymen's associations—the first real labor unions. The function of these organizations seems primarily social, but there is sufficient evidence to prove their early use for raising wages. The problem of capital and labor, which was to become one of the burning issues of our life today, had sprung into existence before the end of the Middle Ages.

So also had arisen the problem of just prices. When each family no longer made all the articles for its own consumption, and things must be bought and sold, then the problem of exchange value in terms of money became a matter of everyday importance. The various guilds attempted to regulate prices, upon the theory that no article should be sold for more than its cost of production; but to determine all the things which entered into the cost of production was a difficult matter. It soon became evident that the guild regulations on the staples of life, such as meat, bread, and ale, were grossly unjust. The power to set such prices was therefore turned over to the city magistrates. By the beginning of the sixteenth century the guilds were deprived of even the right to set prices on their own goods, and it became the general practice to settle prices by higgling (that is, by private bargaining) between buyer and seller. Thus early was it worked out that the fairest price to both consumer and producer resulted from their mutual agreement on the basis of the free adjustment between the supply of and the demand for each article of trade.

The domestic system. Toward the end of the fifteenth century there sprang up in rural communities a type of manufacture which practically superseded the handicraft system and became the forerunner of the modern factory system. The keynote of the new manufacturing was that it was done in the home again instead of in craft shops, and, what is vastly more important, the products were not made for direct sale to the consumer, but went instead into the hands of a middleman These men, called clothiers, since most of the manufacturing done in this way was in the textile industry, bought up raw materials, especially wool, and gave it out to the country craftsmen. Each part of the productive process—carding, combing, spinning, weaving, and fulling—was performed in a different home. The clothier then saw to the selling of the finished product. The clothier was really a capitalist, using a system very similar to that of the "sweated" industries of today.

Several definite results were noticeable: a slow shift of population and wealth from town to country; greater competition for jobs among the workers, and hence lower wages, frequently poorer conditions for working, increased employment of women and children Since most of the workers became combined artisans and peasants, they turned out poorer work, but they acquired the status and spirit of economic independence.

Many of the laborers were, however, unable to hold their independent position They borrowed money from the merchant capitalists for tools and for debts contracted during periods of sickness or unemployment When they were unable to pay back their borrowings they were often forced to give up their homes and small fields, thus becoming as dependent upon their wages as their town brethren.

As long as the English peasant combined agriculture with his trade, he was fairly sure of a roof and some kind of food;

but when he became dependent on wages only, his condition was far less secure. This was the status of production and society when the Industrial Revolution swept away the old order and established the modern factory system.

In Commerce

The revival of trade. The ninth to the seventeenth century brought even greater economic changes to commerce than to industry. The era began with almost no exchange of goods and ended with a world commerce well established. The early manorial village was notable for its economic self-sufficiency, which ordinarily made commerce unnecessary. But there were many years in which bad harvests reduced the yield below the necessary minimum. As commercial facilities were lacking since the decay of the Roman roads, starvation resulted. In good years, on the other hand, there was a surplus which cried to be marketed or exchanged for goods not obtainable within the confines of the manor. These two needs operated to reestablish the flourishing trade of Roman days.

The first exchange of goods came between the scattered manors owned by one lord. On one manor most easily reached by all a local market was opened periodically, perhaps once a week for a single day. Country produce was here bought and sold: straw, wood, ale, cattle, bread, leather, dairy produce, and fish. Desire for articles from afar and for a wider market in which to sell the surplus led to the establishment of another kind of trading place called a fair.

Fairs. The fair was usually held in the open fields with a semblance of streets produced by the rows of booths and stalls, which were assigned to the various merchants. Here could be found not only the neighborhood producers but salesmen with luxuries from afar: woolen cloth from Flanders; linens and laces from France; wines from Italy; drugs, spices, and silks from the Orient. The fairs not only offered a place to buy and sell, but afforded opportunity for amusement in the way of side shows of trained animals, actors, musicians, and dancers. These great social and economic events were institutions throughout Europe from the twelfth through the fourteenth century. In France the great fairs were those of St. Denis, near Paris, and several in Champagne; in Flanders at Bruges, in Germany at Cologne, Leipzig, and Frankfurt; in England at Cambridge, Winchester, and St. Ives; and in Russia at Nizhni Novgorod. They were annual or semiannual affairs lasting from two to six weeks. They were very frequently centered about some great religious day and hence accompanied by feasts and festivals. During the fifteenth and sixteenth centuries fairs began a definite decline. They were no longer the chief marts of trade, for the markets of the towns became permanent and replaced periodic exchange.

The overcoming of trade obstacles. There were many obstacles in the way of trade during the Middle Ages, such as lack of proper nautical devices, piracy at sea and incessant warfare on land, impassable highways with excessive toll levies, and a scarcity of money. Piracy flourished with scarcely a check until modern times, and highway robbery was almost as common. Robbery became, in fact, an almost respectable profession for whole bands of outlaws, sometimes of noble blood. Little was done to repair the old Roman roads, and no new ones were constructed. Traveling merchants banded themselves together into caravans to reduce the danger from assault and robbery and to afford mutual help and cheer along the way.

Even when a trip was free from illegal pillage, it was beset by endless feudal tolls. Every feudal lord over whose territory a traveler passed demanded fees for the upkeep of roads and bridges which were not kept up. If an economical merchant tried to reduce the high cost of travel by going under or around a bridge, he was nevertheless forced to pay the toll. There were about twenty different kinds of tolls assessable on the traveling merchant, and in return for all of them he was given neither safe nor comfortable passage. The building of new roads was discouraged by avaricious lords, and trade in general was burdened, constrained, and heavily hampered by this system of legalized robbery.

As time passed something was accomplished to better conditions in most of these respects, and trade became less risky and difficult as a result. The compass, which had been known in the Far East for centuries, came into common use in European waters by 1300 and made navigation between continents possible. It was early recognized that commerce cannot flourish in war or civil turmoil, and the market cross soon became the emblem of peaceful commercial intercourse. At first kings proclaimed a special peace, with increased damages for violation, during the period of many of the fairs. Later there were established special courts in market places, called, in England, piepowder courts.[1]

These courts gave speedy settlement to commercial disputes on such matters as debts, contracts, and sales. This new law was called the law merchant, and was the beginning of modern commercial and business law

Another thing which hampered all trade transactions was the scarcity of money and the regulations of both State and Church restricting lending Money was believed to be a sterile thing, which, like sterile soils, could not bear anything. Hence it was decreed that although money might be lent, no additional amount could be asked for its use. The whole institution of interest, so scientifically practiced in ancient times, had been lost when Roman business went down at the end of the empire.

The thing which we call interest today was known as "usury" and as such was forbidden [2] Since Jews were not members of the established church, and hence not bound by its decrees, they became the money lenders of the Middle Ages. In countries where there were legal as well as ecclesiastical prohibitions on usury the Jews usually were able, in return for repeated

---

[1] "Piepowder," French *pied poudreux* ("dusty foot") *Curia pedis pulverizati*, "court of the dusty foot", that is, a court for peddlers

[2] The fate of a medieval usurer is most picturesquely presented in Hamilton's "Current Economic Problems," No 17.

gifts, to secure an exemption from the king The unpopularity of the Jews was increased during these centuries because of the exorbitant rates charged by them for loans and their frequent ruthlessness in collecting to the last cent upon the set day. Business was thus greatly hampered by the difficulties and hardships of securing capital. Commercial expansion would have had distinct limits had not some way of getting around these difficulties been invented.

The credit for this device goes to the Italians, who, in the thirteenth century, came into England and set up money exchanges and banks. These Lombards, as the Englishmen called them, brought in a clever innovation. It was a device to evade the usury laws of the land, and it was called interest. They would lend a sum of money to a feudal lord, merchant, or even to the king for a set period, say one week, without charging usury, but with the understanding that it was not to be returned for perhaps one month and one week, and on the month period interest would be charged as damages for not having returned the sum at the date specified in the contract. Other money lenders soon adopted this clever ruse. Before long interest was generally charged, and the term "usury" came to mean excessive rates of interest.

In this way interest, without which modern business could not be carried on, came into use. Without interest modern men of capital would do exactly what many medieval men did, hide their money in secret treasure-troves for a time of great need, or spend it recklessly for whatever they most wanted. Without interest we should have few loans and investments, and modern industry is founded on the lending and investment of money.

Early business organization. The hardships of trade in the Middle Ages led to the establishment of business associations, among which the old Roman partnership was at first the most popular. Usually the partnership consisted of one man who furnished money, wares, and perhaps a ship, and another who gave only his personal services, for which he received approximately one fourth of the profits. As trade flourished the need for a stronger and larger association produced the *regulated company*. By this device many merchants could cooperate through mere payment of a fee and obedience to certain rules. Each merchant furnished his own capital and kept his own profits, there was no pooling of resources. But there was a gain through protection from attack by transporting cargoes in fleets or pack trains and through the sharing of losses due to storm or fire. Examples of famous English regulated companies are the Moscovy Company for Russia and the Levant Company for Turkey.

The Hanseatic League. The most famous continental combination for commerce was not a regulated company, but a loose organization of groups of merchants from such German cities as Hamburg, Bremen, and Lübeck. This Hansa, as it was called, possessed franchises for operating in all the northern countries and maintained trading posts, known as "factories," at London, Bergen in Norway, Bruges in the Netherlands, Novgorod in Russia, and some seventy other places. The leaguers were bound by defensive and, at times, offensive alliances for trade purposes. This potential power, brought about by coöperation, won for the merchants lenient concessions from the European states, with the result that the Hansa dominated the north-European trade from the end of the fourteenth into the early seventeenth century.[1]

The joint-stock company. A more advanced form of commercial organization which became popular and practically supplanted the regulated company in European countries was the joint-stock company. By this device merchants pooled their capital and shared their profits. Management was placed in the hands of a few efficient participators, thus allowing such people as women and children to contribute to the enterprise by investment of capital without actually engaging in the busi-

---

[1] For a map of the Hanseatic Commercial Empire see Day's "History of Commerce," p 106, and, for a fuller description, Osgood's "History of Industry," pp. 169–173.

ness. In addition to this advantage of more available capital there was a wider distribution of risk and a gain in the permanence of the company. The joint-stock company was so efficient in overcoming the obstacles to trade that at least a hundred of such organizations developed into noteworthy undertakings. They added political power to their commercial functions and became as a result the chief actors in the colonial dramas which led to over a century of commercial wars. The joint-stock principle later became the basis of the modern corporation.

Not even the keenest man living in 1600 seems to have stopped to generalize on what the economic events of the Middle Ages really meant There was no abstract reasoning as to the relationships of causal and resultant events. But we of today, who have many carefully formulated economic laws and principles at our command, can look back and see that during these centuries certain natural laws were in operation; that, for instance, supply and demand played an important part in everyday life, although their presence was unrecognized. When, for instance, a pestilence reduced the labor supply, wages rose; and when inclosures lessened the demand for labor, wages fell. When droughts reduced the food supply, prices mounted, and when ambitious master craftsmen produced more than the local market could consume, prices fell. Even money was proved to be no different in its value variations from other commodities; for when it was virtually increased in supply through the repeated debasing of coins by the kings in the sixteenth century, it fell in value. But since its supposed value was stamped on its face and did not therefore lend itself to easy change, that face value was maintained, while its decreased real value was expressed in terms of the smaller quantity of commodities it would buy, or, in other words, in increased general prices.

Another lesson of the past which might well have been deduced from the passing of events was that *no governmental regulation made contrary to natural laws can be enforced except at a great cost, with complicated machinery, and then only for a short time.* Repeated enactments of the Statute of Laborers failed to reduce either wages or prices, and laws against forestalling, regrating, and engrossing failed to kill off the middleman in the infancy of his functioning. Conditions are not greatly changed today; economists have formulated economic laws pretty clearly, but governments are still acting as if man's will expressed in a statute law could successfully combat the operating force of a natural law.

SUPPLEMENTARY READINGS

CHEYNEY, E. P. Industrial and Social History of England (revised), chaps. ii–vi.

DAY, CLIVE. History of Commerce, Part II.

HAMILTON, W. H. Current Economic Problems, Nos. 3, 4, 12, 14, 15, 17, 75, 78.

OSGOOD, ELLEN. A History of Industry, chaps. vii, viii, xvi.

ROBINSON, J. H., BREASTED, J. H., and SMITH, E. P. General History of Europe, pp. 211–214, 248–258.

WEBSTER, W. C. A General History of Commerce, Part II, chaps. v–xiii.

ZIMMERN, HELEN. The Hansa Towns, pp. 30–47, 82–125.

SEARCH QUESTIONS AND PROBLEMS

1. What kind of agricultural implements are used in your community? Are any of them practically the same as those used in the Middle Ages? Observe carefully and report to the class.

2. Is your community a self-sufficient economic unit? What is produced there in entirety? Would you suffer if all the railroads near you were destroyed? Why, and how much?

3. Can you think of any practice of today similar to the subinfeudation of medieval times? What difference is there?

4. Do we have any theories or practices today which infer that possession of property may confer ownership? Has such a theory ever greatly influenced American history?

5. If one third to one half our population had been swept away by the Spanish influenza, what would have been the effect on wages, prices, and labor legislation? Was an effect comparable to that of 1350–1380 brought about in 1917–1918 by other causes?

ECONOMIC CONTRIBUTIONS OF MIDDLE AGES

6. Does your state make laws on wages? If so, what? If not, find out the wage laws of the nearest state having them. What national legislation has there been on wages? How do all these laws differ in purpose from the Statute of Laborers? (Consult yearbooks.)

7. Name two commodities upon which the national government practiced price regulation during the war. What device did it use concerning sugar which served to keep its price down?

8. Write a report of the medieval fairs based on several of the following references. *Harper's Magazine*, Vol XLVI, pp 376ff, Bowine's "The Romance of Trade," chap III, Walford's "Fairs Past and Present"; Osgood's "History of Industry," pp 123–126; Ben Jonson's "Bartholomew Fair"; Bullock's "Selected Readings in Economics," pp. 325–331

9. Does your county hold a fair? your state? If so, contrast them with those you have just studied.

10. On an outline map of Europe trace the various important medieval sea and land trade routes, locating about twenty important trading ports or centers Underscore those cities which are still of commercial importance Compare your map with a railroad map of modern Europe. What do you find?

11. Let some member of the class construct a rude compass by magnetizing a steel needle and floating it on a cork in a basin of water. Check its accuracy by means of a modern compass.

12. Contrast the sending of a crate of oranges from Florida to your home town with the medieval transportation of a case of wine from Orleans to London, in such matters as time, expense, danger, convenience, condition upon arrival, etc.

13. Do you think it would pay a modern small American town to keep a village common similar to those of medieval communities? Why?

14. Read an account of the Jacquerie in a French history. Was anything whatever gained? How do you explain this?

15. Do you know of any kind of home craft now practiced which is really a return to the domestic system?

16. Is the milliner who makes a hat to order still in the handicraft stage of production?

17. Is it necessary for you to serve an apprenticeship if you want to enter a trade in America today?

18. How did the guilds differ from the present trade unions? from employers' associations? from a chamber of commerce?

CHAPTER III

MEDIEVAL SOCIAL AND POLITICAL GAINS

What legislator cannot see that the history of our American municipalities throws light upon the republics of the Middle Ages, and derives light from them?—ANDREW D WHITE

SOCIAL ORGANIZATION AND IDEALS

Class divisions. The Middle Ages witnessed great changes in the organization, ideals, and general welfare of society at large. At its beginning the complicated social organization of the Roman Empire had almost entirely passed away, and the peoples of Europe were everywhere living in the simple clan and tribal groupings of a primitive age. There were no such things as class divisions. Every man was every other man's equal unless his age or valor put him on a higher level, and even then there were no barriers to set him off permanently from his fellow men.

This social equality was entirely destroyed by the introduction of the manor system. One whole group of people set themselves up as a superior class The line between nobility and non-nobility was drawn with a forbidding sharpness. Most of the non-nobles were reduced to a status of semislavery known as serfdom, although some few remained freemen. The serf, or villein, could not own land, travel off the manor without consent, or desert the land. He was not, however, an outright slave, for he possessed personal property, could not be deprived of his right to cultivate some land, and could not be sold on the block as the American negro was later. He was inferior to all freemen, but superior to the outright slaves, who continued to exist in small numbers in England until the eleventh century. The gross injustice of such a system of class division is obvious when we recall that the serf had often been before his conquest superior in character, intellect, and holdings to his conqueror.

As time passed the basis for class division changed from might to blood. The son of a serf was doomed to serfdom, and the conqueror's son remained always noble.

Social subdivision. Among the nobility themselves there grew up social subdivisions. The smaller landholders and in England the younger sons of the great barons became the gentry. They mingled with the non-noble freemen and later with the freed serf. Intermarriages occurred, and eventually it came about that in interest and status the gentry, as they were called, belonged rather to a new middle class than to the higher nobility. In fact it was their union with the rising freemen which made for England the substantial middle class upon which her governmental democracy was to be founded.[1] Above the gentry the major nobility graded up imperceptibly to the king himself, who was the greatest noble of all. The many officials of the Church formed together an ecclesiastical class by themselves. Social equality had no place in the manorial and feudal régime

Social lines continued to be clear-cut in the rural districts even after the downfall of the manor system. As we have seen, the old lords and their descendants became owners of the soil, while the freemen and ex-serfs became renters or day laborers. In England these class lines have existed down to the present time.

With the growth of the towns there came a revival of class equality The freed serfs worked and played together with no thoughts of class distinctions. But this spirit of social equality was short-lived. With the growing importance of capital in

---

[1] The best picture we have of the life of the English gentry is in the Sir Roger de Coverley papers It must be remembered, however, that this portrays the life of an English country gentleman several centuries after the period we are here studying

economic life, the possessors of capital began to set themselves up as a wealthy middle class superior to the common laborers. This distinction was not completed without the aid of the new factory system of manufacturing, but it was without a shadow of doubt begun before the modern era.

Changing ideals. The changes in the organization of society were reflected in the changing ideals of the Middle Ages. Under the simple clan life brotherly kindness and coöperation combined with a deep respect for one's elders were the virtues to be inculcated in children.

During the feudal era the ideal of the servile class seemed to be nothing more than merely a desire to exist, tinged with a faint hope of regaining freedom. The nobility, on the other hand, developed highly complicated standards of conduct and thought, some of which have remained to the present time the objects of admiration and emulation. When one speaks of a man as "gentlemanly" or "chivalrous" one adopts the terms as well as some of the standards of feudalism. The ideals and practices of knighthood are generally known as chivalry. In the beginning the ideals were only those of a Teutonic warrior, such as courage and loyalty to one's lord. As time progressed during the eleventh and twelfth centuries, certain ideals tinged with Christianity crept in, such as brotherly love, courtesy, fidelity to a lady-love, to one's plighted word, and to God, with protection of the weak and generosity toward the needy. Honest work was no part of a knight's code.

Both the good and the evil of knighthood have come down through the ages. A man is chivalrous who gives up his seat to a woman, or who protects her in an emergency. Courtesy demands that people rise when their elders enter the room, and that they follow instead of precede them through a door. Charitableness to the weak and needy is admirable. Fidelity to his word is the mark of a gentleman. Most people do not go to extremes in their observance of these ideals, and many people have not advanced beyond the crudest medieval concept of virtue. For instance, most people think of physical bravery as the meaning of the word "courage." And during the World War there were people who quoted with approval the motto "My country, right or wrong."

The idea of class distinction in etiquette is still to be found One has seen men who offer their seats in crowded street cars to women of their own social standing, while scrub-women continue to hang to a strap. Such men still hold the ideal of the medieval knight, who acknowledged the claim to courtesy of his own class of women only.

The chief shortcomings of medieval chivalry were, then, a courage chiefly physical, a blind loyalty, and a limiting of courtesies to one class. Chivalry was in truth the flower of feudalism, but its fragrance was only for a chosen few.[1] The ideals of chivalry became the social code of rural England.

The townsman's ideals. But with the growth of towns new social ideals appeared. Trade and industry held out the promise of wealth and power. Labor took on dignity and became honorable in the eyes of the townsmen. The yeomen farmers or renters in rural England possessed this same view of work, and joined with the townsmen to form a substantial middle class from which came many of the founders of America. Thus the new town ideals became the very corner stone of American life American conditions favored their retention and development The vast lands of the new continent demanded labor from all. So American ideals place honest work in a high place and condemn idleness, whether it be caused by laziness or by great riches. England has not been so fortunate in her heritage There the attitude of early nobles and gentlemen has come down through the ages and proved a great stumblingblock to social democracy However, the economic changes of recent times have modified the old stratification even in England, where there is now more shifting from class to class than formerly.

[1] Chivalry at its best is portrayed in the tales of King Arthur and the knights of the Round Table Cervantes, in "Don Quixote,' has given us the best satire on the subject, although most American boys prefer Mark Twain's "A Connecticut Yankee in King Arthur's Court"

Social Welfare

The centuries of the Middle Ages witnessed many ups and downs in the general welfare of society at large. Some people would have us believe that the primitive clansman living his simple life was better off than any of his later brothers in more civilized times. In that early period no one ever starved unless the whole group starved; all were equally well off or ill off. But few of us today would be willing to go back to such a life of monotony, discomfort, and ignorance.

Manorialism brought to a few people added comforts, leisure time, and varied ways of refreshing and educating the mind. But what of the many? The condition of the serf on the manor was inferior to that of the free villager who preceded him. He had no hope of ever becoming more than his father had been before him. It took only a few generations of this sort of life to produce degraded mortals robbed of their self-respect, villeins with no political rights and with very limited civil privileges. A serf's life was narrow and filled with few joys. He had only to live from day to day, eking out an existence. There was no incentive to accumulate a surplus, because he must always share it with another who had in no way helped to earn it. Pride, ambition, thrift, could find no rooting-place in so barren a soil.

But even with so few comforts, there were some advantages not possessed by the freed serfs in the centuries following the break-up of the manor system.

Alleviation. Many of the villeins in England threw off the bonds of serfdom at a peculiarly propitious time, when wages were abnormally high owing to the fact that all labor had been materially reduced by the great plague (1347-1349). At first prices were equally high owing to the food shortage, but nature soon furnished a normal supply, and the real wages, that is, the amount of goods the money wage will buy, remained high until into the sixteenth century. The ratio between wages and the cost of the necessities of life was so favorable that this period might be said to be the Golden Age for English labor Wealth was so abundant that the artisans or town workers were able to accumulate capital without being forced to overwork. Never were wages so high nor prices so low.

Defects of the age. But Utopia was by no means reached; the age had some very decided drawbacks. Very little was done to produce or safeguard health. Vegetables were not eaten in sufficient quantities nor in all seasons, and the lack of preservatives, excepting salt, necessitated the use of tainted meat. These two errors in diet produced such diseases as scurvy.[1] Contagious diseases were common, and science had as yet invented no means of preventing their spread. Yet the picture painted by some historians, of excessive typhus and leprosy, is probably not true. There was probably more general good health than there is today, for people's bodies were stronger and did not succumb to slight diseases as they do now.

Another defect of the age was the recurrence of famine. Usually there was food enough for all, but when droughts or insect enemies ruined the crops in one region of the world, there was no well-organized system of transportation to secure the surplus of another region. However, there rarely occurred such a thing in the fifteenth century as may be found today a family starving in one place, while a few miles away another family throws into the garbage can enough to feed half a dozen mouths.

The houses of that day were not so well built nor so comfortable as a standard house of today, but there were plenty of them. In the country they were given rent free, with a garden plot thrown in, to the agricultural laborer as well as to the tenant. There were as yet no rent profiteers in the towns.

A period of decline. In the sixteenth century the lot of the workingman began a gradual steady decline which lasted well on into the middle of the seventeenth century. Everything

---

[1] A parallel case of the present time is the prevalence of beriberi among the Chinese because they eat polished rice as almost their only food The minerals in the rice are in the outer coat, which is lost in the polishing process Americans are just now coming to realize this and to demand coated, or whole, rice.

combined to make prices high and wages low. Money was cheapened by the inflow of precious metals from South and Central America and by the repeated debasing of coins by kings from 1527 to 1551. The royal purse gained by this procedure, but the common people suffered. If a coin had only half as much silver as formerly, then the storekeepers would consider it worth only half what it had been before. Since its face value was fixed, the easiest thing was to double the price of commodities. In this way a dollar may be said to shrink in value.

Prices rose not only because money fell in value, but because commodities declined in supply. In England agricultural produce was lessened by the converting of wheat lands into inclosures for raising sheep. Since the amount of wheat produced was less but the population remained the same, each bushel was worth more than formerly.

The inclosures for grazing lowered wages. Peasant proprietors lost their holdings to the wealthy landlords and became hired laborers. The supply of laborers thereby became too great, because it takes fewer men to carry on grazing than grain-raising, and the towns had no industrial openings to employ the surplus labor. When laborers tried to change this condition by combining to ask for better terms, the upper classes passed through their parliament in 1550 a law prohibiting all meetings, combinations, and contracts which sought in any way to advance wages.

At the close of the medieval era peasants and artisans possessed their independence again, as they had at its beginning; but with most of them owning no homes or land to produce the needed supply of food, with prices of everything high, and wages both low and uncertain, it is not to be wondered at that some historians feel that seven hundred years of so-called progress had done little to make better the lot of the common man.

Sharing the King's Power

Clan government. The opening of the Middle Ages found the peoples of Europe living with no more thought of the great governmental institutions and practices of the Persians, Greeks, and Romans than they had of their economic or social life. It was as if man were to begin all over again on his march of advancement. The simplicity of clan life did not demand anything in the way of complicated government. Whenever there arose problems, such as whether to take part in the warfare against a neighboring tribe, or how to punish some member of their own clan who was suspected of practicing witchcraft, the men of the clan gathered together in general meeting, discussed the question pro and con, and acted in accordance with the will of the majority. There were no written laws, no policemen or sheriffs, and no prisons.

Development of real government. As the social unit grew through the union of clans for protection or the conquest of whole groups of clans by one fighting tribe, this simple type of informal government came to be insufficient to meet the expanding needs. Peoples were no longer grouped on the blood basis into small and separate clans, but associated in large geographical units (which had been again evolved from the earlier blood divisions). At the head of each nation was the greatest military leader, now universally called king. When need arose for common action this king called unto him a number of great and wise men from all parts of the realm. With the advice of these chosen few, he proclaimed the customs of the past as the law of the land. Enforcement of these so-called "dooms" was left to local groups of important men.

In England—and we are most interested in this country because it is from her that most of our governmental practices and customs have come—this process of making a strong centralized state with a monarchical government was hastened and made successful by the conquest of William of Normandy. He assumed a real and active headship over all England, and with a group of his military favorites who became his land tenants in the feudal régime he worked out a central government composed of the king and a council called the Curia Regis.

Now it was obviously impossible for such a small group to carry on without assistance all the governmental functions needed in so large a state To begin with, the feudal age was primarily an age of warfare, and the greatest service needed from the State was protection from enemies abroad and wrongdoers at home. To meet this first need the king required from every one of his tenants forty days of military service for each knight's fee (that is, for each piece of land large enough to produce an income sufficient to equip one knight with steed, armor, and war trappings). The king's tenants in turn made a similar demand from all the underlords to whom they sublet land. Thus it was that the army at the command of the king for protection or conquest was not a national army, drawn from all classes by means of volunteering or conscription, but a feudal army based on private contracts between the nobility and the king. This remained the case until the slow death of feudalism necessitated a change.

So it was also as regards the keeping of law and order at home. All aggrieved persons could not travel to London to present their cases in the king's courts, so each feudal lord was allowed the privilege of administering justice on his own estates. As the years went on and the need for courts to try cases between freemen and lords increased, the government did establish public courts, so-called king's courts, throughout the land. Because of the greater justice obtained there these courts grew rapidly in popularity, but it was not until feudalism passed away in the fifteenth century that the administration of justice became wholly a public affair.

As the centuries of the Middle Ages rolled by the machinery of government grew more complicated. In addition to the feudal courts there were local justices of the peace, traveling king's justices, juries for accusation and trial, and an ever-increasing number of public officials. Laws were no longer confined to the "dooms," but included now not only the unwritten customary practices of the past, called common law, but a new set of statute laws enacted by legislators sitting in parliaments.

Government had become by 1600 a necessary and beneficial thing. It maintained peace and order; it protected private property; it made some provision for supporting the poor; it made unnecessary the blood revenge and clan feuds of tribal days. True it had not yet progressed far enough to protect public health or morals, it did nothing to foster free public education, and in its operation it always favored a small, privileged social class. Much had been accomplished, but much more was left for the modern age to do.

The genesis of limited monarchy. English feudalism must be credited not only with the honor of assisting in making a strong centralized government but with contributing an idea which outlived feudalism and resulted in changing the absolute monarchy of England into a limited monarchy That idea was the contract principle, and its establishment through feudalism, in the words of the great American historian George Burton Adams, "has made the [English] constitution as it exists today possible."[1]

When William the Conqueror introduced Norman feudalism he did not consciously or purposely modify it, but the very conditions of the Conquest tended to make the terms of the feudal contract between lord and tenant much more clear-cut and uniform than on the Continent, where they were the outcome of centuries of varying development instead of the result of a five-year conquest. It was impossible for a king, bound down by contracts, no matter how tyrannically inclined he might be, to demand more of his subjects than the terms of their agreement. But the contracts were not written, as are most contracts today, and so there were frequent disagreements as to just what were the exact terms of the original

[1] G B Adams, "The Critical Period of English Constitutional History," in *American Historical Review*, Vol. V, pp 651–652.

agreement. This happened repeatedly in the decades and centuries following 1066 and led to frequent troubles.

When disagreements arose during the reign of a strong king, such as William I or Henry II, then the nobles were the losers. Under weaker sovereigns, however, the barons made good their claims and even won from Henry I a written acknowledgment.

The crisis of this century and a half of struggle over contract terms came in the reign of John. He was a weak, unpopular, and unwise king. He broke every provision of his feudal contracts, and alienated the affections of the clergy and of non-noble people. The revolt which came in 1215 was not wholly a feudal revolt, therefore, though it was chiefly carried out by the barons; and most of the provisions in the great written contract of Magna Carta which John was forced to sign are feudal in character. It has now been proved that the charter of Henry I was produced at this time by a clergyman, and no doubt suggested a solution of the problem. The Great Charter contained provisions for the creation of a group of twenty-five barons to see that the king kept his word.

It has been said by some historian that England has been peculiarly blessed by having good sovereigns and bad sovereigns mixed in just the right proportions and at the right times. The years following John's reign illustrate this well. If strong kings had come, then this charter, like the earlier ones, might have fallen into disuse. On the other hand, at John's death his eldest son was but nine years old, and during that long minority the charter was reissued three times. The rule of the country was, moreover, in the hands of the feudal council of tenants in chief, which, since the days of the Conquest, had acted as an advisory body as well as a judicial court for the king. When Henry III did grow to manhood he was mean, extravagant, and weak, being just the kind of king who would call forth renewals of the charter.

It was well for the rapid progress of constitutional government that Henry III broke the charter quite as frequently as he pledged to obey it. By 1258 the barons gave up hoping to hold Henry to it without the aid of a specially appointed group to watch over him. They again resorted to the device used in Magna Carta, of a group of barons. This device failed, but the idea remained that a king was bound to preserve customs and was not an arbitrary creature responsible to God alone. There is no regret that the baronial council provided for in the Provisions of Oxford failed to hold the king responsible. It was an aristocratic device, and had it solved the problem it would not have led to the entrance of the middle classes into the government nearly so soon, and democracy, therefore, would have been slower in coming.

In 1311 the device of putting the government into the hands of a group of nobles was tried once again. It worked no better than it had before, and as a last resort the king was deposed. This new device for holding a king to account was not forgotten. In 1399 Richard II was deposed. Feudalism was waning; soon the group of people holding the king to account were no longer his own vassals, but Parliament, a body supposedly representing the nation at large. It must always be remembered, though, that popular representation would have done the people of England no more good than it did the fourth estate in France, had it not been that out of the feudal-contract idea had arisen the genesis of limited monarchy.

The Extension of Self-government

The beginnings of local self-government. Government, as we have seen, developed hand in hand with the system of feudalism, and in England that development was ever toward greater and greater centralization. Now within the growing state there was one group which was unalterably opposed to all that feudalism stood for. This was the towns. They stood for peace, so necessary to industry and trade, whereas feudalism was a system dependent on wars for vitality and usefulness. The feudal lords wished to treat the townsmen as serfs, the townsmen were bound to assert their personal freedom. Thus there grew up a feeling of enmity which resulted in two centuries of warfare, from 1100 to 1300. To gain their ends required not only the military prowess of the townsmen, but their accumulated wealth also. Success came to the towns in the form of liberal grants of privileges, usually secured by a city charter; and thereby was born local self-government.

Townsmen were usually given the right to elect their own local officers (provost, mayor, burgomaster, etc.) and to pay their dues, rents, tolls, and fines to the national government in a fixed lump sum. This meant that the royal officers could no longer increase either valuation of property or percentage of taxes in their canvass of the town. Henceforth the town's own officials apportioned and collected the taxes as they saw fit, and presented them to the royal emissary at the gates. Another important concession was that townsmen were to have courts of their own (called burghmoots in England), free from both royal and feudal domination, wherein all their cases should be tried.

Variety of town institutions. It would, indeed, be interesting if we could make some general statements on the status of actual government within the towns, but on this it is impossible to generalize. Almost no two towns or cities had the same form of internal government. Many of the smaller ones retained the pure democratic features of their Greek prototypes; others, such as Venice and London, became oligarchies in which small groups of people were allowed the franchise and a smaller number yet held the offices. Sometimes magistrates chose their own successors and thus insured an even narrower rule. In some cities, especially on the Continent, "tyrants" seized control (as in Milan) and established absolute monarchy.

No matter what the form of the government, the degree to which it controlled the inhabitants is a surprise to us of today. When the "curfew" (*couvre feu*) rang at eight or nine o'clock, fires and lights must be put out. The medieval townsman could buy his wife no richer jewels, nor have more candles at her funeral, nor plant more trees in his garden than was allowed by law. Such regulations were no doubt irritating enough to the citizens, but they were far more welcome than the bondage of serfdom under which most of the townsmen had once lived. Very little complaint seems to have been made, at least for a long time, against the exactions of the local government. What the townsmen did strive for was noninterference from feudal or royal sources.

The chief aim of all towns was complete independence. They seemed to be conscious of the fact that they were alien units in a feudal civilization, forerunners of an advanced age. They also saw that their progress depended on complete isolation. On the Continent this goal was obtained. In France the period of isolation was short-lived. First, the kings allied themselves with the "communes," as they were called, in order to crush their common enemies, the powerful independent nobles; later, strengthened in their absolutism by the decline of feudalism, the kings turned against their helpers. As early as 1400 the French towns had become subject to the absolute monarchy.

In Germany, where the government failed to become centralized, the cities remained independent. They were sovereign members of the various German confederations, and three of them (Lübeck, Bremen, and Hamburg) kept their separate governments even after the formation of the modern German Empire (1871).

In Italy they secured absolute independence and maintained powerful separate governments down into the nineteenth century. In fact there is no history of Italy as a whole, except for the last one hundred years, her earlier history is a combination of the histories of her city states In England the goal of isolation was never reached, but the towns were able to keep their local self-government and eventually to gain a place in the national government. This was a peculiar happening and was attended by very fortunate results for the success of democratic government.

Popular representation in central government. The townsmen in England, as we have seen, were allowed to carry on their local government very much by themselves, but they had no place in the Curia Regis or Parliament, which limited the power of the king in the central government. It is sometimes stated that the first time the townsmen had the right to attend a national assembly or Parliament was in 1295, when Edward I called the Model Parliament. This statement conveys two wrong ideas. In the first place we have proof that the townsmen were represented in national assemblies in 1265, in 1273, and in 1283. In the second place, it is incorrect to speak of the "right" to sit in Parliament: the burgesses meeting in 1295 and earlier were called because they had money which the king greatly needed to carry on his wars. They were not called for the purpose of being asked to consent to the new taxes which were to be laid, but because Edward knew that if he took them into his confidence they would be more willing to help in assessment and collection. Those towns which sent their quota of two representatives did not do so because they considered it a great honor, nor because they had the slightest idea that here was the beginning of popular government. Since representation did not exempt a borough from taxes, there seemed little to be gained by attending. Many boroughs, therefore, received exemptions from attendance from the king; others simply did not go, and were not punished for it. The result was that there grew up a definite and limited class of boroughs, to which summonses to Parliament were sent.

Toward the end of the fourteenth century, when representation became a desirable thing because of the increased power of Parliament, many boroughs attempted in vain to regain what they now termed the "right" to be represented. But representation had by that time become a privilege to be guarded jealously, and with a very few exceptions the list of represented boroughs at the opening of the nineteenth century was identical with the list of five hundred years earlier. Limited though it was, the townsman had gained a place in the central government of England. Henceforth the goal of the English town would not be complete isolation, but rather local self-government plus an ever-increasing power in the management of the central government.

Another group was called to Parliament at the same time as the townsmen. This group included two representatives of the petty nobles or knights of each shire. At first these county representatives sat with their distant relatives the barons, while the clergy formed a second house and the townsmen a third. Had Parliament continued to be organized thus, the government of England would have remained in essence aristocratic. For on every issue the knights would have been outvoted by the barons, and hence only conservative and aristocratic measures could have passed the upper house. Moreover, the clergy, whose views and interests were more nearly akin to those of the barons, invariably cast the vote of their house on the side of conservatism Thus these two classes could always overrule by their two votes the one vote of the townsmen.

The changing Parliament. Two shifts in the make-up of Parliament were of great importance to popular government The first was the withdrawal of the clergy as a separate estate, and the second was the decision of the knights to leave their noble friends and relatives in order to make common cause with the townsmen The economic and social interests of these groups of people were akin. Moreover, as time went on non-noble freemen as well as the noble knights were allowed to represent the shires. Thus was formed a bicameral (two-house) assembly, of Lords and Commons, with opposing interests.

Hand in hand the townsmen and county representatives set out to wrest power from the king and the barons. It was a long, uphill struggle, not yet finished in the twentieth century. Immense strides were made toward the acquisition of power in the fourteenth and fifteenth centuries. From a body whose duty it was to give information and consent to taxes (never to refuse them), the House of Commons grew into an assembly which controlled the purse strings of the government, which made laws, and which exercised occasional control over such executive matters as the expenditure of money and the appointment of ministers.

The power of taxation was secured first, and through the use of it the others followed. When the king wanted certain things in the way of money grants, the commons also had their demands; and if the king and the lower house both went home pleased from the session, it was because they had bargained together to their mutual advantage. To bargain until the king consented to their own enterprises gave to men a feeling which they would hardly have dared to define as equality with the king, but which bordered very closely on that. Not only did the townsman, with his partners the knight and the freeman of the shire, secure actual powers, but he also won valuable privileges, such as freedom of speech for all things said in Parliament and freedom from arrest during sessions. During the fifteenth-century wars the House of Commons gained control over the king at a rapid rate. In the course of the Wars of the Roses the House of Lords lost in power and prestige as well as in numbers. This was because the greater part of the old nobility, with its tradition of feudal power, was killed in the wars; and the new nobles were subservient to the king.

At the close of the medieval age the government of England was set in the mold of limited monarchy, and the powers of limitation were not to be a monopoly of the aristocracy. For all that, it can scarcely be said that popular government had begun. The town representatives were invariably the wealthy men, even in those few cases where the workingmen were allowed a choice in their selection. In the counties, after 1429, no one had a right to vote for shire representatives unless he possessed a "free tenement to the value of 40 shillings by the year." At best this meant that only the upper tier of the middle class was represented in government, but there was a beginning in popular government which only awaited the modern era for completion.

SUPPLEMENTARY READINGS

ARCHER, T A., and KINGSFORD, C L. The Crusades, chap xxviii, "Results"
TRAILL, H D Social England, Vol I, pp 274–299, 319–388, 396–411, 415–490, 548–564; Vol II, pp. 117–129, 265–274, 416–438, 565–573, Vol. III, pp 6–34, 85–114, 131–167, 245–274, 372–398.
TUFTS, J H The Real Business of Living, chaps vii, ix
WALSH, J J The Thirteenth, Greatest of Centuries, chaps xx–xxiv.
WHITE, A B Making of the English Constitution, pp 104–109, 123–166, 220–238, 253–285, 306–317, 322–341.

SEARCH QUESTIONS AND PROBLEMS

1 Cite proofs of the claim that any honest work is considered honorable in America

2 Is your town or city represented in state and national government? By whom? How chosen?

3 Do congressmen have any privileges that ordinary men do not? (See the Constitution, Article I, Sect. 6) Why?

4. Can you think of a noun in common use today which comes from "villein"? Look up such words as "blackguard," "knave," and "vulgar." What can you deduce from comparing medieval and modern usages of these words?

5 Who performs the functions of holding courts and raising armies today? What services does your father owe in these two lines, and to whom?

6. What conveniences found in a workingman's home in America today were not in the noble's castle in the Middle Ages? Does this mean that the modern workingman is better off than a medieval noble?

7 Give concrete examples of practices of today based on the ideals which have come down to us from the days of chivalry. In what ways have both the ideals and the practices been modified?

8 Exactly why was it not a good policy to pay men wages too low for the support of their families, and supply the necessary addition from taxes or charity funds, rather than to pay a living wage in the first place?

9. To what extent does your village or city have self-government? Has it a charter? Who granted it? What was paid for this charter?

10. Do you know men whose chivalry is as fine as that of any medieval knight? Are there as many of such men living now as there were in medieval times? How do you explain your opinion?

11. Do you know any young men of "good" families who choose to do manual labor because that is the kind they can do best? Do you know others who, to satisfy family pride, are trying to make a living in some profession requiring high intellectual ability, when they might be happily working in a machine shop or tending a counter? What kind of ideals are shown here?

12. Has your town a curfew bell? Is it observed? Do you think the practice a good one?

13. Explain why the clergy and the nobles acted in unison in early English parliamentary affairs. Why did the knights join the townsmen?

CHAPTER IV

AN ERA OF REVOLUTIONS

So all in vain will timorous ones essay
To set the metes and bounds of Liberty.
For Freedom is its own eternal law
It makes its own conditions, and in storm
Or calm alike fulfills the unerring Will
    For ever in thine eyes, O Liberty,
Shines that high light whereby the world is saved,
And though thou slay us, we will trust in thee! — JOHN HAY

CHANGES IN AGRICULTURE

A revolution need not be a bloody encounter of armed troops In reality some of the most important revolutions in the world's history have come about silently, without bloodshed or triumphal march. They have been the work of long decades of time, and are usually not heralded as revolutions until long afterwards, and then first by historians Such revolutions, affecting every side of life, occurred during the seventeenth and eighteenth centuries, and ushered in the modern period.

Agricultural methods. The first great changes in economic life occurred in the basic industry of agriculture. Toward the end of the seventeenth century the disadvantages of the convertible-husbandry system became so apparent that men with a bent for experimenting began to try out new methods of cultivation. As a result of their initiative and courage the old system was soon replaced by a true, scientific rotation of crops, and the modern era of diversified agriculture was begun.

By careful crop rotation it was found that it was not necessary either to allow one third of the land to lie fallow each year or to convert it into pasture at frequent intervals. Careful observation taught the farmer experimenters that wheat takes from the soil much more nitrogen than either barley or oats; that beets and turnips, by drawing their nourishment from the subsoil, can thrive even with a depleted topsoil; and finally (most valuable discovery of all), that clover not only uses the subsoil but actually supplies the surface soil with nitrogen, the food so essential to the growth of wheat.

Knowledge of these discoveries was scattered slowly and quietly throughout England through the influence of Lord Townshend, popularly known as "Turnip Townshend," and by the writings of Arthur Young. Farmers began to plant wheat one year and barley or oats the next, a root crop the third, and clover the fourth. Thus they increased their efficiency as farmers by conserving the soil.

Other experimenters discovered new facts as to the comparative value of marl, lime, and manure as fertilizers. A Warwickshire farmer proved that fen and swamp lands could be made arable by simple drainage systems.

Stock-breeding. Still another group of experimenters turned its attention to animal culture. The old idea had been that breeds must be mixed, but these men produced the same or better results by proper inbreeding. After the experiments of Robert Bakewell became known, the aim of stock-raisers was no longer to produce large-boned sheep but rather to produce animals that yielded as much wool as before and, at the same time, more and better mutton. In the same way cattle were improved, and through experiments the milch and beef breeds were differentiated. For over a quarter of a century one Coke of Holkham held great farmers' meetings, in which the knowledge gained by the few was scattered among the many, and England went into stock-breeding as a scientific business. The meetings became world-famous and were attended even by gentlemen farmers from America.

Agricultural machinery. The agrarian revolution brought about not only improved breeding methods but also new tools. To Jethro Tull belongs the credit for the two most important mechanical inventions—the drill and the horse-drawn hoe. The drill was not at first popularly adopted, but Lord Townshend soon saw its advantages in the saving of seed and in the increased ease of later hoeing as compared with the old inefficient method of scattering seeds broadcast on the top of the ground. The horse-drawn hoe was the forerunner of the modern cultivator Other inventors experimented with plows, harrows, mowers, and even threshing machines. The perfection of most of these instruments was not accomplished until well into the nineteenth century. The most famous invention of all was the American reaper of Cyrus H McCormick. This reaper, with its later additions of a self-binder and gas power, is sold today all over the world. The machinery for farming today is a vastly different thing from that of 1600.

Land tenure. Inventions of farm machinery brought increased returns; consequently there arose a greater demand for lands to cultivate. In England this resulted in a new inclosure movement. Wool and cattle-ranching gave way to wheat-raising, and additional village commons were inclosed Between 1760 and 1844 about five and three-quarter million acres were changed from commons to inclosed fields. This time the peasants were paid an inadequate sum for their rights, but they soon spent this pitiful remuneration and sold also their small remaining plots, and moved to the growing cities. Thus was the yeomanry of England reduced to landlessness and wage dependence [1]

The farm land of England is still mainly owned by a few thousand nobles and wealthy gentry. Some of the estates are immense, as, for example, that of the Duke of Bedford, who has thirty thousand acres in eastern England. One estate in Northumberland contains over one and a third million acres Four hundred nobles own each over fifteen thousand acres. Very few of these landlords cultivate or even directly oversee their estates. A new class of agriculturists, known as tenant-farmers, rent the land at high prices in farms of several hundred acres and oversee the actual tillage.

[1] Goldsmith's "Deserted Village" pictures the conditions of this period

The advantage of this system is that men with moderate means may thereby farm. Moreover, these rich landowners often introduce improvements in machinery, farm methods, buildings, and fences which few small owners would have the capital to obtain. Recent tenancy laws have made it possible for tenants also to put improvements of their own upon the land, with the knowledge that should they, for any reason, give up their tenure they are to be reimbursed adequately. As a result the rural districts of England present a well-kept, trim, even beautiful appearance which our American countryside too often lacks. Other laws have lessened other abuses of the tenancy system, until the "farmers" of England have become in some places a really prosperous class. They cannot have that sense of social well-being, however, which comes from owning one's own farm, and there is grave doubt whether tenancy as a whole results in as wise a treatment of the soil as is given by personal ownership. The present tendency is for the great estates to be carved up into small patches for sale to actual farmers, since the high taxes caused by the war make landlordism unprofitable.

The agrarian revolution in America. The agrarian revolution in America introduced new methods and machinery that increased production quite as it did in England, but as there were then great tracts of free land still to be had, the effect upon land tenure was different. The first effect was to make land more desired by the common people. Aided by government homestead acts, the workers of the East were able to acquire Western farms of a hundred and sixty acres for something over a dollar an acre. Landowning became the custom. Even after the West grew more settled it was not hard for men to buy land. Thrifty farm hands could become renters and even owners in a few years. The tenancy problem in the United States, therefore, rose late and from another kind of agrarian revolution.[1]

[1] This change is described in Chapter XVIII.

The Industrial Revolution

Changes in the textile industry. The inventions which were most to revolutionize society came not in agriculture but in the industries, first of all in textile-making. Under the domestic system the father and sons wove cloth with handmade looms, while the women of the family spun thread, first, upon a distaff and spindle, and after Queen Elizabeth's time on a spinning-wheel. Since only one thread was spun at a time, the weavers found themselves continually out of thread. It took six spinners to supply two weavers. This disproportion was practically doubled in 1738, when Kay invented a drop box and flying shuttle, whereby one man could throw the shuttle both backward and forward.

The weavers' necessity called forth inventions. First came Hargreaves's spinning machine (1764), named for his wife the "jenny." By this machine eight and soon sixteen threads were spun upon one wheel with the same time and energy that had spun one before. The peddler Richard Arkwright began the use of rollers instead of spindles, each pair running more rapidly than the previous pair, so that the thread was continually being stretched out finer. He also applied water power to spinning, for which the king knighted him in 1786.

Meanwhile Samuel Crompton, a weaver, had combined the jenny and the water frame, calling the new machine a "mule" because of its mixed parentage. By this device one spinner could produce two hundred threads at one time, and so the weavers were swamped with thread and could not weave fast enough to use the thread output. The Reverend Edmund Cartwright experimented in 1784 to find a remedy for this state of affairs, and produced the power loom, which threw Kay's flying shuttle back and forth automatically. Water power was applied, and now the weavers were the equals of the spinners in the race of production. Hundreds of additional inventions in a few years increased production 200 per cent over what it had been for centuries. The greatest of these was Eli Whitney's American cotton gin in 1793. The product of one man's labor per day before this invention was six pounds of clean cotton; after it, one thousand pounds. America then became the great source of cotton supply for the English mills.

When Bell invented brass cylinder stamps run by power, which printed the whole design in all its colors as it passed over the cloth, the time used in stamping designs on cotton cloth was reduced to a hundredth of that used by the old method of dipping wooden blocks in dye and pressing them on the cloth by hand. At about the same time white cottons were made less expensive by improved methods of bleaching. Heretofore the sun and air had taken months to do what chlorine now did in a few days. Textile-making had become thoroughly revolutionized.

A revolution in power. Machinery for the new inventions was largely made of iron or steel. England had vast resources of iron, but her equipment for transforming it into usable form had been inefficient. The hand or water-power bellows used in the process gave place to a steam-operated apparatus which produced a steadier blast. The wood charcoal at first used to produce steam was supplanted by coal, of which England had a supply to match her iron resources. Iron and steel industries stood second only to textiles now, for iron and steel are necessary to all other industries; and coal-mining grew in importance with them.

Hand and foot had furnished early power; somewhat later human energy was supplanted by horses and oxen attached to treadmills or pulleys. Neither of these met the needs of the new machinery, nor was water power wholly satisfactory. It did not exist everywhere; industry was forced to move into the north and west of England, where there were streams. In times of drought or extreme cold the power supply vanished. The great need was met by the steam engine, which was invented by an Englishman, Newcomen. His first steam engine was used to pump water out of mines and had only a vertical movement. James Watt, a Scotchman, perfected this clumsy instrument and applied it to wheels which drove the new machinery. By 1800 the new power had supplanted all others for textile manufacture. The industries still remained in the northwest, for the coal needed for steam power was found there. England's Industrial Revolution was in full swing and had begun to produce those changes in the life of men which make it more important than any political revolution that has ever happened.

Scope of the revolution. Industrial invention was not confined to England, but swept over to the Continent and across to America, literally flooding the world with thousands of brand-new things and hundreds of thousands of improvements on first inventions. Every country has benefited more or less India, Russia, and China have only recently begun adopting the new ways, whereas Germany, on the other hand, has contributed her share in such processes as are found in the dye industries and beet-sugar making. The Revolution cannot be said to be complete, for every year brings new inventions in widely scattered fields; but the first century of inventions in Europe and America has worked such great changes in the economic organization that we speak of the results of the Industrial Revolution as if it were a thing of the past.

The social importance of the Industrial Revolution lies in the fact that by it the amount of wealth produced by a unit of human energy in a given amount of time was multiplied many times over what it was before the invention of the new machinery. This has produced much temporary suffering, because it threw workers out of their old jobs, but its net and final result is largely to free men's energies and time from the tasks of producing the material goods of the world, and to enable them to turn their attention to other things

The factory system. The Industrial Revolution ended the domestic system of manufacture and introduced the present-day factory system. From an economic point of view alone this inaugurated more changes than any other event in the history of industry. Production was tremendously increased, and this meant that there was more wealth which could be used as capital for more production. Very large amounts of money were now needed to purchase the expensive equipment and the stocks of raw materials required for the more extensive manufacture. Hard money was added in immense quantities between 1849 and 1855 by the discovery of Californian and Australian gold mines, but even this was not enough to meet the demands of the time. Credit was therefore resorted to, and a new era in finance began

Capital was now no longer furnished by one man, but by new forms of business organization on the principles of the old joint-stock company. Thousands of people might invest their money in a single concern, and business was done on a scale that meant the employment of thousands of workers. These workers rarely saved enough to enable them to invest in the enterprise to which they gave their skill and from which they drew their wages.

A Revolution in Commerce and Transportation

In the world of trade, as in agriculture and industry, revolutionary changes took place during the seventeenth and eighteenth centuries. They showed themselves in the working out and the subsequent abandoning of an all-permeating theory upon which all large-scale trade was based.

The theory of mercantilism. By the time the joint-stock company had become a common business device, merchants and statesmen had begun to form theories which resulted in definite policies. The most important of these, the mercantile theory, has greatly affected the course of history, and still influences thought, although long ago exploded as economic and political doctrine. The practices which formed the basis for this theory had been growing up gradually during the Middle Ages, and by the seventeenth century the conception was pretty clearly formulated in the minds of European merchants and statesmen. It was a complicated theory of the nature and causes of prosperity, which may be summarized briefly as follows:

1. Wealth consists only of gold and silver, especially gold and silver coined into money.

2. The prosperity of any country depends upon the amount of money in the land, therefore a country that wants to prosper must plan its business so as to bring in all the money possible and prevent its leaving the country That is, it should manage to have what we call today a favorable balance of trade, selling a greater total value of goods to other countries than it buys from them.

3 Now goods become more valuable every time a man expends labor upon them For instance, a bushel of flour is more valuable than a bushel of wheat, and a fleece of wool is more valuable cut from the sheep's back and washed than it was when on the sheep, and still more valuable when spun into yarn, and still more valuable when woven into cloth So if a country can raise raw materials and manufacture them and sell them abroad for foreign gold, that country will be prosperous. If it has not enough raw materials for all its manufactures, then it should buy raw materials abroad, make them up into more costly products, and sell them back to the first country or some other at a profit. Manufactures are thus seen to be a basis for prosperity, as they add value to the finished product.

4. In order that the country planning to be prosperous may make money, it must have ships with which to import raw materials and to carry its goods to foreign ports. These ships should be controlled by the nation concerned; for in this way exports and imports may the better be regulated, to the end that all may help to accumulate gold within the country Moreover, as such ships need protection, a good navy is desirable. And as fishing trains men for a seafaring life and provides a home food supply with some surplus for export, fisheries are to be encouraged.

5. If there be a tendency to import manufactured goods, thus reducing home manufactures through competition, the government should prevent such competition by levying import duties high enough to keep them out. Export duties may also be levied if, because of higher prices in some foreign market, raw-material producers are inclined to export what might be used at home. The restriction of trade is justified because the prosperity of the country demands the piling up of gold. Besides, and this is the more usual argument, export duties provide a revenue for the government. Producers and traders must not be allowed to do what they please, but rather what is for the good of the country at large. Moreover, the export of gold must be made a serious offense, in order to keep it within the country. This leads to the passing of laws forbidding or limiting the export of gold.

6. It may be that the desired amounts of raw materials do not flow readily into the country, or that the countries from which they come put export duties on them to make their prices high. Then it will be an advantage to the nation to have colonies in which those raw materials may be produced, so that their importation may be assured and their prices controlled to some extent. Colonies, therefore, may help the mother country by producing raw materials, but they should not be allowed to manufacture for themselves, for then the mother country's manufactures will lose a good market.

Application of the theory. It will be seen that this theory when put into practice would affect many things. Not only would it dictate the commercial and industrial policy of the country, but it would encourage shipbuilding, control production and trade by imposing duties and other excises, and modify, if it did not create, the colonial policy of the nation. It did all these things in England during the eighteenth century, when the theory was so generally subscribed to that it appeared in many ways as national policy. The American Revolution was only one of the results of the colonial policy which grew out of the mercantile theory—not wholly, as there were certain influences in the new land which might have brought about independence in any case, but certainly very largely. On the other hand, it should not be forgotten that the mother country helped the colonists by assuring them good markets for their raw products. It was in accord with the later and truer doctrine of special fitness, moreover, that the thickly populated mother country should manufacture, while the colonists, living where land and natural resources were plentiful, should produce raw materials.

Good results. While this mercantile theory held its own, much progress was made in the arts of trade. The dominance of the theory at least had this good effect: it encouraged popular support of the government on a theory of general welfare rather than on one of divine right or mere parliamentary authority. With its emphasis upon production, it helped the nations accepting it to produce more and better goods. This stimulated improvements in transportation and communication. At the same time there was a development of commercial law and of a judiciary especially equipped for civil cases The postal system became better during the eighteenth century, although cheap postage was not introduced until the nineteenth. In securing these helps for their business, the merchants secured helps for society at large and made the course of living surer and pleasanter for all.

Failures. Although the following of this theory yielded immediate advantages in many ways, in others it failed notably. It did not give to any of the countries which based their practice upon it that surplus of gold and silver which it aimed to produce. Perhaps this was because all the great producing and trading nations believed in it so thoroughly that their efforts practically balanced and canceled each other. "It is noteworthy," says Day,[1] "that Spain, the country which had the best chance apparently to accumulate treasure and which pursued a policy of exaggerated mercantilism, was always complaining of the dearth of gold and silver, while Oriental states, which had

[1] Day, History of Commerce, p 170.

never heard of mercantilism, accumulated large stories of bullion." It was very fortunate for Europe that the money metals were not all cornered in one kingdom, and that all the effort directed toward making economic practice comport with a theory based on a false understanding of wealth was not able materially to change the working of natural economic laws.

Mercantilism defeated its own ends, also, in that it eventually injured prosperity through too much regulation. Trade is a thing which, like prices and supply, depends on economic conditions; and economic conditions cannot be created by statute, although statutes may help to produce or to end them. Spain killed her extensive shipping in time through her detailed and intricate shipping laws; for shipmasters preferred to build and own ships in countries which gave them more freedom.

The era of commercial wars. The interfering habit also influenced foreign policies and helped to bring on those wars for commerce and empire which ran through the sixteenth, seventeenth, and eighteenth centuries. In these wars Spain and Holland first won from the Portuguese. Then the Dutch were displaced by the English, chiefly because the latter were supported by a strong national government, whereas the Dutch had only the support of individual cities, each one the rival of the others. England also won a commercial victory over Spain, as decided as the better-known victory of the Armada in 1588.

The last great rival for commercial England was France. The struggle between these two was fought out in a series of wars on two continents, from 1689 to 1763. In Asia, India was won for the British by the superior organization and support of the merchant forces and by the British navy. In North America the deciding factor was the character of the colonists. The French settlers were a stolid, peasant type, uninterested in the government either of their mother country or the new lands; whereas the English settlers, although desirous of local self-government, were ready to fight for the mother country in her time of need. The Peace of Paris in 1763 closed the era of commercial wars, leaving England in control of India and of practically all North America except Mexico, veritable "mistress of the seas" and master craftsman to the world.

England had come out of these wars the commercial victor, not because of the mercantile theory, but in spite of it. Her success was due to the hearty support given to commerce by a united national government, and to the comparative freedom in production and commerce of her merchants

The death of mercantilism. Early in the nineteenth century England came to see the errors in mercantilism, and abandoned it. The chief honor for discrediting the old theory and popularizing the new goes to a Scotchman, Adam Smith by name. The idea was not original with him, but was copied from a new school of economists in France, among whom Turgot was the most practical. In 1776 Smith published a famous book called "An Inquiry into the Causes and Effects of the Wealth of Nations." This book propounded the laissez-faire theory, which means "let alone", that is, allow people to manage their own affairs with as little government regulation as possible. Smith said that this policy not only allowed men to please themselves better but was also better for society at large, because the invisible hand of God so directed men that while they sought their own happiness they served society at the same time, in the best way. Adam Smith, who is sometimes called the Father of Economics, applied his doctrine of freedom to industry and commerce and pleaded earnestly for the overthrow of mercantilism and the establishment of a policy of free trade. "The Wealth of Nations" was widely read, and its policy of laissez-faire came to be accepted as the theory of the day.

The laissez-faire theory and free trade. The new doctrine appealed to producers and traders because they thought it offered a chance for greater personal gains, it appealed to consumers because they hoped that free competition would bring lower prices; and it appealed to people in general because in the late eighteenth century liberty was coming to be thought of as the natural right of all men. The new policy was first accepted by the government under the ministry of William

Pitt, 1783-1801. Pitt made an arrangement with France which today would be called "reciprocity", that is, each country reduced import duties in favor of the other, thus insuring greater freedom of trade for merchants on both sides of the Channel. It was a small beginning toward free trade.

Some years later Richard Cobden became the great champion of free trade. He was aided by a group of men known as the Manchester School. In 1820 the merchants of the London Chamber of Commerce asked the government to reduce the customs duties to a "revenue only" basis, and the Edinburgh chamber followed suit. The distress caused by the protective duties on grain produced great popular agitation, culminating in the Anti-Corn-Law League of Cobden and Bright, and in 1846 the customs duties were finally removed. First Robert Peel and later Gladstone supported the movement against the tariff, with the result that by 1860 Great Britain was a free-trade nation. At the present time she has a few revenue duties on such commodities as sugar, tea, coffee, tobacco, and liquors, but protection as a policy has been abandoned.[1]

American commerce. Since early colonial times American commerce had been alternately encouraged and restricted by the British Navigation Acts. England wanted her colonies to develop production and trading facilities—provided always they did not interfere with her own. In general, the restrictions were made in accord with the very sensible idea that England should manufacture and the colonies produce raw materials; but as manufactures produce a greater profit than raw materials, the colonists did not always meekly agree with the mercantilist limits set to their production.

Nature had richly endowed America for commercial purposes. Her deep forests of oak and pine furnished timbers and

---

[1] Joseph Chamberlain, however, led a movement for a return to a protection policy Many people think that the threatened return to protection, which would have put German manufactures at a disadvantage in Canadian and some other markets, had much to do with bringing on the late war German manufactures were not seriously rivaling those of England in 1860, but by 1900 the situation had quite changed.

AN ERA OF REVOLUTIONS

naval supplies of the best quality and of seemingly inexhaustible amount. Her indented coasts invited ships to port in a dozen places, where goodly trading cities sprang up. The Yankee sailors were the best in the world, for they combined keen intelligence with hard and varied experience. The untouched stores of a new world offered to the extractive industries unlimited opportunities; and as the teeming populations of Europe offered a ready market, it was most natural that shipbuilding and carrying should become a great interest in the colonies. England needed not only the cargoes but the ships as well; and many a Yankee shipmaster sold both ship and cargo in Great Britain, to return and engage in new ventures with his ample profits. The enforcement of the Navigation Acts was not strict, and up to about 1760 the commerce of the colonists was very prosperous indeed—a prosperity based often very largely on smuggling. It was the sudden resolution of the English government to enforce laws that had always been practically dead letters which helped to bring on the Revolution.

Methods of transportation. After the American Revolution the shipping industries recovered rapidly and fully, and during the early part of the nineteenth century our merchant marine was wonderfully prosperous. During the heyday of its power there was taking place another kind of revolution, the practical revolution in methods, which corresponded to the new methods in manufactures. It began with the ordinary wagon roads, which people began to improve late in the eighteenth century. Two Scotchmen, Telford and Macadam, taught men how to make a solid roadbed topped with layer on layer of crushed stone and having a final smooth surface rounded to shed water. The cost of transporting freight was reduced to less than one half by these improvements. People learned from Telford that it takes about four times as much force to draw a ton on a muddy dirt road as on a hard macadam road.

But there are even more economical ways of transporting burdens than on smooth wagon roads. It has been estimated that with the same expenditure of energy a horse can draw sixty times as heavy a load through still water as on a highway. Recognizing this fact, English experimenters initiated a period of river and canal commerce, copied in part from that of France and the Netherlands. In 1761 James Brundley made the first English canal, for the Duke of Bridgewater. It ran from the duke's coal fields at Worsley down to Manchester; later it was extended to Liverpool. In the next seventy-five years England was so filled with a network of canals that there was scarcely a place more than fifteen miles from a waterway. Canals inevitably declined in importance with the coming of faster inland transportation, but waterways have by no means seen an end to their service. With railroad congestion a return to water transportation for heavy, bulky, and nonperishable goods is bound to come.

The application of steam. The application of steam power to transportation came first on the water. The *Clermont*, the first commercially successful steamboat, made the trip from New York to Albany in two days with her efficient little Watt engine from England. In two decades steamships were to be found on the important rivers of both countries, and before long ocean-sailing vessels began to add engines to their sailing apparatus. The *Savannah* crossed the Atlantic in 1819, with both sails and steam, and in 1833 the *Royal William* (Quebec to London) made the passage without the use of sails. In 1838 the screw propeller came into use for ocean vessels, but sidewheels still remained the chief device for river traffic.

There were "railroads" before the invention of the locomotive. In England they were used, late in the eighteenth century, for making the pulling easier for the horses that drew heavy loads, especially loads of coal in or near a mine. The rails were of wood, sometimes capped with a strip of iron. To George Stephenson goes the credit for operating the first locomotive, the *Puffing Billy*, which, in 1814, carried coal for nine miles from a mine head to Liverpool. By 1830 Stephenson was running an improved model, *The Rocket*, from the cotton works of Manchester to the port of Liverpool, at the unheard-of speed of twenty-nine miles an hour. By 1840 the locomotive had become the accepted means of transportation in England.

In America John Stevens had been trying since 1811 to interest men with money in his plan for a locomotive. After news of Stephenson's success reached these shores, deaf ears became alert; and on July 4, 1828, Charles Carroll of Carrollton, the last surviving signer of the Declaration of Independence, drove the gold spike which opened work on the Baltimore and Ohio Railroad. English engines were used at first on this road, but Matthias Baldwin and Peter Cooper soon began to construct American engines. Improvements in construction and rolling stock came rapidly on both sides of the Atlantic. The iron-capped wooden rails were soon supplanted by those made entirely of iron, and after the Bessemer process came, by rails made of steel. Their shape was changed from flat to T-shape. Coaches were made larger, more comfortable, and finally of steel construction. In America they soon lost their coach shape, but in Europe the idea persisted in the shape of compartments. Roadbeds were made smoother and more solid. Engines increased in weight ten times and in hauling power from forty to twenty-four hundred tons. The age of steam, in short, removed the world-old restriction on transportation and brought the carrying agents of the world fully abreast with the production powers of a machine age.

A Revolution in Social Conditions

The changes in social conditions from 1600 to 1800 or a little later were so great as to warrant the application of the word "revolution." The seventeenth century opened with pitiful conditions for the working-people. Wages were very low, while prices were rising, and unemployment was rife. There was widespread distress and vagabondism, and frequent epidemics of plague, fever, and smallpox. In marked contrast to the lot of the common people was the idle and extravagant life of the leisure classes. The English court in the days of the Stuarts was a hotbed of intemperance and immorality. Only during the brief period of the Commonwealth was the Puritan influence strong enough to curb the excesses of the upper classes.

The ups and downs of social well-being. With the Restoration (1660) the lot of the workingman was made harder than ever by the enactment of corn laws, which shut foreign grain out of England and so raised the price of foodstuffs. As these laws were reënacted after the "glorious" Revolution of 1688, the early decades of the eighteenth century found the poor in a sad case indeed. In years when the English harvest was poor, bread became so high that poor people actually starved. Wages did not provide for decent living; for prices had risen in the ratio of 1 to 2, while wages had gone up only in the ratio of 1 to 1.2.

The Poor Laws of the time of Queen Elizabeth were still in force, and were creating economic and moral paupers out of those who had before been poor but self-supporting folk. People found that they could live without work on parish funds, which gave them a better living than they could earn. The Poor Laws were the worst enemies of the poor. By the second decade of the eighteenth century so many people had come to depend upon the poor rates that Parliament created "workhouses," and decreed that only those housed in them should receive public charity. The law seems to have been a dead letter from the day of its enactment, and between 1742 and 1784 the public money spent for the poor increased six times as much as the increase in the population. This was partly caused by the Law of Settlement, which forbade the poor to move from county to county. This law was enacted to protect counties from being overridden by roving paupers, but in operation it served to prevent the poor who wanted to work from going where work was to be had, and thus greatly increased the poor rates in counties where there was little industry, which were, of course, the counties that could afford it least.

About 1730 there was a decided improvement, owing mainly to the increased productiveness of agriculture. Returns from farming were now, thanks to the agrarian revolution, four times what they had been in the thirteenth century, and the population had increased only from about two and a half to a maximum of eight millions. For once production had outstripped population. Real wages increased greatly, although money wages were raised but slightly. The standard of living became higher.

Most classes were happy and contented at that time. The landowners complained that rents were low because prices were low, but as they had much influence in Parliament they got themselves relief in the shape of bounties to farmers, which the landlords then secured for themselves by raising the rents of the farms.[1]

But this period of prosperity was short-lived. About 1765 there began a time of poor harvests, followed by years of actual shortage. The population was increasing rapidly; by 1850 it was eighteen million, or four and a half times that of 1700. Thus supply was reduced while demand increased, and prices jumped accordingly. A second period of inclosures, begun at this time, saw thousands of people dispossessed of their holdings. They became either farm laborers or city workers, and many now depended on charity who before had earned their living.

The farmers had no pity on their laborers. Their landlords had no pity on them; but they could pass the burden on to their workers, while the farm hand had no one lower down to whom to transfer his burdens. The farm hand had now lost his old rights to free fuel, garden ground, and common pasturage. His money wage was low. In 1795 the rural worker was in straits so dire that the justices of Berkshire decided to wash their hands of the matter by giving up their ancient right to set wages in the quarter sessions. They turned over the responsibility to the individual farmers, with the humble request that a living wage be paid. In case the farmer did not see fit to pay this living wage, the justices provided that the difference

[1] Nearly ten million dollars in bounties were secured in eleven years, a very large sum for those days.

between the wages received and the amount necessary for existence was to be paid to the workers from the poor rates. Other counties followed the example of Berkshire, although the justices were nominally the wage-setters until 1814.

This action further depressed wages and increased pauperism. Employers deliberately cut wages to the starving point, knowing that official charity would step in and pay the deficit in wages. When a man became an outright pauper, the parish sold out his labor at a nominal rate and paid him the difference in poor rates. This atrocious system of official charity degraded everyone connected with it. It penalized self-supporting men, who must pay the taxes which supplied the poor rates. It encouraged employers to cut wages. It demoralized the workers by putting a premium on sloth and improvidence; they need take no thought for the morrow, for society would see to it that they did not starve in old age, illness, or mere indolence.

Effects of the Industrial Revolution. The town artisan did not receive poor relief like his rural cousin. The days of his transition from the handicraft to the domestic, and from the domestic to the factory régime, had been hard ones. The highly skilled workmen had, on the whole, suffered most, as they could not command nearly such high wages as machine workers as they had formerly earned at home. The entrance of women and children into factory production tended further to reduce wages. Perhaps the weavers felt the hardships of the change more than any other class. This was largely their own fault, for many of them refused to accept the change as inevitable and continued with their hand looms to wage a losing fight. No man can turn the clock of progress backward by refusing to admit that it has moved forward.

Even for those who were wise enough to admit the change and try to adapt themselves to it, there were many hardships in store before the ultimate advantages appeared. A chief trouble was that they must move into crowded industrial centers. The work must all be done in one place now, since heavy machinery and power were needed. The great industrial centers of England grew up, fed by a steady stream of workers from the country. In 1770 about 50 per cent of England's people lived in cities, in 1911 it was 78 per cent. In the United States the percentage was 29.5 in 1800, 46 3 in 1910, and 51.4 in 1920.

The concentration of hundreds of thousands of people into a radius of a few square miles raised innumerable problems. Their water supply, their lighting and heating facilities, their communication and transportation devices, all became too often examples of poor administration and selfish exploitation. The building of homes for such multitudes—the housing problem—became a matter of serious import.

The growth of great cities has not created a multitude of social problems, but it has increased and complicated them, and by making them extremely serious and perfectly apparent to all, has aroused mankind to them. The thousands of workers who are dependent for daily bread upon their wages have created complicated problems of profits and wages, and have made the question of distribution perhaps the most serious one of modern times.

If one cause were to be selected as the fountainhead of most of the evils of the social life of any age, that cause would surely be the lack of proper home life. The country cottage of the old worker, with its garden plot and playground for the children, was superior to the tenement home of the new cities. The mother who spent her working-days in a factory could not train her children; she could not cook, mend, clean, or direct. The long hours, insanitary conditions, and standing-work often made her unfit not only to care for her existing children, but to bear others who were either in body or mind a valuable addition to the race

Children suffered most of all from factory production in its earlier years. They could work the new machines when as young as six years old, and were eagerly sought because their wages were lower even than those of women. The most inhuman conditions existed in their employment.[1]

[1] For details see Cheyney's "Readings in English History," pp 690–697.

Economic factors. The evil of economic insecurity followed the introduction of machinery. The serf could not be taken from his land, and the craftsman had a degree of security in the protection of his guild. If he fell ill or was injured, his guild or journeyman's association came to his assistance. The artisan-peasant under the domestic system could always make a bare subsistence with his small piece of land, a cow, and a pig or two, even if work failed him. But with town and factory production all this changed. The worker found himself in competition with crowds of others, with no by-occupation to fall back on if he lost his job. His contract was a short one. His sickness and accident risks were greater than formerly, and he belonged to no fraternal group with insurance provisions. He had no personal relations with his employer to win him loans or concessions. He had become, in short, economically insecure. With the Industrial Revolution this economic insecurity had increased for the employer as well as for the employee, but not nearly to the same degree. The laborer lost a permanent association with the tools of production. They had now passed entirely out of his hands.

It is true the laborer under the factory system gained the tremendous advantage of freedom of movement. He could meet his fellows and talk over with them his grievances, and exchange ideas with them as to remedies. After a long struggle he won the right to organize into societies for mutual benefit. But in most crafts he had lost the hope of becoming a master, although in some there was still hope of advancement to a master's position for the talented and enduring. For the most part the poor laborer had become economically dependent; he had only his wage to depend on, his wage was small and uncertain, and society did little for him in the way of offering him opportunity.

The modern type of class warfare. The factory system set the two classes of employer-capitalist and hired workingman against each other. The former furnished the capital and the brains, the latter only his hands, for he had no surplus capital to invest. If his mind, stultified from the dreadful monotony of his work, ever evolved a suggestion, it was rarely welcomed by his employer, and his suggestion was often worthless, because he could not see the enterprise as a whole. A few clever men, often arisen from the laboring class, formed now a new middle class between the proletariat and the landed gentry. This class was for a long time the sole profiter of the new régime. Class consciousness bred class antipathy, and class antipathy breeds class war if not checked in time. Class antagonisms, coming down from the Middle Ages but vastly increased during the Industrial Revolution, have given to the world of today a bitterness and an obstacle to progress which only good will and justice can overcome.

In the preceding pages only a slight sketch of the social conditions of the working-class has been given. Many other things entered into the sum total of social welfare during the two centuries. There were religious movements which affected fundamentally the history of England and of America, there were literary and philosophical achievements of the first importance; and there was artistic development which meant much to the culture of the world Among the most important of all these changes was the change in the political complexion of the English-speaking peoples.

Changes in Politics and Government

The nations of western Europe and the American people saw great and fundamental changes in political life wrought between 1600 and 1800. Germany, passing through the Thirty Years' War and slowly recovering from its ravages, failed to make the progress of France and England. France failed to make the slow and steady growth in liberalism that took place in England, but under an absolute monarchy became so bankrupt and so discontented that modern ways were introduced only through a bitter struggle entailing bloodshed at home and war abroad. Untrained in self-government, her people fell victims to the self-interested genius of Napoleon Bonaparte, who deliberately traded upon the vanity of an imaginative nation to make himself a conqueror and an emperor. Through the years of the Napoleonic régime and of the Bourbon Restoration, which followed, the French learned little of popular participation in government. But each recurring revolution of the nineteenth century, proving the underlying discontent of the French people with the sops of military glory forced upon them by changing dynasties, brought to that nation a clearer sense of political values, until today the Third Republic stands proved and solid. But the seventeenth and eighteenth centuries in France were years of absolutism in government and restriction in thought, carried finally to such an extent as forced a long-delayed revolution, with incalculable loss to the nation and to the world. They give history's most classic example of what happens when selfish, law-intrenched interests are allowed their way too long.

A "business administration" for England. In England there had been in the same time much liberal development. During the time of the wily Tudors Parliament had, almost without realizing it, lost much of the power gained slowly in the centuries then past, but this was regained by force and skill from the tactless and inefficient Stuarts and was confirmed by the liberal William III. During his brief but brilliant administration Oliver Cromwell had given to the middle-class business men of England a share in national policy which they never again lost, and which was slowly extended during the reigns of the earlier Georges. The gentlemen of Parliament might affect to despise trade, but they realized that national prosperity depended upon its being kept alive and listened respectfully when the great merchants made their demands. The upper middle class won freedom of speech and of worship, the right to protection of property and life, and at least theoretical equality for all men in the administration of justice. It also secured fairer taxation and improved conditions for shipping and manufacturing.

One other thing which the business man introduced into government was business methods. The good business man kept books carefully, and knew where every penny of his money came from and went to. But when he entered politics, he found that the government, managed by gentlemen, was not nearly so well run as it should be. Letters were not answered; money disappeared, no one knew where. The business man demanded better-kept accounts, and accounts were kept more accurately He demanded reports, and reports were made, to someone, although not thus far to the public at large He wanted his letters answered, and an army of clerks was employed to indite and copy replies. He wanted duplicate copies of important documents, and multiplying devices were finally invented to meet this demand Wherever the business man went, he introduced business methods into government, and government was improved thereby.

The English political revolution only started. After 1688 there was no more danger of divine-right rule. Absolutism was dead and gone in England, but political control was still far from being equally distributed among the people. The House of Lords still exercised almost equal power with the Commons except in matters of taxation and was composed of the hereditary landed nobility only. Even the House of Commons did not really represent the common people, for the freed serf's descendants were excluded by the Disfranchising Statute because their tenure was not freehold, while the free artisans of the towns rarely had the right to vote. Even master workmen were rarely found in Parliament, because there was no salary for such service, and few except gentlemen could afford to live in London and devote their time to legislation. In 1800 the lower-class townsman and the rural non-gentle freemen had much yet to gain before they became a part of the self-governing body of Englishmen.

In America. The English colonist along the Atlantic seaboard in the seventeenth and eighteenth centuries found himself between two great expanses of free territory, the wide-stretching sea on the east that separated him from the restricting government of England, and the endless, mysterious land reaching westward to unknown places, where was no white man's government whatever. Perhaps it was natural that, situated between two such freedoms created and maintained by nature, he should find even the comparatively liberal rule of the motherland irksome. At all events each colony sturdily insisted on its self-governing rights and had won, before the Revolution, practically every liberal privilege then desired by men. The Revolution, when it came, was not so much a revolution as a further extension along lines of self-government that had long been followed in the colonies. Independence was the last step in a long progress away from absolutism in government, in which the English colonies had in some ways outstripped their home-staying brothers.

Independence once gained, each of the thirteen states declared itself sovereign, made itself a constitution (often adapted from the former charter), and considered itself a little nation. But this happened while the Revolution was still being fought and when some kind of union was very necessary indeed. So, after several joint meetings of an emergency nature, the thirteen commonwealths joined in a union under what they called "Articles of Confederation" (1781). The weaknesses of a confederation were shown up so clearly during the next six years that the thinking men of that time were forced to devise something more satisfactory.[1] A centralized type of government, such as existed in England or France, was impossible among states so jealous and so various in interests as those of the new nation; therefore a compromise was arrived at in the Constitutional Convention of 1787, which gave to the United States the federal form of union.

This kind of government as worked out by our forefathers was a composite arrangement in which the separate local units are kept as in the confederation, but without sovereignty; and a strong central organization is established as in the centralized

[1] See Muzzey's "American History," pp. 136-142.

government, which has many important but definitely enumerated powers. This plan gives the advantages of local self-government plus the strength of an effective centralization. It was a happy combination, which not only met the needs of the United States, but has since been adopted by the dominions of Canada, Australia, and South Africa, by several South American states, by the German Empire, and by several states organized after the World War.

Division of powers. The distinctive feature of the Federal system is the division of powers between the central government and the member states. The basis of this division in the United States is laid down in the Tenth Amendment to the Constitution: "The powers not delegated to the United States by the Constitution, nor prohibited by it to the States, are reserved to the States respectively." To the United States were delegated seventeen specific enumerated powers and the more elastic right "to make laws which shall be necessary and proper for the carrying into execution" of the delegated powers.[1] These enumerated powers concern the United States as a whole, whereas the residual or remaining powers left to the states concern the daily life of the citizen in such things as education, suffrage, police power, and commercial law.

English features. Although the new state diverged in general type of government from its mother country, it did not entirely ignore English governmental traditions. Bicameral assemblies were established both in the several states and in the nation, and the civil rights won in the struggle of 1603–1688 were incorporated in the first ten amendments to the Constitution. Washington and Hamilton both liked the English tradition, and copied details of administration from the older government.

But although we must never forget that American institutions are the product of English progress and thought and struggle, we shall see that in the nineteenth century, in the free and ample environment of a new continent, the English

[1] This is the famous "elastic clause" of the Constitution.

mind ran ahead of itself, so to speak, and developed in some respects much faster than the stay-at-home-in-England mind of the older country. In other respects, notably in budget management and responsibility, England has set us an example of efficiency.

Summary. The whole Western world, then, underwent a multiform revolution during the seventeenth and eighteenth centuries. It began with its economic and political systems still predominantly under the tradition of the Middle Ages; it looked out upon the nineteenth century with its production fundamentally changed, its society organized in new ways, its thinking stimulated with new ideas, and its governments upon the verge of an epochal change—the experiment of democratic participation. What was accomplished in the century last preceding our own will bring the story of the changing world to our own times.

SUPPLEMENTARY READINGS

BULLOCK, C. J. Selected Readings in Economics, pp. 331–333.
CHEYNEY, E. P. Industrial and Social History of England, chaps. vii, viii.
HAMILTON, W. H. Current Economic Problems, Nos. 24, 25, 27, 29, 30, 32.
OSGOOD, ELLEN. A History of Industry, chaps. x–xii, xvii.
ROBINSON, J. H., BREASTED, J. H., and SMITH, E. P. General History of Europe, chaps. xxviii, xxxii–xxxiv, xxxvii.
TRAILL, H. D. Social England, Vol. IV, pp. 143–172, 310–325, 472–497, 581–609; Vol. V, pp. 99–155, 301–358, 452–500.
WEBSTER, W. C. General History of Commerce, chap. xxiv.
WEST, W. M. Modern Progress, chaps. iv–vii, xii–xiv, xxiii–xxv.

SEARCH QUESTIONS AND PROBLEMS

1. Name ten recent inventions in your schoolroom; ten at home. How recent are they? Do they involve any really new principles?

2. What invention can you think of that is now needed?

3. Are there any more kinds of power yet to be discovered?

AN ERA OF REVOLUTIONS

4 Does your county have any macadamized roads? Are they a good kind of road for America? Why? What is the most economical and serviceable road for your part of the country?

5 Why is it sixty times as hard to pull a load on land as in water?

6. What new canals are proposed or under construction in America?

7 Make a parallel-column chart, showing every process in the production of wheat flour from preparing the ground to the retail sale of the product Let the first column represent the tools and methods of 1700, and the second column those of 1920. If time allows do the same for cotton

8 What are the great manufacturing centers of your state? What do they make? What is it worth?

9 Make a simple experiment in division of labor and report the results in time-using to the class This might be done, for instance, in the writing of sets of fifty invitations Let one section write the whole note and send it; let the other divide up the writing, folding, addressing, stamping, sealing, etc

10 Where is there a natural reservoir of nitrogen? Can it be extracted and applied without the clover rotation now needed? What does chemistry show one about this?

11 What is the usual scheme of crop rotation in your state? Are artificial fertilizers used? Is diversified agriculture practiced in your county? Is it successful?

12. What are the average yields per acre of the staple crops in your state? Compare them with those of other states and nations Are your farmers efficient? See a recent yearbook for statistics

13 On an outline map of the world, color differently the parts which are now under machine production, those which are being industrially revolutionized, and those in which machine production is unknown What do you find?

14 Are the societies which encourage handicrafts in this age of machine production doing society a real service? Why?

15 Do you ever hear mercantilist ideas advanced today in arguments? Read pages 453-456 and the last paragraph on page 472, in Bullock's "Selected Readings in Economics"

16 Bogart and Thompson's "Readings in the Economic History of the United States," pp. 529-537, describes New England factory conditions during our Industrial Revolution. Has the social quality of the workers improved since then? Why?

17. Does the United States have free trade with her island possessions?

18. Is a new revolution in transportation due with the development of air navigation? Should it be cheaper or dearer than land and water carriage?

19. With what period of the past would you compare the social life of today as most like it?

20. Osgood's "History of Industry," p. 199, gives a diagram showing the functions of middlemen in the mercantile period. Find out how closely it corresponds to the present method of marketing wool. Has any improvement been made?

21. Adam Smith's opinion of guilds is of interest. It is given in Bullock's "Selected Readings in Economics," pp. 104–114.

22. The eighteenth century saw the business man become a power in politics. Has the twentieth century a parallel movement?

23. Was there an ethical revolution to correspond with the revolutions in other fields?

24. How much stock raising is carried on in your county? Do local farmers believe that blooded stock is a paying investment?

CHAPTER V

NINETEENTH-CENTURY PROGRESS

Let the great world swing forever down the ringing grooves of change —
TENNYSON

SOCIAL PROGRESS IN ENGLAND

In the previous chapter the pitiful condition of the working-class in the early years of the Industrial Revolution has been noted The bad effects of changing the mode of production when the workers are too ignorant and conservative to adapt themselves to new ways had never a better illustration. Added to industrial causes for suffering there were several wars which upset normal production and imposed heavy taxes. Farmers enjoyed a period of artificially stimulated prosperity during the Napoleonic wars, for which the town population paid dearly in expensive bread This period covered the first quarter of the nineteenth century

Improved conditions after 1830. Beginning with the third decade of the nineteenth century the curve of social well-being for the working-classes began a steady ascent. There were three causes· (1) enlightened legislation, including repeal of some of the bad economic legislation of the past; (2) cooperation of workingmen for their own benefit, and (3) competition of employers for labor, owing to the disproportion of supply and demand.

The repeal of obnoxious economic legislation was due to the acceptance of Adam Smith's doctrine of laissez faire It included not only the repeal of the Corn Laws, but the repeal of the wage clauses of the Statute of Apprentices, the Law of Settlement, and the degrading Poor Relief Act of Elizabeth. Labor was now no longer forced to serve a seven-year apprentice term, or to stay in a county where there existed a surplus of labor while another close by suffered from a dearth of it. The new Poor Law gave help only to the truly incapacitated, and to them only when they went to public charity institutions. One sixth of the people of England were no longer to live on starvation wages from their employers and piecemeal charity from the government.

By the middle of the century the English workingman was well on his way to recovery of the position he had held for half a century a hundred years before. But instead of the setback he had received in the late 1780's, he was in the nineteenth century to keep on with gains in every phase of his life, economic, social, and political, until he reached his present position.

Enlightened legislation. As early as 1802 legal limits were put to the hours of child labor in cotton factories; night work was prohibited, a maximum of twelve hours' labor per day was set, and nine years was made the youngest age for factory apprenticing. Numerous other acts were passed within the next half century, all bettering the social and health conditions in the factories. Working-hours for women and young people were limited to ten, while children were to spend half time in school. Women, and boys under thirteen, were forbidden to work at all in underground mines. In 1878 the varied and overlapping factory laws were supplanted by a new code which covered over fifty pages in the statute book. Children under ten could no longer work, and the maximum working-hours of all youths up to eighteen was ten hours per day. Minute regulations as to sanitary conditions, safety devices on machinery, and physical fitness for work were outlined.

Coöperation. The English laborer is a firm believer in the adage that "the Lord helps those who help themselves." He saw very early that strength lies in unity, and so he has taken various methods of coöperation to better his own condition. After the repeal in 1824 of the Combination Acts, which had prohibited them, he began making trade unions. The first strong unions of harbor men and London builders were able in 1853 to shorten their hours and increase their wages 10 per cent. The history of trade and labor unions is one story after another of gains for their members. With improvement of the condition of the laborer, however, the device has brought class consciousness and industrial strife, of which we shall hear more later.

Besides the cooperation of unified action against employers, English workingmen have worked together in business undertakings in which they became both capitalist and manager. Thus a group of townsmen may begin a general dry-goods shop, or the farmers of a dairy region a creamery. They invest their savings in the enterprise as capital, and either divide up the duties of operation or hire workers whose wages are deducted before the profits are divided among the owners. There are many difficulties connected with this sort of coöperation, they may be summarized in the maxim that "too many cooks spoil the broth." Often no one man is boss, and therefore many try to manage the matter, with the usual result of disunion and failure. In spite of all difficulties many coöperative ventures have succeeded thoroughly in England. They have never met with great success in America, where the economic pressure is less, except in two fields: fruit-marketing and dairying.

Another kind of union that has succeeded in England is the mutual-aid or welfare society, by which workingmen secure aid for one another in times of sickness, death, or need. These societies serve the modern worker as the guilds did their members in their earlier and more democratic days.

Recent events have in some ways improved the conditions of the English laborer. The acquiring of immense foreign markets for English manufactures, the war-time scarcity of labor, and the great needs of early reconstruction days all resulted in competition between employers for labor. The movement was checked by the hard times of 1920–1921 and the slow adjustment of labor (stimulated by the abnormal wages of war time) to a return to normal conditions

Social Progress in America, 1780–1860

The condition of working-people in America has always been different from that of England because of the different proportions of the factors of production. That factor which is most scarce may control the productive process; and since labor has always been until recent years the most scarce factor in America, its condition was always a comparatively good one. The equality of opportunity and the abundance of food in America made the gaining of life's essentials an easy task.

The call of the cheap land, which the government was willing and anxious to sell to anyone who would settle upon it and make it productive, was the secret of the scarcity of labor. There was always a keen competition between the factory owner in the East, who wanted hands, and the farmer in the West, who needed hired men to work the land he had taken up. So, although the money wages of workers was low (as money is not plentiful in new countries), the cheapness of food and clothing, and the simplicity of life, made their living conditions very good compared with those of European workers. The American worker could secure a comfortable cottage, with a garden and yard, for a low rent. Wood to burn was cheap; when coal supplanted wood as a fuel, it also was cheap. Many workers had a potato patch and kitchen garden, with perhaps a chicken yard, and a pig or two fattening for winter meat. Workers who did not have these things were regarded as shiftless by the New Englanders, who knew that it was possible to acquire them with thrift and care. In short, the worker in the early American days who did not live comfortably had himself to blame, for his wages were sufficient to supply him with the necessities and comforts of life.

Conditions of factory life. The first marked change came between 1800 and 1825, when the factory system was becoming a fixed institution in American life. Naturally many of the customs of English factory life were transferred with the factory into America. The operatives, many of them women, earned a very low money wage and lived in cheerless quarters. As these operatives were more intelligent than the corresponding workers in England, and as the abundant land kept food cheaper, their conditions were, however, never so bad as in England. The hours were very long—from sunrise to sunset, with short recesses for breakfast and luncheon, both cold meals brought from home. Lowell, Massachusetts, was considered a town with very fine conditions, for there the working-day was only fourteen hours long, beginning at 5 A.M. and closing at 7 P.M., and having forty-five minutes for noon dinner. This was the town in which many very fine New England farmers' daughters worked, leading a life of cultured activity outside their factory work. To them long hours and simple living were natural enough, for they were used to such a discipline on the rocky farms from which they came.

The reduction of the working-day was first asked for children, who put in almost the same inhuman hours as their elders. Grown people began to realize that these children were growing up ignorant and therefore dangerous citizens, and from 1825 on the laborers waged a campaign for free public schools, thus greatly strengthening that institution of America which has meant and now means more than any other to the life of the nation. To secure their demands, the laborers organized in labor unions, like their English brothers.[1]

Mid-century social betterment. The history of labor organization in America is reviewed briefly in Chapter VI, and will not be given here, but the gains in social welfare secured by union action should be noted. Between 1825 and 1837, when labor organization was lost in the general confusion and suffering, the ten-hour day won some victories in Baltimore (by strike) and in Philadelphia (by example of the city government); but in general the ten-hour day came about between 1840 and 1850

---

[1] They were strengthened by two early labor publications the *Workingman's Advocate* of New York, edited by the Evans brothers, and the *Mechanics' Free Press* of Philadelphia. The press in general was not favorable to the labor movement.

except in New England, where it was not generally adopted until the Civil War. The public-school system, for which workmen persistently agitated, became an accepted policy in the new Western states, in which democracy grew with indigenous freedom. Indiana, in 1816, made provisions for a complete state school system in its constitution, other states did the same in some way or other With the example of the West before it, the East gradually established free schools also For a long time the private academy gave the only opportunity for secondary education, but after the Civil War, the high school, which had been known here and there by 1830, became a widespread institution. So labor, working with the more broadminded Eastern leaders and with the West generally, won even in the Eastern cities its contention for free public schools.

During the same period other reforms, not directly connected with any labor movement, took place. Duelling became disreputable, even in the South, where it held its own longest. Lotteries were no longer conducted by Church and State as formerly. Imprisonment for debt was gradually abolished by the states. The condition of prisons and asylums was improved greatly, largely through the efforts of Dorothea Dix As the land became more settled there gradually took place that accumulation of surplus wealth which carries a thrifty people over the crisis of a year of bad crops or of an industrial failure. Men could now spare some time from their frontier tasks for the higher interests of life.

Materialism versus the higher life. In general, however, culture had to yield first place to the conquest of the land The economic opportunities were so great that the best brain and brawn of the nation were bent to the task of realizing them. This meant that while rents, wages, and profits yielded the essentials of existence abundantly, the higher things of life were often neglected. In the hard years of 1837-1845 Americans were busy overcoming the suffering caused by overspeculation; in the "booming 40's" and the crowded 50's there was work and excitement for everyone, with westward expansion and new farm machinery and railroads to create new jobs, increase production, and extend markets. But the better elements in society combined high thinking with plain living. It is safe to say that never, in all the world's history, had there been so large a proportion of poor people with fair intelligence as there were in America in those middle-century years. Simple and practical religion was general. People were morally in earnest. In practical ways they worked for prison reform, for hospitals and asylums and missionaries, for the extension of suffrage, for the abolition of slavery, and for temperance laws.

"An help meet for man." A characteristic of American life in all its aspects was that women always worked with men. They did not do the same things that men did in the fields or in the factories, unless it became really necessary, but they planned and coöperated with men in almost everything In the Western schools and colleges (led by Oberlin, which opened its halls to women students in 1830) they studied side by side with men. As a consequence American men learned early to look upon women as equals and companions, and for that reason the entrance of women into industry and the professions has been easier in America than in Europe.

Progress of the colored race. Great as was the improvement in the social condition of the white people of the nation, a far more wonderful thing was taking place during the nineteenth century among the colored people of the South. Before emancipation the negroes were receiving a kind of training and discipline at the hands of their masters which, unaided by the conditions of absolute control thus exercised, they would not have experienced in centuries. Slavery was wrong in principle and bad in results for the slave-owning class; but it benefited the negro, for it short-circuited a period of race development which would have taken immeasurably longer without white tutelage, if, indeed, it had taken place at all. When freed during the Civil War, the negro at first found himself lost without the close control and discipline of the plantation system, and for a time he stood still or deteriorated, but after a time there arose negro leaders who have wrought nobly for their race, and under their leadership, at the present time, the colored population in both North and South shows signs of real and permanent progress. It is probably true, as has been claimed, that the negro race in America has made more progress in a century than any other race was ever known to make in like time.

A Second Period of Progress

The struggle over the existence of slavery and the relative powers of state and Federal government occupied the middle of the century, and it was not until about the centennial year that the nation was again free to take up the improvement of social conditions in general.

At this time machine production on a larger scale began to attract a new immigration of foreigners, who became factory hands and also did the unskilled labor previously performed by the great numbers of Irish immigrants. A new campaign for better conditions and wages among laborers began with the effective reorganization of the laboring forces of the country, labor organization having become largely inactive during the period of struggle over slavery.

Labor has cooperated more or less with religious organizations, women's clubs, interested individuals, and welfare organizations of various sorts, such as the National Child Labor Committee. The welfare work of these many forces has been directed toward (1) better working-conditions, (2) better living-conditions; (3) better human beings; (4) building future well-being.

Much of this welfare we shall discuss in other connections, since welfare is a matter that concerns so many sides of life that it is necessarily hard to confine under any one subject, but in addition to the treatment elsewhere we shall outline here the recent and present status of the more important phases.

Who shall work? In an ideal society all the men work at some really productive job, all the married women keep

NINETEENTH-CENTURY PROGRESS 107

house in comfortable, clean homes, and all the children study and play between square meals and nine-hour slumbers. In our far-from-ideal world women and children are still forced

CHILD LABOR IN A TENEMENT HOME

The National Child Labor Committee, with headquarters at 105 East Twenty-second Street, New York City, is the organization through which opponents of this evil work. The photograph reproduced here was taken in 1917 by Mr. L. W. Hine for the Research Department of the committee. The mother, with four of her five children (aged ten, nine, seven, and five years), inserts patriotic flag pins into cards. They are paid three cents per gross, which nets them $2 per week. The mother works irregularly, for she does the janitor work for the building in which she lives, receiving in return the rent of the family home of three small rooms, but no money wage. The husband is a laborer, who had work at the time the picture was taken. The New York law prohibits the employment of children under fourteen in tenement home work, but it is hard to enforce the law, not only because of the expense of adequate inspection but because the low wages usually paid adult labor make child labor necessary if the family is to live

to work outside their homes. But this much has come to pass: everybody, except a few employers whose interests blind them to obvious fact, now acknowledges that all children should be allowed to grow up, not without light and reasonable work, but without work which robs them of health, of school, and of reasonable playtime Our laws do not yet effectively prohibit child labor everywhere, and public opinion is not sufficiently aroused to prevent it; but the repeated efforts of child-labor opponents will eventually put an end to child labor in the nation, so far as its industrial phases are concerned. There will still remain the child labor of farms, which is as serious a problem as child labor in factories, except that the open-air work is less harmful to health, and the moral risks are perhaps less.[1] Too many farms in this country derive their small profit from the contribution of the children, whose parents take them from school for the spring planting or the fall corn-picking, and must sometimes ask of them tasks too heavy for youthful strength. Some real work each day, such as the lighter farm chores, cannot hurt healthy children; but labor that takes the place of that done by a grown man or grown woman is as wrong on a farm as anywhere else.

The disadvantage of woman labor in industries is that it takes women away from home-making. When mothers must leave home and either commit their children to strangers or leave them to shift for themselves, woman labor becomes a menace to society. In America the coming of prohibition has already worked much relief in this respect, there is less going out by the day than in former years, and less factory work by mothers. Adequate wages for the natural wage-earner of the family is the ultimate solution of the mother-in-industry evil; so this question, like so many others, is reduced finally to the question of the distribution of the returns.[2]

Better working-quarters. We come now to the matter of working-conditions. What are the reasonable demands of labor with regard to working-quarters? A worker has a right to ask that his health shall not be endangered by unnecessary

---

[1] For discussion of child-labor bills see page 122, for conditions on farms see *Rural Child Welfare*, by the National Child Labor Committee.

[2] This question is discussed in detail in Chapter XI

dirt, by close and fetid air, by extremes of temperature, and by dangerous machinery. He has a right, if his work be of a necessarily dirty character, such as mining and coke-making, to rooms for washing and dressing that will enable him to make a self-respecting appearance in the street. He has a right to abundant light, and sunshine if possible rather than artificial light. He has a right to an adequate noon-hour for luncheon and rest. He has a right to proper sanitation and ordinary comfort in his working-quarters

These conditions are being furnished increasingly by employers; indeed, the scarcity of good labor makes necessary a certain amount of bidding for it, in the more skilled industries, through attractive working-conditions Those employers who will not give their workers improved quarters find themselves under increasing condemnation by public opinion and in increasing difficulty of finding good workers.

One of the reasons for poor working-conditions lies in the fact that conscious planning for the welfare of workers has not kept pace with the development of industries. Working-quarters are often very old, and capital begrudges the great outlay necessary for constructing new ones. Obviously the later-established industries enjoy a great advantage here. Industrial centers, carefully planned for efficiency, make the best working-conditions possible.

Better living-conditions. Housing and feeding are the two great aims of the campaign for better living. Better clothing is important, but as good clothing is now to be bought ready-made, this part of better living is very closely dependent upon higher wages. But good wages will not of themselves produce better housing or more wholesome food. Careful thought and effort must go into these two problems

Food and welfare. Good cooking means first a balanced ration, with all the elements needed included, and second, attractive dishes well served. Formerly American girls were trained in housekeeping at home, and in their turn trained their daughters. But today there are multitudes of foreign women who do not know how to use the new foods of their new country, or how to manage a gas range, or how to buy economically. They need to be taught in social-settlement centers, or at a night school, or by their daughters who attend such classes. Cooking is a regular study in thousands of high schools, and when the girls now attending them become housekeepers they will know the principles of nutrition and the art of preparing food. Better food is an important part of the better living-conditions which America has made possible for thousands of Europeans.

Better human beings. All these improvements in living will of themselves, in time, produce a sturdier, healthier, finer race; but in the meantime there are agencies at work directly to improve the quality of human beings. Without discussing the means for intellectual and spiritual improvement, which are discussed elsewhere, let us summarize the helps to better bodies that are now offered to the people.

The better-babies movement begins at the beginning in teaching people how to take care of babies and in encouraging them to look carefully after babies' health. Babies are measured and weighed to find out whether they grow properly, and their mothers are given expert advice as to their food, clothing, sleeping, and everything else that can affect their growth and health. Some cities have a better-babies week, in which general public interest in the care of children is fostered.

The better-babies movement is much needed. In 1919 alone two hundred and fifty thousand babies died of diseases caused by ignorance and poverty, diseases that might have been prevented or cured by proper care. Not only the babies but the mothers too die, or suffer long invalidism, because they do not have the care and rest that they should have. Twenty-three thousand mothers was the death toll of ignorance and poverty in 1919, according to the statistics of the national Children's Bureau, which is working for better conditions for mothers and children. The record of the United States in the matter of infant mortality and mother mortality is not a good one; almost all the greater nations show less loss than we. Federal help is needed in this as in other reforms, and is provided for in the Towner-Sterling Bill.

When children reach school age they are looked after, in the best school systems, by the school physician and the school nurse. Dental clinics are held, that teeth may be kept in good condition and so the general health preserved and improved Calisthenics and supervised play give exercise under intelligent direction. Everything that can be done is done to cooperate with parents in bringing up healthy, strong children; and when parents are too poor, ignorant, or indifferent to look after their children personally, the school does its best to supply the need. All this is, at the present time, more an ideal than an accomplished fact in a majority of our schools and towns; but it is a growing custom, and within a few years school education in physical health will be as accepted and universal as school training in intellectual things is now. There is now a strong movement along the line of the socialization of medicine, a movement as new today as the socialization of mental training was four hundred years ago.

Nor does the making of a better, stronger race stop with schooldays. Free dispensaries and hospitals are today more numerous and more efficient than they ever were. The libraries furnish books for self-education in the laws of health, lecturers and periodicals labor to the same end Young peoples' organizations of many kinds stress physical fitness, and not only preach but furnish the means of recreation out of doors and healthful living indoors. The laws of health are published in many ways, and the standard of health is constantly rising Despite the wailing of pessimists statistics show that the death rate is declining and that one disease after another is yielding to scientific treatment.

It was Jacob Riis who brought the housing problem seriously before the American people. As a result of appeals made by him and by other reformers, many cities became interested in their tenements and slums, investigated conditions, and passed housing ordinances. People began to think what bad housing means to society, and how the bad conditions might be remedied. The remedies fall mainly into two groups: those connected with securing the passage of the necessary ordinances by city councils, and those involved in securing the enforcement of these ordinances.[1] Once a building which is really too bad for human habitation can be removed, it is possible to rebuild in a way to meet the needs of decent, comfortable living. What often happens in growing American cities is that old dwelling-houses are torn down to make way for business houses, thus creating a demand for new dwellings in some other place.

This is the opportunity of the housing expert. If only public opinion, municipal law, and farsighted capital can be made to coöperate, new homes of the best type can be built, usually in residential suburbs, which will bring about better living among the tenants. The greatest trouble with most tenements comes from the fact that they were never planned for the purpose to which they are put. Almost all tenements were once either the mansions of the wealthy or the cottages of single families in moderate circumstances. The original owners moved away as the neighborhood changed, and the properties were remodeled to make them profitable for renting purposes. Large rooms were subdivided by means of thin partitions, additions filled up all available empty space on the lots, and the houses were crowded with all the people who could be jammed in.

Aims of a good-housing campaign. The main aims of a good-housing campaign are as follows:

1. *Sanitation.* Cleanliness is put first because it secures health wherever it is observed, and because its lack causes the worst conditions possible. Rubbish heaps in alleys and courts,

---

[1] Chicago, for instance, passed very good housing regulations in 1910, but an investigation showed that they were being flagrantly ignored. The series of articles describing actual conditions in Chicago, published in the *American Journal of Sociology* in 1913–1915, may be taken as an account of typical American slums. The series is valuable because it discusses results as well as conditions.

poor plumbing or none at all, an infected water supply, and a lack of garbage service are some of the disease-breeding conditions found in the poorer parts of our cities and villages.

A SWEATSHOP HOME

One of the major problems of social progress is to establish such control of working-conditions that production becomes a process of life and health rather than one of suffering and death. To this end the abolition of the sweatshop system is an aim of labor organizations and of social workers. This picture, made from a photograph taken in New York City by Mr. Hine of the National Child Labor Committee, shows a mother who lives in a rear house on Mulberry Street. She makes a pittance by finishing trousers; the work of four days is shown on the trunk. When this picture was taken the father was out of work because of rheumatism, and the mother must finish the work she was doing and receive her pay before the family could eat, as there was no food in the house. Two organizations working for the abolition of sweatshop work are the National Consumers' League, 44 East Twenty-third Street, New York City, and the National Women's Trade Union League of America, 311 South Ashland Boulevard, Chicago. The Woman's Bureau of the Department of Labor at Washington is also interested in this reform and sends out up-to-date information upon conditions

2. *Room.* Overcrowding is an evil almost equal to that of dirt in the slums. Large families living in two or three rooms,

lodgers sharing rooms with the family, and rooms too small to allow of comfort, characterize tenements. Chicago makes four hundred cubic feet of air space per adult, and half that amount for each child under twelve, its modest minimum.[1] Closely related to the actual size of the dwelling is the amount of privacy to be had This depends partly upon good planning. There should be strict ordinances limiting the number and relationship of people who can live in houses of given sizes, which would prevent much of the evil springing from the taking of lodgers among the families of the very poor and among foreigners.

3. *Cleanliness, neatness, and beauty.* These depend largely on the state of repair in which the buildings are kept, and on the general standard of appearances in the city in question. Some wealthy tenement owners, because they never see the houses from which they draw their income, and do not realize their responsibility or do not care, spend no money on repairs. Others are poor, and hope soon to sell their property at a gain, which would be reduced by any money spent in keeping it up. In either case the tenant may suffer from a leaky roof, rickety stairs, broken windows, or fallen plaster. Good, clean living is very hard to achieve under such circumstances. And yet visitors to slums are often surprised to find efforts at cleanliness and beauty amid the squalor. There are snowy beds, scrubbed floors, pictures on the wall, and needle-worked covers on the furniture. The housekeeper has done her part, and deserves better of the landlord than she is receiving.

4. *Light and ventilation.* The window space necessary for health is put conservatively at one tenth the floor space of the room, that is, if a room measures twelve feet by ten, there should be at least twelve square feet of window in that room. A window may be almost useless for light and ventilation if it cannot be opened or if it faces a narrow, sunless air shaft. Artificial lights in the halls at night should also be required by law.

[1] City of Chicago, Revised Building Ordinances, Article IX, Sect 447

5. *Fire protection* Buildings should have iron escapes from the upper stories, and stairways wide enough and straight enough to lessen the danger of accident in case of sudden panic.

6. *Garden and play space* In the crowded city these are, of course, impracticable, their place being taken by the neighborhood playgrounds But in suburban tenements, which as time passes may more and more supplant those of city centers, it is possible for each family to have a little plat of its own, in which the children may be kept off the street and may find good employment for spare time in gardening. Such a spot will add somewhat to the rent of the dwelling, but it may be made to pay for itself in produce. "Garden cities" have been made in England for working-people for some years and have proved very successful.

Bad housing is not a city evil alone. Some of the worst conditions are found in country districts, especially in the poorer farming regions. Discomfort, ugliness, and squalor abound where there should be simple beauty, cleanliness, and health Ignorance is the cause of these conditions rather than poverty, for although the people have little money, they have space, time, and independence. They need friendly advice, pictures of beautiful country cottages from which to copy ideas, and incentives for bettering their condition. Here is a field for social work that is open to country and village people Here is a chance for the country doctor or the country parson or the country teacher to do some constructive work of permanent value. The simplest facts about drainage and the disposal of manure must be taught; garden pictures (especially of the beautiful country cottages to be found in some parts both of Old and of New England) should be exhibited; if possible, prizes should be given for improvement in premises; and economical ways of securing good results should be shown. For instance, the planting of shrubs gives beauty, with a minimum of yearly attention; neat walks save hours of floor-scrubbing, a well, located in the right place, prevents typhoid; and screening keeps food clean from flies.

The outlook. All these things contribute to a brighter prospect for the future. The most hopeful aspect of social conditions today, perhaps, is not actual accomplishment along any one line, but the general attitude of care for the future, the feeling of responsibility for coming generations. The human race, so long struggling blindly against adverse conditions caused by the selfishness of an exploiting minority, is at last more thoughtfully considering its problems and more effectively solving them Intelligent thought will in time overcome the two greatest obstacles of all to social progress: the shortsighted selfishness of the exploiter, and the blind, ineffective, destructive resentment of the exploited. It will substitute for both intelligent and friendly cooperation.

Political Progress in England

The reforms of the nineteenth century were not confined to changes in the social life of the people. In some ways the political progress of this age seems even greater than that accomplished in the era of revolutions. The march toward democracy was marked in England by less spectacular events than those of the two preceding centuries, but was none the less steadily directed toward great ends finally accomplished.

Reform in suffrage and representation. The first advance toward democracy in England was the equalization of representation and the extension of the franchise The story of the gradual increase in justice which came with the doing away of pocket and rotten boroughs, and the addition of new classes of voters by the three reform bills of 1832, 1867, and 1884, is told in all the English histories. It is the story of a steadily marching tendency toward more and more complete democracy in English government The process was almost completed in 1918, when women of thirty or over were granted the franchise. Doubtless in time the age qualification for women will be made the same as that for men, as it is in America. A strong movement for this final reform occurred in 1922.

The growing power of the Commons. But all this reform of the franchise applied only to local affairs and to the lower house of Parliament, while the other house has remained a non-elective, hereditary body. One may well ask of what use a democratic lower house can be if an ultra-aristocratic upper house is always present to check and modify legislation to its own liking? England has realized this situation and has met it. The House of Lords has been slowly deprived of its powers until today it remains but a hollow shell of its old self. The titles, ceremonies, and social prestige are still there, but the power is gone.

The weapon used by the Commons during the nineteenth century, in winning its victory over the House of Lords, had been used as far back as 1712. It was the creation of liberal peers by the king (who, since 1688, has been subservient to the Commons). By this device the Commons have forced the Lords to give in on every important point through their fear of having their house packed with liberal peers.

The Commons, however, finally grew weary of this roundabout method of securing liberal legislation; and in the twentieth century, after the Lords' refusal to pass the Lloyd George Budget Bill, by the Parliament Act of 1911 they swept away every vestige of the Lords' power over money bills and reduced their power in other measures to a delaying of their passage for two years.

Cabinet and responsible government. While the lower house was gaining control over the upper, another development was taking place which likewise made for democracy. This was the growth of what is called "responsible government." By this term is meant the responsibility of the cabinet, in whose hands lies the chief executive and legislative power, to the lower house, and the responsibility of that house to the voters of the nation. The cabinet is the only great invention in the English constitution since 1485. It originated in the Privy Council—a sort of inner clique of the old Curia Regis, which really possessed most of the administrative power. After the members of this group of ministers came to be chosen by the Commons instead of the king, they made a cabinet in the continental use of the word. Custom decreed that they be all members of Parliament and, except in rare cases of coalition, of the same party When the Liberals have the majority in the Commons, the king offers the prime ministry to their chief leader. This premier then collects a group of prominent Liberals to be secretaries of foreign affairs, home affairs, labor, finance, etc. These men conduct the government. They not only carry on all the administrative departments, but, acting in unison, they formulate and introduce most of the legislation.

The cabinet is always responsible to the Commons. If its actions either in the executive or the legislative fields displease the members of the lower house, they may cause the fall of the cabinet either by voting down one of its important measures or by passing a resolution of lack of confidence in "the government." If the cabinet does not then mend its way to suit parliamentary wishes, it is forced to resign, and the king offers the premiership to the leader of "the opposition." This leader then gathers together a cabinet which controls the government until it is superseded.

If the party whose cabinet has fallen out of power believes that the country as a whole favors its policy, it may demand an immediate election on the chief question at issue between the two parties. The king issues the announcement of a general election, and the nation chooses the men who shall carry out its preferred policy. In this way the British people keep many of the forms of the old monarchy, while in reality the control which the voters have over their lawmakers is democratic and direct to a surprising degree. This system of republican constitutional monarchy is the most important of the many noteworthy contributions to government made by England.[1]

---

[1] Americans often wonder why the British keep their king, since he has become so purely a figurehead The chief reason is that he is so integral a part of the government that they cannot conceive of his being supplanted Perhaps the memory of their failure to work out a satisfactory form without him in the

British colonial self-government. Political progress was not confined during the last century to the mother country. Several important possessions of the crown have become during this period self-governing dominions. These are Canada (1867), the Commonwealth of Australia (1900), the Union of South Africa (1909), the Dominion of New Zealand (1907), Newfoundland (1832), and Ireland (1921). These dominions are almost completely independent of imperial control and have within them a responsible system of democratic government copied after that of England. They really form a confederacy of British peoples, independent under ordinary circumstances, united in an emergency. Their ties to the mother country are five

1. The sympathy and good will which comes from common blood, speech, and temperament.

2. The governor, a direct representative of the crown (and usually a native Englishman), who symbolizes the unity of the empire.

3. The power of the governor or the crown to refuse consent to legislation. This right is exercised with care and reluctance.

4. The regulation that dominion laws cannot be made which violate existing imperial statutes.

5. The right of the Imperial Parliament to legislate for the dominions. These laws are few in number, never bear on taxation, and are usually about such matters as the position of aliens, copyright regulations, and merchant shipping

In theory these are fairly binding ties, but in reality it is only the first, nonlegal one which operates continually and effectively. The action of the dominions in declaring war against Germany in 1914 is the most striking proof of the existing unity of the empire.

days of the Commonwealth helps to keep the king on the throne A king in name only serves the justifiable purpose of giving a concrete symbol of government, a rallying point for loyalty and patriotism In the United States we have only the flag, the eagle, and the Constitution—none of them personal The president is partisan, and so cannot serve for all Moreover, he changes frequently, while the present English royal family dates back to before the time of Alfred the Great

Although bound by centuries of conservatism, England has worked out her governmental salvation. From an absolute monarchy in form and an aristocracy in spirit she has progressed to a constitutional monarchy in form and a representative democracy in spirit and working. Her political progress has been of the greatest value to the world, because she has worked ahead of other nations; and these nations, including our own land, have copied the valuable results of her experiments with necessary modifications. In the words of Willis Mason West, "The splendid story of England . . . is, also, . . . the story of the foundations of American liberty."

Political Progress in America

The opening of the nineteenth century found the United States an infant nation with a new national constitution and an untested government. In the hundred years following we were to discover that the document made at Philadelphia was an adequate one to serve our rapidly expanding needs with only nine essential textual changes.[1]

During this time the federal form of government changed greatly both in operation and in spirit, but withstood every attack upon it and, as a type of government, stands today tested and approved.

The centralizing movement. The drift of events has taken the United States away from a loose union or confederation toward a stronger, more centralized government. This change has been accomplished, first, through the enforcement of the second paragraph of Article VI of the Constitution; second, through the position given to the Supreme Court as final interpreter in all cases of conflicting powers; and third, through the so-called elastic clause of the Constitution,[2] which provides that Congress may make all "necessary and proper" laws.

---

[1] Of the nineteen amendments it will be remembered that ten were enacted in 1791 as a bill of rights and are practically a part of the original document.
[2] Article I, Sect. 8, clause 18.

Article VI provided that "this constitution, and the laws of the United States which shall be made in pursuance thereof; and all treaties made . . under the authority of the United States, shall be the supreme law of the land." On the basis of this provision the following order of rank and authority has been worked out and universally accepted:

1. The Constitution.
2. United States laws and treaties [1]
3 State constitutions, whether made before or after the United States Constitution
4. State laws.
5. County, town, or city regulations.

The courts of the land enforce this relative ranking. If a city ordinance or a county by-law is contrary to a state law or the state constitution, the supreme court of the state may declare it unconstitutional and therefore null and void. So also the United States Supreme Court declares state laws which are contrary to Federal enactments, and national laws which are contrary to the Constitution, to be null and void. These pronouncements do not come as a general expression of opinion, but as the result of some specific case—a "test case"—which has come to the courts under the questioned law. After one decision of this sort regarding a law, it is thenceforth considered inoperative and wiped out of existence.

Schools of constitutional interpretation. The power of the Supreme Court to declare state and Federal enactments unconstitutional has led to a great modification of the Constitution by means of interpretation. Early in the history of the nation, when John Marshall was Chief Justice, he established what is known as the "loose" or "broad" construction of the Constitution and of the powers of the central government This was done by interpreting the words "necessary and pioper" in the elastic clause loosely to mean necessary *or* proper, which means not necessary at all but "appropriate" or "suitable." From

---

[1] Federal laws and treaties are on a par; when one conflicts with the other the one most recently passed is considered to supersede the other

that day to this the Supreme Court has been inclined to allow Congress to legislate on more and more matters not specifically delegated to it in the enumerated list. Such laws as the Sherman Anti-Trust, the Interstate Commerce Commission, and the Federal Reserve Acts—none of which are within the seventeen delegated powers mentioned in Article I, Sect. 8—have resulted from this latitude in construction.

Occasionally the Supreme Court holds up a law which is based on a construction too lax; as, for example, the Keating-Owen Child Labor Law of 1916. When this much-needed law could not be passed under the pretense that it was an intercommerce act, it was repassed in 1918 as a part of a revenue bill. This was in turn declared unconstitutional on May 15, 1922, which left the matter of child labor again subject only to state control. The child-labor situation is an illustration of how old safeguards of liberty may in time become blocks in the way of social welfare.

Thus it has come about that Congress legislates on many matters besides the seventeen enumerated and specified powers (Constitution, Article I, Sect. 8), and the separate states of the Union find themselves more limited in power as the years go by. Experiment has brought about a more centralized union than would have been possible in 1789. But many local matters are still the province of state legislation; and in many cases the local enforcement of Federal law has become better and better through the coöperation of state officials.

Suffrage. In the matter of suffrage the United States made progress faster than the mother country. Each of the state constitutions of the original thirteen states contained clauses disfranchising various people. In some cases landownership was required for the voting privilege; in others, personal property only. It is safe to say that not one fifth of the white men were allowed to vote in 1780. At the forming of the Constitution the right to lay down suffrage regulations, even for the election of national officers, was left to the states. The first constitution to contain provision for full manhood suffrage was that of the Watauga community, afterwards reunited with North Carolina. This frontier state—a little independent nation with truly American institutions—allowed all its citizens to vote in 1772 When Louisiana removed its property qualification in 1845, manhood suffrage prevailed throughout the United States

When the time came for the extension of the electorate to include women, the West was once more the pioneer. Eleven states west of the Mississippi adopted this extension before one east of the river enfranchised its women. There was a reason for this difference of opinion growing out of the difference in the make-up of the population and of the conditions of living in the two regions. A long campaign, at first mainly educational in its methods, but later more active and aggressive, was carried on by women who believed that they should be allowed to vote. It extended through the forty-eight years between the granting of woman suffrage in Wyoming, in 1869, to the grant made by New York, the first Eastern state, in 1917. After that suffrage champions began a campaign to have the Constitution amended for them, as it had been amended for the negroes. Its later stages were marked by many militant episodes, such as picketing the White House, burning the president's speeches, and refusing food in order to secure release from imprisonment. Whether it was these methods, copied from English militant "suffragettes," or the more peaceful and convincing proofs abundantly at hand that women deserve political power for their faithful and efficient service to mankind, which won the fight will never be absolutely settled. The Nineteenth Amendment, having been ratified by the necessary three fourths of the states, became a part of the Constitution in 1920. Women are now enfranchised fully for any unit in the nation.

Although suffrage in the United States is now practically universal, the various states still set reasonable limits. Three that are almost universal are age, citizenship, and residence. The accepted age for voting is now twenty-one Obviously this excludes many who are able to vote intelligently, and admits many to a share in government who are unworthy of it. In most states full citizenship is a prerequisite, although a few allow newcomers to vote who have taken out first papers only.

There is some agitation for the postponing of the suffrage right of naturalized citizens until they prove themselves worthy of exercising it. It is more likely that the giving of citizenship will be deferred and subjected to more stringent requirements. The wisdom of a residence requirement lies in its power to check the fraud of plural voting, which is not legal in the United States. In elections where such questions as prohibition came up, it was the custom for outside voters to be shipped in by the interests affected for election day. The will of the people in any locality could be thwarted by this device. Now every state demands residence in the state for a period varying from three months to two years, while shorter periods of residence are required for counties, cities, and even city wards.

There are two other fairly common voting restrictions: those requiring the voter to prove that he can read and those requiring him to pay a poll tax. An educational test was adopted by Connecticut, Massachusetts, Maine, and Wyoming during periods of agitation against foreigners. Fifteen states require the voter to be able to read.

In order to see that their qualifications are being observed, most states now demand registration of the voters before election. Various persons, such as paupers, Indians, soldiers, and people who have been convicted of bribery, are disqualified from voting in one state or another. Some changes will doubtless be made from time to time in suffrage regulation, but the great battles for a democratic electorate have been won in America An intelligent electorate is the next great national goal, now that a representative electorate has been secured.[1]

[1] For a complete chart of the state qualifications for voting see the World Almanac for 1920, pp 788–789

Elections

Changes in voting methods. The method of voting saw changes almost as radical as those in the voting body. In colonial times voting was at first carried on by a show of hands in open meeting. The first use of slips or ballots in political business was in 1634, when Governor Winthrop of Massachusetts Bay Colony was put out of office. The idea was borrowed from English borough practice. This secret method of voting was seen to be such a protection to voters that in less than three years it was made compulsory in the Bay Colony, not only for town elections but for elections to the assembly in Boston. By the time of the Revolution all the colonies had adopted the ballot.

The Constitution left the conduct of elections almost entirely to the states. It did lay down the complicated scheme of the "electoral college" for electing the president, and it authorized Congress to alter the regulations of the states in the matter of the choice of members of Congress. But for the most part the Constitution ignores election methods. The result has been that elections have been almost entirely state affairs. The oral method of voting was retained for a long time in some states, voters came to the polls and announced their choices, and the judge scratched down their vote. The value of a secret vote in preventing vote buying and intimidation resulted in the general adoption of the ballot method, but even this failed to secure honest elections in some cases. Ballots were printed on colored papers, and a watcher could tell by the color of the ballot cast the party which it supported. Corrupt election judges sometimes counted out or destroyed part of the ballots.

The Australian ballot. By 1888 dissatisfaction with the evils of this system led to a trial of the English adaptation of the Australian ballot. By this approved method a voter goes through these steps in voting:

1. He has the election official find his name on the registration book to prove that he is a legal voter in that division.

2. He receives a ballot upon which are printed the names of all candidates of all parties.

3. He carries the ballot into a small private booth, where he marks it by crossing the squares after the names of his choice.

4. He carries the ballot folded to the official, who, in his presence, puts it into the ballot box, after assuring himself that it is the official ballot and the only one being cast. The official or a clerk then checks off his name in the list as having voted, thus preventing a plural vote.

The Australian system has proved superior to previous methods of voting, but even it has some drawbacks. Voting machines have been invented which are ingenious and economical of time and clerk hire, but as yet they are not in general use.

The means of choosing a president. The Constitution provides for an executive chosen not by the people, but by a group of men selected in each state, known as electors. They were to meet (as they still do) at their state capitals in the January after each election. There they were, after due consideration, to cast their votes for president, choosing the man they deemed best for the position. Nominally this is still done, but today each elector is a mere machine for recording the will of his district. The character and training of electors is of small moment, for they must cast their votes for the chosen candidates of their parties. This is an example of unwritten law that is as strong as the most iron-bound statute; no elector is ever known to vote contrary to the instruction given him by the popular vote. Therefore today the nation knows, as soon as the election returns show who have been chosen as electors, who will be the next president.

Nominations. The method of nominating presidential candidates has been changed quite as radically as the method of election, and likewise without amending the Constitution. The framers of the Constitution planned to have the president both nominated and elected by the electoral college, but when the voters organized into parties it became necessary to agree upon party candidates before the election. The first nominating device was the "caucus," in use in 1790 in all the states for nominating state officials. Six years later the Federalists adopted it for the purpose of choosing John Adams as a party candidate for the presidency By this device the leading men of each party in Congress met in caucus and informally selected their candidates. Since these men had been elected to office some years previously and upon entirely different issues, their choice of candidates might not be the choice of the people.

Dissatisfaction with the caucus increased yearly as the electorate was enlarged and more men of presidential caliber appeared. In 1832 the device of the national nominating convention was adopted, a method which has been used ever since. The delegates to these conventions are chosen by a complicated and unsatisfactory method, usually under the control of the party machine. As a rule a state convention selects four delegates at large and their four alternates (twice the number of senators from the state) Then each congressional district holds a convention for choosing its two delegates and two alternates. Frequently the members of the congressional-district conventions are chosen not by the people, but by county conventions. This hierarchy of conventions makes it easy for politicians to thwart the will of the people. The delegates who finally assemble at the national convention are not really there to express the choice of their constituents They often cast their first vote in favor of the man who is the first choice of their state, after that they usually feel free to vote as they please. There is often much trading and bargaining in votes. The balloting is often very long drawn out. for instance, in 1880 the Republicans cast thirty-six ballots, in 1860 the Democrats (who require a two-thirds vote) cast fifty-seven ballots, and in 1912, forty-six.

Altogether, the national nominating convention falls short in many ways of giving an ideal method for the selecting of candidates for the two highest executive positions, but imperfect as it is, it comes far nearer to being an expression of popular desires than the caucus, which was in use a century ago.

Examples of change might be multiplied, but enough have been given to illustrate the general movement toward a closer touch and a more general participation of the people in the political affairs of the nation than existed in the early years of the Republic. Political progress during the last century has been toward a people's government; toward a nearer realization of the dream of the citizen who sees in his government the collective will of society, at work for the good of all its members. In extending participation in government to poorer, more ignorant, less experienced men than the aristocratic leaders of a century ago, something of dignity, purity, and efficiency in government has been lost. This is the cost of democracy, which is often expensive of quality. But if in the end the quality of government can be brought as high as once it was, or higher, while it remains the possession of a whole people instead of the plaything of a privileged few, then men will have accomplished a thing of epic scope to which future generations may well look back in admiration and gratitude.

SUPPLEMENTARY READINGS

BRYCE, JAMES. American Commonwealth, Vol. II, p. 353.
CHEYNEY, E. P. Industrial and Social History of England, chaps. ix-xi.
OSGOOD, ELLEN. A History of Industry, chap. xiii.
ROBINSON, C. M. Improvement of Towns and Cities, chaps. ii, iii, v, x.
ROBINSON, C. M. Modern Civic Art, pp. 250-251, 257-259.
ROBINSON, J. H., BREASTED, J. H., and SMITH, E. P. General History of Europe, chaps. xli, xliv.
SPEARE, M. E., and NORRIS, W. B. Vital Forces in Current Events, pp. 34-44, "Western Democracy and Big Business," by Frederick J. Turner.
TRAILL, H. D. Social England, Vol. V, pp. 591-622; Vol. VI, pp. 45-103, 192-242, 404-445, 599-643.

SEARCH QUESTIONS AND PROBLEMS

1. Do you see anything significant in the fact that at the times when the social well-being of the workers was at low ebb there was a movement to dispossess them of their land?

2. Do you know of any employer who furnishes his help with a house and perhaps a garden plot and fuel? Is this of any very great aid? Why?

3. Exactly why is the charity given through the provisions of the Elizabethan Poor Law considered wrong, whereas the work of our modern Associated Charities is considered highly commendable?

4. Prepare a special report on the effects of child labor on the child, on industry, and on society (see Towne's "Social Problems," pp 68–74)

5. Do you believe that if everyone were allowed to do just as he pleased his actions would always be for the good of society as a whole? Give concrete examples of what would happen if parents and teachers applied a laissez-faire theory to you or to some of your acquaintances

6. Has your state enacted effective laws on the following points (use a Blue Book or yearbooks). minimum wage for women, limitations of hours of work for state employees, for women, for men; age requirements to prevent child labor, workmen's compensation act, factory and mine inspection regulations

7. If there is a cooperative store or creamery or a fruit-selling organization in your community, have someone make a full report on its organization and success

8. What lodges or clubs does your father belong to which would aid you in case of his illness, injury, or death?

9. Consult the newspapers and work out the ratio between the jobs offered and the jobs wanted Is there a shortage or a surplus of labor in your community? If there be employment bureaus, consult them for statistics

10. What is the difference between money wages and real wages? Illustrate by the increase in a stenographer's salary from 1914 to 1920

11. Compare the ordinary comforts of your homes with those of your grandparents, or even your parents, in their youth. Is the growth in comfort an improvement, or a sign of decay, like the growth of luxury among the Romans? Do you know any old people who regard modern comfort as an evil thing? Do you think people can live comfortably and still retain strength and endurance of character?

12. Who has charge of the housing inspection in your town or city? Has any report been made recently? Are conditions good? If not, whose business is it to improve them? What ordinances are there? Read them. Are they adequate? Are they enforced? Why?

13. What are the better-health agencies in your community? Has your state passed any laws recently bearing on this question? What does your school do for the health of its pupils? Why does it not do more? Do your newspapers do anything for the improvement of health conditions? What did your state and county or city agencies do in the last epidemic?

14. Do the working-people of your town have any voluntary organizations for the study of their own problems? How many students, say of university extension, are there near you?

15. Morgan Park, a suburb of Duluth, is a remarkably planned industrial suburb. The *Monthly Review* for April, 1918, of the Bureau of Labor Statistics, United States Department of Labor, tells about it. What changes in the standard of living should you expect people of foreign birth and little education to make in such homes in one generation?

16. Much of the welfare of any group of people or of individuals depends upon their own efforts, and especially upon their thrift. What has the United States government done to encourage thrift? Write to the savings organization of your own Federal Reserve District for circulars as to savings and their care. Ask your postmaster what he can do to help people to save. Do you know any people who spend freely when wages are good and have to accept help when work fails or wages are reduced? What proportion of your own allowance, if you have one, do you save?

17. There were three European nations in the nineteenth century in which democracy was fighting for a foothold. Special comparative reports based on history references should be made on the following subjects:

 a The vain attempt to liberalize and unite Germany in 1848.
 b The Sardinian constitution of 1848.
 c. The second French Republic, 1848–1852.
 d. The third French Republic, 1871–1875.
 e Suffrage provisions of Prussia in the constitution of 1848 and of the German Empire in 1871.

18. The other great political movements of the nineteenth century were for national liberty—the right of a people of one nationality to be free from the domination of people of another nationality. Special topics:

 a The War of Greek Independence, 1822–1828.
 b. The revolt of the Spanish-American colonies, 1812–1825.

 c Belgium's freedom from the Netherlands, 1830
 d The unification of Italy, 1848–1870.
 e The success of Hungary and the failure of the Slavs against Austria in 1848 and the years following.
 f The Balkan nations of Serbia, Montenegro, Rumania, Bulgaria
 g The vain attempts of the Poles to secure their freedom in 1830 and 1863

 19 Make a brief of the voting methods in various countries from Charles Seymour's "How the World Votes."

CHAPTER VI

PRODUCTION

The way to wealth is as plain as the way to market. It depends chiefly on two words: industry and frugality.—BENJAMIN FRANKLIN

The world's business. Nature provides man with an endless variety of raw products, but the amount and variety of usable commodities he has depends mainly upon his use of brain and brawn in what is called production. Production is the changing of the world's natural resources to things useful and valuable to man; without creating matter, it appropriates it to human needs. And it is not an end in itself; its great value lies in the fact that it enables the human race as a whole to progress toward a fuller and nobler life. Centuries of experience have shown that abundant wealth, if well distributed and wisely used, stimulates men to new endeavor and better relations. In the world's beginning man was naked and ignorant and helpless; at some time in the future we conceive that man will have become wise, good, and exceeding powerful, and in between lie centuries on centuries of cumulative production, making this evolution possible.

All society is divided into producers and nonproducers. Nonproducers may be normal human beings, such as children not yet old enough to be self-supporting, or old people who have served their day well and deserve a restful old age; or they may be idle people who manage in some way to live upon the production of others. In America there is a wholesome contempt for idlers, whether they be rich or poor, and this contempt is as sound economically as it is ethically. A healthy world has no place for the idler. Producers may, however, contribute their part either directly or indirectly, and sometimes workers do not draw their incomes from the work they do. A maker of nails or flour is a direct producer; the physician who keeps him in good health, the editor who provides him with a newspaper, the teacher who helped to educate him, are all indirect producers of nails or flour Their function is to help in production by adding efficiency to the direct producers.

The producer deserves, of course, a return in proportion to his production The farmer who raises thirty bushels of wheat on an acre of ground, because he works hard and knows how, is generally considered a better man than the farmer who raises only fifteen bushels. Society does not take from him the extra fifteen bushels, which is the reward for his pains. But even then he can rarely keep all the thirty bushels himself, he must divide it with the indirect producers who enabled him to produce more than his neighbor, and he must also divide with the people who are normally dependent upon him. He may have to divide with some lazy or unfortunate people who have no direct claim upon him, rather than see them starve. The surplus of the efficient producers goes partly to support inefficient producers and dependents.

Kinds of industry. Industries are divided into classes according to the way in which they produce goods. Those which simply take what nature has provided are said to be extractive. They include mining, lumbering, fishing. Formerly farming was included in this group, but recent writers classify those industries depending for their product upon man's control of the multiplication of plants or animals as genetic industries. This would include also forestry, fur-farming, and fishing in stocked waters.[1]

Following these industries come manufacturing, in which the raw materials are changed into more useful forms; transportation, by which they are carried to places where there is a demand for them, storage, and selling. The last three, which bring the completed product to its users, are grouped by economists under the term "exchange." They complete the processes

[1] Carver, Principles of Political Economy, chap. xvii.

that have to do with material goods, except the final one of using them, called consumption.

The four factors of production. The four factors in production, as we have already seen in studying the early human economies, are land, or natural resources; labor, which appropriates the materials that nature offers; capital, or tools for work; and organizing ability, the brains of production. Two of these are material, two are human. Each is valuable in proportion as it contributes to the desired result of a plentiful and varied production. And each factor must be distinguished from the agent, which offers it, if we are to think clearly and truthfully; that is, we must think of land and not the landowner, labor and not the worker, capital and not the capitalist, when we are studying the process of production. Only in this way can we gain a clear conception of the process and its laws.

THE MATERIAL FACTORS: LAND AND CAPITAL

Land. Land, in the economic sense, includes the ground, with its minerals and oil, rivers and lakes and the ocean, with their fish and water power; forests and swamps and blowing winds. Whatever man finds ready to his hand, to adapt and use, that is land. It is the only factor in production which is limited; the amount of land and water cannot materially be increased. If the population grows too large for the land in any country, food must be brought in from outside, land cannot be made and piled up in convenient places for the surplus population to use. This using up of land has created one of the world's great problems.

But while the amount of land is practically fixed, the output of land is very elastic. Its efficiency in production depends upon location and fertility. By fertility is meant not only richness for farming but richness in ores, in oil or salt or fertilizer—in anything that is valuable. And available fertility varies much with the intelligence of the landowners: a clever man discovers riches in land that an ignorant man thinks poor or worthless. Location has much to do with available fertility, for rich land far from markets really brings less to its owner than poorer land situated where its products can readily be sold. It is the net marketed product that counts in reckoning the fertility of land.

Capital. Except in such simple forms of production as picking berries from wild bushes or catching fish with one's hands, capital is always combined with land in production. A goodly supply of capital means ample production; limited capital limits production. And since capital is goods left over from necessary consumption, it follows that ample capital depends upon ample production. Ample production depends, in its turn, on three things: on the number of workers, on the amount of time they devote to their work, on the degree of skill they possess. Many men, or a few working long hours and with skill, produce much goods; and all that is left over after consumption needs are provided for may become capital.

This surplus may become capital, but it does not always. It may be turned into excessive amounts of consumers' goods for gluttonous people who use more than they need, or it may be thrown away or allowed to decay in idleness. It may be wasted in many ways, and so miss becoming the nucleus of new wealth. Production alone will not insure capital. There must be also the foreseeing spirit, which refuses to consume what would give immediate gratification, in order that it may grow greater through further use. So waiting adds itself to working as a factor in the making of capital; and with waiting comes also the element of sacrifice, the willingness to "go without"—that fine art which so many Americans have never learned or have forgotten.

Forms of capital. But much capital may accomplish little. It must be in the right place and in the right form. Originally capital was in the form of tools, seeds, draft animals, and so forth. For centuries money has been the common means of buying all forms of capital goods, and so is often spoken of as "capital." The distinction between money capital and capital goods, or producer's goods, is still a useful one. Free capital is capital which may be used for many different purposes—as, for example, sewing machines and hoes, which can be used to produce different kinds of sewing and different crops; while specialized capital can be used for one set purpose only—as, for instance, a cotton-boll-picking machine. Circulating capital changes its form (it "circulates," that is, from form to form) and, once used, is destroyed so far as that form is concerned. Coal is a good example. Fixed capital can be used again and again. The pen with which a merchant keeps his books is fixed capital; the ink is circulating capital. A farmer's spade is fixed capital; the lime he sprinkles on his field is circulating.

Power. Power is an important special form of capital—so important that its production makes whole industries in itself. It is the force that "makes the wheels go 'round" in industry; and since it comes originally from the sun, whatever its form, and is being constantly renewed, it is far less limited than land, nature's other gift to production. Man has advanced in his use of power from his own strong right arm, through the appropriation of the strength of animals, to the use of the strength of flowing water, of wind, and of steam. The use of steam made fuel more valuable than it had been before; coal became a great factor in production. To the present time man has not been able to utilize directly the power in the sun's rays; that invention, as well as the storage of the heat of summer to be used in winter, will doubtless come in the future.

Invention. Great amounts of capital of the same kind do not help production so much as less amounts specialized to perform varying functions in a very exact, economical way. This gives the inventor his chance to contribute his great gifts to the world. Varied tools make varied products. In primitive times, for instance, people dressed much alike—one cave man's skin coat was much like another's. Even in American colonial days there was little variety in dress. But today we have literally thousands of colors, textures, fibers, figures, weaves, breadths, and thicknesses of cloth from which to choose material for clothing, and scarcely two people in the country dress alike. For all this infinite variety, giving interest and pleasure to life, we have to thank the patient, sacrificing inventors, in all ages the prophets of newer and better things. Invention adds specific new applications to common forms of capital, and so adds new form to the product.

Who shall own capital? The question of the ownership and control of capital has been agitated by socialists for a long time and is one of the most important matters before the world today. Shall individual men own it, or shall it be the common possession of society, as embodied in the State? The State already owns a few enterprises, controlling their capital completely, as, the Alaskan railroad and the postal system. The extreme Marxian socialists say that the State should own all the tools of production, or capital, as well as land They base their contention partly on the theory that all production over what is needed for consumption should belong to society, since society makes it possible for men to produce a surplus.

But the individualists reply that all society does not produce that usable surplus, for society includes many inefficient people. Therefore, they say, the person who produces a surplus has a right to control it. He is most interested in it, and if used as his capital, it is more likely to be well used than if turned into a common fund, which may be managed by someone who could never have mustered the energy and farsightedness to save it himself. Society itself, they say, would not be helped by social ownership or management of capital; indeed, since the result would in all probability be less production, society would suffer in the end We may consider it a principle, until something better is proposed by human experience, that *that agency, be it individual or social, which has the greatest interest in the use and effectiveness of capital is the best agency for its ownership and control.* The best user of capital is the man who loses most if that capital fails to produce results.

In the case of education the social body has a stronger interest than the majority of individuals, for the future of the

State and of society depends upon the kind of training given to children. Therefore the State in our country has taken education into its own hands. It requisitions the necessary capital through taxation and carries on the enterprise with, on the whole, marked success—certainly with far better results than ever were or ever could be attained by the majority of private individuals. Here is a case in which, the predominating interest being social, the ownership and management of capital should be social. But in the management of a factory or a dry-goods store it would be impossible to develop a very convincing social interest. It is not possible even in the greater enterprises, in which society as a whole is really concerned. People are not, for instance, sufficiently interested in good service from street-car and railroad companies to complain when the service is bad, except as they may impotently grumble. They growl at conditions, but do not organize any kind of effective protest. Society is interested, man by man and woman by woman, in the thing it can understand; and it does not yet understand railroad and factory organization. Perhaps some day social ownership of the tools of production may be a wise thing; certainly that day will not come until society knows much more about great enterprises than it does today. Its personal interest and interestedness are not at present great enough to insure effective and efficient results.

The Human Factor of Labor

The output of labor. What are the qualities of labor as a factor in production which make it maximally effective? How can labor make itself felt and respected by everyone—not by sheer numbers, but by force of character and value in service given?

Solid, conscientious workmanship is the first requisite of honest, effective labor. The workman who takes pride in his work, and makes a thing of permanent usefulness and perhaps of beauty as well, gives dignity to labor and strength to the cause of labor; he demands the respect of men as surely as does the statesman who labors for the good of his country in more prominent ways. The labor unions have not emphasized this quality of the output so much as did the medieval guilds.

Sabotage is destructiveness practiced by laborers during the productive process, it delays or prevents production or injures the output. The term seems to have originated among French workmen of the last century, whose slang verb for scamping work was *saboter*. It is a policy of certain radical labor organizations, and is used with the object of forcing society to grant their demands. It involves a cowardly, secret revenge and brings down upon the whole laboring class the distrust of society.

Mobility of labor. Mobility makes for a large and varied production and so is of distinct advantage not only to labor but to society as a whole The word is a name for the quality of being moved easily from one employment to another, and it applies both to the place and to the kind of work. A mobile workman will go to another town if work fails him in his own; or if a machine be invented which does his work and throws him out of a job, he quickly finds something else to do and goes at it. Employment bureaus, which put employer and workman into touch with each other, are a prime help to mobility. In every large city there are regions where such bureaus are to be found; and there may be seen, usually gathered about huge placards announcing work, the workers looking for their next jobs. These men are often marginal workers, and the bureaus offer them a possible escape from idleness.

The employment bureau tells workers of jobs in distant parts of the country (often with free fare provided) and tells something of hours, wages, and conditions of work. The private bureaus charge fees either to employer or to employee, and sometimes to both; but the state, in its various units, gives free work-finding service to its citizens.

Cheap and easy transportation is another help to mobility. People who have traveled little are often very nervous and timid about it, and the ignorant dread going into strange and unknown places. But if the railroad fare is cheap the sacrifice and risk seem much less, and workers are much more willing to move to work-offering localities. Of course the prospective wages are a great factor; a workman often quickly overcomes his dislike for moving if the wages offered are high enough to make it profitable for him to move.

Checks to mobility. Several things operate against the mobility of labor. One important obstacle is the "closed shop," or the impossibility of a nonunion worker's finding work in a union-controlled shop. Some workers are kept out of work altogether by this rule; as, for instance, high-school boys who want to work at a skilled or semiskilled trade during their summer vacation, but either do not want to pay dues to a union or object to unions on principle. It also prevents movement from place to place, since nonunion men cannot enter a closed-shop factory or town, no matter how much they may be needed. In the third place, it prevents the easy filling-up of an undermanned trade and the easy shifting from trade to trade at need. Suppose an intelligent carpenter is out of work, while the bricklaying trade is in need of workers. The carpenter knows how to lay brick and could help out for a few days with advantage both to himself and to production, but he will not pay the dues and go through the process of becoming a member of the bricklayers' union for the sake of a few days' work. Instead he goes idle for those few days, thus lessening production and denying his family the wages that he should have earned.

Many workers cannot adjust themselves readily to new conditions because they have not mastered the language. When our Americanization workers have succeeded in teaching the English language to everyone who does not already speak it, the workers will find it much easier to find a new place if work fails them. A more general form of the same factor is the breadth of general training which workers receive, usually in the public schools. If it be helpful for a laborer to know how to communicate with others through the medium of a common language, it is still more helpful for him to have a store of ideas common to all the people about him and to have known the common experiences of his fellow men and to share some of their attitudes. The more of such general ideas the worker has, the easier it is for him to adjust himself to a forced change in his work.

Training the worker. Of recent years certain employers, eager to have plenty of easily managed and efficient workers in their plants, have advocated the establishment of special training schools similar to those in which Germany trained its army of docile, skillful workers before the World War. Such schools would take boys and girls while still very young and, without trying to give them more than the barest rudiments of a general education, would train them in specific trades. While still young, such workers could earn very good wages at their trades, because their pliant minds and muscles would have been concentrated on their specific kind of skill-getting; but if in middle age that work happened to fail them, these workers would be helplessly stranded. They could not turn their highly specialized skill into other channels; they would not have general intelligence enough to take up another kind of work or quickly to effect a changed attitude. They would very probably join the army of disappointed, embittered marginal workers, or even become paupers. For this reason, if for no other, workers should all have a good high-school education. The liberally trained man is a more mobile worker than a narrowly trained one.

LABOR ORGANIZATION

The *right kind* of labor organization may be a great help to a large and varied production. There are labor organizations which hinder production far more than they help it, but this is because they have fundamentally wrong ideas of the relations of capital and labor. Those which are sane and which recognize the established economic laws have done much to better the industrial system, and may do as much more in the future.

There were labor organizations in the ancient world and in medieval Europe, although their functions usually differed from those of modern unions. In the United States the movement began in the second decade of the nineteenth century when certain New York organizations, notably those of the printers, were able to secure considerable political and economic concessions. Then for many years the movement amounted to little, for the demand for labor was so brisk that labor had a comparatively ample return without resorting to organization. After the Civil War, however, a change came. The cost of living had become so much higher during the war that some relief in the shape of higher wages was needed and nothing but united action could reduce the long hours then customary. A national congress of workers met in Baltimore in 1868, and the next year saw the organization of the secret order of the Knights of Labor. This order grew rapidly until 1886, when the more effective American Federation of Labor supplanted it as the leading organization.

This federation, under the able leadership of Samuel Gompers, adopted a plan of organization copied from that of the national government. It kept out of politics,—adopting collective bargaining and the strike as the most effective ways of securing its ends,—and it has been in the main successful in its policies. Starting in 1886 by amalgamating with the earlier (1881) Federation of Organized Trades and Labor Unions, the Federation has grown until, in 1920, it numbered 4,078,740 members. Since 1877, when the first big strikes occurred among the railroad men, the strike as a weapon has on the whole (although some strikes have been engineered in the interests of organizers rather than of workers) succeeded in gaining for labor many things which would probably have come very slowly, if at all, by other means. Strikes have been called for higher wages, shorter hours, and better working-conditions. The Federation has usually shown a willingness to arbitrate, and a majority of the strikes have been settled by this reasonable and progressive means.

Types of organizations. There are three distinct types of labor organization in America, besides the now small and uninfluential Knights of Labor. The most numerous are the trade unions, with a membership of workers in one trade only. Such are the waiters', the cigar-makers', the carpenters', the bricklayers', and the painters' union. A second type is the industrial union, which includes all workers in a single industry, no matter what their trade. The United Mine Workers of America is an example of such an organization—it includes all the laborers who in any way help directly to produce coal. The third type is the labor union, which exemplifies the "One Big Union" idea—a society of all workers, no matter what their trade. The Industrial Workers of the World is a labor union in the exact sense of the word, as were the Knights of Labor in their day.

The American Federation of Labor differs from the I.W.W., not only in the greater conservatism of its policies but in the nature of its organization. It is a federation, not a union; it allows the local unions to keep control of local affairs as much as possible, using the central authority only in such matters as are of general concern.[1] The units of federation are a hundred and eleven national and international unions in the United States and Canada, with state federations, central city bodies, local department councils, and local trade unions. The Federation has grown steadily in numbers and influence; it has become a real power in American affairs, owing to the sanity and conservatism which, for the most part, have marked its management.

Aims of labor organizations. In America labor organizations have sought mainly for three things—higher wages, shorter hours, and better working-conditions. In all these they have gained signal successes, although conditions are yet far from satisfactory in some places. In the performance of certain other functions which some people think belong to unions, they have fallen short of what their friends hope for them. Socially they do not do so much for their members as the guilds of the

[1] See the diagram of organization in Marshall, Wright, and Field's "Materials for the Study of Elementary Economics," p. 193.

Middle Ages; but as there are now many social agencies which were not in existence then, this is not an adverse criticism. It is better, in fact, that in his social life the worker shall meet as many people as possible who do not work in his own field, in order that his mind may be broadened by contact with those having other interests. But the failure of labor organizations to set up high standards of workmanship in many trades is a notable shortcoming. Some of them actually encourage sabotage and "soldiering on the job." So far American labor organizations have not evolved a satisfactory apprentice system which shall allow a young workman to advance as fast as his ability allows him, but which shall have strict standards of trade preparation.

As yet the unions are working toward greater and better production indirectly; but when they have won good working-conditions and an equitable wage, and have thus raised the quality of the human agents in production, they will perhaps turn their attention to the quality and quantity of the output. They cannot do everything at once.

The weapons of labor. Unions have employed three weapons with great success. The first is the compulsion of the closed shop, used to bring all workers into the unions. If nonunion men (or "scabs" as they call them) are employed in a shop, the union members may refuse to work, or may make the lives of the "scabs" so miserable that they are glad either to join the union or withdraw. Sometimes sabotage is directed toward the "scab" product. Whatever the method, the spirit is the same. It is the use of force to effect what should come as a voluntary action, if at all, and partakes of the intolerance shown by any other organization which tries to force human beings to subscribe to its doctrines whether they will or no. It destroys the freedom of labor, but this is justified by its advocates because of the benefits of union membership and the control of the situation which a monopoly of workers gives to labor.

The second weapon is collective bargaining. One laborer bargaining with an employer is weak, especially if many men are waiting for his job. The employer usually has money to live on and can wait for his terms to be met, and he knows how to make the law support his cause. He can dismiss a worker who is troublesome and can hire a more docile man. But a whole body of workers organized into a society that agrees to act together is quite another thing, it cannot so easily be dismissed, for that means the shutting of the factory or shop. So labor has tried to make itself equal to capital by the device of collective bargaining, which provides that wages are to be set by union representatives, in conference with the employers' representatives. The bargain made is called a trade agreement, and all concerned are bound by it.

If employers refuse to give the wage demanded, the unions may go on strike, thus using the third weapon. The mill closes down, the mine is shut, the machinery stands idle, raw materials deteriorate through disuse and neglect. It means a serious loss to labor and to investors, and rather than face this loss, the employer sometimes yields and grants the higher wage asked. More often the case is arbitrated and a compromise reached [1]

Strikes became very common during the World War, when cost of living and wages both rose very high. Up to that time the general public had usually been in sympathy with strikers, because it saw that they were striking for what they really needed and should have. But during the war people began to say that since many of the striking workers had an income larger than the majority of the general public, and since higher wages tended to inflate prices to still higher levels, the strike was a matter in which the public was vitally interested and had a right to interfere.

Upon the passage of the Adamson Law in 1916 there was a distinct turn in opinion. The press echoed constantly a growing conviction that there are some strikes which deserve public support, and others which should be considered crimes against public welfare. Governor Allen of Kansas in the case of coal

[1] Marshall, Wright, and Field, Materials for the Study of Elementary Economics, pp 204–205.

strikers in his state called for volunteers from the ex-service men. The response was such as to show plainly the sentiment of the public toward those who hold up the production of a necessity. Governor Coolidge of Massachusetts, when the policemen of Boston went on strike, ordered them back to work, and established a generally accepted theory of who can and who cannot strike. This theory is that workers in private enterprises which do not directly and essentially affect public welfare have the right to strike, but people upon whose work public safety and welfare depend have no right to stop work in a body, thus interfering with the established order of things upon which our daily living is premised. Policemen, schoolteachers, mail clerks, and government officers generally have no right to strike, and the right of the producers of such necessities as wheat, corn, iron, and coal is open to grave question. The vital question in connection with this theory is of course whether the just rights of these classes can be assured without the right to strike. Will the public always treat its servants fairly, knowing that they cannot protest in the practical way that other workers can? Other questions concerning the ethics of strikes remain for answer; the matter is fairly before the public.

The Labor Supply

The amount of labor available is a factor of the utmost importance. Labor may be intelligent and honest, well-organized, and mobile, and yet fall short of the desired output simply because there are not enough workers. America for many years suffered from a labor shortage; there was more land than there were farmers to till it, and vast resources were undeveloped because labor was lacking. Even today farm labor is untrained and difficult to find, while the upper grades of skilled labor are never crowded. Under normal conditions there is a great supply of unskilled labor. The families of the very poor, the very ignorant, and the very stupid are usually larger than those farther up the human scale; so there are usually plenty of men to dig fence postholes by hand, fewer who can operate a digging machine, fewer still who can manage the erection of a modern wire fence in the proper way, and still fewer who can survey the lands that are to be fenced. The typical modern problem is to find skilled labor—men who can operate expensive, intricate, but economical machines, and who can direct big enterprises. The schools do all they can to train workers, but of course they cannot make ability—they can only develop what they find in their pupils. The great problem of securing a social order in which the superior part of mankind multiplies at least as fast as the inferior part is as yet unsolved. At the present time American economic and social conditions are against this happy condition.

Failing an adequate supply at home, we have encouraged immigration. Employers have sometimes secured foreign labor by tales of high money wages. Until recently Americans have used the work of these foreign-born people without attempting to teach them how to live and think as Americans; and so we have the problem of an un-American, and sometimes of a very anti-American, labor supply. Such laborers are often discontented and unhappy, and are far from maximally productive. If one counts the trouble from strikes and sabotage and inefficient work, this foreign supply is found to be in the end a very expensive one. And yet many of the great industries of the country could scarcely have been built up without it.

These facts about the labor supply should be remembered:

1. There must be a supply of the different grades of skilled and unskilled labor. If not produced at home, they must be supplied by immigration If immigration lowers the standard of living, the native supply of unskilled labor fails, thus perpetuating the need of further immigration.

2. A smaller number of skilled workers takes the place of a larger number of unskilled. Therefore every agency which adds to intelligence tends to keep immigration down, provided those intelligent Americans stay in production. Good public schools, therefore, are a help to good labor conditions.

3. As invention adds constantly to the processes carried on by skilled labor, and reduces those carried on by unskilled, the proportion of workers needed per unit of final production is reduced. The more highly evolved and efficient the method of production, the fewer workers are needed.

Organization

Some economists think there are only three factors in production—land, labor, and capital. They include in labor not only all workers who earn wages—by whatever name and in whatever amount—but also the man who undertakes the organization of enterprises and who risks his own and sometimes other people's capital in them. The older economists called this man an undertaker; this word has now, however, been succeeded by the French word *entrepreneur*, which means the same thing and has no funereal associations. The entrepreneur links up the three basic factors into an integrated enterprise, and assumes the responsibility of placing the capital and hiring the labor and directing the whole. If his judgment is poor, failure may result. An entrepreneur must be openminded, keenly intelligent, tactful in his dealings both with labor and with capital. If he be not honest, he soon loses the confidence of the people he deals with; and confidence is the entrepreneur's greatest capital.[1]

The Processes of Production

Review of early production. The early stages of production have been outlined in the earlier chapters of this book. They are, briefly:

1. The purely extractive stages, in which men with little or no capital make a living by hunting and fishing.
2. The pastoral stage, in which genetic industry begins with the care of animals, which, however, graze on wild grass.

[1] See "The Present System—Organization," in Chapter XI.

3. The agricultural stage, which adds the cultivation of plants to the care of animals and tends to settle man in a permanent home.

4. The handicraft and trading stage, reached when men produce a surplus, first unconsciously and then purposely, which they trade with others for their surplus. Money economy succeeds barter, and capital grows.

5. The industrial stage, in which we now live, characterized by the multiplication of production by machinery, by the most advanced division of labor, and by world commerce.

While modern production is infinitely vast, varied, and evolved, there still exists much of the earlier types of production. Not only are there whole tribes of people who know nothing of modern methods, but in our own country the old ways persist in great measure. Every housekeeper is a domestic producer who adds to the value of raw materials by manufacturing processes, but few of these products ever reach a commercial market. The family that has a garden and puts up its own vegetables and fruits is to that extent living in the domestic era, and we know that to do that is in most cases good economy. In our discussion we shall be thinking of factory production, not because we have forgotten the important domestic production still carried on but because the more modern production involves many serious problems, while the domestic production very neatly takes care of itself.

Intricacy of modern productive processes. Large-scale production is extremely intricate. In the making of such a thing as a motor car or a piano, raw materials from the ends of the earth are used. Many types of labor contribute, and months of time are required. If every part of the process is timed just right, done just right, is assured of fine workmanship and sound materials, the work goes through economically and efficiently. If one cog of the wheel is bent or missing, the whole may be badly skewed or work halted. Cooperation is the key to modern production. *Thousands of people must directly or indirectly coöperate in the making of a pin.*

Several things may operate to stop the machinery of production. If a skilled worker who alone can do a delicate piece of work fails when his turn comes, the process is halted. The meaning of a strike of many skilled workers is therefore apparent. If capital is lacking when materials are cheap, cost of production may be raised to a prohibitive point, or it may reduce the returns or lower the quality of the product. Changes of fashion or delays in production may render the product almost valueless. The main causes of poor production are forms of poor coöperation, and may be summed up as follows:

1. Understaffing: too little labor A large "soldiering" staff may be as bad as too few workers.

2. Underequipment: too little machinery, or poor machinery.

3. Overexpansion, which uses up raw materials too soon.

4. Production wrongly timed, which puts out a product when it is not wanted, because the entrepreneur has foretold the market mistakenly.

Apportionment of factors. Not only must all the factors coöperate, but they must be in the right proportion if production is to be efficient. In the early years of our country there were much land and few laborers, and the carelessly tilled farms yielded far less than land so rich might have brought forth. Under the domestic system there was too little capital per worker, and so each man produced less than one man should. In overpopulated countries land is the scarce factor, and a combination of skilled labor and great capital may produce so little that both laborers and capitalists suffer. Different parts of the world are rich in different factors, only a true world economy, with the utmost freedom of movement of factors from place to place, can even up the uneven combinations and give maximal production to all countries

Now factors may be substituted for each other. In countless industries capital, in the form of improved machinery, is constantly taking the place of labor, and even of land If capital fails, labor may again be put in its place. This gives the law of variable proportions: *The ratio of the factors in production*

PRODUCTION

may be varied, just as in an automobile the mixture of air and gasoline in the carburetor may be varied. If the amount of gasoline is increased, the mixture is said to be "rich"; if the ratio of air to gasoline is greater, it gives a "lean" mixture. So

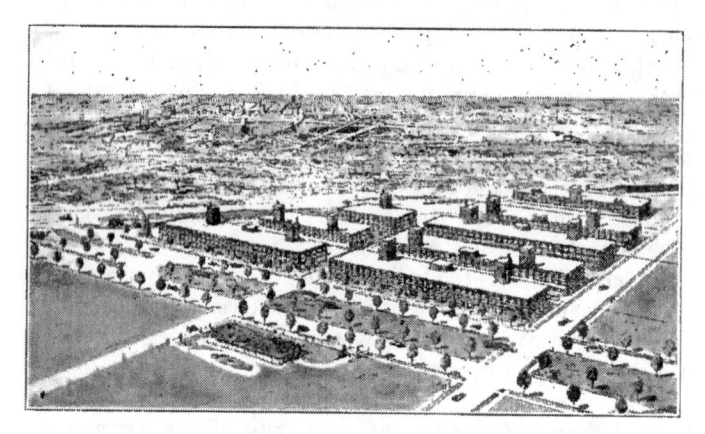

A CAREFULLY PLANNED MANUFACTURING DISTRICT

Most industrial districts have "just growed," like Topsy; and they have as a rule grown remarkably ugly. Of late years some business men have seen that it is possible to make a manufacturing district both beautiful and efficient by planning it as carefully as a first-class residence section is planned. The picture above shows a manufacturing district in Minneapolis, as it will be when completed. The land was truck land in 1916, when it was bought by two hundred and fifty business men of the city and laid out for beauty and use. The heart of the system is a freight station served by all railroads entering the city, each plant connected by underground tramways which obviate a large part of the heavy street traffic. The streets are parked and planted; the central cafeteria stands in a little park; and all buildings must reach a high standard for light, cleanliness, and permanence of structure. The district is typical of many in America which recognize the workers' rights to beauty and comfort

production may be rich in capital or land, and lean in the other factors. The amounts in the combination will vary with circumstances and times.

But when a change in proportion of factors takes place, there is usually something left over which cannot be used in the revised process In the Industrial Revolution it was labor, which found itself out of work because machinery had taken its place. In the last few years many a farmer has found some of his capital invested in horses or machinery idle and unproductive because he cannot find labor with which to use it. The ratio of labor to capital has changed, and some of the capital is waste capital. This waste of factors makes entrepreneurs conservative in changing the producing processes.

Law of diminishing returns. But just as there is a limit to the amount of air which may be added to gasoline for combustion, so there are limits to the variable proportions which will give efficient production. This limitation is stated in the law of diminishing returns.

Let us take diminishing returns from land first. Suppose a farmer found that by adding nitrogen to his acres he could increase his yield without adding land or labor. If wise, he would add capital in the form of money spent for nitrogen. If he kept on adding nitrogen and observed the yield, he would find that for several years his crop increased, but that eventually more nitrogen did not bring more grain. The land would have reached the stage of maximum returns from nitrogen applications. Even before this time it would be evident that each additional pound of nitrogen failed to add as much to the crop as the first pound had done. The point at which the added yield began to be smaller,—not in total amount but in proportion to the amount expended,—that point is the beginning of diminishing returns. At that point it is more economical for the farmer to stop adding nitrogen and to use more land if he can

The law applies to land used in industry but not so quickly. There comes a time when it ceases to pay to add more stories to a factory rather than build on additional land. Foundations and walls must be so strengthened to support the heavy machinery that it is cheaper to buy more land. Before that point is reached, the added returns diminish In like manner, a millhand who tends one machine may tend additional ones and so increase the net product, up to a certain point At that point the ratio of increased output becomes less, for the worker has too much to do. Here the law applies to labor, and it will apply to capital as truly.

It is the task of the entrepreneur to watch the returns from additional units of land, or labor, or capital in the business he organizes, and adjust the proportions used accordingly. Sometimes he can change them at will, more often he can only approximate the ideal ratio. A farmer, for instance, works at a special disadvantage, for land is not so elastic in amount as labor and capital, and often he must go on applying labor and capital to his land far past the point of diminishing returns. Malthus and his followers thought that as population increases faster than food can be produced from a fixed amount of land to support it, a point would be reached some day when the world would starve. But science is really increasing the amount of available land to some extent already, and much more may be done in the future.[1] The point of diminishing returns has probably not yet been reached in the agricultural production of the world as a whole.

Security in Production

Confidence. As civilization advances, the guards and insurances of production become greater and greater, so that the risk element decreases. This means greater production and less worry, which in turn may mean a higher quality in the race. Confidence is first aid to production, and confidence is the result of a conviction of the honesty of the people dealt with. The man whose "word is as good as his bond" is the man with whom everyone wants to do business. But since all business men are not to be trusted, and one cannot always know ahead the character of the other party to a bargain, society has invented the contract. It helps to a good understanding in business, and safeguards those who make it. A contract is an

[1] Marshall, Wright, and Field, Materials for the Study of Elementary Economics, p 21 Malthus (1766-1834) lived before the day of those inventions which promise a permanent agriculture.

agreement, usually reduced to writing, stating definitely what the two parties to the agreement promise to do. Oral contracts are unreliable and unsatisfactory; written ones are more easily and surely enforced, and so have a legal standing not given to most oral ones. A contract involves three essential things:

1. The contracting parties must be free (that is, not forced) and responsible.

2. An exchange of values must take place between the contracting parties. The assumption is that no sane person will give something for nothing, and so a nominal price at least is paid for what the "party of the first part" gives to the "party of the second part."

3. Accrediting data, which will help to prove the truth of the agreement made, such as date, place of making, and signatures, should always be included Some kinds of contracts require the signatures of witnesses and seals.

The part of the State. Society, organized in formal governments, engages to provide business security that shall make production regular and sure. It does this by making and enforcing laws which forbid theft and cheating in their many forms; by protecting property with policemen, courts, and prisons, by providing a civil code and courts for the settling of business differences, by assuring settled order to the buying public and means for the collection of debts; by all the multitude of ways, in short, in which governments make it safe for men to go freely about legitimate business.

Besides the restrictions and regulations that have been enacted in law, there are others which rest on public opinion. Production is made safe by the prejudice that men have against "wildcat" investments, sharp practices which manage to keep within the law, and severity toward helpless debtors. While there are some men not amenable to the force of public esteem or contempt, the more sensitive majority keep production fairly safe by holding men to their contracts and to business custom.

Insurance. All production involves a certain amount of risk, which the entrepreneur must assume. Some men make a business of assuming part of this risk for the producer, exacting a small fee for their service. This system has become a regular and recognized method of buying security. Losses which are of a legitimate and unavoidable nature—such as those from fire, earthquake, shipwreck, and tornado—occur on an average so many times per year over any given area By studying the records a specialist can tell just what the chances are that a building will be burned during the next five years. Upon this estimate of chances the insurance man bases his charges for insurance. A hundred men pay money to the insurer, knowing that probably one barn out of their hundred barns will burn during the year. One barn does burn, and the insurer pays the farmer the amount for which his barn was insured, keeping what is left over as his pay for the risk he takes. The calculating of the probability of losses is called actuarial calculation; the payment per thousand dollars for insurance is the premium, and the paper—a contract—in which the insurance company promises to repay the loss is a policy. Insurance is a science, now very fully and carefully developed, and it gives one of the most practical and valuable of all means of security. The insurance of health and of life gives the same sense of provision against emergency to the individual that property insurance gives to business, and so reduces worry and adds to confidence in the future.

Speculation. Another factor in security is the elimination of illegitimate speculation and gambling. Markets are legitimately controlled by supply and demand, but they may be manipulated so as to cause sudden, unlooked-for fluctuations in price, enabling the man who has foreknowledge of what is to occur to make a large profit. Of course when this gambling affects raw products which are essential to industry, it makes the buying of materials very uncertain, therefore it is to the interest of sound business to prevent such speculation as much as possible. The legitimate speculator deals in actual economic goods, while the gambler deals in "futures"; that is, in fictitious values of market commodities, or in values represented by the marks on cards or dice or other devices, or on the chance or manipulated speed of a car or a horse. Legitimate speculation is the use of judgment as to the future values of actual economic goods, which secures the social or time increment for the speculator; gambling is the staking of gain on a chance or manipulated shift in values which involves no production.

Good judgment of entrepreneurs. In these days almost all production takes place ahead of demand. A century ago the man who found his boots in holes went to a shoemaker, ordered a new pair, and received them when finished; but today the man whose shoes show signs of giving out goes to a shoe shop, where, from hundreds of ready-made pairs, he selects one pair that was made months before by some man who had faith that someone, somewhere, would buy that pair of shoes. The entrepreneur has to estimate far ahead, from all sorts of data that he learns how to gather and interpret, what the demand will be; and then he must gather his materials, employ his labor, superintend the making of his product, and see that it reaches a market. A business is secure, then, partly in proportion to the good judgment of the organizing entrepreneur in estimating future demand.

But not only must the entrepreneur estimate demand and meet it; he must also produce at such a cost as will come within the price he can demand for his product. The return must be enough to warrant his production. He must pay the wages of his workers, the bill for raw materials, the interest on the capital he uses, and the running costs of manufacture out of the price he gets for his product. Otherwise the business is a failure, and the entrepreneur a bankrupt.

Marginal production. The producer who barely makes ends meet in his business is known as a marginal producer. If his ends at any time fail to meet, he will be forced out of business.[1]

---
[1] As a matter of fact, producers often keep on even when they are losing money; the reasons for this are explained in Chapter XI. Free competition

Then the man who made just a little more than he becomes the marginal producer, before his less fortunate competitor went out of business he made a little more than enough to enable him to keep going, but now he is barely able to meet expenses A little fall in the market price of his commodity would put him, too, into the discard But suppose the market price goes up instead of down. now the man who went out of business because his cost of production touched the market price, leaving him no profit, is encouraged to enter the lists again. If the market price goes still higher, some other man with still less capital than he, but with enough to make him think he can "make it," will enter the field of competition. Now the man who was marginal producer is so no longer, another man is nearer the margin of no profit than he.

Under free competition there is a shifting class of marginal producers in any line of production. When their cost of production can no longer be kept below the market price, they stop producing; but when their cost of production is low enough to leave them a profit, they are encouraged to produce again, and their numbers increase The diagram on page 158 shows how this law operates in the case of wheat. A has level, well-drained land close to town, and plenty of capital; therefore it costs him only a dollar a bushel to raise wheat B's land is not quite so good, not quite so near a market, but still good enough to put his cost of production at one dollar and a half. The others raise wheat at a lessening profit until we reach F, G, and H, who may or may not raise wheat at all. This is because their land is hilly and poor, and unless the price of wheat meets their cost of production, of course they produce at a loss. The relation of marginal production to price will be taken up later.

The control of production. Who controls production? If three men on a holiday had an automobile and wanted to go from down-town Chicago to a South Shore hotel for dinner. but had no gasoline, they would be delighted to find a fourth

and mobility of production are premised here—ideal conditions not always true in business life.

A	B	C	D	E	F	G	H	I
$1.00	$1.50	$1.75	$1.85	$1.95	$2.00	$2.10	$2.20	$2.50

Marginal Producer | Non-Producers

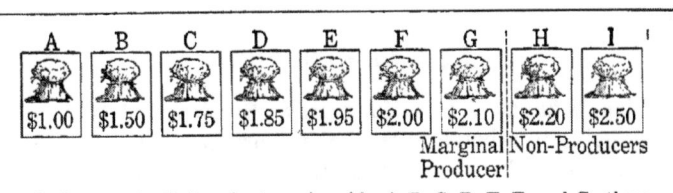

1. Society needs all the wheat produced by A, B, C, D, E, F, and G; therefore it will pay $2.10 a bushel for wheat, or enough to induce G to raise and market wheat. G is the marginal producer, and H, whose land is so poor that it costs him $2.20 per bushel to produce, raises none.

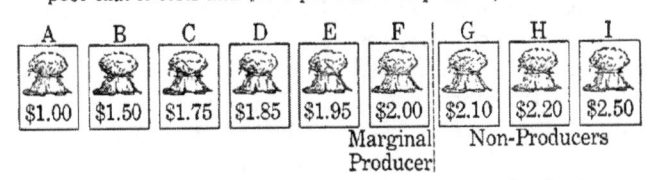

A	B	C	D	E	F	G	H	I
$1.00	$1.50	$1.75	$1.85	$1.95	$2.00	$2.10	$2.20	$2.50

Marginal Producer | Non-Producers

2. Because of a substitution of other cereal foods or a reduction in population, the market demands less wheat. It no longer needs G's wheat, therefore it will not pay for it, since A, B, C, D, E, and F can raise all they need at $2. So the market price of wheat is $2, and G stops producing. F is now the marginal producer.

A	B	C	D	E	F	G	H	I
$1.00	$1.50	$1.75	$1.85	$1.95	$2.00	$2.10	$2.20	$2.50

Marginal Producer | Non-Producer

3. But the population grows, and more wheat is needed. Society now needs the supply of more producers, including even H, whose cost of production is $2.20. Therefore it will pay H his price, $2.20, to raise wheat. There are now no idle producers except I, whose land is so hilly and rocky that it costs him $2.50 a bushel to raise wheat.

4. War breaks out, and the need for wheat is unprecedented. What will happen? Finish the diagram in your notebooks and explain.

DIAGRAM SHOWING THE RELATION BETWEEN DEMAND, SUPPLY, AND PRICE

The set of diagrams given above illustrates the relation which theoretically exists between demand, supply, and price. Actually the process is much more complicated, as many factors not shown modify conditions. The diagrams show fundamental relations, however, and will explain why the older schools of economists used to say that price is set by the marginal unit produced

friend who had a plentiful supply. But if that friend insisted on going to a hotel on the Lake Shore Drive, the three would have to yield, for it is clear that the car could not be taken anywhere without gasoline. Now in the industrial journey there is always one man of the four who has the gasoline. He is the man who holds the most-needed factor—either land or capital or labor or organization. The man who controls the factor of the four which is scarcest can control the situation if he has the necessary intelligence. He can demand almost what he will from the others and get it. Usually capital has been the scarce factor, and so has controlled production, lately labor has often been hardest to find, and so has often been able to dictate terms to capital. In an ideal world no one factor will be so lacking as to give its owners dominating power; there will be such a balance of factors as will give the control to no one class and will subject no class to the domination of another.

SUPPLEMENTARY READINGS

ABBOTT, LYMAN. America in the Making [Industrial responsibilities.]
BEARD, MARY A Short History of the American Labor Movement, especially chaps i, iii vi. vii, ix, x, xi
BULLOCK, C J Selected Readings in Economics, pp 668–681 "A Socialist Idea of History," by Karl Marx and Frederick Engels Criticize.
BURCH, H R , and PATTERSON, S H Problems of American Democracy, chaps xxviii, xxix, xxx
CHEYNEY, E P Industrial and Social History of England, chap iv.
HENDERSON, C. R The Social Spirit in America, chap viii, "The Way to Industrial Friendship and Prosperity"
OSGOOD, ELLEN A History of Industry, chap xix.
Current National Child Labor Committee bulletins.

SEARCH QUESTIONS AND PROBLEMS

1 Copy the table on page 49 of Carver's "Principles of National Economy" Which of these does your state prohibit and punish? Which does it permit, but regulate by law? Which are practically free of restriction? As practiced in your state, are there any now free of restriction which should be socially controlled for the social good?

2 Famine has been a recurring event in human history. Famines are still frequent in India, China, Russia, and southeastern Europe What causes them? How can they be prevented? Is there any danger of a famine, at any time, in America? What is America doing to prevent them in other parts of the world? See *National Geographic Magazine*, Vol XXXII, pp 69-90

3 Is a farmer a landowner, a capitalist, or a laborer? Are these distinctions between men or between economic functions? When several functions are united in one man, does that man have trouble with himself over his conflicting interests? Do you know of any men besides farmers who unite several functions in themselves?

4 It is calculated that three acres of land will produce food enough for one person for one year. Find the number of acres in the land area of the earth, exclusive of arctic and desert regions, and the number of people in the world as accurately as you can from the latest atlases and yearbooks at your command Can the earth support its population?

5 The article "The Nation's Wheat Supply," in the *Contemporary Review* for July, 1920, pp. 71-78, shows conditions in an old and crowded country. Read it, explain to the class, and show how English conditions illustrate (1) marginal production and (2) government help to production

6 Is there a United States free employment bureau in your town, or in the nearest large city? Where is it located—in a district which is frequented by the unemployed? Compare the location of the state bureau with that of the private bureaus. Find out what amount of service the state bureau gave during the last year What kind of jobs does it find? Would it be of use to a high-school boy or girl hunting a summer job?

7 Why should the state conduct labor agencies, thus depriving citizens of a legitimate way of making a living? Does the state have any more right to take the business of conducting a labor agency from a business man than it has to take a dry-goods business from him? See "Public Employment Offices in the United States and Germany," in Commons's "Trade Unionism and Labor Problems," pp. 603-626, and Hamilton's "Current Economic Problems," pp 526-528.

8 On page 147 is the statement that the typical modern problem is to find enough skilled labor. But in 1914-1919 unskilled labor was very hard to find in the United States Production was halted repeatedly for the lack of the most common kind of labor. Can you explain this? Is it still true? Why?

9 (1) From material found in recent yearbooks complete the table on page 705 of Marshall, Wright, and Field's "Materials for the Study of Elementary Economics" (2) Can you detect any rise or fall in the use of the strike? If so, graph it.

10. Teamsters give relatively unskilled labor, and yet their unions, first organized in Chicago in 1899, helped to establish several important practices What are they? See Commons's "Trade Unionism and Labor Problems," pp 36-64

11 When labor and capital disagree, is it better for them to decide between themselves what they will do or submit the matter to the arbitration of a third party? Read Commons's views in "Trade Unionism and Labor Problems," pp. 1-12.

12. The extreme division of labor in the butchering trade that has come with the great packing-plants, and the consequent problems both to employer and men, are described in Commons's "Trade Unionism and Labor Problems," pp 222-249. Find the causes of the strike described

13. The Mergenthaler linotype machine may be said to have done for printing what the eighteenth-century spinning and weaving inventions did for textiles: it produced an industrial revolution in the trade. Therefore the problems and conditions following its introduction may be studied as a modern example of what usually follows an important labor-saving invention See Commons's "Trade Unionism and Labor Problems," pp. 250-273

14 Should women be paid as much as men for the same or equal work? Should an industry be self-supporting, or else stop producing to permit a self-supporting industry to take its place? When is a man self-supporting? When is an industry self-supporting? Read Commons's "Trade Unionism and Labor Problems," pp 371-434 (perhaps dividing the reading among several members of the class), before answering

15 Has labor, as a class, ever entered into political life in the United States? If so, make a list of the campaigns in which it has figured. Compare this record with that of recent years in England See Schapiro's "Modern and Contemporary European History," pp 347-348, 393-394, 597, or other history of recent England Does labor influence international relations? See the article by John A. Fitch in *Survey* for January 19, 1918, pp 439 ff , *Literary Digest*, December 20, 1919, p 20; *World's Work*, Vol XXXVIII, pp. 124-125; *Current History Magazine* for May and June, 1919.

16. Is your home insured against fire? What is the rate per thousand paid? Compare the rates for residences and for down-town business buildings. Why the difference? Find the actual difference between rates for a wooden and a stone or brick building in the same district.

17. How does the actuary decide on the rates for life insurance? Of the factors age, present condition of health, and heredity, which would you consider most important? Ask a good life-insurance agent to explain the different kinds of policies to you so that you may present them clearly to the class.

18. Will a farmer whose land is being slowly "worked out" reach a point when it ceases to pay to farm? Has this ever happened in the United States? If so, when and where?

19. In the *Christian Science Monitor* for December 10, 1919, is a diagram with explanations of the economic scheme of soviet Russia as it existed, in theory at least, at that time. Put the diagram on the board for class study, and explain it. Compare this system with French syndicalism, as described in the *International* and other recent encyclopedias. How does it compare with a blood basis for organization, and a geographical one? Is such a system, if carried out in actual practice, favorable to plentiful and varied production? Do you know what the actual results were?

20. What has been the economic effect of prohibition in the parts of the United States in which it has been enforced long enough for one to judge? See *Literary Digest* for June 12, 1920, p. 86, and more recent articles on the subject.

21. Construct (preferably on the board) a map showing the production areas for the ten leading products of the United States. Use the latest yearbooks. Compare the productiveness of East, Middle West, South, and West, and explain.

22. How many of your class live on farms? Of this number how many receive bulletins from Washington or from some state experiment station?

23. Of what importance to farmers are the life habits of birds? Is there a bird refuge in your county? Where?

24. Do you have any streams near you which are large enough for fish, but which have no fish in them? What can be done about it?

25. Why do not Americans eat more fish? Can this industry be organized as effectively as the meat-packing industry? See "The Harvest of the Sea," in *Leslie's* for August 14, 1920, Vol. CXXXI, pp. 179ff.

26 Where does the material for binder twine come from, and where is it made up? Suppose this raw material were cut off, what would happen? Is Kentucky at present a hemp country? See *Outlook*, Vol CXIV, pp 822–828, and *Scientific American*, Vol LXXXVII, p 356

27 What proportion of the water of Niagara Falls is used for production? Are the beauty and grandeur of the Falls marred by this use? See *Literary Digest*, Vol. LII, pp 963–964; December 29, 1917, p 29; January 17, 1920, pp. 27–28

28 A change in the location of iron industries is taking place. Why?

29. Farmers who move from large Middle West farms to irrigated districts have some trouble adjusting their ideas and methods. One man from Illinois bought eighty acres and began to raise English walnuts and dates What happened? The old riparian law that we inherited with other parts of the English common law was at first applied to irrigation projects Why not now? See *Annals of the American Academy*, Vol. XXXIII, pp. 658–663, 664–676

30 Read the January, 1916, number of the *National Geographic Magazine*, which tells "How the World is Fed," and answer the following questions

a What food industries have gone furthest in the division of labor?

b What food industries are not yet developed to their maximum efficiency?

c Is the United States a self-sufficient nation?

d. What are the true criteria for pronouncing food "good" or "bad"?

31 Find the retail cost of gasoline in your part of the country in 1916 In that year the average price of oil at the wells was $1 10 per barrel of forty-two gallons Calculate the cost of refining and transporting the oil, with all middlemen's profits, until it reached the purchaser

32. Are the national parks productive land? Why?

33 Study the production of coal, a basic industry. See articles by W. J Showalter, in the *National Geographic Magazine*, Vol. XXXIV, pp 407–434, and C F Talman, in the *Mentor*, May 1, 1918

34 What is the relation of space used in making a living to the quality of that living? to the civilization it supports? In other words, how much space is needed for the successive stages of human culture? Why were fewer than a million American Indians often reduced to starvation, while over a hundred million now find ample support in America? Read Carver's "Principles of National Economy," chap. xix.

CHAPTER VII

PRICES, THE MIDDLEMAN, AND CONSUMPTION

A liberalist in economics . . . believes that the interests of the public are expressed quite as accurately on the market and through the price lists as through the ballot box and the statute books.—THOMAS N. CARVER

All the machinery of production is set in motion in order that the people of the world may have what they need and want; or, to speak technically, production is stimulated by consumers' demands. But between original production and consumption there lie several obstacles to be overcome: commodities cannot be given free to consumers, nor are they made where they are to be consumed, nor are they conveniently sold to the consumer just as they are turned out from the farm or factory. Therefore we have now to consider how goods are transported, stored, and handled before they reach the ultimate consumer, how prices are fixed, and the principles that govern consumption itself.

PRICE

No question is of more interest to mankind than what causes the prices of the things that we buy from day to day. We have seen in Chapter IV that the problem of the high cost of living is not a new one. Ever since men began to make goods in excess of the demands of their families and to sell them in markets, there has existed the question of the reasons for "high" prices.

Some of the things most desired and needed by men, such as fresh air and sunshine, can be had for nothing. These things are called free goods by economists. Other things, which because of their scarcity command other goods or money in exchange, are known as economic goods. Economic goods have money value because they are useful to man and because they are scarce. Personal associations might make an heirloom or a piece of handwork done by a friend of very great value to the possessor, but this is a subjective or personal value and, like free goods, is not a subject of interest in the science of economics. It is the value put upon an object by a whole group of people which determines what they are willing to pay for it. Therefore *price is the expression in money terms of social value.*

Price theories. Economists have worked out many theories as to why economic goods command prices varying from a few cents to thousands of dollars It must be remembered that these theories are theories, and that they will not explain specifically why any one article sells for a certain price on a certain day, at a given place. They deal almost entirely with the wholesale price, thus ignoring the additions for transportation, storage, and other middleman's services, and the differences in retail prices due to the fact that the retail markets are local. Practically there is no one universal price for any commodity.

In spite of these deficiencies in price theories, they are well worth our careful study, because before we can remedy any injustices in daily retail prices, or before we can know there are injustices, we must know what sets the original producer's price. And much of the reasoning used in the price theories is applicable to local retail prices.

One of the oldest theories of price and one often quoted by entrepreneurs today is the "marginal cost of production" theory. According to this theory prices are never for very long either higher or lower than the marginal cost of production; that is, than the cost at which the producer with the poorest equipment and resources can put goods upon the market. For if they mount higher, then people who could not afford to produce before now enter the field, supply is thereby increased and the price falls. If, on the other hand, the more favored producers lower the price below the cost for the marginal producers, the latter will drop out of business to avoid bankruptcy. Their ceasing to produce lessens the supply and thereby causes a rise in price, back to the cost-of-production level.

The newer school of economists do not deny that the cost of production affects the supply of any commodity. They are quite willing to admit that entrepreneurs will not continue to produce indefinitely at a loss and that therefore the cost of production will probably be the lowest limit at which producers will offer goods. In other words, they say the cost of production serves to define a minimum supply price. But they point out that frequently, owing to high wages, popular fads, habit, and public ignorance of economic costs, there will exist a wide range of difference between the minimum supply price and the maximum demand price which consumers are willing to pay. Take, for example, the price of bicycles: when the patents expired so as to open manufacture and make the supply price less, the market was flooded with many bicycles, but the price did not go down to ten or fifteen dollars, which was the cost of production. It remained far above that level, although it was below the old $100 price. There are some kinds of goods for which people actually prefer to pay a high price rather than a low one, because of the prestige that inheres in such purchases.

In these cases consumers set a demand price that is far above the lowest possible supply price. Producers, seeing this willingness of consumers to pay high prices, do not need to compete with one another. The point at which the supply price and the demand price coincide is called the point of equilibrium, and sets an equilibrium price. Actual price is nearer the maximum demand price than the minimum supply price. This point is the market price.

At this point the thoughtful student asks, What keeps other producers from entering the field if the market price is so far above the marginal cost, and, by increasing the supply, causing prices to drop to a cost basis? There are several preventives. To begin with, for some time possible producers hold off for fear of a changing demand. Then in many fields it requires years to construct factories, equip them with proper machinery, and secure skilled labor, in order actually to put goods upon the market. In reality the market wholesale price is not likely to be far from the marginal-cost basis, because sellers tend to keep underbidding each other as long as the price is above. In spite of this it is not true to say that the cost of production sets the price. Rather the theory should be stated thus. *normal market price depends upon the relative amounts of supply and demand*

The two foregoing theories both make the important assumption that free competition exists; that many producers are competing with one another to drive down the supply price, just as many consumers compete with one another, thus pushing up the demand price. Now this status of free competition does not exist, as we shall see in the next chapter As a result we have another theory of prices known as the "utility theory." It holds that price is fixed at a point just below that at which people would absolutely refuse to buy at all, because they would rather go without than make so great a sacrifice. This was the theory used by the railroads, which charged "all the traffic would bear," and by all monopolies and profiteers, who charge all they dare charge for things they know people want Of course, under free competition some producer charges less and brings the price down, so the utility theory of price-fixing can be used only by firms which have a monopoly of some kind.

Complicating influences. There are certain factors other than monopoly which tend to make prices other than equilibrium points between demand and supply at any one time One of these is interference by the government. This may be by adding taxes, such as excises upon tobacco, drugs, and toilet articles, or it may be by forcing out foreign competition through protective duties, or it may be by actual price-setting such as was carried on in war time by the Federal government.

More natural interferences with the working of supply and demand are to be found in the operations of speculators and in the complications caused by by-products. A speculator who knows how to foretell changes in demand or supply can steady prices by creating a countermovement on either side, previous to the coming of the change he foresees. Suppose, for instance, that a cotton buyer finds out that a storm is about to sweep the cotton belt which will do great harm to the cotton crop. That means that the crop will be short and cotton will be higher, so he buys cotton. His buying of cotton tends to make the supply less, the demand greater, and hence the price rises. This checks the immediate consumption and leaves a larger supply after the storm has come than would otherwise have been the case. Suppose, also, that a wheat buyer finds that an importer intends to bring in a large amount of Canadian wheat to compete with our own wheat. He knows that this means a fall in price, so he sells his wheat ahead of the fall. His selling helps to bring the price down, and if a farmer about to plant spring wheat notes this fall he will probably plant less wheat. This decrease in production tends to keep the price up later, so that the price does not fall so low as it would have fallen had the full quota of American wheat had to compete with the imported wheat. So legitimate speculation is a market-steadier and a production-guide. It does not overthrow the theory of supply-and-demand price, but works through it to secure a lessening of price fluctuation.

Last of the factors which deflect prices from the equilibrium of supply-and-demand price is the existence of by-products. By-products often cover the cost of production of the main products, which enables a producing company to cut prices either on the main or the by-product, and so undersell their competitors. After securing a monopoly the price is, of course, raised, and the usual rules governing prices set by utility to the consumer apply. A packing-company may be able to set its prices where it will, within the buying ability of its customers, because of the extra profits it makes on soap and toothbrushes.

It is clear, then, that although normal price is set by supply and demand, in actual life there are many factors which deflect price from this point. In the interest of the consumer it is an

PRICES, MIDDLEMEN, AND CONSUMPTION

advantage to reduce such factors as raise prices; in the interest of struggling producers it is helpful to reduce factors which lower prices below the marginal cost of production. This balance of interests is recognized in the efforts of a good government to control monopolies and reduce tariffs and other taxes to the point of need

Transportation and Storage

When one goes down to the retail grocery to buy potatoes, let us say, the price paid consists not only of the equilibrium price between what the potato-growers want for them and what the wholesalers will pay for them, but also of an added amount which is the sum of the charges of all the people who have handled them. Consumers frequently call all the men who handle the products between the farmer or manufacturer and themselves "middlemen," and they object to their increasing the price by each of their transactions. Exchange (as economists call all these processes) is to them an intermediary affair coming between production and consumption, and they question its necessity. Much is written nowadays about doing away with the middleman. Let us see if this view of the case is a right one.

Secondary production. To begin with, the economist insists that these men—or at least many of them—are really producers. They add more usefulness, and therefore more value, to the original commodity If production is defined as the creation of utilities or kinds of usefulness, clearly they are producers They do not give *natural utility*, as the farmer does when he raises the potatoes, or *form utility*, as the manufacturer does when he makes them into potato flour, but there are other kinds of utility just as necessary to the consumer as natural and form utility. Place and time utilities enter into the value of most goods. The former is added by transportation, which takes the product to the place where it is wanted; and the latter by storage, which keeps it until it is wanted.

Transportation. We have seen how transportation grew in scope and changed in means during the early history of man. Today there are so many different means of carrying goods that producers can often make choice of several in getting their goods to market. They will choose, of course, the kind of transportation which gives them greatest efficiency, or the greatest service for the least cost. For transportation is good or bad according as it is safe or risky, cheap or expensive, quick or slow. Safety varies with the kind of transportation and with the temper of the workers in that field, as well as with the laws which safeguard the freight to be carried. Transportation is notoriously risky in America; even in transporting people, the most precious of all freight, the ratio of loss through death and injury is very high. Commercial insurance safeguards the shipper at a nominal cost, and safety-first propaganda and laws are helping somewhat in the passenger services. Unfortunately the American temperament is one which takes risks lightly.

The cheapness of transportation has, of course, a direct and calculable bearing on the prices consumers must pay, and so enters into the reckoning of the business man. Cheapness depends upon several factors, notably:

1. *Operating ease and cost.* The greatest factor in this field is the consumption of the carrying agent. If the gasoline used by a motor truck costs less than the food eaten by a horse, and the carrying power be the same, then it is cheaper to use the truck. But the entrepreneur must also know whether he can find a man who can drive the truck as readily as a man to drive the horse, the relative wages for the two, and the relative dependability of the two men.

2. *Relative carrying power.* If the horse, even with its greater expense for upkeep, carries so much more that the additional cost is more than balanced, the horse is the cheaper carrying agent.

3. *Durability.* Which will live and work longer? Is the risk on one greater than on the other? Which is more liable to happen—that the horse will die, or that the truck engine will

explode some day and scatter the truck and its contents over the adjoining country? Which is the safer investment?

These elements are present in different kinds of transportation in varying degrees. Trucks appeal to farmers in these days of high food prices, because they consume gasoline only when they work, while a horse eats every day of the year; but for a farmer with small knowledge of mechanics, horses are more manageable than trucks. Each shipper, be he small or large in his interests, must weigh the elements of cost for himself. In general, mechanical power is today cheaper than animal power, and water carriage cheaper than land carriage, for the same distance and load. Friction is the great obstacle in land transportation; this explains the ease and cheapness of water carriage. But water carriage is slower; and so for perishable freight, land transportation is preferable unless some method of effective refrigeration is possible. Canals, which are notably slow, do very well for wheat and coal, they are out of the question for, say, the carrying of bananas.

The function of giving place utility to goods is an indispensable one, and one that deserves compensation. But the exact amount of this payment is a difficult question. Much has been said in recent years of high freight rates as a chief cause of high prices. As is shown in Chapter XII, the government now considers transportation so thoroughly a public utility that it has virtually taken over the control of rates charged for this service.

Storage. If one buys potatoes in April he must pay not only the producer's selling price plus transportation charges but an additional sum for storage during the winter. The man who has added time utility to the original commodity has made it more useful to the consumer, and deserves a return for his service. One may perform this service for himself if he can buy potatoes when they are dug and store them in his cellar. In this case one keeps the money for himself which the spring buyer pays to the storer. But for many things it is impracticable or impossible for the consumer to act as storer (as, for example, for ice), and here it is legitimate that the middleman should be paid for his service, which is a real and a valuable one.

Modern storage is accomplished by means of warehouses, usually conveniently located near the terminals of transportation systems and near markets. This means, of course, that great warehouses are found chiefly in large cities. An exception is found in storage elevators for wheat, which are often built in the open country along railroads. Food warehouses, of course, must have special equipment for keeping the food in good condition; hence the cold-storage plants, which now play so large a part in our food supply. When food is really well kept in such plants, they add utility to the product and therefore deserve a reasonable profit. But cold-storage plants need careful supervision and regulation.

The cold-storage man is not loved by the public. This is partly because he has often put badly deteriorated food on the market, usually of fair appearance and thus easily salable. This is the result of criminal neglect or carelessness in management, for it is possible to keep food a reasonable length of time without harmful changes. One year has been found to be a safe storage limit, and some states have made laws to that effect. Another reason for the storage man's unpopularity is the high price often charged for stored goods. Storage men have sometimes made an outrageous profit on stored eggs or chickens or fruit. But the number of such cases is overestimated by the public, and it must be remembered that large profits in one commodity may be balanced by an entire loss in something else. A reasonable control through state commissions is practicable, and the honest storage men accept such control in good spirit.

The legitimate objections to storage are augmented in times of shortage or high prices by much simple and unhealthy prejudice. It is hard for some people to see that the saving of food until the time when it is needed really adds utility to it. It is much easier to see that a farmer has added utility to a chicken by feeding it until it grows large and fat than to see that another man adds utility to the same chicken by keeping it in an ammonia-coil room until Christmas time. The one secures natural utility, the other time utility, and one utility is as real as the other. The storage man equalizes the supply and makes possible variety and steadiness in consumption.

Marketing

The third part of exchange is marketing. By this is meant all the processes, aside from carrying and storage, that take place between the producing and the consuming of a commodity. Strictly speaking, all the men who handle goods during the period of its exchange are so-called middlemen, whether they transport, store, or buy and sell goods. The term is commonly used, however, only of those who actually possess the goods at some time between its production and its consumption; for example, the wholesaler, the jobber, and the retailer.

Possession utility. Now many people who are willing to grant that the transporter and the storer are actually producers deny that the men who merely buy and sell are adding any utility to the product. But many economists insist that any act which brings the product nearer to the consumer makes it more useful to him, and that hence the adding of *possession utility* deserves a return. A pound of coffee in the bin of the grocer is of no use to the consumer, but that pound of coffee wrapped up and exchanged for money by the retailer becomes full of utility for the consumer. Most fair-minded people think it right to pay the retailer and all other necessary handlers for their addition of possession utility, but they are somewhat skeptical as to whether the long array of wholesalers, jobbers, commission merchants, and retailers is all necessary. There is a general feeling that the number of owners between producer and consumer is larger than it should be.

It is impossible in this book to deal with the middleman's functions in detail, but the general rule can be laid down that when a selling middleman actually performs a service by adding necessary possession utilities or by distributing the risks of production, he deserves a return equal to the cost of his service plus a fair profit. But if his expenses and profit together exceed the amount of value he adds, then he is no longer a producer; he has ceased to be profitable to society.

It is a well-known fact that in the complicated production of today, involving the carrying of products thousands of miles from the spot of their original creation, there is a great need of middlemen, and also that there are many chances for the abuse of the middleman's function. The recent high prices and the positive knowledge that some men have taken middlemen's profits without performing legitimate services have led many people to object to middlemen *in toto*, and to urge either their entire abolition or else drastic remedies for the abuses they practice.[1] When, however, men have tried to do business without them, they have never succeeded very well. It takes so much time and capital and trouble that after a trial the consumer is willing to allow the middleman to keep his job. He is not willing to allow him his own will, however, in the matter of profits. Regulation by the State has been found the best solution, so far, of the problem of extortionate middlemen's profits.

Two other remedies are of some avail. The first is publicity. The middleman of the past could sometimes extort undue profits because no one knew just who he was, where to find him, and what he did. Today such facts are to be had, and people who really feel that there is something wrong in the middleman's field can ascertain where the wrong lies and publish the facts. The press may or may not be willing to print information about middlemen, but the State is willing, in a number of cases, to undertake regulation when informed of the need.

[1] For instance, a Federal investigation carried on during the war proved that in a certain large city the middlemen devised a clever trick by which to outwit the government in its price control of sugar. The law allowed only one cent profit per pound to each handler of sugar, but the middlemen sold and resold sugar back and forth among themselves until they had piled up a handsome profit.

PRICES, MIDDLEMEN, AND CONSUMPTION

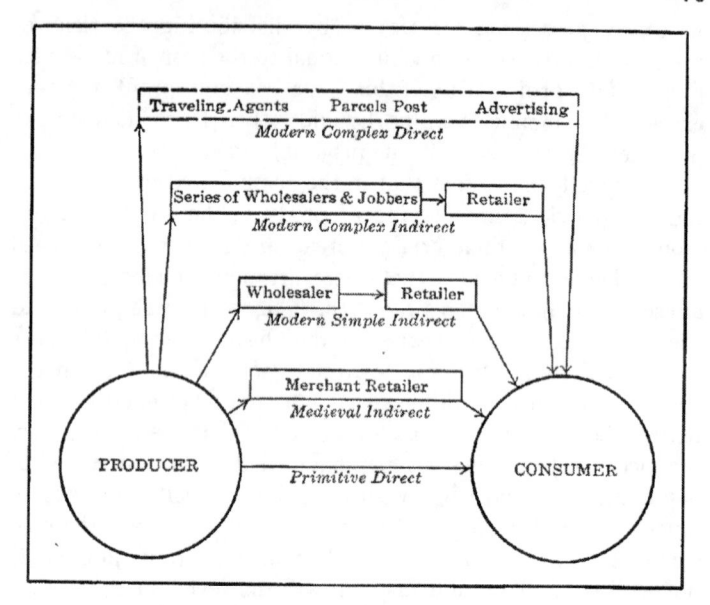

SELLING METHODS

The producer and the consumer are the constant factors in exchange. Early barter and sale took place directly between them, while the modern transactions of truck gardeners and peddlers, custom tailors and milliners, show that the system is a permanent one, although relatively less important each year. In the Middle Ages craftsmen often turned their product over to a retail merchant to sell. The functions of production, wholesaling and retailing, became definitely separated in early modern times under the domestic system. As time passed the system became more and more complex, the multiplication of middlemen adding greatly to the final price. This has given rise recently to a tendency to seek more direct selling methods. Large-scale production and the widespread market usually make a return to primitive direct methods impossible; therefore such devices as advertising and traveling agents are used. Notice that although a personal middleman may be eliminated, his function must still be performed by some agency. From your own community life make a list of illustrations of each type of selling method

The other means is the reduction of the number of middlemen. The elimination of one man in the series means the elimination of his profit from the consumer's price unless some other man at once appropriates it to himself. The United States postal service has recently undertaken to eliminate middlemen by advertising free the names of farmers near large cities who will sell direct to consumers what they produce, sending the product by parcel post. Such business can be carried on only on a small scale; large-scale industries are impracticable without middlemen. Large public markets in which the farmers meet the consumers have sometimes been successful as money-saving institutions in the United States, but they have never supplanted the retail dealer to any great extent.

The intricacy of exchange. In this matter of food selling, as in other respects, the middleman's usefulness and functions spring from the size and intricacy of the business world. Products are made so far from the point of their consumption and pass through so many processes of acquiring utility that middlemen are simply indispensable. The three sets of relations to the product are not in neat, consecutive order nor divisible into exact steps. Suppose that one uses a cup of coffee as an example of a consumer's good. The coffee is raised in Brazil, sold to a local buyer, and by him to an exporter in Bahia. The coffee is handled by many middlemen aboard ship, at the docks, in the warehouse, and on the railroad. It lands in a wholesaler's warehouse in Chicago and is sold to a roaster, who sells it to a packer of fancy-named brands. The packer grinds and blends it, packs it again, and sells it to a jobber. The jobber sells it to a retailer, the retailer to a hotel buyer, and the hotel buyer hands it to the cook. The cook makes it up, and it is finally served to the consumer. In its journeys the plantation owner, the roaster, the grinder, the blender, and the cook gave it natural or form utilities; the transporters (including the waiter) added place utility; the storage men who kept it between moves added time utility; the wholesaler, the jobber, and the retailer gave it possession utility. It is impossible to separate all these steps and deal out strict economic justice.

The next decade will see much careful investigation into the practices of middlemen in many industries; and we have a right to hope that if these investigations are carried on in a scientific spirit, and the remedies suggested are carried out by a government supported by public opinion, the present practices of "profiteers" will be corrected.

Consumption

The satisfaction of human wants comes from consumption, which is the destruction or using up of the utilities created by production. We have seen that in the beginning man's wants were few and simple, they were merely existence wants—food, shelter, clothing. Becoming more cultured, man added to his desires the culture wants the desire for religion, beauty, education, recreation and greater physical comfort, ease, and convenience These things, which are not existence essentials, are progress essentials, for man is a stagnant and unambitious creature without them.

The order of consumption. Even with all the goods that civilization has given to the world, any sane man with his purchasing power in his hands will choose first to buy and use the prime necessities of life What is left over after providing necessities is spent according to the taste and habits of the consumer It is in this class of consumption that the differences in human nature appear. Some men spend their surplus in things that make them more efficient, and thus the surplus tends always to become larger. Others, the slaves of tradition, habit, or ignorance, spend it for that which decreases their efficiency as producers or leaves it at a standstill. Their surplus remains stationary or grows less. *The order of consumption is always from more to less necessary things, with choice becoming more varied as the amount of the surplus increases*

One does not continue indefinitely to consume articles of the same nature. Suppose you come home from school very hungry, desiring a piece of bread and butter above all earthly goods. Bread and butter has most utility for you, at that moment, of all commodities, and you proceed to secure some at once. But having eaten one piece, you are still hungry—not quite so hungry as at first, but still hungry enough to eat another slice. Even a third slice may tempt you to postpone a set of tennis or a half hour with a new magazine. But the third slice has lost the fine satisfying flavor of the first piece, and perhaps before you are through you wish you had not cut and spread it. Nothing could induce you to eat a fourth; you have reached satiety. In this experience you have illustrated one of the fundamental laws of consumption, called the law of diminishing utility. The first slice of bread and butter had great utility, the second less, the third very little, and the fourth you did not want. An economist would say that the third slice had *marginal utility*— a term applied to the utility of the last unit consumed—and that the fourth had disutility. The utility of all three slices taken together is, of course, the *total utility* of your lunch. We may state the law as follows: *If there be an unlimited supply of an economic good for consumption, units decrease in utility as they are used, and the last unit used has a utility on the margin of no utility at all.*

Relative utility. People nowadays have a great variety of wants, and no two people consume exactly the same things. The returns of production come to us in money, and this gives us the precious privilege which our remote ancestors did not have, of much choice in the commodities we consume. Now when anyone goes into the market to buy what he will with his money, what he always does is to see which of the goods that his money will buy will have most utility for him, and to take those. That is to say, he balances utility and cost and takes what will give him the most satisfaction for his money. Suppose, for instance, that a clerk receives $20 per week for her services in a department store. She makes out a budget of her weekly expenditure, in which she puts down first of all her expenses for the existence essentials—$7 for board, $3 for room, and $6 for clothing allowance. This leaves her $4, which she divides as follows: $1 is saved, 70 cents goes for car fare, 30 cents for amusement, $1 for laundry work, 25 cents for church

GRAPHIC REPRESENTATION OF THE LAW OF
DIMINISHING UTILITY

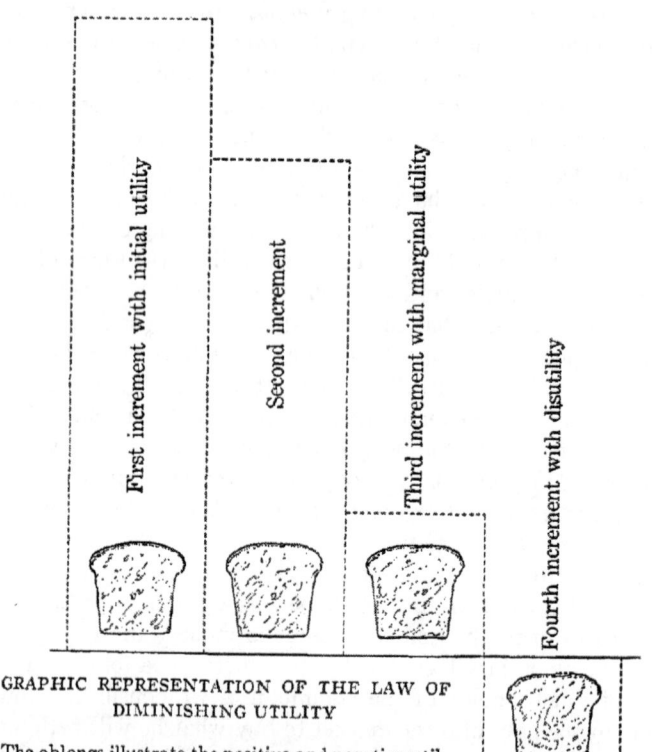

The oblongs illustrate the positive and negative utility of the four slices of bread and butter, and are labeled with some terms often used by economists.

But suppose that when you reach home you find only two slices of bread, which you proceed to eat; then the second slice becomes the marginal slice, and its value is still, of course, greater than a third would be, if available. Suppose, again, that with plenty of bread and butter available your pet dog comes up to you and begs mutely for a "hand-out." You then "consume" that fourth slice by giving it to Fido; of course its use is still less to you than the use of the third slice, since it gives you vicarious satisfaction only. But now it has become the marginal unit, or increment, of bread and butter. From these illustrations we see that the utility of the marginal increment changes, and, other things being equal, it will vary inversely as the supply of the goods.

State this fact in a definite law

contribution, 25 cents for a little sister's spending money, and 50 cents for emergency expenses of her own. In making out this budget the clerk followed the law of the economic order of consumption. She figured that she would win the greatest utility out of such a division. Tabulated, her expenditure reads:

Item	Amount	Percentage of Income
Food	$7.00	35.0
Clothing	6.00	30.0
Shelter	3.00	15.0
Laundry bill	1.00	5.0
Saving	1.00	5.0
Transportation	.70	3.5
Charity and gift	.50	2.5
Incidentals	.50	2.5
Pleasure	.30	1.5
Total	$20.00	100.0

Let us now suppose that this clerk is advanced to $30 per week. Her budget under the higher salary reads as follows:

Item	Amount	Percentage of Income	Increase or Decrease in Percentage
Food	$8.00	26.66	− 8.34
Clothing	8.00	26.66	− 3.34
Shelter	5.00	16.66	+ 1.66
Laundry bill	1.00	3.33	− 1.66
Saving	3.00	10.00	+ 5.00
Transportation	1.00	3.33	− .17
Charity and gift	1.00	3.33	+ .83
Incidentals	1.50	5.00	+ 2.5
Pleasure	1.50	5.00	+ 3.5
Total	$30.00	100.00	

Everyone whose income increases readjusts his consumption in a similar way. If we compare these two personal budgets we find some interesting facts: first, that with more income this clerk slightly increased the absolute but decreased the relative amount she spent for food. Perhaps the added dollar represents a little better surroundings, or more pleasant company, rather than better food or more of it. Her room now cost her slightly more and her clothing slightly less in proportion than before: but the relative amount spent for pleasure, charity, and incidentals increased, while the percentage saved was doubled. The last column in the second budget shows the increase and decrease in existence and progress essentials.

Engel's law. Although she probably did not know it, this clerk was changing her expenditure in accordance with Engel's law of expenditure, which holds whenever an income is really increased. Of course if costs keep pace in their rise with wages, there is no change, for then there is no real increase in income. Dr. Ernest Engel found that when incomes increase (1) the relative amount spent for food decreases; (2) the relative amount spent for clothing and shelter and other existence essentials changes a little; (3) the relative amount spent for the progress essentials—saving, charity, culture, amusement, and health—increases.

Characteristics of wholesome consumption. There are three characteristics of the consumption of people in advanced civilization which we do not find among savages. The first is that consumption is ample compared to that of savage life. This does not, of course, include war time, for war is a reversion to savagery and brings a return of savage conditions. But under ordinary, peace-time production under the modern division of labor, production is so ample that there should be plenty for everyone. The cause of a lack lies in poor distribution and in unwise choice of productions. The efficient person consumes enough for his needs, he has enough nourishing food, good enough clothing, a comfortable and attractive home, and ample satisfaction for his spiritual needs.

Consumption under high civilization is, in the second place, varied. No two people have to eat or wear or read exactly the same things. There is ample opportunity for that delightful variety in consumption which means interesting individuality in the people one knows. We may choose our food from the cargoes of the seven seas, our clothing from all the looms of earth, our books from every mind of every age, and our pleasures from half a hundred ready recreations. Life is full of variety for the highly civilized man of initiative and interest.

The third characteristic of wholesome consumption is that of steadiness. We know that American Indians, or any savage race for that matter, ate ravenously when there was a feast and then starved until the next big hunting party brought in another deer or bear. There were no refrigerators, no cold-storage plants, no great granaries, no facilities of any kind for the deliberate saving of food. The same rule applied to other commodities. But in the modern world there are countless ways of saving all sorts of goods until they are wanted, and people have learned to consume steadily. A habit of eating set meals each day is one of the earmarks of a high civilization. In the same way we count it a sign of weakness for people to make a great display at one time and to deny themselves ordinary comforts at another. When consumption is steady no one need either go without or consume more than is good for him at any one time.

The Standard of Living

The term "standard of living" is used in two ways. Some economists consider it to be the sum of the desires of an average member of any given class—the amount and kinds of commodities that such a person must have before he will be contented and happy or will marry and support children; but the more common use of the term is that in which it stands for the actual consumption of the members of a given class—the sum of the goods that they use in their living. So when we say that a class has a low standard of living we mean that they use relatively few and cheap commodities. A class with a high standard of living uses a great deal of varied goods. The term is used in this book in the latter sense.

There are three things which affect the standard of living. There are, first, one's desires—what one *wants* to consume. These desires depend upon what one is used to, first of all; for some people have always had and accept as a matter of course things which others have scarcely dared to dream of. One wants some things just because he knows that other people enjoy them, and he thinks he would enjoy them too So he who goes about among people or who reads interesting novels and books of travel is likely to have more and higher wants than those who never read or travel. A few original and imaginative people even think of new things which they have not heard of as actual used goods, but which they can see "in their mind's eye" as the sources of happiness, and they want those things. Perhaps this first influence of desire is strongest of all.

But two circumstances act to limit the satisfaction of these wants The first is income; the second, market price. They act together and conversely, each unit of income tending to add to the chances of securing what one wants, and each unit of price making one's wants less easy to get. To illustrate· people in a low state of civilization do not care for lights at night. They go to bed and sleep until dawn, for they do not read, or go to the theater, or attend church, or visit with their friends. When they become more intelligent they sit around a fire and tell stories, later they want candles or kerosene lamps, as they begin to read and to play interesting games after the day's work is done. Finally, because the other people of their acquaintance have them, and because mother is tired of cleaning and filling lamps and wants more time for her sewing or for riding in the Ford, the family wants electric lights in the house. But here the two limiting factors make their appearance. Can the family afford electric lights? The father of the family thinks it can, because his wages have been increased twice in this last year; on the income side he is sure it can be done. But upon making inquiry he finds that while his wages have been increased twice, the price of wiring, fixtures, and current has been increased three times, and that electric lights are now at such a price that the augmented income will not cover it. So for the time being that family remains on the kerosene-lamp level, although it wants to be on an electric-light level of living.

Standard of living and prices. Of course this standard of living affects prices in its turn. It is because so many people want electric lights, as well as because materials and labor have "gone up," that the electricians can charge so much. If most people were content to live with kerosene lamps, electric lights would be cheaper, in order to induce occasional buying. When the standard of living rises without a corresponding rise in production, the cost of living becomes higher; that is to say, as the people of a community come to the point at which most of them demand electric lights, the price of the equipment and current will go very high unless there is another plant installed or more fixtures and current brought in from outside. The higher standard of living, which has been very noticeable in the last few years in America, combined with the reduction in production of many things wanted because of the World War, has been one of the chief causes of the much-discussed high cost of living.

Classification of societies. We have now considered the great complementary processes that make up the greater part of human activity in production (with exchange) and consumption. These processes are opposite in nature, and if production does not approximately balance consumption in any nation, that nation soon falls behind in wealth and progress. If a nation is constantly creating a surplus, and so accumulating wealth, it is called an accumulating society. Such a society is adding to its capital all the time, and eventually it will be able to produce by using much capital and little human effort, for it will more and more substitute capital for labor. This will release human effort for the production of works of art, great books, great teaching and thinking. Much of its capital will be fixed capital, capable of repeated use through many years, such as houses and furniture, books, household linen, machin-

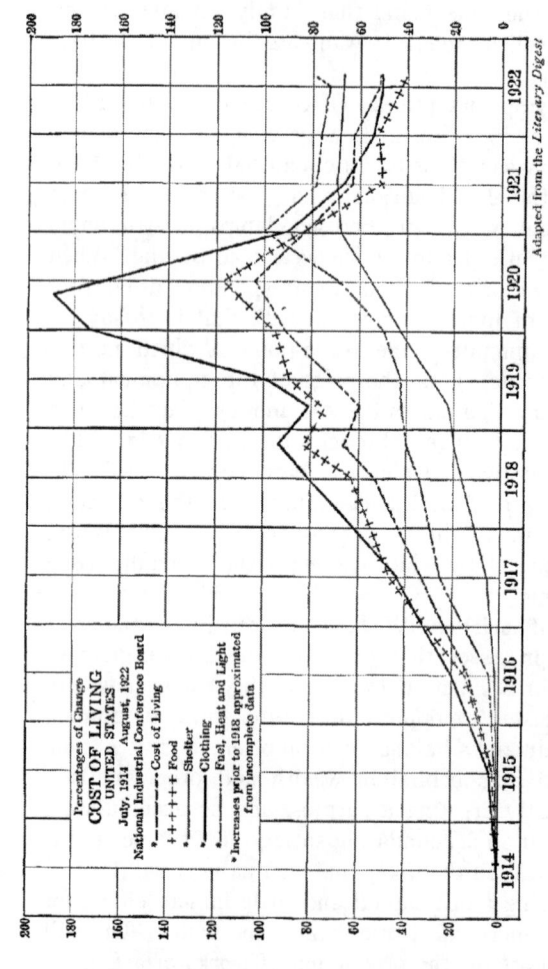

RELATIONSHIP BETWEEN FACTORS IN THE COST OF LIVING

Adapted from the *Literary Digest*

This graph shows the close relationship between the various factors in the cost of living; it should be studied with a view to finding out which factors are most affected by a war — the great political fact largely conditioning the abnormal rise — and which factors tend to remain comparatively stable. Note the effect of the armistice

ery, utensils, and tools. The money capital that in another society must be used to produce such capital goods can then be used as investment to produce consumer's goods. The advantages of an accumulating society might be enlarged upon at length, but it is clear that they mean prosperity to all classes in proportion as this capital is divided among all classes.

A society which uses up its production as fast as it makes it is a static society. Many American individuals are economically static; they make good wages, but they save nothing. Such a society can live as long as crops are good, business runs along "as usual," and peace reigns; but if war or a season of hard times comes, it is reduced to suffering because it has no reserve. Moreover, a sudden forced change in the variable proportions of the factors of production finds it helpless and confused. It provides nothing for future generations, and so insures that its children must work as hard as itself, under conditions no better. It leaves the world no better, economically, than it found it.[1]

A losing society is one which is using up the accumulations of past years of production. Any country in time of war is liable to be a losing society; a country torn by dissensions or famine or a general strike is in such plight. It is not self-supporting; it is reducing the earth again to the nonproducing conditions of the lowest savage life.

Manifestly any efficient individual or nation belongs to the first of these classes. The efficient man adds something to the social surplus, to the sum of capital which, accumulating from generation to generation, makes for a constant rise in the standard of living and for a constant rise in human quality. This last aim is the object of all our improvements—the production of a better race of men on the earth.

---

[1] Strictly speaking, of course, there is no such thing as static society, just as a human being is never the same from day to day, but is always a little worse or a little better off today than yesterday; but if through a period of years a society cannot be seen to have gained or lost, the term is used and is justified because of its approximate truth and convenience.

PRICES, MIDDLEMEN, AND CONSUMPTION

Summary. The secondary producers, or middlemen, add place, time, and possession utilities to goods. For these services they are entitled to a fair remuneration. The consumer pays for a commodity a price based upon demand and supply, but greatly affected by many other influences. Societies are classed according to their habits of consumption, and are good or bad, economically, according as these habits affect the present and the future of mankind.

SUPPLEMENTARY READINGS

CARVER, T N   Principles of Political Economy, pp 461-485
Causes of price-change:
BABSON, R W., in *Annals of the American Academy*, Vol XXXVIII, p. 492, summary, pp 493-497
TUFTS, J H   The Real Business of Living, chap xxv   [Fair price]
WEBSTER, W. C   General History of Commerce, pp 237-241   [Price-fixing in the French Revolution]
The farmer and the middleman.
BAILEY, L. H   The Country Life Movement in the United States, pp 149-164
CARVER, T N   Principles of Rural Economics, pp. 271-288
Cold storage ·
Annals of the American Academy, Vol L, pp. 48-56.
American Review of Reviews, Vol XLIII, pp 474-475
Good Housekeeping, Vol. LII, pp 343-344
Independent, Vol LXXIV, pp 348-350

SEARCH QUESTIONS AND PROBLEMS

1 For how many different purposes do you use paper in your home? Which of the several utilities thus illustrated is the marginal utility? What is the marginal utility of salt on a farm? of iron in a blacksmith's shop?

2. Money has perhaps the slowest rate of diminishing utility of all the commodities   Why is this?

3. List ten things of fairly general utility that are now scarce and high in your locality. Now refer to the diagram showing causes for scarcity in Carver's "Principles of Political Economy," p 282, and see whether you can assign the cause of scarcity in each case.

4. It is one of the "paradoxes of value" that diamonds and rubies, which have little real use, are far more expensive than bread, which possesses great usefulness. Explain.

5. On June 10, 1920, a dry-goods merchant offered ten ladies' suits, which had cost him from $23.50 to $52.50 and which had sold from $40 to $100 when first offered in February, at the flat price of $25 each.

   a. Did the merchant use cost or utility principle in fixing this price?

   b. Why did he not keep the suits until the next spring?

   c. What kind of utility had been added to them between February and June?

6. Mary Smith knit herself a sweater. When asked how much it was worth, she said: "The wool cost $10, and it took me three full days to knit it. My work was certainly worth $4 a day, which is what mother pays the seamstress. That would make the sweater worth $22." Her questioner said, "I can buy one down town for $20, but I like the color and design of yours; I will give you $17 for it." Mary thought for a time, and then consented to sell it, meaning to buy more yarn and make another sweater.

   a. What theory did Mary use in setting her price on the sweater?

   b. Did she gain or lose by the transaction?

   c. Was the $17 price set by demand and supply alone, or did other elements enter in?

7. How many public-utility monopolies are there in your town? Does the town regulate their rates? Are the rates reasonable? How do they compare with the rates of privately owned and controlled public utilities?

8. Are high rentals a problem in your town? Can the landlords be limited by law? See *American City*, Vol. XIX, pp. 147–149, for a legal opinion on this subject. Has your city council gone as far as is indicated for Baltimore?

9. What is the remedy for very large profits that come as the result of abnormal—say war—conditions? See *Outlook*, Vol. CXIX, pp. 250–251; *Literary Digest* for August 31, 1918, p. 15.

10. If low-cost producers are limited in their profits by government regulations, what becomes of the high-cost, or marginal, producers? See *World's Work*, Vol. XXXVI, pp. 453–454; *Bellman*, Vol. XXV, p. 61. For the report of the Federal Trade Commission see *Nation*, Vol. CVII, pp. 32–33.

11. How did the government regulation of wheat prices during the World War affect farmers? See *Literary Digest* for March 16, 1918,

pp. 18-19, *World's Work*, Vol XXXV, pp 12-13, *Scribner's*, Vol LXIV, pp 80-86

12 Is government price-fixing a good thing? Read an unusually good article in the *Unpopular Review*, Vol. IX, pp 312-327; also, *Outlook*, Vol CXVIII, pp 531 ff, and Vol. CXIX, pp. 341-342; *Century*, Vol XCIII, pp. 605-611, *Independent*, Vol XCII, pp. 134 ff Arrange a class symposium or debate on the subject.

13 What kind of production is the drying of vegetables for winter use?

14 Are housekeepers and cooks producers or consumers?

15 What was the attitude of the past toward middlemen? Why has it changed? See Hamilton's "Current Economic Problems," p 161

16 The open market of Seattle is one of the show places of that city Has it reduced the high cost of living there? See *Overland Monthly* (N.S.), Vol LXII, pp 407-408 Do you think that if municipal markets were established in your town the housewives would take advantage of them to reduce the high cost of living? Note what happened in New York, in *Journal of Home Economics*, Vol VII, pp 241-245, and in *Independent*, Vol LXXXIX, pp 450-451

17 How large should a city be before it is wise to install a city public market? Why? Under what plans are public markets conducted? See *Journal of Home Economics*, Vol VIII, pp 343-347; *American City*, Vol XVIII, pp 315-316 Has the municipal-market idea been really "tried out"? Does it work? See *Craftsman*, Vol. XIX, pp 125-131; *American City*, Vol. XVI, pp 132, 167-168.

18 Suppose the boys and girls of your community doubled the food supply by making vacation gardens in every vacant lot and back yard Could they market their vegetables profitably? Note how six widely separated American cities solved the problem. *Century*, Vol. XCVI, pp 398-403

19 If you had to give up successively all the things you possess, which would you give up first? List the privileges, advantages, habits, and possessions that you would give up, putting the most valued things last. Now make a set of lists to include what you would buy if your whole income were (1) $1 per week; (2) $5 per week, (3) $10 per week, (4) $20 per week; (5) $100 per week; (6) $1000 per week Tabulate this information, and calculate the percentages of each weekly income spent for food, clothing, shelter, fire and light, pleasure (including travel and beautiful surroundings), charity and religion, saving,

legal, medical, and other personal service, etc. Compare the two lists. What interesting things do you discover?

20. Read Carver's "Principles of Political Economy," chap. xlii. What do you think of the efficiency of the standard of living of your own family? Do you as a family produce more value for the world than you use? Consider the case of your friends: does the "set" to which you and your parents belong produce more than it consumes? Is its standard of living a luxurious and inefficient one, or do the items in its consumption give back value to the consumers and to society? What do you think of the efficiency of the standard of living of the Japanese race? of the German people? of the French? of Americans? In view of these things what are the chances for each of these races in the matter of holding their own economically and politically?

21. A house decorator was paid $25 per week in 1914, and spent about 25 per cent for house rent, including fuel and light; 50 per cent for food; 20 per cent for clothing; and 5 per cent for incidentals. In 1920 he was paid $55 per week, and spent about the same percentages for each item. His son, who attended high school, told him that Engel's law said that they should then be spending less for rent and food and more for saving, charity, and pleasure. The family was much puzzled, as it did not know how to spend less for necessities and live at all. Can you explain what had happened?

22. Said A to B, "Thirty thousand dollars' worth of corn was consumed in our state in 1915 in the making of whisky; I am a prohibitionist." Said B to A: "Yes; and forty thousand dollars' worth of corn meal was consumed in the same time. Economically whisky cost the state less than corn meal did in material resources destroyed. I am not a prohibitionist." Criticize the attitudes of A and B.

23. Complete the following table and then tell what it means in terms of the standard of living:

Year	World Cotton Crop in Millions of Pounds	World Population in Millions	Average Pounds used per Capita
1800	500	640	0.8
1850	1,490	1,075	
1900	7,566	1,570	
1918	10,280	1,729	

What other factors besides the amount of the cotton crop entered into the increased use of cotton during this period?

24. During the war Herbert Hoover gave this table of substitutes as a guide to economical home consumption:

THE SOLDIERS NEED	THE FOLK AT HOME CAN USE
Wheat	Corn, oats, barley, and rye
Butter and lard	Cottonseed oil, peanut oil, corn oil, and drippings
Sugar	Molasses, honey, and sirups
Bacon, beef, mutton, and pork	Chickens, eggs, cottage cheese, fish, nuts, peas, and beans

a. Of what use is such a table in time of peace?

b. What relation does such a table bear to the high cost of living? to permanent agriculture?

25. Is the United States government interested in what you serve at your home table? Why? Send to the Superintendent of Documents, Washington, D.C., for a copy of Price List 11, "Foods and Cooking," which will show how the government advises its people in making their home consumption more economical and efficient

26. Does your family use a family budget in apportioning its expenditure? What proportion is spent for the various items? Make a list of all expenses for one week. What do you find?

CHAPTER VIII

THE TRUST PROBLEM

> Notwithstanding all the law against agreements in restraint of trade, the present generation has seen the greatest movement toward consolidation which is recorded in economic history.—BRUCE WYMAN

THE GROWTH OF BIG BUSINESS

Statement of the problem. One of the most pressing problems which has developed in the field of production is the trust problem. That expression is used to include all the problems which have grown out of the formation of a bigger business unit. Before the Industrial Revolution, when production did not necessitate expensive machinery or power, and the market was confined to a more narrow area, the problems of big business were fewer and easier. But today, with one concern hiring thousands of men, using millions of capital, and supplying not only a national but in many cases a world market, the problems of big business are many and varied.

The organization of business. In a preceding chapter we saw that the fourth factor in production is organization, or, as it is sometimes termed, management. Without the organization of land, labor, and capital into a business undertaking there could be no production. The earliest organization was the single entrepreneur or "one-man" business. This form of organization still meets the needs of the custom tailor, the pop-corn and peanut vendor, and a number of other small enterprises. So also does the second form of business organization, the partnership, serve well enough when the size of the business is limited and its need for capital is small. Many corner groceries and suburb drug stores are still under partnership form.

The corporation. But after the Industrial Revolution the processes of production were so changed that the old forms of organization no longer served the needs of industry any more than they had satisfied the needs of trade after commerce had begun to expand. Business men seized upon the principle of the commercial joint-stock company and originated the corporation. By this device a group of producers can join together in an enterprise instead of running small competing establishments They can also add to their accumulations of capital by selling shares to stockholders.

These shares may be either preferred or common. Preferred stock receives a set rate of annual return or dividends of from 5 per cent to 7 per cent on the face value, which is usually $100. In case the corporation does not earn in any one year sufficient to pay the preferred-stock dividends, the stockholders may receive less than the set amount for that year, and only in case their stock is "cumulative preferred" will they receive the arrears in the following year. Since the dividends on common stock are not paid until after all those on the preferred stock, the rate is likely to fluctuate greatly from no percentage in poor business years or weak concerns up to far above the preferred rate. All the holders of stock, common and preferred, are members of the corporation. In other words they are entrepreneurs, although the actual managing of the business is done by a small group elected annually and called a board of directors.

Every corporation receives a charter from a state government granting it a legal entity, or the right to act as an individual in such matters as buying and selling, and suing or being sued at law.[1] The charter frequently lays down certain restrictions as to the granting of stock. Almost every state in the Union, the

---

[1] The corporate form is used by other private organizations whose aim is not profit—as, for instance, colleges, lodges, churches, etc—and also by public organizations A city is a corporation For the form of a typical charter see Marshall, Wright, and Field's "Materials for the Study of Elementary Economics," Nos 65, 66, and for splendid diagrams of various ways of organizing business see No 61.

exceptions being West Virginia, Delaware, and New Jersey, has forbidden overcapitalization.[1] A company may be said to be overcapitalized when the value of the business is very much less than the outstanding stock issue. If thousands of shares have been distributed gratis among a few originators of the company, or if stock is sold to the public and the proceeds not invested in the business but divided up as profits among the original shareholders, then the company's stock is said to be "watered." If, of course, the value of the enterprise has risen greatly owing to a general rise in values or to some discovery of natural or artificial resources, then more stock can be issued without a corresponding investment, and the company cannot be said to be overcapitalized. Excessive overcapitalization often results in bankruptcy, and even a small amount of watered stock draws dividends away from regular stock paid for in cash.[2]

Advantages of incorporation. The advantages of the corporate form of organization are many. In the first place coöperation means the accumulation of more wealth for business uses. Widows, orphans, teachers, professional men, may become capitalists, reaping profits without having to enter business themselves. They need not assume liability for the debts or failure of their undertaking, beyond the sum total of their amount of stock.[3] This is a big advantage over the partnership, wherein each partner is limited only by the extent of his whole fortune for the debts of the business, even those which are accumulated by his partner without his knowledge.

Another advantage of the corporation is its permanence. When one member dies his stock is simply passed on to his heirs or sold as he himself wills. The corporation as such is in

[1] New Jersey during the governorship of Woodrow Wilson passed laws against overcapitalization which have since been repealed.

[2] For a detailed explanation of stock-watering and corporations in general see Marshall, Wright, and Field's "Materials for the Study of Elementary Economics," Nos. 71, 72, and Hamilton's "Current Economic Problems," Nos. 90, 95.

[3] In a very few corporations, such as the national banks, a man is liable for twice his amount of stock.

no way affected, for it may continue to do business for dozens of years, building up a large trade and a well-known name.

The characteristic of permanence produces another advantage of incorporation by making a safe place for the investment of savings. If money is lent to a corporation, the lender receives bonds which are in reality mortgages on the buildings and equipment. In case the corporation goes bankrupt, the bondholders are the first to be paid. During solvency they also receive interest before stockholders receive dividends. Even for those who invest money in the enterprise by purchasing stock there is a large degree of safety furnished by means of preferred stock, which is paid back in full before the common stockholders receive a penny.

Another great advantage of the corporation is that such an organization allows business to be conducted on a large scale. This is highly desirable, since it cheapens production by making possible the purchase of expensive machinery, the minute divisions of labor, the purchase of raw materials in great quantities, and the elimination of waste in the duplication of buildings, machinery, advertising, office and selling forces. Large-scale production, moreover, makes possible an output of better quality due to the fact that big business units are able to employ the most highly skilled labor and still have a surplus which can be used for experimentation with new machinery and methods.

Finally, large-scale production means the utilization of by-products which formerly were thrown away. Packing-plants, for instance, no longer cure meat only but are manufacturers of lard, buttons, soap, cleaning powders, medicine, and fertilizer, thus justifying the boast of one of our great American packing-companies that it utilizes everything "except the squeal." Not only is a great source of waste stopped by the utilization of by-products, but the primary products themselves may become cheaper and hence within the reach of more people. Frequently a comparatively cheap by-product may serve as a substitute for an expensive primary product; as, for example, cottonseed oil in place of olive oil.

The advantages of incorporation are so great that most businesses, except those needing careful and skillful personal supervision and those serving only a small market, have adopted the corporation form. By 1890, incorporated organizations were turning out 65 per cent of the output of all the manufacturing concerns in the United States, and by 1910 this percentage had increased to 80 per cent.

The beginning of combination. The aforementioned advantages of large-scale production led business men to realize that even more gain would result if they could combine companies into still larger working business units, as they had combined individual organizations into corporations. This led to combinations of various kinds. The first were the loose forms of the gentleman's agreement and the pool. In the gentleman's agreement the chief officers of several competing companies met and agreed among themselves, usually over their dessert, to limit the output of their product or to raise its price. This form of combination proved unsatisfactory, for jealousy and suspicion soon entered; moreover, there was no legal contract binding the parties, and usually one of them failed to be a "gentleman." So also in the pool, where the companies bound themselves to pool their profits or the territory for purchasing and selling, mutual jealousy and distrust soon dissolved the combination. Moreover, when the members of a pool tried to punish disobedient members, they found that many of the state courts refused to enforce the provisions of the agreement on the ground that pooling contracts were illegal. In 1887 the United States government prohibited all pooling by the railroads.

The Trust and the Government

The weaknesses in these loose forms of combination led to a new and closer form, known as the trust. By this device a board of trustees consisting of the chief directors of the combining firms took over the stock of all the concerns, giving in return trust certificates. The earnings of all the combined companies were divided on the basis of the trust certificates. It was possible now for one plant to shut down entirely for the purpose of pushing prices up by limiting output, and yet receive its share of the profits of the trust as a whole. Complete unity of action was secured through the board of trustees. This form of combination was rapidly adopted throughout the country.[1]

Monopoly prices. To a small degree the public had felt the evils of combinations even when these organizations were of the loose type, but it was not until the trust form became prevalent that the startled public grasped the significance of this new turn in the affairs of big business. When the price of oil rose 46 per cent and tobacco 43 per cent, the consumers became alarmed and irritated. The injustice was all the more keenly felt because it was known that by cooperation the cost of production had been reduced. They turned to economists for an explanation and were not comforted by the result of their inquiries. For prices were now based not on the cost of production but upon the utility principle, that is, all that the consumer would pay. This was possible, of course, only when the trust had grown to such an extent as to drive out most of its competitors and had become in reality a monopoly. Sometimes it happens with an article for which the demand is elastic that a lowering of price will bring in a greater total profit from the greatly increased sales than a higher price would produce with the resulting lessened demand. In such cases the trusts lowered prices below their old competitive level, but nowhere did they approach a cost-of-production basis.

Excessive profits. Consumers knew this and began to wonder what became of the great difference between the cost and the selling price. The account books of the trusts held the answer. In a ten-year period the United States Steel Trust paid out $650,000,000 in dividends, largely on watered stock, the profit on tobacco per pound rose from twenty-eight cents in 1899 to ninety-eight cents in 1907. When companies wanted to con-

[1] Marshall, Wright, and Field's "Materials for the Study of Elementary Economics," Nos 86-91.

ceal their immense and ill-gotten profits they issued stock dividends to their stockholders, thus increasing the "water." Some trusts would not produce their books when they were brought up in court, or if they did these were in such shape that no one could make out the status of the company. Even when the courts were able to find gross evils there were often no laws by which to punish the offenders, since trusts were not incorporated by law.

Prosecution of the trusts. In order to remedy these conditions many states enacted antitrust laws. These limited or forbade overcapitalization (an evil indulged in to a greater extent by trusts than by the ordinary corporation). They also taxed excessive profits, prohibited unfair methods of driving out weak competitors, and in general tried to check the evils of the trust. Some of them actually forbade the trust as a form of combination. These laws differed in every state. They often conflicted with one another, and some of them were so drastic that they were declared unconstitutional. Only Federal legislation could meet the situation.

In 1890 the United States Congress, therefore, passed the famous Sherman Anti-Trust Act, which prohibits "every contract, combination in the form of trust or otherwise, or conspiracy, in restraint of" interstate commerce.[1]

Now the wording of this statute is so all-inclusive that by applying it literally not only would every trust and pool be illegal but so also would every corporation in restraint of trade. But what did restraining trade mean, and who was to be the one to say what was and what was not restraint, since the statute itself was not explicit? In our country interpretation of

[1] Notice that the only way in which Congress could legislate against trusts was in their relationship to interstate commerce, because the Constitution does not give Congress the power to regulate ordinary industry. Since the products of every trust or even big corporation are sold in other states than the one in which they are manufactured, this law made practically every trust illegal. For this statute see Marshall, Wright, and Field's "Materials for the Study of Elementary Economics," No. 93, and Hamilton's "Current Economic Problems," No. 24.

law is left to the courts, and in the case of a Federal law the ultimate decision rests with the Supreme Court.[1] That body declared that the only way in which the statute could operate without destroying all business was for the courts to read the word "unreasonable" before "restraint of trade," and that in each case the Supreme Court was to decide whether any specific combination brought up before it was practicing unreasonable and hence illegal restraint of trade.

For about ten years nothing was done to enforce the Sherman Law. Then under Theodore Roosevelt the United States Department of Justice began a policy of trust prosecution for which Roosevelt earned the titles of the "Trust Buster" and "Theodore the Meddler." In reality little actual "trust-busting" was accomplished, with the exception of the Northern Securities Company (a combination of the Northern Pacific and Great Northern Railroad systems). In Taft's administration the prosecutions continued with somewhat better results. In 1911 the Standard Oil and American Tobacco Companies were dissolved.[2] But the trust problem continued unsolved. Many powerful trusts remained, although most of them, fearing the fate of the Standard Oil, hastened to reorganize their combinations so as to evade, if possible, the penalties of the Sherman Anti-Trust Act.

Trusts in reality but not in form. The Standard Oil Company had dissolved into thirty-three supposedly separate companies. The public, therefore, settled back, well satisfied. But the price of oil did not go down. The Standard Oil Company of Indiana did not compete with the Standard Oil Company of Nebraska, nor the Crescent Pipe Line with the Eureka Pipe Line. Investigation proved that a new form of combination had

---

[1] See pages 120-122 and 516-518

[2] For the order dissolving the Standard Oil Company into thirty-three separate companies see Hamilton's "Current Economic Problems," No 216 Good articles on the formation and conditions of these trusts before dissolution are to be found in Marshall, Wright, and Field's "Materials for the Study of Elementary Economics," Nos 86, 87.

followed the trust. The Standard Oil Company of New Jersey had issued immense quantities of new stock with no backing whatsoever and had exchanged this stock for the stock of the other Standard Oil companies. In other words, the New Jersey Standard Oil Company had now become a *holding company*.[1] By holding the majority of stock in each of the other supposedly separate companies the Standard Oil Company of New Jersey could dominate business and eliminate competition. In point of fact a form of combination more consolidated than the trust was now the foe to public interest, and the name "trust" continued to be used for all combinations in restraint of trade.[2]

Another device of combination, the interlocking directorate, was invented to evade the Sherman Anti-Trust Law. A number of corporations supposedly independent have on their boards of directors the same group of men. For example, Company One has A, C, E, F, G, X; Company Two has B, C, G, H, L, Y; Company Three has E, F, J, L, K, Z; Company Four has G, F, L, A, C, Q; and so on. There is no definite form of combination, no board of trustees, no contract in restraint of trade. And yet when some ten or twelve men form the overwhelming majority on each of the boards of directors of numerous companies, it is obvious that these companies will not compete with one another and will act in unison on all important matters.

Legislation against all combinations. The Sherman Act had failed to solve the problem of monopoly combination. Through ineffective enforcement the old trust form still remained, and through clever invention new forms of combination avoided punishment. Knowing little of the laws of economics the average consumer ignored such causes for high prices as the depreciation of gold and therefore blamed the trusts (as he now called all monopolistic combinations) for the increased cost of living.

[1] For diagrams see Marshall, Wright, and Field's "Materials for the Study of Elementary Economics," No. 239.
[2] An evaluation of the Sherman Act is given in Hamilton's "Current Economic Problems," No. 218.

In answer to popular demand, therefore, the Democrats pledged themselves in their party platform of 1912 to enact such legislation that private monopoly could henceforth no longer exist in the United States. The Republican administration was condemned for not invoking the criminal penalties of the Sherman Act against the officers of the Standard Oil and Tobacco Trusts, and regret was expressed that the Act had received such judicial construction that it was no longer efficacious. Upon winning the election the Democrats set about fulfilling their campaign pledges in the form of two important laws: the Clayton Anti-Trust Act and the Federal Trade Commission Act.[1]

The first of these was a supplementary antitrust act. It forbade companies to discriminate between purchasers when the object was to lessen competition, a practice which had been a common device of huge corporations. Holding companies, with the exception of railroads, were prohibited, and interlocking directorates were limited by the provision that after a period of two years no person could be director of more than one concern (except railroads and banks) whose capital equaled one million dollars.[2]

The enforcement of the Clayton Act was placed in the hands of a Federal commission created by the second act. This commission was given wide powers of investigation and the right to issue an order forbidding any practice by a corporation. The company could then take the case to court, or if the directors simply ignored the order the commission could force the case to court. The criminal penalties of the Sherman Act, which juries had been so loath to apply, were now supplanted by civil procedure.[3]

[1] For these two acts see Hamilton's "Current Economic Problems," Nos 219, 220, and Marshall, Wright, and Field's "Materials for the Study of Elementary Economics," No 93, Parts II–III

[2] A special clause limited directorships in United States banks, and another exempted labor organizations from combination prohibitions

[3] Review the difference between criminal and civil cases in any good civics text.

The Federal Trade Act also stated that unfair methods of competition in commerce "were unlawful and should be attacked by the Trade Commission."[1] Once more we see legislation faulty in its vagueness, for no attempt was made to define what methods were unfair. The Clayton Act had forbidden "local price-cutting" and also "tying agreements," that is, the sale of goods upon certain terms in return for a promise from the purchaser that he will not use any of the goods put out by the seller's competitors.[2] This was well enough, but there are other doubtful methods of competition; such as, for example, deceiving the public by similarity in names, slandering one's rivals, persuading their employees to betray trade secrets, and making it impossible for them to secure raw materials and banking credits. Threatened lawsuits also have often killed competition. Therefore the law is not all that could be desired, but it is a big step in the right direction. Abolition of "bad trusts" now depends very largely upon the commission.

Present status. Too short a time has passed since the passage of these acts to say with any degree of accuracy how much yet is left unsolved in the "trust" problem. The war interfered with its operation, since in that case of dire necessity for production no one stopped to investigate the organization of an industry so long as it kept its production up to maximum. Since the war the trade commission has dealt with two important cases. In one instance it succeeded in getting the five great packing-firms voluntarily to give up such side lines as groceries and creameries.[3] In the other it brought the United States Steel Corporation before the Federal courts. The Supreme Court's decision was that since the corporation was not using unfair methods of competition, it was a "good

---

[1] For practices of unfair competition see Marshall, Wright, and Field's "Materials for the Study of Elementary Economics," Nos. 209, 210.

[2] See Hamilton's "Current Economic Problems," No. 219. For other questionable competitive practices upon which the Federal Trade Commission has taken a stand, see *New Republic*, Vol. XXVII, pp. 140–142.

[3] See *Literary Digest* for January 3, 1920, Vol. LXIV, pp. 11–13.

trust" and not subject to dissolution [1] In view of the fact that this corporation controls some 80 to 85 per cent of the steel industry in the United States, it is evident that the courts of our land are not going to take a stand against combinations, even if they are monopolies. There are, in the words of Theodore Roosevelt, "good trusts" and "bad trusts," and only the latter are to be exterminated.

Recently many combinations have grown tired of being continually subject to legal prosecutions and have adopted a new form, or rather readopted an old form. They have dissolved as combinations and reëstablished themselves as mammoth single corporations. When one of the parts of an old combination buys out the other parts, the enlarged corporation is known as a merger. When a new corporation under a new name buys out the old units of the combination, it is called an amalgamation. Economic evolution has brought business organization back to the corporation, its first form under the factory system. The latest phase, then, of the trust problem is what shall be done not only with the combinations which remain but with the mammoth corporation.

The Solution of the Problem

The abolition of monopoly. There are two entirely opposite attitudes as to what should be done with monopolistic business. The one is that it should be abolished, and the other is that it should be tolerated but kept under closest supervision. Advocates of the first policy point out that the evils are many and insurmountable. prices are raised, class divisions sharpened, civic and social responsibilities are passed from directors to shareholders and back again with no good results, and political corruption is sure to be an accompaniment.

Advocates of trust dissolution differ widely when they come to suggest what form of business organization should supplant the trust. Some would have coöperative undertakings in which

[1] See *Literary Digest* for March 13, 1920, Vol LXIV, pp 17-18

the laborers unite to furnish both the capital and the entrepreneurial functions of organization and risk-taking. There are few examples of coöperation in production in America, because of the shortage of capital among laborers. The most successful attempts have been made in the line of farmers' creameries. The chief difficulty outside of the capital shortage is to keep personal prejudices and passions from wrecking the coöperation.

Government ownership. Other trust opponents would have the government take over the ownership and management of industry. In the United States the Federal government now manages the postal system, the Alaskan railway, and several other enterprises. As a war measure the United States government took over the operation of railroads, telegraphs, and telephones, but these have since all been returned to their owners. This experiment did not serve to popularize government ownership. The effect was rather to stifle almost all sentiment for government ownership except among the rail employees and a remnant of socialists. Ownership by local units of government has proved much more popular. Many cities own and operate one or more of their public utilities, such as waterworks, plants for gas and electricity, and systems of transportation. Such services as these have often been termed natural monopolies. They call for a great expenditure of money in establishing the plants, and duplication is a needless waste of money. No one desires the streets torn up for the laying of additional tracks, sewers, or gas pipes. It is highly inconvenient to have several street-car or telephone companies. Either these utilities must be let out to some one firm by means of a franchise wherein the city retains certain rights of control to protect the public, or else the city must itself become the entrepreneur.

Until a large majority of our citizens come to possess a higher degree of intelligence and a keener sense of public morality, wise leaders do not urge the general adoption of public ownership for even these natural monopolies. The only safe course for the present is that each case should be dealt with separately on the basis of its peculiar circumstances. Government ownership eliminates the abuses growing from personal greed, but too often it also prevents the betterment of the service or the product. It would seem, therefore, that the socialist party is disregarding the results of past economic experiences when it advocates government ownership of grain elevators, stockyards, storage warehouses, mines, and banks in addition to all communication and transportation companies.

Other people who favor the abolition of private monopoly and big business combinations will have nothing good to say of either coöperative undertakings or government ownership. They insist that matters should be restored to the good old status of free competition among small business units. The objection to this is that no amount of legislation will ever make business men give up the advantages of combination, and, moreover, it is an open question whether the unavoidable disadvantages of combination, so far as the public is concerned, are not offset by the wastes of competition.

Close supervision of big business. For this reason many students of the problem advocate the retention of combinations and big corporations, for they hold that the public can be safeguarded by close supervision and the elimination of the chief dangers. If it is true that big business has come to stay,—and it looks that way,—would it not be better to accept it, to legalize it, but to purge it of its evils? Some of the remedies which have been proposed are as follows:

1. Laws forcing all units doing a large business to open their books for public inspection, as the railroads must now do. This would reveal excessive profits and unwarranted prices.

2. Reform of the tariff to allow foreign competition and the consequent lowering of prices.

3. Federal incorporation for all firms doing interstate business, with strict provisions as to overcapitalization. This would make uniform the requirements for big business.

4. Detailed Federal laws prohibiting unfair methods of competition, and rigid enforcement by a powerful nonpolitical commission.

Summary. The organization of industry, taxed to its uttermost by the demands of the factory system and the ever-widening market, has adopted numerous forms in its struggle to secure efficiency in its output and large profits. The weak forms have been supplanted by the stronger, with an ever-increasing tendency toward growth in the size of the business unit. No amount of legislation has been able to stop this growth, for restrictive laws have served only to tax the brains of the corporation lawyers into devising new forms. Today it is quite generally believed that big business has come to stay. It remains for society to work out schemes by which all the advantages of this kind of coöperation may be kept, while all its evil effects are cast away.

SUPPLEMENTARY READINGS

BULLOCK, C. J. Elements of Economics (revised), chaps. iv, ix.
CARVER, T. N. Elementary Economics, chap. xii.
CARVER, T. N. Principles of Political Economy, chap. xiv.
HAMILTON, W. H. Current Economic Problems, Documents 90–95, 203–208, 213–221.
HANEY, L. H. Business Organization and Combination, pp. 81–144, 193–255, 365–414.
MARSHALL, L. C., WRIGHT, C. W., and FIELD, J. A. Materials for the Study of Elementary Economics, Nos. 71–72, 84, 90–93.
Quarterly Journal of Economics, Vol. XXXIV, pp. 473–519.

SEARCH QUESTIONS AND PROBLEMS

1. List examples in your community of single-entrepreneur businesses, of partnerships, and of corporations.

2. Since bondholding is safer, why should any man wish to become a stockholder?

3. State which of the following articles you would expect to find produced on a large scale, and why: paintings, ready-made clothes, hand-tailored suits, farm machinery, cut glass, pins, trimmed hats, orchids.

4. Find out what laws there are in your state regulating corporations. Do you have a commission to investigate new companies before stock can be sold to the public?

5. If there is in your community any large-scale-production establishment, visit it as a class, taking notes on the following: the division of labor, the use of by-products, labor-saving machinery, kinds of power; whether wages are by the day or piece; sanitary conditions, safety appliances, lunch rooms, rest rooms, medical aid, and recreational facilities for employees.

6. It is often said that "tariff is the most intrenched of trusts." To what extent do you think this is a true statement?

7. Why is it that if a corporation or trust has not a monopoly the utility principle of price-setting cannot be used?

8. Is there any limit to prices a trust can charge? See Hamilton's "Current Economic Problems," No. 208.

9. Explain each of the facsimiles of investment securities given in Marshall, Wright, and Field's "Materials for the Study of Elementary Economics," No. 70.

10. If any of the following books are on your English reading lists make reports of what their value is for this chapter. Edward Bellamy's "Looking Backward"; Thomas Lawson's "Frenzied Finance"; Winston Churchill's "Coniston"; Upton Sinclair's "The Jungle"; Frank Norris's "The Octopus" and "The Pit", William Dean Howells's "The Rise of Silas Lapham."

11. If there are any cooperative organizations or enterprises in your community, find out what you can about their operation and success. If there have been failures, analyze them by the tests given in Marshall, Wright, and Field's "Materials for the Study of Elementary Economics," No. 264.

12. How is each of the public utilities in your city managed?

13. Construct a series of diagrams that will illustrate the various forms of organization and combination.

CHAPTER IX

THE TOOLS OF BUSINESS

The degree of specialization which characterizes modern industry could never have been reached under a system of barter; it is too minute, too complicated, too extensive both in space and time; the increasing use of money was both sign and cause of the transition from the primitive to the modern economy.—HENRY CLAY (an English economist)

MONEY

We have seen how money originated and the forms which it took in the ancient and medieval worlds. In our own day exchange is so universal that we could not carry on our civilization without it. Money serves us two useful purposes, just as it always has: it is a medium of exchange and a measure of value. The exchange may be immediate, as when we sell a dozen eggs at the general store and turn around to buy a yard of muslin; or it may be long delayed, as when the farmer sells his wheat crop and buys, perhaps five years later, a new house.

Forms of money. This delayed exchange of the wheat for the house brings us to the question of the forms of money. Suppose the general storekeeper pays thirty-six cents for the eggs, which you at once repay to him across the dry-goods end of his counter. He has probably given you a silver quarter, a dime, and a copper cent. This is money. A Greek of the days of Pericles or a native of farthest India would instantly recognize it for money and hold it of value, although he could not read the inscription or know what government issued it. Such money, made of metal and coined into little tablets and stamped, is called "hard money," or "specie," and is used in all normal times and places by civilized people. But the farmer who sold his wheat for a house probably never handled a piece of gold or silver in the whole course of the transaction. If you had asked him how much money he received for his wheat or how much he paid for the house, he would have told you, and yet he neither received nor paid a cent of metal money for either. The two transactions illustrate the two great methods of exchange by which modern business is done. They are money and credit. The bank, the mint, and the clearing house are institutions which deal in these two great exchange commodities

Gresham's law. Mankind has made many experiments in its dealings with money and is not yet in possession of an absolutely ideal system in any country. Some definite things have been established, however, in the course of these experiments. Perhaps the surest conclusion of all is that money must have real value, either in itself or in what it represents. At one time a theory was held that a government could make money by simply saying that something, anything, *was* money. This "fiat" money was made of paper, since paper was cheap and could be cheaply printed. The effect of the introduction of such money into general currency has always been the same. debtors paid in paper money the debts which they had contracted when real, "hard" money was the accepted medium of exchange. If they had any hard money they hid it, in order to have it for a greater need, for they had more confidence in its value than in that of paper money. As more and more fiat money was issued, everyone did the same thing, and hard money disappeared from use. Part of it actually left the country, for in international trade nothing but gold is good, since gold can be melted down and recoined into the money of any land. As hard money became scarcer its value greatly increased, for there are always a few things for which hard money alone is usable, and always a time ahead when hard money will again come into use. Paper money then *depreciated*; that is, it was worth less and less in terms of hard money When the United States issued irredeemable greenbacks during the Civil War their value fell until in some places two paper dollars could be exchanged for one silver one, and at one time the value was as low as thirty-nine cents. When the government provided for their redemption, the greenbacks promptly *appreciated*; they went up to par value because the government had made them worth and exchangeable for silver and gold. The invariable action of fiat money or any kind of poor money is expressed in Gresham's law: *Bad money drives good money out of circulation.*

Characteristics of good money. The second requisite for good money is that it shall be convenient in form. Gold and silver are good metals for money, because a considerable value can be carried in small space and weight; but diamonds, which are valuable enough to make good money, are not easily changed in form and are therefore not good material for money. The metals can be melted and pressed into any form desired, and they can be measured accurately and so divided into convenient amounts for the measurement of any value down to a conveniently small approach to nothing. The convenience of metal money as a measure of value depends upon this divisibility; it can be made to fit any transaction from the purchase of a stick of gum to the payment of a national debt.

A third characteristic of good money is that it be standard in form. During the Middle Ages, when governments were greedy for gain or powerless to control money, it was subject to so many abuses that no one knew how much a given coin was worth, and merchants and money-changers had scales in which they weighed all coins, and methods by which they ascertained the amount of precious metal in each. Today no one thinks of weighing a coin or of testing it for validity beyond the most cursory examination for nationality or for holes. This is because our government has the most severe penalties for tampering with or mutilating coins. People everywhere consider the making of money one of the necessary and legitimate functions of government. A government can insure uniformity in style, weight, and value of the coins it issues; it can protect the people from counterfeit production; and it can control the forms of money in agreement with popular demand as perhaps no private corporation could.

United States specie. The metal coins used in the United States conform very well to these standards of efficiency. They are

1. Gold dollars,[1] eagles (ten-dollar pieces), and half, quarter, and double eagles.

2. Silver dollars, which pass at the value of a gold dollar. They contain 412.5 grains of silver, $\frac{900}{1000}$ fine. The value of the actual silver contained in a dollar varies, of course, with the market price of silver. For many years it was less than the face value, so that part of the worth of a silver dollar was fiat value—the word of the government that the silver dollar was exchangeable for a gold dollar, irrespective of the value of the metals in the coins. In 1902, 1909, and 1915, for instance, the silver in a dollar was worth only forty cents, in 1919 the value of the silver in a dollar passed par.

3. Silver subsidiary, or "token," coins, which are fractions of the dollar in convenient denominations of fifty-cent, twenty-five-cent, and ten-cent pieces. These, like the silver dollar, have a conventional value guaranteed by the government and are not dependent on the value of the silver they contain.

4. Minor coins: the nickel, or five-cent piece, weighing 77.16 grains and made of 75 per cent copper and 25 per cent nickel; and the one-cent piece, weighing 48 grains and made up of 95 per cent copper and 5 per cent tin and zinc.

The superintendent of the mint buys silver, copper, nickel, and zinc at the market price or from the lowest bidder, and the coins are then made up in the government mints at Philadelphia, Denver, and San Francisco. As the token coins pass at face value and are rarely presented for redemption in gold, the government makes a very goodly profit from this transaction. It is therefore able to render various services to the people in matters pertaining to money; as, for instance, its service in recoining worn specie and in laundering soiled notes.

---

[1] Not minted for many years, as the coin is too small for practical use. The other gold coins contain 25.8 grains to the dollar (23.22 grains of pure gold with a little alloy).

Paper money. We have seen that fiat money is money which states that it has a value which it very patently does not have, and that the penalty of this falsehood, which is no less a lie because a government vouches for it, is depreciation and the driving out of good money. There are, however, many forms of paper money which are as good as hard money and form a regular part of our currency. At the present time the United States issues or authorizes the following forms of paper money:

1. Silver certificates. These are issued to anyone who deposits silver, either in bullion or coins, with the Treasurer of the United States. When presented again silver coin will be paid for them.

2. Gold certificates, issued in the same way as silver certificates.

3. Treasury notes, issued under the Sherman Act, authorizing the purchase of silver bullion in 1890. The amount of these is constantly decreasing because they are being redeemed in gold or silver dollars.

4. United States notes. The government makes a promise to pay just as a private individual might, and these promissory notes pass as money. When these notes were issued during the Civil War there was no gold or silver deposit to insure the payment which was promised, and they depreciated with Union failures in the field or appreciated with Union success.[1] They were pure "fiat" money. They have been as good as gold since the operation of the Specie Resumption Act of 1875. These are the "greenbacks" of popular parlance.

5. National bank notes. Formerly, with loose and inefficient government control, any bank could issue notes, the value of which depended upon the reputation of the bank. In 1863 the national government found that it could not readily sell its bonds issued to finance the Civil War, and so banks were induced to buy them by the expedient of requiring them to deposit government bonds as security for their notes. Banks issuing notes under this system were called national banks, as they were

[1] See the chart on page 320 of Thompson's "Elementary Economics."

chartered by the Federal government and their notes secured by deposits in the national treasury. State bank notes could not be driven directly out of currency by the Federal government, but they could be taxed out of use. This expedient was adopted, and the 10 per cent tax operated to stop all note-issuing by state banks. At the present time there are practically no state bank notes, and the number of national bank notes is decreasing as the Federal Reserve and Federal Reserve Bank notes increase in circulation.

6-7. The notes issued under the Federal Reserve Act of December 23, 1913, will be described later.

Legal tender. Some money is declared by law to be "legal tender," or legal payment when offered as payment for any debt. Other money has not this legal standing, but practically all money now current in the United States is so sound that it passes freely at par. Thus gold and silver certificates and Federal Reserve notes are not legal tender, but they pass at face value in payment of debts. The legal-tender laws of the United States make the subsidiary coins payable only for small debts—the cents and nickels up to twenty-five cents, the silver coins up to ten dollars. This is merely to secure convenience and not because the small coins have any less value.

The decimal system. Following the independence of the United States, it was necessary for the new government to select a system of money. The most natural course of action perhaps would have been simply to copy the English system, to which the colonists were used. They were, however, about as familiar with Spanish money as with English, in fact, one of the chief grievances of colonial business men was the scarcity of English money in the colonies. The Spanish "piece of eight," beloved of pirates, was the most common coin in many parts of the colonies, and this naturally became the standard for measurement of values, or the *monetary unit*, in the new nation. This coin, which in some form or other has come down to us from very ancient times, was therefore adopted, with a German name (*thaler*) and a Spanish value and a French fractional division. Thomas Jefferson was the farsighted statesman who urged the decimal division into ten dimes and a hundred cents.

In 1792 Alexander Hamilton fixed the content of the gold dollar at 24.75 grains and that of the silver dollar at 371.25 grains. This meant that gold and silver were coined at a ratio of fifteen to one, or that one silver dollar had fifteen times the amount of metal in a gold dollar; or, again, that gold was fifteen times as valuable as silver. The ratio changed to 15.9 to 1 in 1834, but after a time it appeared that this ratio did not actually represent the difference in market value between gold and silver, for silver bullion was worth more than silver coins. Naturally everyone who had silver coins had them melted into bullion, and so silver coins disappeared from the currency.

The Worth of Money

The struggle for bimetallism. In 1873 Congress decided to discontinue the coinage of the silver dollar, because for several years little bullion had been brought to the mints owing to the scarcity of the metal. But shortly after, new silver mines were opened, and silver was produced in large quantities in the West. The silver-miners protested against the demonetization of silver, for they needed every possible market for their product, and the government ratio made silver worth more than its market value. Moreover, there were not enough silver dollars for the business of the country. So Congress bought silver and coined it.[1] This did not put an unlimited amount of silver into circulation, but only a fixed, although generous, amount each year. The country had what is called a "gold standard" for its money, for gold was coined free and all values were measured in gold-money terms. This gold standard is the standard of the leading nations of the world; and it is sensible, because it is simple, easily controlled and understood, and almost uni-

[1] The Bland-Allison Act of 1878, in force to 1890. For exact provisions see any good United States history.

versal. But the silver men of the Far West wanted a wider market for their silver than the limited government purchases gave them, they clamored for "free and unlimited coinage of silver in the ratio of sixteen to one." They were supported by the Western farmers, who needed more money and saw in silver a solution to their problem. Yielding to popular demand, Congress passed the Sherman Silver Purchase Act of 1890, directing the Treasurer to purchase four and a half million ounces of silver per month. The result was the accumulation of a "silver hoard" and the depletion of the gold reserve. This bill had to be repealed hastily in 1893; whereupon the champions of silver roused themselves to renewed efforts. Free silver became the issue of the national election of 1896. But the silver men were defeated, and the nation remained a gold-standard nation. This basis for our coinage was secured by law, March 4, 1900.

If the silver men had won in 1896, and laws had been made allowing the free coinage of silver on the same terms as those for gold coinage, the nation would be said to have a bimetallic standard, since the two metals would be considered equally standard. As it is, the United States is monometallic in its money system; it measures all values in gold and makes all other metals subsidiary. This single, or monometallic, standard is the world's standard for money.

The relation of the value of money to prices. Money, like every other commodity, has its ups and downs in value. These rises and falls come from supply and demand, just as in every other kind of goods. If there be a great deal of gold in the world, gold bullion will naturally fall in value, if the amount of gold be reduced, it will rise in value This rule is called the quantity theory of money. The world demand for gold, like the world supply, is singularly steady, but the demand in any one country varies a great deal. At long intervals a great discovery of quantities of gold really affects the supply by launching into currency so much gold that the additional supply is really felt, this happened when gold was discovered in California, and again when the South African fields were first worked.

Now gold and, of course, the other money metals as well are used for many things. All the gold used in the arts subtracts that much from the available amount which can be coined. Any great increase in the use of gold in jewelry or in chemistry or in medicine or in dentistry reduces the amount of money. In spite of these many uses, the world supply for money is fairly regular. But when the amount of gold in any country becomes reduced, and the supply of things for which it is exchanged remains about stationary, the amount of gold for which any given article is exchanged will be smaller, since demand remains the same and the supply is less. Conversely, if the supply of gold becomes much larger, and the supply of goods for exchange remains the same, those goods will exchange for a larger amount of gold than before. As the "amount of gold" is the price, this means that *prices and the value of money vary inversely.*

A very good illustration of this law has recently come into our own national experience. During the war the production of the war-ridden countries was reduced at the same time that their consumption was vastly increased. They needed food, leather, metals, horses, ammunition, and clothing, which the United States could supply. The vast amounts of gold which flowed into our country from abroad, with no returning flow for the imports which in peace times come to us from the Old World, piled up an immense gold surplus. This gold surplus made prices very high here. It was not by any means the only cause of high prices, but it was an important one.

This late rise in prices has been general; that is, the required amount of the medium of exchange became greater for practically everything. Things have not changed in their value when compared with each other: a silver spoon is still worth more than a tin one, and a linen tablecloth is still worth more than a cotton one, but they all cost more money than they did before. The *price level* has risen because the purchasing power of money has declined.

Index numbers. All people know when prices have advanced or declined by the prices charged for the things they buy.

THE TOOLS OF BUSINESS

But there is a more scientific way of judging price fluctuations, which is more practicable for the student of economics than the unauthoritative but vivid testimony of one's own experience. We measure the changing values of all other commodities in money, since money is the universal measuring tool for value; but we cannot measure money by itself, nor can we measure it by any one of the commodities which it measures, for it might happen that that commodity would vary at one time directly with money but at another time inversely with money. But by taking a fairly large number of staple goods, which are always on the market and always subject to fluctuation, and averaging them, we can arrive at a very fair measure of the purchasing power or value of money. Several authorities on finance give this information, expressed in what is called index numbers.

Index numbers are made by taking a standard amount of the several staple goods decided upon and averaging their prices for a whole year; then these prices are added, and that sum makes a standard for comparison. The sum of the prices of the same goods in the same quantities in any other year can be expressed as a percentage of this standard, and this is the index number for that year. For instance, in our country the year 1913 is taken as the standard year: its index number is therefore one hundred. Different authorities reckon their index numbers in somewhat different ways and take somewhat different staples for their measuring averages, so that index numbers vary more or less. For instance, here are estimates of the price level for twenty years:

Year	United States Bureau of Labor	The *Annalist*	Bradstreet's
1900	80	71	86
1910	99	98	98
1913	100	100	100
1914	100	104	97
1918	196	205	203
1919	212	211	203

The social service of money. The gold available for exchange depends on two things: the actual amount in existence at the time and the amount and rate of circulation. These two factors are complementary; that is to say, a small amount of gold may do an immense amount of business if it passes quickly from hand to hand; while a large amount will accomplish very little business if it remains stationary, piled up in someone's safe, for weeks at a time. Therefore the man who saves his money in a secret hiding-place is hurting public business. Actual money should never be kept in safes or secret hiding-places; it should be deposited in banks, where it is available for use at any time and under well-controlled and safe conditions.

It goes without saying that there should be enough money in a modern country to avoid a return to general barter, which is a certain sign of serious shortage. All small-scale buying and selling, and most wage-paying, should be done in coin or paper as a matter of general convenience. But the volume of business changes a great deal from time to time, and so the regulation of the amount of money becomes a big problem, in which everyone has an interest whether he is interested or not. Of this regulation we shall speak later.

Credit

We have now studied the kinds and value of money. If, however, business had to be transacted entirely with real money, it would be greatly curtailed, for the volume of business is estimated at from seven to nine times the amount of money in circulation. The volume of business not transacted on a money basis is done "on credit," and we shall now take up the study of this second method of providing a medium of exchange.

Credit is the reputation of having the ability and intention to pay, which makes a promise equivalent to the deed in the business world. It rests on faith in the creditor and honesty in the debtor; and since everyone is both creditor and debtor in modern business, credit may be said to be the joint agreement of society to carry on business, whether local or world-wide, upon the basis of the word of honor.

The simplest form of credit in common use is called book credit. It is simply the trust which a dealer has in his customer when he gives him the goods he wants and sends in his bill at the end of the month or the year. Farmers, for instance, are paid for their crops after harvest, but they need to eat and to wear clothing all the year round. Therefore the storekeeper gives them groceries and cloth whenever they need it, if their credit is good, and receives his pay when the farmer receives his. Payment once a month is a common way of doing business which is based on credit. It is so common that most wholesale merchants allow for delay in receiving their pay by adding a little to the price of each article and then taking it off again in the form of a "discount for cash" for those buyers who can and do pay cash.

Notes. Another form of credit is represented by the promissory note. Vast amounts of goods change hands yearly for which the buyers cannot pay at the time, they give instead a note for the amount, which they must pay, usually with interest, on or before the date of its maturity. Banks or other corporations and the government, as we have seen, may issue notes, including a special form of note which is called a bond. A bond is a note which is, so to speak, issued before the debt is contracted; that is, the bond-issuer advertises that he wishes to borrow so much money, usually in denominations of one hundred dollars, five hundred dollars, or one thousand dollars. People who have money to invest buy the bonds, which pay interest like any other note to the time of their maturity, when the principal falls due. This form of note, used largely by nations to finance their enterprises, contributes to the stability of governments, since everyone who owns bonds will want the government to remain solvent and responsible at least until his bond loan is paid back.

Checks and orders. A third form of credit in general use is the *order to pay*. A person who has money on deposit in any institution may order that institution to pay money to his creditors instead of paying it himself. The most common form of the order to pay is the check. A depositor in a bank orders his bank to pay any sum up to the amount of his deposit. By keeping an account on the stub of his check book the depositor keeps track of the amount of money he has in the bank and pays his bills without the risk and trouble of carrying money around with him.

Drafts and bills of exchange. The personal check is used mainly for payments to people in the same town with the depositor. If a check is cashed in a distant town with which the banks do not have daily exchange of checks, a small fee, called the exchange fee (or simply "exchange," for short), is charged. In order to have this fee paid in advance and to save the trouble of looking up the individual depositor in a town in which he is not known, money is usually sent from place to place by means of a draft. A draft is an order to pay given by one bank to a "corresponding" bank in another city, bought by the person remitting (sending) the money and sent to the payee or receiver. The bank which issues the draft balances the amount of all drafts sent to, with the amount of all drafts received from, its correspondent bank and pays or receives the difference at regular intervals. The three cities of New York, Chicago, and San Francisco serve as centers for draft exchange in the United States; a draft on Chicago banks is cashable anywhere in the Middle West, and drafts on the other two financial centers in like manner in their own districts, while a New York draft is cashable almost anywhere.

A bill or letter of exchange is a draft for foreign use. It does not differ essentially from the draft; in fact, the word "draft" is simply an American term for a domestic bill of exchange. The "corresponding" banks pay the drafts or bills of exchange drawn upon them and so keep a stream of credit flowing from country to country. A bill of exchange may be drawn upon a merchant firm or any established firm, as well as upon a bank, and is often in such a case drawn for a date some time ahead.

The Use of Credit

These forms of credit money save the handling of actual cash and so leave more cash free for the smaller transactions of everyday life and for the use of people who do not have enough money to warrant their having a bank account. Therefore they add materially to the available money supply. Their usefulness depends upon their quality of *convertibility*, which means that they are changeable at will into real gold (or some metal or paper substitute for gold which is in turn as good as gold and convertible into it) If a man checks out his entire deposit, of course a future check is no longer convertible and will be returned by the bank as a worthless check.

Rating authorities. We may pause here to describe the means by which everyone in American towns and cities is listed as to his credit. Often the local bank takes the responsibility of rating the citizens of a town, in larger places the Employers' Association or a Municipal Credit Association makes up the lists. The names of the citizens are sent in from the retail shops with which they have accounts, and people are listed as in class A, B, C, or D A class-A man pays his bills promptly, within the first ten days of each month, and is not only absolutely reliable in his business dealings but also businesslike in his methods. Class-B people are reliable enough, but are careless about allowing bills to run into the middle or last of the month or even until the beginning of the next month. Class-C people pay eventually, but buy carelessly and do not keep careful accounts, and allow bills to run so long that they inconvenience sellers and raise prices. Class-D people are absolutely unreliable, they probably could not negotiate a loan at any bank, and retail dealers will be very careful about allowing them to open new accounts. What the local rating bureau does for the citizens of a town or city, Dun's and Bradstreet's do for the business firms of the nation.

Discount. Now banks have found by long experience that not nearly all their deposits are called—that is, checked out—at any one time. They therefore lend out their surplus cash and so earn through interest the money which enables them to do various services for their patrons. This money is lent on regular notes which business men make, secured either by the deposit of collateral[1] or by indorsers who pledge the payment of the debt. Bankers do not wait until these notes fall due for their interest, but secure it at the beginning by the method of discount, which is the prepayment of interest. Suppose that a retail merchant has a bill falling due October first, for which he has no ready cash. But he does have a promissory note from a responsible man, which falls due on November first. He takes this note to the bank, which pays him the cash for it minus the interest which would accrue during the month yet to pass before it falls due, and minus also a small fee for the accommodation. The sum which the bank thus subtracts from the face value of the note is called the discount. When the note falls due the original maker must, of course, pay the bank which now owns his note its full face value plus interest. This function of banks, by which they aid production by furnishing money on notes ahead of the date of their maturity, is one of the most valuable of their many services. It stabilizes the business world by making resources available when they are needed.

Cancellation. Suppose a druggist to have bought a bill of lumber for a garage amounting to $544.38, while the lumber dealer has a bill at the drugstore for medicines and toilet articles which comes to $76.25. If the lumber dealer sent in his bill on January 1, and the druggist sent him a check for $468.13, both men would consider their accounts settled. If money had to be used in the payment of all bills, $620.63 would have changed hands in this case. If there were no instruments of credit, but the device of cancellation were understood, then

---

[1] "Collateral" is the term applied to anything of value which is deposited as a guaranty of payment. Stocks and bonds are a very common form of collateral; they are valued according to their market price at the time of the loan, but not at the full current quotation. Farm mortgages are another common form of collateral.

a saving of $152.50 in the amount of money actually used could have been made. But because the druggist had a bank account he gave the lumber dealer no actual money at all, but transferred instead $468.13 of his credit at the bank to the lumber dealer, who may or may not have turned his check into cash. The process of balancing debts and paying only the difference is called cancellation, and it is a device used in business of small and large scale.

Commercial paper. Closely connected with cancellation of a simple nature, such as has been described, is the use of instruments of credit as actual money. If the lumber dealer with the druggist's check in his pocket passes the automobile dealer's, he may be reminded that he has an unpaid bill there. He goes in, inquires at the desk, and finds that he owes the automobile dealer $522.50 for repairs and parts. He takes the check of the druggist from his pocket, indorses it, and hands it to the automobile man with a check of his own for $54.37. Let us say that the automobile man takes the druggist's check and the lumber dealer's check and starts out for the bank, but on his way he passes the grocer's, and remembers that he has not paid his bill for the month. The grocer's cashier tells him the bill is $73.28, and he pays it by indorsing the lumber dealer's check for $54.37 and adding $18.91 in cash. Going on toward the bank, he meets a man to whom he owes a hundred dollars, and tells him to come on with him to the bank, as he now has money to repay the loan made the week before. But his friend in need is in a hurry, and they step instead into a hotel lobby at hand. The automobile man has very little cash with him, but the man of ready money has plenty.

"Give me your check for $468.13," he says, "and I'll give you $368.13 in cash." This is quickly done, and the dealer in cars goes on to the bank.

In this series of transactions, debts to the amount of $1316.41 have been paid, but only $387.04 in actual money has changed hands. This is because checks made by reliable people in their own community pass as the full equivalent of money.

We have seen how the possession of credit economizes hard money and increases the business of the country by increasing purchasing power. It substitutes itself for money to such an extent that a comparatively small amount of money may serve to do a large volume of business. This supplementing power of credit has in modern times actually grown to be the chief means of trade; a conservative statement of actual conditions is that at least three fourths of modern business is done by means of credit, the other fourth being transacted with specie.

But credit serves another great purpose in its steadying effects. If men had to wait for hard money before they could proceed with their business, the world of production and exchange would run by fits and starts according to the amount of money available day by day. Through credit, business is kept steady and continuous, future consumption is pre-provided for, and men in temporary straits are tided over to more prosperous times. Consumption, as well as production and exchange, is steadied; but for credit, half the world would be starving in winter and feasting in summer, like our remote ancestors or like the American aborigines in times gone by.

A third service of credit remains to be noted; that is, its effect upon human character. The need and the use of credit have exalted truth and honesty as no other practical device of man has been able to do it. For all their elaborate codes the knights of old were guilty of dishonesty and bad faith in many ways, as legend and history show, without apparently greatly injuring their social, military, or political reputations; but the town man's insistence on business dependability, on the necessity of playing straight even when one played sharp, has brought into common acceptance a new level of business honor. Moreover, the standard of honesty is being constantly raised; things that fifty years ago, or even twenty-five, were considered creditable in business are now condemned, often by law but most effectively by public opinion. A favorable reaction upon personal honor in other fields does not always follow, but here also there has been a notable gain.

It is only fair to add that credit has been responsible also for some very discreditable things. Watered stock, extravagant speculation, and "frenzied finance" of many colors and forms may be laid at its doors, and this shows that while credit is a good friend to man it may become a bad enemy if not wisely supervised, limited, and controlled.

Banks and their Functions

Banks in the United States. The United States has had much experience with different kinds of banks. In its early days it had two national banks, the second of which was destroyed because of the Western prejudice against well-regulated institutions of finance connected with the government. That is to say, the Western bankers, who wanted to carry on business without due regard to safety, rebelled against the disadvantage to which they were put when they met well-secured Eastern banks in competition. They objected to the National Bank because they thought it dabbled in politics. Their own connection with politics was usually fairly close. They found a champion in Andrew Jackson, who used his power as president to end the National Bank. After that the country had only such regulations, often most inadequate, as were furnished by the states. These regulations were usually conservative in the East and very liberal in the West, where frontier conditions made banking a more hazardous undertaking.

In 1846, after the destruction of the National Bank, the government established the Independent Treasury system. It built a treasure house at Washington and branches in several cities, and in the vaults of these places, for the most part, it kept the moneys of the nation This method of caring for national funds has been followed to the present. It has the same disadvantage, nationally, as the wool-stocking habit has in individuals · it ties up money needed for business where it cannot circulate. On July 1, 1910, over $317,000,000 lay idle in the United States Treasury; on the same date in 1918 the amount was over $356,000,000. The power of the Federal Reserve banks to act as fiscal agents for the United States will in time reduce this idle treasure to a reserve insuring safety but not hindering free circulation.

During the Civil War the national banking system was established, as has been said, for the double purpose of creating a market for bonds and of making a stable, dependable banknote currency. This system was a distinctly different thing from the two national banks of 1791-1836. It was a system, not a bank, and the operating banks were neither owned nor managed by the government.

A national bank is incorporated by five or more persons who receive a charter from the Comptroller of the Currency. The required capital varies according to the size of the city, from $25,000 for cities of three thousand people or less to $200,000 for cities of fifty thousand and over. The banks buy United States bonds with part or all of this capital, and deposit the bonds with the national treasurer. The Comptroller of the Currency then issues them an equal amount of notes, engraved with their own names, which they can circulate as money. Anyone who holds one of these bank notes may present it for redemption in hard money, and if the bank does not pay its debt the national treasurer may sell the bonds he holds in trust for that bank and so redeem the debt. In addition to its United States bonds, each bank keeps, in legal money at the national treasury, 5 per cent of the value of its circulating notes to insure their prompt redemption. There were $725,522,045 in national bank notes in circulation on March 1, 1924.

Banks are more or less familiar institutions, although they are not used by the people at large so much as they should be. Almost everyone has cashed a check at a bank at some time, and many people have bought Liberty Loan bonds through banks or have a savings account in one. The very first function of a bank is to serve as a safe place of deposit. People put their money in banks to make it safe from two dangers: the danger of theft and the danger of unwise and extravagant spending.

There are two ways of depositing money in a bank. It may be deposited on a checking account, in which case a check book and a pass book are issued to the depositor. The pass book contains entries of all deposits made, with date and the initials of the receiving cashier; while the check book shows, if properly kept, the amount checked out with dates, purposes, and payees. Money kept on deposit in this way, unless over one hundred dollars, usually draws no interest; it is assumed that the service of the bank in keeping the money safe and relieving the patron of its care pays for the use the bank has of the unchecked balance. Some banks charge a small fee, usually the interest on a hundred dollars, for checking accounts which average less than that amount.

The second way of depositing money is to put it in a savings account Such money cannot be checked out, although it may be drawn out by the depositor. The bank pays interest at a low rate, and then combines the small amounts thus intrusted to it to lend for a higher rate of interest to business men and wage-earners. In this way people who can save only a little at a time receive some interest for it, and the bank makes enough on the margin between the two interest rates to pay it for the labor of care and handling. The rate, terms, and period of compounding for savings accounts vary greatly at different banks and in different sections. At present 4 per cent is a common rate, and interest is compounded either quarterly or every six months. Of course, when the depositor has saved a large enough sum it is better for him to invest his money in something which will pay him a higher rate of interest than the savings account offers. The United States government has in recent years opened savings accounts in its post offices, thus encouraging saving in places where there is no bank to suggest and reward thrift.

The funding of capital. The second function of banks has already been touched upon. Banks gather up capital in sums too small for effective use in modern enterprises, and by combining these sums make large amounts which can be used to finance business. Moreover, by their expert knowledge they put this money where it is safely and productively used, and so increase the prosperity of the country and provide employment for labor. The money that would otherwise lie idle because it is too small an amount for any business man to borrow and use, and because the saver probably would not know how or where to invest it, thus becomes useful not only to the saver but also to a whole series of persons and to society at large. As the amount of money in the country approaches complete utilization it also nears maximal usefulness. Idle money is a slacker, and no one should be guilty of owning any. The savings bank is a recruiting station for money; it gathers it up, organizes it into companies, and sends it out on campaigns for prosperity.

The function of the exchange of money. The third great function of banking is that of exchange, of which we have spoken in dealing with the instruments of exchange. Banks are the central offices through which the checks, drafts, and letters of exchange pass and in which they are balanced. Every city which has several banks and which, moreover, serves as the financial center for small town and country banks has a *clearing house*. The clearing house is an institution of credit which was started by bank messengers in an interesting way. At the close of each day's business any bank will have on hand checks drawn not only on itself but also on other banks of the city and vicinity. Messengers were formerly sent out after business hours with these checks, each messenger to carry to other banks from his own what it had received in the day's business. The messengers found that the easiest and quickest way to transact their business was to meet in some convenient place and exchange checks. Every clerk gathered in all the checks that were due his own bank and gave to the other clerks what was due them. On finding out how their employees had saved time and trouble the bankers organized the clearing house, which now meets every day at noon and "clears" the day's checks. Then each bank, by means of checks, pays the balance due to banks to which the day's transactions have left it a debtor and receives the balance due from banks to which it is a creditor. The clearing house thus becomes a bankers' bank. In time the clearing house will probably give place to the clearing system inaugurated with the Federal Reserve system, but at present it remains a very important part of the business life of any city.

Foreign trade. Payment for foreign exchange is carried on through the great banks of the business centers of the countries concerned. The products exchanged are those which each country is best fitted, either naturally or by some artificial means, to produce. Let us say that the amount of annual imports from France comes, as it did in the year ending June 30, 1918, to $75,638,078, while our exports to France for the same year are $890,481,513. Now if we had no money and no credit system, we should say that France had paid us, by an exchange of goods, for $75,638,078 worth of her imports from the United States and that she still owed us the remainder. In that case France would try in some way to send more exports to us to balance the debt she owed. In the case of the unusual balance of 1918 (caused, of course, largely by war conditions) there would have to be sent over something to balance the huge debt; and as France could not send goods, she must send gold, or, failing gold, securities. The flow of gold into the country which has the balance of trade gives to that country what is called *favorable exchange*.

The payment of goods sold is usually in the form of a bill of exchange, drawn for some months ahead.[1] This bill of exchange is subject to discount, of course, and becomes commercial paper; that is, an instrument of credit which may be used instead of money. It is indorsed by each firm which uses it as

---

[1] Before the World War, when London was the world's commercial center, bills on London were the favorite means of payment in international trade, for a London bill of exchange could be cashed almost anywhere. Now New York bills hold a preeminent position, although they may not keep it after the return of normal conditions.

a payment for debts, and finally it comes into the hands of a banking firm. The banking firm probably has many more like it, from various countries. It puts all those payable in England, all those payable in France, all those payable in Italy, together in groups and offers them for sale to the men to whom they are most useful; namely, the importers of goods from those countries. Let us revert to the case of the Franco-American trade of 1918: in such a case there will be many, many bills of exchange piled up in New York for which there are no balancing bills in Paris, for the trade has been a very one-sided affair. The claims that Frenchmen have against Americans will not nearly balance the claims of Americans against Frenchmen. American bills of exchange will be at a premium in Paris, because they are scarce and hard to get, and so men will be willing to pay a bonus for a bill that will save them the trouble and expense of sending gold across the ocean to pay their debts. The French importer will pay more than a thousand dollars for a bill in New York for one thousand dollars, because such bills are hard to find; American dollars will therefore be quoted at over one dollar each in the French market reports. Conversely, French bills of exchange in New York will be so plentiful that they will sell at a discount. Men will be anxious to sell them rather than have gold shipped; therefore they will be willing to sell a bill for one thousand francs for less than one thousand francs, and the value of the francs will accordingly fall on the American market. In this way the comparative value of foreign money fluctuates according to the amounts of imports and exports and the balance of trade.[1]

Law of the equal distribution of metals. Another reason for the rise and fall of money values grows directly from unequal foreign trade. When great amounts of gold are centered in one country the purchasing value of gold goes down in that country, which, of course, makes its quotation in the terms of other

---

[1] Ordinarily the fluctuation falls within what are called the "gold points," but this did not hold during the recent war. Read Clay's "Economics for the General Reader," p. 211, for an explanation of gold points.

coinage lower. When there is little gold in France, for instance, it will purchase more than when there is a normal supply.[1] Thus commodities become cheaper, and foreign trade is attracted to the bargains offered. This brings in gold again, equalizing international trade. So throughout the commercial nations *exports, imports, and the distribution of gold tend always to become equal* Every country must pay for its imports with exports and give service in return for services received.

Recent Improvements in the Banking System

Inflation and contraction. When the supply of money becomes so large or so small as to affect the whole price level, it is said to be inflated or contracted When inflation comes from a real increase of the amount of gold the results are not so serious as in the case of artificial inflation through the making of fiat money, for in the former case there is a more general and permanent rise in the price level. But any inflation of the money supply means higher prices and lower money values Since people who have lent money or have supplied goods on credit are then paid in a medium of less value than that which they advanced, inflation helps a debtor but injures a creditor On the other hand, if the money supply is reduced or contracted the debtor is hurt, for he has to pay in money which is worth more than what he borrowed. Until recently it has been easy to inflate the currency but difficult to contract it at will, and the bad results of inflation by means of paper money have made governments chary of using it. The need of some means of controlling the amount of money in circulation led to a new kind of banking, now to be described.

We have seen that the functions of banking include the receipt and care of deposits, the paying of interest on small sav-

---

[1] The student is warned against drawing general conclusions from the facts of trade during war time, as a war upsets all ordinary economic relationships and introduces so many abnormal factors that no reliable conclusions can be drawn from what happens at such a time.

ings, the funding of capital, the exchange of money and credit, the discounting of commercial paper, and the issue of bank notes, which are part of the currency. There are three other functions of banking which until recently were imperfectly fulfilled; namely, providing a source of lending power for borrowers, pooling bank resources so that they may be used whenever and wherever they are most needed, and influencing the amount of money in circulation at any one time.

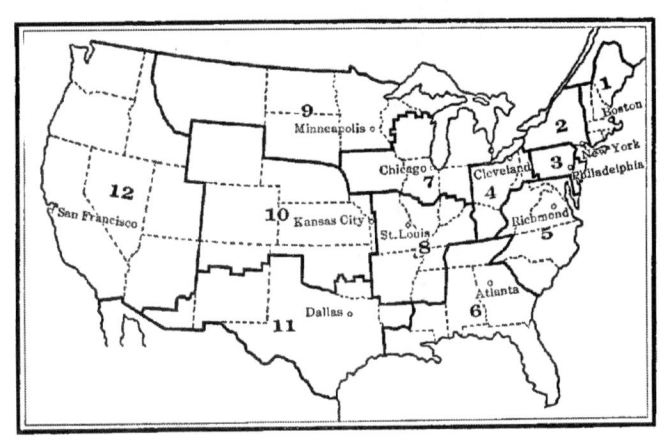

FEDERAL RESERVE DISTRICTS

The Federal Reserve Banking Act. These three problems were carefully studied by financial experts, with the result that in December, 1913, Congress passed the Federal Reserve Act, which has given to the United States as good a banking system as exists anywhere in the world. The plan adopted was to divide the country into twelve districts of about equal financial resources.[1] Each district has a regional Federal Reserve bank in the leading financial center of the district, which does not do ordinary banking business with the citizens of the district,

---

[1] In practice this proved an impossibility, and today, although the state of New York alone was made into a district, it represents about 40 per cent of the financial resources of the country.

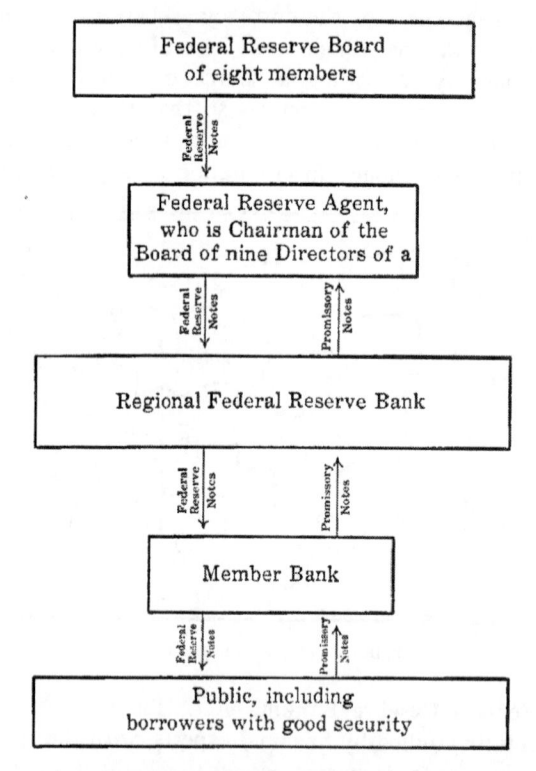

```
┌─────────────────────────┐
│   Federal Reserve Board │
│    of eight members     │
└─────────────────────────┘
            │ Federal Reserve Notes
            ▼
┌─────────────────────────┐
│  Federal Reserve Agent, │
│   who is Chairman of the│
│ Board of nine Directors of a │
└─────────────────────────┘
      │ Federal      ▲ Promissory
      │ Reserve      │ Notes
      ▼ Notes        │
┌─────────────────────────┐
│ Regional Federal Reserve Bank │
└─────────────────────────┘
      │ Federal      ▲ Promissory
      │ Reserve      │ Notes
      ▼ Notes        │
┌─────────────────────────┐
│       Member Bank       │
└─────────────────────────┘
      │ Federal      ▲ Promissory
      │ Reserve      │ Notes
      ▼ Notes        │
┌─────────────────────────┐
│    Public, including    │
│ borrowers with good security │
└─────────────────────────┘
```

THE FEDERAL RESERVE SYSTEM

This diagram shows the exchange of promissory notes for money through the Federal Reserve system. Credit is thus nationally transformed into money, which is the most efficient use for credit yet found. The promissory notes are rediscounted at the regional Federal Reserve bank, where the Federal Reserve agent serves as their custodian until they mature and are redeemed. When they are canceled, Federal Reserve notes are again brought into the member banks, which return them to the regional bank. Here any surplus over what is needed is kept in reserve until business demands call it out into circulation again. If the surplus were allowed to remain in circulation, it would raise prices above the normal level made by supply and demand

but which acts as a central bank for all the banks in the district which belong to the Federal Reserve system. All national banks must become member banks; and as many state banks as desire, and can conform to certain requirements, may belong. The regional bank is controlled by a board of nine directors, six of whom are elected by the member banks (each bank having a vote) and three appointed by the Federal Reserve Board.

The Federal Reserve Board is the controlling body for the whole system. It conducts its business at Washington. It has eight members: the Secretary of the Treasury, who is ex-officio chairman; the Comptroller of the Currency; and six members appointed by the president and the Senate for a ten-year term. The duties of the board are to supervise the system, to publish reports, to examine the twelve banks, to supervise and regulate the Federal Reserve notes, to compel any or all of the twelve banks to loan to each other when need arises, and to suspend the reserve requirements when necessary. It will be seen that with an official governing body composed of experts from all over the nation, wise financial policies are much more probable than under the old lack of system.

Elasticity of credit and currency. Now let us see how the new system meets the needs of the country. The needs begin with the individual farmer, business man, or firm wanting money for some legitimate enterprise. The borrower secures money at his own local bank, giving, of course, good security. Many other firms also borrow money; and when the bank, which is a member of the Federal Reserve system, has a number of notes and needs more money for the demands in its vicinity, it sends them to the regional Federal Reserve bank. This central bank takes them over and returns Federal Reserve notes, which it in turn has received from Washington through a special agent authorized by the Comptroller of the Currency. The amount of Federal Reserve notes is further regulated by the rule that each bank must provide a 40 per cent gold reserve for the redemption of its notes. In this way additional money is sent out for circulation just when additional money is needed. There is a constant and controlled market for promissory notes, which are returned to the member banks when due and redeemed by the return of Federal Reserve notes. The member banks also keep their required reserve at the regional bank and are subscribers to its capital.

More money is needed in the spring, when farmers are buying seed and machinery and hiring extra help, and in harvest time, when farm expenses are especially high; it is needed by certain manufacturing concerns at the season of the year when they produce for their big sales, say those for Christmas, and by the building-trades during building-weather. When these seasons of special activity are past, contraction is needed to bring the money supply back to normal, as the money demand has been brought back to normal. Certain years, also, are years of great activity, while others are comparatively quiet; and in these longer periods there are varying needs for money.

When desirable, contraction of the currency is advised by the Federal Reserve Board. This board has such facilities for securing accurate knowledge of conditions that it can ascertain when contraction is needed. It will then suggest caution to the twelve regional banks, which in turn advise the member banks; the member banks then become more conservative in issuing loans, and advise their patrons to call in their promissory notes and redeem them.[1] As the Federal Reserve notes accumulate in the member banks in response to this advice, they are gathered up and sent to the regional banks, which store them until needed again. The unfit are destroyed. Thus this new banking system has originated a new kind of money, which is just as good as any other money (being redeemable in gold at the national treasury and payable for taxes and customs duties), but which is issued when needed and retired when not needed. Money which appears and disappears by the magic of good

---

[1] The process of paying up debts, gathering in assets, and generally settling up old business without contracting for new—in short, of clearing the decks for a fresh start—is known as "liquidation."

business sense is a new factor in the world of affairs; and although the system is too recent to be judged as yet, it seems to answer several long-felt needs and to give a safeguard against panics. Of course contraction must be managed very carefully, with due consideration for all the interests involved.

Another kind of money is provided by the Federal Reserve system—the Federal Reserve Bank notes, issued in return for the deposit of United States bonds, much as ordinary national

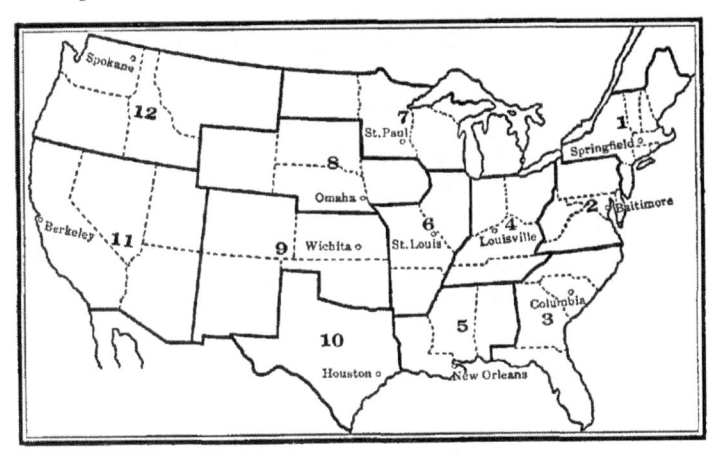

FEDERAL FARM LOAN DISTRICTS

bank notes are. Being based on these bonds of steady value rather than on the fluid supply of commercial paper, these notes are not elastic as are the Federal Reserve notes. There were over twelve million of these notes in circulation in 1924, but they were then being retired.

The Federal Farm Loan Act. The Federal Reserve system, with all its excellences, did not quite meet the needs of the farmers of the country, who are passing through a transition period in farming methods in their efforts to put agriculture on a permanent basis. They need capital for the introduction of improvements, but often find it hard to secure that capital when they need it. There is plenty of money in the country,

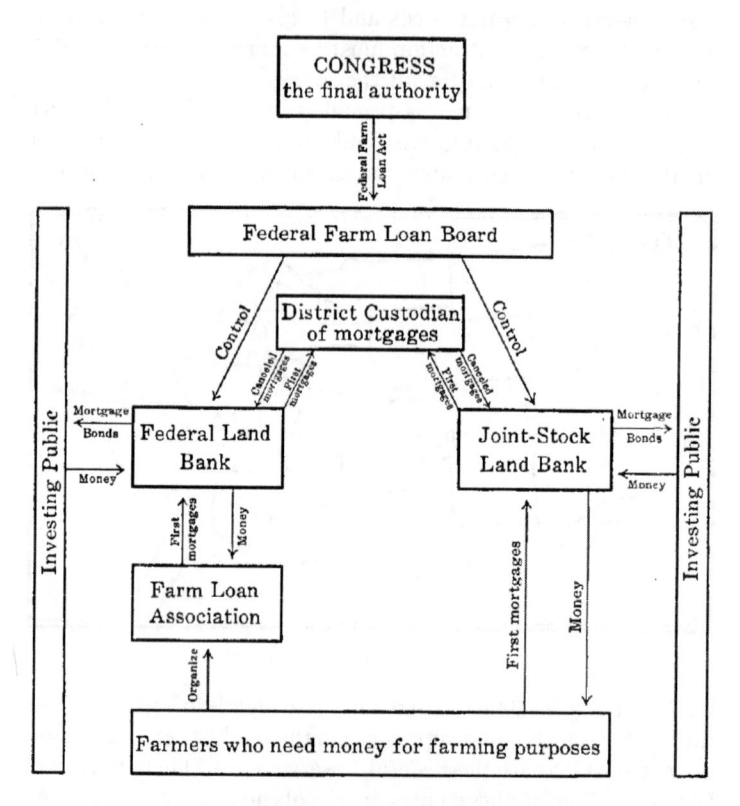

THE FEDERAL FARM LOAN SYSTEM

The needy farmer who can give a mortgage on his land as security may either borrow direct from a Joint-Stock Land Bank, or with nine other farmers form a Farm Loan Association, which may borrow $20,000 or more from a regional Federal Land Bank. This money comes from the sale of mortgage bonds in denominations of from $25 to $1000, which bear not over 5 per cent interest, and run twenty years unless redeemed after five years by the issuing bank. The mortgages are reduced by a partial-payment plan which pays off the debt in about thirty-five years. Federally appointed appraisers fix the value of the land which secures the debt but until lately there was no effective way of bringing borrowers and lenders together. The surety for farm loans is naturally the farm land, pledged in a mortgage. The mortgage is a safe form of investment if certain precautions are taken, but the nature of these precautions is so technical, and the laws governing them vary so in different states, that a man who is not a specialist hesitates to put his money into mortgage loans.

What was needed, then, was some official agency which would examine and pass upon mortgages offered, and secure capital on them when that capital was needed; and which could organize the lending and borrowing forces of the country in an economical and advantageous way. The answer to this need came in 1916 in the form of the Farm Land Bank System (see diagram, p. 237), which did for the farmer what the Federal Reserve System had done for the business man and the manufacturer.

SUPPLEMENTARY READINGS

CARVER, T. N. Principles of National Economy, chap. xlix. [Emergency financing.]

TUFTS, J. H. The Real Business of Living, chap. xxi, "Good Faith in Business."

VAN WAGENEN, T. F., in *Popular Science*, Vol. LXXIII, pp. 267–276. [The history of silver.]

WEBSTER, W. C. General History of Commerce, pp. 61, 102–104, 109–110, 126–128, 130–132. [Money history.]

Current Opinion, Vol. LXI, pp. 382–383. [Origin of the Federal Reserve.]

"Latin-American Monetary Systems," in *Bulletin of the Pan-American Union*, September, 1919.

SEARCH QUESTIONS AND PROBLEMS

1. Ely and Wicker, in "Elementary Economics," p. 198, give these nine qualities which they say money must have: (1) commodity value, (2) high specific value, (3) stability of value, (4) uniformity of value, (5) cognizability, (6) durability, (7) portability, (8) malleability, (9) homogeneity. What do these words mean when applied to money? Does United States money have them all?

2. Why has China abandoned the iron money she used so long? Why do the older Chinese coins have a hole through the middle? Do

THE TOOLS OF BUSINESS

you think the comparative prosperity of Sparta and Athens was at all influenced by the kind of currency used in the two cities? See Davis's "Readings in Ancient History for Greece," p 104, and Breasted s "Ancient Times," pp 299, 346

3 Find in your United States history the time and way in which the greenbacks were made as good as gold. Who suffered? Why?

4 It is generally conceded that the salaried classes fare worst in a time of increased cost of living Why is this?

5 On July 14, 1920, Mrs Drake found in an old traveling bag three English sovereigns which she had mislaid and forgotten while in England in October, 1918, when exchange was at $4 866 On looking at the daily paper she found that exchange that day was at $3 93 She took the sovereigns to the bank and had them exchanged for American money. What did she receive? What did she gain or lose because of her carelessness? Can you explain why British money changed so in its relation to American money?

6. Find in today's paper the market quotations for the pound sterling, the franc, the lira, the guilder, the German mark, and the Canadian dollar Compare them with the quotations for a month, three months, and a year ago. If you had money to invest would you buy foreign money and wait for it to appreciate in value? Which of these foreign coins are below and which above par? What does this show?

7 Do you own a Liberty Bond? How did you acquire it? Why were these bonds issued? What interest do they bear? When do they mature? Why is a government bond a safer investment than a commercial bond?

8 The value of gold at the United States mint is always $20 67 per fine ounce; that is, per Troy ounce of pure gold An ounce contains 480 grains, and there are 25.8 grains, nine-tenths fine, in a gold dollar. If the United States coined $18,525,026 in gold in 1916, what did the government pay for the gold bullion used? What did it make, if anything, on the transaction?

9 In 1917 the coinage of gold fell to $10,914 Why?

10 The United States coined for the Philippine Islands, for the year ending June 30, 1918, the following silver coins. 2,502,166 peso pieces, 6,255,656 twenty-centavo pieces, and 8,210,519 ten-centavo pieces A centavo is worth half a cent, a peso, fifty cents What was the value of the coins made for the Philippines in that year?

11. With silver bullion worth 69.0242 cents per dollar at that time, what was the bullion value of this money made for the Philippines?

12. Find the bullion value of silver for the year 1920 and the number of silver dollars coined that year. Does the government gain or lose by this coinage? How much?

13. From 1700 on for almost two centuries the coinage ratio between gold and silver remained between fourteen to one and twenty to one. It first passed the 20.1 mark in 1886, and reached 39.84 in 1915. How do you explain this change in the relative value of gold and silver?

14. The story of silver is only partly sketched on pages 214–215. Outline it more fully, giving the causes and results of the chief events. Dewey's "Financial History of the United States," J. L. Laughlin's "History of Bimetallism in the United States," A. D. Noyes's "Forty Years of American Finance," Marshall, Wright, and Field's "Materials for the Study of Elementary Economics," and Bogart and Thompson's "Readings in the Economic History of the United States" all contain information on silver.

15. In what way does the Federal Reserve Act provide for elasticity in the working of the system? See Hamilton's "Current Economic Problems," Nos. 126, 127, 128.

16. Does any nation now have a bimetallic standard? Is the statement true that the United States had a silver standard to 1853 and has had a gold standard ever since? See Clay's "Economics for the General Reader," pp. 158–161.

17. Can barter be substituted for money economy in the modern world? Read "A Concrete Example of the Possibilities of Barter," in the *American* for July, 1920, Vol. VI, No. 10.

18. What will happen if silver remains for any great length of time above par in value?

19. *The Economist* gives the index number for all Europe in 1910 as 90 and in December, 1919, as 287. Was the price level higher in Europe than in America for these two years?

20. Some very interesting facts about gold are given in the *Literary Digest* for March 20, 1920. Study page 52 and tell the class:

a. How gold flowed into and out of the United States during the war.

b. How the production of gold varied from 1912 to 1918 inclusive.

c. Whether there was gold enough to make Federal Reserve notes safe during the war period. (Note the use of the word "cover" here.)

THE TOOLS OF BUSINESS

21. Is the popular contempt for Mexican money justified? See *Literary Digest* for May 15, 1920, p. 36.

22. Explain as well as you can these fluctuations in the value of the world's gold output for the years indicated:

Years	Ounces Fine	Value
1841–1850	17,605,018	$363,928,000
1851–1855	32,051,621	662,566,000
1856–1860	32,431,312	670,415,000
1896	9,783,914	202,251,600
1897	11,420,068	236,073,700
1898	13,877,806	286,879,700

23. Suppose a young man of twenty-three years, of excellent character and earning a yearly salary of $1500, needed to borrow $500 in order to send his mother away for her health. He has no real estate, but rents a flat for himself and mother. He expects to pay back the loan from his salary. Can he borrow the money at a local bank?

24. In what Federal Reserve district do you live? What is its central reserve city? How many banks in your town are member banks? Where is the regional Farm Land Bank of your district? What plan for handling loans to farmers is used in your part of the country? To date, has the system functioned to any extent in your neighborhood to help farmers improve their working-plants and produce more?

25. The Federal Reserve banks must carry 40 per cent gold reserve for the redemption of their outstanding notes, but are they required to hold a reserve for the redemption of deposits? See extracts from the act in Marshall, Wright, and Field's "Materials for the Study of Elementary Economics," No. 159.

26. The Federal Land Banks do not take care of the short-time money needs of farmers. To meet the need for loans running from six months to three years, the system of Intermediate Credit Banks has been established. Write to the Treasury Department, Washington, or to your district Federal Land Bank, for information, and report your findings to the class.

27. How small an amount will start a savings account in your local post office? How old must one be to start an account? Is your post office much used as a savings bank? Who uses it? What rate of interest is paid?

CHAPTER X

CRISES AND HARD TIMES

The crisis is an acute malady to which business appears to be increasingly subject To understand the social organism completely we must study it in disease as well as in health —EDWARD D. JONES

In the past chapters we have studied the present economic organization of society. Its efficiency is proved by the fact that it supports an ever-increasing population in more comfort than the world has known before But ever since village and town economy were replaced by metropolitan and national economy there have appeared at varying intervals jars in the peaceful and efficient working of the machine. It seems at times that a cog has slipped in the wheel of production, throwing the whole machine out of order. A few years back economists placed the blame on the shoulders of those few whose ill fortune it was to be in charge when the breakdown occurred. More recently the tendency is to blame the machine itself and to seek a reason for the slipping of the cog by studying the inner workings of economic organization.

CRISES IN THE PAST

The first financial crises or panics came in the early sixteenth century. In the days of ancient Rome there had been commercial emergencies which might warrant the name "crises," but they did not develop into real panics. The medieval crises, like those of later times, originated in metropolitan centers. They followed fast on the heels of the establishment of "exchanges", that is, places where men met daily and, without real commodities, made exchanges by means of paper securities representing their wares. The Flemish city of Antwerp was one

CRISES AND HARD TIMES

of the first to establish such an exchange, with pepper featuring as one of the chief wares on the slips of sale and purchase. In addition to securities for produce, men began bringing to the exchange papers which represented capital. Merchants and traders could now come to the exchange and secure the money they so much needed, giving in exchange securities on their goods. Even princes used to secure loans at the exchanges. It was not necessary for them or for the men who possessed available capital to appear on the floor of the exchange, the whole transaction might take place through the medium of agents. Thus it is said that the king of France borrowed money from the Sultan of Turkey without either of them stirring from his royal palace.

Stock exchanges. It was only a question of time until the shares of the newly created joint-stock companies came to be bought and sold in exchanges, which now gave up the handling of produce and became solely money and stock exchanges. Shares of the English East India Company could be bought in Paris and Amsterdam as well as in London. At first these stock exchanges served a real need: people with small means would not have known where to invest their meager savings without them. The prices quoted on the exchanges also gave the best indication of the value of the various stocks for sale.

Soon, however, trading in shares for the sport of it began to seize men's fancies. Speculators began to buy stock, not for the purpose of investment but because they believed that it was going to rise in price in a short time and that then they could sell out at an enormous profit. They sought no longer a safe place to invest their surplus wealth for the purpose of safe-keeping and a normal return of interest and profits. They now bought because they thought they could pick up a fortune overnight by sudden rises and falls in the value of the stock itself. Soon many of these speculators went so far as to bet that certain stocks would rise or fall without bothering actually to buy the stocks. This practice was pure gambling. Unfair methods were not uncommon. Leaks of political events, such as the concluding of peace at the end of wars, would be used by the speculators to their own advantage. False rumors were even started of impending wars or political and economic disturbances so that advantage could be taken, by those who were in the inner circle, of the hurried sales of the timid and credulous.

The stock exchange had its good as well as its bad points. It made possible lending for legitimate purposes, as exemplified

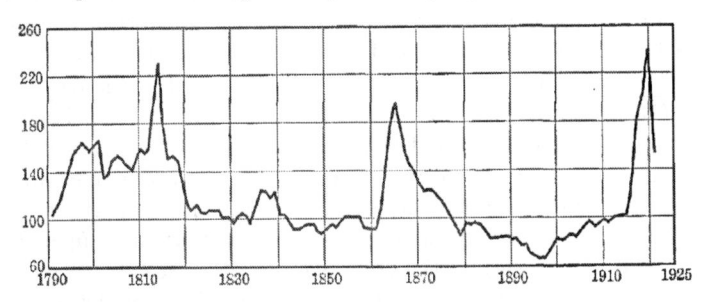

RISE AND FALL IN WHOLESALE PRICES

This graph, by Alvin H. Hansen, combines several sets of index numbers for some twenty staple products for over one hundred and thirty years. What historical and economic events might have produced the three high-price peaks? Can you trace any relation between the periodicity of crises and the prices shown here? In view of the following facts what deductions can you draw as to the connection between labor movements and prices in the United States? Between 1790 and 1820 local unions arose; between 1833 and 1837 these unions joined into groups known as city centrals; and from 1850 to 1866 some thirty national unions were formed and began to adopt aggressive measures. Between 1866 and 1873 these nationals met in an industrial congress, which after 1870 advised and promoted aggressive action. From 1873 and 1880 three fourths of the trade unions died out, to be reborn in 1880-1883. In 1886 the American Federation of Labor was formed, with a policy of collective bargaining and strikes as means to secure its ends

by the fact that most of the money which rebuilt the city of London after the fire of 1666 came from Holland. It facilitated the launching of the joint-stock companies, which were doing so much to foster commerce. On the other hand, the exchange made possible the floating of enterprises of a very doubtful and even utterly fictitious nature, in which some people lost their all to clever fakirs. The money which should have gone to the upbuilding of society might therefore go to swell the private purses of swindlers.

Human credulity. The stock exchange catered to an instinct that seems to be inherent in mankind. By nature most people are gullible to a surprising degree. Experience and training tend to reduce this trait, but at times it becomes uppermost, and nothing can hold it in check. So on the stock exchange, when times were good and money was plenty, contributors could be found for schemes that, when viewed in the coolness of afterthought, seemed literally harebrained. Participation in such schemes resulted in some fourteen financial crises between the years 1520 and 1720. None of these panics were long in duration nor widespread in their effects, and none of them seem to have taught the wisdom of caution in financial investments. Rather, the credulity of people seemed to be on the increase, as proved by one adventurer who offered stock on the London exchange in "a company for the carrying on of an undertaking of great advantage, but nobody to know what it is." The amazing result of this piece of effrontery to intelligence and common sense was that the originator was able to collect £2000 in five hours of stock-selling. Another company was launched for the purpose of "milking the wild cows of South America."

In 1720 there occurred almost simultaneously two panics unequaled in the preceding years and not to be paralleled until over a century and a half later. Two whole nations, the English and the French, became reckless gamblers overnight These twin panics contain lessons which the business men of the last two centuries might well have studied and applied.

The Mississippi Bubble. In France the panic of 1720 is called the Mississippi Bubble, because it resulted from excessive speculation in the stocks of a company which had been granted a royal monopoly in trading with the French province of Louisiana on the western bank of the Mississippi. John Law, the clever Scotch gambler who launched the company, was a personal friend of the Regent of France. He received from the Regent a further trading monopoly in the French East Indies. With these anticipated economic resources at his command, Law promised a yearly dividend of 40 per cent. The people of France had faith in the clever foreigner who was supported by their ruler and who the year before (1716) had miraculously solved the bankrupt condition of their country merely by issuing paper in the form of bank notes.[1] Trade and business were flourishing anew by his great additions to the currency, optimism had succeeded depression, and the populace was ready to invest its newly acquired wealth in any "get rich quick" scheme.

In addition to public faith in the times in general and in Law in particular, and to the desire for a 40 per cent profit, there was another reason for the enormous purchase of stock: Law allowed the shares to be paid for in government paper money at par value. Since this money was greatly depreciated, the stock of the company was largely "water," and the 40 per cent promised return really meant about 120 per cent on the actual money investment.

The country entered into a frenzy of speculating unequaled in all history. Six times as much stock was sought for purchase by the French people as had been at first issued. Law, with the advice of the Regent, yielded to the demand and printed three hundred thousand new shares. Twice that number could easily have found a market. Everyone, from dukes to street cobblers, was scrambling to obtain Mississippi Company stock. Informal stock exchanges on the streets were established where not only were shares bought and sold, but gambling on their rising and falling prices took place on an enormous scale. Shares jumped to forty times their par value. Cooks and footmen became rich overnight. All the world seemed to have

[1] These notes were at first backed by 25 per cent specie and 75 per cent of the depreciated government paper money accepted at par value. Later Law had been forced by the Regent to issue a thousand million livres of notes without any backing.

gone mad. Law's own coachman was soon competing with his master for a servant to drive him about the boulevards of Paris. As is always the case in a time of great speculation, there seemed to be prosperity everywhere buildings were erected, business boomed, and commerce flourished. Elegance and luxury were broadcast. The bubble of faith was at its biggest.

The first prick came from a man who had a personal grievance against Law because he had refused to sell him any stock in the Mississippi Company. He sent three wagonfuls of notes to the bank and demanded specie payment. Through royal influence he was later forced to return two thirds of the specie But the damage was done Clever stockbrokers "smelled a rat" and began at once to play safe for themselves. While still playing the game for the public, they quietly sold their stock and either turned the bank notes into specie or else purchased gold plate and valuable jewels to send into hiding in foreign countries.

Before long it became evident that there was insufficient specie in the country. Rumor ran like wildfire. Again the populace emulated a flock of sheep Everyone hoarded what hard money he could secure and tried in every way to turn his instruments of credit into coin The government tried to stop the panic by forbidding the buying up of plate and jewels and by limiting the amount of specie any one person could legally hold This edict only served to fan into flames the smoldering fears of a now aroused people, and stock began to fall in value rapidly.[1]

Nothing could stop the foredoomed crash. In vain additional bank notes were issued, and the bank and the Mississippi Company joined. Every move only served to increase public fear Credit and faith were demoralized. After a parade of

[1] An amusing story is told of a doctor who, while taking a patient's pulse, murmured, "It falls! it falls! Mon Dieu! it falls continually!" The lady began ringing frantically for her family, moaning meanwhile, "I am dying! My pulse! my pulse!" This brought the doctor to his senses and to the embarrassing necessity of explaining that it was the stock he owned, not the pulse he was observing, which was taking its precipitous flight downward.

some six thousand working-men, supposedly bound with their picks and shovels for the Mississippi mines, the Law stocks rose for a short time; but when most of these men returned to the wandering street crowds of the Paris unemployed, the price of stocks slumped only the more. An attempt to check a run on the bank by the specie-hungry mob was not helped by closing its doors; for after the reopening, dozens were squeezed to death in the crowd. The shares of the company became wellnigh worthless, and paper money was irredeemable. Fortunes made overnight were gone, and savings hoarded for years suffered the same fate.

Quite naturally the fault was all placed on the author of the two schemes, but it does not justly belong there. Law was no knave, or he would have escaped the crash with a fortune stored away in some other country, whereas his wealth had been invested in French estates which he must leave behind when he fled. He was more deceived than deceiving. He left Paris a penniless man save for one valuable diamond. He had made serious mistakes no doubt: he had a confused idea that paper money meant more wealth—at least he allowed the Regent to act upon the erroneous theory that credit is inexhaustible. Then he had erred in allowing the bank to be united with a doubtful commercial company, thus endangering the bank notes, which all people must accept. The issuance of stock not backed by actual resources or full investments was another great error, but its excessive overvaluation by the public, for which Law was not to blame, played even greater havoc. He had not reckoned on the human passions of confidence and distrust. The blame should rather be placed on the ignorance, credulity, and avarice of a whole people.

The South Sea Bubble. In England the colossal gambling spree of 1720 was in the stock of a South Sea trading company. It, also, was connected with the government by its assumption of the national debt. Inflation and crash were similar to the French episode, but the depression period following was not so severe, owing to the work of England's first prime minister,

Robert Walpole. He confiscated the estates of the directors of the company and was thereby able to pay back about one third of the par value of the stock.[1]

American crises. Later crises have proved that it is not necessary for the speculation to be in companies operating beyond the seas, nor is it necessary for the speculators to be connected with the government in order to produce acute panics In 1837 in the United States the mania took the form of vast purchases of public lands and the overissuance of unsound paper money In 1873 it was the uncurbed construction of railroads which caused the panic, both because of their initial high cost and because in new and sparsely settled areas the returns must of necessity be slow.

The result of unrestrained speculation and overconfidence is always the same. when men sow a whirlwind they reap destruction.

The Business Cycle

In the two hundred years following 1720 there have been some fifteen crises. In the European countries there seems to be a gradual decrease in their frequency and force. In the United States in the last half century, while the period of panic is shortening in duration and is accompanied with less suffering, the period of economic depression which follows in the trail of every panic seems to be lengthening and increasing in severity.

Failures in solving the problem of panics. The attention of progressive business men is being drawn more and more to a close study of panics in the hope that these financial emergencies may be prevented or at least mitigated. Until a short time ago little had been accomplished. There are two chief reasons which account for this inability to solve the problem of crises. In the first place, economists have erred in trying to find one sole cause to account for panics, and in the second place, both business men and economists have been so occupied with a

[1] For the South Sea and the Mississippi Bubbles see Charles Mackay's sketch, "Commercial Delusions," in the "Library of Commerce," Vol I

study of the spectacular or acute phase, which expresses itself in the panic or crash, that they have neglected to analyze the more chronic characteristics of the malady—the flush times which precede and the depressed times which follow. The most recent belief is that the causes of panics are many and varied and that to understand them we must analyze the period preceding the crash. To prevent or mitigate the panic we must remedy mistakes made in the periods before and after.

Erroneous theories. Several erroneous theories as to the cause of panics have been so widely accepted that they deserve mention in passing. One of these is that crises in business and hence panics are due solely to crop failures. One economist, W. S. Jevons by name, would have us believe that he has even found the cause for the crop failures. In his book "Investigations in Currency and Finance" he sets forth the theory that spots on the sun so affect climatic conditions that crop failures result. Henry Moore of Columbia University, without accepting the "sun spot" theory, does affirm the sole cause of panics to be crop failures. Insufficient rainfall, according to him, must bear the blame for our financial emergencies. Moore has studied the matter sufficiently to realize that there is a cycle of business activity of which the panic is only a part; but instead of looking for causes within this cycle of industrial activity, he is satisfied with affirming that "the fundamental persistent cause of the cycles in the activity of industry is the cyclical movement in the yield per acre of the crops, which in turn is due to the cycle of rainfall."[1]

Another theory quite as erroneous as that crop failure is the sole cause of a panic is the belief that a political event may produce a panic. There are books in existence today which state that the panic of 1837 was caused by the actions of Jackson, the panic of 1893 by the election of a Democratic president, and the panic of 1907 by the Roosevelt investigations into the evils of trusts. Such statements are false and mislead-

[1] Cf. Hamilton's "Current Economic Problems," Nos. 120–121.

ing. This does not mean that political events cannot help to precipitate a critical condition into a panic. The specie circular of 1837 and the announcement of the empty treasury found by the Democratic administration in 1893 both played their parts in turning a crisis into a panic, but to say that any one political event caused a panic is not only incorrect but harmful. When anything beyond the control of society as a whole is blamed for the evils of our civilization, then men cease to try to remove the cause, and reform is accordingly at a standstill.

Real causes in the business cycle. Thus it was that no real progress was made in the prevention or mitigation of panics until economists recognized that their causes lie within the cycle of activity in which modern business moves. Careful study of this business cycle has revealed many of the causes and suggested many of the remedies Much may yet remain to be discovered about panics, but of this we feel sure · we are at last on the right track in tracing their origins and remedies Let us see what science has so far discovered.

A number of concise descriptions have been made of the business cycle. Perhaps the most succinct is that of Lord Overstone· "State of quiescence, improvement, growing confidence, excitement, overtrading, convulsions, pressure, stagnation, distress, ending again in quiescence." Frederick Engels has likened the cycle to a race in which after a stillness "production and exchange begin to move again, little by little the pace quickens. It becomes a trot. The industrial trot breaks into a canter, the canter in turn grows into a headlong gallop of a perfect steeplechase of industry, commercial credit, and speculation, which finally, after breakneck leaps, ends where it began —in the ditch of a crisis. And so over and over again."

A period of good times. Careful study of great panics has proved without a doubt that so-called good times precede every crash. Prices are high, but money is so plentiful and is flowing so freely that no one minds the high prices. Everyone buys more of everything than he has ever bought in the past, and begins buying things which he never thought of possessing before. Every concern does a record-breaking business per month.[1]

Not only do old-line business concerns sow big business and reap big profits, but thousands of new enterprises begin. In 1837 it was land that was acquired by all investors, in 1873 it was the construction of railroads that ate up capital, and in 1893 it was the construction of big-scale factories. In all these lines of investment free capital is transformed into specialized and fixed forms. Money cannot be realized quickly from railroad cars and rails or from factory buildings and specialized machinery. It is invested to stay some time. Moreover, it is liable not to earn an immediate and ample return. While there is still a surplus of free capital, neither of these characteristics troubles the investor; but when the stringent times come, both of them operate to cause him hardships.

No small part of the reason why men talk of good times in the days preceding a crisis is that money seems so plentiful. Never does ready cash seem so easy to get. There are several reasons for this. In the first place, money may be moving so rapidly from person to person that the supply is virtually increased, because one dollar performs the services of many in a given period of time. In the second place, there may actually be a greater supply of money than in the years previous. This may have come about (1) through the issuance of paper money, as in 1837, when the many state banks increased their note issue from $95,000,000 to $140,000,000; (2) through the increased purchases, as in the years before 1893, of a cheap metallic currency such as silver; (3) through the increase of gold, as from the South American and Alaskan output before 1907; or (4) from a favorable balance of trade such as existed in the United States from 1914 to 1920.

---

[1] Take the case of steel, for instance, which is a barometer of construction and equipment. In 1872 the amount of steel manufactured jumped from 1,911,608 tons to 2,854,558 tons per year. Again, just before 1893 it jumped until the production exceeded 9,000,000 tons in a year, and in 1905 and 1906 it increased almost 3,000,000 more, to over 25,000,000 tons output in a year.

The dangers of good times. When money is plentiful it becomes cheap. Cheap money encourages much borrowing. Public and private extravagance knows no end. People borrow to begin new businesses or to expand old ones; they borrow to buy luxuries that they have done without before, they borrow in order to speculate in stocks or bonds. Exchanges are the busiest of all busy places in the months preceding a crisis. The increased demand for stocks and bonds sends them mounting in price, but still people continue to buy, either because the returns are abnormally high or simply because of anticipated higher market values. Speculation runs rife, for credulity and gullibility spread like wildfire among the populace

Much has been accomplished by legislation to check the evils of speculation. No Mississippi Bubble could be staged today. Our stock exchanges are not public institutions yet, but their rules and regulations are carried out with a surety that puts to shame much of our legal nonenforcement. Most exchanges prohibit the sale of fake stock and make their prohibitions effective by punishment in the form of canceled membership, which means no more exchanging for the offender. Others, such as the great New York Exchange off Wall Street, punish the breaking of rules by forfeiture of a deposit required of all members. Contracts for purchase and sale, sometimes involving as much as thousands of dollars, are made on little slips of white paper. They are made without the formality of a legal contract, but they are as binding as if they had been drawn up by a lawyer and sworn to under seal. Perhaps in no other place is a man's word so sure to be as good as his bond as on the New York Stock Exchange.

But all this careful regulation is powerless to prevent speculation Regulations may be made as to fake companies and the keeping of one's word, but so long as human nature remains the same, men will love to take a chance and will possess implicit faith that some day luck will bring in to them the ship of fortune. In the period preceding a crisis optimism grows like a weed As the days progress, interest and faith are replaced by an excitement which displaces sound business judgment. Confidence drives out reason. Desire overwhelms ethical standards. A fortune may be made overnight, and what matters it how it is made! With this human factor no law yet devised has been able to cope.

The crisis. Cheap money makes for other evils than speculation. Higher prices are due to its depreciation in value. This works a peculiar hardship on the laboring classes.[1] For although as a whole their wages have risen, they have not gone up in proportion to the prices of the necessities of life. Real wages, in other words, seldom increase as much as money wages. In the period of transition there are always firms who do not raise even money wages as quickly as others. These are often the marginal producers, who are afraid to increase for fear the price of the product will not remain high and they may go bankrupt. Sometimes they are profiteers who see a chance to reap additional profits. The first sign, then, of hardship in the midst of good times comes to the working-man. The result is that there are liable to be strikes, riots, and general unrest—clouds as small as a man's hand on the horizon of prosperity, but forerunners of the storm about to come.

Frequently the approaching storm is hastened by a crop failure. The effects of this natural emergency are many and far-reaching. First, the farmers need and demand less help to harvest their crops. Unemployment results. Next to the laborer railroads are hit, for they have less to haul away from the farms and less to haul to them in the way of manufactures which the farmers buy with their crop money. The ultimate result of the crop failure will be to raise the high prices further still. This may mean increased suffering for laborers, deeper discontent, and more strikes.

---

[1] Professional people also find that their returns do not increase as rapidly as the cost of living. They do not, however, suffer as soon as the laborer, because their margin of surplus over cost of living is usually higher to begin with. They may be pinched for money to spend on luxuries, but they will have sufficient to meet necessities.

In addition to these hardships a failure of crops may operate in such a way as to disrupt the system of credit, which has become the lifeblood of modern commerce. If the farmer does not get an adequate return from his crops he will not be able to pay his debts to the retail grocer, the dry-goods dealer, and the machinery firm. They in turn cannot meet their obligations to the wholesalers, and so the wholesalers in turn cannot cancel their indebtedness to the manufacturers. The bankers who have lent to all these men are hard put to it for money and are forced to stop loans

This breakdown of credit may, however, come from other sources than crop failures. Manufacturers may fail to get out their orders, owing to strikes, or, having produced their output, they may find that the demand of the public has ceased to exist for their products or that the prices have dropped to such an extent that a deficit results instead of a surplus. In any of these cases the manufacturer goes to the banker to secure loans for meeting his obligations Now if the bankers of the country have made too numerous loans for expansion and development, they may be unable to accommodate those who need credit in order to survive as solvent business concerns Moreover, if they have extended credit for speculative or nonproductive investment purposes, they will not be able to call in their loans, and a panic is almost sure to be the result.

The panic. The event which precipitates a panic is not the mere continued failure of a group of farmers or manufacturers to meet their obligations. It is usually, as it was in the days of Law, some event which pricks the bubble of human faith. In 1720 it was the act of the spiteful man who sent back his three cartloads of paper money to be redeemed in specie In 1837 in the United States it was the specie circular put forward by President Jackson, saying that the government would no longer accept the paper money of the state banks in payment for public lands. In 1873 it was the bankruptcy of the Jay Cooke Company through its overinvestment in Northern Pacific Railroad stock. Owing to its connection with government officials and its successful handling of Civil War government bonds this company had won the reputation of being as sound as the government itself; therefore when it fell the panic of mental doubt and fear seized everyone far and near, from New York to San Francisco.

After the prick of the bubble the balloon of credit and faith collapses in a miraculously short time. As in 1720, so in 1837 everyone began crying for specie in place of his paper money. Not only those who desired to purchase Western government land, but everyone else wanted to have hard money—to have something which in itself had value. People rushed to the banks and demanded redemption of their paper money, but all in vain. The state bank notes had been issued with little or nothing behind them. They were "fiat" money, and the faith which had given them their only value was now gone. So they became worthless. Without them business activity could not go on; the country was plunged into the slough of depression. In 1873, when Jay Cooke went to the wall, everyone was possessed to rid himself not only of all his Northern Pacific stock but also of any of his credit securities which might not be sound. Selling on the New York Exchange outrivaled all past rushes. The lower stock fell, the faster people sold it, until the Exchange finally closed its doors for ten days—an unprecedented event. Everywhere banks were called on to make loans and to pay out money to their depositors, until they too went to the wall and had to close their doors. Within forty-eight hours some thirty banks went down in ruin. Manufacturing concerns and railroads followed fast in succession. When they could get no money at the bank they could not pay their employees, for no firm of today carries any considerable amount of cash on hand. Many of the firms that failed had more money owing to them than they owed to all their creditors, but since they could not collect, it did them no good.

Depression, the aftermath of panic. The next period of the business cycle now begins. Depression is everywhere. Closed factories, bankrupt railroads, and decreased sales of all sorts mean lack of employment. The laborer suffers more acutely than any other element in the population, because as a rule he has no savings to fall back upon. Poverty runs rife, institutions of charity are taxed to the limit, and such outdoor help as "soup kitchens" must be established.

At such times capitalists also have their hardships: interest rates drop because there is no longer any call for money to invest. Much capital which has been invested in the failing banks and factories is lost entirely. Entrepreneurs have their grievances also Even those who have not gone bankrupt are forced not only to accept low profits but to live in daily fear that they will be the next to go to the wall. If for any reason their firm comes under the breath of suspicion, they will see their stock sold on the market for a song, while the stock which they hold in other companies drops far below the price they paid for it. Landowners bear their share of the hardships through decreased rents. Demand for goods is reduced even below the reduced supply, with the result that prices fall. Falling prices predict small returns for the future, so enterprise is checked, and the depression is felt by all. Conservatism and discouragement prevail, no one buys anything unless he has to. All business slows down. This period of overcaution and contraction may last from one to four years.

Revival. But just as we saw that the causes which brought on crisis and perhaps panic were existent in the period of greatest prosperity, so now we see in the period of depression promises for a brighter future. When only necessary buying is indulged in and prices are low, good results are bound to follow, because people cease to borrow but instead begin to accumulate a surplus, and the shortage of money gradually disappears. In the business world the lower prices of raw materials and capital make production cheaper; so also do the somewhat lower wages and the increased efficiency of labor, owing to the fact that there are more laborers than are needed and hence each man struggles to do his best in order to keep his job. With decreased cost of production, modest profit-making becomes possible. With profits comes the willingness of the more daring to invest capital again. Confidence grows when no more failures are reported in the morning papers. People decide that they have worn last year's styles long enough and that it is safe to buy anew. Banks have accumulated surpluses in the time of caution, and so they begin making loans. Timid investors creep out and risk a little, which they soon increase when no bad results follow. Soon all evidences of the panic and its preceding crisis are wiped away. Memory is short; and the race begins again, passing through the trot and canter stages up to the gallop. Prosperity reigns once more. Good times are come, awaiting only overexpansion of business, credit, and confidence to create another crisis and perhaps, if the overexpansion is great enough, another panic. The business cycle is thus complete.[1]

Periodicity of crises. As we look over the list of the world's crises it would appear that men completely forget the lessons of the past every twenty years, and even at the end of every ten years there seems to come a period of partial forgetfulness which causes a semicrisis. Perhaps the business men who underwent the hardships of the preceding crisis are not completely oblivious to the danger of their actions, but there have come into the business world during the intervening ten or twenty years enough new and inexperienced men who have not themselves learned the lesson of overexpansion to dictate the policies of the times. The fact that crop yields run in cycles contributes an additional, although not a fundamental, factor to the causes of the periodicity of crises.

Some people have doubted that there was any regularity in the occurrence of periods of commercial and financial emergency. A glance at the following table should settle this point of dispute.

[1] For a detailed description of the rhythm of business activity see Hamilton's "Current Economic Problems," No. 101.

LIST OF ECONOMIC CRISES AND PANICS

United States	England	France
1814	1815	1813
1818	—	1818
1825	1825	1825
		1830
1837[1]	1836–1839	1836–1839
1847	1847	1847
		1855
1857[1]	1857	1857
1869	1866	
1873[1]	1873	1873
1884		{ 1882 { 1884–1885
1890	1890	1890
1893[1]		1893
1903		
1907		

Prevention of Crises through Better Banking

Now when people overeat, nature punishes them by illness, which must be cured by abstemiousness and rigorous physical discipline. People who regulate their diet wisely, however, eat regularly and enjoy their food. It is so in business: the unreasonable profits of wildcat enterprises, the spectacular fortunes made in speculation, the gambling in stocks and commodities, and the undue inflation of money that precede a crisis are unhealthful, unsafe, and overplentiful food for the business organism—these things are overdoses of false prosperity which cannot be digested. If the business world can be saved the foolishness of overindulgence, then it will not have to pay the penalty of deprivation later on.

The impending panic of 1920. The belief that panics may be completely avoided has been strengthened by the events of the past few years in the United States. For some time the

[1] Especially severe panics.

country had been riding on a wave of apparent prosperity. This was caused by the commercial impetus which the war gave, through the opening of the markets of half the world to us at a time when our great trade rivals, Germany and England, were in no position to compete with us. Demand for raw materials and manufactures outstripped supply. The inflow of gold and the new issues of the Federal Reserve notes made money the cheapest thing in the country, and prices rose by leaps and bounds. The signs were unmistakably those of good times preceding a crisis.

Numerous reasons have been advanced as to why the impending panic of 1920 never passed beyond the stage of comparatively mild hard times in financial and industrial fields. The reasons deserving most careful attention are the operation of the Federal Reserve Banking Act and the intelligent coöperation of business men and the public.

Mobility of resources. Under the national banking system the financial reserves of the country were decentralized and highly immobile. If the Knickerbocker Trust Company of New York had been able to secure specie, the panic of 1907 could have been averted, for it was not until the National Bank of Commerce refused to clear for the Knickerbocker Company that the company fell under suspicion and suffered a withdrawal of twenty-eight million dollars of deposits in one day alone. Some students of finance insisted that the inability of the company to secure specie was due to a peculiar situation,[1] but others began to realize that immobility of money reserves accompanies every financial crisis. Since every bank under the old national bank system stood by itself, with no obligations

---

[1] It was thought by many that the Knickerbocker Company was deprived of specie by the great Wall Street bankers as a punishment for its daring to establish itself as an independent financial power. Others believe that the specie shortage was framed up in order to set in motion the conservatism which follows a panic and thus choke off the wave of reform which had been begun by President Roosevelt and the progressive wing of the Republican party. It is because of these suspicions that the panic of 1907 is often spoken of as a "manufactured panic."

to assist other tottering banks, it was quite possible that in one bank there were resources which would have saved the situation if they could have been mustered to the service of the needy concerns; but since every bank might itself become the object of suspicion and be the next to experience a "run," it was only to be expected that the minute the bubble of overconfidence was pricked by the failure of some big concern, each bank would begin to hoard specie. So the money resources of the country were scattered in hundreds of unconnected banks.

This cause of panics was eliminated almost entirely by those provisions of the Federal Reserve Banking Act which provide for the centralization of deposit reserves in twelve centers and for mobility between these centers in times of need.

Elasticity of currency. The second way in which the Federal Reserve Act operates to prevent panics and lessen crises is by remedying the inelastic money supply of the country. Now it may seem like a contradiction to say that inelasticity of money supply is a cause of panics when we have just pointed out that one of the underlying causes is the overexpansion of the money supply by means of credit. But there is no contradiction in these two statements. In the first place, it is evident that when the first prick in the bubble of faith comes, the increase in the supply of credit money stops at once; there is an instant decrease in the supply of available capital. Further loans are refused by banks, and all outstanding loans which are due are called in. Thus supply decreases at just the time when a further increase is necessary to cope with the situation. The second fact to remember is that when the panic of doubt and fear strikes into the hearts of men they no longer wish to accept money in the form of credit: they want instead a sounder measure of value—either hard money, which has intrinsic value, or else a paper money whose backing is as sure as the government itself. No panic can make such money worthless or even greatly depreciate it. But hard money cannot be increased in a short time, so the needed supply must come from sound paper money. We have seen that the only flexible paper money—the national bank notes—necessitated for their issuance 105 per cent backing in gold. Any bank which had sufficient gold to warrant note issue on such terms would have sufficient specie to meet an emergency, and there would be no object in sending its hard money to the Treasury and being allowed in return to put out 5 per cent less in bank notes. Inelasticity of currency was, then, a direct cause of panics.

The Federal Reserve Banking Act, by providing for an elastic but none the less sound currency, has wiped out this cause.[1] Even in the smaller cycles of activity occurring within each year, money tightness during planting and harvest has been remedied by the ease of increasing the currency.[2]

Curtailing unnecessary credit expansion. The Federal Reserve system has further contributed to the curbing of crises by its provisions for curtailing the excessive supply of credit in the months of feverish activity preceding the crash. The Federal Reserve Board not only sends out letters warning bankers to curtail credit but it may actually set the rate at which money may be lent for speculative purposes. This it did do several times in the years 1919 and 1920. By raising the rediscount rates, excessive speculation may be checked. If higher rates do not sufficiently decrease the amount of speculation, the Board may ask the bankers to confine their loans for investments to necessary transactions only. It may urge that no money be lent for speculation. Investment enterprises can be checked in the pre-crisis era by the Board's refusing to accept commercial paper for note issue which has been given to the banks as security for unnecessary loans. This proceeding was used in the spring of 1920. Bankers were, however, cautioned not to curtail loans for agriculture nor for necessary manufacture and construction. Legitimate business may thus continue while risky enterprises are starved out for want of funds.

[1] Review these provisions as discussed on pages 234 ff

[2] The new banking system is not able, however, to prevent failures of state banks, as was proved by the wholesale casualties during 1923–1924 in the wheat states. See *Literary Digest*, February 9, 1924, pp 11–13.

Prevention of Crises through Better Business

A panic in 1920 was averted not only by the operation of the Federal Reserve Act but also through the cooperation of speculators, business men, and the general public. All these groups of people must acquire sound business and financial knowledge and must put this knowledge into daily practice if panics are to be averted and crises mitigated.

How the speculator can help. Next to the banker comes the speculator in the matter of power to cause or prevent panics. To deprive him forcibly of the resources of the Federal Reserve member banks is not enough. Unless he is converted to a policy of wisdom, he will secure money elsewhere and continue to gamble. The ways in which the speculator may help to bring on panics are numerous. He must learn that to base his actions on "tips" or "hunches," or to buy on too small a margin, or to try to make a fortune overnight with only a small capital is to court ruin. Speculators with unscientific knowledge of conditions who buy on small margins in the expectation of winning great riches can, if there are enough of them, be the sole cause of a panic.

On the other hand, the speculator may serve as a great force in preventing panics if he has a goodly supply of capital upon which to work. It is impossible to lay down any rule as to what percentage of the value of the stocks bought should be paid for in currency or checks, and what percentage may be by the book credit given by brokers. Each transaction has its own safe margin,[1] and it is the duty of the wise speculator to study until he has learned what this margin is. He must realize that the big fortunes reputed to have been made on the Exchange were the result of vast expenditures of money and time. In order for the speculator to prevent critical conditions he must know when to buy and sell. This knowledge he can gain only through careful study of past transactions and present

[1] For an explanation of buying on margin see Hamilton's "Current Economic Problems," No 83

conditions. The study of the present must not be confined to open and obvious appearances When "everyone" is buying stock may be the very time to sell. It is upon unseen factors and future developments that the future depends. Wise speculators, seeing in "the good times" the seeds of a crisis, may do much to ward it off by curtailing their own buying and by selling their more hazardous stock. This must be done slowly and in advance of the crash, or of course it would operate to enhance rather than to mitigate the crisis. Slow contraction of credit and business will prevent sudden contraction, just as in a balloon a slow and guarded outlet of air at the opening will prevent a collapse following overinflation

The speculator may not only help to prevent panics but he may ward off periods of hard times. If crops fail, speculators will begin to offer high prices for future deliveries of foodstuffs. These high prices tend to decrease the present consumption and thus leave a greater supply for future use. In some cases a large future demand for certain commodities anticipated by speculators tends to encourage producers to increase the supply. Thus it is possible for intelligent speculation to prevent wide and abrupt fluctuations in prices. The top and bottom periods of the business cycle may be so compressed by the wise speculator that the rhythm of business activity will resemble a mildly undulating curve rather than a series of jerky changes.

The business man's duty. Business men may do their share in averting hard times and stabilizing business activity. They too should have accurate knowledge of finance. They should make it a part of their daily routine to study official reports of prices, of conditions in industry (especially steel), of the number of business failures per month, of the amount of railroad traffic, and of the conditions of labor. Their study should extend to bank statements in order to see the relation of trade to credit. If they find that there are more loans than deposits and that the specie reserve is low, then they must conclude there is inflation. The greater this inflation, the nearer there looms a crisis. No matter how prosperous the times appear to be, the wise business man will begin to liquidate. He will ascertain his individual or corporate indebtedness and pay outstanding debts before incurring others.

There are other things besides liquidation which the ordinary business man may do to stabilize industry. A study of most crises has proved that in almost every instance there has been overproduction in some lines and underproduction in others. In 1920, for example, there was underproduction of food, necessary wearing apparel, and building materials, while at the same time the market was swamped with the luxuries of jewelry, furs, rich cloth, fancy brands of soft drinks, and cinema films. Business men who are wise and willing to take precautions against the coming storm will turn from these surfeited industries to the manufacture of staples for which the demand is not so spectacular but more steady.

Knowledge of existing conditions does not usually point to a change in occupation, but it does make possible changes in business activity. In the period of overexpansion the wise man will curb his investments, purchases, and debts, on the other hand, in the days of depression which follow a panic he will have the courage to buy sound things at the low prices. He will let out contracts for construction and will not hesitate to begin new and staple enterprises. By his activity he will help to relieve unemployment, money tightness, and the psychological factor of discouragement and ultraconservatism. In other words, he will go slow when the rest of the world is traveling at a breakneck speed, and will shift into high gear when the others, less wise, have stopped to pull themselves out of the ditch or to find their way carefully along the precipice.

Coöperation of the public needed. The banker, the speculator, and the entrepreneur are not the only ones who have duties in changing the trend of business activity to a more moderately undulating curve. The laboring-man and the professional classes can help by their knowledge and wise actions. It is they quite often who precipitate a crisis into a panic. Someone has said that financial troubles are often due to the fact that "at particular times a great many stupid people have a great deal of stupid money." This money they invest foolishly in unsound schemes with the idea of making sudden wealth, or else they spend it lavishly on unnecessary luxuries. This creates an unhealthy demand and thereby an unwise and unbalanced production which can command abnormal prices. There should be some way of convincing the public that crises are partly the results of their own extravagances and miscalculations It is they who spend when they should be saving and borrow when they should be lending. It is they who mistake dangerous times for good times. It is their demands which establish unwise production and excessive expansion of credit.

Not only is the public largely responsible for the critical conditions preceding a panic, but its sudden loss of faith precipitates the crash. People yield to a mob impulse. Perhaps no amount of knowledge on the subject will completely prevent human beings from acting in mob fashion. It behooves us, therefore, to remove the conditions which motivate a run on a bank This means the establishment of wise buying, wise saving, and sound investment. When these become the habits of people at large the business cycle will be robbed of its peaks of apparent prosperity and its depths of real depression, and panics will be no more.

SUPPLEMENTARY READINGS

BOGART, E. L, and THOMPSON, C M Readings in the Economic History of the United States, pp 729–737 [Panics of 1873, 1884, 1907, and crisis of 1914]

BURTON, T. E. Financial Crises.

CARVER, T. N. Elementary Economics, chaps. xxv–xxvi.

HAMILTON, W. H. Current Economic Problems, Nos. 84. 97–117, 120, 122, 124–132.

MITCHELL, WESLEY CLAIR Business Cycles.

American Economic Review, Vol. V, pp 499–533

Annals of the American Academy of Political and Social Science, Vol. LXXXIX, pp. 234–246.

System, Vol XXXVIII, pp. 31–33, 204–209, 235–237, 1031–1035

SEARCH QUESTIONS AND PROBLEMS

1. From the current newspapers follow the stock-exchange price of several important industrial stocks for one week. Do the same for several staple commodities Report your findings.

2. What does the United States government do through the Post Office Department to check bubble companies?

3. What has our Federal government done to protect the people from foolish speculation? What has your own state done? Why are such protective laws called blue sky **laws**?

4. Do you agree with the distinction made by Harry J. Howland, in "The Twilight Zone" (Hamilton's "Current Economic Problems," No. 83), as to the differences between speculation and gambling?

5 Of what value are modern stock and produce exchanges? See Hamilton's "Current Economic Problems," No. 88.

6 What effect may irrigation and scientific farming have on crises?

7. Give special reports on the panics of 1837, 1873, 1893, and 1907 As far as possible secure data to prove or disprove the business-cycle theory of crises Sources for this are any financial history of the United States, F. L. Paxson's "The New Nation," (chap. iv), and Hamilton's "Current Economic Problems," Nos 96–132.

8 Give a special report on how a panic was averted in 1913, based on Hamilton's "Current Economic Problems," No 125. Why was it felt necessary to pass a new banking act after one panic had been so successfully prevented?

9 How many of the business barometers recommended by Wesley Mitchell in Hamilton's "Current Economic Problems," No 131, do the business men of your community study in order to keep posted on the trend of business conditions?

10 Why has the business cycle been more severe in America than in Europe? See Hamilton's "Current Economic Problems," No. 132

11. For the variety and amount of stocks for sale on the New York Exchange see the World Almanac for 1920, pp 512–513.

12 Write a theme of five hundred words on the phase of the business cycle which the United States is now in, basing your conclusions on evidence as to investments, profits, turnover, financial conditions, employment, etc, which you can secure from conversations with bankers and business men and from articles in the daily papers and weekly magazines.

CHAPTER XI

DISTRIBUTION

The first aim of any economic society should be the production of a large amount of wealth. . . . The second aim should be the just distribution of wealth.—Roscoe Lewis Ashley

General Principles

Distribution is the dividing up of the combined product of the four factors of production: labor, capital, land, and organization or management. It is no longer divided in kind, as in primitive times, but in money, the common denominator of value. Each of the agents furnishing a factor in production wants at least his fair share in the return; some want as much as they can get of it, irrespective of justice. Justice in distribution is a very obscure thing, less understood than perhaps any other phase of economic relations, and yet it is the very crux and center of economic life and the most fundamental problem of modern times. Men generally agree that there is something wrong with our present system of distribution; but what it is that is wrong, and how to remedy that wrong, it is hard to say. If only distribution could be made fair, many other problems would straighten themselves out easily, as a Chinese block puzzle arranges itself readily once the center key blocks are in place.

In the past, as a rule, the control of production has been in the hands of the agents controlling land and capital. These men paid out what they must to labor and kept all that was left. Frequently these agents controlled three of the four factors, and so received three of the four parts of the return, leaving to labor only what labor was able to demand in the way of wages. Consequently most of the widespread discontent with distribution is on the part of labor, which feels that it has been cheated out of its fair share. Of recent years, when

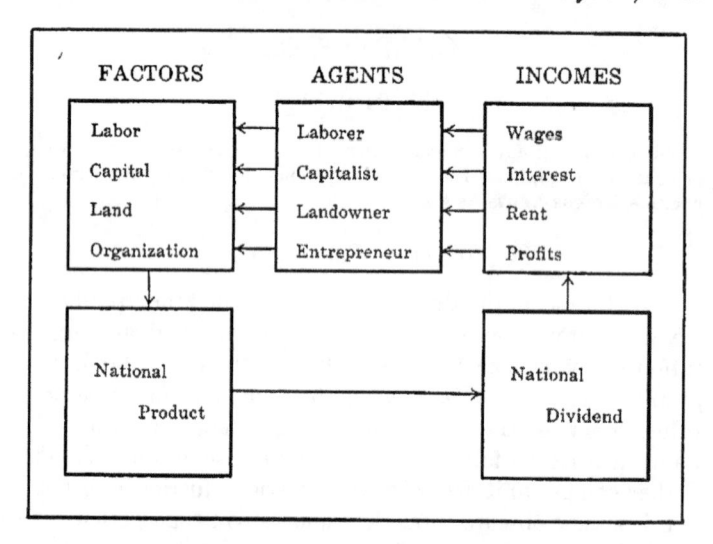

```
FACTORS          AGENTS           INCOMES
Labor       ←   Laborer      ←   Wages
Capital     ←   Capitalist   ←   Interest
Land        ←   Landowner    ←   Rent
Organization ←  Entrepreneur ←   Profits
     ↓                                ↑
National Product  →           National Dividend
```

DISTRIBUTION OF THE NATIONAL INCOME

The sum total of the production of any people is called its national product. This product is the result of the combination of the four factors of production; that is, labor, capital, land, and so-called organization. The national product when sold brings in the national dividend or income. This income must then be distributed to the agents who have furnished the factors for production. Wages go to the laborer for his work, interest to the capitalist for the use of his capital, rent to the landowner for the use of his land, and profits to the entrepreneur for his exercise of the organizing and risk functions. If one man furnish all four factors for an enterprise, he is a combination of laborer, capitalist, landowner, and entrepreneur, and as such he receives an income which — no matter what he or society may call it — is in reality a composite of wages, interest, rent, and profits

thinkers who are not laborers have developed a keen sympathy for labor, and when many people in every walk of life are seeking the principles which will enable men to reform the whole producing machine and make it just and socially profitable, the search for the laws of distribution has grown more and more earnest, and more and more general.

The attitude of labor. The natural attitude of labor, which sees itself living in poverty while the organizers and investors of industry enjoy much more of the goods of production, is that the employer has kept more than his share because he receives the return, and hands out the various parts of it to the agents in the form of wages, interest, rent, and profits. Labor says that the employer sets the price of the product and therefore determines its amount, and that he sets wages also and so determines the proportion received by labor. Recently, with labor practically controlling some phases of production, the high wages have given some color to this idea; it looks as though the controlling agent could have things all his own way. Therefore labor has subscribed in some cases to a theory that it should manage industry itself, thus combining management with labor, whereas in the past management has usually been combined with capital and land. In some places actual experiment of workingmen's management has been made. Very few workmen and far too few employers have attempted to find out what is known of the principles of distribution in order to answer the question in accordance with economic law. Any other answer is bound to be but a temporary expedient.

The principles of distribution. Now the principles governing a just distribution are not yet thoroughly understood, and good authorities differ widely about them; but as nearly as they can be stated at the present time, they reduce to these brief statements:

1. Distribution is not, under normal conditions, controlled by any one agent of production, but is the result of the comparative value of the factors contributing to production.

2. Factors, not agents, are rewarded; that is, the laborer is paid, but labor is paid for.

3. The market value of the factor determines its compensation.

DISTRIBUTION

4. This market value depends, with free bargaining, on supply and demand.

5. Wages and interest make up the cost of production. The surplus left after paying these two may be divided between rent and profits. When production is taxed, the taxes are included in the cost of production Production cannot be carried on for long unless the selling price equals the cost of production, but it may go on without meeting profits or rent.

6. At present distribution is based on the theory that all four factors of production share in the return Various changes are proposed which hinge on different theories, especially that of omitting one or more factors in the distribution

7. The more generally accepted programs do not propose to change the basic theory of distribution, but to readjust by various devices the present very unequal proportions of the shares.

8. Social and economic justice do not always coincide.

9. If the human worth of the agents of production be considered more important than the economic worth of the factors they contribute, then (1) the agent may be paid more than the market value of his factor, (2) this investment on faith in a future return seems, from the limited trials so far given, to bring about an increased value in the factors contributed, which eventually warrants the investment.

The assumption of free competition. The first thing to be kept in mind is that it is impossible to calculate distribution except under a system of free bargaining. Free competition and bargaining is the basic condition under which economic law works. It is the basis for justice; without it powerful agents may impose on weaker ones, and the workings of well-established laws may be so warped and diverted that it is hard to recognize them.

In the matter of distribution, for instance, under free competition the employer does not set wages, nor does he set the price at which his product is sold. That is done for him by supply and demand. Under such a system each agent receives what his factor is worth economically. The return may not suit the agent, but at least it is economically just. But if any one agent secures a monopoly, this economic justice is circumvented and the whole process bent out of plumb to favor the one agent who has secured the unfair advantage. An employer may, by combining with all other employers in his field, destroy the normal competition for labor, and so fix wages at a point below what they are really worth in a free market. A labor union likewise may by a closed-shop policy raise wages above what they are economically worth, destroying the normal result of competition for work. Any monopoly destroys the chance for economic justice, and so the first duty of all citizens who want to see justice come to industrial life is to secure economic freedom in production—to see that all producing agents, whether they contribute land, capital, labor, or organizing ability, compete in a fair field and receive their reward according to the actual worth of what they contribute. The absence of monopoly privilege of any kind is the first condition of just distribution.

Market value of the factor. Suppose that this condition of free competition is secured. Then each agent is paid according to the value of his factor in the entire cost of production. That value will not depend on the personal character of the agent, nor on his needs, nor on his ambitions, nor on his demands; it depends solely upon the value of what he gives toward producing the finished article, compared with what every other agent gives in added value to the product. *Factors, not agents, are rewarded.* A miserable, ignorant, dirty workman may do as good work as a refined, high-minded workman whose personal needs cry for higher wages than those of his less evolved brother; their wages will be the same. This is economic justice, although it may not seem fair to the man who is denied books and concerts and good clothes by his small wage. Economic justice gives its reward in proportion to the value of the contribution made to production.

The law applies to the entire field of production. The producing process is very complicated, and it is not possible to analyze it so as to know just how much of the whole is due to this workman, that machine, this dollar of capital, or that piece of land. The only measure there is of the producing value of the different factors is their market value, or what each costs. Thus, if the market value of labor is low, then the laborer will receive low wages; if the market value of capital is low, the capitalist receives low interest. Each factor gets its economic deserts, whether each agent receives his personal worth or not. And this market value, as already shown, depends upon supply and demand.

The effect of substitution. There is always some demand for each of the four factors, as each is necessary to production. But the proportion changes, for they may be used in varying proportions, as we have seen. As a result, demand for the factors is changed from time to time without a corresponding change in the total demand and supply of production. Suppose the demand for labor is high and the supply limited: labor has then a high market price, and wages are high. But if this continues long the entrepreneur, whose business it is to produce as cheaply as possible, substitutes capital for labor, perhaps in the form of machinery This lessens the demand for labor, and its market price goes down. So we see that the entrepreneur's power to substitute in production makes for an unstable and changing demand, its range limited only by the law of diminishing returns. When it ceases to be profitable to substitute capital for labor, the employer goes back to hiring more laborers. Then wages rise again, and interest grows less.

If the student finds, then, that in any specific case he studies, the laws given do not seem to apply, he should examine the conditions to see if any form of monopoly power or any kind of substitution is "queering" the working of the laws. The first condition is not legitimate, although it is very common today; the latter is fair and inevitable and tends to keep the balance in the world of production.

Wages. Now, in production, wages and interest must be paid, or the business is a failure. If nothing remains over with which to pay the landowner and the entrepreneur, the enterprise is said to be a marginal one; if something does remain over, this surplus of production is paid to land and management for their share. Wages and interest comprise the cost of production; rent and profits are paid from the surplus of production, and business may be carried on without them.

The Present System—Labor

Wages are that share of the returns of production received by the agent, the laborer, for his factor, labor.[1] They include all pay for work of whatever grade, including the routine management of business by entrepreneurs (often carried on hand in hand with their function of deciding business policy), the salaries of professional people, and the work of farmers on their own land. Wages are either money or real wages, but only money wages are discussed here; for since real wages depend so largely upon the spending wisdom of the laborer, money wages give the only fair measure for all labor of the same class at the same time.

Wages are paid either by the piece or by some time unit. The piece method allows workers to receive more for added industry, but sometimes leads to overspeeding. Progressive wages allow for a minimum guaranteed wage with additional amounts for increased or superior turnouts. Under scientific management the normal time for the performance of each task in the plant is first found, and the workmen are expected to make a daily turnout on this basis for a set daily wage. Then they are given bonuses (which sometimes run as high as 60 per cent of the basic wage) for all they accomplish in addition.

---

[1] See Marshall, Wright, and Field's "Materials for the Study of Elementary Economics," Nos. 187-191, and Hamilton's "Current Economic Problems," Nos. 272-280, 305.

High wages do not necessarily mean high labor cost. The amount and the quality of work turned out for high wages are often so far ahead of that secured for low wages that the cost to the employer per unit of production is less. His wage bill is higher, but his return is higher still, and the difference is the amount by which his labor cost has been lowered The economy of high wages has been proved by many entrepreneurs.

In studying the return to labor, each grade of labor must be considered separately, for the different grades do not compete with each other. If there be a small supply of plowmen and a large supply of bookkeepers, the wages of plowmen may run higher than those of bookkeepers, for each class of laborers receives the market value of its offering. *The price of labor in any one grade varies directly with the demand and inversely with the supply.*

Factors influencing the supply of labor. Now the supply of labor depends on many things. It is not so elastic as the demand. Its chief source is the natural increase of population through the birth of new workers, and an increase from this source is not effective for about a score of years If wages are not high enough to warrant an increase of potential workers, the supply declines In America our standard of living—the kind of living conditions under which people will rear children to carry on their work after them—is so high that native labor has had to be supplemented and largely supplanted by immigration.[1] The cost of producing another worker has been made more for Americans by the custom of educating children for a higher grade of labor. The final result is not so much an increase in the amount of the supply as a change in the composition of the different grades. The lower grades are less and less American in character; the higher grades less than formerly, but still mainly American.

In America there has been a steady upward movement in families as to grade of labor. The first generation is usually unskilled, the second slightly skilled, the third often greatly

[1] See Hamilton's "Current Economic Problems," Nos. 232, 235, 237.

skilled. During recent years, when the wages of manual labor became greater than those of the holders of "white-collar jobs," many college-trained men and other skilled workers shifted to the lower ranks. But this shift is never so rapid nor so great as that upward, for it involves many sacrifices of the by-products of skill in labor—shorter hours, social standing, comfort, and responsibility. It is not in line with the general trend of industry away from muscle power toward brain power.

The upward shift in labor is, however, limited by unwillingness to study, the expenses of higher education, limited native ability, and the artificial barriers to mobility set up by trade unions. As a rule an increase of machinery results in greater mobility, although not at once; and the bright worker may make this shift an upward one, especially as machinery is for him a stimulation to greater skill.

Other limits on the labor supply are the destructiveness of war, disease, famine, and plague. It is also kept down by late marriages and immigration laws, laws forbidding the labor of women and children, physical and mental deficiencies, and plain laziness. Geographical immobility often operates as effectively as an actual scarcity. Even with every help from labor agencies, labor is not so mobile as capital, which can be sent quickly and safely from place to place by mail or telegraph. The laborer and his labor are inseparable, and the worker thinks twice before he breaks social ties and tries his fortune in a strange place.

Limits upon wages. There are limits to the range of wages. If wages are higher than the productivity of labor—that is, if the cost of production is greater than the selling price of the product—the marginal producer has to go out of business; he is bankrupt. There are then unemployed workers who make an oversupply, and an oversupply lowers wages again. So wages do not go above the productivity level, or if they do, the mistake quickly corrects itself. On the other hand, if wages go below the cost of production of labor or below the line of the accepted standard of living, then the decrease in labor supply will eventually bring wages up again. So we have the law limiting the range of wages: *Wages do not, over a long period, exceed the productivity of labor nor fall below the cost of production of labor.*

Before passing to capital's share in the return, we should note the advantage secured to labor by the laws of our land. It is placed first in the order of distribution. The worker makes a contract with the entrepreneur for his labor, and this the entrepreneur is bound to keep. Wages must be paid before interest on borrowed money or profit dividends. If the firm fails, the law provides that wages shall be paid before any other creditor receives a cent. The worker has a "mechanic's lien" on the raw materials, machinery, and buildings. The sale of these properties usually covers the debt to labor.

THE PRESENT SYSTEM—CAPITAL

The agent capitalist receives interest for his factor, capital. If his capital be in the form of machinery or buildings, he is paid a return which is commonly known as rent, but which is not rent in the economic sense. It is not usually thought of as interest, as it is not expressed as a definite percentage of the value used; but it is still, for all that, as truly interest as the return on bonds; it is a premium paid for the use of capital.[1] Again, an entrepreneur who furnishes part of the capital for his enterprise receives interest from his invested money, although he commonly calls this return his "profits." Really only a part of the dividends on stock is pure profit; the rest of it is economic interest. In the case of preferred stock the dividends are usually so low as to be little more than interest.

---

[1] The rate paid for buildings and machinery is logically somewhat higher than that paid for money capital, for it must include replacement for the deterioration resulting from the use of this form of capital—the wear-and-tear decrease in value. It is really a return of part of the principal in another form. Money rarely deteriorates in this way, and when it does, the government makes it good. There is no need, therefore, to exact an impairment fee for money.

The demand and supply of capital. What determines the amount or rate of interest? Exactly the same control which regulates wages: market value, dependent on supply and demand. If much capital is offered for investment, interest will be low; if capital is scarce, interest is high. If demand is great, high interest is offered to attract capital into investment, if demand falls, interest falls with it. Demand for capital is great in a new or sparsely settled country, where there are many undeveloped natural resources. Capital is needed to cut forests, to dig mines, to build railroads, to stock farms, and to start factories When business activity is very great, and at times when money is very "tight," naturally the demand for capital is high. At times of labor shortage, when entrepreneurs plan to substitute machinery for too expensive labor, they will call for additional capital.

The supply of capital, as we have seen before, depends both on the amount of production and the willingness to sacrifice the present to the future—the saving ability of those who possess wealth. In old and settled communities where working and saving have been going on for centuries, we may expect to find a goodly supply of capital unless it has been destroyed by wars. Some people are notably thrifty, others spend foolishly[1] Such events as fires, tornadoes, floods, storms, and war decrease the stock. The San Francisco earthquake, the Chicago fire, and the frequent floods of the Ohio and Mississippi are examples of catastrophes that reduce the amount of capital and so raise interest rates. Many of these catastrophes are preventable. In general a low rate of interest indicates a normal, healthy economic condition in an old community; high interest rates indicate some upsetting cause. In a new community rates are normally higher.

The rate of interest itself influences the supply of capital. When rates are high, people save money that ordinarily they

---

[1] Look up the miracle of the woolen stockings in the trying years after 1871, when the French peasantry poured forth their wealth to pay the German indemnity demands.

would spend; when the rates fall, only the most thrifty continue to save. In the last Liberty Loans, for instance, the rates of interest were raised to induce people to save and invest who had not been persuaded by the lower rates of the first issues. *The rate of interest varies directly with the demand and inversely with the supply*

As with wages, there are upper and lower limits beyond which interest rates cannot go without setting into operation reactive forces. If the rate of interest becomes so high that the marginal producer of goods cannot afford to use capital and is forced out of business, the capital he has been using is set free for other use. This adds to the available supply, thus reducing the rates. On the other hand, the rate cannot go so low that the marginal investor, the last man whose capital is needed to supply the needs of business, is not willing to make the sacrifices of present enjoyment for the hope of future reward, for if this were to happen, the supply of capital would be less than the needs of necessary production, and the rate would rise accordingly. Thus the forces of supply and demand are equalized and a normal rate of interest established.[1]

The element of risk. The element of risk is a factor affecting the rate of interest quite aside from the general supply and demand of capital. If an entrepreneur undertakes a risky enterprise, he must offer a rate of interest higher than the normal to secure capital, since the supply for that particular enterprise will be short. Since frontier enterprises depend much upon the chance of booms, discovery of metals, government aid, and other uncertain contingencies, risk enters largely into the determination of rates there. European capital invested in America, and Eastern capital invested in the West, secure

---

[1] There are short-time loans, known as call loans, which bankers make to speculators and business men in emergencies. The rates vary from 1 per cent to 100 per cent and change rapidly within a few hours. Their rate depends upon the supply of cash reserves of the lending bank, not upon the amount of capital in the country; hence the variation and lack of normal rates based on the working of economic law. See Marshall, Wright, and Field's "Materials for the Study of Elementary Economics," No. 218, p. 775.

higher interest than at home because the investors consider that they risk entire loss of principal in sending their capital so far from old, settled conditions. When a rate higher than the prevailing norm is offered in any enterprise, the element of risk is usually present.

The Present System—Land

Rent is that share of the return which goes to the agent, the landowner, for the contribution of the factor land. No production takes place without this factor, although the amount used varies greatly, being large in agriculture and small in city enterprises as a rule. Existing economic theory grants land its share, based on the current value of the contribution made, but makes it wait until wages and interest have been paid; and business may go on even if rent remains unpaid, as we shall see later.

The economic rent of any enterprise may be masked under different names. A farmer who owns his own land does not separate the part of his return due to land from that which comes from his labor, or from his capital invested in machinery and seed, or from his profits resulting from good management. But the rent does form part of his return. Nor do factory owners always distinguish the part of the return owed to the factory site. The popular custom is to lump all the net return, after paying expenses, and call it "profits."

But all land used in production does not receive a rent return. Rent is paid only when the producer is able to produce goods at a cost below the market price. The marginal producer pays no rent. If he did, his cost would exceed the selling price, and he would be forced out of business. It seems strange on first thought that any landowner is willing to allow his land to be used without receiving a return for it. But let us examine the case in farming, where no-rent land is found most often. Suppose a renter has made a contract to pay so much rent for the land he uses, and the crops fail. If his landlord be well-to-do and merciful, he will release the renter from his contract, knowing that the renter has lost the interest on his own capital and much of the wages of labor in the venture. The land is here clearly no-rent land. But suppose the landlord sees fit to enforce his contract. The courts will support the landlord in enforcing a contract, and the renter must pay the amount out of his capital if he has any, or, failing that, sometimes with his labor. In any case the land is still no-rent land, it has not paid the rent, which has had to be made up out of capital or labor. If the land fails repeatedly to bring forth its rent, renters will stop risking the loss of their capital on it, the owner cannot rent it, and it is now acknowledged to be no-rent land. The renter who has capital will not knowingly use it in so risky an enterprise, for he can lend the money and be fairly sure of interest on it. If the owner of the no-rent land is wise, he will allow it to be worked without charge for a few years, knowing that soon it may be so improved through cultivation that the cost of producing crops will be below the selling price.[1] The renter is then no longer a marginal producer; he has a surplus and can afford to pay rent.

Differences in rent. But probably he can pay very little rent at first. When the land first begins to be worth paying for, it is called marginal land. As it produces more, it becomes worth more. In agriculture rent value is increased by fertility and nearness to good roads or railroads; in mining it is the richness of the mineral deposits and their nearness to the surface; in manufacturing it is nearness to water power, fuel, raw material supply, and markets; in business it is nearness to the city's center. These elements of "superiority" reduce to two: natural gifts and location. They are never the results of man's labor or of the investment of capital in them; the returns from such "improvements" would be economic interest. The demand

[1] This is, of course, providing that the soil really has in it the elements that feed crops. Much land in Kansas, Nebraska, and other Western states has had exactly this history. Today it produces rich crops, but fifty years ago it did not pay for its cultivation.

for land, and hence the rent it pays, is always greatest for those pieces which are "superior" because of natural gifts or location.

The demand and supply of land. The supply of land is very stable. It can be increased somewhat through irrigation, reclamation, and flood control, and is decreased very slightly through the loss by floods, sea encroachments, and earthquakes. For all practical purposes it is fixed, and so rent depends upon demand.

Demand is decided by the two measures of superiority, natural gifts and location. It is proportionate to the amount of superiority which the piece in question has over the poorest piece which it pays to use at all; that is, over the marginal piece. The cost of production (labor plus capital) of a bushel of wheat on poor land is more than the cost of production on an equal amount of good land; extra cultivation and better seed must be used on it to produce what the good land produces with less investment. Suppose one piece produces wheat at $1 a bushel, another at $1.25; the difference of twenty-five cents is the difference in productivity of the two pieces, and so the former piece is worth twenty-five cents more in rent than the latter, for every bushel raised.

But the greater productivity of a piece of land may be balanced by its distance from market; if the dollar-a-bushel land is so far from town that it costs twenty-five cents for drayage for every bushel raised, clearly the cost of production is equal to that of dollar-and-a-quarter land which is close to the elevator.[1] *The amount of rent is determined by location and by the superiority of the piece of land in question over that of an equal amount of marginal land.*

Rents not a cause of high prices. There exists an idea that high rents make high prices. The truth is that high rents exist only when there are high prices; they are the result, not the cause. Marginal land sets prices, for prices must equal the

[1] The effect on rent of railroads, street-car lines, and concentration of population is shown in Marshall, Wright, and Field's "Materials for the Study of Elementary Economics," Nos. 181, 183, 184.

cost of production on the poorest land which must be used to furnish what society demands. Every advance above this rent is a premium which the renter pays for a piece of land which will reduce his cost of production If he can manage to pay a little less than that difference, he makes something for his shrewdness—a profit. If society demands a great deal of the product in question, he may have to pay very high rent for good land. If he miscalculates and pays more than the productivity plus location of the land will warrant, he must make up the difference from his interest or wages. Now he has lost. Profit and loss, economically speaking, are both due to judgment in management.

The rent money actually demanded by landowners is based on productivity plus location, as shown above, but practically the amounts are not accurate measures of the worth of the land, because human knowledge and judgment are so fallible. A farm landlord demands and receives what the crop records of the past few years make him think his land worth, an unusual season may show him to have estimated wrong. If a man leases a house and gardens opposite a pleasant meadow for five years, he agrees to pay what the place promises in producing pleasure for himself and family; but if during that time a cemetery is opened in the meadow and he objects to the view, the rent value of his grounds falls in his estimation, and if he renews the lease it will be at a reduced price. But in a general way rents in money and kind follow the law of economic rents.

The "**unearned increment.**" The paying of rent is sometimes said to be an injustice because it is an unearned income. The landowners do not devote time nor energy to production as do laborers, nor do they sacrifice as do the capitalists. Hence some students think that rent should not be paid. Once more we must remind ourselves of a fundamental principle: factors and not agents are paid. The landowner may not have earned the income, but the factor land has, without land no production could take place. Nor could the payment of rent be eliminated from the process of production; men would always be willing to pay for the advantage of better land, even as employers after the Black Death were willing to pay for labor what the law prohibited. Economic law holds. The landholder, however, may be changed, and so the rent diverted. The State may confiscate all land with its rent, for instance, or society may take the rent from the landholder in the form of taxes. This course has been urged by single-tax adherents, and will be considered later.

The Present System—Organization

The agent, the entrepreneur, receives profits for his organization of the other three factors and for assuming the risk of the enterprise. The word is loosely used for the whole return of an enterprise after the payment of wages and overhead expenses, but profits are not properly credited until wages of routine management, interest, and rent have been provided for. The farmer and the small shopkeeper, who usually combine all four functions in one person, inaccurately call their entire net income their "profits."

Critics of the existing system of distribution object to profits as they do to rent and sometimes to interest. The answer is the same: brains used in organization make a real and an indispensable contribution, and so deserve a return. Brains are so rare that the man or woman who possesses them can demand a return for their exercise; if the return is refused, and the three remaining factors try to manage without brains or with such small supply as can be mustered from less gifted people, enterprise fails, wholly or partially. Then the other three factors suffer for their stupidity. Long human experience has shown that it pays all the factors to use managing ability to the utmost and to allow it all that remains after the other factors have been paid their market value.

Why profits are a necessity. It must be remembered that true entrepreneurs have two functions: organization of the factors and risk-assuming. If a man manages routine matters only, he is simply giving a high quality of labor to the enterprise, and should receive only wages—called in this case a salary, and perhaps very high. Men who manage cooperative creameries and large plantations often belong to this class; they have invested no money of their own in the enterprise, they do not decide the proportion of factors, they are not responsible financially for failure. A true entrepreneur assumes the responsibility of organization, not only in the beginning but daily as the business progresses and changes. He must judge what proportions of land, labor, and capital to use from time to time; he makes decisions, and if he decides wrong he is responsible. He must estimate future demand, supply, and markets. Clearly there are not many men adventurous enough to assume such responsibilities unless they have a chance—dependent on their own skill—of realizing something in excess of the salary they could get without risk of loss. Profits must be offered as a lure to enterprise.[1]

In recent years there has been much discussion of labor management of enterprise. Some men have thought that profits might be eliminated from the division of the return, or rather that they might be diverted to labor, by having the workmen manage their own labor and control the producing plants The profits would then be divided among the workers. The experiments so far made have largely failed, but this does not prove that the idea is wholly bad They have failed because men of small ability have led the movements, because mob power is liable to gain the control of affairs once the traditional forms are abandoned, and especially because management vested in committees and crowds tends to lose unity and authority. The fact is that good management depends on brains, and brains are not too common a possession. Landowners and capitalists know this, long experience has taught the "ruling" classes of society that efficient administration is centralized administration. Labor, less experienced, has not always seen that to vest

[1] Marshall, Wright, and Field's "Materials for the Study of Elementary Economics," Nos. 225–226.

management in the whole body of workmen is as foolish as to vest it in all the stockholders.

On the other hand, management of sections of the enterprise by labor is entirely practicable. Department superintendents are practically entrepreneurs when they are held responsible for the planning and output of their sections of the enterprise. Such men are paid more "wages" than the men they manage; and this "wage" is really composed partly of profits, which they have earned by assuming responsibility and by producing results that pay wages, interest, rent, and something over. A good administrator recognizes the varying degrees of managing ability possessed by his abler workmen, and makes them managers of parts of the enterprise, as he is of the whole. This is the form of labor management which is practicable and wise, since it resides in the men of proved ability, imposes responsibility, and is individualized enough to secure unity of action among the workers.

No-profit enterprises. But as the landowner may receive no rent, so the manager may have no profits. There are no-profit enterprises, as there is no-rent land. Profits come only when the enterpriser can produce goods below the market price. If the marginal entrepreneur were to take profits, he would have to make them out of an increased selling price. But since he is the marginal producer, his price is already the highest obtainable, and the addition of profits would make his price so high that no one would buy of him. Now if the enterpriser had known when he entered the business that things would go so hard with him, he would probably not have risked it; but once in, he goes on, hoping always that things will take a turn for the better. Much of his capital is invested in buildings and machinery, on which one cannot realize quickly or adequately. The entrepreneur is able to live on his interest and his salary as routine manager, and he prefers being independent to being a hired worker. His pride counsels him not to acknowledge that he has not succeeded. And, above all, his faith is always telling him that conditions will soon be better for him and that next year he can produce for less than the market price. "Hope springs eternal" in the breast of the marginal producer; there are always enough of him in the field, producing at or slightly above cost of production, to supply the market with goods at cost price—providing always that no monopoly exists. The more skillful or fortunate producers make a profit; therefore, we may say that *profit is the return for the exercise of superior managing ability and for assuming risk*, plus chance gains from sudden changes in supply and demand.[1]

Amount of profit. As rent depends on the superiority of the unit of land over the marginal unit, so profits depend upon the superiority of the ability of the entrepreneur over that of the marginal manager Some economists classify managers in four grades: those with genius, those with unusual ability, those with ordinary capacity, and those with marginal ability respectively. Managing ability includes organizing skill, knowledge of business conditions, scope of outlook and insight (the knowledge of those obscure influences which the ignorant lump together and call "luck"), and the clarity of thinking which sees the end from the beginning. No small part of business success may be due to judgment in the use of patents. Entrepreneurs have often been very unjust in their taking of profits from patents for which the inventors had been inadequately rewarded. When managers buy patents at a fair price or agree to pay a set royalty for their use, there is no injustice in their profiting by their good judgment or courage.

When competition prevails, profits are not a cause of high prices, but a result of them. For this reason it has been justly said that, barring monopolies, "anger at the great captains of industry on account of the pure profits which they acquire is not only groundless but insane. Rather it is the stupid and unsuccessful undertakers who deserve the blame for sinking capital and starving laborers."

[1] The rule of superior ability does not always hold, accidental factors may modify it For instance, a fire, a drought, or a tornado may destroy the profits that a skillful entrepreneur has earned.

The Apparent Conflict of Social and Economic Justice

We have seen that the present system of distribution does not exist because the employing class has selected it as the one most favorable to itself; it is a circle of compensation in which each agent receives pay for what he has contributed to the coöperative work of production, and is so enabled to live and to go on contributing. The process stops if any factor is wholly withdrawn, but if a factor is partially withdrawn another may be substituted for it within certain limits. The compensation is in proportion to the value contributed, provided a state of free competition exists.

It may also be said that the present system of distribution exists because men are allowed to bargain freely, contracting to accept not what they should have, but what they in their ignorance or helplessness are minded to take, for their contribution to production. It always exists with free bargaining and can be destroyed only by forbidding it.

The problem of social justice. But uncounted numbers of people who look about them and see that under the present system there are millionaires and paupers say decidedly that something is wrong. However just economically, the present system is unjust socially. It is not right that a small number of human beings should have so much that they are bored and burdened taking care of it and cannot possibly use a fraction of it in any useful way, while vast multitudes have not enough food and clothing and must see their children grow up without a chance for education and wholesome recreation. A society that allows children to grow up without a fair chance is an unjust society. Why is it that social justice and economic justice are so far apart? How can both social and economic justice be attained? Is it necessary to abandon the present system and adopt a new one, or can the present one be made to work for righteousness if reformed? If so, what reforms are needed? Who can make them?

There are several reasons for the present lack of social justice, owing to the "queering" of the distribution machine by several unfortunate conditions. If these conditions were removed, social and economic justice would at least more nearly coincide. One cause has already been mentioned—the absence of free competition. Under present conditions this works an injustice, some people think that combination and cooperation may in the future bring better results than competition, but this remains to be seen. In any case cooperation must be complete and secure full production if it is successfully to replace competition.

Altogether, the question of reformed distribution centers in that of dealing fairly and wisely with labor, which, up to the present time, has suffered more than any other factor from the blunders and sins of bad distribution.

The concentration of functions. Besides the unhappy effects of monopoly, extremes of distribution are due to the fact that three of the factors of production are very generally concentrated in the hands of the employer class, while labor can sell but one. Less than one fourth of the population controls most of the land, capital, and organization. Having land and capital, men are able to develop whatever abilities they have in the way of management; or having great gifts as organizers, men are able to win and accumulate land and capital. One group of people in our social whole (and that group a numerical minority) receives three returns, while the laborer has his wages only But there is no economic injustice here. Land and capital are not, as some people have said, "dead" factors, they function in a very live way in producing goods, and deserve their share of the return, irrespective of the human agents that control them Economically speaking, on the other hand, no worker deserves a living wage who does not contribute the worth of his living to the business of production; which explains the low wage of many workers. Sociologically speaking, the inefficient worker may have an excuse for his failure to do his share in really *earning* a living. It may be true that the worker has done his best and yet is not economically worth a share of the returns which will make him socially efficient.

Labor has other peculiarities which further complicate the situation. The supply is not so elastic as the supplies of other commodities, being slow to increase and still slower to contract. It lacks the convertibility of capital. If increased rapidly through immigration harmful social effects follow, both for old and for new workers.

Proposals for new systems of distribution. There are many suggested remedies, most of which propose to throw overboard the system of distribution on the basis of economic value and substitute an entirely new basis. Of those willing to include all the agents, one group wants the returns of production divided equally among all citizens.[1] This idea is preposterous; to grant a share of the return to babies, criminals, vagabonds, and the willfully lazy would only encourage shirking and fault-finding. To insure a return to all would soon set all but the most conscientious capitalists to using their capital in pleasure, while laborers stood idle in the assurance that they would not be allowed to starve.

Others, more reasonable, want distribution on the ground of personal desert in character. But who is to decide what makes desert? Ideas differ as the poles. This idea is so impracticable that it need not be seriously considered. Nor is the distribution on the basis of needs more sensible, for the same difficulty arises of deciding what needs must be considered first. If "needs" be limited to existence needs, then every creature would receive what would keep him alive, whether he worked or not. History has shown repeatedly the foolishness of supporting a population in idleness; it is a biological law that the creature, human or otherwise, which is supported without effort deteriorates. A pig fattened for market serves well enough for slaughtering, but it could not possibly take care of itself if

---

[1] Dr. King, in "Wealth and Income of the People of the United States," estimates that such a division would give each person in the country only $332 per year.

pitted against an animal which had been forced to fend for a living. Society in general agrees that the man or woman who has never had to make an effort for a living is an undesirable being. To increase the number of these undesirables by making a living dependent on needs alone and not the worth of one's contribution would be to bring on the physical and mental decay of the race.

Other proposals. Then there are those who would eliminate, or divert, one part of the return. About 1870 an economist named Henry George advocated the single tax as a remedy for social ills. He called attention to the "unearned increment" of value in lands which pay high rents because of the population on or near them, and claimed that landlords deserve a return less than any other agents, since they do nothing to earn their share. Mr. George did not propose that the increment be divided among laborers, but that it be appropriated for all society by means of a single tax on land, which should equal the economic rent of the land. This tax he proposed to substitute for the various taxes now paid and so lighten the burden of the poor.

Some socialists want to put enterprise into the hands of the government, thus eliminating private risk and making all bear the loss or share in the gain of bad or good management. The State would not need to be paid for taking risk; that would become part of its regular functions. The objection to this is a very pragmatic one; State enterprises, with certain exceptions, have not succeeded so well as private ones, and the losses which would have to be made up out of taxes would probably be greater than the gain from division of the profits from fortunate ventures. Probably as time passes and people gradually learn how to coöperate better and better, the number of enterprises which can be successfully operated by governments will increase. It is foolish to say that government operation of railroads, for instance, can never succeed, but it is just as foolish to plunge society into government ownership before people have learned to work together unselfishly and intelligently.

It is the sort of experiment that should be made gradually. Its success so far has been limited to local governmental units except in the case of two notably successful social undertakings: the public schools, managed by local and state agencies, and the postal system, controlled by the Federal government. Neither of these is run for profit, and both are services for which people are willing to be taxed. That a self-supporting business would continue to be a self-supporting business under government management remains to be proved.

The extreme (Marxian) socialist has a still more radical program. He would take not only rent but interest and profits also, leaving the returns from production to labor alone. He would "eliminate" rent and interest by establishing common ownership of land and productive capital. He would like to return to the primitive conditions in which land was as free as air. He says that the introduction of capital in great quantities into the productive process which came with the Industrial Revolution has divided society into two great classes, the upper one using its power to exploit the lower. Employers, he says, force wages down to a low level and keep them there because labor is helpless in bargaining, and deals in a commodity that is perishable and must be sold at once, without waiting for a favorable market. The only way to remedy this, says the extreme socialist, is to take from the employer class the sources of its power, or land and capital, and to give them to society at large. This would be done by instituting State ownership. Of course the "elimination" is not true elimination here, but a transference of the ownership, and consequently the earning power of land and capital, from private to State hands.

Anarchists differ from socialists in that they would vest all property in a local commune instead of in the national State. Syndicalism will have no State ownership of any kind, but wants each industry to be independent and managed by its own workers. The syndicalists, who are strongest in France, do not believe in trade unions, in legislative reforms, nor in revolutions, but advocate strikes, sabotage, and boycotts for the purpose of overturning capitalists.

A knowledge of the principles of economics reduces to absurdity the theory that the return should be appropriated by labor alone At the present time it is not held except by a minority of extremists, and it is mentioned here partly to show how far from the truth theorizers may go by not looking fairly at all sides of a question.

Improving the Present System

Most economists seem convinced that it is better to right the old machine of economically just distribution than to throw it overboard and install a system of distribution on some other basis. No new proposal seems both sound and practical. At least men may make those repairs and readjustments which are clearly indicated, whereupon it may be found that a system has been evolved that will yield an increasing dividend of social justice.

The most fundamental help must come from a change in the status of labor. This should spring, not from the theft of the share of some other factor but from an enhancement of the economic value of labor's own contribution. Since his share, like everyone else's, depends on the value of his factor, it behooves the laborer to make his contribution so valuable that it will deserve and therefore command more return. This can be done by believing and practicing the slogan "A full day's work for a full day's pay", by increasing skill through attending night schools, trade schools, and shop classes in regular schools, by correspondence courses in some subjects and by private study in others. Employers should, and in countless cases do, allow time for such study when good results can be shown in a reasonable time

But technical education is not enough to help labor out. Labor needs also general education for two reasons · without it, it is impossible to understand the most fundamental laws that underlie the relations of employer and employed; and with it, labor has a fluidity and mobility that enable it to adjust the proportion of workers in the different callings and to keep all at a point where demand and supply balance to give a living wage. Suppose there are too many coal miners, and mining wages are too low. if part of the miners are intelligent enough to transfer their services to farms, where laborers are almost always scarce, wages in both fields will support the workers fairly; but if the miners know nothing but their one trade and will not vary their work, they cannot expect a good wage— the oversupply of labor makes their factor a cheap factor.

But it is not enough that labor become more valuable. The laborer must also, if he is to become the equal of other agents, add to his one function other functions. The employer class wins a large return because it unites several functions in one agent. The laborer may do this too if only the adequate surplus over living expenses is assured. With a wage that allows saving he may buy land—especially government land, of which much remains unappropriated in the United States. Land unused and held for future profits may be heavily taxed to force it upon the market. Further to help labor a scheme of State loans might prove practicable. Workmen can be helped at least to own their own homes, with kitchen-garden and playground through building and loan associations. The same conditions exist as regards the entrance of the laborer into the capitalist class: he must earn more than he absolutely needs to live on.

But many workmen will not save money. Hundreds of workmen saved their first fifty dollars for investment when the Liberty Loans added patriotism to thrift as a motive, and people began to feel sensitive to public opinion if they did not save and buy a bond. And yet the rate of interest on other safe bonds is higher, and there are plenty to be bought. Every man who owns a fifty-dollar Liberty Bond and cashes the coupons as they fall due is a capitalist. When each laborer has a pile of such bonds, or pays rent to himself for his house and garden, he will find that the advantage of contributing more than one factor to the production machine may be enjoyed by labor as well as by capital.

But at this point the size of the "if" conditioning this rosy state of affairs confronts one. Labor may do all this, providing it is intelligent and thrifty *and has a living-and-saving wage.* But what of the laborers who do not earn such a wage or who, by some trick of monopoly control, are not paid what they earn? Some employers have solved the problem by paying their employees more than they were economically worth. Knowing that their contribution was not worth, say, five dollars a day, they nevertheless paid five dollars a day, setting certain conditions as to personal improvement in the laborers; that is, on faith they invested an extra, unearned wage in their labor, hoping that some day the labor would be worth what they paid. And they have not been disappointed Men will do much for money, they will even earn it The human agent in whom other men had faith has justified that faith. Money that was at first borrowed, so to speak, from profits or interest, to be added to wages, soon becomes actual wages, the return earned by the increased value of the factor contributed. But it must be observed that incentives were held out in these successful trials to make the quality of the agent and the factor higher. The high wages were not a permanent misrepresentation of the value of labor: they were an encouragement, an effective proof of the confidence that capital had in labor's good sense and honesty; and labor, which for so many generations had no such courtesy and faith shown it, responded nobly and generously.

Varying methods of wage increase. The form of the advance in wages varies. It is common to pay bonuses for extra skill, regularity, or long service. One company gives its employees bonuses of 5 per cent of their wages if they have worked every day in the month, 4 per cent if they have missed one day, and 3 per cent if they have missed two days. Another concern gives a 5 per cent bonus to all who have been in its employ five years,

4 per cent for four years, 3 per cent for three years, and so on. The most common bonus is for extra-quality or additional output. The bonuses based on time of service may be unearned and so have been thought unwise by many, but those for output have no such objection. The bonus has, however, sometimes been used to speed up production, with the extra returns going into the form of entrepreneur's profits altogether, because the bonuses are dropped, while the acquired speed and skill are still demanded for the old wages.

Profit-sharing. Many employers offer stock to their employees, sometimes at reduced rates or on time. But the most popular way of helping workers to become two-factor agents is profit-sharing. There are many methods, differing on the following points:

1. *Time of sharing:* annual or semiannual.

2. *Amount:* All the earnings of the company after providing for wages, interest, and sinking fund; or the surplus after paying set dividends on outstanding stock. A large Boston department store divides the earnings of the company into two equal parts to be distributed equally among shareholders and employees.

3. *Those who share in the division:* All employees, or only those listed on an honor roll, dependent upon length of service (six months to five years) or efficiency of work. Two Massachusetts concerns, one a manufacturer of woolens, the other a public-service corporation, include only the workers whose work is satisfactory in amount and quality. Henry Ford goes a step farther and refuses to include any man who will not give up vicious habits of drink or drugs and whose family will not adopt cleanly, decent habits and find decent places of abode.

4. *The basis of the shares received:* This may be the unique form originated by Henry Ford, whereby every employee has a sum of money called profits added to his weekly earnings sufficient to bring the two combined up to at least five dollars a day. The smallest wage-earners may thus receive the largest "profits." Or the "profits" may be simply a percentage of the

wage of each worker, or it may follow the plan of combining wage and output for the basis

5 *The form of the shares·* A Philadelphia company manufacturing soaps pays straight cash; other firms combine cash in various ratios with stock. A manufacturing company of Evansville, Wisconsin, gives 15 per cent in cash and 85 per cent in stock. The laborer has now become an entrepreneur; he too is risking and earning profits on his venture in the form of stock dividends on his share. He has become a partner in the business and sees that his employer and he have interests in common

Some employers who have tried profit-sharing have been disappointed in the results. They say that laborers do not appreciate the help given them, and they ask why they should sacrifice to give something that their workers do not really want. Many workers will not trust their employers' motives, and accuse them of underhanded schemes for furthering their own ends under a pretense of brotherliness—which means, of course, that labor has been kept ignorant and resentful for so many generations that it cannot believe in a spirit of fairness when it shows itself. Again, workmen have defeated the purposes of increased wages by spending their profits in cheap automobiles and other foolish and extravagant things. They have not grasped the opportunity to become landowners and capitalists, they have spent large wages lavishly and are as poor as ever when hard times come But a class of people which has never had money enough to develop a tradition of thrift cannot be expected to learn saving habits in a year or two of prosperity This is no reason for throwing the whole experiment overboard; it is a reason for patience and for the propaganda of thrift.

The employer as well has made some blunders that made profit-sharing experiments fail, he too is inexperienced in the more generous treatment of labor Perhaps (noting, for instance, that one of the first companies to try profit-sharing has had no labor trouble in more than thirty years) an employer adopts the scheme for the purpose of quieting labor unrest. In such cases there is warranted suspicion and often failure, actual interest in the welfare of the men is lacking, and labor wants justice rather than charity.

Other problems remain to be solved in the practical working of profit-sharing schemes. Economists have objected that it is impossible to distribute the profits on a strict basis of deserts. This is true; but some firms have used boards of apportionment with very satisfactory results. The objection that because of the shifting habits of labor profit-sharing firms may find quantities of their stock held by employees scattered about in other plants is answered by the tendency of workmen to stay with the firm in which they hold stock.[1] Some firms have found that their employees are too ready to sell the stock they have earned, and so have imposed the condition that the employee shall resell to the company in case his stock must be disposed of. Premiums for retention of stock for a given number of years may be paid. One company that has succeeded well with profit-sharing has the stock left in its hands in trust, the laborer holding receipts. In fact, there are none of the present defects in the schemes for holding out added incentives to labor to earn a greater return, and to add to itself other functions in production, which cannot be adjusted with patience and experience. And there are none which do not improve upon the system of paying labor nothing but its actual economic worth; for labor, given a social square deal, tends in a majority of cases, if not always, to justify the faith put in it.

Summary. The return from production is divided among the factors in proportion to the economic worth which each con-

---

[1] In the Nelson Manufacturing Company of Edwardsville, Illinois, over a fourth of the plant is owned by present employees. When, in 1910, Mr Nelson gave a party to celebrate the coming of age of the company, he found that there were so many employees who had been with the company ten years that he had to raise the service qualification to fifteen years in order to accommodate the guests in his home.

After Henry Ford adopted his scheme of profit-sharing, which is really akin to bonuses, the number of "floaters"—that is, those who work only for a week or two—fell from 55 per cent to less than 5 per cent

tributes. Labor and capital are paid first, because when business fails to pay them bankruptcy results. Wages and interest make the cost of production; when prices fall below the marginal cost of production the marginal producer stops producing. Supply being less than demand, price rises. Therefore price is always high enough to pay wages and interest. Only when the cost of production is below the market price are the landowner and the entrepreneur paid their shares. There will be a surplus over wages and interest only when land and management are superior to the land and management of the marginal producer

The present scheme is unsatisfactory because (1) it is hindered in its workings by the lack of free competition from many causes, and (2) economic justice for the factor may not produce social justice for the agent. The first deterrent is best remedied by government control of monopolistic combinations. The second condition is best remedied by practically lending the agent laborer additional pay from the three better-paid factors, so that he may improve his condition and become really worth a greater return Such an advance has justified itself repeatedly by making labor worth more and by enabling the laborer to unite in himself several of the productive agencies.

The whole problem of distribution remains, after much study, one of the most difficult confronting men. Every member of society owes it to the world not only to add as much as possible to production but to do his part in helping to meet "the primary and most urgent need of our time—the attainment of greater justice in distribution."

SUPPLEMENTARY READINGS

Bullock, C J. Elements of Economics, chap xii
Carver, T N Principles of National Economy, chaps xxxiii, xxxiv, xxxvi–xxxix
Hamilton, W H Current Economic Problems, Nos. 352–353, 366, 370, 374.
Hayes, E C Introduction to the Study of Sociology, chaps vii–x
Marshall, L C., Wright, C. W , and Field, J A Materials for the Study of Elementary Economics, Nos 224–227, 236, 258–267.

Quarterly Journal of Economics, Vol XXXIV, pp 114–137, 138–160.
 [Theory of profits]
"Two Years of the Rockefeller Plan," in *Survey*. Vol. XXXIX, pp. 14–20
"The Cooperative Movement," in *Independent*, Vol LXXIV, pp. 357–358.

SEARCH QUESTIONS AND PROBLEMS

1. How do the contributions of the legislator and the policeman enter into the making of a pair of shoes?

2 Show how prices affect the problem of distribution.

3. Why is the problem of distribution so much greater now than before the Industrial Revolution?

4. From the Statesman's Yearbook find out the birth rate in the United States, Great Britain, France, Japan, and Germany. What deductions as to standards of living can you draw from these statistics?

5. Find out what executive department the Bureau of Immigration is in. What does this show?

6 Discuss the following statement: "The employer's interest is in money wages, but the laborer's interest is in real wages."

7. Can you see any objection to a minimum wage set by law?

8 Why should organized labor object to the wage methods used in scientific management?

9 State for which position you should expect to receive greater wages, and why· (1) a fast-train conductor or a motorman, (2) a skilled surgeon or a physician; (3) a digger in a mine or on a road

10 Make a table showing all the different factors which tend to limit the supply of skilled and of unskilled labor.

11. Can you think of any production which does not require capital?

12 What money wage did a cook or general servant earn when your parents were young? What does such a helper earn now? Why? What general truths about labor does the "servant question" illustrate? Why do most women prefer other work to domestic service?

13 Why is the interest rate almost twice as high in northwestern Canada as it is in the eastern part of the United States?

14 If a community gains the habit of storing a surplus, what effect will its new precaution have on interest rates?

15. State to what extent, if any, the income received from the following is to be called interest (1) a United States bond, (2) a share of common stock in the United States Steel Corporation; (3) an apartment block, (4) a rented piano.

16. What would happen to the prevailing rate of interest if all immigration to the United States were prohibited?

17. Find out from some yearbook how much money was raised in the United States by the five Liberty Loans. How many people subscribed? What was the average subscription? What would the average have been if everyone had bought an equal share throughout the country? Is it as great as the average of money spent on cinemas, candy, or tobacco in one year? Was this money simply shifted from bank and savings deposits, or was it saved from what had formerly been spent? See *Literary Digest*, May 31, 1919, p 124.

18. Why were the people of the United States willing to lend so much to their government at $3\frac{1}{2}$ per cent and 4 per cent interest, when they could obtain twice that on other loans? Does the economic interpretation of history explain this?

19. Why are the rates of interest paid by local transportation corporations higher than the prevailing rate of interest in their localities?

20. In the *Outlook*, Vol CXXI, pp 742 ff, T H Price describes a new method of wage-setting. What do you think of it? See also *Literary Digest* for September 4, 1920, pp 83–84.

21. Does your state have usury laws? Are they wise and just?

22. Labor Banks are described in the *Literary Digest*, February 3, 1923, Vol LXXVI, p 10, the *Nation*, November 14, 1923, Vol CXVII, p 545, the *Atlantic Monthly*, June, 1923, Vol CXXXI, p 815, *Collier's*, June 30, 1923, Vol LXXI, pp. 5–6, and the *New Republic*, December 19, 1923, Vol XXXVII, pp 89–91. What effect will this movement have on the distribution problem?

CHAPTER XII

SOCIAL CONTROL

> Freedom is valuable only as a means to an end. That end is the liberation of the powers of all men equally for contributions to a common good No one has a right to do what he will with his own in such a way as to contravene that end It is only through the guaranty that society gives him that he has property at all —THOMAS HILL GREEN

MODERN DEVELOPMENT

The theory. Society permits and approves of private ownership and management of property, because it has been found that more and better production results from this form of control of wealth than from communal holding, which was the custom with some tribes in primitive stages of civilization. Private ownership permits men to carry on a competitive struggle for their own betterment, and this struggle develops ability and a surplus production which react in a good way upon society as a whole. All society is better off because its ambitious, capable members are able under a private-property régime to make the best and the most of themselves; but if the individual members who have been helping society through their freedom use that freedom in a way that hinders social betterment instead of helping it, then society, which gave the right of private property, has the right to take away the privilege it gave. By this time (since all such processes take place through centuries of slow change) the individuals who have the property have entirely lost track of the fact that it was originally allowed to them by the social group, and they do not propose to give up to the group what they have. So there is inevitably a struggle between these "vested" (that is, established) interests and the social group, which proposes to take back what it gave *conditionally.* When the social group has won back as much of its original control or ownership as it needs for the purpose of insuring the supreme object of human betterment, it stops, leaving the greater part of property still under private control and ownership.[1] If society takes too much, it destroys the incentives for production; if it takes too little, it may have an increased material production but a reduced human product. *The problem of society is, then, to find the happy mean between pure individual control and complete communal control, neither of which by itself has proved successful in practice.*

The right of eminent domain. The right of eminent domain is one of the oldest of the ways in which social control has been exercised. This is the right of the government to take for itself the land which it needs for its enterprises, whether the owner wants to sell it or not. In our country the government must pay a fairly appraised price to the dispossessed owner for the property taken; otherwise this practice would be simple confiscation [2] The right is exercised when land is needed for the building of railroads, for the erection of public buildings, or for any other cause from which a general public profit may be expected.

The period of class control. Other forms of social control came slowly in the modern world, except as they might happen to coincide with kingly or aristocratic control. At certain periods, indeed, there were minute and galling restrictions on freedom of enterprise, these were not made by society for its general good, however, but rather by a privileged group for the sake of increasing its own wealth and power. Then Adam Smith wrote his epoch-making "Wealth of Nations," effectively puncturing the essential tenets of the mercantile theory. The

---

[1] The text must not be taken too literally here For instance, much of the property of European landholders was seized by force during the Middle Ages; society did not at that time grant it, but rather submitted to being robbed. The statement refers more to the earlier time when private property was first granted to individuals—the times referred to in Chapter II.

[2] See Amendment V of the Constitution.

business men of the incoming order of factory production welcomed the freedom of the laissez-faire theory. For about a quarter of a century they were allowed to carry on their enterprises without serious interference, employing whom they would, paying what they must, and resorting to any device they pleased for reducing the cost of production.

The period of no control. All students of English history know the shameful story of those years of laissez faire: the employment of "apprentice" children, the inhuman treatment given them, the unspeakable conditions in the mines, and the use of women in the mills at starvation wages is a tragic phase of the early nineteenth century. Early and lonely voices of protest were unheeded, but finally the reformers won. The "free" employers were forced to yield to a new era of social control, in which they carried on their business according to laws and regulations as in the old days of the mercantile theory. The difference lay in the source of the new control and in its motive.

Social control for social welfare. For during the nineteenth century there was growing up a social consciousness that recognized the duty of society to its members. It held that good and happy men, women, and children are the prime interest of mankind, and that society prospers only as it secures the welfare of its members. It did not propose to interfere with the freedom of business for the sake of piling up a gold surplus, or controlling colonial trade, or building an empire, but it would do whatever might be needed to protect its human materials, the stuff of which the future is made.

This attitude grew in acceptance very slowly. Of course it met a strong resistance from those who had profited by the old order—the factory-owners, who had exploited orphan children; the mine-owners, who had built fortunes out of human misery and disease, the ship-owners, who had winked at the kidnaping of sailors, and all the women and children who had profited financially by these acts of industrial piracy. From the day when manufacturers became indignant at Elizabeth Barrett Browning's "Cry of the Children" to the present day, when they oppose a Federal child-labor law and expensive safety devices, the vested interests of the old order fight the welfare schemes of the new

The eternal struggle between conservative and liberal. The fight takes every conceivable form. It may manifest itself in the quiet contempt of prosperous, authoritative, and influential people against the "wild" schemes of idealists; it may be done by quiet tax dodging on the part of someone who objects to paying his share for social enterprises; it may be the skillful legal fight of intrenched interests against welfare legislation; or it may be a clever manipulation of supposedly liberal forces in the real interests of selfish property-owners. Good will is not strong enough by itself to combat the selfishness of property-owners who propose to use their property not for social welfare but solely for their own interests; good will must call to its aid the keenest intellectual service, the funded experience of years gone by, and the united support of the people who have at heart the good of the race.

Limiting the Right of Contract

The present economic order is built on two things the right of private property and the right of freedom of enterprise. The first puts material things into the hands of individuals (or corporations, which, of course, act in business like individuals), and the second gives to every land-owner, laborer, capitalist, or entrepreneur the right to dispose of the particular factor which each has to sell, as he sees fit. But in each case the freedom which theoretically exists is limited by law and custom For instance, a man is supposed to own and control a house and lot on a good residential street; but if he chooses to turn his property into a glue factory, he very soon finds out that society has a right to control his property rights. A man is supposed to be able to sell his labor freely to whomever he will, for any purpose whatever; but if he hires himself to a counterfeiter, he may be put into prison for exercising his "right," since it interferes with social welfare. In actual practice there is no such thing as *absolute* human freedom, there is freedom only for those who choose to work in accord with social welfare. Unrestricted freedom, without regard to its effects upon society, exists only among the lowest savages, if it can now be said to exist at all.

Freedom of contract. With these two rights there goes the contract, which is the record of the bargain struck between "free" bargainers. A contract between the buyer and the seller of a house which changes owners is called a deed; the contract between employer and employee, which may or may not be written, is a trade agreement There are numberless kinds of contracts, to suit the endless variety of businesses carried on by the "free" bargainers, privileged to make their own agreements as to the terms upon which they will buy and sell the things in which they deal

Contracts are either absolute or conditioned. The absolute contract is one in which the bargainers decide between themselves just what their transaction is to be; no one interferes with their "freedom of contract" in any way. The conditioned contract, which is by far the more numerous kind, is one in which the parties are limited as to their bargaining by society. Society does this through its organized agency the government, which agrees to enforce contracts, but with certain exceptions. It excepts contracts which would, if carried out, break laws. The laws are a measure of society's feeling of responsibility toward itself and its children. Thus, fifty years ago no one interfered with a woman's right to contract to work twelve hours a day, society did not then realize that the number of hours a woman works per day has a social significance. But today the employer who contracts with a woman to work twelve hours per day cannot enforce his contract by law in any state which has adequate labor laws, because such hours affect the health of the workers and so indirectly affect the quality of the future citizens of the nation, the children of these workers.

Of course there is the greatest difference of opinion as to how far society should go in limiting the right of free contract among its people. Many laws passed are afterward held unconstitutional by state or national Supreme Courts. The principle supposed to be followed is that individual freedom goes as far as social welfare will allow and no farther. One finds that a supreme court has upheld the freedom of women to work over eight hours, in Illinois, of bakers, to work over eight hours in New York; of laborers, to assume the whole risk of injury while at work; of employers, to make unlimited deductions from wages, and of mine-owners, to screen coal, mined by weight, before weighing it as a basis for setting the wage. Such decisions indicate a narrow view of what will hurt society; but when New York limits women elevator operators to nine-hour days, and forces the employer to give forty-five minutes' luncheon hour and wash-room facilities, with no night work, it takes a very liberal view of what is necessary to social progress.

Modern social control had its origins, as we have seen, in England. In the United States the resentment toward governmental control inherited from Revolutionary days, together with the economic conditions of a new land so rich as to offer plenty to all without exploitation of the poor, produced an unusual freedom of enterprise in all fields. This was in the early years. But gradually, as labor became more plentiful and land more scarce, it became necessary to make laws for the protection of labor and of the poor—laws referred to elsewhere.

Another set of laws controls wealth for the benefit of consumers. These include pure food and drug laws, especially the fairly effective ones passed about 1906, when the country became really aroused concerning its food and medicines; laws and inspectorships to regulate and standardize weights and measures, which make dishonest dealers afraid to cheat too grossly, and all the many safeguards thrown about professional services, usually by private or semiofficial associations.[1] There has been as yet little control of the businesses of making clothing, building materials, or other things which do not greatly or directly affect health.

Prohibition the latest control. The legal prohibition of the manufacture and sale of intoxicants, which is now part of the United States Constitution, is the most radical and far-reaching exercise of the right of social control that has ever been put into law by any nation. Imperfect as enforcement is in some parts of the country, the results have amply proved that this bold move is justified by its increase in human efficiency and happiness.

The growth of social control may be traced in many fields, but in none is it clearer than in the great business of transportation. If we take this as an example we shall see how society passed from one degree and method of control to another, and is still laboring with the problem of how much, what kind, and by whom.

THE GROWTH OF A NEW IDEA

Early control over transportation and communication. The roots of this control go far back of the days of railroads to times when wagon roads were the only paths for travel. The making of roads was one of the first functions of organized, formal governments. Long before men thought of forming any theory to justify it, they had the custom of taking from privately owned land a narrow edge for a public highway. Indeed, by the right of eminent domain they might cut a road straight through a man's land. The establishment of communi-

---

[1] The rules of medical associations, for instance, which tend to protect the public from ignorant and conscienceless quacks, largely take the place of legal restriction, and in some states the examination and certification laws are strict enough to make the path of quacks a thorny one. In general, however, society has not as yet adequately protected itself from ignorant and dangerous practitioners of various kinds, who exercise their "freedom" at the risk of human life and health.

cation between social groups, or between individuals, seemed naturally to be a social function, since it concerned everyone, and the keeping of these means of communication open and in good condition followed naturally. So road-making has been an activity for which society appropriated wealth,—sometimes money in taxes, sometimes labor for repairs and improvements.[1] And from the making of land roads for common use, it is a logical next step to waterway improvement—dredgings in shallow rivers, improved harbors, jetties, and all sorts of undertakings that make water travel safer and more profitable.

It is felt that the means of communication should be under social control not only for actual travel but for the sending of messages as well. Recognition of this principle led civilized nations to take over the postal service more than a hundred years ago and to add to the sending of letters, in recent years, the parcel-post system, which carries parcels for less than did the express companies. All this carrying is done for the public at so low a rate that the post office rarely pays for itself; the deficit is met by taxation, and the tax on private wealth for a business carried on by the government for all the people is justified by the social service of the postal system.

Although everyone realized the right of society to control the roads on which society traveled, no one thought in the early days of our nation of extending social control to the vehicles that carried goods or human freight over those roads. Such vehicles were distinctly private property, and to control them would have seemed, to our grandfathers in their youth, like impertinent interference with freedom of private enterprise. Of course the same principles applied to canals and railroads when they appeared in the 40's and 50's.

Evils of railroads. Railroad-building became a rage over the country, and east of the Mississippi more roads were built than the business of the country at that time needed. Conse-

---

[1] For the Federal road law see Magruder's "American Government," p 13, *American Review of Reviews*, Vol LIV (1917), pp 275-280, and Yearbook of the United States for 1917, pp 127 ff.

quently there was fierce competition between roads, which reduced their rates below the actual cost of service in their efforts to attract patronage Of course this loss had to be offset in some way, and it was made good at the cost of those parts of the country in which there was no competition. Thus, freight might be sent at a ridiculously low rate between Chicago and New York, which had several connecting roads, but the small towns in Wisconsin or Illinois which had but one road to Chicago made up the difference. This seemed very unjust to people.

Rates based on what the traffic will bear. This cutthroat competition in the eastern part of the United States was partly done away with after the panic of 1873. Moreover, when the poorer and shorter railroads failed and were bought up by the richer lines, there grew up pooling arrangements in the East. These tended to raise rates even more than the consolidation of railroads, without giving an equal improvement in service. The old cutthroat, below-cost rates were now supplanted by rates "as high as the traffic would bear." In the West, where the roads remained few in number, the old high rates continued. Everywhere the farmers began to cry out that the cost of transporting their crops to market swallowed all their return. It was under the stress of a strong resentment toward the railroads, which had been built largely from the proceeds of land grants from the public domain, that the farmers began to talk of social (that is, government) control of railroads.

The granges. The Western farmers were organized in local nonpolitical lodges calling themselves Patrons of Husbandry. These local granges were united in a national association, the National Grange, later identified with the Farmers' Alliance. The movement was most popular in Illinois, Iowa, Wisconsin, Minnesota, Kansas, and Nebraska, and when it had reached its height, in 1874, it numbered over a million and a half men, grouped in about twenty thousand granges. These farmers, talking over their affairs at their meetings while the women prepared supper, decided that railroads were not private businesses that could do as they pleased, but that they were quasi-public enterprises, affecting the public prosperity and therefore rightly subject to public control They called them common carriers, that is, carriers open to general public patronage and therefore to public regulation They said the railroad had no right to make a secret rate to a large shipper, charging him less than small shippers were charged. They said that railroads had no right to help one town by low charges to its shippers, and to hurt another by maintaining a high rate for goods shipped to and from it.

The Granger laws. As the granges often sent their members or their lawyer friends to the state legislatures, between 1871 and 1874 they secured a series of state laws known as the Granger laws, which established this new attitude toward railroads. The Eastern capitalists called them confiscation laws, but East and West have now come to accept the principle they represented—that of social control of common carriers.

Wisconsin passed a law which fixed railroad rates in 1874. Illinois, in 1870, had established a state railway commission with power to fix maximum rates and to control administration Other states followed with other control laws, all showing the weight of farmer resentment toward the Eastern-owned, "profit-grabbing" railroads. Most of these laws were very crudely framed, as is likely to be the case when amateurs try their hand at lawmaking. The railroads, with the help of skilled lawyers, attacked them at once, and they ran the gamut of court trial until they reached the United States Supreme Court. In 1877 this final authority gave the important Munn v Illinois decision, which said that such quasi-public businesses as railroads are "subject to the power of the body politic to require them to conform to such regulations as might be established by the proper authorities for the common good." Thus was the principle of control acknowledged by the highest authority on American law, although most of the Granger laws themselves were in 1887 declared unconstitutional.

Federal Control of Railroads

The question then arose, Who shall administer the control of railroads? To leave the matter to legislators would be awkward, slow, and often unfair. The state commissions helped a little, but their powers were often hampered by the fact that railroads run through more than one state, and can annul the effect of regulation in one state by their powers in another. The national House tried to apply the principle of control to interstate commerce in 1878, but the bill was defeated in the Senate. Finally, after much agitation, the Interstate Commerce Act was passed in 1887, creating the Interstate Commerce Commission.

Some of the regulations of this law were noteworthy. It prohibited extortionate rates, and forbade unreasonable discrimination in rates between shippers and between towns. If the spirit of the act could have been carried out, it would have been impossible for the great corporations to continue to receive such preferential rates that they could drive their competitors out of business and so secure monopoly control of great industries. So, also, would it have been illegal for hauls of a longer distance to be charged with lighter rates than those of a shorter included distance. In addition, the practice of pooling was prohibited. On paper the law was an admirable one, making public control over the evils of the railroads a reality.

The working of the interstate commerce law. In actual practice the Interstate Commerce Commission found that it was thwarted on every side in its attempt to abolish the evils at which the act aimed. In the matter of discriminations against shippers, the railroads conspired with the large corporations, and the result was the payment of *rebates* at the end of the month or quarter-year. These repayments of part of the regular rate were in essence discriminations, but they were not condemned by the letter of the law and hence stood the test of the courts. In the matter of discriminations in favor of places, the act had stated that short hauls should be charged at no greater rates than long hauls *under the same conditions.* This offered the railways a loophole: it was soon decided that any competition, water or rail, made conditions dissimilar, and hence the railroads were permitted to do the very thing that the act was meant to abolish—to cut rates excessively where competition existed and to make up by exorbitant rates where there was none. As for the attempt of the act to prevent the evils of combination by prohibiting pooling, the railroads simply set about to combine in other ways than by pooling. These combinations were more thoroughly organized and more effective in eliminating competition than any kind of pool could have been.

The law therefore failed in many respects. One ever-operating reason for the ineffectiveness of the work of the Commission was that its recommendations were not binding. When complaints were made they were taken to the courts, where issues were confused and presentation of new evidence was permitted. Thus the Commission was made to appear futile and almost ridiculous.

Notwithstanding these defects the Act was of very great importance. It gave publicity to railroad rates, it awakened the public to a realization of the evils of transportation, and, most important of all, it established firmly the principle that railroads were of a semipublic nature and hence subject to public control. Thus the foundation was laid for future acts which were drawn with more care and enforced more effectively.

Amendments to the Interstate Commerce Act. In 1906 the first important amendment was made to the Interstate Commerce Act. By this Hepburn Act, as it was called, the practice of both giving and taking rebates was made a misdemeanor punishable by law. The Commission was given increased powers which allowed it actually to set rates rather than, as heretofore, merely to declare certain rates unreasonable. It was also given power to enforce a uniform method of accounting, so that when the books of a suspected railroad were inspected, it was possible to know the exact status of its affairs.[1] In addition to freight and passenger service control was now extended over private express, sleeping-car, and pipe lines.

Four years later devices for communication (telephone, telegraph, and cable) were put under the jurisdiction of the Commission. Other modifications were made to strengthen the effectiveness of public control. The burden of proving the reasonableness of a rise in rates was put upon the shoulders of the railroad desiring to raise. Heretofore the Commission had had to prove that the new rate was unreasonable. The loophole clause of the long-and-short-haul section was eliminated by striking out "under substantially the same conditions." At present, therefore, short hauls cannot be charged at a higher rate than long hauls, except by specific permission of the Commission.[2]

The Esch-Cummins Act further enlarged the powers of the Interstate Commerce Commission (then increased to eleven members) by giving it the control of securities issued by the public-service corporations under its jurisdiction. Rates were to yield a return of $5\frac{1}{2}$ per cent on the actual estimated value of the railroads. Thus the social control of wealth used in transportation is not only acknowledged but put into daily practice. The old state commissions are still operating to control intrastate commerce, and the problems of conflicting jurisdiction leave much still to be worked out, but the principle is established.

[1] The practice of giving free passes for the purpose of winning political favors among legislators and judges was done away with at this time by limiting the pass privilege to employees and dependent members of their families

[2] One attempt to remedy old abuses proved a failure A Commerce Court was created to review the decisions of the Commission, in the hope of avoiding the apparent lack of sympathy of the Supreme Court in its final decisions; but in less than three years a judge of the Commerce Court had been impeached for having improper relations with the railroads, and before the end of that year (1913) the court was abolished

A War-Time Experiment

In less than a hundred years, then, the United States changed from a policy of unrestricted private ownership, operation, and control to a policy of private ownership and operation but with control vested in the government. During the years 1917–1919 a new system was tried. Ownership still remained with private individuals and corporations, but operation in addition to control was now given to the Federal government This new policy was not a socialist experiment, nor an attempt to remedy railroad abuses, it was purely an emergency measure for the purpose of securing the quickest and most economical transportation of troops and war materials.

Viewed in the light of its objectives, government operation was a success. It did not, however, succeed in keeping up the standard of service to civilians which private operation with competition had established Moreover, in spite of the fact that both passenger and freight rates were materially increased, the government incurred a deficit of some eight hundred million dollars during its period of operation.[1]

No fair-minded person claims that government operation was given a fair trial during those few months of abnormal war conditions. It is also to be remembered that although the Secretary of the Treasury was made the director general, the men who were in positions of actual management were the men who had formerly operated the roads for private corporations —men who as a rule were not interested in proving government operation a success Moreover, students of the railroad situation prior to 1917 realize that the higher wages paid by the government would have come inevitably, during the war, under private management.[2]

[1] During the same time the expenditure for upkeep and replacement of deteriorating roadbeds and equipment was inadequate, and railroad property deteriorated

[2] A tie-up of the railroads of the whole United States through a nation-wide strike was barely averted in 1916 by the passage of the Adamson Act, which although purporting to be an act on hours operated as an increase-in-wages law.

These facts are not taken into account by many people who assume that government operation has been tried and found woefully wanting. The disapproval of the American people at the delays, increased cost, and poorer service has been such that they will probably frown upon further experiments in government operation for years to come. The American public thinks that government management has failed, and so to all intents and purposes it has; for there is nothing good or bad, as Shakespeare says, but thinking makes it so. Entirely aside from that war-time experiment, there are many strong arguments offered against government management or ownership of railroads. Among them are the faults of state ownership as seen in Canada and in certain European countries.

Defeat of the Plumb Plan. When in 1919 the time came for the government to give up its emergency operation and adopt a new plan for future control of the railroads, it was not surprising that many schemes were urged as better than the old private control. One of these schemes, the Plumb Plan, provided for government purchase and operation by a board of fifteen men. Five of these men were to be appointed by the president, to represent the people, five were to be elected by the operating officers, and five by the classified employees. The surplus earnings were to be divided between the government, the employees, and the managing force. The government was to use its share of the profits in retiring the bonds issued to purchase the roads, and in making improvements and extensions, for which regions benefited were to pay their share also. A purchasing board, composed of the Interstate Commerce Commission and three of the directors of the new corporation, was to buy the roads for the government. The plan is of interest because, with its syndicalist features, it caused much discussion and had some popular support; mainly, however, among the railroad employees themselves

The Esch-Cummins Act. After much discussion Congress passed a compromise measure, the Esch-Cummins Act, which provided that

1. The roads were to be returned to private management (this was effected March 1, 1920).

2. General control was to remain with the Interstate Commerce Commission, but a special Railway Labor Board was to deal with labor disputes. The nine members represent equally labor, employers, and the public.

3. The railroads might consolidate.

4. The Interstate Commerce Commission was to fix rates according to the earning capacity of the different roads, enabling them to make 5½ per cent on the total valuation of their property. If more than 6 per cent were earned, the surplus until rates could be reduced was to be divided equally between a Federal fund to aid needy railroads and a reserve fund for the railroad itself. This arrangement was for two years only, from September, 1920; subsequent plans are in the hands of the Commission.

A clause eliminating strikes was struck out in conference, as it involved difficulties with the railroad unions. Of course it would have been unfair to have forbidden strikes in one industry while others were allowed to use this weapon, but the original inclusion of this clause is significant of the changing public opinion on this subject. The law is far from perfect, but it affords a chance for experiment which ought to prove useful to the American people in deciding what degree of social control is wise in the case of the greatest of our public carriers.

Local Control of Natural Monopolies

Social control the only safeguard for local public utilities. The root of the feeling that society has a right to control railroads lies in the fact that railroads affect so critically the lives and fortunes of everyone What effects everyone, everyone has an interest in and a certain right of control over. The same thing applies to local affairs which affect the lives of all the people, such as the water supply, broadcasting, the milk supply, the street-car service, street-cleaning, and lighting arrangements. Many of these things are natural monopolies; that is, in the nature of things there will be but one enterprise of the kind in a community. Two parallel street-car lines would be the height of absurdity; two water plants in any but the large cities would mean a wasteful duplication of expensive machinery. Consequently, whatever company elects to furnish the people with some commodity which is generally used becomes a monopolizing company in that field.

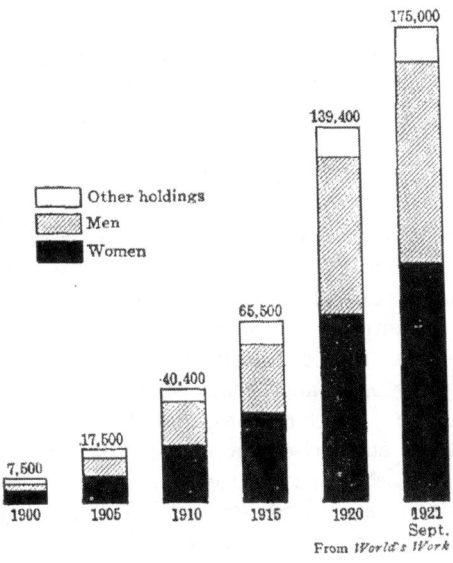

PUBLIC OWNERSHIP OF TELEPHONE STOCK

The growth in public ownership of a leading telephone company is shown in this graph. The company urged its patrons to buy enough stock to pay the telephone bill from dividends on telephone stock. How the public liked the idea is shown by the increase in subscribers, few if any of whom owned as much as 1 per cent of the stock. Many economists think that such ownership of stock in public-utility companies is a better way of securing social control than the state socialization of quasi-public businesses. The stockholders are intelligent people who have a real, if small, stake in the business management as well as the service of the company; they will see to it that both phases are fairly managed

But in case the company shows a disposition to take advantage of its position, where there is no competition there is no weapon by which such a company can be made to offer fair terms and treatment to the public. So the public, which in the case of competition withdraws its patronage from the unfair company, must in this case make laws compelling the monopoly to grant it certain terms. Or it may adopt an even better plan, since it avoids certain technical difficulties. it may fix the terms of the charter granting the monopoly, in such a way as to secure the best ends.

Changing attitudes toward public utilities. The consciousness of society's power to do this arose slowly. At first, when business men proposed to put up waterworks, a power plant, or a heating plant, the people were so pleased at the idea of having this "modern convenience" in their homes and places of business that they granted very liberal terms to the enterprisers. It was only as they saw, or thought they saw, immense profits, outmeasuring any usual and "reasonable" percentages on investments accruing to the companies, that they began to question the right of the enterprisers to all they could make. Sometimes they forced the companies to invest some of the returns in improved service or more service, but often they were unable to force a change until such time as the charter or franchise expired. In such cases the citizens are liable to be very wary about renewing the franchise, and do not grant a new one except on improved terms.

Franchises to water, gas, electric, street-car, and telephone companies are granted by the city councils or corresponding bodies, which represent the citizens. Naturally the companies dealing in the public utilities mentioned above will do all they can to secure the election of men favorable to their interests, whereas the people at large are interested in what they receive from the company rather than in what the company receives from the public. Consequently such companies are usually much interested in local politics. The history of public utilities is largely the story of the growing determination of the public to secure fair treatment. In other words, what started out almost as private businesses are now regarded generally as quasi-public ones and rightfully subject to social control.

The growth of public interest in, and control of, public utilities, together with an increasing investment of small savings in such utilities, points toward economic unity.

CONSERVATION

Americans have always been wasteful. Free-handedness has always been considered a virtue, and miserliness one of the most contemptible of traits. The Yankee, bred on stony soil and unused to the prodigal returns of Southern and Western farming, has developed much thrift, but on the frontier and in the rich regions of the South and Middle West the great plenty has made Americans careless and improvident. There was a time, well within the memory of people now living, when Westerners refused to trouble themselves with copper cents: nothing less than a five-cent piece passed current in the region west of the Rockies. We have not yet passed the stage when American farmers burn their straw and cornstalks, feed white bread left over from the table to the chickens and hogs, and leave wide margins of untilled ground in their fields.

The era of wastefulness and exploitation. Closely related to the wasting of what is now possessed is the failure to provide for coming generations by the thoughtless using of resources that should be sufficient for many years to come. From the close of the Civil War, when Western land began to be taken up both in large and in small areas, the American people recklessly exploited the soil for all it would yield. The farmer on his quarter section skimmed the soil of its richness with successive crops of maize and wheat, while great timber and mining companies secured the most richly stored tracts of land and ruthlessly took from them immense fortunes in lumber and coal and oil.

The work of Roosevelt. This waste did not exist without objection and warning. Public protest against the private exploitation of forests was loud enough to secure in 1891 a law for forest reserves. In 1905 interest was sufficient to secure a Bureau of Forestry in the Department of Agriculture, under the enthusiastic direction of Gifford Pinchot, who became the leading conservationist of the country. Cleveland continued the work of reserving public forests, so that Roosevelt, when he became president, found some forty-five million acres of valuable wooded land set apart.

Roosevelt was an Eastern man who had spent much time in the West, and he realized how serious was the robbery of the resources of the land in the interests of a few individuals who had been able to buy great tracts of land for exploitation. He used his power as president to withdraw temporarily some sixty-four million acres of public lands from the market, and then urged Congress to pass laws that should establish a national policy of conservation, or saving, of these national riches, until an economical method of using them for the good of the people at large could be devised. He called a conference of experts in 1908, which outlined a program for conservation which correlated the closely interwoven matters of forest preservation, floods and navigation of rivers, and mineral exploitation. The points in this program were as follows:

1. As to minerals, the United States should sell the surface of its public lands and the minerals that might lie beneath separately, thus correcting the abuse of purchase of lands ostensibly for farming, but really for the minerals which had been secretly discovered to lie beneath the surface. The nation should retain mineral rights to oil, gas, coal, or phosphate rock lands, but allow private capital to mine them under national control. This would not retard the settlement of farm lands, but would retain part of the great profits of mining for social uses.

2. Forests, which retain the water in the soil and so prevent destructive floods, were to be retained, especially at the sources of the great streams. Special means were to be taken to prevent the destructive forest fires which cost so tragically in property and life. This conservation of forest life necessitated the care of trained men, and therefore scientific forestry became a part of the conservation program.

3. Besides the protection of the sources of streams from deforestation and washing, some unified plan for the development of a waterways system was needed. Therefore the Inland Waterways Commission was charged with preparing a plan for

a system of inland transportation by water which should answer the needs of commerce.

4. Each state was asked to appoint a commission on the conservation of its own resources which would coöperate with the national agencies.

The conservation laws. These ideas found legislative sanction early in 1910, when a series of laws, drafted by Richard A. Ballinger, Secretary of the Interior, made a working reality of the conservation program. Ballinger added to conservation a revision of the land laws, which had not been essentially changed since early in the century, and which were not adapted to the sale of the Western lands that now remained to be disposed of.

A special law passed in 1911 provided that mountain lands in the Appalachian system should be bought by the government, and so reforested as to prevent floods and keep the streams flowing from them in good condition for commerce. With this addition and with Porto Rican and Alaskan forests, the national forest area now amounts to about 154,541,700 acres. The expense of caring for it is some four million dollars in a year without great fires, but the forests yield a revenue of over that amount from timber, grazing, and other sources.[1]

Reclamation. Parallel with the movement to save forest and mineral wealth has been the movement to make dry lands available for cultivation. In 1900 it was estimated that there were four hundred million acres in the United States which would produce good crops if only they could be watered. In tracts of forty acres this land would furnish homes and living for ten million families. As the good farming land in districts with a normal rainfall was taken up by 1900, there was a strong movement to secure some means of providing water for this arid land. Of course irrigation offered the solution; but

[1] The extra cost of fire-fighting in 1918 was over a million dollars Many states shortsightedly understaff their force of forest rangers, only to suffer great losses later from forest fires Minnesota had this experience in the severe fires of 1918

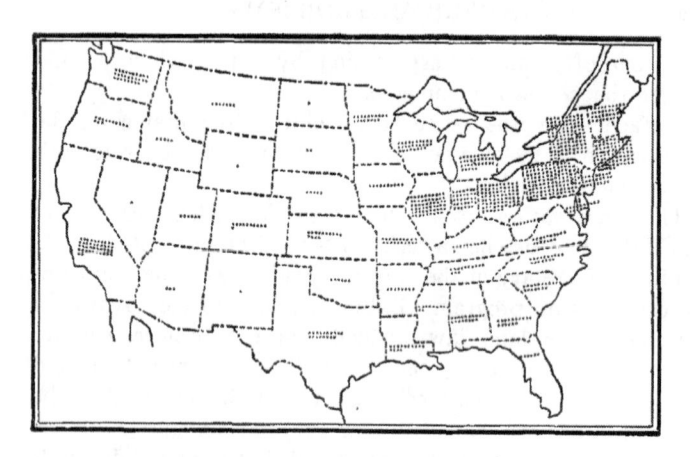

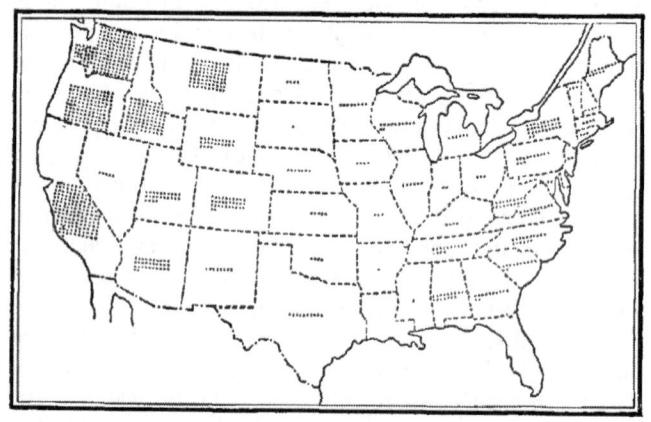

MANUFACTURING POWER AND WATER POWER

These two maps illustrate a condition of affairs which would present an unsolvable problem but for the degree of social control which has now been reached. The upper map shows the distribution of power-driven machinery now in use in manufacturing in the United States; the lower map shows the units and distribution of water power. As coal becomes more expensive, water power must increasingly take its place; but water power exists mainly in the West, while manufactures are in the East. What is to be done? Can you suggest any possible solution which does not involve some public control? How is this public control actually secured?

irrigation has a very high initial expense. A great many privately financed irrigation projects had failed in the West, especially before the era of state irrigation began. This era was marshaled in by California, which passed a law in 1887 that became a model for many state laws during the next few years.

This California law provided for the organization of irrigation districts, which could erect the necessary works and manage them. Money was raised by the issuing of bonds, the sinking fund for which was to be raised by taxation. Between 1900 and 1910 many such districts were organized. In the meantime, however, the Federal government had come to the help of the arid West with the Carey Act of 1894, which stimulated state interest by the gift of land. It provided for the ceding of irrigable tracts up to the amount of a million acres in each state, provided the state would resell the land to actual farmers at a low price, and let out irrigation contracts to responsible parties who should sell the water at a reasonable rate to the farmers.

But there was need for greater projects than any one state felt itself able to finance, and so, after a preliminary survey begun in 1889, the Western interests secured the passage in 1902 of the Newlands Reclamation Act. The administration of this act is in the hands of a Reclamation Service, which was organized in the Department of the Interior within a few days after the passage of the act. It has charge of three million acres in the seventeen arid and semiarid states.[1] Thirty separate projects have already been launched. The service carries on an immense business, which includes the mining of coal, the building of railroads, the digging of canals, the manufacture of cement, and the construction of the huge dams by which the water is conserved.

[1] Texas, Wyoming, Washington, Utah, North and South Dakota, Oregon, Oklahoma, New Mexico, Nevada, Nebraska, Montana, Kansas, Idaho, Arizona, California, and Colorado Crop value of these reclaimed lands per acre averages about double that of the rest of the United States

As nearly as possible this business seeks to be self-supporting, as recommended in the Newlands Act and the Reclamation Extension Act of August 13, 1914. The funds are derived from sales of public lands in the states concerned after a 5 per cent reservation for education has been subtracted. The tracts are usually forty acres in extent. The cost of building the irrigation plant is repaid by the farmers, usually in twenty annual installments, without interest. When these farmers have paid their installments they take over the management of the plant. The payments go to swell the reclamation fund, which is used to carry on the next project. The largest area irrigated by Federal funds is the Boise Project, in Idaho, which covers 327,552 acres.

Conclusion. We have traveled a long road since the day of Adam Smith and his doctrine of laissez faire. Momentous changes in practice and opinion are evidenced by the present-day control of public utilities, natural resources, and even private business.[1] These changes prove that the conviction of social responsibility has struck deep into the fabric of American thought. Back of any wealth-controlling laws passed and supported by the American people is the feeling that wealth is given to men to be used wisely for race improvement, not for selfish individual enjoyment. Those people who do not realize this yet, and who do not practice it willingly in their lives, are thinking in terms of a past generation when individualism was the accepted mode of thought and life.

The justification for all this control of private wealth for social uses is a pragmatic one. It works. Although tried for a few years only, and in limited and imperfect ways, the permanent and growing forms of social control have paid such dividends that unprejudiced people cannot deny their advantages. Perhaps under conditions of a remade, wholly normal, and efficient race, and a just and scientific scheme of distribution, individualism may be a better working-plan for society than that of the social control of wealth for welfare; but at

[1] As described in Chapter VIII.

present economic justice alone will not bring happiness and progress, and so society resorts to the social justice of a fair chance for all, secured through the control of private enterprise.

SUPPLEMENTARY READINGS

Control of railroads.
Nation, Vol CX, pp 716ff.
Outlook, Vol. CXXIII, pp 564-565
Survey, Vol. XLIV, p 247.
Control of agricultural lands for the future
BAILEY. Country Life Movement in the United States, pp 44-54
Outlook, Vol. XCIV, pp 659-667.
Forest control.
American City, Vol XXIV, pp 121-124, Town and Country Edition, Vol. XXII, pp. 563-566.
Current Opinion, Vol LXIX, p 546
Independent, Vol CII, pp 201 ff
Scientific American, Vol CXXIII, pp 62 ff, 540.
Good Housekeeping, Vol LII, pp 334-339, "The Government to the Rescue." [Making the tradesman honest]
TUFTS The Real Business of Living, chap xxiii. [Control of private business for public welfare]
KELLEY, FLORENCE Some Ethical Gains through Legislation, pp 3-45, 58-99, 105-125 [Control of family life for general welfare]

SEARCH QUESTIONS AND PROBLEMS

1. Do you think that the right of eminent domain should be claimed by a city for the use of idle lots as garden plots by people who own no land?

2 What employers today claim laissez-faire rights in the treatment of their employees? Give examples

3 What was the moral justification of the draft levied during the last war?

4 Do you know of establishments in which state laws concerning hours of labor, age of workers, and safety devices are habitually broken? Whose business is it to report such cases? To whom? What can be done about it?

5. Under what circumstances, if any, is it right for society to deny some men the right to drive their own motor cars? Do you believe in making every driver pass an examination before being allowed to drive on the highway?

6. List the quasi-public enterprises in your city and county, and note the amount of public control in the case of each. Which are most closely controlled? Which are the least controlled? What is the relation between the amount of control and the age of the enterprise?

7. Of how great importance is the Grange, in rural affairs, in your state? What function does it perform? Are there other farmers' organizations which undertake the same work?

8. Why should not the government take over the press education as it has the school education of the people, and furnish each citizen with a daily news-sheet, paid for by taxation?

9. Is it to the interest of the public that franchises to street-car and other public-utility companies be made for a long or a short term? What do the companies want? Why? What do you consider a good term, and why?

10. Are the citizens of the large city you know best allowed to cut down the trees in their own lots and parkings without permission from the park authorities? Do you consider this right?

11. How much land is included in the area of the Florida Everglades? Is it practicable to reclaim these swamps and make them fertile? See *Scientific American*, Vol. CIV, pp 67–69, *Collier's*, Vol XLIV, p 19, and *Putnam's*, Vol VII, pp. 796–802.

12. How did President Wilson seek to secure a degree of social control of the Peace Conference at Versailles? Was there more social control of the Disarmament Conference? Why?

13. It has been claimed that teachers and policemen have no moral right to strike. Why?

14. The United States government would not feed starving Russia until American prisoners had been released. Was this control of the affairs of another nation justified? Give reasons.

15. What moral right had Lincoln to free the slaves, who constituted legal property in 1863?

16. Debate: *Resolved*, That the government should own and operate our great natural resources.

CHAPTER XIII

TAXATION

Taxation has generally operated in such a way as to make the injustice in the distribution of wealth greater instead of making it less as it might easily do.—EDWARD CARY HAYES

THE JUSTIFICATION OF TAXATION

In our discussion of the distribution of the income from production we ignored entirely the fact that part of the shares going to the agents of production are taken away by the government in the form of taxes. Taxes were first imposed by rulers to support their governments; they were continued by popular governments because they furnish the means for coöperative social enterprises carried on by those governments; and some students of economics and sociology think that, pending the coming of an ideally just system of distribution, they may be used to correct some of the social injustices of the present practice in economic distribution.[1]

It is necessary for governments to collect revenues from their peoples in the form of taxes, because the other sources of revenue are not sufficient to meet running expenses. In some countries public properties and industries bring in a good revenue, but the United States receives little from such sources. The nation once owned vast stretches of land, but sold them at very low prices—usually $1.25 per acre—to its citizens or gave them to homesteaders. Our government operates few industries. The Alaskan railroad is but recently completed, and since 1850 the postal department has had only eleven years in which it has earned more than expenses. Local

[1] Hamilton, Current Economic Problems, No. 338.

units of government operating gas works, street cars, etc usually aim to "come out even." Government units charge fees for coinage, customs entrance, court services, consular returns on passports, motor-car, shooting, and marriage licenses. All these combined do not begin to meet the expenditures of the government. The last source of nontax revenue is gifts and donations made usually to the local units of government. These are frequently in the form of libraries, art collections, and museums, or of money to support such institutions Adding all the returns from public property and industries to these fees and gifts, we still have a great deficit in meeting the running expenses of a modern government.

The justification of taxes. The government, therefore, resorts to taxation. In most civilized countries of the world today the taxes are voted by the elected representatives of the people, who therefore talk about the "injustice" of taxation much less than they did in France before the Revolution, or in the American colonies. But some few people still insist that governments have no right to take a levy from the private property of individuals for governmental expenses.

The justification of taxation rests on two points: the first is the premise that the right to hold private property is not based on possession nor labor, nor even on natural right, but upon the sanction of society given because experience has proved that private ownership of property tends to promote social welfare. In other words, society grants the rights of private property for the sake of general welfare, and may of course except any portion of it which yields more social welfare by being used in common.

This doctrine implies that since the purpose of the dominance of society over the individual is to protect and forward public welfare, the ways in which taxes may be expended *must be for the public good* This use of taxes gives their second justification. It is not morally right for the government to collect taxes from one group of people in order to enrich another group, or to expend public money for private enterprise. The fear that a powerful section of the country may exploit the weaker sections is evident in several clauses of the Constitution; for example, in the provision that excises and customs must be uniform and that direct taxes must be apportioned according to population. As years progress the meaning of "public use" is being extended to include such internal improvements as roads and schools and such services as preservation of public health and safety and the care of dependents and delinquents. These uses are assuredly in the larger sense of the word for the public welfare, and do not smack of the old-time tax expenditures to keep up an extravagant and useless court.

Characteristics of a good tax. For the time being we shall assume that the government is to spend its revenues in an enlightened way, with the good of the public as its aim, and shall study the problem of the best ways to assess and collect these taxes. There are a number of attributes of a good tax:

1. It is collected at set times, in a definite manner, with the amount clearly understood by the contributor.

2. It is easily administered. If the machinery of collection is complicated, then too much of the money goes for expense in collecting and too little into the public treasury.

3. It must be suited to the unit for which it is assessed. For this reason a general property tax for the United States government is not good.

4. The chief characteristic of a good tax system is justice.

In practice legislators have added a fifth characteristic— that the tax should be as little felt as possible. As Colbert once said, taxation has become "the art of so plucking the goose as to procure the largest amount of feathers with the least possible squawking." This is because taxes are regarded as a necessary evil—a feeling summarized in the old saying that "nothing is sure in this life except death and taxes." This attitude may have been well enough in medieval days, when an arbitrary government was taxing unrepresented peoples for the support of extravagant courts and nonsocial enterprises. Today, however, we should be past this stage of pulling the wool over the public's eyes. Premium should not be put on ignorance, the public should feel that taxes are an investment, not an imposition. So informed, the contributor is more liable to see to it that he receives returns, not as an individual but as part of society, for every cent he pays to support his government He will demand wise expenditure and economy. There will be, in other words, less squawking and more feathers.

The Problems of Taxation

Justice a prerequisite. It is not easy to find a wholly just method of taxation. No one tax can be equally just to all, but systems can be devised that as a whole operate justly. In the first place, justice implies the ability to pay. A tax which is out of all proportion to the people's ability to pay will bring social and economic havoc such as we saw in the days of decadent Rome. A just tax does not penalize the production of socially valuable articles, as might a too stringent profits tax or an excessive tax on land.[1]

A just tax takes into consideration not only the ability to pay but the methods by which the taxable goods have been acquired. It is not fair to tax an income which has been earned by labor, either manual or mental, at as high a rate as one which comes merely from the possession of inherited wealth in the form of lands and capital. Property privileged by special governmental grants, such as public utility corporations, should be taxed at a higher rate than ordinary property. Many political economists say that private property possessing valuable resources in the form of minerals, timber, or water power should pay higher taxes. These resources of nature should not fall wholly to a few lucky men If they are not made the possession of the State, as the socialist wishes, their owners should at least be made to acknowledge their semipublic nature by sharing with the State their increased incomes in the form of heavy tax payments.

[1] Hamilton, Current Economic Problems, No. 353.

The problem of just distribution. The problem of justice comes up again in connection with just distribution: which factors of production, or which returns of production, shall be taxed and which exempted, and shall the rates be uniform or progressive? Political economists differ widely in their replies. The single taxers claim that any tax on labor (wages) or on capital (interest) penalizes production, and hence that land alone should bear the burden. Land, they say, is not the product of any one man's effort: its rental is dependent on the value given it by natural resources and by society's demand. Those who do not believe in a land-only tax point out that under such a system only a part of the community would contribute to public expenses: that many people who own forms of wealth created by the modern credit system would pay nothing toward common enterprises and burdens. They remind us that the land tax as it is now administered puts a premium on the dishonesty of township assessors, who grossly undervalue land in order to make the local burden light and curry favor with their constituents. These men believe that taxes should be largely or wholly on articles of consumption and on enterprise.

Between these two extreme schools are many who think that all forms of taxation now used should be kept and others invented to meet the growing needs of society.

Another phase of the problem of distribution of taxes is the question whether taxation should attempt to even up the inequalities resulting from the present distribution of industrial return. This involves a social use of taxation which frightens those students of politics and economics who exclude all consideration of ethics from their discussions. But since governments are coming to spend their money more and more for social uses, there is no great innovation in their accomplishing social ends by readjusting the net returns of the various factors. Whether this will help or hinder the coming of social justice is an open question.

The last problem of distribution is neither economic nor ethical, but political. There are five units in the American government: the national unit, the forty-eight states, and the local units of city, township, and county. Each one of these has its separate expenses of government, each serves the public in a different capacity; each deserves some share in the taxes. Once again we run into a great variation of opinion, but the following seem to be the generally accepted principles for a basis of distribution between the units of government. The Federal government needs an elastic revenue. It is this branch of government which supports wars, the present source of sudden demands for vast revenues; hence the need for elastic sources. The states, on the other hand, and the local units are subject to more definite and steady demands. At present the state and local taxes are drawn largely from the same sources, with a division of the revenue on the basis of needs. This is proving very unsatisfactory and must soon be changed. Clearly the steady sources of revenue should provide for regular expenses, leaving emergency means to the Federal government.

With this general discussion of the problems of taxation let us turn to our units of government and see how truly their expenditures and methods of collection answer the demands of public welfare and individual justice.

Expenditures of the United States government. The uses to which the Federal government puts its yearly taxes of over one billion dollars in peace time are considered by most people wise and conducive to the public welfare. The only very serious objections come from those people who point out that nearly four times as much is spent on preparing for war and paying the debts (including pensions) of past wars as is spent on all the peaceful operations of the government. These people claim that more money should be expended in scientific research, on reclamation and irrigation, on aids to agriculture, commerce, and education. They insist that if the United States continues she will soon be loading the backs of her people with war burdens like those of European countries. Their opponents, the militarists, hold that peaceful pursuits depend on prevention of wars, which in turn depends upon a high degree of expensive preparedness. The first part of the statement is obviously true, but intelligent people are beginning to wonder if there cannot be some way to preserve peace without excessive expenditure for a possible war. Out of experiments such as the Hague Tribunal, the League of Nations, and the Disarmament Conference some successful arrangement may be worked out.

The Tariff

As a source of revenue. One of the chief sources of Federal revenue is from a tax or "duty," known as the tariff, levied on certain goods imported into this country. Of some two thousand kinds of imported goods only about half are usually taxed. Congress has made new tariff laws from time to time, varying the articles on the free list, and varying the rates on the others from $7\frac{1}{2}$ per cent to over 50 per cent.

When we consider the tariff solely as a means of raising revenue, we find it meets rather admirably the characteristics of a good tax as listed on page 330, especially in the matter of the ease of its collection. Two thirds of all the customs dues in any year are collected at the New York port of entry. The tariff, moreover, has the advantage of being little felt. As Colbert would say, many feathers may be plucked without much squawking because the man who really pays the tax is usually unaware of the fact that included in the retail price of the article he buys there is a sum equivalent to the tax which the retailer has previously paid to the wholesaler, the wholesaler to the importer, and the importer to the customs officials at the port of entry. This kind of tax is called an indirect tax and is the best example of the consumer's paying without knowing it.

The tariff without doubt falls with a comparatively heavier hand on the poor or fairly well-to-do than it does on the rich. This evil can be remedied, however, by combining tariff with income, inheritance, and excess-profits taxes.

The question of protection. From the very first American tariff law, enacted in 1789, the tariff has been used not only as a source of revenue but as a device for giving advantage to domestic producers over their foreign competitors. This was accomplished by taxing the importation of articles of the same kind as were produced in this country. Up to 1812 this protection to American production was incidental, that is, of secondary importance to the raising of revenue. As the nineteenth century progressed the customs duties were increased by succeeding Congresses until many imports were checked, the revenues therefrom accordingly decreased or even in some cases ceased, and protection became of primary importance.

As a result of this change in the use of the tariff, the problem became primarily a question of industrial policy. The great political parties took opposite sides, and the tariff became a political issue of more or less importance in every election.

Arguments for high protection. Advocates of high protection offer the following arguments in its favor.

1. We need a protective wall to prevent newly established industries from being driven out of existence during their infancy by foreign-made articles which can be sold for less owing to the presence in Europe of cheap capital and cheap skilled labor.

2 A protective tariff encourages the development of resources and the diversification of industry so necessary for national economic independence and so valuable in times of war.

3. A policy of high tariffs will bring prosperity to the country by creating a favorable balance of trade; for imports will be lessened while exports are increased, thus retaining in the country the largest possible amount of gold

4. Protection will enable American products to sell at a high price, and therefore American labor will receive high wages. This argument has been popularized in political campaigns by the slogan, "Vote for the tariff, and you will have a full dinner pail."

Arguments against protection. People who oppose the use of the tariff for purposes of protection are advocates of tariff for revenue only, or free traders. They claim that the various arguments of the protectionists are economically unsound and that one class of people is benefited at the expense of all others.

Their answers to the protectionist arguments may be summarized as follows.

1. The infant-industries argument obviously should not be applied to manufactures of today which have outgrown their infancy, and it should never be applied to newly established industries for which the country is not aptly fitted.

2. It is economically unwise to develop in any country industries which are better adapted to other countries. Each country, like each region within a country, should produce what it can best and cheapest, and exchange its surplus with other countries International geographical division of labor is economically ideal. True, it may cause some hardships in times of war, but war itself is not ideal. A policy of high protection by encouraging international bitterness plants the seeds of war. Free trade would be a stepping-stone toward international peace Why not work toward an ideal goal instead of perpetuating imperfect economic and political conditions?

3. The balance-of-trade argument is based on the false reasoning of the mercantilists of old. When more gold pours into a country than flows out of it, money shrinks in value, prices rise to offset this depreciation, and foreign buyers seek other markets. In the long run exports must to a large extent be paid for by imports.

4. The fact that the American workingman has a full dinner pail is not the result of protection but, instead, is the outcome of the workings of the laws of wages, which were presented in Chapter XI. Wages were high in America long before we adopted an outright policy of protection, and they have always been higher in free-trade England than in high-tariff Germany. The tariff, instead of causing high wages, produces lower real wages by raising prices and thus lessening the quantity of goods obtainable from any set amount of money wages. The true effect of the tariff is to reduce the real income of all people who are not producers of the protected articles.

In addition to the rebuttal of the protectionist arguments many free traders insist that the tariff has been "the mother of

the two countries When this is made it will be found that the big difference so talked about reduces to a very small one, and that that small difference is due largely to the greater scarcity of the supply of labor in relation to the demand and to the high standard of living [1]

OTHER FEDERAL TAXES

Internal taxes. The second great source for Federal taxation comes from internal taxes. Since 1911 these have exceeded the customs revenue, rising from $322,520,201 in 1911 to $3,694,703,334 in 1918, while tariff returns dropped in the same period from $314,497,071 to $179,990,383. Since 1918 the trend of taxation has been to increase the revenue from tariffs while decreasing it from internal sources. At the end of five years customs duties had more than trebled, amounting in 1923 to $561,928,867, whereas the amount drawn from internal revenues in that year ($2,621,754,227) was over one billion dollars less than the returns in 1918 The reasons for these changes are to be found in the high tariffs of the Harding administration combined with the removal or reduction of many war-time taxes on profits, incomes, and luxuries.[2]

Internal revenue taxes are of two kinds: indirect and direct The indirect are usually *excises* Originally the chief source of excise income was from liquors and tobacco Even in 1918 the return from these two sources was over half a million dollars, but with the eighteenth amendment to the Constitution, prohibiting the manufacture of liquors, this source of revenue is almost cut off New excises have been placed on many luxuries, such as cameras, guns, pleasure boats, jewelry, automobiles, etc. The old tax on playing-cards has been supplemented by a tax on tickets into places of amusement. Levies on transportation, however, have now been abolished except on transporta-

---

[1] Hamilton, in "Current Economic Problems," No 343, reproduces pamphlets used in English campaigns against protective tariffs Other arguments used in the United States are given in No 344

[2] Statistics from World Almanacs, given on page 338, illustrate these taxes

SOURCES OF NATIONAL INCOME

	1916	1918
A. Unnecessary Indulgences		
Spirits and liquors	$141,333,668	$443,819,544
Tobacco	85,324,094	156,188,160
B. Food		
Sirups and extracts, unfermented juices, and mineral waters		1,221,503
Oleomargarine	924,670	2,336,907
C. Amusements		
Amusement places		28,299,028
Playing-cards	819,654	1,276,544
D. Consumption and Luxuries		
Tax on club dues		2,259,056
Automobiles and motor cycles		23,981,268
Pianos, jewelry, films, perfumes, medicines, gems, cameras, yachts	4,086,161	12,995,732
E. Transportation and Communication		
Freight tax		30,002,163
Express		6,458,995
Passenger		24,306,350
Tax on parlor seats, berths, staterooms		2,236,700
Oil by pipe lines		1,433,324
Telephone and telegraph		6,299,017
F. Miscellaneous		
Tax on insurance		6,492,025
Corporation taxes	56,993,657	37,917,689
Inheritance		47,452,880
Munition manufacturers		13,296,927
Income and excess profits		2,839,083,585
Total	$512,723,287	$3,694,703,334

tion by water to foreign countries. All these taxes, like the tariff, are indirect; that is, the ultimate payer of the tax does not hand over the duty into the hands of the government official in a lump sum at certain times in the year. Instead he adds the amount of the tax to the ordinary price of the commodity or service, and the person who receives this passes it on to the government. This is usually done by means of internal-revenue stamps, which are attached to the article. These are purchased by the handler of the commodity and attached to it in such a way as to be broken when the article is used. Since the war, excise taxes have been largely reduced, and the present trend of taxation is quite clearly away from indirect internal sources.

Some of the same objections may be brought against these taxes as against the tariff: they do not instill enough interest in the use to which the government puts the revenue thus raised, and they fall unevenly on the rich and the poor. A tax of a few cents on soap, powder, or medicine is scarcely felt by the man with an income of ten thousand dollars a year, but an accumulation of such taxes works a real hardship on a man with an income of one thousand dollars and a family to support.

The income tax. In order to even up this injustice Congress, in 1892, incorporated an income tax in the Wilson tariff bill. This provided for a tax of 2 per cent on all incomes of over four thousand dollars. Before this law went into effect the Supreme Court of the United States, reversing a former decision, declared it unconstitutional because it was a direct tax not apportioned among the states according to population.[1] It was not until 1913 that a constitutional amendment was passed exempting taxes on incomes from the prohibition put on direct taxes. Congress immediately passed a law imposing a tax of 1 per cent on all incomes over $3000 for unmarried people and $4000 for married ones. In addition a graduated tax, ranging from 1 per cent to 6 per cent, was put on incomes of over $20,000. In 1916 both of these rates were raised: 2 per cent was the normal, and the surtax ran to 13 per cent. In 1917, because of the war a new law was passed. This added a 2 per cent regular tax and an additional surtax ranging from 1 per cent to 63 per cent. These were to be paid in addition to the 1916 rates This double system caused a great deal of confusion in administering, so in 1918 a new measure was passed combining the rates

---

[1] During the Civil War such a tax had been levied, and in 1875 it was declared constitutional by a unanimous vote of the Supreme Court

into one unified system. As modified by later legislation the rates are now 2 per cent on incomes up to $4000, 4 per cent to $8000, and above that 6 per cent. Surtaxes are not levied under $10,000 and reach their maximum at 40 per cent on incomes above $500,000. Moreover, for the first time, distinction is made between earned and unearned incomes, the former being given a 25 per cent reduction up to $10,000.

As a device for raising revenue the income tax has proved a decided success. In 1918, $663,183,000 was raised in this manner. As a device for equalizing the burdens of taxation it has, however, not been so successful. It is pretty generally felt that the rich have not borne this burden, but have by various devices shifted the tax to the shoulders of the general public in the form of increased prices. Some economists criticize the law, too, because, they say, by retaining high taxes on big incomes it offers no encouragement for the transfer of fortunes from tax-exempt securities to investment in business enterprises.[1]

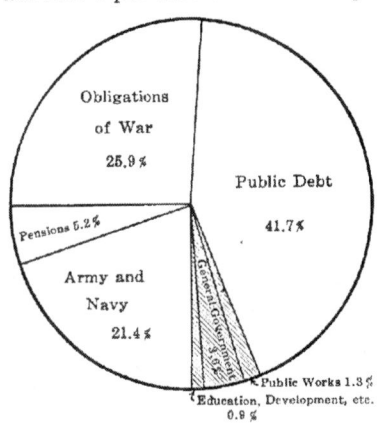

FIG. A

Fig. A is based on statistics of Federal expenditures in the year 1920. Notice that only the barred portion, which is 5.8 per cent of the total, is spent for normal civil activities, and that of this only 0.9 of 1 per cent is spent for such purposes as education, research, and the work of the women's and children's bureau. Included in the 94.2 per cent appropriated to military purposes is 25.9 per cent used to meet obligations arising from war, such as various Philippine expenses; and 41.7 per cent for principal and interest on the public debt, which Mr. Rosa of the United States Bureau of Standards said represents "the expenses arising from that part of the cost of past wars which is not yet liquidated"

[1] Hamilton, Current Economic Problems, No. 348; Marshall, Wright, and Field, Materials for the Study of Elementary Economics, No. 253.

TAXATION

Corporation taxes. There are several kinds of internal indirect taxes which have been used to an increasing degree of recent years. One of these is the *corporation tax*. It was first enacted in 1909 and amounted to 2 per cent of the net income of joint-stock companies and other industrial corporations. But during the years 1914–1917, when, on account of the disrupted conditions of Europe, America became for the first time in her history a great exporter nation with international markets, a new condition arose. Demand outran supply. Prices rose with a leap. Some manufacturers became millionaires overnight. Meantime war had come to us with its need of increased revenue. There was an urgent demand that those who were reaping fortunes out of these conditions should share in the added costs of the government. The result was a 10 per cent corporation tax and an excess-profits tax placed on every business organization, profession, and occupation which received profits in excess of 7 per cent.[1] The rate ranged from 20 per cent to 60 per cent.

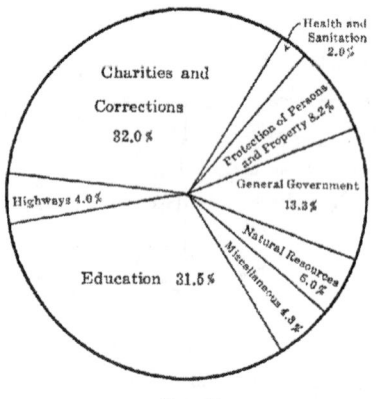

FIG. B

Fig. B shows the expenses of the state of Illinois in 1919. Compare the amounts spent for preventing and curing public evils. Secure data for your own state's disbursements and compare the percentage with that of Illinois. In what respects does your state seem to be using its income more wisely and in what repects less wisely than Illinois?

As in the case of the income tax, the corporation and excess-profits taxes were a real attempt to make the rich bear their share of the support of the government under which they had acquired their fortunes. The financial return from them was

[1] In some cases as high as 9 per cent was allowed to those concerns which had earned a high rate of profits in prewar days.

immense. In 1918 the corporation tax brought in $37,917,689 and the excess-profits tax $2,227,500,000, the largest amount of revenue ever received from one source in the history of the United States. Many objections were raised to these various taxes on business. The laws initiating them were extremely complicated, and the result was much confusion, many errors, and great expense for collection. Moreover, it was commonly believed that the burden was not being borne by the rich as was the intention, but was passed along to the general public in the form of increased prices.

In 1921 the excess-profits tax was repealed by a special session of Congress called by President Harding for the express purpose of revising the revenue laws. The corporation tax, however, was retained and raised to 12 per cent. The 1924 law made no changes in this field of taxation.

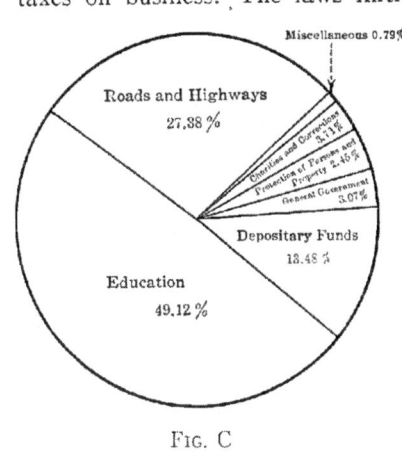

FIG. C

Fig. C is adapted from a chart made by the county expert of Fresno County, California. Notice the proportion spent for education and roads. Secure statistics from your county clerk and compare the expenditures of your county with those of Fresno County. Wherein does your county differ, and why?

Estate and gift taxes. In 1918 the Federal government found a new source of internal revenue in an estate tax. The rates ran from 1 per cent on estates over $50,000 up to 25 per cent on those exceeding $10,000,000. This differs from the inheritance tax, popular in so many European countries, in that the basis for taxation is not the amount inherited by any heir or beneficiary, but is instead the valuation of the entire estate of the deceased. The 1921 tax law made no change in this provision, but the 1924 law raised the maximum to 40 per cent. The same law initiated a gift tax, with rates similar to the estate tax, to prevent evasion of the latter law by gifts previous to death.

Opponents of the estate tax point out that many estates are called upon to pay a number of state inheritance taxes in addition to the Federal tax, and that the combined sum is so great as to be truly confiscatory. Moreover, they say that since the tax must be paid in cash or liberty bonds a real injustice is done to the heirs. Since the largest part of every fortune is not in cash but in bonds, stocks, and business equipment, it necessitates the sudden sale of great amounts of the most liquid assets. The forced nature of the sale is bound to result in a smaller return than the true value. In addition, since only the most liquid assets can be realized on in short order, the estate is left in a bad way for ready capital. This of course is not only a hardship for the heirs but a detriment to general business. Economists offer another criticism of the estate and gift taxes. They point out that the government is using this money, which is really capital of the country, to meet current expenses, and then they utter a warning to any person, concern, or government which lives on its capital and not on its income.

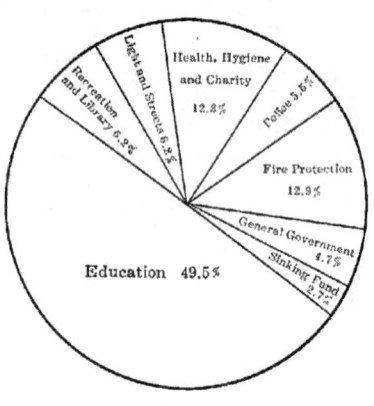

FIG. D

Fig. D is based on the picture of a dollar which the city of Grand Rapids, Michigan, stamps on the back of every tax receipt it issues. This picture shows every taxpayer where his money goes. What items appear to be abnormally high? How do the annual disbursements of your nearest large city compare with those of Grand Rapids?

Outlook for Federal taxes. Doubtless the estate and gift taxes will undergo many changes in the years to come. It is quite possible that a true inheritance tax may take the place of the estate tax. The changes may be varied and many, but it seems safe to predict that taxes on the transmission of wealth in large quantities have become a permanent part of our tax system

These internal taxes, combined with those on corporation and personal incomes, bid fair to continue the mainstay of our Federal revenue for years to come The present outlook would indicate that the tariff will remain for some time a considerable source of income, but it is quite evident that it will never again be able to meet the greater part of the expenses of a rapidly expanding government A nonpartisan tariff commission created by Congress, with a membership of three Republicans and three Democrats, has in recent years been investigating the financial and industrial effects of the tariff. It has collected volumes of statistics and information, but it still remains to be seen how much use will be made of this in the construction of new tariff bills by the financial committees of Congress. Should an efficient political federation of the world ever be adopted, it is possible that all tariffs might be abolished

The only alternative to high taxes on incomes and wealth is a general sales tax on every article of consumption. The farming and laboring classes oppose this violently. Each group of people seems to feel that the only fair taxes are those which fall heaviest on other groups. But since every citizen benefits by the expenditures of the national government, every citizen should contribute his share to its support. It is the duty of every educated, fair-minded citizen to work for a system of taxation that exempts none, burdens none, and calls for just proportions from all.

State and Local Taxes

On property. At the present time more than half the state and local revenue in the United States is raised by general property taxes This includes real estate, "tangible" personal property, such as animals, machinery, and household possessions, and "intangible" property, such as stocks, bonds, mortgages, and notes. In reality intangible personal property is so easy to hide that it bears very little of the burden.[1] This means that the country districts, where there is little of this kind of property but much of the tangible kind in the form of live stock and machinery, bear more than their share of the state taxes on property. Moreover, undervaluation is practiced everywhere, but especially in the cities, in order to escape having to contribute in large amounts to the upkeep of the state. The present operation of this tax is therefore characterized by perjury, deceit, and inequality.[2]

Dissatisfaction arising from the inequalities of assessment has led some states to create equalization boards to hear complaints. In order really to remedy the situation they must be given power to reassess the whole state, but this has always proved highly impractical. Professor Seligman of Columbia University says: "In short, the general property tax is so flagrantly inequitable that its retention can be explained only through ignorance or inertia. It is the cause of such crying injustice that its abolition must become the battle cry of every statesman and reformer." Although forty-six states still retain the tax, it seems to be a universally accepted belief among economists and financiers that it should be given up, at least as a state tax. If confined solely to a local tax, the chief motive of undervaluation would be removed.

State taxes on corporations and inheritances would then become of more importance. Many states now tax insurance, express, mining, banking, and telegraph companies. Only Pennsylvania and New York tax every corporation. Other states are sure to develop this form of taxation further in the near

[1] For the Minnesota plan of taxing intangible property see Marshall, Wright, and Field's "Materials for the Study of Elementary Economics," No. 250.

[2] Since the amount of undervaluation depends upon the willingness of the individual assessors to cheat the state, great inequalities are found; undervaluations in some states run from 20 per cent to 80 per cent, and within some cities vary in the different wards as much as 100 per cent. For the defects of the general property tax see Hamilton's "Current Economic Problems," No. 345.

future [1] The only problems are so to arrange this tax that every corporation is taxed once and once only, and to make the various states adopt similar rates so that corporations will not move from one place to another in order to avoid high taxes.

Miscellaneous taxes. At present forty-three states in the Union have some form of inheritance tax. One reason for the popularity of this tax is that it is easy to collect through the probate courts, another is that it does not penalize the incentives to industry.[2]

In 1913 the forty-eight states of the Union realized almost $21,000,000 on liquor licenses; other business licenses brought in over $8,500,000; while nonbusiness licenses, such as game, marriage, and automobile, brought in almost $6,500,000 more. With the cessation of liquor licenses others are likely to be substituted. Several states already have increased their automobile licenses tremendously in order to raise money to build hard-surfaced roads.

In some states the poll tax is still used. It is not a source of much revenue, but is used rather as a means of controlling the right to vote. It sometimes leads to the buying up of votes of ignorant whites and negroes, and should be abolished.[3]

Another possible source of revenue to take the place of the property tax for states is a tax on valuable resources in the hands of private individuals. This is yet a very new idea and therefore has not met with wide acceptance Even without it states may be able to meet all their expanding needs and not have to keep the general property tax, which has worked out so unsatisfactorily.

Local taxes. If confined to counties and townships the property tax could be operated without great evils The rate would then be lower, there would not be so great an incentive to

---

[1] Hamilton, Current Economic Problems, No 347; Marshall, Wright, and Field, Materials for the Study of Elementary Economics, No 251

[2] Hamilton, Current Economic Problems, No 349; Marshall, Wright, and Field, Materials for the Study of Elementary Economics, No 252.

[3] For the operation of the law in Virginia see Magruder's "American Government," p. 360.

undervaluation, and the inequalities would be slight when limited to one unit of government. Municipalities would add returns from natural monopolies to the general property tax. These might come in the form of profits from efficiently conducted public enterprises, such as gas or waterworks, or from increased returns on franchises of street railway and electric companies. Local licensing and special assessments for paving, sewerage, etc. should fill out the rest of the needed revenues. Newer forms of taxes, such as taxes on unused lands and on unearned increment, may be tried out in the states which are more advanced in social thinking.

Summary. The next decade will witness a continuation of the great changes in our tax system which have begun during the last few years of war and postwar necessities. The problem is not only to pay off our war debts but to provide more revenue for such things as national highway systems, educational progress, increased aids to dependent and defective people, reforestation, public parks and playgrounds. This can be done by turning our peace-time war expenditures into these channels, provided war can be prevented; otherwise it must be done by raising more revenue. With the internal revenues greatly reduced by national prohibition and the majority of economists condemning the tariff, the need for other sources is clear. The touchstone for every new tax must be justice to the contributor on the basis of value received for revenue paid, and of a fair relation between his taxes and his income.

In some cases only experiment can dictate a wise policy, but in others the opinions of financial experts, such as the tariff commissioners, can well be used. More simple tax laws must be enacted to avoid confusion and extra expense in collection. Expediency points to the wisdom of separating state and local taxes.[1] Whatever the changes that are to come, we should al-

---

[1] The need for simplification of our state tax system is well brought out in No. 248 of Marshall, Wright, and Field's "Materials for the Study of Elementary Economics," and the advantages of the separation of state and local taxes in No. 254.

ways remember that the taxpayer is not an ignorant goose to be plucked of his feathers without squawking, but is rather an intelligent human being who will contribute his share willingly if it is clear that his share is a just one, and that he is to receive invaluable returns in the form of protection, education, and numberless helps in the business of living.

SUPPLEMENTARY READINGS

BULLOCK, C. J Elements of Economics, chap xv
CARVER, T. N Principles of National Economy, chap. xlvi.
FORMAN, S E. The American Democracy, chaps xxxiii–xxxvi.
HAMILTON, W H. Current Economic Problems, Nos. 343, 345, 348–349
MAGRUDER, F A American Government, chaps. x, xxvii.
MARSHALL, L C, WRIGHT, C. W, and FIELD, J. A. Materials for the Study of Elementary Economics, Nos 238–255.
Journal of Political Economy, Vol. XXVIII, pp. 499–504

SEARCH QUESTIONS AND PROBLEMS

1. Find out from the World Almanac what was the United States revenue from land sales in 1918 How do you account for the fact that it more than doubled since 1916?

2. From the table in Magruder's "American Government," p 137, figure out roughly what percentage of the income of the United States in 1916 came from sources other than taxes, and from the table on page 387 do the same for state revenues in 1913.

3. What group of people was the Constitution protecting when it forbade taxes on exports?

4 How could a congress before 1850 made up largely of Easterners make a tax that would favor New York and discriminate against New Orleans?

5 In Boston the city was prohibited in 1872 from issuing bonds to rebuild private buildings after the fire. But after the forest fires of 1918 Minnesota gave almost $260,000 in relief, much of which was spent in replacing farm buildings and animals. How do you account for this?

6 Why would it not be fair for New York City to have all the taxes which are collected at her port of entry?

TAXATION

7. Congress in 1914 laid a tax of $300 a pound upon the manufacture of opium. Two years earlier a tax was put upon white or yellow phosphorus matches equal to twice the retail selling price. Would you consider either of these an unjust tax in view of the fact that they both practically destroy production? Justify your answer.

8. Make a special report on the Lloyd George Budget of 1909 drawn from Cheyney's "Short History of England" (Revised Edition), pp. 680 ff., and elsewhere. Discuss each one of these taxes as to its justice. What is the significance of the purpose for which these new revenues were to be expended?

9. Upon what ground did the Minnesota state legislature pass a bill to tax the iron-ore tonnage of the northern iron ranges? (See the article by E. R. A. Seligman in *Annals of the American Academy*, Vol. LVIII, pp. 3-4, and 8.) Why was not this bill unconstitutional, since Article I, Sect. 10, clause 3, of the Constitution prohibits the laying of tonnage by states? Most of the money to be raised by the tonnage tax in Minnesota is to be spent on the state education system. What is your opinion of this?

10. What is the difference between a "tariff for revenue only" and a protective tariff?

11. Work out special reports based on American histories of the tariff laws of (1) 1816-1833, (2) 1842-1857, (3) 1860-1887, (4) 1887-1920. In each case bring out the rates of duties, the types of articles taxed, and the arguments for and against political party attitudes. After the above reports are given in class, answer the following questions:

a. What is meant by the "American system"?

b. Why was the tariff of 1828 known as the "Tariff of Abominations"?

c. Why did South Carolina take the stand she did in 1832?

d. What new argument was brought forward in 1842 by the supporters of tariff?

e. What was the condition of public finance in 1887 which led Cleveland to denounce the tariff as "vicious"?

f. In what campaign did the Republicans adopt tariff as a sworn party policy?

g. To what measure in the McKinley tariff of 1890 did the farmers most object?

h. Why did Cleveland call the Wilson Bill of 1892 a measure of "party perfidy"? Why did he not veto it if he felt that way?

i. How did the Democratic platform of 1908 purpose to stop the tariff from bolstering up "trusts"?

j. What effect did the Payne-Aldrich tariff of 1909 have on the Republican party?

k. How did the Democrats keep their campaign pledges in 1913?

12. Compare the rates of the Payne-Aldrich Law and the Underwood tariff, as given in the World Almanac for 1919, pp. 824–826, for some half a dozen things used in your home or in your father's business.

13. Why have such manufactured articles as harvesters, threshers, and sewing machines been on the free list for years?

14. What conclusions can you draw from the charts given in Marshall, Wright, and Field's "Materials for the Study of Elementary Economics," Nos. 239 and 240, p. 839?

15. E. B. Rosa, chief physicist of the United States Bureau of Standards, analyzed the nation's expenditures for the year ending June 30, 1920, as follows: public welfare, including education, public health, labor, and agriculture, 1 per cent; public works, including harbors, roads, rivers, and parks, 3 per cent; administration of the government, 3.2 per cent; war expenses, 92.8 per cent, including 25 per cent for present armaments and 67.8 per cent for debts caused by past wars. Make a bar diagram on the blackboard showing the proportionate expense for these items, and discuss the significance of the showing. Compare this with the charts in *Literary Digest*, Vol. LXXI No. 7 (November 12, 1921), pp. 16–17.

16. On the basis of current-magazine readings make a report on the Fordney-McCumber tariff of 1922. Among others try to read the following:

American Economic Review, March, 1923, Vol. XIII, pp. 14–33. *Literary Digest*, April 22, 1922, Vol LXXIII, pp. 5–7; September 2, 1922, Vol. LXXIV, pp. 7–9; September 16, 1922, Vol. LXXIV, p. 21; October 7, 1922, Vol. LXXV, pp. 11–13; May 26, 1923, Vol. LXXVII, pp. 12–13. *Review of Reviews*, November, 1922, Vol. LXVI, pp. 505–509. *The World's Work*, August, 1922, Vol. XLVII, pp. 363–371.

CHAPTER XIV

THE ELEMENTS OF POPULATION IN THE UNITED STATES

Above all, humanity.—Woodrow Wilson

Humanity is the most precious thing in the world. All the changes which add to the value of things and make the material wealth of the world, all the activities which keep the world busy and interested, all the achievements which make so much stir and create satisfaction for us, in fact all that we call civilization, amounts to nothing if it does not bring the great result of an improved race. The end and aim of all production and all consumption is a higher quality in human beings. The criterion for judging a nation is not the riches of its material resources, not the ability it shows to excel or conquer other peoples, not its art treasures or its learning or its majestic buildings, but the character-quality of the people who make up the nation. Civilization is but the outward expression of this character-quality—the "outward and visible sign of an inward and spiritual grace."

The supreme interest of Americans. Socrates' famous motto, repeated as a piece of good advice to each succeeding generation, was "Know thyself." The modern American citizen may adopt the same motto with profit, and add to it a socialized generalization—*Know thy people*. Young Americans, especially, preparing themselves for the duties of citizens in a time troublous and critical, should study the make-up of their country as it was in the defining period of early nationality, as it is now, and as some day we hope it may be. The destiny of America depends upon the quality of its citizenry far more than upon any resources of its well-stored land, or any political machinery it may contrive, or any business success it may achieve. The nation can be no better than its individual citizens.

THE OLD STOCK AND ITS STANDARDS

The original composition. When the United States became a nation, late in the eighteenth century, it had a more or less homogeneous character. Practically everyone spoke English, and all had lived under English rule so long that they were familiar with English institutions and customs, while a majority—probably three fourths—of the people were of English blood. On the whole these people were a strong-minded race. They had opinions so definite and convictions so deep that they had more or less difficulty in getting on together; and their native strength of character, exercised freely in an exceptionally free environment, developed strong traits that in an older, more highly conventionalized country would have been weakly developed, if at all. Each region of the narrow strip of Atlantic coast line which made the United States of 1783 had its peculiar type of people and its own distinct stock of American ideas. As the people spread westward and intermarried and moved from section to section, these sectional characteristics became American characteristics. "Americanisms" are the joint result of certain racial traditions and tendencies and of climatic and economic conditions which were peculiar to America.

The New England contribution. The New Englander on his rocky farm or in his fishing-village was perhaps, on the whole, the greatest shaping force in American life. The people of New England were very religious, intellectually alert, and thrifty in management. Shrewdness and sobriety united themselves in the Yankee. Not all New England people were of the typically New England tastes and habits, but the influential majority fixed the character and reputation of its section. Practically all the people were of British ancestry and cherished a more than English love of liberty. Deep conscientiousness and devotion to duty, strict habits of life, and penuriousness that grew from actual poverty were the rule in the northeast. The "New England conscience" is a proverb in America.

Men of the Middle States. In the Middle States there was a variety of peoples and modes of life. The Dutch along the Hudson and the German Mennonites of the interior of Pennsylvania, known as the "Pennsylvania Dutch," were phlegmatic but industrious people, taking small part in the intellectual and political life of the nation, but living in solid comfort upon their productive farms. The Quakers followed many callings—going into business and trades in the cities and farming in the fertile valleys, and carrying everywhere their kindly toleration, their peaceful and just relations with others, and their good-natured, quiet efficiency. The wiry, intense, keen, and enduring Scotch-Irish seeped through the settlements where life was easier, and made up the vanguard of civilization on the frontier, at that time in western Pennsylvania and Virginia.[1] The few descendants of the Swedish settlers of New Jersey were an uninfluential group. Scattered here and there were groups of Huguenots, high-minded and mentally keen, setting a standard of simple but elegant living that has contributed much to the refinement of American life.

Their contributions. In a section so mixed in its racial elements there was, of course, great variation in living and ideas. The gulf of character between the easy-going Dutch patroon and the tense, ascetic Scotch-Irishman—the one drawing a simple plenty from the soil without undue exertion, the other strenuously engaged in putting the starch and iron into American life—was a deep and wide one. Variety in the national

---

[1] Distinguish accurately between the Scotch, the Irish, and the Scotch-Irish. The Scotch-Irish were not Irish in blood, but were Scotch people who had lived for a few years in the north of Ireland, whence they migrated to America. See Farrand's "Development of the United States," pp. 12–13, and H. J. Ford's "The Scotch-Irish in America."

inheritance was assured. The Middle States had many descendants of indented servants. On the whole the cultural level (save in Philadelphia) was not so high as in New England. But, on the other hand, the mixture of traditions produced a better balance, a wider outlook on life, than was usual in New England.

The South. In the South the population was mainly English, although in South Carolina especially there were many Scotch and French people. The stratification of classes and the range of culture here was much greater than in the middle section. The Virginia and Carolina planters of cavalier descent set the social standards for the South, emphasizing those aspects of life which had seemed most important to them in England. Below them in the social and economic scale were the poor whites of the mountain regions and the backwoods, descendants of the submerged classes of England or the shiftless offscourings of more prosperous and intelligent communities. Some of them were descended from deported criminals. Many of these people had a great contempt for the culture of the cavalier planters of the tidewater, men who could spend their time in hunting and reading and arguing cases at court. And there was a great gulf fixed also between them and the slaves of the planters— the still almost savage Africans, whose presence so largely controlled the ideas and lives of their masters. These three distinct layers of society in the South—the courtly planters of British or Huguenot blood, the poor whites of the uplands, and the ignorant slaves, whose savagery reacted strongly on the characters of their owners—fixed on the South the control of a political and social aristocracy.

Standards and ideals. It was the racial and sectional groups briefly outlined above that set the standards and ideals of the old-stock Americans. Among these standards and ideals four stand out clearly as definitely characteristic of the American people at large. The first of these is an unusual mental alertness, which showed itself in countless manifestations, but in nothing more than in shrewd business dealings. The "grit," resourcefulness, energy, and pure intellectuality of the New

Englander and the courage and patience of the Scotch-Irishman have combined to build up what popular parlance calls "gumption"—an eloquent expression for a quality of character that was supremely necessary in the opening up of a vast continent. The success of American business men, the energetic way in which Americans go about everything (even their recreations), the alert air and carriage of the typical American, and the unparalleled growth of the nation in wealth and civilization are all outgrowths of this Yankee gumption, this American alertness, quickness, shrewdness, and determination.

High standard of living. In the second place, Americans from colonial days have maintained a higher standard of living than Europeans of a corresponding class. The plentiful land gave food in abundance when cultivated with any care at all. Life was simple and work was hard, and the wives and sisters of the settlers must do their own housework. Since they shared the mental ability of their men, they did this necessary work as well as they could, and thus built up the American tradition of good housekeeping. American women, with the exception of Southern women who have had negro servants, are proud to be called good cooks, no matter what their social and intellectual standing. The Dutch, New England, and German housekeepers built up the good-cooking tradition, having brought with them sensible bourgeois pride in their skill in preparing food, and having plenty of good materials to work with.

In like manner the tradition of good dressing grew up, perhaps mainly through the influence of the prettily dressed Huguenot women, who added little elegancies to their dress that English Puritan women were denied and for which the German and Dutch women had not the skill and taste. Cleanliness was almost a religious rite with New England and Dutch women, and cleanliness became a social standard in America wherever women did their own housekeeping. Manual labor was honorable everywhere in the North, where men despised the shiftless and inefficient and admired the thrifty and skilled. American women understood that their chief business in life was not to be beautiful or learned, but to make a clean, attractive home for their husbands and children, to dress neatly and attractively, and to cook good meals. Men took pride in being "good providers," and their wives were equally jealous of their reputation as housekeepers. So the American standard of wholesome, ample living grew up, a standard that has made our race taller and stronger than Europeans of the same ethnic stock.

Righteousness and wholesomeness. A third trait of the American people is that from the stern Puritans there filtered westward and southward a standard of righteousness that has kept American life clean of many evils that have corrupted and weakened the Old World. The Sabbath was kept with strictness wherever the New Englander set the social customs; and as a rule the New Englander set the social customs wherever he went because of the force of his character and the depth of his convictions. And although Americans have not always lived up to their conventions, the single standard of social morals is generally subscribed to Clean living in both men and women has made a stronger and more virile race in America than the nations of the Old World know, and has given wholesomeness to our social life. Puritanism sometimes made people afraid of good times and imposed a sternness on life that was hard on young people, robbing youth of its heritage of joy; but if it took something from life, it also gave great treasure of sound judgment, wholesome habits, and righteous convictions.

Democracy. Most distinctive of all the American ideals and practices was democracy. America is known among the nations for many things, but most of all for putting into actual practice the ideal of the brotherhood and equality of man. This virtue was not clearly understood and accepted at the time of our independence except by a few idealists, led by Thomas Jefferson, but it grew and clarified under the influence of American conditions upon the fertile English mind. The New England Puritan believed in and practiced democracy in his church and in his town meeting; the man of the Middle

States imbibed ideas of Quaker simplicity and equality from the dominant Friends, even if he did not belong to their body; the Southerner limited his equality to his own class, but within that class he was even more democratic than the New Englander or the man of the Middle States. And all classes, of whatsoever section or belief, were influenced by the primitive demands of the frontier for helpfulness, simplicity, and the sloughing of artificial, man-made distinctions between man and man. There were, of course, as there always must be, economic and cultural classes in America; but *equality of opportunity, which is the very essence of democracy*, was such that distinctions were elastic, allowing any man to belong to the class to which his ability and industry entitled him.

Independence. A fifth American trait that has given notable strength to our national life is self-respecting independence. Americans, even when very poor, want to be self-supporting, and consider it a deep disgrace to have to accept charity. It is more respectable to live plainly and to earn what one uses than to depend on relatives and live at ease. Self-support is consequently regarded as a virtue. High-school and college students, for instance, who earn their own way receive unusual respect and consideration. This feeling is responsible for the unpopularity of unemployment doles and other tax-supplied charities given in some other countries. The American hesitates long before adopting a policy which would destroy the independence and self-respect of the poorest citizen.

Chivalry. Another American trait deserves mention here, although it is not so common as could be wished. It is the greatest contribution of the cavalier element in American society—the chivalry of American men. The ideal of the knight of the medieval world, brought down to colonial times by English gentlemen, was transferred to Virginia and the Carolinas during and after the English Puritan régime. It was not a new thing; in fact, it had survived storm and change through centuries because it was intrinsically true and fine. But what was new, and what constitutes one of the most beautiful and hopeful things in American development, was its adoption by men of every class and inheritance on the Western frontier. Puritan, poor white, and plain Middle State citizen of mixed blood and tradition adopted and adapted the cavalier's chivalry and applied it in his relations with those weaker than himself. This democratization of the knight's ideal, this extension of fine sentiment into the lives of simple people, has sweetened and refined the manners of the American nation.

THE OLD IMMIGRATION

From the Declaration of Independence to the middle of the nineteenth century, when American ideas began to be influenced by new stocks of European peoples, was about seventy-five years, which in this new country was three generations. In that time the American ideals had become strengthened and diffused pretty thoroughly. English and French travelers, journeying in the new and strange America and writing their impressions in journals and letters, give us a very clear idea of the strength of these American ideals by the middle of the century and of the impression they made upon Old World visitors The Americans themselves thought very little about their own characteristics, for they were so busy making the virgin soil into farms and building new cities upon the waterways that they could not stop for introspection and criticism of themselves. And so, almost before the Americans found out that they were a peculiar people, having ideas and attitudes that were in some ways far ahead of what the rest of the world believed, new peoples began to enter America These newcomers added their ideas and their racial customs and attitudes to the American mixture, complicating and enriching, while at the same time they destroyed the homogeneity of, American character.

The Irish migration. Of course English and Scotch people had continued to come to America to some extent after the Revolution, but their ideas were so like those of the English and

Scotch already here that they did not change American character. The first new people to enter in large numbers were the Irish, who flocked to America after 1845, following the potato famines of the middle 40's. These unfortunate people, starved out of their own land, became day laborers on railroads or in city-building. They were bright and ambitious, and in the second generation largely manned the police forces of our cities, or farmed their own land, or practiced law in our courts. The third generation often saw them political leaders, judges, or governors of states, or prosperous business men. The Irish brought with them an almost ineradicable resentment toward England, a talent for political organization, and good, healthy physical powers which, under the influence of plentiful food and American cleanliness in housing, developed the race into splendid specimens of humanity. Their feeling for liberty was intense rather than rational, owing to their long struggle for independence from English domination; and they manifested a tendency to take possession of the government, especially in the cities, and to operate it in their own interests. They have been energetic and influential in many fields, exerting an unusual influence because of their readiness and quickness of assimilation.

The "forty-eighters." The Irish immigration had been of the peasant class. A very different class of people came to us after the unsuccessful revolution of 1848—the most liberal and cultured people of Germany, who had been driven out by the shortsighted conservatism of the king of Prussia and his reactionary fellow monarchs. These able, progressive, and highly educated Germans settled largely in the cities of the Middle West or bought farms in the fertile Mississippi Valley. They helped to win the Civil War for the North, built up educational and cultural institutions, took an active and intelligent part in politics, and in general added much to our national worth.[1] Their ideas were not essentially different from those of

[1] A most interesting tale of one of these "forty-eighters," who escaped prison by way of rope ladders and sewer exits, and who did more than any

the other North European peoples who had already come; they contributed much to qualities and institutions already existing in our country, bringing to us the ability and breadth which Germany lost through her blind conservatism.

The Scandinavians. One of the most interesting immigrations has been that from the Scandinavian countries, which, although never reaching the great numbers of some other peoples, has been notably influential. There was a fairly steady inflow of Swedes, Danes, and Norwegians from the early years of the nineteenth century, but the immigration was small until after the Civil War. Then shiploads of Scandinavians began to pour rapidly into the fertile Middle West and north and westward into the new lands of Minnesota and the Dakotas. Used as they were to a cold climate and to hard work, they gave our nation a service in the development of the great grainfields of the Northwest that can never be repaid.

Some of their young men went into professions or business in the second generation, and in the regions which they took almost solidly for their own they have shown an aptitude almost Irish for certain phases of practical politics. On the whole they have not affected American thought so much as certain other peoples, as they have settled in country districts and in a few cities, in which their ideas and customs have formed patches of foreign life rather than permeating influences. There are many differences between their ideas and those of the older North European peoples, but although the process must be slow, the final amalgamation will probably be more thorough than in the case of many of the more sprightly peoples, who are superficially more quickly assimilated.

THE NEW IMMIGRATION

Up to 1870 very few people from the southern and eastern parts of Europe had come to us, but by that year a very noticeable addition from the many races of Austria-Hungary was

other one man to save Missouri for the Union, can be found in the Autobiography of Carl Schurz.

apparent. By 1880 the Russians had entered, and their numbers rose quickly until they passed the Germans, the Scandinavians, and the British. At about the same time the Italians began to

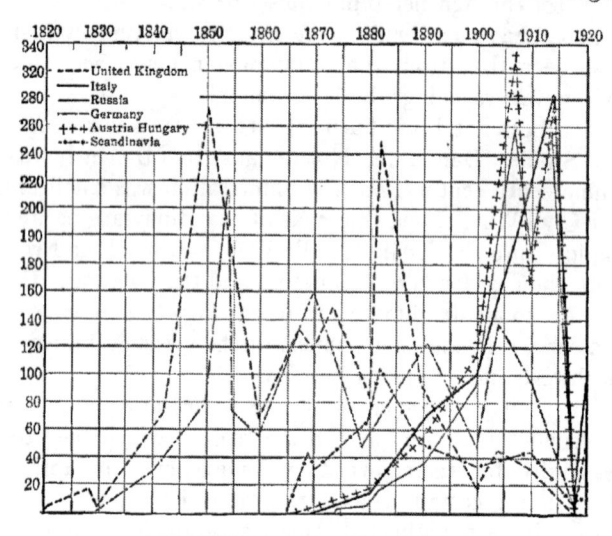

A HUNDRED YEARS OF IMMIGRATION

This graph shows the immigration in units of thousands from the chief European countries for the last century. France has never sent many people to our shores; the twenty-thousand point was reached in 1847 and 1851, but the average has been only 5238.06 per year. Belgium, the Netherlands, Mexico, Portugal, Rumania, Switzerland, Turkey, and the West Indies have given few people to America. The Poles and other peoples formerly in the Russian Empire and the many peoples of the former Austro-Hungarian Empire have not been separately listed. Owing to the back-and-forth movement between Canada and the United States it is impossible to say just what the Canadian contribution has been, but it should be noted that great numbers of British people emigrate to Canada, stay there a few years, and then come to the United States. From your knowledge of the history of the Old World and of America can you explain the peaks and depressions in the line of migration for each country?

flock to our shores in ever-increasing numbers. They had always come to us to some extent since Thomas Jefferson brought over the first Italian stone-carvers to decorate the classic halls of his beloved University of Virginia. By 1889 the whole character of our immigration had changed, the new elements greatly outnumbering the old The high point of foreign immigration was touched in 1907, when 1,285,338 foreigners came to us, of whom 338,452 were from Austria-Hungary.

New ideas with new people. The people who came after 1870 were essentially different in many ways from the North Europeans who had preceded them. Their languages, their standards of living, their traditions and customs, their ideals and ambitions, and their political experiences and aims were such that they could not so easily understand American ways and adapt themselves to them as could the earlier immigrants. The United States had never made any systematic efforts to Americanize its new citizens, and until the South Europeans came the need for it had never been clear to a majority of the people. Sociologists and social workers realized the need for a definite immigration policy and efficient Americanization work before the World War, but it took that catastrophe to show the ordinary citizen that a great un-American force had been admitted into the nation which had powers for good and evil that needed to be guided, guarded, and controlled.

The melting pot. Moreover, the entrance into our country of these new peoples in such great numbers has shown us that America has not yet a fixed and definite character. Israel Zangwill, in his great play "The Melting Pot," gave to the world the idea that America is a mixing-bowl for all peoples and ideas, a place in which the best of many races may be fused into a new race, which shall give to the world new treasures of thought, new achievements and ideas, and a greater civilization than it has yet known If this be true the process is now but begun. The people of the new immigration of the period since 1870 have gathered in isolated groups in the cities or in the country and have not sufficiently mixed with the older Americans either to gain or to give helpful qualities of character and habits of living. Some exchange of ideas there has been, often of the worst and not of the best in each; and the old American ideals have been already greatly modified by the newer peoples. This has happened almost unconsciously, and has not been guided and controlled by a conscious determination that each group shall appropriate the best in the other, so as to build up a greater, stronger nation than we have known in the past.

Two kinds of assimilation. The process of making foreigners into real Americans, so that they shall not think and act in any essential way differently from ourselves, is called assimilation. There are two kinds of assimilation, one of which must, with few exceptions, precede the other. Environmental assimilation is produced by the exposure of our new citizens to such contacts with American institutions and ideas that they learn to think and act as we do. It is produced by such means as schools, newspapers, clubs, social settlements, public meetings, and, above all, by friendly intercourse. The foreigners who come into this friendly contact with American ways and people cease to wear queer foreign clothes, to eat strange, foreign dishes, to live in uncomfortable quarters, to speak an alien tongue, and to think in terms of the Old World's problems; they become in very truth Americans, because they are part and parcel of American life, and their interests are right here among us.

The second kind of assimilation follows the first; as yet it is comparatively uncommon in the United States. It is ethnic, or blood, assimilation. With some exceptions peoples do not intermarry until they have a community of interest. This explains why intermarriage took place between the old-stock American and the old immigrant, but has not taken place to any great extent with the new immigrant. Whether such intermarriage would be a good thing or not remains to be seen, but at all events there is as yet comparatively little blood admixture of essentially different races in America. Environmental assimilation has begun, and should go on much farther than it has as yet, before ethnic assimilation will be possible or wise.[1]

---

[1] What the final ethnic American will be like is not yet known. Some anthropologists think that Americans tend to look more and more, as generation succeeds generation, like the native Indians.

Why immigrants come. The great American ideals have appealed with varying force to the peoples of Europe. In general, Europeans have admired Yankee shrewdness, and it is this trait which has often drawn the more ambitious and able people to us. Universally, the American standard of living and the ease with which comfort seems to have been secured by successful relatives and friends has been America's greatest drawing-card. Foreigners have not come to us because this was the land in which women are treated best, or in which children are most appreciated and petted; they have not come as a rule because of any high standards of personal conduct and character; but a majority have come in the hope of bettering their condition. Many of the best of our immigrants have come because this is "the land of liberty." Many immigrants do not know the meaning of the word "liberty," nor where liberty should begin or end; but they usually know it is something good that they have not had, and they want to live where there is reported to be plenty of it.

Let us see how the great ideals established by our fathers have been affected by the new immigration.

The Yankee wit survives. The American ideal of "smartness," of shrewdness, and keen ability to make the best of any situation has not been changed. Indeed, in many ways it has been deepened, for the Yankee who seemed so clever to his earlier countrymen finds himself less than a match for some of the newcomers, who bring with them a sharpness made keen by generations of struggle against great odds and unhampered by Puritan traditions of justice. The stolid transplanted peasant sometimes catches the spirit of American vim and gumption, sometimes submits to it, and is exploited by his intellectual superiors. In earlier days the ability to bargain to an advantage was considered a good joke, for there was bread enough for all, and only the shiftless need really suffer from sharp practice. But with increasing population and the filling of great cities with wage-earners, with the passing of cheap land and cheap food, the fruit of American sharpness is bitterness and resentment, a fruit filled with the seeds of shameful deeds—riots, strikes, sabotage, and class war. There must be a change in this ideal, which is no longer a matter for amused tolerance, or sorrow and defeat will come of it. The high mentality of America can be exercised in nobler ways than in "getting ahead" of others.

A higher standard of living still exists. Nor has the American ideal of a high standard of living been essentially changed. Greater wealth and the development of tastes for the elegant and beautiful things of life have rather made it higher than ever. Foreigners who came here mainly to share in this better living feel, when they have compassed it, that the object of their coming is gained. But the first and second generations of newcomers need careful teaching as to the essentials of our higher standard of living, for otherwise they copy what they see, without knowing at all about the more intrinsic details of our ways.

Difficulties in copying the standard. For instance, an immigrant mother sees American children on the street, dressed in smart, well-made clothes, well-fitting shoes, and pretty hair-ribbons. She has no time nor skill to make such clothes for her own children, so she tries to buy them in a store. Her stock of money is small, and she probably wastes much of it in her effort to buy what will imitate good American clothes at cheap shops. No one shows her how to buy materials, how to cut and make garments, or how to keep them in good condition. She knows nothing of the American housewife's skill in sewing, cooking, cleaning, and in making the house cheerful and pretty, for in her own country she has not had the materials to work with that American women have had for generations. Her children see American young people at the motion-picture theaters and in the parks; they do not see them reading about the lamp at night or singing around the piano. If our new citizens are to understand the real home life of America, they must be shown these things by friendly visitors and entertainers, for they cannot see them on the streets or at work. It is the adoption of the home life of America that will bring them most surely and quickly into the fold of true Americanism

The actual standard of living has been brought down in our large cities by the influx of foreigners, while the foreigners who have settled in the country have generally been able to bring up their standard approximately to that of the native Americans. As wages rise and intelligence increases among the new Americans, the tendency is to raise the standard to American levels even in the cities.

Changed standards of manners and morals. Puritanism in American life has been greatly affected by the influx of new peoples, mostly from South European lands. The old strict Sabbath, for instance, has definitely disappeared in certain parts of the country and has been modified everywhere. In the cities moral conditions are worse than they were before the foreign influx; but science and law, under the impulse of awakened consciences, are giving us new weapons against evil which may yet keep America from the ruin that follows general moral laxity. Of course the higher moral standards of America were never universal; they characterized the Americans who were heard from by foreigners, and so came to be regarded as typical of the nation. Unless the whole mass of Americans, new and old, can be made to conform to a new Puritanism, more rational but just as effective as the older form, the nation can never hold its own in influence and strength. This new Puritanism is one of the aims of all our efficient social forces.

We come now to democracy, the thing for which America is most known and honored The new immigration has reduced democracy in our land. There is, first, the inevitable gulf between the old-stock Americans and the newer peoples, each group somewhat scornful of the other, each lacking friendliness because each lacks knowledge. The new races have brought race antagonisms with them that introduce new discord into our national life. They have helped to create a wealth in which they very rarely share; and this wealth has paid for fine homes, country clubs, beautiful restaurants and theaters, great and luxurious hotels, and seaside resorts made for the rich alone. All these things have destroyed that fine simplicity of living which used to be the common-sense, effective basis of democracy. Economic extremes foster suspicions and jealousy and contempt. No matter how much they may want to do so, very rich men and very poor men do not understand and like each other.

A treasure to be worked for. All this means that if democracy is to exist in the future here in America, it will exist only through the efforts of determined and intelligent people. The first American democracy was a thing that grew up unconsciously in the lives of a free, happy, hard-working, and simple people. The most of these people thought very little about it; having it, they never realized its value. But today a hundred influences combine to destroy our democracy, and if we keep it and perfect it, it will not be through the gift of cheap and productive land, as in the past, but by the thoughtful and sacrificing zeal of intelligent citizens devoted to a fine ideal. Although we probably now have as much or more democracy than any other nation, the second American democracy is not yet ours.[1]

---

[1] The same may be said for other "lost" qualities. Without doubt the chivalric attitude of Americans has suffered a sad drop within the last century, and much of this is due to the influx of new peoples whose ideals were not those of the founders of the nation. The decline has come not only through the infusion of great numbers of peasant-bred peoples, with neither the chivalric traditions nor the ready imitative facility of the earlier Americans, but also indirectly through great changes in economic conditions. Chivalry is a reaction to helplessness, and the American woman has shown herself anything but helpless during the last fifty years, in which she has been forced out of her home and into the industrial and professional world. Even American children, trained and sharpened in the public schools, often seem to the observer more able to take care of themselves than their bewildered parents, especially if those parents do not know our language. The new chivalry, which we may believe is to come, must rest upon a basis different from the old; and the working out of this ideal is one of the tasks of the new generation.

The Immigration Policy of the United States

Strictly speaking, there has never been a real immigration policy in the United States. Our policy has been a negative rather than a positive one, and has consisted mainly in the passing of certain restrictive measures whenever the pressure from any one interested quarter became so great that it could not be longer resisted. When the Western laborers, led by Dennis Kearney, demanded the exclusion of Chinese labor with unmistakable determination, the Chinese Exclusion Act was passed in 1882. When organized labor grew strong enough it secured the Contract Labor Law, prohibiting the immigration of laborers under contract. There has been no constructive policy—no scientific comparison of the needs of the country with the needs of foreigners, no attempt to fit the newcomers into the niches which they could best fill.[1]

Present United States laws. Nevertheless the United States has passed certain restrictive laws which limit entrance into our country. Control is vested in a Federal Bureau of Immigration, which is, logically enough, a part of the Department of Labor. This bureau has a highly organized service at Ellis Island, where about three fourths of our immigrants enter, and at other ports. The steamship companies must take back

[1] The case is quite different with several other New World nations which need immigrants Canada, realizing that her need is for farmers and not for city dwellers, has made skillful bids for North European immigration to her wide-sweeping western plains Her immigration laws are elastic, giving great authority to the immigration officials, who judge whether the applicant for admission is a desirable settler or not As a result of this policy Canada has been able to control immigration more than we, in 1913 only 3 per cent of her immigration was from southeastern Europe Canada also acts as an agent to bring orphan children from the British Isles to Canadian farms, where the children have a far greater chance for education and eventual landowning than they could ever have in the British Isles Over sixty thousand children were given a chance in this way between 1850 and 1910 Argentina and Brazil offer the greatest help to newcomers, who are mostly from Italy, Spain, and Portugal: Argentina exempts new citizens from taxes and military service and transports them free to their destination, Brazil furnishes ship and train transportation, free seeds and tools, and medical care in case of illness

excluded persons.[1] The following people are at present excluded from entrance: oriental peoples not of the upper classes, all those likely to become public charges (such as orphans, criminals, paupers, those either mentally or physically diseased, immoral persons, and anarchists), and (since 1917) those who cannot pass an easy literacy test. Immigrants must have a supply of money and pay a head tax of eight dollars each.

A law was passed in 1924 limiting the immigration in any one year to 2 per cent of the population of each foreign nationality in the United States in 1890. After July 1, 1927, immigration is to be limited annually to 150,000, each country having its quota according to its representation in 1920. Consuls in foreign lands are to issue certificates to those entitled to come to America.

A constructive policy. The present policy of partial exclusion is good as far as it goes. In addition, sociologists and Americanization workers and the American Federation of Labor think that immigration should be stopped altogether for a period long enough to enable the nation to catch up with the problem; that is, to Americanize our present foreign-thinking and foreign-living population. Such a period of exclusion would permit systematic effort, uncomplicated by constant new additions of foreigners always undoing part of what has been done, and would give to America a people with at least superficial homogeneity. The shortest time that would suffice to produce such a result is perhaps thirty years. Unfortunately there is small prospect of any such respite.

Another needed improvement in our immigration policy is the addition of some kind of machinery by which newcomers can be admitted with regard to the place they are to fill in our economy. When farm workers are needed, then such men should be sought in the Old World, and the conditions of their labor truthfully set forth by authorized government officers,

[1] This regulation results in much suffering, as the steamship is likely to drop the would-be immigrant at some port in which he has no friends and in which he has difficulty in earning a living or finding the means of again reaching his home.

who would act as agents between needy farmers and peasants who want to better themselves. When factory hands are needed, they should be encouraged to come. The present hit-or-miss admission gluts the labor market at times and produces much suffering among the marginal workers. It is wasteful and unsatisfactory.

Still stricter requirements as to mental ability are needed. Now that mental testing is no longer an experiment but a device of proved value, mental testing of immigrants would save the country the problem of dealing with the many morons who slip in under ordinary unscientific inspection. The requirement of the presentation of certificates showing the civic record of entrants would serve to keep out certain malcontents and trouble-makers who now complicate our civil life. Some European governments in the past have sent as many of these undesirables as possible to America, thus relieving themselves of responsibility and expense.

Few if any of these improvements can be introduced under the present mode of administration. A Federal commission is needed, composed of trained experts under civil-service regulations, to which a large discretion would be granted in deciding individual cases upon their merits. Only the general policy can wisely be decided by law. Our consuls in foreign ports could coöperate with this commission to prevent the sailing of emigrants unlikely to be accepted. In this respect conditions have been much improved by the 3 per cent law.

Immigration and native increase. The greatest need of all is open-mindedness and frank study of population problems. Such a study shows many things not at first apparent. One of these facts is that the great foreign influx since about 1870, when growing factory and railroad needs suggested to capitalists the use of docile foreign laborers, has not really increased our population and labor supply; it has simply changed its quality. For while the number of foreigners has increased, the birth rate of native American families has steadily gone down. The old-stock Americans are scarcely holding their own in natural increase, for the burdens of partially supporting great numbers of ignorant and often dependent newcomers prevent the normal increase of the North European stock. Without immigration the native Americans would have kept up, not the frontier rate of increase but one sufficient to meet the nation's needs. Immigration has therefore been the means of substituting a South European increase for a native American increase of population.

There is also to be considered the effect upon Europe of its policy of dumping its surplus population upon our shores. In this way Europe has eased itself of what was becoming a serious problem of overpopulation, by simply pushing the problem across the ocean to us. Perhaps we are better able to solve it than they; certainly that is not proved so far. Transference has postponed the solution of the problem. And if in the interval between consciousness of the problem and its ultimate solution we can improve the quality of the races in question, we shall have helped matters.

The foremost practical help in sight for our own present condition is the shifting of foreign peoples who are suited to it into farm work. Hebrews rarely succeed in agriculture, although there is a prosperous colony at Vineland, New Jersey; but Italians have proved their farming ability in many places and ways. Such immigrants as come from the country districts of their own land could be recruited to help American farmers if there were an effective agency of contact. Italians, once given a chance, usually work hard, save steadily, and finally buy little farms of their own. What is still more encouraging, they take an interest in local matters and make good citizens.

The evolution of a farmer. Many workers who begin as seasonal workers in berry patches or harvest fields afterward work as all-season farm hands, finally earning patches of land themselves. Too often these foreign-born workers have bought worn-out lands in the East, which, with all their industry and skill, they cannot bring into paying operation.

The Poles, Bohemians, Finns, and Hungarians have all gone upon the land in small numbers, but never in the same way that the earlier North Europeans did. Very often this is because the new immigrant is not a true immigrant, expecting to own land and to stay here, but a temporary worker tempted to America by promises of high wages and anxious to stay in cities where the temporary rewards are greater than in the country. He saves all he can by keeping his Old World low standard of living, and hopes some day to go back to his own land, where he can live in comparative affluence the rest of his life.

Americanizing our Population

It is a matter of common comment that the human race is far more willing to take medicine to cure an ill than to take proper precautions to prevent it. So although it would probably be impossible to persuade the nation that it should forbid immigration until the foreign-born and foreign-thinking elements now in the country are better assimilated, it has been easy to interest people in efforts to Americanize these people. Many agencies have coöperated and many methods have been adopted to the end that our new citizens may learn how to live successfully in America. Sensible Americanization work has centered about three efforts:

1. To teach the language, thus giving the newcomer a means of expression and communication with his fellow citizens.

2. To teach American ways, and especially to teach such arts of living as will bring health and happiness and prosperity to the new American home.

3. To teach American ideals, ideas, and standards, and to instill a real love of and loyalty to the American government, which is the American people organized for the common good.

Helps and agencies. The agencies used in Americanization work are many, both public and private. The public schools in many cities hold night schools for the foreign-born, in which the students are taught the language and the things they need to know as citizens. Churches and social settlements hold classes for mothers and children, in which practical arts of housekeeping and the proper care of children are taught by trained nurses and domestic-science experts. Some factories organize classes for their foreign-born employees in which the main facts in the history of the United States and the characteristics of our government are taught. Some of this work is superficially done and amounts to little in real citizen-making; but it at least shows a friendly interest in the newcomer and so tends to establish that brotherly interest which is the greatest tie that can bind the hearts of compatriots. At last Americans are becoming conscious of the fact that it is neither safe nor Christian to allow great numbers of people to come to our shores in whom the older citizens take no interest whatever. If we let them come we must help them to become real sharers in American life and ways.

Americanizing Americans. But it is not the foreign-born alone who need Americanizing. There are people in America whose ancestors for generations have lived in this country who have no more idea of what it means to be an American than has some peasant newly arrived at Ellis Island. He is a poor American who bases his citizenship on his residence or his birth record. America has given too much to the world, America owes too much to the world, to remain unconscious of a national mission among the nations—of the responsibility that inheres in conceded leadership. That American who does not feel the necessity of helping his own nation to take her place honorably among the nations as a champion of fairness, truthfulness, clean living, and equality of opportunity is a poor citizen. He needs Americanization more than the foreigner who cannot speak our language but is in sympathy with our spirit.

The native Americans who need Americanization are to be found everywhere. Many of them are in mountainous or other very isolated districts; they have been left in the backwaters of national life and have lost track of national movements or never heard of them. Others are well-to-do folk who are so busy making of spending money that they have no interest in the affairs of their country. Others still are too poor and miserable to care about any troubles but their own. The most contemptible of all are the clever, insolently selfish people who have received richly of the advantages of American institutions, perhaps having been educated in free schools and colleges, but who delight in breaking American laws, violating American traditions, and shaming their country before the nations of the earth. Whatever the cause, these Americans, who never think of what it means to be an American, should avail themselves of the means at hand for finding out about their country and entering into its affairs. They need to read American history, or to join a current-events club, or to investigate the city council, or to organize a campaign for better roads in their county—they need to do anything, in fact, which will make them think what America means to the world and what America can do to make that world better.

Sectional consciousness. Another enemy to America which should be mentioned here is sectionalism. The United States is so large that it is idle to hope for such unity among its people as is possible in small, compact countries like Belgium or England. Uniformity would be as tiresome as it is impossible in our country. There will be always New Englanders, Southerners, and Westerners to rally each other on their peculiar pronunciations and their distinctive customs. But there is a type of sectionalism, unhappily too common in some parts of the country, which works against American unity, good will, and efficiency. This is the sectionalism which narrowly considers itself superior to other parts of the country and fancies itself the special custodian of the culture and standards of the nation. Nothing could be more foolish, and few things are more ridiculous in the eyes of really cultured and broad-minded people. There is no part of America which is intrinsically superior to the other parts, as those who have traveled know. There is no region of America whose traditions and history warrant its people in substituting loyalty to it for loyalty to the whole nation. The provincialism which makes men more proud of being New Englanders, or Southerners, or Californians than of being Americans is an enemy to the national unity which we need so much.

E pluribus unum. National unity does not mean national uniformity in nonessentials. It makes little difference how men of different sections pronounce their *a's* or roll their *r's*, but it makes an immense difference whether they are united in eliminating political corruption and solving the race problem. It is through intelligent and earnest work on common problems, through faith in the established principles of American life, and through a firm belief in the mission of America to give freely toward the welfare of all the earth that the many and various elements in our population may hope some day to become a homogeneous whole.

"America has an unparalleled opportunity to serve the whole world," says the National Committee for Constructive Immigration Legislation. "She must refuse to be either Europeanized or Asiaticized. She must admit to her land no more of any people than she can Americanize. And she must find a way by which to treat all peoples and races as brothers and friends."

SUPPLEMENTARY READINGS

BOGART, E. L., and THOMPSON, C. M. Readings in the Economic History of the United States, pp. 777-779, 779-783. [Growth and changes in population.]
DODD, W. E. "The Social Philosophy of the Old South," in *American Journal of Sociology*, Vol. XXIII, pp. 735-746.
JOHNSON, J. W. The Autobiography of an Ex-Colored Man.
LOW, A. M. The American People. Especially chaps. vi-xiii.
WARNE, F. J. The Tide of Immigration, chaps. xiv, xx. [The clash of old and new.]
WASHINGTON, B. T. Tuskegee and its People. Especially Part II.
WILLIS, H. A. The Japanese Problem in the United States, chap. xi.

SEARCH QUESTIONS AND PROBLEMS

1. Tabulate the following data for your own high school, or if the high school does not offer a fair cross section of the community, use the grades also. Number of students born abroad, with nationality, number whose parents were born abroad, with nationality, number whose grandparents were born abroad, with nationality, number whose foreign-born ancestors go farther back than three generations, with note of nationality and number of generations in America. Number of pure nationality; number with two nationalities; number with three; etc. Number of children in foreign-born and native families, number of children in pure-bred and mixed-nationality families. Having tabulated all these facts, what do you know about your community that you did not know before? What conclusions can you draw?

2. The immigrant bank offers a problem in itself. Read about such banks in Jenks and Lauck's "Immigration Problems," pp. 104–118, and explain and discuss the matter in class.

3. Another interesting matter is the formation of fraternal societies among foreign-born citizens. Jenks and Lauck give a list in "Immigration Problems," pp. 121–123. Inquire which of these organizations exist among the foreign-born population of your own vicinity.

4. Suppose that literacy and the possession of a small amount of capital are criteria of desirability among immigrants. By the use of the table on pages 510–511 of Jenks and Lauck's "Immigration Problems" graph the comparative desirability of the various peoples entering the United States in 1912.

5. Debate. *Resolved*, That all immigration into the United States should be stopped for ten years.

6. What are the desirable qualities which the Southeastern Europeans may contribute to American life which the North European races do not have or have but in small degree? Will these qualities, added to the good ones already belonging to the American character, make a well-rounded, symmetrical national character?

7. Examine the last census returns for your town or city, and note what per cent of each nationality there is. From your tabulation prepared in problem 1, note whether the native-born or foreign-born youth seem to be attending high school in larger proportions.

8. What inducements brought the foreign-born population to your city or state? Are these inducements still operating?

POPULATION IN THE UNITED STATES

9. What emigration from the United States has there been in the last ten years? (See a recent yearbook.) To what countries? Why? What is the American opinion of expatriots?

10. Do you know any Americans who are living in China, the Philippines, Hawaii, or the West Indies? Do they intend to come back to the United States? Do you think this is wrong? What do you think of Chinese who come here to earn a little fortune in gardening or laundry work and then go back to China to spend it?

11. On page 358 is the statement that twenty-five years made a generation in the early history of our country. That is four generations to the century. How many years make a generation now in America? Why?

12. What "forty-eighter" might have been nominated for the presidency but for his foreign birth? Cite the clause in the Constitution that debarred him.

13. What was the history of the literacy-test bill? Why was it repeatedly vetoed?

14. Why do the Californians object to the Japanese in that state? Note this table of Japanese births registered in California from 1906 to 1918:

1906	134	1912	1467	1916	3721
1908	455	1914	2874	1917	4108
1910	719	1915	3342	1918	4219

How do you interpret it?

15. Can you explain the movements of the peoples named in the table below? It shows the immigration and emigration of certain races for the year ending June 30, 1919. What general movements can be seen?

Race	Admitted to United States	Departed from United States
Armenian	228	11
Croatian and Slovenian	23	154
English	20,889	9,406
French	12,598	5,472
Greek	813	1,934
Japanese	10,056	2,127
Mexican	28,884	17,793
Scotch	10,364	1,687
Slovak	85	1,150
South Italian	2,137	36,980
Spanish	4,224	7,489

16 Organize a class symposium on the foreign elements in our country, based on the series of articles which ran in the *Literary Digest* in 1919–1920.

17 Show, by means of colored chalk on a large blackboard outline map of the United States, the location at the present time of the foreign-born population of the country See *Science Monthly*, April 3, 1919, Vol. VIII, p 380

18 The declining birth rate of the old-stock Americans is one of the most serious problems of our country Read the article "Count the Baby-Carriages," by P W Wilson, in the *Independent* for August 9, 1919.

19 In an article entitled "Discouraging New Citizens," in the *Literary Digest* for July 10, 1920, p 64, some reasons for the lack of naturalization among the foreign-born are given Do they apply to your own community?

20. Perhaps the best recent presentation of the race situation in the United States is that of the *National Geographic Magazine* for February, 1917. Study its maps and charts, compare them with the still more recent statistics given in the last World Almanac or other yearbook, and graph any important changes that have occurred. What relation do you find between the character of the population and the character of the industries in various parts of the country?

CHAPTER XV

POVERTY

> Find out the cause of this effect,
> Or rather say, the cause of this defect,
> For this effect defective comes by cause.—Shakespeare

The problem. Of all the host of problems arising from the mixed population of the United States, those of poverty and crime cause most suffering and degradation, and therefore it is most necessary to understand their causes and remedies. The unfortunates who become a burden on producing society have been classed by sociologists as (1) dependents, who, without apparent reason, do not take care of themselves; (2) defectives, whose minds or bodies or both are not normal; (3) delinquents, who have transgressed social law in some way.

We find all three among the very poor. Now poverty, a problem as old as the race, may result in pauperism, but the two must be sharply distinguished. Poverty is the condition of all who cannot obtain for themselves those things which are needed to maintain a state of physical efficiency. Paupers are those who depend upon public or private charity for a living or for part of their living. This is the legal use of the term "pauper," and excludes those moral paupers or parasites existing on the fortunes piled up by their ancestors or provided by relatives, who do nothing to earn an honest living. The rich pauper is less respectable in reality than the poor one, but he is less of a problem to society at large, which does not have directly to provide for him.

Extent of poverty and pauperism. The United States has less poverty and pauperism than the rest of the world. But even in this especially blessed country there are about 395,000 dependents in institutions. It is impossible to say how many receive "outdoor" relief (that is, relief outside of institutions), but probably four and a half million would be a conservative estimate. Some sociologists think that 10 per cent of our population live below the poverty line.

Attitudes toward poverty. The solving of the poverty problem depends a great deal on the attitude of society toward it. An old and still popular point of view is that poverty is a necessary evil which will exist as long as the world lasts. Some people holding this view deny any personal responsibility or interest in the matter, others hold that the State should relieve suffering in a reasonable way, and rest easy thereafter. Another view is that poverty is a necessity in order that the spirit of giving shall not wither and die in the hearts of the well-to-do. In other words, charity is so lovely a virtue that nothing should be done to kill it, and thousands of human beings exist in misery in order that others, more fortunate than they, may properly cultivate their souls. This was taught by Christian teachers in past ages, but is held in its entirety now chiefly in the South American states. But it still colors philanthropic thought greatly in our own country.

The most recent attitude toward poverty is that in America at least, with its great resources, its free education, and its faith in men, poverty is unnecessary and should be ended. No one thinks it can be done in a day or a year, but good authorities think it can be reduced rapidly and ended eventually by curing the causes. And every advance toward curing poverty will help to cure its related social evils.

The causes of poverty. Men are the product of two great sets of creative influences, which we call heredity and environment respectively. And the causes of poverty are to be found in abnormalities which are either inherited or acquired from surroundings. The abnormalities may be either physical or mental: a mind or a body that is not up to the normal human standard, that puts its owner at a disadvantage in the struggle of life, will bring on poverty.

Hereditary Causes

Hereditary physical defects. Whether physical or mental, inherited unfitness is due to the weaknesses or sins of ancestors. Recent science has proved that there is far less of this inherited weakness than was thought probable a few years ago. Tuberculosis, rheumatism, cancer, and other diseases have been shown not to be directly inheritable. No characteristic, mental or physical, which has been acquired during the lifetime of the parent can be transmitted to children; but if the life cells are undernourished or poisoned and the child is therefore undervitalized, an inherited weakness or predisposition may bring on the same disease from which the parents suffered, or some other. Many such weakened children grow up into weak and lazy adults, who become a burden on society.

Some defects are, however, directly inheritable, and these include deaf-mutism and blindness. Less than 18 per cent of the world's deaf were born so, but about 10 per cent more become deaf before they are two years old as a result of inheritance. These children become dumb also, unless given special training, since they hear no sound to imitate. In the case of blindness only 12½ per cent are born with the defect, but from 20 per cent to 30 per cent become blind within a few days of birth through infection from a diseased parent.[1] With a few exceptions this completes the list of congenital physical defects.

Hereditary mental defects. Mental weaknesses are much more easily inherited than physical ones. Certainly two thirds of the cases of feeble-mindedness—the commonest kind of mental weakness—are due to heredity; some scientists put the proportion as high as 75 per cent.[2] The defect must be distinguished from insanity and retardation. Insanity is a derangement of a formerly normal brain; retardation is the slow

---

[1] The "babies' sore eyes," which so often result in blindness, can be cured by a 2 per cent silver nitrate solution applied to the eyes at birth. Most states require that this solution be applied to every baby's eyes at birth.

[2] Other causes are intemperance, immorality, abuse, falls, blows, and such diseases as diphtheria, scarlet fever, meningitis, brain troubles, and convulsions.

development of the mind due to such physical conditions as malnutrition, bad sight or hearing, adenoids, overwork, or too little sleep. But feeble-mindedness is lack of mental development due to the arrested development of the brain. These people, whose mind growth has fallen behind their physical growth, are divided into three classes

1. Idiots (composing almost 10 per cent), who have minds of not more than two years.

2. Imbeciles, with minds equal to those of normal people three to seven years old. They can talk, play, and sometimes write their names.

3. Morons, the largest division. They have the minds of children of seven to twelve, can read and write, and often earn enough for themselves when grown, although they can rarely support a family. It is estimated that about 2 per cent of the school children of America are morons, and about 10 per cent of the inmates of institutions of relief. Morons are commonly addicted to intemperance, vice, and crime; our reformatories and prisons are filled with them.

Treatment. The first thing to be done for the feeble-minded is to separate them from normal people and from other dependents, defectives, and delinquents. It is not fair either to them or to others that they mix freely in society. If they go about freely in the world they almost invariably are led into vice or crime, and in time they are punished for wrongdoing from which society should have saved them and itself. They cannot really be reformed, as they are too simple to be morally responsible, and if freed after serving in prison, they usually fall into worse and worse crime.

Detection. Morons often appear quite intelligent, having good imitative powers, and for a long time it was very hard to pick them out from others They are often fluent talkers and physically energetic. But since 1908 there have been worked out psychological tests which ascertain mental age. These have nothing to do with acquired information or attainments, but are means of testing purely native ability. These tests should be used in every reformatory, prison, insane asylum, and poorhouse to select the mentally deficient. They should be used in every school and by every charity organization in the country, in an attempt to locate every feeble-minded person for confinement in a separate institution.

The great objection to this program is its immense cost. No one knows the number of feeble-minded in the country, although it is estimated that there must be at least three hundred thousand. To keep such a number at public cost means a heavy tax burden. But when one examines the question fairly, one realizes that part of this number are already being kept by charity, in one way or another. Transferring this number from one kind of institution to another more adapted to their care would not increase the cost, but would increase their happiness and the safety of society. And the confinement of those at present free would vastly reduce the burdens of the future, for they or their descendants will eventually land in large numbers in our prisons and reformatories. And as the moron is very prolific, the total number of defectives, dependents, and delinquents in the next generation would be so greatly reduced as to cut the cost of public support and care of them into a fraction of what it now is.

But the cost of confinement in institutions scientifically managed need not be so great as is feared. The first two classes of feeble-minded cannot earn a living and are therefore a complete burden. But the larger number, the morons, can be taught to do many useful things. With proper training and under constant care some 30 per cent may become entirely self-supporting, who, if left to themselves, would drift into complete or partial dependence. They learn occupations of routine character easily. Broom-making, carpet-weaving, carpentry, painting, basketry, and farm work are some of the things they do well in institutions. The State may market these products and services to offset the upkeep, and give the worker an incentive for effort, besides, in the small sum of spending money that can be allowed him from his earnings. By this housing in institutions, the moron labor which is now largely a waste product may be utilized, many abused and miserable human beings made happy and healthy, and the ultimate number of criminals decreased By the prevention of propagation the whole social fabric may be immensely improved within a few generations. Pauperism, intemperance, immorality, and crime can all be materially reduced if the feeble-minded can be eliminated.

In the meantime marriage laws forbidding the union of the feeble-minded will help the situation, and the general education of the public to the seriousness, both from a social and from an economic point of view, of the present lack of control will pave the way for a solution of the problem later on.

Insanity. Next to feeble-mindedness in the list of mental defects comes insanity, "a disorder of the mind, due to disease of the brain, manifesting itself by a more or less prolonged departure from the individual's usual manner of thinking, feeling, and acting, and resulting in a lessened capacity for adaptation to the environment."[1] This is almost wholly a disease of adults. It is estimated that there are over a quarter of a million insane in the United States, of whom there were 199,340 in special institutions in 1916. The remainder are in prisons, poorhouses, or at large. Statistics show that the number of insane is increasing in our country.[2]

Causes. About two thirds of the cases in American institutions are congenital, although it is a predisposition to the disease rather than the actual malady that is inherited. The offspring of abnormal parents are often subject to extreme nervousness, hysteria, or general mental instability, which later develops into insanity.[3]

---

[1] Cyclopedia of Education, article "Insanity"

[2] In 1890 there were 170 in every 100,000 of our population; in 1910 the number per 100,000 was 204 2, and in 1917 it had become 227 6 Part of this increase is due to better commitment laws, part to actual increase of insanity

[3] Other causes are (1) intemperance, including the use of such drugs as morphine, cocaine, and heroin, (2) immorality, which accounts for the greatest number of men in insane asylums, (3) diphtheria, meningitis, typhoid, tuberculosis, kidney and artery troubles; (4) exhaustion, great nervous stress, un-

The attitude of the general public toward the insane has passed through four distinct phases. The first was neglect; the second, detention with accompanying cruelty; the third, detention with more humane treatment; the fourth is the period of scientific investigation for causes, cures, and prevention. We know now that the insane should be separated from all other abnormal people, treated with the greatest kindness, and given treatment for cure if cure be possible, as it sometimes is. Osteopathy, massage, and other nonmedical treatments, including suggestion, may effect a cure; but cures are rare, and the hope for the future lies in prevention.

Prevention. And since the causes seem to lie mainly in intemperance and immorality, prevention becomes a matter of education and legislation. The greatest enemies to the prevention of insanity are those who object to the right of society to regulate the lives of citizens in the interests of self-control and morality. In addition to the strict enforcement of prohibition and the cleaning up of moral conditions in towns and cities, two things are needed: the education of all the people in the facts concerning the wages of sin, and strictly enforced marriage laws forbidding the union of those known to be insane or to have a tendency toward the disease.

Moral hereditary defects. Inherited moral defects are closely allied to physical and mental ones. Indolence results from undernourishment and undervitalization; incompetence is the usual trait of morons; quarrelsomeness is found among the children of drunken parents; shiftlessness is frequently the outcome of some congenital social disease. It is not yet known to what extent moral traits not connected with physical conditions can be inherited. The willingness to get all one can from the world without giving anything in return, which is the essence of pauperism, seems to run in certain families, but how much of this is transmitted and how much is absorbed from

controlled grief or excitement, and great shocks. Of all these the social diseases resulting from intemperance and self-indulgence, either through inheritance or participation, account for the majority of cases.

the environment is not known. Sociologists agree that a predisposition to be sensitive to social approval or disapproval can be inherited. If parents have not this predisposition to hand on to their children, those children must often lack ordinary self-respect and so may easily become paupers. The interesting studies of the Kallikaks by Goddard, the Jukes by Dugdak, and the Ishmaels by Warner all go to prove that pauperism and degeneracy are hopelessly intertwined and that they increase and diverge through heredity.

Physical Mishaps

Poverty springs from causes in the environment, from the training and opportunities known collectively as "acquired" conditions, as well as from inherited handicaps. These conditions are physical, economic, and social, but all are closely interrelated and often inseparable.

Deafness and blindness. Deafness, for instance, in children may come from meningitis, adenoids, or scarlet fever; among adults catarrh, influenza, and old age operate to bring it on. Prevention and cure are impossible in a large proportion of cases, and therefore the education and care of the deaf become very important. They can be made happy, useful, self-supporting citizens. The methods of teaching the deaf are not yet as fully developed as they will be, and there are too few good schools for these unfortunates. Many pursuits in agriculture, manufacturing, and commerce do not require hearing for efficiency, courses for the training of deaf persons in vocational schools should put all otherwise normal victims in positions of self-support. So far the deaf seem to succeed best in farming.

Blindness, except when congenital, comes usually after maturity. It comes from industrial accidents, poor lighting, cataract, old age. Blindness in children is from poor lighting (sometimes in the schoolroom) or from scarlet fever or measles. State inspection of schools and factories with a view to correcting their defects in lighting and forcing the installation of safety devices would do much to prevent blindness. The blind may be self-supporting; libraries of raised-print books and vocational training will make them capable of taking their places as citizens among their fellows. Again, agriculture offers a good field for those thus handicapped; about one half the blind now earning a living are in this occupation. They make good brooms, brushes, baskets, mattresses, and rugs. A number have become good piano tuners. The State owes it to the blind to train them for useful lives and to help them if necessary to buy raw materials and market their finished products. Such help costs the taxpayer less than to support the blind in institutions and makes those thus afflicted self-respecting and independent.

Accidents. When we realize that accidents cause a death every sixteen minutes and an injury every sixteen seconds of every day among the workmen of the United States, we are face to face with another great cause of poverty. When the accident causes the death of the breadwinner, or costs him his eyes, hands, or feet, pauperism for his family is almost surely the result. Even when the injury means but a few weeks of idleness the result is often dire want, for few laborers have a money reserve.

In 1915 the United States Department of Labor estimated that in 1913 there were 25,000 deaths from industrial accidents and 57,530 deaths from other accidents. Seven hundred thousand other accidents resulted in over four weeks' disability each. In the nineteen months in which the United States participated in the war, over two and a half times as many Americans were killed in peaceful pursuits as there were soldiers who gave their lives. And in the United States there were almost two hundred times as many citizens injured as were wounded in Europe. All this loss of health and life costs tremendously, not only to the injured and their families but to the public at large. New York State alone paid $146,000,000 in compensation in 1910. And at least half this loss is avoidable.

Causes. Transportation produces more accidents than any other one source. Certain railroads have vastly improved conditions in this respect, but the country as a whole is little if any better than before the "Safety First" slogan became popular. In the 90's the number killed per year was usually under 6500 and the injured numbered less than 40,000, in 1917 there were 10,087 killed in railway accidents and 194,805 injured. It is true that the number of passengers carried and the number of employees have both about doubled in that time, but this fact does not fully account for the increase in accidents.

Over 50,000 deaths and 53,000 injuries during the past ten years have come to trespassers on railroads. The amount of pauperism was not increased in many of these cases, as the victims were tramps; but when the accident resulted in a permanent disability the injured often became a burden on the State. Another prolific and tragic cause of such dependence is the "train-hopping" of venturesome boys, or the "bumming" trips sometimes taken by youths who want to see the world. Town councils, policemen, and parents can help prevent sorrow and suffering by warnings and severe punishments, for usually the boy hurt has turned the trick successfully a few times before he is caught. Sometimes the victims are self-supporting workingmen with families, yielding weakly to the appeal of a cheap method of travel or taking a short cut home through railway yards. No one should be allowed on or near railroad tracks who has not real business there.

In cost of life and limb mining comes next to transportation. Between the ages of fifteen and thirty-four more miners die from accidents than from all diseases put together Metal-mining has taken its toll, but it is in coal-mining that most accidents occur. Statistics show that in recent years one man in every three hundred gives his life to his work. Open shafts and unsafe overhead structures have taken many lives every year, but the chief cause of mining fatalities is explosion In the twentieth century there have been fifteen cases in which over a hundred lives were lost at a time.

Construction comes next to mining, and then manufacturing in furnishing accidents to labor. Unguarded machinery, boiler explosions, and contact with electricity cause most accidents in manufacturing. Children, according to the National Child Labor Committee, are three times as liable to accident from machinery as adults.

On the employer's part the lack of guards and safety devices causes many accidents; but the worker is as often to blame, for his carelessness, chance-taking, or mind-wandering. By far the greatest cause is ignorance, as is proved by the fact that non-English-speaking foreign-born workers have the highest industrial accident percentage of all workers. They cannot understand the directions for handling the machinery. Inexperience also plays its part; a large majority of injured men have been employed less than six months in the plant where the injury is received.

With careful employees and conscientious employers doing all they can to prevent them, there will always be some accidents. The question arises, Who shall bear the burden? Formerly the family of the injured or killed had to bear the loss, or if it was unable, charity was the only alternative. The common law exempted the employer from bearing any part of the burden if he could prove that the accident was the result of negligence on the part of the man hurt or any fellow employee, or whenever the risk was known to the employee or was an integral part of the industry itself. It was a stupid employer who could not prove one of these to be the case. Lawsuits are expensive things, especially for workmen. Employers escaped practically all responsibility.[1]

Today many people go to the other extreme and put the entire responsibility upon the employer. This may be fair enough so far as making him responsible for the risks and dangers inherent in the industry itself, and even for those acci-

---

[1] See Marshall, Wright, and Field's "Materials for the Study of Elementary Economics," No. 214, and Hamilton's "Current Economic Problems," Nos. 262–266.

dents caused by other employees; but it is very unfair when applied to accidents caused by the carelessness of the injured one himself. The new view has had, however, the good result of lessening the number of accidents through the introduction of many safety devices.

Insurance. Many American employers are not in a position financially to bear the whole burden of liability, and so the device of insurance was copied from European practice.[1] Arizona in 1912 was the first state to adopt a workmen's compensation act. Since then forty-three states have followed with more or less adequate laws. The laws vary much as to industries affected, means of raising the insurance fund, and methods of placing the insurance (whether in state or commercial companies), and the amounts for medical care, for partial and permanent disability, and for death benefit differ. But the principle is the same: every industry has its characteristic kinds and proportions of unavoidable accident, the responsibility for which is very hard if not impossible to fix, and therefore the industry is compelled, in the interest of justice to the killed or injured, to share the risk through insurance systems. Even if the employer shifts the burden of insurance upon the public by classing it as part of the cost of production and therefore making it a determinant of price, there should be no complaint, providing he has used every device known for reducing the chance of mishap. The public pays for the cost of material and labor, why should it not pay for the cost in life?

[1] In 1838 a Prussian law was passed compensating injured railway employees. In 1871 there was passed a general liability law for the whole empire, embracing accidents in quarries, mines, and factories as well as on railways In 1884 a more efficient law covered industrial accidents of practically all kinds, involving a scheme of collective and cooperative responsibility of employers, who form associations for the sharing of the costs of indemnification of injured workers The law was brought up to date in 1900, and worked efficiently until the World War The Scandinavian countries adopted the principle of compensation to injured workmen and enacted laws during the 90's England, after experimenting with several half-measures, passed the British Workmen's Compensation Act of 1897, which makes employers pay for the insurance of their workmen against accidents while at work

Nonindustrial accidents. During the World War period almost three times as many lives were lost out of industry as in it. The causes are so many that they cannot be listed fully. An ever-increasing number of street accidents comes from congestion of traffic due to the increase of automobiles and trucks. It has been estimated that eleven thousand deaths per year come from this cause, as often as not the fault of careless pedestrians. Human nature loves to take a chance. Good traffic direction and strict enforcement of traffic rules can reduce this number.

"One of the most popular methods of getting into the grave is to fall into it," says someone. In 1917 almost 15,000 persons were killed by slipping, falling, and tripping. "Watch your step" is a popular phrase that should be taken more seriously. Then the toll of lives from burning is heavy, amounting in 1917 to almost 7000. Most of them came from careless handling of matches or gasoline. Over 5500 more were drowned. A large number of these accidents befell children and old people, so that only part of them may be said directly to increase poverty.

Prevention. The startling thing in the story of accidents is that so many of them—perhaps 90 per cent—are avoidable. The knowledge of this, plus the knowledge of the steady increase in the number of accidents, led in 1907 to the initiation of the Safety First movement. Wherever the slogan has been taken seriously there has been a decided decrease in accidents, but there is still great room for improvement. City and state agencies should coöperate more. An adequate program of Safety First must contain

1. The institution of such safety devices as danger signals and automatic couplers on railroads, the use of goggles in the steel industry, inspection of props in underground mines, insulation of electrical apparatus, etc.

2. Education in avoiding danger, through pamphlets, lectures, street-car advertisements, and the motion pictures.

3. First-aid training in the treatment of sunstroke, drowning, suffocation, arterial bleeding, and other accidents.

4. Adequate (that is, severe) punishment for criminal carelessness, such, for instance, as workhouse sentences for automobile speeders.

In addition to all these it is well to remember that no program can succeed unless grounded in a deep reverence for human life and health [1]

Disease, a Potent Cause

Industrial diseases. Illness that comes from work is called industrial or occupational disease, and it is estimated that there are thirteen and a half million cases of such disease in the United States. Some of the commonest are lead poisoning in smelting and refining and in porcelain and tile plants; lung diseases in the dusty industries of mining and the first stages of cotton and woolen manufacture, poison from fumes such as hydrogen in making storage batteries, or sulphur dioxide in vulcanizing rubber, or wood alcohol in brush and felt making; eczema from baking and sugar-refining; cancer from soot in chimney-cleaning, skin rashes from the plugging up of hair glands by oil in the making of lubricants, and anthrax, a disease which increased suddenly among men working in tanneries and hide and skin concerns along the lower Mississippi and Delaware Rivers in 1915.

Prevention and treatment. In many cases these diseases are absolutely unnecessary. They may be avoided by such simple precautions as the wearing of respirators, or the use of adequate suction apparatus, or the spraying of water when drilling in mines. But it is hard to persuade workmen to use these precautions. They object to the trouble. Respirators are uncomfortable, and splashing mud plasters up the clothing when miners use a spray. Some men even boast that they can eat dust or breathe gas; and these are the men who die young.

[1] In the *American* of July, 1920, in a very readable article entitled "What Fool Things do *You* do that Endanger your Life?" Keene Sumner tells of several unique punishments to speeders in the form of sentences to visit morgues or to sit by the victim of the speeder's carelessness.

In oil rashes all that is needed is frequent applications of hot water and soap with stiff brushes to keep the pores open. Complete disinfecting of hides, hoofs, hair, and wool prevents contagion in anthrax.

In many cases simple treatment in the early stages of the disease will cure; but where the worker has contracted a tenacious malady, such as tuberculosis, time and money are needed,[1] which shows the bearing of the whole matter of occupational diseases on the poverty problem.

Insurance. In 1883 Germany adopted compulsory health insurance for workmen, and since then practically every country of Europe, except Russia and the Balkans, has followed suit. The funds are variously provided by the workmen, the employers, and the State. In some cases the insurance includes any disease which causes a loss of employment.[2] In America there has been a strong sentiment against insurance, on the ground that it is better to raise the workers' wages and let them insure themselves in a commercial company if they wish, or else save their extra wages for illness.

But this policy no longer solves the problem in the United States. There are too many ignorant workers, unused to exercising personal responsibility. They neither save nor insure. Probably a compulsory insurance system which will force workers to provide for the rainy day will be found a good temporary expedient for a few years; and in the meantime the raising of wages and education in thrift will bring about a condition of things in which it will be unnecessary to force men to plan for their future and for emergencies.

It is not only the illness of the breadwinner which brings on poverty; the illness of some child or other non-wage-earner

---

[1] An example of the simplicity of treatment which is sometimes effective is that of white-lead poisoning, in which it has been found that submerging the hands and feet in tubs of salt water, with the pole of an electric battery in each, will rid the body of the lead. The current carries it through the man, who acts as a conductor, and deposits it on the electrodes.

[2] See Hamilton's "Current Economic Problems," No. 268, for arguments on insurance, and No. 269 for the British National Insurance Bill.

AMERICAN PROBLEMS

keeps many thousands of families on or below the poverty line. Irving Fisher estimates, in his "National Vitality," that if the illness in America were equally divided, every person in the country would be too ill to work for thirteen days out of each year. Much of this disease is concentrated among the very poor, because of ignorance, insanitary homes, and lack of medical attention. It perpetuates the poverty which has largely brought it on. The New York City Charity Organization thinks that from 55 per cent to 60 per cent of the poverty in that city is due to illness.

Fatal diseases. Since the death of the wage-earner is the most frequent cause of poverty through disease, it is worth while to know wherein lies most danger and what may be done to better conditions. The following table shows the chief causes of death in the year 1920.

Cause	Number of Deaths	Rate per 100,000 Population	Percentage[1]
Organic heart disease	124,142	141.9	10.9
Pneumonia	120,108	137.3	10.5
Tuberculosis	99,916	114.2	8.7
Acute nephritis and Bright's disease	78,192	89.4	6.8
Cancer and other malignant tumors	72,931	83.4	6.4
Apoplexy	70,780	80.9	6.2
Accidents, sunstroke, etc.	62,492	71.4	5.5
Influenza	62,097	71.0	5.4
Whooping cough	10,968	12.5	1.0
Suicide	8,959	10.2	0.8
Measles	7,712	8.8	0.7
All other causes	424,261	483.0	37.1

Tuberculosis, formerly the greatest menace to health, has decreased. In 1913 the number of deaths from the Great White Plague was 147,600; in 1917 it was 110,285; in 1920, only 99,916. This includes only the approximately 73 to 83 per cent

[1] Statistics from United States Health Reports, November 4, 1921, Vol XXXVI, pp 2723-2725. The death-registration area covers thirty-four states and sixteen cities in nonregistering states.

of the population from which statistics are available. The disease comes from overcrowding, overwork, and underfeeding and from improper housing and living. It must be cured by increasing vitality, which means that milk and house inspection should become a regular part of the duties of cities or counties, that antispitting ordinances should mean more than dead-letter signs, and that people must learn to sleep with their windows wide open. Cases must be found in the early stages and subjected to institutional treatment, which the states are now providing in free or part-payment hospitals. By preventive measures and scientific treatment the number of cases has been reduced greatly—from 15 per cent of all deaths in 1909 to 8.7 per cent in 1920. This is doubtless due to organization both in preventive education and in treatment. It is the result of a social campaign for the control of a common enemy.

Pneumonia is very prevalent, often fatal, and easily communicated. Unlike tuberculosis it increased seriously from 1910 to 1920. It comes after measles, scarlet fever, influenza, and whooping cough, and from such habits as alcoholism. It takes its toll between the ages of twenty-five and fifty-four and hence is the cause of the loss of many wage-earners. Prevention is secured through the prohibition of liquor, the building up of the devitalized through good food and rest, keeping children from catching preparatory diseases, and careful disinfection where the disease exists.

A high and entirely preventable death toll is taken by the social diseases of syphilis and gonorrhea. It is almost impossible to say how many die yearly of these diseases, or how many more are affected by apoplexy, softening of the brain, or locomotor ataxia as a result of them. Possibly fifteen thousand deaths and four million diseased is not an overestimate. Both diseases are highly communicable through such channels as drinking-cups, towels, and kisses. These diseases, with their dread results of insanity and poverty for the diseased and possible physical and mental defects for their children, are curses which well deserve the name of the Great Black Plague. Before society can hope to cut down the number of paupers and defectives it must wage a war upon them in the open, quite as it fights the White Plague of tuberculosis.

The 180,000 cases and 18,000 deaths from typhoid fever in 1913 were cut down, through education and care, to 6805 deaths in 1920. The decrease came mainly from care of milk, water, and sewage in large cities. In the country there is much typhoid from contaminated drinking-water. Country authorities rarely inspect wells, or mark dangerous springs for the protection of picnickers and children. It should be unlawful to use milk utensils that are not sterilized or to transfer milk from one container to another on the street. New York has reduced her typhoid cases by chlorinating the entire city water supply. Inoculation will prevent this disease. As most of the fatalities come between the ages of fifteen and twenty-four, the wage-earning part of the population is hard hit by typhoid. It so reduces resistance to other disease that other maladies often follow it, and lowered vitality may result in a long period of small earnings or none.

Children's diseases. Among the troubles that keep wage-earners from saving and from comfortable living are the numberless so-called children's diseases. Diphtheria and croup secure 88 per cent of their fatalities before the age of ten, and scarlet fever is a children's disease in about 82 per cent of its cases. Fatality has been reduced greatly in diphtheria and croup through care in the handling of such carriers as handkerchiefs and by the use of antitoxin. Measles, which is a more dangerous disease than most people think, takes a toll of over ten thousand lives annually. Like whooping cough, measles is often a forerunner of tuberculosis, and often brings on deafness and blindness. Scarlet fever is even more dangerous in this respect.

Prevention. Old-fashioned mothers used to think that the sooner a child caught and recovered from these children's diseases the better. They were regarded as necessary evils, if not quite a normal part of a child's life. Some mothers purposely exposed their children in the summer, when the illness would entail no loss from school. This antiquated and barbarous practice is passing away, for medical science has shown how really dangerous and at the same time preventable these diseases are. Good mothers now see to it that their children are kept from contagion if possible, and a good government helps them by (1) strict school care and isolation of children who have headaches or other symptoms, (2) immunity through vaccination and inoculation, (3) strictly enforced quarantines, and (4) the spread of general education as to contagion and the result of disease.

Prevention is the policy which will in time remove most of the acquired physical defects which produce poverty. If society really wants to abolish poverty, here is the point of attack which will bring the first and easiest results. Accidents may be prevented by proper precautions, and care in the matter of contagion can make tuberculosis, typhoid, diphtheria, and the other common scourges of life as rare as typhus was in the United States before the World War. A war against these causes of poverty is a sensible one, fought to bring life rather than death, and fought against a mighty enemy within our gates. The weapon is education, combined with surveys and clinics and free treatment when necessary. No matter what such a program might cost the public, it could not cost what disease and death now cost it.[1]

Economic and Social Causes

Economic causes. Some of the chief economic causes for poverty are (1) lack of sufficient natural resources, as in certain parts of India and China; (2) the sudden destruction of property, as in the San Francisco earthquake and the World War's devastation in northern France and Belgium; (3) sud-

[1] The work done by the Ford plant in cleaning up the twelve thousand homes of its employees in Detroit is told in *System* for March, 1917. Magruder, in "American Government," p. 5, describes the United States Public Health Service.

den changes in money values, as in the case of the resumption of greenbacks whereby the Western debtors found their debts increased 100 per cent; (4) bad economic policy which produces starvation wages, unemployment, and strikes; (5) poor home management.

This last cause of poverty is far more important than is generally realized. A man may have a good wage and every chance to provide for the future, but if his wife is a wasteful housekeeper and home manager he has small chance for a happy, peaceful old age. The bad management may lie either in buying the wrong things, or in failing to make them up so that they will yield their value to the family. Money needed to buy meat, oatmeal, bread, and milk may be spent instead for pickles, candy, soft drinks, and coffee. If the housewife knows nothing of the relative nourishment of various articles of diet, or allows herself to pander to perverted tastes, undernourishment and disease lead the way to poverty. Classes in buying will help teach housekeepers to make the most of their husbands' money. In clothing there is too often a wish to purchase smart style instead of good quality, and flimsy silk when honest flannel is needed. Few mothers know how to tell shoddy in wool, or what makes leather long-wearing, or how to test silk for weighting. Too many homes are furnished with showy curtains and rugs but lack good mattresses and plenty of household linen. In all family expenditure the same principle holds. the buyer should know what will give solid service and add to health and happiness, and should buy that, whether it makes a great show or not.

Quite as important as the quality of purchases is the principle of buying adopted. The family income should be divided among the various needs as carefully as possible, and a fixed amount allowed for each. Any change from this plan should come only in case of emergency The family which keeps books thinks twice before spending money. Many parents find it wise to give each child an allowance, which is increased as he grows older; and from this allowance he is expected to provide certain specified things for himself. So each child learns gradually how to spend money economically; and as he learns he is trusted with more, until he can look after his own expenses with good judgment.

Fathers and mothers often need education in how to manage a home. This is offered in classes in social settlements, Y.M.C.A.'s, and similar organizations, in night-school classes, and through household and farm papers. Banks are glad to give advice on money matters free. Doctors can often suggest needed changes in diet which will bring about better health and efficiency. Harder to correct is the bad management due to family jars, discouragement, spite, and despair. Only removal of the causes of the mental attitudes will serve here.

Social causes. The fundamental social unit is the home. If the home is not normal, it becomes a breeding place of troubles. Paupers, social malcontents, and even criminals come from it. Every condition which destroys the happiness and wholesomeness of homes is a condition that society does well to fight and overcome in its own defense.

Broken family ties. The incomplete family is a result of death, desertion, or divorce. When the father, who is the normal breadwinner, dies, leaving wife and children unprovided for, their efforts are often unable to keep them above poverty. They may become actual paupers. The state of Illinois led the way in providing widows' pensions, and since 1911 some twenty states have followed. They feel that it is better to provide money with which mothers may take care of their children in their own homes than to take the children away from their natural guardian and rear them as paupers in public orphanages, and that the cost of the pensions is less than the cost of the socially unfit who result when mothers must work and children are reared on the street. Many cities have day nurseries and playgrounds where mothers may leave their children when they go out to work.

The willful breaking of family ties is a crime—a crime especially bad when it results in leaving dependents upon society.

The State is not usually strict in punishing this type of crime, although it injures society at large in many ways. If men who deserted their families were sought out and punished, the evil would doubtless be greatly lessened. Widows or unmarried mothers who desert their children, and those who shamelessly throw aged parents upon public support, are harder to deal with Law can do little to solve these dilemmas, education in moral responsibility is the best means of prevention, and public opinion the best agent for punishment. In the meantime the homeless and resourceless ones must be cared for by charity.

Even legal divorce may result in pauper dependents. Of 74,893 wives who were granted divorces in 1916, there were 31,606 who had children. Support of these mothers and their children can best be secured through laws forcing the father to pay alimony and to contribute to the support of his offspring. The .real solution of the divorce problem goes back to the marriage problem, hasty and ill-advised marriages are easily contracted in America.

Sometimes through their own wastefulness, but often after lives of hard toil and sobriety, old people find themselves unable to earn and facing want. Their children, if they have any, may be earning too little to provide for extra mouths, or they may even refuse to do so. England pensions her poor who have reached the age of seventy, although the weekly amount is so small as to provide a minimum for existence wants only. In 1913, five years after the passage of the Old Age Pension Act, almost a million aged people were receiving this aid Germany has used a system similar to her accident insurance system for workers earning up to about $500 per year.

Pensions. Although the government pensions old soldiers and Federal civil-service employees, and some cities pension their policemen, firemen, and teachers, the pension idea is not popular here. The accepted theory is that workmen not in government employ should be paid sufficient to permit of saving, and educated into thrifty provision for old age But facts do not tally with theory; wages do not provide both for living and for saving, and many a workman who is not pensioned by his union or supported by his children becomes a public charge in a poorhouse or old people's home. If he has been a hard worker and careful spender, this is not fair to him. The alternative faces us: America must make facts tally with theory by securing intelligent saving from adequate wages, or else must provide some kind of old-age relief.

Bad habits and associations. Among the many other social causes of poverty are bad habits and associations, defective education, unrestricted immigration, and unwise philanthropy. Parents who do not bring up their children to feel keenly the moral responsibility of making one's own way provide for future pauperism. Immorality and intemperance seem to cause the greatest proportion of poverty; they reduce the productive power of the wage-earner, increase his expenditure for non-essentials, and add to his liability to discharge from employment. It is impossible to say how much of the world's poverty comes solely from such habits as alcoholism and drugs, for almost always other causes—such as disease, feeble-mindedness, and broken home ties—exist along with them. This fact illustrates the mesh of social evils that must be cleared away before better times can come.[1]

Evil thoughts and associations break down personal morale and prepare the way for poverty and pauperism. They may come from the crowding of tenement life, from hours spent on the street, from attendance at bad motion pictures or time given to pool rooms and loafing-places, or they may come from

---

[1] Note that the immediate effect of doing away with one social evil is often to increase others, and that freedom through mastery may come only when time enough has elapsed for the good effects of the first reform to have worked out. Persons weakened by years of alcoholism, for instance, upon the enforcement of prohibition took to drugs. Nothing else could be expected; the mere removal of food for their depraved appetites could not remake the men and women whom society had allowed to degenerate through the existence of a harmful institution. The uplift of society is not an overnight process; in many cases a new generation must come before the good effects of reform legislation are felt.

reading immoral novels. The standards acquired by many a man in a saloon have made him a pauper quite as surely as the liquor itself.

REMEDIES

Education. Since homes often fail to teach the habits and ideals that prevent poverty, schools find it their duty to do as much as they can to correct wrong impressions and establish positive standards of right conduct. The dignity of labor and the crime of willful idleness should be part of the creed taught in every school. General education must be made compulsory in all states, and the period of school attendance made longer than it is now in many states. School-training, if it is to function in social betterment, must be more practical than it is at present in some schools. This does not mean that cultural subjects should be taught less, but that the regular school subjects should be so taught that they help in solving the real problems of life. For instance, history and civics should throw light on the political and social questions of today, the study of English classics should enable boys and girls to tell the good new novels from the poor ones, and arithmetic should teach pupils how to keep a family budget. More trade schools and vocational guidance are needed in America, a beginning only has been made so far.

Many men fail to achieve the success they should because they are vocational misfits. One man is a dentist who should be a plumber, another becomes a city clerk, although he might have made a good farmer. There are two reasons for misfits: occupations are seldom picked out scientifically, but are rather the outcome of chance openings or obvious opportunity, and differences in wealth send the rich man's son into business or a highly trained profession, while the poor man's son learns a trade by apprenticeship or practice, irrespective of their relative abilities.

The first step in vocational guidance is to ascertain the mental ability of the boy or girl who is looking forward to a life work. No matter how financially able a boy's family may be to send him to the best schools, it is foolish to try to make a lawyer or an engineer of one who has not a first-class mind. Knowing the capacities of students, the well-trained vocational adviser sets before them a wide range of possibilities, bringing to them books and magazine articles which show the nature of many kinds of work, the hardships, risks, advantages, and remuneration and, when possible, making it easy for them to observe the work itself and to talk with the workers. Very talented but poor boys and girls may be helped toward a college education by honor scholarships and after-school employment.

Controlled immigration. Our present immigration laws aim to exclude all who may become public charges, by keeping out cripples, diseased, mental defectives of a pronounced kind, criminals, orphans, and illiterates. With all this care many immigrants become paupers within a few years, as they seldom have any surplus funds to fall back on in an emergency. By their very numbers they lower the wages of unskilled labor and make the chance of employment for themselves and their kind less.

Wiser philanthropy. Unwise philanthropy may not be a direct cause of poverty, but it adds greatly to pauperism. The needy poor must sometimes be helped; but almsgiving for its own sake is a great evil, since it neither teaches nor incites to self-help and independence. Any charitable project which destroys the desire to be self-supporting defeats its own ends, for it creates paupers instead of eliminating them. To give money and food to beggars without requiring some honest return encourages the lazy and shiftless in the habit of getting a living without working for it.

Such help as must be given in emergencies is best administered by trained and organized social workers, who have means of telling the worthy from the unworthy poor. Associated or organized charities make thorough investigations, incite the poor to strive for economic independence, and act as central stations for bringing the needy and the charitable together.

They prevent overlapping of relief and imposture as far as possible.[1] Organized charities also serve as research centers for the scientific study of social evils, as they keep careful records of all cases.

Government inspection by intelligent agents not politically appointed is the best means of insuring scientific and kind treatment of the poor housed in institutions managed by lodges, churches, and other semipublic societies. Such institutions have done much to build up brotherly sympathy for the unfortunate by interesting their members in the work carried on. There will be need for philanthropy for some generations to come, and no wise person would destroy it. But it must be wiser than it has often been in the past, or it will continue to perpetuate the evils it seeks to cure.

Curing poverty. Our discussion has shown that poverty is the symptom of abnormalities and evils in society. Charity may relieve it temporarily, but only the removal of its causes will cure it and bring permanent happiness and usefulness to the whole race. A constructive program against poverty must include the following features:

1. Liquor and drugs must be done away with. Both are now legally abolished in the United States, but the ignorance, self-indulgence, and self-interest of thousands of citizens still make the law a dead letter in some places.

2. Sexual immorality must be curbed by education in its tragic results, by the creation of high ideals of personal character, by severe punishment of offenders, and in extreme cases by segregation.

3. Defectives whose abnormal traits are inheritable must be put into institutions and kept from propagating their kind.

4. Sanitation and medical science should be given a chance to correct evils through education and where necessary through

---

[1] A Brooklyn organization found one woman who was receiving help under nine different names, while others were suffering for the want of any help at all. Every city and many small towns have professional poor who shamelessly exploit the kind-hearted but careless giver.

compulsion. Housing reform, pure-food laws, examination of school children by nurses and doctors, strict quarantine regulations, inoculation and vaccination, are all included in this program.

5. Education should include character development and vocational training and guidance, that every man may earn a living and every woman keep a home efficiently.

6. Marriage, divorce, and desertion laws should be made uniform throughout the country and stricter than at present, with a view to establishing wholesome marital unions and forcing men to support their families.

7. Some sort of insurance against sickness, old age, and accidents should be worked out which will not pauperize the working population.

8. Unnecessary unemployment must be eliminated by better economic management secured where necessary by wise laws. This includes the reform of our present system of distribution in some way to make social and economic justice more nearly coincide.

This is a staggering program, and to accomplish it means that all the intelligence and good will of a great nation must be mobilized. But the poverty stricken are inefficient producers, political malcontents, a source of degeneration in the race, and a cause of suffering to the industrious and worthy. To neglect the fight on poverty means to spread its harm and perpetuate its tragic fruits. The citizens of the United States must choose between an active fight for better conditions and the suffering of the results of a great social disease. Certainly no right-thinking man or woman can hesitate in choosing. The evil can be cured if we seek and apply the remedies.

SUPPLEMENTARY READINGS

BURCH, H. R., and PATTERSON, S. H. American Social Problems, chaps. xiv, xvi–xvii, xx, xxii.
Fatigue and welfare:
Current Opinion, Vol. LXIV, p. 39.

Independent, Vol. XC, p. 210; Vol XCI, p 427
New Republic, Vol. VI, pp. 173–175
Scientific American, Vol CXVII, p 378, Vol. LXXXII, p 250.
ELLWOOD, C. A. The Social Problem, chaps iii, iv
FORMAN, S E. The American Democracy, chap xlix
HAMILTON, W H Current Economic Problems, Nos 256–274
MARSHALL, L C, WRIGHT, C. W, and FIELD, J A Materials for the Study of Elementary Economics, Nos 21–26, 207–208
Survey, Vol XLIII, pp. 280–281, 357–362; Vol. XLIV, pp. 90–91, 245, 526, 707–708, 725–726

SEARCH QUESTIONS AND PROBLEMS

1 Does your state require an application of silver nitrate to the eyes of newborn babies?

2. Are mental tests used in your school?

3. Does your state make special provisions for the feeble-minded, or are they kept in prisons, reformatories, insane asylums, and poorhouses?

4 Does your state prohibit the marriage of mental defectives?

5 Where are the deaf and blind of your state educated? Are they taught to make their own living?

6 What are the statistics of mental and physical defectives for your city, county, or town?

7 For one week keep track of all the accidents mentioned in your city daily. From this study, what do you find the chief cause of accidents in your vicinity? What percentage of them could have been prevented? How? What safety devices are used by motorists, railroads, and industrial plants in your region? Are these compulsory or voluntary?

8 What is the liability of employers for accidents and illness in your state? Compare with a neighboring state (World Almanac for 1920 or later) What does the United States do for its ill or injured employees?

9. Write to your state Department of Health for statistics on the amount and causes of death in your state What is being done to prevent unnecessary loss? Ask the Department for the literature which it distributes

10 In what direction should you look when you start to cross a street? when you reach the middle?

11. How are the ill who are too poor to employ a doctor taken care of in your state? Who assists their families?

12. How much money was raised in your community last year for war against the White Plague? Who raised it?

13. Are there common drinking-cups, towels, or bars of soap in your school or stores?

14. Why does not vaporized steam shot into milk-bottles and cans sterilize them? What is live steam? How should these containers be sterilized?

15. In 1863 a Nebraska farmer mortgaged his land, worth $1000, to a New York capitalist for $500 in "greenbacks." When he was ready to pay his debt, the value of the greenbacks had risen from 50 cents to 90 cents. Who lost, to what extent, and why? What political party was formed by the people situated as the Nebraska farmer was? What were their views on the redemption of greenbacks, and later on the free coinage of silver? Why? What has all this to do with poverty?

16. Make a list of wise expenditures and one of foolish ones for a girl earning $15 per week.

17. Ask students in the domestic-science department to make out a chart of, say, twenty foods and drinks which are most economical on the basis of their value to the human body and their market price.

18. Why have most of the Federal employment bureaus opened in war time been closed? Does your city conduct a free labor exchange?

19. Debate: *Resolved*, (1) That cities should house the poor; (2) that cities should aid the unemployed in times of depression.

20. Look up the story of Brook Farm. Was it a success?

21. Debate: *Resolved*, That the United States should adopt a compulsory old-age insurance policy. For references see Shurter and Taylor's "Both Sides of One Hundred Public Questions."

22. What are the poorhouses and old people's homes in your county like? Would you be willing to spend your last days in them if there were no disgrace connected with it? Can you bring any joy into the lives of the inmates?

23. How thoroughly is prohibition enforced in your state? If not enforced, who is to be blamed? What has been the effect of prohibition upon the number of inmates in municipal lodging-houses, workhouses, and poorhouses?

24. To what extent is your city, county, or state following the program recommended in this book for ending poverty?

CHAPTER XVI

CRIME

"Good" people and "bad" people represent groups of tendencies, altruism or selfishness preponderating as the case may be, but in the extreme complexity of human nature, men can never be divided sharply into "sheep" and "goats," for none attain absolute virtue, any more than any descend into unmitigated villainy.—GEORGE IVES

For many years it was accepted as a fact that there were certain people who were incurably bad—a truly criminal type. In 1876 Cesare Lombroso, an Italian criminologist, went so far as to assert that these inherently criminal beings could be distinguished from normal men by the physical features of the body, head, and face.

The "criminal type." Since that time many men have adopted and elaborated the idea, until one may read that certain kinds of noses, chins, and foreheads are signs of criminal instincts, and even that "tattooing has great criminal significance." But at present the majority of scientific authorities have ceased to accept this belief. Many men who are in prison have crooked noses and receding chins; but there are also many men bearing these characteristics outside of prison, many of them holding high positions of influence and honor.

Thomas Mott Osborne has aptly remarked:

To list men who commit all sorts of different crimes arbitrarily in a group and proceed to generalize about them, is as ridiculous as it would be to generalize about the habits and character of any chance assortment of men—legislators or theatergoers; or to draw conclusions as to the psychological characteristics of blue-eyed men, or of those who wear tan shoes. . . . The truth is that, while it is often convenient to speak collectively of the men who commit crimes as criminals, there is no such thing as "The Criminal," and no such group as a "criminal class." A criminal is after all only an ordinary human being who has more than a normal amount of weaknesses, follies, or vices to which all men are subjected to a greater or less degree.

A soluble problem. The reason that those who commit crime present a bigger problem than those whose weaknesses lead them into poverty is that criminals in their operations harm others more than themselves. They attack the most fundamental idea of all healthy social life, that of coöperation. Their cost to society in expense of capture and detention and in loss of property and life is so great that more study has been awarded to crime than to any of the other abnormal activities of man. The results of this study are available in the form of data on the kinds and amount of crime, of analyses of the causes of crime, of suggestions as to the prevention of crime and the proper treatment of convicted criminals.

At first the investigators and experimenters in this field were beset by pessimism, but in recent years a hopefulness has been creeping into the writings of sociologists and criminologists until now we may read such positive statements as the following by Charles Ellwood, "The problem of crime is, then, not insoluble." Since the recognized end of all civilization is to produce healthy, happy, right-thinking human beings, it behooves us to wage ceaseless war against crime of all kinds while at the same time we strive to bring back the criminal to the paths of sane, straight living and to keep his potential brother from following in his footsteps.

KINDS AND EXTENT OF CRIME

Social crimes. Crime, according to the Encyclopedia Britannica, is "a failure or refusal to live up to the standards of conduct deemed binding by the rest of the community." Under this broad definition many things not punishable today would come into the category of crimes. The employment of laborers at starvation wages in the sweating industries, the deliberate warping of children's minds by unclean stories, the housing of hundreds of human beings under one roof with insanitary sleeping and eating conditions and immoral living conditions, are all crimes in the broader sense, but they may or may not be crimes in the narrow sense of "an act or omission which the law punishes in the name and in behalf of the State." Any person who accepts the privileges of society, who demands rights as a member of that society, and then refuses to meet the obligations which those rights and privileges involve is in reality a social criminal His avoiding of responsibility may be due to intentional unwillingness to meet his obligations or it may be due to ignorance. In either case he fails to live up to the standard of conduct binding on the rest of society, and he is therefore a criminal in the broader sense. Not only do many social criminals escape punishment by the law, but so also do vast numbers of spiritual criminals, who are guilty of many sins in their hearts and wrongdoings in their homes.

Statutory crime. Although some of these social and spiritual crimes are greater than those punishable by law, their very nature makes it impossible for society to deal with them. We shall confine ourselves to those acts which have been stamped by the law as criminal. This condemnation may come as a result of statutory law, or by "common law," which makes certain acts, obviously dangerous to society, crimes without specific enactment.

Classifications of crimes. There are numerous classifications of crimes on the basis of their degree, their motive, and the object against which they are directed In one classification we have the division into big crimes, or *felonies*, and little crimes, or *misdemeanors*. No two states are alike in their classification of crimes under these two divisions, but most of them place murder, rape, arson, burglary, robbery, grand larceny, forgery, bigamy, and perjury in the class of felonies. Various degrees of crime within the class of felony are recognized; as, for example, murder in the first, second, and third degrees, or arson and burglary by day or night and with reference to whether the building is a dwelling-house or not. Misdemeanors are less serious crimes, such as petty larceny, assault and battery, disobedience of city, town, and county ordinances, and disturbing the peace.

Crimes have been classified according to their causes into crimes of impulse and crimes of circumstance, of which more will be said in the discussion to follow. A third classification of crimes is according to the object against which they are aimed. The following table shows the present classification upon this basis and shows the percentage that each class bears to the whole number of crimes committed in the United States:

	Per Cent
Crimes against government (treason, counterfeiting, anarchy)	2.2
Crimes against society (speeding, disturbance of the peace)	22.0
Crimes against persons (murder, assault, robbery)	21.9
Crimes against property (burglary, arson, theft)	45.8
Miscellaneous	8.1
Total	100[1]

The extent of crime in the United States. Much has been said and written about the enormous increase in the amount of crime in the United States. Writers on penology call attention to the fact that the number in the criminal class increased by over 400 per cent from 1850 to 1890. It is true that in 1850 there were only something like 29 people out of every 100,000 in penal institutions, whereas in 1890 there were 131.5 out of the same number.[2] But this does not indicate exactly that much increase in the number of criminals. It must not be forgotten that the development of an effective judicial system is not the first thing to be accomplished in new communities, such as made up at least half of the United States during this period. Even in the older regions of the East the record for the apprehension and conviction of criminals was greatly improved

---

[1] Statistics from Forman's "American Democracy," p. 405.

[2] When prisoners awaiting trial but not yet sentenced are deducted, this number falls to 106.

during the forty years of 1850–1890. Moreover, the number of acts which have been made legal crimes increased enormously during this period. Doubtless, too, the actual amount of wrongdoing did increase greatly, for reasons that we shall see later. But these statistics are as much an indication of the improvement in society's attitude and action toward crime as they are an indication of the increase in criminal acts. Whatever the case between 1850 and 1890, it is true that between the latter year and 1910 there was a decrease. The number per 100,000 fell from 131.5 to 121.2. Therefore we do not need to take so pessimistic a view of the problem.

A pressing social problem. Nevertheless, when we read that 121 out of every 100,000 people were committed to prison during the year 1910, it becomes evident that the total amount of crime in our country is appalling. When we think also of the number of criminals who escape imprisonment through payment of fine or who escape punishment altogether in some way, it becomes evident that here is a problem that demands more serious attention than even poverty. We are startled also to read that in 1904 there were more prisoners in the penal institutions of the country (81,772) than there were undergraduates and graduates in all public universities, colleges, and technological schools in the United States (79,579).[1]

When we come to consider the cost of the criminal element in our society we are again confronted with the difficulty of securing statistics which cover the subject adequately. Various estimates have been made as to the amount of money it costs the United States and state governments to apprehend, convict, and care for criminals. The sum has been put at somewhere from half a billion to one billion dollars per year. This is little more than a guess and, of course, omits the loss of property, time, and private expenditures in precautions and prosecutions. The states bear the greater part of the public burden, and next to education it is the heaviest item for which their taxes are expended.

[1] This ignores the students in private educational institutions

Although the amount spent for this purpose increases we must not assume that this is a bad sign. Like the increase in the number of criminals in institutions, it may mean that better devices are being used to apprehend wrongdoers. In this case it may also mean more efficient housing of them after detention. But after making all due allowances, there is no way of avoiding the conclusion that there is an excessive amount of crime in the United States, and that valuable resources are going into the care of criminals that could do much to upbuild society and foster constructive enterprises, such as education, were this money not needed to deter and punish the destructive elements in our society.

Crime and the Home

Hereditary crime. As in poverty, so in crime, the causes may be either hereditary or environmental. But in crime environment plays much the larger part, hence the remedies are easier and surer.

It is only recently that sociologists have abandoned the idea that criminal instincts as such are directly inheritable, that the sons of criminals commit crimes because their fathers committed them. In spite of this refusal to believe in an inherited criminal type, there is a general recognition that certain inheritances may operate as causes for crime. On the basis of experiments in the Elmira reformatory in New York, congenital feeble-mindedness would rank first among these. Inherited physical defects—such as undervitalized organisms and those affected from birth by alcoholism—play an important part in making an easy path to the police station.

There are also certain inherited spiritual or ethical defects which in themselves are very hard to detect and classify, but which are known causes of crimes. Certain predispositions of the normal man may be lacking; as, for example, altruism (the spirit of group helpfulness) and the instinct to be sensitive to social disapproval. A lack of these two inheritable predispositions may, under favoring circumstances, prove an important cause of crime. Other predispositions may, when found in excess, become causes for crime. Examples are the overdevelopment of the instinct to collect and hoard, which may result in robbery and burglary, and the overdevelopment of the instinct for revenge, which may produce assault, arson, or even murder.

The problem of preventing crimes from hereditary causes must be solved by a combination of preventing the inheritance by strict marriage laws and of offsetting the inheritance by proper education in responsibility, self-control, and altruism. Prohibition laws, good housing conditions, and community centers will all do their part in reducing the amount of harmful inheritances.

Complexity of causes. It is impossible to ascertain what percentage of crime is due to heredity. Probably no crime was ever committed in which hereditary factors played the only part. On the other hand, it is incorrect to assume that certain obvious environmental conditions are the sole causes. Close study has proved that many causes operate to produce almost every crime. The nature of man is very complicated, and in none of its workings more so than in the committing of crime. Future criminologists will do well to give up the idea of locating one cause for each wrongdoing. The following discussion presents merely analyses of many environmental conditions which, in combination with one another or with inherited abnormalities, may produce criminal acts.

Evil home conditions. The first and most important influence in the life of man for good or evil is the home. Not only poverty but also crime may be laid at the doors of disrupted or imperfect homes. Adults who have deserted their families or have never married often have no anchor and no incentive to keep from wrongdoing.

The influence of poor home conditions in making children into criminals is even greater. Children without homes, living in the street by day and in deserted buildings or empty boxes by night, cannot be expected to know the way of the righteous, and sometimes a poor home is as conducive to wrongdoing as no home at all. Homes which contain drunkenness, vice, and quarreling breed crime as surely as can be. In a home possessing no high ideals, no obedience, no coöperation, no self-sacrifice, the ground is being prepared for possible later wrongdoing. Lack of sympathy and understanding between parents and children is another crime-breeding home condition. The queer dress, habits, and foreign tongue of many of our immigrants lead to their losing direct control over their children. This is the chief reason for the fact that the amount of crime among the first generation born of foreign parents is higher than among natives or even among the foreign-born.[1]

Remedies. Since the home is the most private of all our institutions and open to so little control from outside, all that can be done to build up a nation of splendid character-making homes is to work diligently at the slow process of educating potential fathers and mothers. In the meantime the number of broken homes can be reduced by the establishment of Domestic Relations Courts for the peaceful settlement of marital disputes and by the enforcement of strict marriage and divorce laws.

In cases where the homes have already become disrupted every precaution should be taken to keep the children from becoming criminals. Orphans cannot be left to fend for themselves. Up to date their lives in institutions have as a rule been not only dreary and brutalizing but frequently crime-

[1] Much has been written about the high rate of crime among immigrants. It is true that in 1910 they contributed 72.5 per cent of the inmates of penal institutions, while they were only 16 per cent of the population. Several modifications should, however, be noted. Immigrants are very largely between the ages of fifteen to thirty—the very age in which most crime is committed. Then immigrants, especially the newer type, settle in cities, where the amount of crime is always greater than in the rural communities. Moreover, it must always be remembered that the only statistics which we have are of the people sent to penal institutions. The wealthy criminal may often escape imprisonment by payment of fine or even by bribery, while the immigrant, who is usually poor, will have to pay by giving up his liberty, thus swelling the ranks of the recognized criminals. In view of all these things one must be very cautious in assuming that foreigners are greater criminals than natives.

breeding. If orphanages are to be kept as society's solution of the orphan problem, there should be a more earnest study of the best methods of managing them and more care, with less politics, in the selection of their staffs. Many sociologists think that effort should be concentrated on finding homes for orphans wherever legal adoption is possible. Sometimes a well-supervised system of boarding out works to advantage, as in the Coldwater School in Michigan. When managed by intelligent men and women of high character, orphanages using the cottage system provide an environment approaching real home conditions Each cottage is under the authority of a housemother and housefather, and the children, not dressed in uniforms, attend the regular public schools. An orphanage, even when a state institution, should aim to develop character as it aims to provide shelter, food, and clothing The care of orphans in institutions offers a worth-while work for a higher class of men and women than often engage in it. But with every admirable quality, a good orphanage is not so good a place for a child as a private home, and earnest attempts should be made to place normal children with child-hungry people who can give them love and personal interest.

In cases where children have taken their first step on the road of crime much may be done to turn them back and prevent them from becoming habitual wrongdoers. Even those people who do not believe that adult criminals are capable of reform are willing to admit that juvenile delinquents can usually be cured if given proper treatment and training. The first movement in recognition of this belief was the establishment in many states of reformatories for boys and girls, which initiated the important policy of separation of adult and youthful offenders.

Probation supplants reformatories. Reform did not stop at this point. Enlightened judges ceased treating the youthful offenders as criminals. Juries were dispensed with and special juvenile courts were soon established in which the child, his accuser, and the judge met in a room without policemen, reporters, or spectators.[1] The trial has been supplanted by a heart-to-heart talk. If the judge believes the child is guilty, he is put out on probation. That means he may live at home (if his home is decent) and attend school. But he is under the watchful care of probation officers and is bound to report at intervals to the judge. In case the offender does not behave himself, he may be sent to a state industrial detention or reform school.

Since between 25 per cent and 50 per cent of the child delinquents are either feeble-minded or epileptic, it is one of the first duties of the juvenile courts to detect these defectives. If scientific treatment cannot make them normal, then they should be committed by the court to special institutions for permanent custodial care.

In cases where the child is only wayward it is the duty of the judge and the probation officer to build up his self-reliance and to develop a character of honesty and uprightness. No greater opportunity nor responsibility is offered for public service than is here presented. Characters can be molded and lives changed. The success or failure of our attempts to deal with juvenile delinquency lies in the hands of our juvenile-court judges and probation officers.

Juvenile and Domestic Relations Courts. Wherever it is expedient the delinquent is kept within his own home. Miss Friday, a social-service worker, once wrote, "Although the law deals with the child, it is the parents who are often the real probationers." To blame the parents for the delinquency of the child has become a platitude in juvenile courts, although often the parents have not willingly contributed to the delinquency. It is their ignorance or helplessness which has been the root of the trouble. It was estimated by Judge Pinckney of Chicago that 315 of 12,000 cases of child delinquency which came before him were due to parental neglect or incompetence.

---

[1] The first Juvenile Court Act was passed by Illinois in 1899, as a result of the bad conditions in Chicago. In less than fifteen years forty-four states and the District of Columbia had established special courts for children.

Now a juvenile court judge must know home conditions before he can deal justly with a child. There is therefore a movement (strongest west of the Mississippi) to combine in one court the functions of handling domestic relations and child delinquency. The home is a social unit which cannot be separated into parts; hence the argument that its parts (parents and children) should be treated in one court by the same judge. After the judge has investigated the home conditions, he is confronted with two alternatives: either the child may be left in the home or he may be placed out in some other home or detention school. In the first case it becomes the duty of the probation officer to see that the bad conditions are remedied and the home made a fit place for the child. In the absence of other agencies for improving homes the probation officer has had to take on a great deal of this burden. So far as possible this should be transferred to other social agencies, such as home visitors attached to the schools.

Sometimes the judge may decide that the home is hopeless and that the child must be taken away from its influence and placed in a home with the right atmosphere. The courts for the most part use regularly constituted agencies for this home-finding work, although in some cities (Pittsburgh, Chicago, Kansas City, and Salt Lake City) the court does the placing itself.

Since the records of our prisons show that a large percentage of the "long termers" began their life of crime when very young, there can be no doubt that every successful step accomplished by the probation system in reforming juvenile delinquency will reduce materially the amount of adult crime.

Crime and Society

The school. Next to the home, the school is the most important influence in the formation of character. The ideals of conduct and thought which the home fails to teach should be taught in the school. Education in the real business of living was long neglected for much needless drill on the three "R's." Temperance, steadiness, honesty, and altruism should be taught by precept and example.

Children who have inherited any of the predispositions mentioned earlier as potential causes of crime should be discovered by watchful teachers. Their defects will surely show up in their work and play. These children, without its being made evident, should become the objects of the most careful character-molding. If our schools are going to prevent crime they must teach the necessity of obeying law and of changing any errors in it by legal methods rather than by evasion or revolution. Our educational systems may aid further in solving the problem of crime by detecting the mental defectives through intelligence tests and by passing them over to the State for cure or isolation.

Not only one-sided education but lack of schooling may be a cause of crime. This is attested by the high percentage of illiteracy among prisoners. Many sociologists are coming to believe that the large percentage of crime among the negroes is due rather to their illiteracy than to their race.[1]

Influence of the community. Next to the home and the school as factors affecting standards of human conduct come the community at large and the smaller social groups within it. When there is a well-defined neighborhood watching the actions of men and commenting upon them, the natural instinct to be sensitive to social approval or disapproval will exert a marked influence. It is due partly to a lack of this social disapproval that the number of criminals in cities is greater than in village or rural communities. The city wilderness covers up the actions of its dwellers so that they are not subject to the disgrace of facing a disapproving community. But sometimes the community does not disapprove when it should do so. Many crimes, such as speeding, drunkenness, and vice, are winked at by the public. The result is of course an excess of those crimes

---

[1] In 1910 it was found that 34 per cent of the inmates of penal institutions were negroes, although they constituted only 11½ per cent of the population of the United States.

in such communities. In many communities there is a general approval of anyone who can break the law and "get away with it." This attitude is a remnant of school days and a result of an education deficient in teaching responsibility.

Public disapproval of crime can be fostered by the press, but instead the average daily newspaper tends to incite a sentimental interest in crime which is very unhealthy and in some cases positively crime-breeding. The duty of our daily journals is rather to reveal the social crimes which are not yet listed as legal crimes, with a view to securing their outlawry.

The community fosters crime in another indirect but none the less powerful way. By its refusal to accept a "jailbird" back into its midst, with forgetfulness for his past and encouragement for his future, society may make a confirmed wrong-doer out of a man who, through momentary weakness, made one misstep. Many "second termers" tell of their unsuccessful struggle to keep a new job and establish new social ties. Past disgrace seeks out released "jailbirds," and although they commit no new wrongs, they find themselves unemployed and socially disgraced.[1] Ex-convicts should be treated as fellow men who have erred and suffered for it and now need help to begin anew. It is only human nature to want to do and be what people expect you to do and be. If the public expects the returned convict to repeat his offense, it cannot wonder if he lives up to his reputation.

Through the recreation it offers, the community may either check or foster crime. "Satan finds some mischief still for idle hands to do." If the usual way of spending leisure hours is in an indulgence of the appetites, such as drinking, drug-using, or sexual immorality, crimes are sure to result. Amusement in apparently much more harmless form, such as association with

---

[1] The classic story in fiction on this subject and one having many modern true counterparts is the story of Jean Valjean in Victor Hugo's "Les Misérables" It is to be noted that Jean Valjean was not really a criminal, but a victim of laws unreasonably strict Conditions have changed radically from those depicted in Hugo's masterpiece.

bad companions on the street or in pool rooms, the reading of dime novels and yellow journals, or constant attendance at degrading motion pictures and public dance halls, may breed crime. These things corrupt the mind by glorifying wrongdoing. That which is talked and thought about in leisure hours becomes the basis for future action.

Every community that is seeking to reduce crime should furnish its young people with playgrounds, public libraries, and musical entertainments. Besides public entertainments furnished free or at a nominal cost, there should be careful supervision of private amusements to insure wholesomeness and high idealism. Business men's and mothers' clubs are beginning to function along this line.

Economic causes of crime. So far we have seen that the social units of home, school, and community have it within their power to create or curb much crime. They are not alone in this respect, for the economic and political organization of society has great influence on crime. It is a moot question whether actual want has ever been the sole cause of many crimes of robbery and burglary. Since the famous story of Jean Valjean we have heard much sentimental talk of how hunger and dire want force men to commit crimes. It is true that many crimes have been perpetrated by the poor for the purpose of acquiring more of the world's goods, but it is doubtful whether mere hunger or want of the necessities of life ever made a criminal out of a man who otherwise would have been honest. Poverty, however, with its accompanying home influences and physical ailments, is surely a rich soil for crime. Other economic causes, such as lack of steady employment, with its consequent idleness, tempt men to drink and to associate with uncaught criminals. In this way a life of crime may be entered upon as the path of least resistance.

The economic organization of our society into two opposing classes has produced a class antagonism which at times breaks out into crime. Enraged employees have committed assaults, sabotage, and even murders. Employers have in turn been guilty of committing slow murder through the insanitary conditions of work which they force on the laborers, and oi causing sudden death through the gross neglect of dangerous machinery. Crimes of this nature can be prevented in part by legislation, but ideal conditions will be obtained only when all employers and employees come to recognize the community of their interests.

Crimes of the entrepreneur. Our system of business competition is in itself an incentive for crime among employers. When "survival of the fittest" is the only rule, we may expect that foul means will be employed by some to insure survival. Until some form of cooperation has proved itself worthy to supplant the competitive system, we can prevent such business crimes only by making the penalty so sure and so severe that it will far outweigh the gain. Up to date the punishment for unfair methods of competition and undue restraint of trade has been so mild or so uncertain that it has had almost no deterrent effect.

The business man in his position of producer or salesman has it within his power to use numerous criminal devices against the public. He sometimes justifies this by the conditions of the competitive struggle for existence. Many of his tricks, such as adulteration of foods and medicines, have been made illegal. Their prevention depends upon strict governmental supervision. Other business tricks, such as palming off shoddy as real all-wool, cannot be checked effectively by law and hence can be prevented only by raising the standards of business ethics.

Political crimes. In the economic field as well as in the social field we are continually impressed with the fact that many crimes against society are not crimes in the eyes of the law. This in itself might be called a political crime. For if legislators will not enact laws against wrongdoing, the prevention of crime is impossible. As the social conscience of the country develops, we are making great strides in this field. It has been estimated that more additions have been made to the penal code in the past quarter-century than in all the centuries which preceded.

Even when there are good statutes for the prevention of crime, if there is no effective enforcement of law, crime flourishes. Whenever the apprehension of criminals is lax, owing to an insufficient or inefficient police force, then wrongdoing will increase. The recent excess of crime in our big cities has been largely due to this cause. Moreover, technicalities of the law which allow the guilty to escape reduce the certainty of punishment and thereby lessen its deterrent effect. Crime will surely increase where the law really protects the criminal rather than society. Wherever bribery or influence secures exemption from punishment for some individuals, the incentive to crime is doubled, because the man of power does not fear to do wrong and his lesser brother does it in imitation. Robert Ingersoll once remarked, "As long as society bows and cringes before the great thieves, there will be little ones enough to fill the jails."

Our system of apprehending suspects must be efficient, their trial must be fair, speedy, and with equal opportunities for poor and rich, and the enforcement of their punishment must be certain and free from corruption.

Opposition to the enforcement of law. Crimes are committed not only because of the nonenforcement of law but sometimes because of a direct opposition to enforcement. In this class fall the crimes of political and social "reformers": men who preach draft evasion, or revolution as the only method of progress. These people often mean well, but they have adopted methods which are harmful to society, and hence they must be restrained. The disgraceful lynchings which fill the annals of our history to such an alarming extent are due partly to this opposition to law. It is usually not the nonenforcement of law which produces these group murders, but rather an unwillingness to wait for the law to take its course. Sometimes it is dissatisfaction with the mildness of a sentence. To these motives is always added the element of mob passion, with its group violence, brutality, and intemperance. Of the same nature are the crimes committed during race riots.

Crime-producing punishment. One other source of crime is wrong methods of punishment. When the ex-convict goes back into the world with broken health and bitterness in his soul, his one idea is to "get even," and he not only commits more crime, but he is a source of contagion for gangs of susceptible boys and discontented, weak men. No greater criticism could be brought against any system of criminal punishment than to say that it bred criminals, but such has surely been the case with many penal procedures of the past.

The Treatment of Crime in the Past

Tribal treatment of crime. It would be impossible for us to enter into any detailed study of the historical treatment of crime and criminals. But since our present penal code and our methods of apprehending, convicting, and punishing criminals are based on the experience of past ages, it will be worth our while to observe some of the important historical practices before we attempt to criticize our present system.[1]

The spirit which dominated the early treatment of crime in the tribal stage of civilization is well expressed by "an eye for an eye, and a tooth for a tooth." When a man considered himself to be injured by another, he set about to retaliate. When the injury resulted in death, the kinsmen of the victim punished the murderer or, if he had fled, some member of his family. This custom soon developed into the practice of all the members of one tribe setting out to revenge any wrongs done to any of its individual clansmen. This custom of blood revenge led to feuds which have been kept up in some regions (such as, for instance, the mountain districts of Kentucky) long after regular legal methods of punishment by the State were instituted.

[1] It is well to remember that criticism may be both adverse and favorable

Ordeals. In Anglo-Saxon records of England we begin early to have accounts of legal procedure and punishment. The accused was brought by the accuser before some public tribunal and there made to go through an ordeal to test his guilt or innocence. There were a number of different ways in which guilt could be ascertained. The accused might be thrown into a lake with his arms tied: if he sank, he was innocent; if he floated, he was guilty. A rope was fastened around his waist to be used for pulling him up after he had gone down so many feet. Sometimes the accused was made to carry a red-hot iron weight of from one to three pounds, according to the degree of his crime, or to plunge his arm up to the wrist, elbow, or shoulder into boiling-hot water, or to walk over red-hot plowshares. In any of these cases, if after a certain period of time there were no blisters evident, the person was adjudged innocent.

From our modern viewpoint this seems like a very unjust system. Certain physical tricks could be learned by the wise to evade just punishment, while others less clever but innocent were pronounced guilty. In the wager of battle, wherein the two parties were forced to fight out the question, might had surely the upper hand over right.[1] These types of trials would be worse than useless today, and no doubt they worked many injustices in the Middle Ages; but in those days there was a strong belief that God would intervene in behalf of the innocent.[2] This implicit faith in divine intervention did, without doubt, work certain so-called miracles. At best the system was very unsatisfactory, and at worst it was one step above the personal-vengeance stage.

[1] Women, priests, and incapacitated people were allowed to have champions to take their places.

[2] There was one method of ascertaining innocence which depended, not upon divine intervention but on one's reputation. If a man was accused of committing a crime and could get a certain number of men (depending on the degree of the crime and the social status of the persons harmed and testifying) to swear to the *good standing* of the accused,—not his innocence of that crime, but simply his good reputation—then the man was adjudged innocent.

Dissatisfaction with the old methods. Early in the twelfth century great dissatisfaction came to be felt with the whole system of criminal apprehension and conviction. Too often the guilty went unpunished while the innocent suffered. Criminals were often never even brought up for ordeal, since the accusation must be made by the injured person or his relatives. Therefore, if the murdered man had no relatives, or the injured man either did not know whom to accuse or was afraid to bring accusation, there was no attempt at punishment.

The grand jury. Henry II, England's lawyer king, coming to the throne in 1154 after a period of general disorder, saw that it must be a public duty to search out suspected criminals. So he had in every locality throughout the country chosen groups of men who were to keep their eyes open for the commission of crimes. These men were to report their suspicions to the king's justices, who made regular visits to each region. Here was a jury of men whose official duty it was to accuse. This jury was known as an accusing, or indicting jury, and later as a grand jury. At first this jury brought accusations against only those thieves, robbers, and murderers whom "no one will or dares to accuse." Later it became the business of these local jurors to indict all criminals. Accusation was becoming a public affair.

Great changes were taking place in the attitude of men toward law and order. The State, with its ideals of internal peace and its machinery for enforcing peace, was supplanting the personal rendering of justice which dominates all uncivilized communities. If two men got into a dispute and broke the peace, it was no longer a matter solely between them or their relatives. They were indirectly attacking the State, whose chief functions were the preservation of law, order, and justice.

The trial jury. Just as personal accusation had failed to preserve law and order, the ordeal method of conviction failed to bring justice. Dissatisfaction with this method grew as the State grew in power and efficiency. One expression of this dissatisfaction is found in a statute of the twelfth century, which provides that if a man accused of murder or other felony comes through the ordeal unscathed and is still thought to be a criminal by his neighbors, he must leave the country within forty days. Records of the time contain other evidences that the people were feeling their way toward a better method of ascertaining guilt. They were slower at reform here than they had been in the matter of accusation, because they feared to put the responsibility of determining guilt into the hands of mere human beings.

During the reign of Henry II a new device for ascertaining guilt was adopted. This was the trial, or petit, jury.[1] At first only civil suits in the king's courts were tried in this way. Its popularity soon led to the transfer of much business from the local manorial and feudal courts, and later to its adoption in criminal cases. By this device the accused was brought before twelve men of his neighborhood who knew most about the circumstances of the crime. These twelve men gave all the evidence they possessed and heard any others who desired to testify; then they gave a verdict as to guilt. This method of trial was much fairer to the innocent man. It therefore became a very popular form. In 1215 the Pope forbade the clergy to take any part in ordeals, and soon afterward this form of procedure gave way entirely to trial by jury.

Punishments. Not as important as the changes in apprehending and trying criminals in the twelfth century, but none the less interesting, were the innovations in punishment. In the Middle Ages most crimes, even murder, were punishable by fines. The amount of the fine depended upon the nature of the crime and upon the individual harmed. It is surprising to us who believe in social equality before the law to read that the murder of a "thane" must be punished six times as severely as the murder of his social inferior the "ceorl." In the Anglo-Saxon days when a man could not pay his fine he was sold into slavery, made an outlaw, or in rare instances put to death. The whole idea of punishment was to repay the wrongdoer in kind.

---

[1] This jury was usually smaller than the accusing jury, hence *petit*.

In the twelfth century a new idea about punishment arose. The peaceful, order-loving Plantagenet kings believed that a crime demanded not only compensation to the injured but some recognition that the peace of the State had been broken. In other words, crimes were public as well as private matters. So to the old fines of *bot*, paid to the injured, or of *wer*, paid to the family of the murdered, was now added the fine to the State called the *wite* This shows a great growth in the recognition of the social interest in private behavior, a basic idea of civilized government.

In the Middle Ages much trouble was experienced in carrying out the award of the judge. There was no machinery which enforced the collection of the *bot* and *wer*, and a very inadequate arrangement for collecting the *wite* The result was that men were fined for not paying their fines, and then fined again for not paying the second fine, and so on to great length. In some instances the sheriff called around him the citizens and set out to collect the fines by force.

Perhaps it was the ease with which penalties could be avoided that led to the construction of prisons.[1] By 1300 imprisonment combined with a fine was often inflicted on those unable to pay all the original fine. These prisons remained for centuries dreadful places in which the inmates were clothed in rags, bound in chains, and confined in quarters which were ruinous to health The prisoners were, however, in almost all cases spared the cruelty of solitary confinement.

As the centuries progressed more severe methods of punishment than imprisonment were invented. Cruel deaths by hanging, burning, and boiling in oil were administered. Mutilations of hands, legs, eyes, and ears were not uncommon To cause pain seemed often the chief motive. Sometimes the punish-

---

[1] In all the Anglo-Saxon records there are only a few mentions of prisons, and these were used only for temporary detention, pending other treatment Dungeons and towers had served as prisons for political offenders ever since ancient times, but imprisonment as a form of criminal punishment was unheard of.

ments caused even more pain to the spirit and sensibilities than to the body; as, for example, the public floggings or exposure in stocks and pillories.

In early days the punishment of banishment filled the forests with outlaws. Later, when the country grew more thickly populated, it became the custom to ship convicts to foreign lands. Thus some American colonies and, after 1775, British Australia became prison colonies for criminals. Much of the labor of the middle seaboard colonies was performed by involuntary indentured servants. Since many of these people had committed no greater crime than falling into debt, they often became good substantial citizens in their places of banishment; but this was not until they had suffered years of hardship.

The penal code of the eighteenth century. During the early modern period little value was placed on human life. The English penal code of the eighteenth century was as bloody and brutal as can be imagined. In 1800 there were at least two hundred offenses that were punishable by death. Forgery and counterfeiting, shoplifting to the value of five shillings or above, and the pickpocketing of so small a thing as a kerchief, were all punishable by death. The result was, on the one hand, that the populace was demoralized by watching public hangings as an amusement; and, on the other hand, that juries often failed to pronounce a man guilty even when certain of his guilt, because their souls cried out at the injustice of sentencing a petty robber and a foul murderer alike. Hence many an offender escaped scot-free. This encouraged others to evil practices, just as today the laxity in the execution of our automobile-theft laws leads to excessive stealing of cars.

Nineteenth-century reforms. As the eighteenth century drew to a close English statesmen began to realize that the penal code was failing utterly to solve the problem of crime. Therefore by the first quarter of the nineteenth century capital punishment was largely replaced by imprisonment. Forgery, stealing, and counterfeiting were no longer punishable by death; in fact, in most places only treason and murder remained capital crimes. At about the same time reforms began in the prisons and jails Much was done to clear out the filth and contagion. Separate cells were resorted to, and silence was enforced on all. There still remained many defects, for example, the cells were unhealthful because of the dampness and darkness, and the solitary confinement worked horrible results in the minds of men. The idea behind this first cell-reform movement was that if convicts could be made to think, they would reform. The result was quite discouraging: insanity or suicide was the fate of many, and others came out at the end of their terms hating all humanity, their warped souls filled with an over-powering desire for revenge.

The English system of solitary confinement began in this country even before it became well established in England. Philadelphia became the leader of the system in America. Soon afterward there grew up at the Mount Pleasant Prison at Sing Sing a method of treatment known as the Auburn system. This system was widely adopted and remains in force in most of the prisons of the United States today. It entails solitary confinement at night, but allows congregation for work during the day, but with enforced silence all the time. This allows convicts to see each other and to have the mind-saving companionship of combined, although silent, work. This system is built on the theory that if criminals can act right they can be reformed. The ball and chain of the Middle Ages have been displaced, but the convict is incased in a striped uniform which covers his identity and marks him as a degraded being, set apart from all his fellow men. The monotonous life drags on the convict's soul with a weight greater than the chains of old. It means murder of the mind and soul.[1]

[1] If you wish to get an idea of how life in a prison under the Auburn system oppresses even a normal man whose imprisonment is voluntary, read the account given by Thomas Mott Osborne of his life in Auburn Prison, to be found in his book "Society and Prisons," pp 120-138 This entire book—a series of lectures given to Yale students—is a most interesting account of prisons and criminals drawn from the personal experiences of a man intimately connected with them in an official capacity

Criminal Procedure of Today

Apprehension. Let us now see wherein our criminal procedure today is superior to that of the past and in what respects it might be improved.

We have much machinery for the apprehension and accusation of suspected criminals. Cities have their police forces, supposed to guard carefully the lives, property, and welfare of the citizens. Too frequently the police department has been the seat of great political corruption. Too often the public has not cared whether the police force were cognizant of evil and willing to wink at it. Until the community demands that its officers of law enforce the law, it cannot be hoped that conditions even approaching the ideal will prevail. Frequently, too, it is not the individual policemen who are to blame, but the head of the police department, or perhaps even the mayor or council. In the country districts the sheriffs and constables serve as policemen. In addition to these officers of the law a private individual may arrest a person whom he has seen committing a felony or whom he knows to be about to commit one. In a matter of misdemeanor a private person may make an arrest without a warrant only to quell a breach of peace.

Commitment. If a person is haled before a justice of the peace or a city police justice for a misdemeanor, the accusation of his apprehender is sufficient. Even the decision of his guilt is often settled at once by the officer in charge without trial. If his crime is a felony, the magistrate can only decide whether the person is possibly guilty and whether he should be committed to jail or merely told to report before an accusing jury. If he is committed to jail, he can in most cases secure temporary release upon payment of bail.

Formal accusation. A public attorney—either Federal, if the crime is against the United States, or otherwise a state district attorney—investigates the evidence against the committed person. If he believes that the person is probably guilty, he draws up a *bill of indictment*. This written statement of the charge against the suspected he presents to the grand jury. This jury meets at set intervals for the purpose of reviewing the evidence of attorneys, calling in further witnesses, and deciding whether the arraigned person ought to be brought to trial. If it is the opinion of a certain majority (varying in different states) that the case seems a genuine one, the words "a true bill" are written across the indictment; if not, the words "not a true bill" are written, and the accused is released.

Change in the grand jury. It must be noted here that although the grand jury can no longer, as in the days of old, know from personal observation or hearsay whether the suspected person is liable to be guilty, it is still serving much the same purpose of accusation and indictment; only now the chief function of the grand jury is to prevent useless cases from coming to trial, rather than to investigate cases which would otherwise go uninvestigated. This change is due, of course, to the multiplication of our machinery for apprehending suspects.

When an indictment is pronounced a true bill the accused must appear before the court at a specified date. If he pleads guilty, there is no need for trial: the judge simply applies the law and sentences the man to whatever punishment the law provides for that offense. There is often a wide margin in the penalty or even alternative penalties, which allows the judge to use his discretion.

The trial jury. If the prisoner pleads not guilty, a trial jury is impaneled (that is, drawn by lot), and the accused is furnished by the State with a defending lawyer if he is unable to hire one. We have completely thrown over the original idea that jurymen should act as witnesses. In fact we have gone to the other extreme, and provided that each juryman must be questioned as to his knowledge of the case; if he knows anything about it or is prejudiced on the issue at stake in any way, he is not allowed to serve.[1]

---

[1] The extremes to which lawyers go in challenging jurymen whom they suspect are unfavorable to their side is illustrated by the questions asked in the Iroquois Theater fire case in Chicago (Magruder, American Government, p.297).

Jury exemptions. Most states exempt professional men and public employees from jury duty, and a few states exempt men in skilled occupations. This practice and the fact that through the papers most intelligent people secure a knowledge of crimes before the calling of a jury result in making our juries unsatisfactory to the public. Because of this many people are doubting whether the jury method for trial is as fair and as much a safeguard to human liberty as it was in the past.[1]

The verdict. In over two thirds of the states it is necessary for the whole jury to return a verdict of guilty before the accused is considered guilty in the eyes of the law.[2] Sometimes one man of the twelve may hold out against a verdict for hours or even days. If he never agrees with the other members, he is said to have "hung the jury." In this case a new jury must be called or the case dismissed. Because of this rule and the low intelligence of some jurymen, it has become a saying that a guilty man always wants a trial by jury, while an innocent man prefers a decision by a judge. This is the reverse of conditions in early times, when the judges often stood for royal oppression whereas the juries meant popular protection.

The sentence. When the jury returns a verdict of guilty, the judge then pronounces the sentence. Sometimes the jury has recommended which of the punishments provided by law should be applied, but usually the matter is left to the judge's discretion. In the United States we have adopted the fine as a popular form of light punishment. Fines vary from a few dollars up to tens of thousands. It is felt by many people that when sentences offer an alternative between fine or imprisonment the law discriminates against the poor. Imprisonment may be for a few days in a workhouse, or for life in a state penitentiary.

---

[1] Jury trial in civil suits (where the decision depends on technical matters, such as claims for damages, breaches of contract, property-exchange difficulties, etc.) is more and more being dispensed with.

[2] A number of states allow a small dissenting minority in unimportant criminal and in civil suits.

Capital punishment. The extreme penalty under our laws is the taking of life by hanging or electrocuting. This method of punishing offenders is fast losing its hold in America. This is due to many causes: some people consider it a barbarous device at best, and the slips in justice which have resulted in the legal murder of innocent men have shocked people. The alternative between capital punishment and life imprisonment for such felonies as murder, rape, arson, and even burglary and robbery remain in the statutes of many of our states, but in practice the number of executions is becoming less and less every year, and they will doubtless soon be as extinct as the Roman practice of crucifixion or the Spanish devices of torture. With the passing of the belief in a "criminal type," one of the chief arguments for capital punishment is destroyed. But there are still many people who argue that murder will increase if it is not punished by death, and that the protection of society demands that depraved people be inhibited from acting on their impulses by fear of the most severe punishment.

The Question of Punishment

Purposes. The kind of punishment administered should depend very largely upon the end to be accomplished. Originally the only idea was retribution When this "eye for an eye" doctrine prevailed it was only natural that if a man killed another, he in turn should be killed. If he harmed another in other ways, he should be injured in return To some extent the idea of retribution still remains, but it has been greatly modified. Imprisonment, because of the loss of liberty, is considered by many to be a sufficient retribution. Man, meant to be free, deprived of that freedom, has lost his dearest treasure

The second motive for imprisonment is determent. Society must be protected from the actions of its harmful members. While they are imprisoned they can commit no harm themselves, and their imprisonment serves as an example to others who might be tempted to do wrong. People who do not believe in severe punishments object to this argument. In the first place, it is impossible to know how many people have ever been frightened away from crime by the fear of severe punishment. It cannot be proved by statistics that states which have capital punishment or even life imprisonment for many crimes have fewer crimes committed therein. Most students of the subject are tempted to believe that it is not the severity of the punishment but the *certainty* of it which deters.

It is obvious that when a man is imprisoned he can commit no crimes against society at large, but the records of penal institutions prove that he may still commit many against his guards, his fellow prisoners, and himself. Even the total amount of crime in the outside world may not be less because of his detention. If his term is not for life he may go back into the world with revenge in his heart and commit many more crimes before he is again caught; and this may be repeated time after time.

English statistics show that 62 per cent of the people convicted in 1910 had been in prison once before, 38 per cent twice before, and 7 per cent at least twenty times before. If we stop for a moment to consider that in the year 1910 in the United States over four hundred and seventy-five thousand inmates were discharged from our penal institutions, and that we have reason to believe our percentage of repeating criminals is even larger than England's, it becomes plain that the determent basis for punishment, unless coupled with some other motive, cannot justify itself.

Reformation. One other motive for punishment is so to change the heart and soul of the evildoer that he will go back into the world and not only forsake his wrongdoing but act as a positive force for good. In the belief of some people crime is a disease which has its incurable phases. If this is so, then certain criminals are incorrigible and will always remain a source of danger to society. Thomas Mott Osborne, after his years of close association with criminals, urges strongly that we throw over this theory of disease. It is harmful, he believes, because it cancels the responsibility of the criminal for his acts, and, moreover, it is untrue to facts. He insists that these people are only natural human beings who are spiritually ill. They are ill of selfishness, they have a peculiar form of egotism which causes them to be indifferent to the social rights of other people. This weakness is sometimes inherited, but more often it is caused by the evil influences of bad environment, and most often of all by the stupidity or indifference of older people to whose care a precious human life was early intrusted.

The newer school of criminologists would not have us ignore the weaknesses of criminals. They believe in punishment by imprisonment, but would not add other hardships to the greatest of all hardships, the loss of liberty. And they believe thus not so much on the basis of justice to the criminal as that this is the only expedient and sane thing to do for society as a whole

Criticisms of the old system. As a result of his study of and life among the prisoners in Auburn and Sing Sing, Osborne passed these criticisms against the old system of imprisonment:

1. The confinement in cells leads to physical, mental, and moral degeneration.

2. There is no incentive to honest steady work, because preferences and capacities are not consulted and because no reward is offered for efficiency.

3. The attempted enforcement of silence leads to conspiracy and morbidness, for speech is one of the things that lifts man above the level of the brute.

4. The terrible monotony deadens the soul.

5. The frequent executions unnerve the inmates.

6. The system of espionage produces an unstable nervous equilibrium which may be destroyed by the slightest jar (this accounts to a large extent for the amount of assaults among prisoners), and serves to honeycomb the whole community with suspicion.

7. The high-strung nervous condition extends even to the guards, who, because of constant fear of their lives, become brutal.

8. The whole system denies initiative and responsibility to the prisoners. This, above all else, they need for their remaking. In this and in this chiefly do their salvation and the safety of society lie.

The new self-government system. In view of the defects of the old system, Mr. Osborne instituted in the Auburn prison in 1913 a reform system of true self-government. It was worked out through the suggestions of Jack Murphy, an inmate of the prison and a working partner of Osborne's while he was "doing time" under a voluntary imprisonment. Its success was so great that its originator was made warden of Sing Sing, and there worked out a more complete and ideal system. Advocates of the new movement claim that it has resulted in the general upbuilding of the prisoners. Their physical improvement is evidenced by the extermination of the drug habit and by the absence of the usual prison pallor; their mental improvement, by the conversations, recreations, and activities in the self-government organization; and their moral improvement, by the many responsibilities willingly assumed. Supporters of the new movement point to occurrences which have been real tests of the system, such as in 1915, when fifty-four of the self-government officers were entertained at the home of Mr. Osborne without a single prison guard's being posted, and in 1916, when over two hundred Sing Sing prisoners went on parade without guard outside the prison walls.

This new prison-reform movement is not confined to the work of Osborne in New York. Other noted experimenters in the problem of humanizing imprisonment are Tyman in Colorado, Hunt in Arizona, and Homer at Great Meadows, New York. Dozens of other prison wardens throughout the country, although unwilling to adopt self-government in its entirety, have instituted a series of privileges and concessions which prove their firm belief in the wisdom of according humane treatment to the poor unfortunates under their care.

There are still many people who cling to the old idea that criminals are hopelessly "bad" and that their treatment must be solely in the nature of severe punishment. These people have no sympathy with a movement to supplant the old prisons by "universities of another chance." They claim that crime will surely be encouraged if we make our prisons too enjoyable and too tempting.

A compromise. Probably in this, as in other reforms, a common-sense middle path will prove the safest. Prisons should be considered not only places of detention and punishment but of reform also. Wrongdoing warrants punishment for the offender and protection for society, but until it can be proved conclusively that criminals cannot be reformed, it behooves us to try zealously every possible device for sending convicts back into the world better than they came out of it. And this we cannot do if the old motto "Abandon hope, all ye who enter here" is kept as the slogan of our prison wardens. At least for those prisoners whose term is limited, the prison must become a place of training in democratic citizenship; otherwise our prison system is only perpetuating itself.

The following conservative program of prison reform will, if administered wisely, go far toward accomplishing the ultimate goal of all prison reform, that is, the abolition of the need for prisons

1. Establishment of wholesome, natural living conditions, with the cell supplanted by individual living-rooms and by dormitories, and with the prisoners' having the right to converse.

2. Requirement of five and a half days of good honest work per week, at occupations as far as possible suited to each prisoner, and on pay, with the aim of making every man potentially self-supporting.

3. Supervised recreation in the form of outdoor sports, lectures, music, and motion pictures.

4 Replacement of dogmatic prohibitions and brutal punishments by incentives and rewards to do right because it is right, accompanied by punishments in loss of privileges and good standing for doing wrong.

5. Substitution of indeterminate sentences for life and set sentences, except for the most serious crimes. Thus men who are ready to go out into the world may be allowed to go, while those who have not yet reached a stage at which they probably will never again commit a crime willfully may be kept on in the training-school.

6. Establishment of a system of parole for ex-convicts. For several years after the expiration of their sentence they should report to the authorities at set intervals.

7. Creation of a public opinion which will encourage the ex-convict to forget his past errors and to become a normal, useful citizen.

Summary. Both the attitude toward crime and the methods of treatment have undergone a revolutionary change during the last century. Crime is no longer thought to be an inherited incurable disease of the mind and soul which warrants only damnation. Instead it has come to be considered a complex social problem, but one not in the least insoluble. Sociologists and criminologists now spend their time in analyzing the many causes of crime with a view to removing them, and reformers are busy investigating methods of detection, conviction, and punishment which will best serve to curb crime. It is generally accepted that there must be some sort of adequate punishment for the adult wrongdoer; but unless out of that punishment there comes an understanding of why the act was wrong and a positive aversion to its repetition, the punishment is in vain so far as the culprit is concerned. All our treatment of crime must have as its premise the belief that so-called bad people form a group which lacks altruistic tendencies but which has not descended into "unmitigated villainy."

SUPPLEMENTARY READINGS

Burch, H. R., and Patterson, S. H. Social Problems, chaps. xviii, xix.
Ellwood, C. A. The Social Problem, chap. vii.
Forman, S. E. The American Republic, chap. l.
Hayes, E. C. Introduction to the Study of Sociology, chaps. xxxii–xxxiii.

OSBORNE, T M Society and Prisons, especially chaps. 1 and v.
Survey, Vol XLIII, pp 239-240, 619, 765-767, 775-776.
Proceedings of the National Conference of Social Work, 1919, pp. 13-19, 67-69, 99-100, 107-118, 257-259.

SEARCH QUESTIONS AND PROBLEMS

1. Can you find any examples of socially criminal acts committed in your school? Do they come through intent or through carelessness? Are they any less "criminal" if they are due to ignorance? Is there any way in which the good citizens of your school can condemn these acts and punish offenders without having the faculty make school rules on the subject?

2. In one state of the Union a man was tried for grand larceny for stealing a watch During the course of the trial it developed that the watch, although originally marked $55, had been put on sale for $49 75. Now in that state thefts below $50 are petty larcenies. Why could they not continue with the case without a new indictment? Through influential friends the criminal was able to hire a very clever lawyer, who then proved to the judge that he could not be brought up for a new trial. He based his argument on a provision in the state constitution which contained the same provisions as are given in the fifth amendment of the national Constitution. Can you figure out the argument? Is it sound?

3 Ascertain from reports of your state secretary of the treasury and your city treasurer how much money is expended in your state and city to prevent crime and to house criminals Who pays the bill?

4 Follow the chief newspapers of your community for a week, keeping account of the percentage of column space on the front pages devoted to accounts of crime. Is this a good thing? Why?

5 Can you find out from criminal statistics in your state which has the highest percentage for commitment to penal institutions the foreign-born, the native American, or the first generation of American-born?

6. Compare the statistics on pages 135, 148, and 150 of the World Almanac for 1920 to see if density in population appears as a cause of crime.

7 Compare the tables on pages 150 and 152 of the World Almanac for 1920 to see what connection there is between a high divorce rate and the amount of crime, also the tables on pages 135 and 150 to see if lack of home life accounts for crime.

8. What percentage of the white, negro, and foreign-born elements, respectively, in your state are criminals? See charts on pages 138 and 150 of the World Almanac for 1920.

9. Is there any adequate censorship of the motion-picture houses in your neighborhood to prevent the showing of films which might incite people to robbery or immorality?

10. Are the following devices used in the competitive struggle legal crimes in your state: (1) libel, (2) local price-cutting, (3) the use of fraud or violence to induce someone to break a contract, (4) rebates given by railroads to big shippers, (5) blacklisting or boycotting?

11. In what phase of the business cycle described in Chapter X should you expect to find most crimes committed? Why?

12. How clean a record has your state for lynchings and race riots? See the World Almanac for 1920, p. 174.

13. If the census of 1920 had included criminal statistics how do you think they would have compared with those of 1910 in view of the fact that the percentage of the population living in urban communities has increased from 46.3 per cent to about 60 per cent? What other factors might play an important part?

14. Make a visit to some court and try to identify all the methods of procedure discussed in the text.

15. What classes of men are exempt from jury service in your state?

16. Debate: *Resolved*, That the jury system should be abolished in the United States. For assistance see Shurter and Taylor's "Both Sides of One Hundred Public Questions" (p. 30), Reader's Guide, and Poole's Index.

17. Debate: *Resolved*, That capital punishment should be abolished. See Shurter and Taylor's "Both Sides of One Hundred Public Questions," Reader's Guide, and Poole's Index.

18. Visit the nearest state penitentiary and jails with a view to ascertaining the type of treatment accorded prisoners in your state.

19. If you have a juvenile court, try to find out what it is doing in your community.

20. What is the relation between alcohol, fatigue, and crime? See Washington's "Negro Crime and Strong Drink"; T. D. Crothers's "Criminality from Alcoholism"; and the *Journal of Criminal Law*, Vol. IV, pp. 687–697, 768–772; Vol. XXVII, p. 188.

CHAPTER XVII

TRAINING FOR CITIZENSHIP

Good intentions combined with limited intelligence are fatal in high places.
BOSSUET

The business of life. Every man, woman, and child in the world has two responsibilities that overshadow most other duties. These are, first, the duty to make himself as fine and noble as he possibly can; second, to contribute as much as possible toward making the world a better place for himself and other people to live in. People who think a great deal about the second duty need not worry about the first, for they are sure to develop good characters if they are truly interested and active and sane in securing the welfare of others. And since social efficiency is the great business of maturity, education is the great business of youth.

Of the total population of the country there are at any one time from 20 per cent to 25 per cent who are of school age, while many more who are beyond school age still need education and guidance. And since the future of the country depends upon the wisdom and public spirit of a majority of its people, education becomes one of the greatest, if not the very greatest enterprise of the nation. The future of America hinges upon the character of its people; the character of the people depends largely upon the breadth, common sense, and thoroughness of the discipline of education.

What is education? Now education is a very broad thing indeed. It is not schooling alone, it is the sum of all the influences of our homes, our social life, our formal school training, our religious training, and of what we learn on the street, on the playground, in travel and in reading. A live young man or woman learns something "every time he turns around." Life is rich in learning experiences, and if those experiences be chosen wisely the sum of what they teach makes the citizen very valuable to his community and his country. The purpose of this chapter is to afford a review of the various forces that make up our education, and to see how each one may be used so as to make it yield its greatest value to the student.

THE HOME

The home is the original training institution, and society, with all its modern improvements, can never find a substitute for it that can fully serve its purposes. It is the best and most economical of all educational agencies not only because it can do effective work earlier, and so save time and effort, but also because it can use a greater variety of means than other institutions can. Parental love and care, wisely limited by a common-sense apprecia-

A CLEAN-STREETS POSTER

Many people are bad citizens through ignorance and carelessness rather than depravity. The National Child Welfare Association of 70 Fifth avenue, New York City, is one of the organizations which try to educate the public into better training and care of children. The poster reproduced above is one of many which it sells to local child-welfare societies for their educational work. The posters deal with physical care, education, child labor, dependency and delinquency, character-building, and recreation. People who want to do something for the young people of their community should write this bureau for suggestions. Does your town tolerate the practices shown in the picture?

tion of the value of strict discipline, can set the tendencies of character early and set them strongly toward self-control, unselfishness, and justice.

The home we live in. There are three ways in which home training influences children. The material form of the home leaves a lasting impression; if clean, orderly, cheerily but not gaudily furnished, and far enough from the street and the neighbors to insure a fair degree of quiet, the children brought up in it are likely to be less irritable and nervous than children reared in a noisy, crowded, and disorderly place. Specific habits are formed from certain characteristics of the house we live in in early childhood For instance, plentiful ventilation helps to form good sleeping habits, while adequate room and provision for privacy make for considerate habits toward others that further good social relations. Children who are given drawers or boxes for their playthings, and are made to put away what they are not using, learn to be orderly when habit-forming is easy and the results permanent. Cleanliness and sanitation promote good health, and good health means a better chance in life. Beauty in and about the home, in garden and street and view, teaches every day its lesson of good taste, clean thinking, and the appreciation of nature and of man's handiwork.

Then homes influence character by their daily examples. Children love to imitate grown people, and they are bound to do it whether the grown people want them to or not. The stable character of our civilization depends pretty largely upon this tendency that all children have, to imitate what they see when they are little, thus forming habits which they do not break in maturity, but pass on in turn to their own children. Everyone knows that by listening to a little girl playing with her dolls one can tell much of the manners and character of her mother. Children actually learn to be neat or disorderly, energetic or lazy, temperate or self-indulgent, crude and boisterous or tactful and well-bred, by imitating their parents or other members of the home circle. Their whole attitude toward life is likewise often copied. If father is always complaining of the weather, the price of food, the policy of the president, the street-car service, the pancakes and coffee, he must not expect to have his children develop into sunny optimists; and if mother gossips about the neighbors, she must not expect her sons and daughters to be big-minded and big-hearted people when they grow up.

But it is probable that what is taught specifically in the home has most influence of all. Some homes never teach anything in a conscious way; the parents seem to have no conviction of their duty to teach their own children. But when instruction is given, "line upon line, precept upon precept," it lasts through the years and comes to people's minds when they are trying to solve the problems of their own lives later on. That child is fortunate whose parents have strong convictions and devote time and effort to his training. The American parents of times past who taught religion, honesty, self-control, and unselfishness in no uncertain voice have been mighty factors in making our nation strong and free.

Eugenics. Today there are destructive forces in American life which vitiate and weaken the influence of the home. Underlying them is a basic weakness of low mentality and low ideals among many parents—the character shortcomings that are handed down from generation to generation, and which often make homes the source of social problems rather than a chief help in their solution. The most effective remedy for this very fundamental weakness lies in a new science called eugenics, which teaches the laws of marriage and heredity so as to help people to contract such marriages as will produce a better race. Some states have laws limiting marriage to the physically and mentally fit, but in most of our states there are no such laws, as the people do not widely understand or support the new science. It has still much prejudice to overcome before it can operate widely to better the race. It is already powerful in influence among intelligent people, however, and in time will be embodied in law or in accepted custom in a way to reduce the number of unhappy marriages and unsuccessful homes.

All the misfortunes which break up homes are discussed elsewhere. All these interfere, of course, with the educative functions of homes. Poverty-stricken homes, broken homes, neglected homes—such homes as these rarely send good citizens into the nation.

The old type of family life, in which the family did almost everything as a group, is probably doomed. But family life does not depend entirely upon household custom—upon a breakfast eaten by everyone at one time, for instance, or the baking of bread and beans in one's own oven, or the making of the children's clothes at home. It depends upon the saving, in some way, of enough time for mutual acquaintance by the members of the family, upon the keeping of parental authority and of respectful obedience on the part of children, so that the natural order of government is not reversed in the family; upon love, consideration, and courtesy and upon reasonable concessions to the demands of a changing world; and especially upon thoughtful adaptation of the family customs to the new ideas which the young people of a family are sure to have if they live effectively in their own generation.

Wholesome family life is possible today, but it cannot be achieved by merely copying the family customs of past times, when family life is known to have been good Changing times make changing manners, but the essential things can be retained through much shifting of household and social custom. Parents and children can think out means of adapting themselves to the world they live in without sacrificing their common interests, but it requires much thought and considerable firmness and a willingness when necessary to sacrifice popularity and influence outside the home to happiness within it.

THE PRESS

The actual educational power of the press is very great. The newspaper has two potent functions: it gives people the news, telling them of what goes on in the world; and it essays to interpret to society the reaction of its owners or managers to the events and conditions of the time. The modern newspaper devotes far more space to the giving of news than to editorial comment, which is the expression of its reaction to events. But news may either be presented as a plain statement of facts or it may be colored in such a way as to secure in a majority of the readers just the reaction wanted, in other words, it is possible for a newspaper to do a great deal of the kind of teaching that it wants to do without seeming to teach at all. Everyone knows that a political event, for instance, may appear very different when reported in a Republican and in a Democratic paper, and that as a result the reaction of the readers will be very different.

The press and the truth. The value of the press depends upon the truthful presentation of its news and upon the good judgment of its comment. Truth may be literal or intrinsic; for instance, it is possible for a newspaper to present some scandal, the actual details of which it can prove absolutely, in such a way as to make that scandal appear the rule and not the exception in society. Such a news feature will then be literally true, and yet it will misrepresent the social life of a class of people or of all the people of a city.

Not all the truth, moreover, is worth presenting, and the value of the press depends also upon its judgment in selecting the news that is to be presented to the public. Worth-while news is news that people need in order to help them to live with their fellows wisely and well, personal gossip, then, is seen to have little social value, while financial news, political events, and new inventions mean a great deal to society and therefore should find a prominent place in newspapers.

The truthfulness of newspapers, which is the general criterion for judging them, depends upon a number of factors. Most important of these is the freedom of the paper from dictation by special interests—what we call the independence of the press. Newspapers are nowadays business enterprises and must be managed on business principles or they are doomed to failure. At the same time their great influence keeps them from being entirely private enterprises, just as the relationship of railroads to the public weal makes them quasi-public utilities. Now any interest which needs a mouthpiece in these days usually has a newspaper or a magazine for the purpose. This publication may state frankly what it stands for, or it may exercise a great influence because people do not know what animus directs the expression of opinion and the slant given to the news. If the readers know what interests control the newspaper, they are better equipped to judge what it says; if the control is not generally known, partisan presentations may appear to be very fair and so become very misleading.

Periodicals as organs of interests. The most common interests served by newspapers and other periodicals are political or religious. The majority of American newspapers are frankly either Democratic or Republican, while the number of religious magazines and newspapers exceeds that of all other specialized periodicals. Besides periodicals devoted to general political interests, there are some which are owned and operated in the interests of some one man who aspires to political power. Other publications are frankly edited in the interest of some cult, as, for instance, the theosophical periodicals and the socialist press. The weekly and monthly magazines for general reading are cultural in their object, presenting material which adds to the general knowledge and taste—good or bad—of their readers. Readers of any and all periodicals should learn to distinguish sharply between the advocacy which maintains a regard for truth and that which does not. If fair, periodicals will present the truth even though it hurt their cause. They will not represent their interest as altogether righteous and without fault, for no human institution is that; and they will not distort obvious truth for the sake of making a case. They will not leave out important parts of the truth so that the result is a virtual lie. They will not use abuse and appeals to prejudice against their opponents instead of real arguments. They will be honest in their advocacy of their cause.

Aside from the intentions and methods of the editors and writers of periodicals, the sheer ability of the staff counts for much. Editors may be honest and fair and yet affect opinion very little because they lack ability. On the whole, newspapers are much better written today than they were years ago; the literary standard of even the most temporary writing is constantly rising. Unfortunately the same thing cannot always be said of the content as of the style.

This brings us to one of the most crucial tests of newspapers. Some newspapers are said to be "clean"; that is, they present wholesome material to their readers, telling about matters of general social interest and things that people really need to know. Others, which are known as the "yellow" press, deliberately present to their readers not what they need to know but what will appeal strongly to their weaknesses and their lower natures. They are sensational in their content, relying for their popularity and sales upon the excitement they are able to offer. They have little regard for the reticences of civilization or for the morals of children and young people; they want only to present something sufficiently "spicy" to insure a big sale to the sensation-hungry multitude.

Responsibility of the press. It is well known that when great publicity is given to crime, the amount of crime increases, because weak-minded people always imitate what they happen to have presented to them as models for conduct. Now there is nothing sensational about the actions of good citizens who go quietly about the real business of living, and so they seldom figure in the "yellow" press. It is the abnormal and diseased side of human nature that makes profitable "copy" for such papers, and this is therefore presented vividly as the thought-material of weak and imitative people. Newspapers that print long, detailed accounts of murders, robberies, and other crimes lay themselves open to charges of responsibility for other crimes with which to regale their readers. Although such newspapers are corruptive social influences, they can rarely be held legally responsible, because they take care to print what is literally "the truth."[1] They keep within the law.

Another test of the value of a newspaper is the timeliness of its contents. The news should bear a close relation to the real issues at stake at the time of printing. Sometimes newspapers purposely cloud issues or ignore them altogether, because the interests they represent do not want public attention directed to the questions at issue. Perhaps they hope to have a law passed quietly, in a time of popular indifference, which could never be passed if the public were well informed on the imminence of the issue. A political campaign is a case in point: newspapers may carefully avoid discussing the real issue, if there be any, harking back to issues of bygone campaigns in order that their candidates may secure support which they could never receive if their position on the real issue were truly understood. In a similar way many newspapers never mention a great question until public opinion is so aroused that the result of the issue is practically sure. They "straddle the fence" in the hope of placating all interests and making no enemies. They may succeed in keeping their advertisements and their subscription lists by this policy, but they have no value to their readers as factors in their education as citizens.

Making newspapers safe for humanity. These considerations lead to the formulation of some useful rules for young people, and older people as well, who want to use the press intelligently as a means of training for citizenship:

1. Never read one side only of any question; hunt up the best presentation you can find of the opposite view, and study the two side by side, noting the manner of presentation and

---

[1] A certain minimum of crime reports may be necessary for public information, perhaps, in the case of occasional crimes of great social import, such as lynchings, it is best that the public should know the full and terrible details, in order that it may realize its full responsibility. But the average newspaper account of a sensational murder or divorce case can claim no one of the following justifications for the publishing of human sins and weaknesses (1) the effective warning of youth, (2) the scientific study of crime, (3) the protection of society, (4) the arousing of society to effective remedial measures

discounting at once for cheap abuse, ridicule (which is no argument), and extreme partisanship.

2. Check up statements by official or other reliable, disinterested accounts before drawing conclusions. Remember that figures are good liars when skillfully manipulated, and that part truths may be lies in effect.

3. Suspend judgment in unfinished matters until all the evidence is in. Do not make up your mind hastily. But it is better to make up your own mind wrong than slavishly to accept the dictation of others as to what you shall believe.

4. Deliberately refuse to waste time reading sensational stuff that makes you neither wiser nor better. Life is short enough at best.

In these days society is very generous with its means of education There is scarcely a small town that does not have its public library People who want to can add immensely to their culture and to their value as citizens of the democracy by taking advantage of public reading facilities. People who want to be well informed in these days can be; of course it means some sacrifice of time and trouble and perhaps a cherished pleasure. Some people are timid about using the facilities furnished by the public; they should remember that under the new social order the people in the world are engaged in a common enterprise of making better times, and that every single citizen has his right to public facilities and his duty to make himself intelligent.

The Church

Religious influences. The Church deals primarily with individual character through its direction of human relationships to God. Both directly and indirectly the Christian Church has from the first exercised a great educative influence on society. It has directed man's thoughts and activities, inspired him to heroism in great causes, and dictated his ethical ideas. It is perhaps more influential today than ever, although apparently less a controlling power than formerly in America The special service of the Church, from a social point of view, is that because it works through the universal emotions of religion it meets the varied needs of many different kinds of people and holds them to socialized behavior by whatever motives appeal to them most strongly.

As a force in social affairs the Church in its many branches varies according to the attitudes and ability of its leaders. Some churches follow a fixed policy of teaching nothing about secular affairs; others exercise a controlling influence upon the secular as well as the religious beliefs of their members. The Church has sometimes been antiliberal in the extreme, a force clearly associated with retrogression and stagnation. Sometimes it has led its people against an established order into a better one. But whatever its attitude toward the world's problems, no one can question its great influence as a social teacher.

The School

The State furnishes a free education, complete from kindergarten to university in the more advanced communities, to its citizens. This education is sometimes of a very traditional and inefficient kind, but where it has been made effective and valuable it does two things:

1. It enables the youth to take his place in society without disadvantage; it helps boys and girls to catch up with the long development of the race in a few short years, as nearly as their abilities will permit. Those essential habits and units of knowledge which enable people to communicate with each other and to live peaceably and conveniently in the world,—such habits, for instance, as eating three meals a day, reading and writing and speaking the English language, and such bits of knowledge as how to tell time by a clock, how to pass people on the street, and what George Washington stands for,—these things society, through its public-school system, will teach people if they do not already know them and if they will come and learn. In other words, it will educate its citizens to live in the world without serious trouble if its citizens will accept the gift.

2. But society does more than this in its educational work for its citizens. It demands that when grown up every citizen shall be a productive, accumulating unit in the social whole; and that no one may have any excuse for not leaving the world

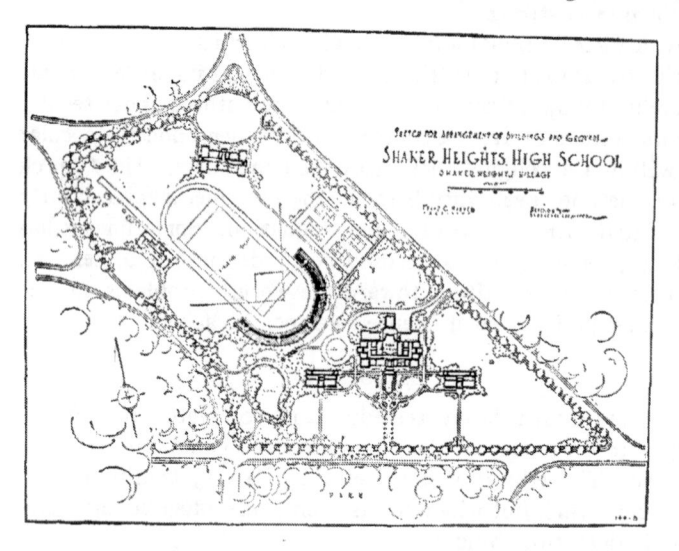

AN AMERICAN HIGH-SCHOOL UNIT

Shaker Heights, a suburb of Cleveland, planned for its educational needs when the village was still very small. Twenty-five acres centrally located were set aside for school purposes, and this campus became a part of the village park system, with drainage and sprinkling for the shrubbery carefully provided for. Two hundred and fifty feet from the road, to secure quiet, the main high-school building was built in this little park. As the number of students increases and money becomes available, a junior high-school plant, tennis courts, an athletic field, a natatorium, and other features will be added. Permanence and economy as well as a keen appreciation of civic beauty characterize such a plan, which looks years ahead and provides for future generations. (From *The American City*)

richer and better than he found it, the public schools are planned to educate people so that they can contribute to the sum of wealth and happiness in the world. To summarize, the public schools are planned, first, to make citizens sharers in existing civilization; second, to make them effective builders in a greater civilization to come.

Development of the public-school system. The public schools of America have not always been so good as they are now. There was a time when education was not free, nor was it at that time elastic and efficient. Then free public schools were established, first for the common-school subjects only and without the careful grading that our schools have today. Later the secondary-school system was added, and later yet kindergartens in the larger places. During the Civil War the Morrill Bill appropriated public lands for agricultural education, and this stimulated the growth of state universities, which, in the last half century, have become powerful and scholarly institutions of which the nation may well be proud. No frank and well-informed American will claim that our free schools and universities are as good as they should be. But they have served this nation well. They compare favorably with the free schools of all other countries in the attainment of their object of educating a whole people for democratic participation in public life, and they are growing better year by year.

As the school system has grown in organization and scope it has grown in the variety of means for the education of its citizens. The school began by teaching just the things that people must know in order to "get on" together—the communication arts, as they might be called; then it began to teach its pupils things that would enable them to earn a living, then it was seen that the school must train its pupils to become socially efficient —to help other people; lastly, it realized its responsibility in aiding its pupils to make the very most of themselves in their private characters.

School studies. This growing realization of the usefulness of the public school and of its function in a democracy has given us these four groups of school studies:

1. The communication group, made up of subjects which help people to understand and work with each other conveniently. This includes reading and writing, literature and history of com-

mon interest, familiarity with conventional manners and customs, the mathematics of everyday life, and all the hundred and one matters which to know means easy adaptation to the life around us and not to know means trouble in social adjustment.

2. The vocational group, which makes people economically independent—able to earn their own living. Such studies come late in school life, since no one should choose his life work until he is old enough to know what he is doing. Many schools now have vocational advisers, who help pupils to choose their life work. Shop work, household economics, commercial courses; music and dancing and illustration, for the especially talented; millinery and salesmanship and dressmaking and catering, for girls—all these things are now taught in the best school systems, if not so thoroughly as to afford a complete training, at least fully enough to enable young people to know whether they care to take them up as a life work.

3. The third group follows logically after the vocational group, which teaches people to help themselves. It is the social-service group, which teaches people to help others. In this group we have history, which teaches us something about the struggles and triumphs of man in the past and helps us to appreciate and understand the world we live in; economics, which teaches us how wealth is made and managed—and mismanaged; and civics, which teaches us about states and about what can be done by common effort through the machinery of government. And with this information the social group of studies should develop a feeling of loyalty to mankind, a keen sympathy with different kinds of people, and a deep conviction of social responsibility. This group of studies is in an especial sense the citizen-training group.

4. The fourth group of studies includes those which make for high personal quality of body and of mind. They are the studies which teach us how to use our leisure time in the very best way. They include outdoor sports and physical training, to give strong and healthy bodies; music, drama, painting, sculpture, and appreciation of what is fine in art, to give us well-

filled minds. These are the studies which enable us to talk with cultured folk freely, which give us worthy friendships, and which fill our evenings and holidays with pleasant and profitable interests. They are the subjects which help us to make our spending-money yield the very greatest return in solid, lasting recreation. The Boy Scouts and Girl Scouts, the Camp Fire Girls, and the "High Y" activities have all stimulated this part of education greatly in the last few years; so have the camera, dramatic, debating, hiking, and tennis clubs, and the high-school orchestras and glee clubs.

At present the American ideal of a high-school education for every boy and girl in the nation is far from realization. But with national aid for the parts of the country which need it, and with an honest appreciation of the fact that democracy succeeds only when there is an intelligent majority of citizens to support it, we may expect this ideal to become a working fact some day. Its coming is associated with the establishment of a Federal department of education which will give to education the same representation in the counsels of the president that is held by agriculture, commerce, and the other great national interests. Such a department, without taking the management of education away from the states, in which according to the Constitution it resides, will unify the national program and give to education the standing it deserves as one of the nation's greatest enterprises.

The value of hard work. In the meantime, no matter how far from ideal the school system may be, it gives pupils the most valuable thing in education, the discipline of hard work. Some really hard work each day, which actually taxes the powers of the student, is the preparation for life which will make grown men and women able to meet the demands made upon them in mature years without dismay and without defeat. To do this hard work successfully, as it comes, is the surest prophecy young people can give that they will not fail as citizens

The worth of a formal education grows yearly, even when measured only in terms of dollars and cents. "The time should come when a young man starting life will be able to borrow money at a bank on the strength of his school record," says Frederick J. Haskin. School records are now so carefully kept in many places that business men telephone the high-school office for the references of a youth who applies to them for employment The books of an up-to-date high school include the mental-test records of its students, their grades in their studies, and their character record—an account of citizenship as shown in school life. Indeed, the State has in the school a means of rating its citizens at the very beginning of their careers, if it chooses to use it.

Recreation

We have spoken of the importance of play as a part of formal education. But aside from the athletics and fun of school life, society is now beginning to understand that it should furnish play facilities for all its citizens. Until recently play was the privilege of children and rich people only. But now we know that everyone, child and adult alike, needs rest and recreation to make him an efficient member of society. Let us see what society offers.

The theater. The theater has been an agent of public education, for good or for bad, for centuries. The ancient Greeks used it to teach religion and ethics, in modern life its use is mainly for amusement, but even so it has an immense influence on manners and morals. Of recent years the cinema, or motion-picture theater, has had a vogue so great that it has come to be one of the world's greatest educative forces As yet it is not consciously used to any extent in the training of citizens in their duties, but with its introduction into public schools, and with the closer regulation of the industry and the extension of its use, we may expect to see it employed more and more for this end.[1]

[1] The picture of manners produced in the average screen play is not the best in the world, but it certainly is affecting American manners in no uncertain way If put into the hands of really fine men and women, the censorship of

Pageants. Another form of dramatic art which has great educational possibilities is the pageant. Towns and societies and community groups organize pageants, usually on subjects of general social interest, such as the history of the region or the service of the Red Cross. Such pageants are not only reminders of what society is working for or of what it has already achieved, but they are almost an education in themselves for the people who take part in them and manage them. When a whole community sets out to represent its history, its ideals, its aims, and its interests in a colorful pageant, it reaps among other things a new appreciation of its corporate self—of the coöperation and friendliness and interdependence that affect its common life.

Long years ago the culture-hungry people of this country established the lyceum bureau and the winter lecture course, which brought to remote country communities as well as to larger places the best talent of the times. Bishop Vincent established the first summer Chautauqua in western New York in 1874, and since then countless tired farming folk and village people have found renewal of life and extension of interests in the music, lectures, classes, and religious inspiration of Chautauqua assemblies.

In addition to the theater, pageants, museums, concerts, etc., there is the amusement of travel, which, of all forms of play, is perhaps the most educational. Travel not only renovates tired nerves and bodies but teaches us how others live and instills a broader, more sympathetic, and more brotherly spirit.

Ceremony. Society has created in ceremony a constant play-element in life, to which we have grown so accustomed that we often forget its true nature. The big events of life are habitually ornamented by this colorful and interesting decoration, which serves to make us realize the significance and importance of the event. A wedding, a funeral, the commencement exer-

---

the motion pictures may in time produce such an art as will really elevate American manners and life At present the censorship amounts merely to an elimination of the extremely harmful features of the plays

cises of schools, the induction of new officers in societies and in the government, the honoring of great men and women, the worship of God,—all these important events are solemnized by

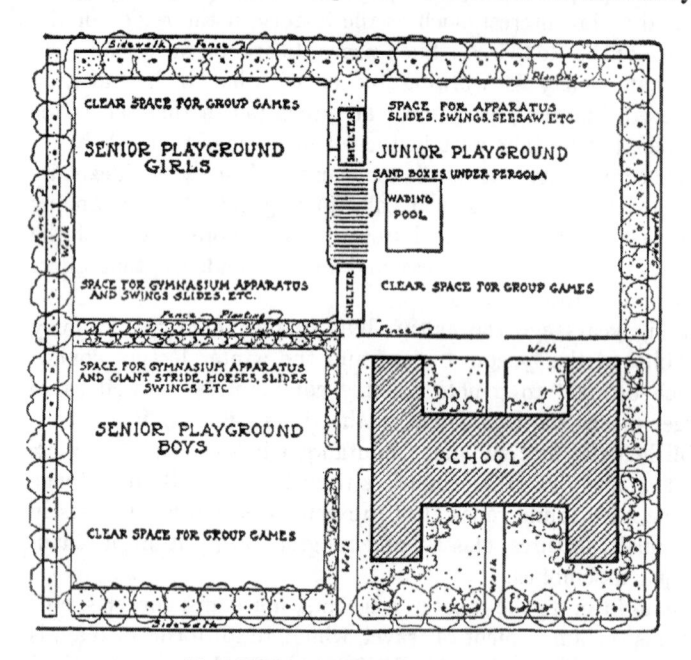

AN AMERICAN RECREATION CENTER

This plan of a school playground is one of those adopted by the unofficial Citizen's Committee on City Plan of Pittsburgh, Pennsylvania. This committee finances its own activities, but coöperates with the city government. It believes in the central municipal control of all public recreational facilities. The neediest parts of the city are to be furnished with playgrounds first, and all playgrounds are to be used the year round. For instance, baseball diamonds are to be given spraying apparatus so that they may become skating-rinks in winter. (From *The American City*)

ceremony. Ceremony is the symbolic expression, in ways as beautiful and impressive as can be devised by the people who plan them, of the special significance of the event in question.

When a ceremony has once become established in connection with a certain type of event, it usually becomes a tradition and so tends to become a permanent characteristic of that event. Flowers and rice-throwing at weddings, processions and addresses when a hero is to be honored, and the formal delivery of a diploma at commencement are all forms of play—picturesque and impressive expressions of what is actually taking place. The actual event is a change in the human relationships of the people involved; the ceremony is a dramatic representation of that change in relationship. Some people like their dramatic expression much more elaborate than do others; the American Puritans distrusted play and had very little of it in their lives, while the Latin peoples who have come to us since 1870 are very fond of it.

The lubricant of good manners. Another form of ceremony which makes life delightful to those who practice it and experience it in others is the formality of courteous manners. People who add to the daily round of routine duties the ornament of politeness give charm and worth to the simplest everyday occurrences. We like to have such people around us; they are welcome to everyone, provided only their courtesy is felt to be the sincere expression of real kindness and consideration, not a pretense assumed for selfish purposes. Young people who express their reverence for old age, or their honor for a person of great worth, by rising when such persons enter the room are adding to the beauty of life by a fine old ceremony that deserves to be perpetuated. Boys and girls who remember to thank each other for favors and to observe the conventions in their social intercourse are increasing the pleasure of life. Ceremony is a good friend to pleasant living and is not to be abandoned without careful thought, and then only when a simpler manner of doing things offers a distinct gain.

The public playground. Out of its collective pocketbook society, when gathered together in towns and cities, offers facilities for play that bring people together in pleasant intercourse. In towns all over our land public playgrounds are now established, with trained play-leaders in charge. The equipment is such as few fathers could afford to buy for their children, since swings and wading-pools and merry-go-rounds require money and space in plenty. The leaders show the children and young people how to play; for although children are born with the instinct to play, they often do not know how to play without being taught. Their tendency is to imitate the life and manners —sometimes very harmful ones—of the grown people about them unless they are taught games and sports that really belong to youth. The play-leaders also protect the smaller children from bullies and teach the ethics of play, the principles of good sportsmanship. They direct children in mastering the muscular correlations that belong to games and sports. They see to it, in short, that play does its part in the education of citizens.

Nor are grown people neglected. Golf, too long considered a rich man's game, has become practicable for people of moderate means through the public links in the great parks. Tennis courts are open for a small fee, or are entirely free. The rowboats and canoes on the lakes in city parks are for rent at rates that make water sports possible for almost everyone. Thousands of people avail themselves of the bathing-beaches supervised by park boards and open, with their bathhouses and showers, to the public. Bands and singers are employed by the cities to give public concerts, free to all, through the summer months. All these lures to outdoor living mean increased health and happiness to the people, and they mean that the people are learning to live together in a kind of municipal family life, which teaches them effectively how many are the interests common to all.

Rural recreation. Country communities are usually behind towns in this matter of common facilities for good times and outdoor living. Although farm people especially need recreation of a social nature, because of the isolation of their work, they are slow to organize for good times in common. The community school or church makes a good center for social life. Too often the ground around these buildings, instead of being neatly kept and attractive, is an unmown, weedy, treeless waste. Tennis courts and croquet grounds, a baseball diamond and a basket-ball floor, might easily be provided, and thus healthful and delightful fun and exercise be secured for everyone. Some communities have made a beginning in this direction, holding picnics in the summer and spelling-bees or chicken suppers in the winter Eight-weeks clubs, fostered by the Y.W.C A, have drawn the girls of villages and farming communities together during the warm weather. Community recreation should be so planned that whole families can enjoy their outings together, with appropriate fun for people of every age. Now that motor cars are owned so generally throughout the country and that good roads are increasing, the recreational side of the education of a citizen need not be neglected. Perhaps the hardest part of the work to be done is to persuade a great many people, especially grown people, that a good citizen is one who not only votes right and feels right toward other people but who can also enter heartily into good times with his neighbors, in good fellowship and good faith.

The national parks. The nation itself has followed the policy of providing for the recreation of its citizens, in establishing the national parks. "For the enjoyment and benefit of the people" is the significant dedication carved in great letters over the entrance to Yellowstone National Park. It is part of the education of a citizen to learn how to rest and re-create his tired body and mind, and the nation does what it can to preserve the most inspiring and beautiful places for the use of all its people. Some states and many smaller civic units follow the example of the Federal government in providing parks for campers and motorists. The habit of camping is a peculiarly American one and, fortunately, a growing one. The custom of spending a part of each summer in day-and-night outdoor living means a total gain of health and good living that will help immeasurably to keep our nation fit in body and mind.

The State may do its part, and countless other social agencies may hold forth all sorts of helps for embryo citizens, but unless the citizen wants to learn and feels the need of learning, these facilities count for nothing. Too many grown people think that their training is finished when they stop school; too many students think that when they receive a diploma they are educated. There is simply no end to the things citizens need to know in order to fulfill their duties to the State and to society in general. A lifetime is not long enough for the attaining of ideal citizenship. Wide-open eyes and a learning heart are the greatest assets of the nation.

SUPPLEMENTARY READINGS

BAILEY, L. H. The Training of Farmers, especially Part II

BRYCE, JAMES. American Commonwealth, Vol II, pp 763–934 [Religion]

FINNEY, Ross L. Personal Religion and the Social Awakening, chap. iv, "The Social Harvest of Materialism."

HART, A. B. National Ideals Historically Traced, chap xii, "I Want to Know"

SHELDON, C. M. "The Modern Newspaper," in *Independent*, Vol LXXIII, pp 196–201

TARBELL, IDA M The Business of being a Woman, chap iv, "Home-making."

TUFTS, J. H The Real Business of Living, pp. 102, 115, 117–120, 171, 358. [The relation of education to liberty]

Literary Digest, June 5, 1920, Vol. LXV, p 44 [The educational rank of the states]

SEARCH QUESTIONS AND PROBLEMS

1 Does your state have eugenic laws? In what states have such laws been passed? How are they administered? See World Almanac for 1920, pp. 369–371

2. How does your state compare with other states in the percentage of divorces? (See World Almanac for 1920, p 154) Why does Nevada have so high a rate?

3 What are the chief causes for divorce in the United States and in your state? Why do you think the proportion in the United States increased from 73 per 100,000 in 1913 to 112 in 1916?

4. Since less than 200 Japanese could enter the United States yearly under the Immigration Law of 1924, why were both Japa-

nese and Americans so excited at the proposal to exclude them entirely?

5. What can be done for children who are not orphans, but whose parents are unable for a time, owing to misfortune, to care for them? Note what New York City did in 1916–1917 in solving this problem, in the *Survey* for January 19, 1918, Vol XXX, pp. 435–439.

6. Why not start a health library? The United States Public Health Service, the Department of Agriculture, the Superintendent of Documents, and the Bureau of Education, all at Washington, furnish citizens with up-to-date information on hygiene and health, much of it free

7. Who censors the cinema plays for your town? Does the Woman's Club have anything to do with it? Do your parents know anything about the quality of plays shown in the motion-picture theaters you attend? Does your state law have anything to say about it? the town board? Does the school use cinema films in teaching? Are the plays you see true pictures of American life?

8 Find out how much the public library in your town has been used during the past year by comparing the statistics of the library as to the number of books read with the number of people in town What sections of town use the library most? Does your library make a systematic effort to furnish its patrons with the information that voting citizens need? Does it specialize in offering timely information on public questions? Does it buy the talked-of books promptly? If its service is not efficient in these respects, is it because of too little public support, or because the librarian is not trained, or because the people are indifferent? What can high-school students do to make the public library more useful to the community?

9. Draw up a set of criteria by which one may judge a newspaper as to its independence and fairness Now select ten of the leading newspapers to be found in your public library and evaluate them as guides for the reading public Do the same for all your local newspapers.

10. Who owns and directs the policy of the leading large city daily newspapers read in your vicinity? Think whether this ownership has had anything to do with the editorial comments and "news slant" in the treatment of (1) the Mexican situation, (2) relations with Great Britain, (3) the policy of the Federal administration, (4) the doings of the city council, (5) the labor situation

11. Why is there no Federal department of education? Read about the programs for a better national management of education in *School*

and Society, Vol XIV, pp 259–263 Which of the two proposals would benefit your own community more?

12 Does your own high-school course give you a good balance of the equipments mentioned on pages 454–456? List your high-school studies for the four years, according to the contribution of each to an adequate equipment for a useful and happy life in maturity. Is your course short anywhere? If so, what can you do to remedy this?

13. Does your high school have a High Y, a Boy Scout, a Girl Scout, or a Camp Fire organization? If not, and you are interested in starting something very worth while, you might write to one or all of the following addresses to find what they have to offer·

a International Y M C A , Secretary for High School Boys, 347 Madison Avenue, New York City.

b National Headquarters, Girl Scouts, 189 Lexington Avenue, New York City.

c. National Headquarters, Boy Scouts of America, 200 Fifth Avenue, New York City

d. National Headquarters, Camp Fire Girls, 461 Fourth Avenue, New York City

Consult with one or more teachers or with the principal concerning the advisability of such societies in your school.

14 What part does play take in the education of animals? Think of kittens, lambs, foxes, wolves, and other beasts Does play help to educate calves and colts? What kinds of play help to educate boys and girls? List the plays of your own childhood which were based on the sober work of grown-ups. What do you conclude? Are the plays of grown-ups based on vocational activities?

15 Who has charge of the Americanization work in your town or vicinity? What methods are being used? Does the public school cooperate? Why? Is there urgent need of more workers than are available? What can high-school students do without sacrificing time and strength that should be used for study, exercise, or sleep?

16 Are the country schools near you as good as the town schools? Why? What is the consolidation movement? Has it succeeded?

17. Do you know of any good teachers who have left teaching to go into other work? Why did they do it? How can people insure good teachers for their children? Do the average parents take any interest in the matter? Do yours, for instance?

18 Debate. *Resolved*, That no citizen be permitted to vote who has not satisfactorily completed the eighth grade.

CHAPTER XVIII

PROBLEMS OF RURAL LIFE

The solution of the farm problem—that is, the holding of a standard class of people upon the land—will be accomplished only when country life is made adequately and permanently satisfying . . . Permanent rural satisfaction comes only through the harmonious upbuilding of the country community.
MABEL CARNEY

TENANCY IN AMERICA

The great problems of rural life center about three things: the tenure of the land, the productivity of the land, and the character of the land-dwellers. Landholding in all times and countries has been a very important matter; the social and political status of the land-tillers always depends largely upon it. In production the interests of farmers are intimately tied up with the interests of all the rest of the world; but if the world finds its economic status to rise and fall with that of agriculture, it is almost equally affected by the social and intellectual status of the farmer class, for town life and achievement are constantly fed from the ranks of the farm-bred.

Tenancy. To speak of a tenancy problem in America is misleading, for America is so large and the conditions in different sections vary so widely that there are really many tenancy problems. Moreover, in studying them one cannot draw conclusions from the experience of Europe, for there the conditions of land tenure for centuries have been essentially different from those of the short period of landholding here. In America the land longest tilled by white men has been worked only about three hundred years. But in spite of its youth there are real tenancy problems in the United States, and as these must be met some day by legislation and by greater industry and coöperation, American young people should study the conditions of land tenure and how they affect production and social life.

European and American conditions. Back of the present landholding customs and conditions of Europe stretch centuries of feudal tenure and varying degrees of landlordism, peasant proprietorship, and rental custom, as we have seen But back of the present conditions in America stretch a few years of ownership, acquired from the government of the nation by actual settlers and workers. In the Middle West and the Far West the present owners are very often the sons or the grandsons of the men who turned the first furrow in the virgin soil some seventy or eighty years ago. These men were never peasants in the European sense of the word; their mental attitudes and ideas were those of independent citizens who acknowledged no one better than they. They were Americans, and although their manners might be crude and their lives simple, they held themselves "just as good as anybody." The sons of such families who had *wanderlust* or for whom there was not land enough on the "home place" went farther west than their fathers, and rented land for a few years from some man who had more than he could work. They saved their surplus, and in a few years they were landowners themselves, and perhaps landlords to other, younger men who were gaining their start in farming. Under such conditions there was no distinct social line between renters and landlords, because they came of the same blood and, in the elasticity of frontier conditions, might easily change places if fortune or disposition so decreed.

The beginning of a tenancy problem in America. This happy economic elasticity, due, like so many other things, to the cheap land of America, has changed. There has grown up, since about 1890, a distinct class of "renters," who rent for their whole lives unless they are unusually able and successful farmers, or unless some windfall in the shape of a legacy or a rich marriage gives them the means of acquiring land of their own. For productive farm land has now become so expensive that a man can scarcely in a lifetime save up enough money to buy a farm. The machinery, seed, and animals required for modern farming cost vastly more than a working equipment did forty or fifty years ago, when the fathers and grandfathers of the present landowners were starting out in life. Capital and labor problems become important factors in the business of farming, as land rent goes ever higher and land fertility grows ever less.

Types of landlords. On the other hand, the landlord also has changed in character. Years ago the landlord was himself a farmer, who rented his extra "eighties" and "quarters" to ambitious young men with a team or two and a working equipment of cast-off plows and harrows from "father's place." Neither owner nor tenant troubled himself about scientific farming, for the land was still so rich that they could count on a good crop in a good year without rotation or fertilization or any such modern devices. The arrangement was very simple and easy to adjust · the tenant received half or two thirds of the crop, and no one asked him questions about his use of the land or his methods.

But although the fields returned large harvests for their tillage, and the farmer's bank account grew accordingly, the farmer's wife was often unhappy and his children discontented. The farm kitchen was the stage on which the farm wife played a lifelong tragedy of hard work, narrow interests, and crude manners. She saw town women, well dressed and leisurely, whose husbands had not so much money as her husband had, but whose lives were enriched by travel, club life, church attendance, and more elegant living than she knew. Her children perhaps attended high school in town, and there heard of good times from which they were largely cut off because of the long drive. The boys and girls possibly wanted to go to college, which meant that for four years their parents could not have their help as they had hoped, and very probably that they would enter business or professions and leave the farm altogether. Thus much pressure was brought to bear on substantial farmers to build houses in town and retire from active work, renting their farms and supplementing this income with the interest on savings. Thousands of farmers did this, and so introduced into the towns and villages, especially of the Middle West, the retired farmer, a type of citizen new to the world and bringing with him his own problems.

The retired farmer as a town citizen. Some of these retired farmers have been godsends to their towns. They have entered into the social life of the place, helping with school, church, and business affairs, have held local office worthily, and have been in the forefront of every progressive movement. But often the story has been quite different. For the farmer in the country has in the past lived an isolated life, independent of others to an unusual degree, and so less conscious of social interdependence than town people are. On moving to town, therefore, he is too likely to limit his social contribution to the building of a good home and to show himself undeniably stingy toward those common undertakings upon which community prosperity so greatly depends. As he is usually an elderly man by the time he has money enough to retire, it is hard to remake him into a socialized being.

The retired farmer as a landlord. As a landlord the retired farmer may be as far behind the times as he is in his capacity of town citizen, or he may develop unexpected sharpness of vision where the buttering of his own bread is concerned. If hopelessly ignorant, he continues to rent his land as his father would have done, but if progressive enough to attend institutes and to read farm papers, he soon learns to supervise the cropping and renewing of his land in a more or less scientific way He now makes such a contract with the renter as secures a rotation of crops, and insists that the manure be spread upon the fields, the cornstalks be turned under rather than burned, and the green fodder be put into a silo for winter feeding. He probably demands a money rent rather than a share in the crops, for he is a better business man than his father, and wants a dependable income. Besides, the use of more scientific methods—as, for instance, dry farming in a dry region—insures to the tenant the means of paying this rent if he farms intelligently. In short, the whole farm-renting business has come to be more scientifically done than formerly, badly as much of it is still done.

Renting is bad for land. In spite of improvements in methods of farming rented lands, the land itself has in almost all cases deteriorated since renting extensively superseded owner-operation. For even the best of renters have not the incentive to "keep up the place" which the owner has; and often renters are ignorant and indifferent men, selfishly bent on making every possible cent out of the land for the limited time they intend to stay upon it, before pulling up stakes for the next scene of their exploitations. Owners who live in town are not so careful about keeping the fences neat and the buildings painted as they would be if they lived on the land. In short, the bad institution of absentee landlordism, the plague of Ireland for centuries, has affected American farms and farming conditions in the same way, although not to the same extent, as in the Old World.

The following table shows the increase of tenant-farming in the United States in the period of the passing of cheap land:

In 1880 the proportion of tenants was 25.5 per cent.
In 1890 the proportion of tenants was 28 per cent.
In 1900 the proportion of tenants was 35 per cent.
In 1910 the proportion of tenants was 37 per cent.
In 1920 the proportion of tenants was 38 per cent.

Causes of tenancy. There are three main causes for the growth of farm-renting shown above:

1. The first is the accumulation of wealth through land-skimming, by the owner-operators during the first half-century of Middle Western and Southern farming. This has changed the status of these farmers from proprietor-tillers to landowners living on rents—has changed them, that is, from a class corresponding to the rich landowning peasantry of the more prosperous parts of France to people who economically, if not socially, correspond to the landed gentry of England. Of course the

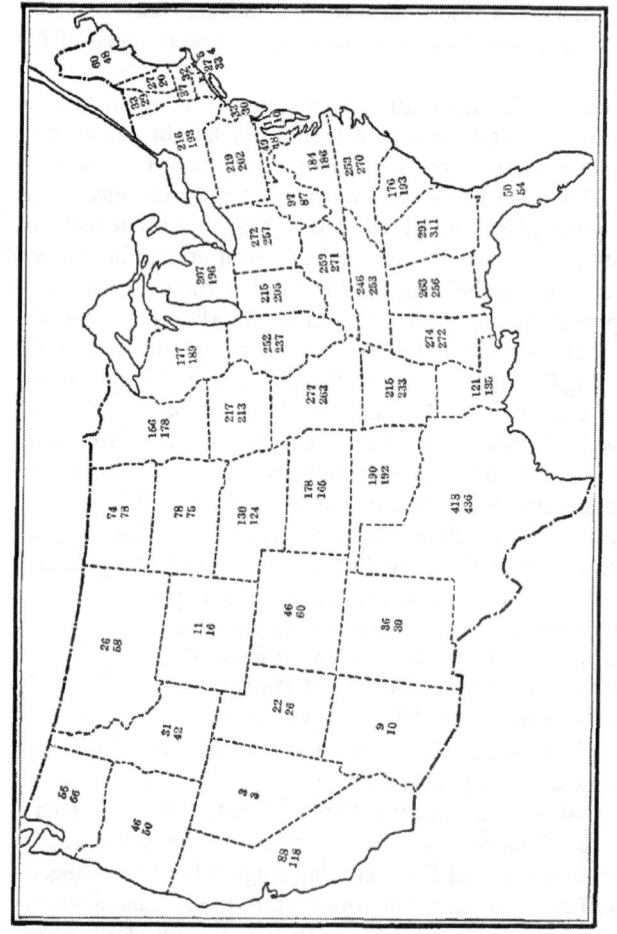

DISTRIBUTION OF AGRICULTURAL ACTIVITIES

The upper numeral in each state shows the number of farms, expressed in thousands, in 1910; the lower numeral the farms, in thousands, in 1920. Explain the changes

increased rental value of the land, which makes it yield enough for a living for two families, does as much to perpetuate the system as the interest-value of the invested money made in farming.

2. The second cause has already been described—the lengthening, often past the span of an active lifetime, of the time necessary for saving enough money to buy a farm. It will be noted that this, like the first cause, is a by-product of the always operating factor of the passing of cheap land.

3. A love of landowning perhaps contributes much to the third cause of tenancy in America, although good American business acumen is also responsible. During the last half-century great numbers of prosperous lawyers and physicians, as well as business men in towns, have invested their savings in farm land. As they do not care to farm the land themselves, they rent it and keep on with their town pursuits, thus adding substantially to their income and insuring themselves a living in old age and an inheritance for their children.

Dealing with the Tenancy Problem

Trouble ahead. The supplanting, by tenancy, of the older American custom of owner-operation will, if carried out generally, result in a decrease in production, a deterioration of land, and a fixing of unwholesome class distinctions. These conditions will bring serious problems to us later on. America should see to it that she never saddles herself with the land and tenancy problems which cause such grave trouble in the Old World. The results of American tenancy are already serious, but by taking thought and by exercising energy and brains in the matter American tenancy can be checked before it goes so far as to become a menace to peace and prosperity. Here are several suggested remedies that offer help in the solution of the problem:

1. Of course the most obvious remedy is for the absentee farmer to move back upon the land, or for his son to do so, allowing the father to spend his old age in town comfort and

ease. With the great rewards that come to the scientific farmer in these days, few men can hope to do better financially than farmers do; and with the modern improvements in farm living, the old reason for retirement to the easier and pleasanter life of towns is passing away Farming is now so specialized that neither the farmer nor his wife need slave, as in days gone by, for a mere living. Modern homes, furnished with modern conveniences and in the best of taste, are as possible now on farms as in town. The motor car and improved roads make driving to town an easy thing, and the old-time isolation need no longer keep the farmer an unsocial, narrow-minded man. The community organization of good farming regions sees to it that good schools, churches, buying and selling organizations, and entertainment courses make prosperity and culture possible for all. In fact, there is every reason, both for their own prosperity and for the good of the country as a whole, that people who own farm land should live on it and work it themselves. It is to be hoped that in the near future society will regard it as a duty for the sons of farmers to learn to farm their own land unless some very special talent justifies them in going into other work. A land made up of farms managed by working-proprietors is a land that produces not only abundant food and clothing for the city workers dependent upon it but also a constant crop of boys and girls who have a good chance to grow into valuable citizens.

2. If owners must rent, then they should make rental contracts which will conserve the land, for they have no moral right either to exploit land themselves or to allow a renter to do so. They should also give the renter a fair chance, allowing him in some way to reap the reward of ability and industry in proportion as he exerts himself. Many of the present abuses of renting can be obviated with a little knowledge and a good deal of consideration on the part of both landlord and renter.

3. Renters hold the solution very largely in their hands, if they could be made to realize it. Renters lose money both for themselves and for their landlords because they do not stay on

one farm long enough. Short-term rentals are wasteful and foolish. If landlords could be made to realize the value of securing an intelligent renter and then giving him such incentives to stay as would bind him permanently to that farm as long as he remained a renter, half the renting abuses would be done away with. Landlords are much to blame for the short-term evil, for they do not value a good renter enough to give him a bonus after he has stayed a given number of years. If renters received, say, partial commutation of rental every five years of their profitable occupancy, the amount to be based upon the profits made and the net increase in the value of the property for the period, they would exert themselves to farm in such a way as to secure a good yearly showing in crops *with* conservation of the soil and the farm equipment. Good renters are not easy to find, and as the problem becomes more acute a good renter can demand more and more nearly an adequate reward for sincere and industrious husbandry of his landlord's resources and his own.

4. The United States has established a system of farm credits by which, on very easy terms, farmers who have little capital can pass from the renting to the owning class. A firm determination on the part of renters not to remain renters, and earnest study of the help which the government offers them, will show the means of taking this upward step.

5. A fifth possibility is not so much a solution in itself as a means of postponing the critical phase of the problem. At the present time one hears much of the passing of cheap land. But as a matter of fact cheap land has not passed; indeed, all that has happened is that the cream of the land has been appropriated, leaving the marginal land still to be made into farms. All the rich prairie is gone, and much of the woodland has been cleared and made into fields; but there are still many embryo farms, even in the Middle West, along streams and in cut-over land, about the lakes of Minnesota and Wisconsin, in the tiny valleys of the Rocky Mountain states, and in the semiarid regions of the Southwest. In the Old World this land

would be profitable farming land; indeed, it would be in this country too, were it not that the American farmer has been spoiled for marginal land by his easy mastery of the ready-spread prairie of the great Mississippi and other river valleys.

If Italian, Scotch, and German farmers of intelligence and industry could be settled on this marginal land, it could in a few years, with the aid of farm loans secured by mortgages, be made into productive farms. The rougher land must be tilled some day, for with the increase of population and the high price of food marginal land must more and more come into use. The sooner the move is made, the better for all concerned.

Whatever the mode of tenure, however, farm land must in the next few years be made to bring forth more than it has in the past if food and clothing are to become plentiful enough to insure comfortable living to a world with an increasing population. This consideration brings us to the farmer's second problem, that of production.

Agricultural Production under Changing Conditions

The economic life of the world depends so largely upon agricultural production that everyone has an interest in what the farmer can bring forth from his acres. The farmer himself knows it for his greatest work; he may not realize just why a good crop means so much to the outside world, but he does know that crop reports affect prices, that political issues often wait on them, and that business is largely dependent upon them. Society at large measures its welfare largely in terms of farmers' welfare; and that welfare depends upon farm production.

The existence point in production. The American farmer has had many troubles in bringing about a full and profitable production. At first, upon the frontier, there was a struggle to make the newly broken ground produce enough food to carry the farmer's family through the coming winter. Virgin soil is difficult to break, even on the prairie, and it was usually about the fourth year before a really adequate crop could be expected. Frontier diseases among cattle and horses and other animals were common; that farmer was fortunate whose animals lived through the first few years and multiplied in such a way as to stock his farm profitably. The existence level was therefore the first goal of farm production.

But of course the frontier farmer, coming from a land in which farmers had produced for a market for centuries, looked forward to the time in which he could not only raise food for his family for the year but also send a surplus to market. The surplus came in due time if he was industrious and fairly fortunate; but then another difficulty arose Marketing was difficult because of lack of transportation. For many years, on the frontier line or just behind it, farmers could not manage to sell their produce for what it was worth in town markets, because roads were few and bad, because railroads and canals did not reach many fertile regions, and because selling devices were not yet worked out. So although there was actual production, the farmer did not receive in exchange the manufactured goods that he needed. Finally the time of adequate transportation facilities came; and although it brought with it its own problem in the way of rates and control, the farmer was now able to market his surplus. His second problem was solved so far as city marketing was concerned. The problem of good roads to town, where shipping took place, was not solved until the day of automobiles, when town and country people united in providing roads that would allow crops to be hauled quickly and economically to the shipping point.

The elements of production. The third and perhaps the greatest production problem has been that of providing and managing the factors of production Land there was in plenty, and good land; the initial factor was not, except in stony New England or used-up plantation regions, a serious question. But labor and capital were big problems. Capital, of course, could be saved from surplus production; so labor became, and still is, the critical factor in production. The very large families of frontier days made the problem less acute; for a man with half a dozen stalwart sons could not only till his own farm but provide his sons, as they married, with seed and animals to start new farms a little farther west. If it were necessary to hire help, he might secure the services of a neighbor's son or, by pointing out the possibility of his becoming a landowner in a few years, induce some factory hand from the East to help him. The diminishing labor supply of later days is partly a social and partly an economic matter, but as it seems to be more social than economic at the present time it will be discussed later in the chapter.

The factor of capital in the form of farm machinery. Fortunately, before the middle of the last century an era of invention in agricultural machinery set in, to aid farming by substituting mechanical power for man and horse power. The effect of machinery on production has been fourfold:

1. It has displaced labor, enabling one man to do what had been the work of several. If barley, maize, hay, oats, potatoes, rice, rye, and wheat—the crops in which machine production has gone furthest—be considered together, it appears that 42.5 per cent of the labor required by hand methods had been displaced by machinery between 1850 and 1895[1] The labor used in 1904 in producing the nine principal crops was only 21 per cent, or a little over a fifth, of the labor that would have been necessary to produce the same crops in 1850. In the twenty years between 1880 and 1900, when horse-drawn farm machinery came into general use, the effectiveness of human labor was increased about 33 per cent.[2] All this means that great numbers of men once used on farms have been freed for town industries, and also that those who remained have been able to add greatly to the total production.

[1] Cotton is a crop in which, owing to the peculiar conditions of Southern labor, there has not been a displacement of labor by machinery parallel to that of the Northern crops See Quaintance's "Influence of Farm Machinery on Production and Labor," p 33

[2] Quaintance, The Influence of Farm Machinery on Production and Labor, p. 16, quoting from agricultural statistics in the twelfth census

It must be remembered that much of the labor which is popularly said to be "displaced" by machinery has simply been differently placed; that is to say, many of the farm occupations of fifty years ago are now carried on in town factories. This has happened to grain-grinding, butter-making and cheese-making, implement-making, and cotton-ginning. This means that inevitably a certain proportion of farm workers must follow their work into town. The work is still done; a greater proportion of town-dwellers does not necessarily mean that farm production is decreased.

2. The increase in production has been marked. If we take maize as an example it has been found that if the laborers who worked on the 1894 crop had used the methods of 1855, they would have produced only 473,528,022 bushels instead of the 1,212,770,052 bushels that were produced, showing that approximately 60.9 per cent of the crop was due to machinery. The showing for the smaller grains is even higher; it is estimated that 95.7 per cent of barley crops and 94.5 per cent of wheat crops were due to machine methods as long ago as 1895, with an increasing proportion as machine methods became more efficient and more general. It will be seen that machines not only save human labor but perform labor; they do the work of many men.

The effect of increased production has been to encourage increase in population, which always depends largely upon the food supply. In the case of the United States this increase has come about largely through immigration; but if immigration were to be stopped, our increased production would function as assurance of support for natural increase in native population. In either case it provides food not only for farmers but for all other producers as well.

3. In the next place machinery lowers the cost of production. Comparing the cost of production in 1850 and 1895, Quaintance found that for fifteen leading crops raised by machine methods the cost was only 53.7 per cent of what it had been by hand methods. This is in spite of the fact that the working-day has

been shortened and that wages have risen greatly under machine production, since a more intelligent laborer, and therefore a more expensive one, is required for machine work. It has been found that for crops raised by machine, wages rose 166 per cent between 1829–1830 and 1895–1896, whereas for crops in which machines were not used, wages fell 6.7 per cent.[1] The farm-laborers who worked with small vegetables, strawberries, apple trees, potatoes, tomatoes, and sweet potatoes (crops in which, in 1895, hand production still held its own) represent the laborers who lose by the introduction of machinery. They are the tragic minority whose sufferings cloud the greater prosperity of the day of new ways and bigger results.

4. The final effect of the introduction of machinery, a result of the first three effects, is the higher level of intelligence and the changed nature of farming which have followed machine methods. Because a skilled laborer using a machine must have more intelligence than is required of "the man with the hoe," stupid men are being eliminated from farming. Brains are required to farm in the modern world, and more and more those brains must be well trained. Scientific farming is making what was once an almost purely extractive industry, dependent upon wind and weather for its success, a genetic industry largely under human control. Farming has become a business; the modern farmer is a business man, as keen in his judgment and as broad in his interests as any other business man.

The passing "independence" of farmers. And because farming is not a grab bag, but a business in which the farmer takes out according to what he puts in, capital and managing ability play an increasing part in it. It is becoming more and more specialized, more and more dependent upon the coöperation of other businesses. People used to talk much of the independence of the farmer; fortunately the independent farmer is

---

[1] The rise in wages from 1914 to 1920 is far greater; but as other factors besides the introduction of farm machinery enter largely into that increase, it is better not to generalize from it. The rise to 1895 was mainly due to machine methods, although not entirely.

disappearing, and the farmer who realizes that he is very dependent upon others, and they upon him, is abroad in the land. He is more prosperous, more cultured, more socially minded than his father, who ran his little kingdom like a feudal baron and never knew how much he missed.

Most American farms were literally like feudal baronies until recently, in that they were so often isolated from neighbors and from town by bad roads. The roads, dusty in summer, frozen into deep ruts in winter, and a mass of sticky ooze in the spring, were one of the greatest bars to effective production that ever robbed farmers of the results of their toil. If a farmer succeeded in hauling his crop to market, he did so by slow stages, often occupying a whole day in one trip to a neighboring town. He lost time from farm work that he could ill afford to lose; he spent precious hours toiling through the mud that should have been spent in mending fences or in painting barns or in seeding his ground. Not only was time lost, but the expenditure of horse power or of gasoline was great.

The economic loss from bad roads. If the roads were, as often happened, so bad that the farmer did not attempt to take his produce to market, he might lose the chance of selling when prices were best. He must sell when the roads were good, or at least passable, not when prices were most favorable. Trips for pleasure, for church worship, or for mental improvement were curtailed or omitted, for the strength of the horses must be conserved for necessary marketing. So the bad-roads problem had its social and intellectual phases along with its economic aspects.

The Eastern states began the movement for better roads in the 90's, followed slowly by the Middle West and Western states State laws passed either under the stimulus of local demand, or after the Federal Aid Road Act of 1916, are giving to most of the states a good system of roads both for business and for pleasure. Main roads are being built first, the less important "feeders" will be improved in time. The saving to farmers is simply incalculable; the private gain hinging on the ability to market crops when prices are best is in itself a bringer of prosperity. In road legislation and in road-building town and country unite their forces, for town and country interests are at one in this matter. The town merchant, whether he sells to the farmer during the day or rides out in his car in the evening, profits as truly as the farmer by improved highways.

Timesaving transforms rural life. The change in life and attitude of farmers who have profited from machine methods is due in large degree to the greater leisure they enjoy. The farmer who has time to read, to motor with his family, to attend farmers' institutes, and to live a normal life should be a broader and happier man than the grubbing farmer of handwork days; but unless he knows how to use his leisure, and unless he extends the advantages of machine-won welfare to his wife and children, he may be no better citizen than he was before. This brings us to the matter of social welfare in the country, a matter quite as important as economic welfare.

SOCIAL PROBLEMS OF COUNTRY LIFE

Since men first gathered in cities, "hayseed" or its equivalent has been a term of contempt. The countryman, awkward in manner and antiquated in dress, ill at ease before more polished folk and domineering toward his helpers, has been the joke of his urban neighbors. In spite of the clownishness, which might or might not be justly imputed to him, the farmer has kept his self-respect, for he has known that his production lays the foundations of economic welfare and that towns cannot exist without him. Nevertheless his life in times past has been a hard and sometimes a dreary one.

The stream of country boys to town. Hard and dreary farm life, in fact, has been the rule rather than the exception in America. But there are now enough farmers leading happy, prosperous, and socially profitable lives to prove that farm life need not be dull drudgery. The revolt against farm life is most common among young men, who refuse to stay on their fathers' farms, or who prefer to work in towns rather than hire themselves out as farm laborers. Such youths give in the main three reasons for preferring town employment and town life:

1. Farm work is unattractive. It means rising at four or five, working until dark, and working hard. The work is monotonous and dirty. City work is for definite hours, is usually easier to do, and a man keeps physically cleaner at it.

2. The wages are too low.

3. There is not enough company, enough fun, or enough adventure. Youth longs for color, romance, and companionship, for novelty and adventure. A farm is an isolated place, with few people—a drab place for a young man. The lights of city streets shine alluringly for him.

Good wages alone will not keep farm labor. But recently the conditions have changed so that the first two of these objections to farm life no longer hold. Farm labor has been so scarce that it has practically fixed its own working conditions and has cut down hours and classes of work performed to a very reasonable basis. Wages have also increased so greatly that a farm laborer is now able in a year's time to save a very fair balance in the bank. The economic advantage today is clearly in favor of the farm worker rather than the town laborer, but the flow of country and village boys to the city continues. It is clear that the cause lies, then, in the personal and social conditions of country life. Men will not work on farms unless farm life is made as attractive to them as city life, or at least not unless the attractions plus the wages make an equal appeal.

The question of comfort is fundamental. Cold, scantily furnished bedrooms are the usual lot of workers, whether they be in city or country, but the city worker can at least find attractive and comfortable places in which to spend his waking hours. If the farm kitchen or living-room can vie in attractions with the cinema shows, free reading rooms, concerts and games and Y.M.C.A. athletics that the city offers, it does well, indeed; but at least it should offer comfort and cleanliness and good cheer.

Bathrooms and furnace-heating are possible in many farmhouses which do not have them; the farmer has money enough —what he lacks is a sense of the duty of furnishing his family and his helpers with the comforts which have become common in modern town life.

Labor conditions for farm women. The average American farm home is still a place in which housekeeping means much hard work. About two thirds of a large and typical group of farms studied recently, located throughout the Northern states (and Southern conditions are worse in this respect), had no water for the kitchen save what was carried in by hand. Only about a fifth of the farmers' wives had any power which could be used for churning or washing or sewing, although almost half of these farms had power for the outside farm work. There were few that could boast a bathtub, and few in which the farm wife was not starter and stoker of the kitchen stove. The care of milk and chickens devolved on her, and she was fortunate if she were never called on to bed the cattle or to milk.[1] These facts explain why farmers' daughters, no less than their brothers, seek work in towns.

The lure of adventure. Perhaps the element of adventure is the one in which it is hardest for the farmer to meet the competition of city attractions. The farm boy imagines that manifold wonderful things may happen to him in the unknown, mysterious town to which he feels so drawn. As a matter of fact city life is, for most city people, a very dull and prosaic affair, for adventure is a matter of temperament and appreciation more than of circumstance. If some scheme of profit-

---

[1] Fortunately things are better than they were. In a recent survey of the Department of Agriculture it was found that 62 per cent of American farms throughout the North have automobiles and that 72 per cent are equipped with telephones. Motor cars and telephones are a very real help in marketing and a means of relieving the monotony of country life. Comfort and sanitation in farmhouses are growing, also, linoleum floors, fly-screened doors and windows, kitchen sinks and washing-machines, show that farm wives are insisting on some lightening of their burdens and on some of the more common household comforts.

sharing which will reward service of extra quality and effectiveness can be offered the farm hand, as such incentives are now offered to many town employees, farm work will acquire an element of adventure which it does not have when its wages are fixed and certain. There are few ventures which appeal to mankind more potently than financial ones, and few profit-sharing plans which do not in the end repay their originators. If to this money venture be added some interest in farm experimentation, such as any intelligent farmer may carry on from season to season, the appeal to intelligent farm labor becomes stronger still. Fortunately college and high-school boys are increasingly spending their summers in farm work, and to such boys farm experimentation should appeal strongly. While the farm does not furnish adventure of a hair-raising kind, its work can be made interesting enough to enlist and hold the attention of live, normal young men and women; and if it offers rewards for unusual intelligence and effort, it must attract a certain number of young people who have in them the spirit of the venturer.

Because many farmers did not indulge in much recreation in their youth, they refuse to supply means for it for their sons and daughters and for their hired men Very few farm homes include a tennis court, a basket-ball field, or even a croquet set, and yet there is usually ground and to spare. Books, magazines, indoor games, and a piano are somewhat more common, but unless there is leisure and good company these helps to pleasant living count for little. Leisure on a farm can come through the spending of money on labor-saving devices plus good management on the part of all. The farm wife or daughter who has a power washer, a cream separator, a gasoline stove, and running-water may manage to finish her work and spend the evening in games or music. Concrete walks and a washroom mean the saving of hours in scrubbing kitchen floors; electric lights mean the saving of time formerly spent in filling and cleaning lamps. The time thus saved may be spent in recreation, and human happiness and content bear a very direct ratio to the time spent in recreation.

The social betterment of country life must, in short, begin at home. Unless the home life of the farm shares reasonably in the advance in comfort and economy and health which modern invention has made possible, inevitably the free younger members of the family will seek those conditions elsewhere. Nor will intelligent free hired labor choose to work where common comforts are lacking Without hired help, and without the interest of children who can and will carry on the business of farming when the present generation is old enough to retire, the farmer loses his two main aids to production.

The Community Idea

Social betterment cannot, however, stop at "the home place " It is not enough that the farm be well run, the community must be well run also if farming is to be established as a permanent and profitable business. In many country communities the farmers learn to work together through coöperative enterprises, such as dairies or thrashing-rings. The cooperative dairy is one of the few such enterprises which have succeeded in this country Thrashing-rings are usually simple in their organization, each farmer helping his neighbors in the "ring" when the thrashing-machine works through a neighborhood. This kind of cooperation is as old as white settlement in America; it is the modern form of the old house-raisings and corn-shuckings, which played so great a part in pioneer social life. Unfortunately, with the coming of machinery and with the necessity of doing as much work as possible in a short time, the modern thrashing-day means less socially than the old handwork gatherings did; but wherever men and women are socially minded the lack may be filled with neighborhood merrymakings.

In union there is profit. The coöperative buying and selling organization is a means to greater profit which American farmers have neglected. It is needed especially in regions where the chief crops are perishable in nature or have not a fixed world-price. Fruit-growers in California and Florida, for instance, are thoroughly organized and prosperous; but fruit-growers who are unorganized often lose a large part of their crop, pay high transportation charges, and fail to realize a profit on their investment. A selling organization bargains for the combined crop of the members, and because it can offer large quantities of standardized quality, it can secure terms that individual farmers can rarely demand. Moreover, it buys containers in quantity, arranges for transportation in the most economical ways, and by interchange of experience and advice among its members helps them to develop the technique of their special crops to a high point of efficiency. In some communities the buying association, which purchases farm supplies at wholesale prices, has succeeded, but the opposition of retailers in neighboring towns, combined with the disinclination of farmers to the management of such companies, has prevented their becoming general.

These forms of association may or may not bring about a closer social *entente* among the farmers and their families. But in the case of farmers' organizations of the type of the Grange, once so widespread in the Middle West and still found in many rural communities, a better social feeling can scarcely fail to be developed. Any neighborhood gatherings, at school or church or Grange hall, in which people talk freely and eat a meal together tend toward friendliness and social unity. Some country-school teachers have done wonders in building up the social life and community loyalty of the districts in which they teach by planning spelling-bees, holiday celebrations, and suppers at their schools.

The antiquated district school. Country schools determine to no small extent the quality of country life, for the rural citizen is trained in them. And country schools are more often bad than good. The district school became fixed as an American institution many years ago, and because it costs less than better schools it is still widely used. The sum of its virtues may be said to be that it is better than no school at all, but it no longer meets the educational needs of the typical country community. Three solutions to the poor-school problem offer themselves to the farmer who wants his children to have as good an education as their friends who live in town.

The absentee pupil. The first is to send the children into town to school or even away to boarding-school. But this solution is

A SCHOOL BUS AND ITS PASSENGERS

About eighty of the hundred and twenty-five pupils of the Colomakee School, near Blakely, Early County, Georgia, ride in this bus daily. It makes two trips, gathering up the pupils from a consolidated district of about thirty-six square miles. The school has four teachers besides the music teacher. Roads used by the school bus are kept in good repair, and even in the worst weather the attendance averages about 90 per cent, the pupils living farthest from school having the best attendance record. This country school in Georgia is typical of thousands of schools throughout our land which have been made more efficient by consolidation and by the furnishing of transportation. (From *The American City*)

not a common one, for not only is it too expensive for the average farmer but it leaves the question unanswered. The poor school remains, probably poorer than ever for the withdrawing of the interest of the man who sees how bad it is. The question has not been answered; it has only been avoided. Besides, the rich farmer who sends his children away is giving them an undemocratic advantage, which will divide them in sentiment and interests from their future neighbors. Except for the higher grades which cannot be provided in country schools, the practice of sending children away is a lazy side-stepping of the issue which brings with it no community good.

The improved district school. The second solution is to improve the district school as much as possible by employing the best teacher available, to make the plant comfortable and well-equipped, and to insure a thorough and practical course of study. Good teachers for country schools are hard to get, for capable, trained, and experienced teachers can easily find positions in towns, where as a rule living is more comfortable and salaries higher Country-school teachers are too often young girls just through high school or perhaps without even that amount of education, or poorly trained older women who either live in the district or prefer rural to town positions. The feeling that a country-school teacher should have as good a training as any other teacher grows slowly; it grows most slowly in the country, where any other idea should first be resented. Fortunately educational authorities are now insisting upon better and better training for rural teachers and also upon improved school premises. Better lighting, better heating, better walks and grounds, and better school furniture are being prescribed, and schools that do not meet the standards set are penalized in some way by the state or county authorities.

The consolidated school. The third solution of the question, and probably the ultimate one, lies in the consolidated school. This is a school which combines a number of district schools in one, centrally located, graded like a town school and taught by a competent staff of teachers under a principal. The teachers are frequently housed in "teacherages," built near the schoolhouse, often on the school grounds. The quality of teaching is usually better than in the district school, not only because the teachers develop professional skill and interest through exchange of ideas but also because the consolidated school, being much more economical to operate than an equivalent number of district schools, can pay higher salaries. Moreover, teachers do not find their lives so lonely in such schools as under the old system. The pupils in the enlarged school district are usually carried back and forth in autobuses; this enables them to help night and morning with light farm work. The social spirit and efficiency of such a school is so vastly superior to that which was possible in even the best of the district schools that doubtless the consolidated school will prove the final solution of the rural-school problem.

The community center. The ideal arrangement for country districts is to have a community center in which school, church, and recreation grounds are combined, with homes for the staff of teachers, the minister, and perhaps the community doctor and nurse. This is a far cry from the typical haphazard, decentralized social life of most country communities of today.

If this ideal be realized, it will be because the people of the community begin to plan, work, and sacrifice for their own community good; because they are no longer content to let things happen as they will, but make them come about as they should No such ideal arrangement can come all at once, and it is not best that it should. It can be built up little by little, each year bringing new features and improving the old ones A consolidated school gives perhaps the best nucleus for the community center, as it builds the community life about an institution which is officially managed by a unit of government —a group of people organized for work

The country church. The problem of the country church is a difficult one, but there are powerful agencies at work on its solution, and there is hope of its being helpfully solved. In some communities the people of several denominations have united in a liberally organized church, have employed a pastor with a practical knowledge of sociology and a great faith in humanity, and have succeeded in creating a powerful agency for the improvement of social and spiritual life. So much in the way of creeds, prejudices, and customs must be thrown aside for the sake of friendly unity, in such cases, that the people practically start out afresh, sans the inherited differences that formerly kept them apart and unfriendly. Recreation and self-culture follow naturally in the wake of such a church, when led by a pastor with broad views of Christian living and teaching

With provision made for educating the children, for public worship, and for social recreation, there is for the whole community a constant stimulus toward the higher life. Materialism in its grossest form is an accusation laid at the door of the American farmer and his wife. This materialism is the natural outgrowth of a life centered in the eternal problems of making money and doing the day's work. People whose thoughts are concentrated on the crops and the bank balance can never hope to see their souls expand very far. The cure for materialism lies, first of all, in the provision of means by which a new vision of social relations and a new joy in living and a new sense of duty to men may be gained.

SUPPLEMENTARY READINGS

GILL, C O, and PINCHOT, G The Country Church, pp 37–53 [A working program.]
GILLETTE, J. M Constructive Rural Sociology. [Social agencies are discussed in chapters xiv, xv, xvi.]
MUZZEY, D S Readings in American History, pp. 519–522 [A famous oration on the South]
TUFTS, J H The Real Business of Living, chap xxxi [Country problems]

Child Labor Bulletin No. 6 (May, 1917), pp 50–56
Outlook, Vol CXXVI, pp 425–429. "The Passing of the Hick"
What can be done in the little country school?
G C SMITH, in *Outlook*, Vol CXIII, pp 717–722
CARL HOLLIDAY, in *American Review of Reviews*, Vol. LIV, pp 69–78.
J. C. MUERMAN, in *Survey*, Vol XXXVI, p 75.

SEARCH QUESTIONS AND PROBLEMS

1. How much land does the United States still own? Is this land surveyed? Can it be homesteaded? Do you know of anyone who has located a claim and secured title? How much time and capital were necessary? Write the General Land Office, Department of the Interior, Washington

2. Do you know of any tenant farmer who has been able to save enough capital to buy a farm of his own? Where did he buy, and at what price?

3. Dividing the following references among the members of the class, make a symposium study of land-tenure problems in different times and countries, with a view to thinking out principles that might apply to a good permanent system for universal use at some future time

ANCIENT HEBREWS *Contemporary Review*, Vol CIV, pp 496-504
MODERN HEBREWS *Public*, Vol XXI, pp. 9-10
MEXICO *American Review of Reviews*, Vol XLVII, pp 741-742, Vol L, pp 373-374
  Outlook, Vol CVII, pp 228 ff
RUSSIA *American Review of Reviews*, Vol XLVI, p 624, Vol L, pp 747-748.
  Public, Vol XXI, pp 211-213, 235-238, 606-607, 798-799.
  American Economic Review, Vol VI, pp 61-68
JAPAN *American Historical Review*, Vol XX, pp 1-23
SCOTTISH HIGHLANDS *Living Age*, Vol CCLI, pp 203-211.
IRELAND *Fortnightly Review*, Vol LXXXVIII, pp 976-990, Vol CVII, pp 1060-1074
  Nineteenth Century, Vol LXVI, pp 618-633
  American Review of Reviews, Vol XXXII, pp 572-573
ENGLAND. *Fortnightly Review*, Vol CVII, pp 868-877.
UNITED STATES *Century*, Vol XCIV, pp 625-632
  Sunset, Vol XXXVIII, pp 16, 20-21, Vol XXXIX, pp 26-27
  American Review of Reviews, Vol LVIII pp 182-184
  Journal of Political Economy, Vol XVI, pp 201-211
  Popular Science Monthly, Vol. LXXII, pp 40-45.
  Annals of the American Academy, Vol XXXIII, pp 647-657
  Quarterly Journal of Economics, Vol XIX, pp 270-286

4 What state agency in your state reports rural conditions? Can you find out what proportion of your farms are operated by owners and what proportion by tenants? (See latest census report.) Are there

any state tenancy laws? What are the terms of tenancy in your neighborhood? Is rent in kind, for instance, or cash rent more common? Do the farm owners dictate the crops to be raised, or are tenants allowed to raise such crops as they please?

5 Read what Young and Mill, two eminent English authorities, thought about renting and landowning about a century ago. Then, with our present American conditions in mind, criticize the wisdom of their opinions See Gillette's "Constructive Rural Sociology," pp. 220–222.

6. In the same way consider those who favor tenancy because of its practicability Remembering the present prices of farm products. do you think tenancy is inevitable because of the impossibility of the renter's saving enough capital for a farm of his own?

7. Who owns the public country roads in your state? Who controls them? Do you know of any closed roads that should be open? Why are they not opened?

8 Does your state charge a fixed road tax per man, allowing the choice of working it out or paying for the labor of another?

9. Do you know of any case in which farm production has changed recently from hand to machine methods, on a farm in your vicinity? If so, secure data which will enable you to compute .

a The saving in labor, counted in number of days' work for equal crops by the two methods.

b. The saving in cost of production. How long will it take the machine to pay for itself?

10 Do you know of any kind of farm work still extensively done by hand because machinery has not yet been invented for that purpose? Do you know of any kinds of farm work in which machine production is quite out of the question?

11. Is the effect of machine production of farm crops to equalize the product, or to produce uneven supplies over a period of years? Give reasons for your answer.

12 What is the usual type of farmhouse in your vicinity? Is it comfortable, commodious, modern, and beautiful, or the opposite? If the farm homes are poor, is it due to poor production and consequent poverty or to indifference and a low standard of living?

13. A few years ago it was said that there were more farmers' wives in insane asylums than women of any other class Why? Does the statement still hold true?

14. If a survey were made of several typical farm communities in your neighborhood, what facts should you consider it most worth while to learn? How is a survey conducted?

15. How many consolidated schools are there in your county? Do the farmers like the idea? Why? What do the educators say about it? the business and professional men in town?

16. How many Chautauqua assemblies were held in your state last summer? What is the function of these assemblies in rural and village life?

17. What provision is there for obtaining a traveling library in a country community in your state? To whom would one write for information?

18. Draw plans for an ideal rural-community center and explain the functions of each feature included

19. Can you see any difference in improvements, upkeep, and beauty between the rented farms and the personally operated farms in your community?

20. American farmers suffered severely after the World War Read in the *Literary Digest* for October 13, October 27, and December 22, 1923, and February 9 and March 1, 1924, and report on conditions.

CHAPTER XIX

PRESENT-DAY PROBLEMS OF DEMOCRACY

Aggressive fighting for the right is the noblest sport the world affords
                                                          ROOSEVELT

EXECUTIVE ORGANIZATION

In Chapter V we saw that the United States had made great progress on the road toward efficient democracy. Many obstacles have already been overcome; more remain to be surmounted. This is a fact which every American should keep in mind. To have pride and faith in our government as one of the best in the world is both excusable and justifiable; but to assume that our present democracy is a perfect one or that we have no disgraceful faults to overcome is counterfeit patriotism and egregious conceit. If we are to continue on our path of progress we must face our problems squarely, recognize our defects candidly, and earnestly apply our best thought in search of solutions.

The need for reorganization. Much destructive and some little constructive criticism has been voiced of late regarding our executive departments, in both state and Federal governments. It is felt that the administrative branch of the government, in growing to meet the needs of the growing country, has become a poorly organized conglomeration of subdepartments, commissions, bureaus, boards, and agents. In many cases the powers and functions of these agencies overlap, so that overhead expenses are needlessly increased. Besides added expense, this poor organization produces decentralized authority and responsibility, and fosters the process of what is popularly known as "passing the buck." When an energetic citizen desires to have something done, he is sent around from commission to board, from board to committee, and often ends by giving up in despair. Just as efficiency experts are needed in business concerns to work out well-correlated organization, so our government executive departments are now in dire need of someone to plan a thorough administrative reorganization.[1]

This need was so keenly felt during the war that an emergency law, the Overman Act, was passed, providing for temporary shifting of powers from one administrative department to another as necessity or expediency might dictate. Almost no attempt, however, to reduce the vast personnel was made, in fact the number of administrative bodies was necessarily increased. One of the pledges of President Harding was to institute as thorough a reorganization of Federal administrative departments as the existing law allowed Such a reform has two purposes: reduction of expenses in response to universal demand, and the equally important purpose of greater efficiency.

Illinois is the best example of what can be done in the way of concentrating power in the hands of a few elective officers. Under Governor Lowden's administration the number of separate commissions, boards, and officers in the state executive department was reduced from one hundred and twenty-five to nine departmental divisions, with directors responsible for the appointment, expenditure, and actions of all members.[2] Nebraska, Idaho, and Massachusetts have since consolidated their executive offices, and other states have movements on foot to administer the people's affairs more effectively and economically.

The need for harmony. Another serious criticism of our executive departments is their failure to work harmoniously with the legislative division. This is due to the device adopted by the framers of the Constitution of separating the powers of government into distinct branches, instead of concentrating them in the hands of a cabinet within the lower house as the English have done. The idea of this separation can hardly be

---

[1] A good illustration is to be found in Ogg's "Social Progress," p 101

[2] A chart of the organization of the Illinois administration is given in Forman's "American Democracy," p. 169

said to be distinctively American, but the practice of it and the sharp lines of cleavage are certainly so. The advantage of the check-and-balance system produced by division of power is stability and rule by the many rather than domination by the few. The disadvantage is that the checks and balances may work out so perfectly that a deadlock ensues, and progress becomes impossible. This danger is enhanced by the attempt to divide the functions of government into water-tight compartments One of the pressing problems of today is to solve this difficulty of departmental deadlocking.

For example, the executive department may stop legislation by a presidential veto, and if the two Houses cannot muster a two-thirds affirmative vote, the measure must wait for an election possibly three or four years distant. When a president does not care or dare to express his disapproval by a veto, he may still block action by failing to enforce the law.[1] In recent times the real efficiency of the Espionage Law and the Federal Trade Commission Act has depended upon the degree to which the executive branch of the government, through its department of justice, has enforced these measures of Congress. Had there been no prosecution of those who willfully obstructed the raising of an army for war, or of those corporations which practiced unfair competition in trade, then the laws on these two matters might as well never have been passed.

Responsible government the solution. Often, whenever disagreement does develop between the departments, each puts the blame on the other, as in the Wilson administration. In this case part of the trouble was due to a difference of opinion on the interpretation of the Constitution. In Article II, Sect. 2, clause 2, the president is given "power, by and with the advice and consent of the Senate, to make treaties, provided two-thirds of the Senators present concur." President Wilson followed in the steps of his predecessors in taking this to mean that the presi-

---

[1] For example, Andrew Jackson made worthless the charter given by Congress to the second United States Bank by removing all the government funds to "pet" state banks

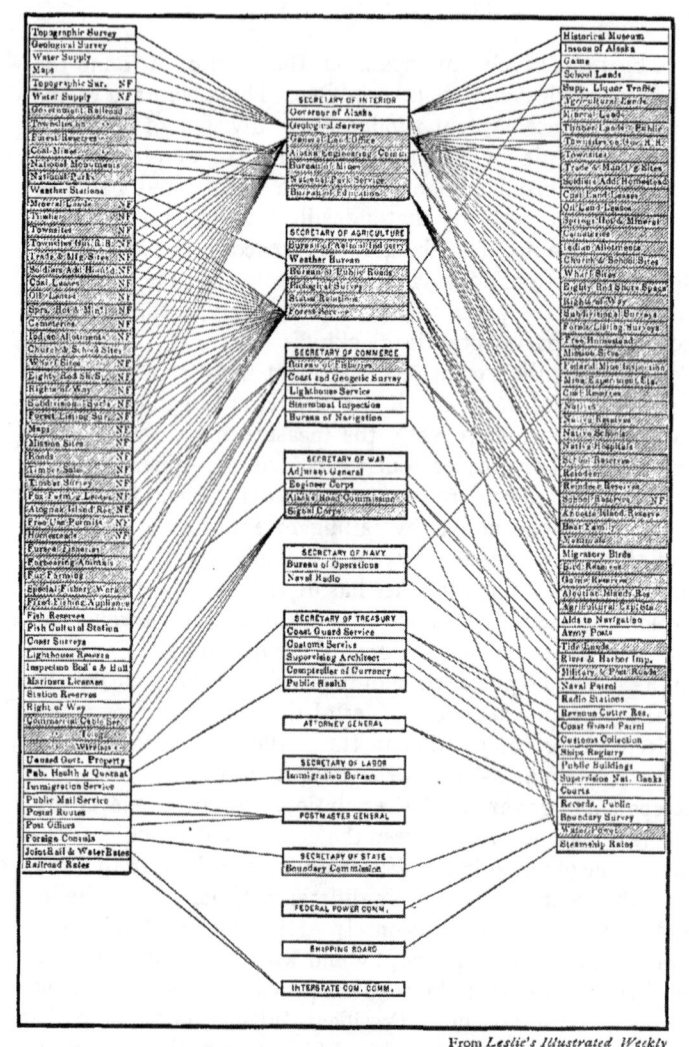

GOVERNMENT CONTROL OF ALASKA

This diagram strikingly shows the wasteful duplication of government agencies and the necessity for reorganizing our executive departments. Bureaus which should be coördinated are shaded

From *Leslie's Illustrated Weekly*

dent was to make treaties and the Senate was to accept or refuse to ratify them after they were drawn up and duly presented to it by the president The Senate in this case, being of another political party, insisted that its advice should have been asked during the process of making, and that therefore, since this had not been done, it would itself make a new treaty. This the President resented, and a deadlock ensued.

Such a condition of affairs is possible only under a three-department, check-and-balance system such as ours, wherein the executive and legislative departments may be of differing opinions and even of different political parties. The obvious solution is to give up our traditions of the separation of governmental powers and accept "responsible government," wherein both executive and legislative powers reside in a cabinet whose members are members of Congress.[1]

Defects in Congressional Legislation

The executive branch of our government is not the only one which presents problems demanding the attention of earnest citizens. Every congressional session offers examples of defects and inefficiencies in legislation. It is easy enough to point out these defects in lawmaking, but it is a more difficult task to suggest the best remedies. But of one thing we may be sure: until satisfactory remedies are worked out, our democracy cannot function perfectly. It behooves us, therefore, to analyze these problems carefully and to canvass the possible changes in

[1] President Harding took the first step in this direction when he invited the vice president, who is also the president of the Senate, to sit in cabinet meetings But before any of the cabinet members, who, in the United States, are purely executive officials, can take a place in Congress there must be an amendment to the Constitution.

There is some prejudice against responsible government in America, due partly to a distrust of anything English and partly to a fear of the concentration of power in a small group In reality the device gives the voters of the nation a direct and powerful check on the administration, which they now entirely lack Cf pages 117-118.

the hope that we may contribute something to the adequate solution of the difficulties involved.

Evils of initiation. The framers of the Constitution laid down no restrictions whatsoever regarding the initiation of bills, except that revenue measures must begin in the lower house.[1] As a result of this policy of nonrestriction we have the evils of excessive and ill-considered initiation of bills and the introduction of improperly worded bills. The cure for the latter is the adoption of a policy of drafting committees composed of legal experts who will see to it that measures contain no flagrantly unconstitutional provisions, no treacherously concealed loopholes for evasion, and no careless, trouble-making ambiguities.

The cure for excessive legislation is not so easy to suggest. But it becomes evident that some cure must be found when we learn that some twenty-five to thirty thousand bills are introduced during each session of Congress This great number is accounted for partly by the fact that some 90 per cent of these bills are of a private nature, bearing on pensions, private claims, etc. Partly, too, it is accounted for by the fact that two Mondays out of every month are devoted to legislation for the District of Columbia. Much of this is of a petty character; as, for example, when the Sixty-second Congress changed the name of 16th Street in the city of Washington to the Avenue of the Presidents, and the Sixty-third Congress changed it back to 16th Street.

We must not stifle the wishes of the citizens of the nation by making initiation of legislation too difficult, but we must find some way to limit the measures introduced into our Federal Congress to those of a national and important nature.

Inadequacy of discussion. Such a limitation on initiation would go a long way toward remedying one of the other legislative defects; namely, inadequacy in the discussion of pending

---

[1] Even this limitation has been abolished by the Senate's custom of amending revenue bills to such an extent that they are virtually new measures An illustration of the power of the Senate in revenue matters is furnished by the story of what happened to the Wilson Tariff Bill in 1893.

measures. As it now stands, it is absolutely impossible for all bills introduced in Congress to receive adequate thought and discussion. Even if the number of bills were reduced materially, it would still be impossible for all members to go into the details of each bill. In order to secure action on all measures it would still be necessary to retain many of the various committees which, in each House, work over the details of all bills. But with a lesser number of bills to discuss there would be more time available for reviewing the findings of the committees and for debating important features on the floors of the two Houses.

Inadequate discussion of even the most vital phases of bills is due not only to excessive initiation but also to the ever-increasing size of the lower house. Many reformers have suggested that we remedy this evil by reducing the House of Representatives from its present number of 435 to something like 200 members. This would mean that each congressman would represent not 211,977 citizens, as he does now, but over twice that number. The first apparent objection to this is that some of our states do not have 500,000 population. This would not, however, debar them from representation, for under our present system neither Nevada nor Wyoming nor Delaware has a population of 211,977, and yet each has the one representative guaranteed to each state by the Constitution. The other and more powerful objection to reduction of the size of the lower house is that once having given a state a certain number of representatives, it would prove difficult to deprive it of part of its representation. It is all well enough to agree that the House is too large for efficiency, but it is quite another matter to be willing to reduce your own state's representation. The recent trend of debate seems to indicate that Congress is about to enlarge our lower house still further, thus catering to the popular desire for increased prestige rather than courageously choosing the wiser course at the risk of incurring unpopularity.

In view of the difficulties of reducing the size of the lower house, other reformers have suggested that we solve the problem of the inadequate discussion of measures by a regular use of the legislative caucus, wherein the members of each party meet together informally to decide which measures deserve their unified support. This device is good in that it permits informal discussion and produces party responsibility in regard to legislation, but it is bad in that every member who attends the caucus is bound morally to vote in the House as the caucus decides. Thus the individual member is made subject to the will of the party leaders.

It is difficult to say without further study of the problem, and possibly without experiment, just what is the best cure for this evil of insufficient discussion of proposed legislation. But some remedy ought to be found soon in order that each succeeding session of Congress may not add to our already long list of inefficient laws and in order that important measures, especially appropriation measures, may not have to be rushed through in the closing hours of Congress. Frequently Congress sits all through the last night of the session and then is forced to turn the hands of the clock back several times as they approach the noontime of closing. In this concluding scramble bills are sure to be passed with unwise or even harmful sections which if they had been given adequate consideration would have been eliminated or modified.[1]

The passage of minority legislation. Inadequate discussion is not the only reason why many measures which should never become the law of the land are enacted into Federal statutes. Since our form of government is a republic of the representa-

---

[1] Sometimes a certain section has no real connection with the rest of the bill and is attached to it in the form of a so-called *legislative rider* in the hope that it will ride through along with the bill, thus avoiding a probable presidential veto These riders are usually attached to appropriation bills because, since money is needed to carry on the work of the government between meetings of Congress, the president usually feels that he must sign the bill no matter how much he disapproves of the rider If the president were not forced to veto the whole of a bill, he might make riders impossible by vetoing merely the rider while signing the main part of the bill.

tive democracy type,[1] the will of the majority should be the basis of our laws. Therefore, whenever we find measures being pushed through Congress which have not the honest support of the majority of the chosen representatives of the people, we may term such minority legislation unfair and condemn the devices by which it is enacted. The two most frequently used devices are *lobbying* and *logrolling*. Lobbying is practiced by persons not members of Congress in order to win over indifferent or obdurate members. Many different kinds of organizations, such as trusts and railroads, labor, liquor, and prohibition interests, keep lobbyists posted in our state and national legislatures. Some of these organizations serve to keep legislators posted on the needs of the country, and if their means be open argument and their purpose one of social betterment, it would seem unwise to forbid them. But in the past corrupt forces, often using threats and bribes, have almost monopolized this device. Wisconsin has adopted a novel remedy, or at least a means of control, in its law requiring all lobbyists to register their names and the organization which they represent. The register is open for inspection, and thus the public may know who has been influencing legislation and something of the extent of the influence.

The practice of logrolling is confined solely to the duly elected representatives of the people and hence is harder to eliminate and more of a disgrace to a democratic people. This term is drawn from the pioneer days of America, when settlers aided each other by rolling logs for a newcomer's cabin or barn. If the same spirit of neighborly coöperation characterized legislative logrolling, the practice would not be an evil one; but instead of friendly cooperation for the enactment of good legislation, logrolling has become a device whereby groups exchange support for measures so questionable that otherwise they would fail of enactment. Logrolling is used in Congress chiefly in

[1] If the United States were as small as the Greek city states of old, we could have a pure democracy, wherein the assembled people make laws without the necessity of choosing representatives.

getting through many private and public appropriations which go to deplete the treasury. Laws which do not express the wishes of the majority of the voters are often passed by the short session of a Congress and signed by a president both of whom represent a party which has been repudiated at the November elections An attempt is now being made to amend the Constitution to abolish these "lame duck" Congresses by ruling that all Federal officials elected in November shall enter office the following January.

Legislative Inaction

Congress, in the same manner as human beings, errs not only in its sins of commission but also in its sins of omission. Many good and needed measures fail of enactment for one cause or another—oftentimes for no better reason than that they were sidetracked during the legislative session. Some bills are deliberately pigeonholed by the particular committees to which they have been referred. Others are reported back to the House, but owing to the excessive amount of legislation never come up for discussion. Still others are discussed at length, but for one reason or another fail of enactment.

The disadvantages of a bicameral assembly. Frequently the reason for legislative inaction lies in the fact that our Congress is a bicameral (two-house) body. If both Houses were elected for the same term and on the same basis of representation, this division would rarely result in a deadlock. But the Senate is more conservative than the House of Representatives, owing to the fact that the term of its members is longer and the qualifications for office higher.[1] Moreover, the basis of representation tends to make the lower house more truly representative of the wishes of the people as a whole, for each state is divided into a number of congressional districts, each of which

[1] Note that while members of the Senate and of the House of Representatives are alike members of Congress, the latter only are usually given the title of congressmen, while the former are known as senators.

sends one representative to the lower house, whereas the two senators allowed each state are elected at large by all the voters in the state.[1] Thus while the minority party in a state may succeed in electing one or more congressmen it cannot hope to elect a United States senator, even though in some parts of the state it be supported by an overwhelming majority. On the other hand, because of the six-year term of senators, it may happen that a majority of the Senate belong to a party that is no longer the majority party. The House of Representatives, the entire membership of which is elected every two years, is much more likely to represent the popular will of the moment In view of all these differences, it is no uncommon occurrence for the two Houses of our Federal legislature to be in opposition on matters of importance. And since a majority in both Houses must favor a bill before it can become a law, legislative inaction can sometimes be laid at the door of the otherwise admirable provision for a two-house assembly.

Filibustering, a weapon of the minority. It has sometimes happened that a majority in both Houses of Congress may favor a measure and that yet it may fail of passage through the Senate. This was possible until a few years ago through the practice of *filibustering*. According to the long-standing rules of the Senate, all members had the right of unlimited debate. Several times in American history senators have taken advantage of this rule to coerce the majority. In one case a man talked for fourteen hours without stopping, and in another a senator threatened to read the collected works of Lord Byron from beginning to end unless the Senate yielded to his desires. In 1917 twelve "willful" senators led by Robert La Follette of Wisconsin talked the Armed Neutrality Bill "to death"; that is, they debated on it until Congress expired at noon on March 4. Not only had the House passed this bill with an overwhelming majority, but some eighty senators had expressed themselves in

---

[1] A study of the Constitution, Article I, Sect iii, clauses 1 and 2, and Amendment XVII will show that prior to 1913 the provision for the election of senators was such as to produce an even more conservative upper house.

its favor in a round robin, and the country at large was crying for its enactment. This inexcusable thwarting of the will of the majority by a mere handful of obstinate men brought the evil of filibustering before the public eye and led to action In the special session of Congress in the spring of 1917, the Senate adopted a cloture rule which provides that on petition of sixteen senators and the vote of two thirds of the Senate, debate may be limited on any measure to one hour for each senator. The wisdom of this cloture rule was apparent in 1920, when the Treaty of Versailles was under discussion.

The obstacle of unconstitutionality. Sometimes Congress is prevented by lack of power from enacting needed legislation. The statement is often made, especially in regard to many social measures, that it is useless for Congress to enact laws on such matters as child labor, for instance, since the Supreme Court will declare such enactments unconstitutional. In order to give Congress more power, some reformers have suggested that we should make amendment of the Constitution an easier process. Instead of the old method of securing a two-thirds vote of both Houses, plus ratification by three fourths of the state legislatures, they suggest amendment by a bare majority vote of Congress plus ratification by a majority of states.

The chief argument in favor of this change is that it seems unfair, when the majority of the people of the country desire Congress to have a certain power, that the process of conferring such power should be unduly slow and difficult. This argument has been partly answered in the last decade by the passage of four amendments in six years. This proves that when textual changes in the Constitution are really needed, amendments can be put through. With these recent developments has come a prevailing opinion that it is better to have stable constitutional provisions favored by a considerable majority than a complexity of changes dictated by temporary public opinion. The movement for a new amendment process may not be dead, but for the present, at least, it is slumbering.

Financial Mismanagement

Congressional appropriations. Among the evil practices of Congress none in the past affected the ordinary citizen so much as our system of financial appropriations. Instead of having one committee, with the income statistics of our government before it, plan in an orderly and scientific fashion what our expenditures for each year should be, we allowed nine different committees to prepare separate appropriation bills and push them through Congress.[1] None of these committees took into account the income of the government, so we had the peculiar practice of appropriating money before it was collected. Each one of these committees considered its own class of needs, with no thought of the pressing needs of the others.

This scattering of financial responsibility led to an extravagant, selfish, and unbusinesslike attitude toward the Treasury of the United States. The public money was thought of not as a fund to be administered carefully and frugally, as are the funds of a business organization, under a motto of "a dollar's worth of return for every dollar spent," but rather as a public "pork barrel" out of which every congressman and senator was to grab as much "pork" as possible. Thus it was that every year saw hundreds of thousands of dollars expended for fraudulent pensions, questionable private claims, and impractical "improvements" on rivers and harbors. The desire of members of Congress was to secure as much of the appropriations for their own communities as possible. The more they received the stronger they thought their chances for reëlection. One congressman alone has introduced as many as 208 bills appropriating money to individuals. In seven days of the Sixty-fourth Congress 4144 private-pension appropriations were made. Almost all of these had previously been refused by the Pension Department because the petitioners either could not give evidence of having served

---

[1] Magruder's "American Government," pp. 97-99, gives the names of these nine committees.

in the Civil War or else had been deserters. There is little doubt that most of the cases were fraudulent.

The pork barrel became so well established an institution that honored senators referred to it without shame, the general attitude being that since all legislators rob the pork barrel, there is nothing wrong in the robbing. Upon one occasion a senator from South Carolina called the attention of the Senate to "a little orphan of a naval station" down in his state for which he was trying "to get a few crumbs of this money which is being wasted."

Congress may err not only by making unneeded appropriations but also by failing to make proper and necessary ones. There are ten different executive departments, all depending on Congress to appropriate sufficient funds to meet their needs. The Department of the Treasury was in 1920 so handicapped for funds that it could not adequately prevent smuggling into the United States from the border countries of Mexico and Canada. Congress at one time refused to appropriate money to take the navy around the world, for once the executive came out ahead when Theodore Roosevelt replied: "Very well. We already have sufficient funds from past appropriations to get the navy on the other side of the world. We'll send them there, and if Congress wants to leave them off the coast of China, why that's its business." The executive department is not always so fortunate in its blocking of congressional short-sightedness, as has been shown in the past few years when the Federal employment bureaus have had to close for want of appropriations.

The budget. The obvious cure for such a condition was the adoption of a budget system, such as has long been used by other nations. But although such a system was advocated by thoughtful people, and although President Taft championed a well-planned movement for its adoption, it was not until June 10, 1921, that an act was approved which established the budget system in national affairs. The act provides for a Bureau of the Budget in the Treasury Department, under a director, who is appointed by the president and is directly responsible to him. This bureau advises the president regarding the actual needs and resources, and aids him to prepare the annual budget. This the president sends to Congress, Congress thereupon makes the needed appropriations. The House and Senate have amended their rules by the adoption of a single appropriations committee each, which enables them to coöperate with the president more effectively. An audit of the government accounts under a comptroller general, appointed by the president with senatorial consent for fifteen years, is part of the new system. Upon its organization the budget bureau promptly created nine boards to handle government business in an economical way by purchases made in large quantities and by interdepartmental coöperation. The success of the scheme is assured if only Congress does not block its operation, as was done in the early days of civil-service reform.[1]

Problems of State and Municipal Government

State legislative defects. Practically all of the weaknesses and defects in congressional legislation are to be found to an even greater extent in the state legislatures.[2] Their organization is faulty, and they are literally ridden to death by private measures. They are sadly in need of expert bill-drafting committees, concentration of financial functions, and devices to insure their responsibility to the public. One great evil in some state gov-

---

[1] General Charles G. Dawes became the first director of the Budget. Under him the work of reorganizing the national finances went forward rapidly. As a result of the budget system the treasury had a surplus of over $300,000,000 for two successive years, and hence a reduction in taxes became possible in 1924. Contrary to the hopes of many the budget system has not abolished the pork barrel, for Congress raised the estimate of the Budget Bureau $15,000,000 in 1922 and $28,000,000 in 1923 for so-called river and harbor improvements. This defect can easily be remedied as soon as public opinion shall demand it.

[2] The lack of harmony between the executive and legislative departments in one state — Oklahoma — became a topic of nation-wide discussion in 1923. See *Literary Digest*, October 13, 1923, Vol. LXXIX, pp. 12-13.

ernments is that the legislatures have taken to themselves many of the strictly administrative functions. They are often the real power in making executive appointments, and since they make the appropriations which these appointees expend, there is "no one to watch the watchman." The practices of lobbying and logrolling work more harm in the legislatures of the various states than they do in Congress.

So, also, is the harm greater from the difficulties of constitutional amendment Eleven of the state constitutions provide that when a constitutional amendment is referred to the voters for their approval or disapproval, anyone voting for one or more officials but failing to vote on the amendment shall have his vote counted as if he had voted against the amendment. Since the ordinary voter often does not take the time to inform himself on constitutional matters, even though his partisan sentiments are strong enough to bring him out to vote for or against some political candidate, many amendments are lost through pure indifference. Some eighteen states have abandoned this requirement and made the adoption of amendments dependent on the vote of a majority of persons voting thereon.

Direct control legislation. Although the shortcomings of state legislation are greater than those of congressional legislation, we must admit that in some matters the states are forging ahead in reform. Since the people cannot always know at election time which man will best serve them after election to office, they often elect men who, contrary to the popular will, enact or refuse to repeal unjust or unwise laws. This condition has led to the invention of devices whereby undesirable laws may be repealed at once, and needed ones initiated by the people, who thus gain a more direct control over legislation.

The two reforms which have made this direct action in legislation possible are the *referendum* and the *initiative* By the former some 5 per cent to 10 per cent of the voters can demand through petition that any law be referred to the people for approval or rejection. Twenty-one states and some three hundred cities have adopted the referendum. All these twenty-one states, except Maryland and New Mexico, and practically all of these cities have adopted the initiative as well. By this device from 5 per cent to 25 per cent of the voters may initiate a law by means of a petition. If the legislature does not feel inclined to pass a bill so introduced, it may then be referred to the people for acceptance or refusal.[1] The chief objection which has been brought against these two direct-control devices is that people act in haste and without due consideration. This country, argue the opponents of direct control, is too large and the average citizen far too busy for any form of pure democracy. Advocates of initiative and referendum say that these measures do not need to become a burden to the voters, who should use their unusual powers only in an emergency. These measures are not meant to supplant the present system of representative democracy. They are only to supplement it, in order that justice and the will of the people as a whole shall not suffer defeat. Ex-President Wilson has aptly said that such measures should be considered only as "a gun behind the door."

The state commission. Legislative inefficiency in state government has led even to the suggestion that a state-commission form of government, with a small lawmaking body of experts held rigidly responsible for the administration of a still smaller body of responsible department heads, may be the ultimate solution of our problem of state control. Whether experts would secure any higher degree of general public welfare than the untrained members who compose most state legislatures is a question that perhaps only experiment can settle.

The question of city home rule. Just as the powers of the Federal government are outlined in the United States Constitution and those of the forty-eight states in their respective state constitutions, so the powers of the hundreds of municipalities are outlined in their various charters. One of the first questions which arises in connection with the government of municipalities is who shall draw up these charters.

[1] In Magruder's "American Government," p 380, will be found a good chart of the progress of the initiative, referendum, and recall to 1915.

Since the right to delegate municipal powers belongs to the legislatures of the states in which the cities are situated, it was the long-established custom for the state legislatures to grant to each city within its borders a specific charter. As time progressed this practice was seen to be defective in several respects. As the cities grew and their needs changed accordingly, the problem of securing charter amendment in the overcrowded legislative sessions became increasingly difficult Moreover, the state legislatures played political favorites among the cities.

As a result of these deficiencies numbers of the Western cities began clamoring for home rule, or the right of each city to draw up and adopt its own charter. A number of states have already recognized the justice and wisdom of this request and have amended their constitutions in such a way as to allow, under certain restrictions, the adoption of home-rule charters.[1]

The need for municipal reorganization. Every municipal charter, whether formulated for a city by the state legislature or by the people of the city under home-rule arrangements, contains a provision for the governmental organization of the city. There are three general forms of municipal government in the United States.

The oldest and commonest form is similar to the organization of the state governments, in that it is comprised of a legislative body, known as a council, and an executive or administrative head, called a mayor. The council sometimes has two houses or chambers, as do the state legislatures, but more often only one. It is elected by the voters of the city, which is divided for the purpose into districts known as wards. Each ward elects one or more aldermen, as the members of the council are frequently called.

The mayor resembles the state governor in that he is elected by the people and possesses in most cases the power to veto the legislative ordinances of the council. He has under him a group

---

[1] Ohio is the only state east of the Mississippi which has incorporated a home-rule provision in its constitution Its restrictions are more lenient than those of any other state.

of men who are in charge of the various administrative departments, such as, for example, the departments of public works, public safety, and public utilities. One of the open questions in cities under this type of government is who should choose these executive officers In some cities they are appointed by the mayor, in others they are chosen by the council, and in still others they are elected by the voters. Cities differ, too, in the control of the administrative departments. Owing to the inefficiency of the average city council the tendency is toward concentrating power in the hands of the mayor. In many cases, in fact, even legislative powers have been transferred from the council to the mayor.

One of the reasons for the inefficiency of our city councils is that ward politics of a pernicious type plays too great a part in both the election of aldermen and their conduct in office. Through the indifference of citizens and the presence of many foreign-born voters unfamiliar with American ways, it becomes possible for corrupt politicians to gain control of sufficient wards to dominate the council. Thus it is that we find graft and corruption running rife in many cities under this type of government.

Severe criticism of the mayor-council type of government is being offered in all parts of the United States. This type of city government is so complicated in organization that there is no way of holding the various officials responsible. When something goes wrong, let us say, for example, with the police system, and some interested citizen makes complaint, it is often impossible to secure action. The head of the public-safety or police department may put the blame on the mayor; he in turn may claim that the council is responsible for his inability to act. As a result of this "passing of the buck" the interested citizen goes home disgusted and does not waste his time again trying to rectify inefficiencies.

New types of city government. Dissatisfaction with the mayor-council type has led many cities to adopt a simplified

PRESENT-DAY PROBLEMS OF DEMOCRACY 513

form of government, known as the commission type. Under this form both legislative and executive powers are concentrated in the hands of a small commission (composed usually of five members). Each commissioner is put at the head of an administrative department and is made responsible for all the activities

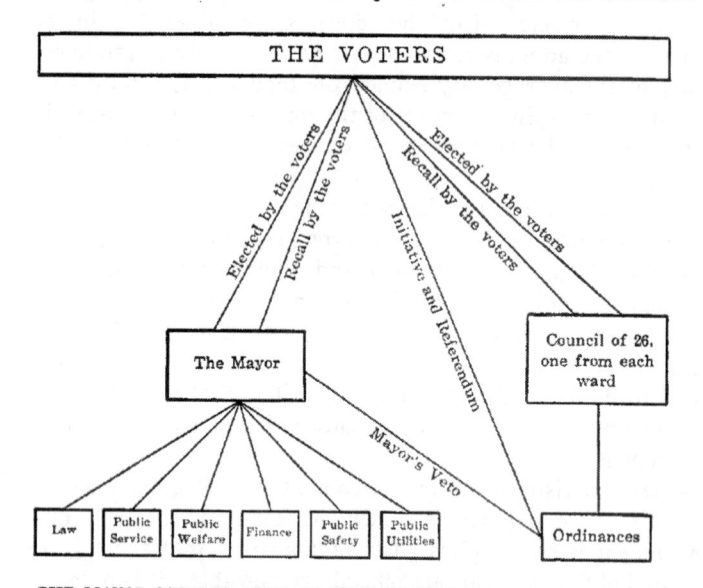

THE MAYOR-COUNCIL TYPE OF CITY GOVERNMENT, AS USED UP TO JANUARY 1, 1922, BY CLEVELAND, OHIO

Note that this scheme is better than the old-time mayor-council type described in the text, in that popular control is secured by means of the voters' recall powers over mayor and council and their legislative rights of initiative and referendum. Compare this plan, however, with those given on pages 514, 515 for simplicity, concentrated responsibility, and economy in administration

of that department. In addition to making impossible the shifting of responsibility, the commission form has another advantage. It does away with ward organization and forces the candidates for office to stand before the whole city. Intelligence, ability, and a clean record usually count for more in such a method of election than in the old ward contests.

In the latest type of city government—the city-manager type—the responsibility is even more concentrated than in the commission type. The voters elect some three or five prominent

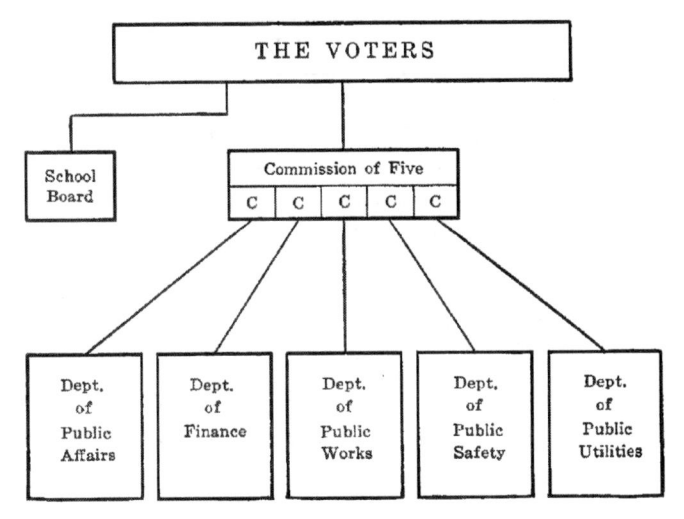

THE COMMISSION PLAN OF CITY GOVERNMENT, AS USED IN DULUTH, MINNESOTA

The direct-control measures of recall, initiative, and referendum may also be incorporated into this scheme, as has been done, for example, in Des Moines, Iowa. Note how in every phase of city welfare it is possible to fix the guilt of waste and mismanagement

business men to serve on a commission or council whose function is to determine the general policies of the city and to choose a trained manager to administer the government. This manager is not only a highly trained man, but he is likely to be a better man than the average mayor because he is chosen without reference to his party or residence. In national and perhaps in state affairs it may be wise and even necessary to choose officials on the basis of party alignment, but it is becoming more and more evident that in city affairs it is neither necessary nor wise. As John R. Commons has so aptly pointed out, a man's views on the tariff have nothing to do with his views on special

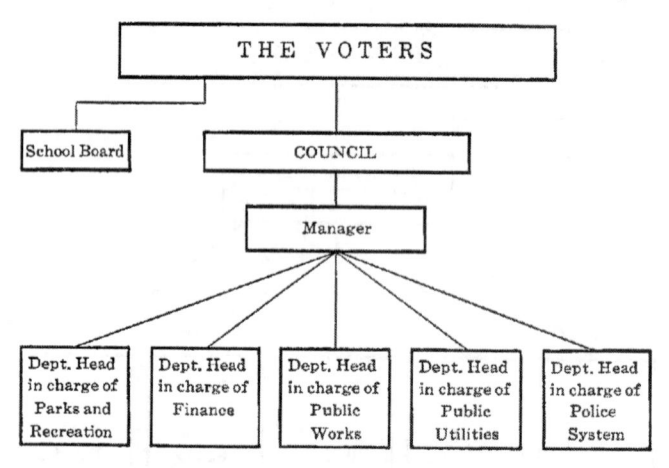

```
                    ┌─────────────────┐
                    │   THE VOTERS    │
                    └─────────────────┘
              ┌───────────┴──────┐
        ┌───────────┐      ┌───────────┐
        │School Board│     │  COUNCIL  │
        └───────────┘      └───────────┘
                                 │
                           ┌───────────┐
                           │  Manager  │
                           └───────────┘
```

| Dept. Head in charge of Parks and Recreation | Dept. Head in charge of Finance | Dept. Head in charge of Public Works | Dept. Head in charge of Public Utilities | Dept. Head in charge of Police System |

A TYPICAL CITY-MANAGER PLAN OF CITY GOVERNMENT

This type of government was first used in Sumter, South Carolina, in 1912. By January 1, 1921, one hundred and forty cities had adopted the plan. Direct-control devices may also be added to this scheme, as has been done by Dayton, Ohio

assessments, health administration, franchise-stealing, or police. Under the manager plan the governing of a city is considered as a business proposition rather than a political game. The one highly trained man at the head is responsible for the entire government. He therefore employs experts as departmental heads that he may secure the greatest efficiency in administration. This scheme is probably the wisest yet devised for eliminating bad politics and returning one hundred cents of the taxpayer's dollar to him in civil service.

Judicial Issues of the Day

The power of the Supreme Court over legislation. There are two great issues before the American republic today in regard to the judiciary. The first pertains to a subject of dispute which we touched on earlier (in Chapter V)—the power of the Supreme Court to construe laws and the Constitution, and thus to serve as a virtual legislator; the second issue is the use or abuse by both Federal and state courts of the power of injunction.

We have seen that the Supreme Court has power to pass on legislative enactments, with a view to declaring them null and void if they appear in the eyes of the judges to be contrary to the United States Constitution; and where not contrary, to interpret them in ways not meant by the authors. This power makes the Supreme Court virtually a lawmaking body. This transfer of powers has met with a great deal of opposition. The socialists have a plank in their platform favoring the abolition of this power. Even such prominent men as the late Theodore Roosevelt have taken offense at this judge-made law. At one time Roosevelt went so far as to compare the people who supported this "divine right of irresponsible judges" to the Bourbons of old, who upheld the divine right of kings.

One of the several objections to this power is that the court is a body appointed for life. This means, its opponents claim, that a small body in no way under the control of the people has more power than the duly elected representatives of the nation.[1] Suggestions have been made that a device used in many of the states, known as the "recall," be instituted to make Federal life-term judges responsible to some extent to the wishes of the voters of the nation.

---

[1] Politics are supposed to play no part either in the decisions of the court or in the choice of the judges But many people do not believe that politics are entirely eliminated As evidence that partisan interests touch even the chief court of the country, they refer to the Dred Scott case and to the fact that three judges who might have retired in the years 1913-1921 remained in office until a Republican president might be in a position to appoint "safe" judges.

Another reason for dissatisfaction with the court is that not all cases seem to be settled on a purely legal basis, judging by the frequency with which important decisions are made by a one-judge majority. Among these were the Owen-Keating Child Labor Law and the New York Bakeshop Case [1] The fact that the Supreme Court has several times reversed its decisions on important matters, such as the Income Tax, the Granger laws, and greenbacks as legal tender, serves further to make people doubt whether the decisions of this body should be taken as the final word in all matters.

The solution of the problem. Like most criticism, this is destructive rather than constructive. It is easy enough to insist that the court has usurped unintended and autocratic power, but it is quite another matter to outline some better plan whereby state laws and constitutions and Federal laws shall be kept from contradicting each other and producing confusion and anarchy in law.

Roosevelt, with his characteristically creative mind, did make a concrete proposal. He believed that to the court must be left the power to interpret and construe, but that the people should have the power to review and change the decision if they so desire. This could be done only by a national referendum, which seems to many an impracticable and unwise solution. In the first place, it would mean waiting until a national election period, a possibly disastrous delay. Then the ordinary voter is far less interested in legislative and judicial questions than he is in the election of officials; and even if he could be trusted to take an active interest, there is little probability that his judgment in legal matters would be sound. The question at issue is not so much justice as legality. Few who are not trained lawyers can judge of this.

Another suggestion is to amend the Constitution so that whenever the Supreme Court declares a law unconstitutional, that law becomes constitutional upon being repassed by the

[1] In this case the ten-hour day for bakers was declared an unreasonable restraint of personal liberty and hence unconstitutional

next Congress. This method is doubtless modeled after Great Britain's Parliament Act of 1911, and really amounts to a simpler method of amending the Constitution.

It is hard to see how the federal form of government, with its constant conflict of powers, could possibly function without some highly trained interpreting body having final decision. Many people use this as an argument for making constitutional amendment easier, so that the will of the people in matters of justice and welfare may be made possible of enactment, while at the same time the present system of legal interpretation is kept.

The use and abuse of injunctions. The second vital problem of the judiciary is the use of the injunction, especially in labor disputes. An injunction is an order by a court, commanding that something shall not be done. It was first used against labor in a strike in 1868, when the posting of placards asking union men to stay away from work was forbidden by the court. The justification for an injunction is that when a person knows that his property is threatened in such a way that money can not compensate for the threatened loss, it seems only fair that he should not have to wait impotently until after the act is committed before having recourse to the law, which, in the very nature of the case, can offer him no adequate compensation. By securing an injunction, irreparable damage is prevented Up to 1890 labor made no objection to this ounce-of-prevention use of the injunction. Since that date, however, laborers believe that the courts of the land have used the injunction as a potent weapon against labor.

There are a number of specific objections which have been brought against the injunction One of these is that it is sometimes issued on false information, with no chance for the defendant to show cause why the injunction should not be issued. Frequently a hearing does not immediately follow the first or temporary injunction. When that is the case injustice may result, for although the court may later set aside the injunction, the injury to the cause of labor through the postponement of the strike may be as great as if the injunction had been upheld.

A second objection is that when violations of the injunction occur, undue power is placed in the hands of one judge. The violator is summoned before the court in order to show why he should not be punished. Evidence is presented, but the decision is made by the judge and is not subject to appeal. Thus it is possible for the violator to be deprived of the right of trial by jury in criminal cases, a right which is guaranteed to him by the Constitution (Amendment VI).

The use of injunctions without recourse to trial was placed upon a firm legal basis by the Supreme Court as the result of a case arising from the Pullman strike of 1894 in Chicago. Since injunctions have prohibited such lawful actions as giving food and money to strikers, peaceful picketing, and boycotting, the laborer feels that this "government by injunction" is an undemocratic and unfair practice. To him it smacks of the dictatorial methods of autocratic government. He asserts, and correctly, that the injunction has been used even against free speech. For example, in the New York cigarmakers' strike of 1900, an injunction forbade the laborers to present their case to the public if the tendency was to vex the employers or to make them uneasy; moreover, it forbade arguing even inside one's home with a "scab" for the purpose of trying to persuade him to desist from being a strike-breaker.

In cases of violation of injunction the judge not only determines the guilt, but without legal limits to guide him he also sets the penalty. The punishment, therefore, may be greater than it would be in a criminal suit, where the maximum is set by law, or in a civil suit, where the penalties cannot exceed the amount of the proved damages.

Another objection formerly brought against injunction was that instead of being used to restrain specific persons named within the document, the injunction was issued against whole groups of people, many of whom were not aware of it. This so-called "blanket injunction" when coupled with the Sherman Anti-Trust Act made it possible for an employer to force men to remain at work and thus, says the laborer, to rob them of their constitutional right of liberty of action.[1] This point was at issue in the Pullman strike; and in the Lennon case in 1897 the Supreme Court held that all persons who have actual notice of the issuance of an injunction are bound to obey its terms, although the order may not be especially directed at them nor served upon them. Thus was the blanket injunction sanctioned.

Action against the injunction. Labor became more and more insistent that this abuse of judicial power be removed. In 1908 the Republican platform contained a plank favoring a clarification of the points in dispute regarding injunctions; the Democratic plank was more specific, stating that the injunction was not to be permitted in industrial disputes unless issued under other similar circumstances, and that contempt of the court's order was not to be punishable without privilege of trial by jury.

In 1914 the Democrats kept their campaign pledges by enacting certain important labor clauses in the Clayton Anti-Trust Act, a law regarded by many labor leaders as the Magna Carta of the American labor movement. Besides exempting labor organizations from the operation of all Federal anti-trust laws, the act contains important provisions regarding injunctions. It provides that no preliminary injunction shall be issued without notice being sent to the opposite party, or without defining the injury and stating why it is irreparable. Thus the blanket injunction is made impossible. Other clauses of the act provide that the accused may demand trial by jury if the contempt of court through violating the injunction was committed outside the presence of the court. Provision is also made for review of the judgment by higher courts as in ordinary criminal cases, and the penalties are limited. Other provisions prohibit injunctions from being used to prevent persons from ceasing to perform any work or "from recommending, advising, or persuading others by peaceful means so to do, or from ceasing to patronize or to employ any party to such dispute (that is,

[1] At this point it would be well to answer question 19, p. 536.

labor dispute), or from recommending, advising, or persuading others by peaceful and lawful means so to do, or from paying or giving to or withholding from any person engaged in such dispute, any strike benefit."

On the face of things the Clayton Anti-Trust Act seems to give labor all that it desires in the reform of the abuses of the injunction, but subsequent court interpretations have robbed the act of many of its seeming concessions to labor. In the coal strike of 1919 the Federal court issued an injunction to the officers of the miners' organization prohibiting them from supplying the striking miners with funds The injunction was upheld under the war-emergency Lever Act. Injunctions are still issued against labor as a conspiracy in restraint of trade under the various state laws In the Duplex Printing case, 1920, the Supreme Court interpreted the Clayton Act as not legalizing the secondary boycott.[1] Labor is therefore far from satisfied with its gains against the injunction.

The Evils of Party Government

Political parties. Our government is not merely a machine made up of legislative, executive, and judicial parts for states and nation There must be human agencies to set up this machine. These human agencies are organizations of voters who work together under the name of a political party to make their aims the laws and policies of the government. All through our history there have been, as now, two outstanding parties and ephemeral third parties of lesser apparent importance. Since the Civil War the two main parties have been the Republican and Democratic parties. Recent "third parties" are the Socialists, the Prohibitionists, the Farmer-Labor party, and others. Processes of nomination and election are all in the hands of these parties, and hence problems along these lines are, in America, problems of party government.

[1] A secondary boycott is a refusal on the part of labor to patronize those business establishments which use the products that labor desires to boycott It differs from the primary boycott by bringing into the dispute a third party.

The necessity of voting. We have already seen in Chapter V how the right to vote has been extended until now it may be said to be universal. The question is, What are we going to do with full suffrage now that we have it? This calls for our most earnest attention. The success of any democratic form of government depends partly upon the attitude of the electorate on the importance and the purposes of voting. Suffrage should be considered by all those who possess it as a duty, unavoidable and sacred. Since the American government is a representative and not a pure democracy (with the exception of certain town governments), the important matter is the election of suitable officials to make, to interpret, and to enforce the law.

Only occasionally in a representative government do the voters have the opportunity to govern directly. They exercise this power when amendments to state constitutions or city charters are submitted to them for ratification and when financial questions, such as the raising of money by bonds or the spending of money for internal improvements, are put to them for acceptance. These cases are few; but when they come, it is the voter's duty to learn all there is to be learned on both sides of the question, to weigh the arguments pro and con, and to vote one way or the other. Most of the needed amendments to city charters and state constitutions have failed, not because they were voted down, but because a majority of those who voted on candidates were too indifferent to vote either way on the charter or constitutional change. Whenever it is possible voting on constitutional and legislative matters should be separated from the election of officials, because where the two matters are put before the electorate at the same time, there is sure to be a neglect of the former.

Election of officials. Even in the election of officials a tragic apathy is often shown by the voters. This is especially true when no great issue is at stake. For instance, in the presidential election of 1904 there were over four hundred and forty thousand fewer votes cast than in 1900, although the voting population had increased in that interval. Representative democracy depends largely for its success on the seriousness and honesty of purpose with which the voting population tackles its job of the election of officers It is the duty of every voter to vote at every election, whether there is an important issue before the people or not Officeholders are elected at intervals of from one to six years, and no one knows what emergency may arise during these terms. No one foresaw the World War in the fall election of 1912.

Bribery and the machine. Each voter should have an opinion which is the basis of his voting, and his preference for Mr. X should not be the result of a bribe in any form. Many a respectable citizen who would scorn to accept money for his vote hesitates not the least in accepting the promise of an appointive position, or of a commercial contract for materials or construction which the government will be desiring during the term of the official for whom he is voting. This is a form of bribery, less direct than the purchase of the votes of newly naturalized citizens or "poor whites," but not less corrupt.

There is a form of giving one's vote away which, in the United States, is more common than selling it. This is voting the way some well-oiled political machine dictates. Now thorough organization of the political forces in a city or state is not in itself bad; only by organization and united efforts can worthy innovations succeed in overcoming the natural conservatism and inertness of the average citizen. But there are good and bad machines, quite as there are good and bad combinations in the business world. The motive underlying the organization and showing itself in its activities is the test of its worth. Bad political machines buy votes with money, secure political "plums" in the form of appointive offices and privileges of many sorts, give poor service, and make threats.[1] In many cities the best

---

[1] They also work in ways less visible than these The whole system of political organization for the purpose of carrying on the government by means of unofficial and often unknown "bosses" and "rings" is aptly called *invisible government* Its workings in New York under Boss Tweed are well told in Rhodes's "History of the United States"

newspapers are under the control of a political boss or machine. If the public allows itself to be blindly guided by the propaganda of the machine, it commits against democracy a crime of needless ignorance.

Party slavery. There is still another electoral "slacker"—the man who votes a straight party ticket, election after election, through traditional devotion to the party of his father. Political parties are an aid to the carrying on of representative government, but when they are held in higher esteem than is public service they become a hindrance to good government. Not many years ago much was said about party desertion's being a "crime." In recent years among intelligent people the "crime" is thought to be blind party voting—the attitude of "my party, right or wrong."[1] Such an attitude appears even less justifiable when one thinks that the two dominant parties in the United States have in recent years sometimes had no great issue between them. In this case the character of each individual office-seeker, his past experience, his general fitness for the task, and his stand on the unsettled questions, should be the bases for his right to win the election.

The question of revolution. And suppose the candidate who should have won the day loses—the man best fitted for the work, the man who stands for the changes one thinks to be in the line of progress and betterment, then it is the duty of American citizens to abide by the results in true American style, to be good losers. If the methods of election are bad, then it is the voter's privilege to convince the majority that they are bad, and a majority may change them by strictly legal means. The ballot box is the American means of registering a desire for a change. In Tsar-ridden Russia the direct method of revolution may have been necessary, but it can have no possible justification under the American form of democracy

---

[1] About half the states are trying to avoid the straight-ticket evil by using ballots on which the candidates for each office are arranged alphabetically, with their party affiliations in parentheses. In the older style of ballot the names are arranged in party columns

Even in revolutions it is not muscular might nor even accumulated wealth that wins the day; it is rather a majority of conviction. The side that can muster a majority of character-power is the winning side. Since this is so, the loss of life and property in a revolution appears more than ever unnecessary and wrong. In spite of this there are many people, who fondly imagine themselves to be "advanced" thinkers, who preach that the only way of setting right the abuses of imperfect government and bad distribution of wealth is by revolution. In some cases the ends they seek are in the natural line of progress. The practices of today were in many cases the objectives of radical propaganda yesterday. Who can say that the programs of progressive minorities today will not be the accepted practice of tomorrow? But they must come in orderly and legal ways as a result of the conviction of a majority.

The Need for Election Reform

Criticism of the elective process. Sharp criticisms have been made to the effect that on account of our methods of voting, the popular will is not allowed to express itself. The four features of our elective process which have received most censure are (1) the indirectness of nomination and election, (2) the expenditure of excessive campaign sums, (3) the method of casting votes, and (4) the lack of proper representation for minority parties.

Indirect election and nomination. Indirect election was common in the early years of the Union. Many of the earliest state constitutions provided that the judges and governors were to be chosen by the legislators. In the days of Jacksonian democracy this indirect election was supplanted by direct election of state officials. Selection of presidential electors by popular vote soon followed. It was not until 1913, however, that the United States senators were directly elected [1]

---

[1] The Seventeenth Amendment Before the passage of this amendment nearly half the states had followed Oregon's device for securing the results of direct election without its form. When the people chose their state legislatures

Although Americans have made great strides toward a direct elective process, they have not gone so far in securing direct nomination of candidates. If autocratic or corrupt methods are used to select the candidates for office, then direct election is of little avail to the voter. His choice may be merely between two or more undesirable men.

The one field in which election remains according to law as indirect as of old is in the choice of our national executive. Even here practice has resulted in making the election direct in effect while retaining the original indirectness in form. This has been accomplished by having the voters at large instead of the state legislatures choose the presidential electors and by binding these electors to vote as directed instead of allowing them, as of old, to exercise their own judgment in the choice of a president. The electoral college has thus become only a mouthpiece for the voters of the nation.

The indirect method of nomination by convention was long used in many of the states. Today over thirty of them have adopted the so-called direct primary. By this device the voters go to the polls and select by ballot the men who shall run as the nominees of their party at the following election. As a rule this direct method of nomination applies only to local and state officials and to congressmen.[1] Some states, however, use the direct primary in choosing senatorial nominees. But the presidential candidate of each party is selected by a national nominating convention, the delegates to which from most states are chosen by state conventions. During 1912–1915 there was much sentiment for making the choice of presidential candidates a matter of direct nomination (either by a preferential primary or by popular election and instruction of delegates to the

---

they expressed their choice for senator The law made it compulsory for the legislators to vote according to the preferential votes This was more binding than the duty of presidential electors to vote for the man who heads their ticket The latter is not a legal duty, but only a customary one

[1] For a list of the states using the direct primary see Magruder's "American Government," p. 368.

national convention). This agitation for a presidential primary law seems to have died down before more immediate problems.

Machine politicians oppose the introduction of the direct primary and insist that it has not worked in an entirely satisfactory way in the states where it has been adopted. They point out that people will not turn out to vote at the primaries, that too many candidates run and hence the minority man often wins a plurality, and that since everybody is responsible for the choice, no one can be held so When Charles Evans Hughes was governor of New York he suggested, as a remedy, that there be a party committee to suggest nominations preceding the primary. In Minnesota, in the 1920 election, an extra-legal convention was held a few weeks before the primary in order to assist the Republicans to concentrate on one candidate at the primaries.[1]

Such uses of party groups to secure concentration and overcome the danger that the minority candidate may win the nomination cannot meet with serious objections. Such devices would not force the voters to a choice between several machine-chosen nominees, as does the nominating-convention method. No doubt in most cases the indorsement of the pre-primary meetings will go to machine candidates, but there is nothing to prevent the minority and unorganized groups from putting up their men for nomination; in fact, an unwise party indorsement should act as a clarion call to the independent voters to turn out for the primary

The direct primary is a more democratic device for nomination than the indirect convention method, and to say that it should be abolished because insufficient voters make use of it is comparable to saying that, since not enough citizens exercise their right to vote, we ought to replace our democracy by an aristocratic or monarchial form of government.

[1] The Nonpartisan League candidate was running as a Republican Had the Republicans split their votes among the seven true party candidates, then the Nonpartisan Leaguers would have succeeded in nominating their man Later the use of a convention preceding the primaries was legalized by the state legislature

Excessive campaign expenses. One of the chief and growing criticisms of our elective system is that too much money is expended in the conduct of political campaigns. We have already spoken of the use of bribery in vote-winning. The public is beginning to feel that even when money is not used for corrupt purposes it is not right nor democratic to spend fortunes on campaigning. Moreover, when corporations give into the tens of thousands to campaign funds, it is felt that they expect to receive in return some special privileges at the hands of those elected. In recent years reformers have secured some legislation checking this evil. In 1907 Congress passed a bill forbidding corporations and national banks to contribute funds for the election of president, vice president, or members of Congress. Many states have enacted similar laws regarding state and local officers. Since 1911 a candidate for the House of Representatives cannot legally spend more than $5000 nor a candidate for the Senate more than $10,000.[1]

But in a country as large as ours expenditures for legitimate publicity must necessarily be great. Congress has therefore enacted laws demanding that records be kept of the contributors to campaign funds and of their contributions, if over $100, and of itemized expenditures over $10. No limit has as yet been set to the amount which can be spent for a presidential campaign. The accusations brought forward by both parties as to the excessive expenditure of funds in 1920 led to a congressional investigation which showed that in the 1920 campaign over $2,500,000 was spent by the Democrats and almost $10,000,000 by the Republicans. In 1923-1924, during investigations of public officials, it was found that the law demanding a record of contributors was being evaded by the practice of campaign committees of incurring deficits, to be made up quietly after election by wealthy men who expected something in return.[2]

---

[1] Review the case of Senator Newberry of Michigan, 1918-1922.

[2] North Dakota has tried the remedy of publishing campaign pamphlets at public expense with one page allotted each candidate See the *Literary Digest* of April 26, 1924, on the national use of this plan.

The short ballot. Criticisms against the method of casting votes are chiefly aimed at the length of the ballot. As our country grew and its governmental functions expanded, the number of offices multiplied until now the voter is in a maze when he attempts to mark a ballot in any other way than as a "straight ticket." It is impossible for even an intelligent and interested voter to know the qualifications of the dozens of men whose names appear on the ballot. In a New York City election a few years ago the voters were asked to mark a ballot some fourteen feet long.

The first move to cure this trouble was the separation of city, state, and national elections, many village and city elections are now held in the spring or early summer, and some states have set their elections earlier than the November date for national elections. This has not solved the problem entirely, because the list of officers for even one unit of government has become too long to handle intelligently. Many cities have gone a step further and adopted what is known as the *short ballot*. The underlying principle of this reform is a reduction of the number of elective offices and an increase in the number of appointive ones. From the voter's point of view this is a good move. From the governmental point of view it seems on the face of it to be an undemocratic step, because election is the first-hand choice of the people, whereas appointment smacks of monarchy or aristocracy. But when the appointments are made by officeholders who themselves have been chosen directly by the people and who are responsible to the voters for the appointments they make, then the short-ballot method is not undemocratic.

One objection to the adoption of the short ballot is that the past history of appointments has not been of such a nature as to encourage us to increase the number of appointive offices. Previous to the passage of the Pendleton Civil Service Act, in 1883, appointive offices were distributed among the favorites of the party in power under the theory that "to the victor belong the spoils." Even since that date appointment to nonelective offices has been far from satisfactory. It is impossible for any written examination, such as is provided for by the civil-service system, to ascertain the real capacity of a man, and it is especially hard to judge his ability to handle other men or to get along with them. Consequently there are many misfits in the civil service. Moreover, when men do not have to come up from time to time for reëxamination, they are likely to remain in office after they have become incompetent because of old age or inability to progress. It is hard to see how the first criticism can be overcome, but the second will probably be partially remedied, so far as antiquated Federal civil-service officials are concerned, by the Retirement Law of 1920.[1]

For those appointive offices which are not filled by examination the only safeguard is to make the appointer wholly responsible for the actions of his appointees, in the same way that many city commissioners in the commission form of government are responsible for the official acts of every man in their departments.

Direct control through the recall. When responsibility is concentrated in the hands of a few men whose terms of office may run several years, there is danger that they will abuse their power. According to the law, officers may be impeached, but only after a legal crime has been committed or corrupt conduct proved. Moreover, it is very hard to obtain a conviction in impeachment cases, since it requires a two-thirds vote of the Federal or the state senate trying the case. More effective methods of removing officers are therefore deemed advisable by many people. Since 1906 ten states and some three hundred cities have adopted the direct control of officers through the "recall."[2] By this device whenever a certain number of voters, varying from ten to twenty-five per cent, are dissatisfied with

[1] By this act the United States government pays annual pensions of from $180 to $720 upon their retirement to all civilian employees who have been in government service for at least fifteen years. The age limit for letter carriers and post-office clerks has been reduced to sixty-five years and for railway postal clerks to sixty-two years. Retirement is made compulsory only for those beginning employment after January, 1922.

[2] In Idaho, Louisiana, Michigan, and Washington judges are excepted.

the official conduct of any officer they may, by petitioning, force him to stand the test of a new vote on his fitness for office The recall sometimes is in the form of a new election, in which the old official runs against some new opponent. The danger of the recall is that the people will use it unwisely to remove a man who is doing his duty, albeit an unpleasant and unpopular one. Especially may injustice be done in the case of judges, who are forced to make decisions on the basis of the law, regardless of what they may personally think right or wrong The recall is very seldom used in the states and cities allowing it, but it works as a good stick to hold over lax or corrupt officeholders.

The need for a new basis of representation. Democracy and justice in government grow by fits and starts, as the people become conscious of evils or lacks. A hundred years ago the poor man was clamoring for representation, a decade ago women were demanding the franchise, at present it is minorities which feel the injustice of being excluded from government, and ask for a share in State affairs Majority rule, once regarded as the very touchstone of democracy, is now seen to involve a very great injustice to the minority, which may be the most intelligent and devoted part of the nation. Moreover, when there are more than two political parties, the party which secures the largest vote in an election and therefore secures the administration may not comprise a majority at all, it may simply be the largest single party. A representative government should represent all the people, each section of opinion influencing legislation in proportion to its numbers.

Our present system of dividing up the states into districts, each represented by a single member, makes it impossible for the members of minority parties in a district to have any voice in the government, even though their numbers mount up to within a very few of the majority party. It is possible, although rarely has it ever happened, that one or two votes may be the deciding factor as to which party sends its candidate to represent an entire district. The result of this system, which allows a bare majority to monopolize the representation from any district, leads to the practice of unfair districting. Districts are supposed to be composed of contiguous and approximately equal amounts of territory, but in many cases where one party is in control of the state government its leaders so juggle the boundary lines that the opposing party is cooped up, with overwhelming majorities, in a few districts, while the party in power secures most of the districts by small majorities. This practice of gerrymandering, as it is called,[1] is in common use and works rank injustice in representation.

The geographical basis for representation works a further injustice on new or third parties. Their members are likely to be so scattered that they can control a majority in no one district and hence are deprived of all voice in the government. If they go to the polls and cast votes for their own candidates, their votes are really thrown away. This is also the position in which the independent voters are placed. The result is that many of them simply stay at home and are accused of indifference to public welfare when in reality they have the public welfare very much at heart. Occasionally there is a great popular reform movement with a regular landslide away from the old-line parties, but this must of necessity be a rare occurrence, to be soon followed by a return to political apathy.

Proportional representation. As citizens have come to realize the injustices and evil effects of a purely majority representation, there has arisen a demand that our units of government— nation, state, and city—should represent all the people, each section of opinion influencing legislation in proportion to its numbers. This means that the basis of representation must be changed from the straight geographical district electing a single representative to some form of voting district that will accord recognition in proportion to its numerical strength to every important group of people with similar ideas on social and economic problems.

[1] The term "gerrymander" was first used in 1811 (when Elbridge Gerry was elected governor of Massachusetts) to describe sarcastically the district of Essex, whose shape had been made so peculiar as to resemble a salamander

Many countries of the world have experimented with devices for securing fairer representation. These devices vary in many details which we must not stop to consider here. A number of them—such as, for example, the Illinois Cumulative Vote—give fairer representation to the minority without helping out third parties in any way.[1] The scheme, which seems to give the fairest representation to all parties, has the following provisions:

1. Consolidation of the present single-member voting districts into larger districts, each electing a number of candidates

2. Each voter to cast as many votes as there are candidates to be elected.

3. Each party to have the right to elect a number of candidates proportional to its vote. This number is determined by dividing the total number of votes cast by all parties by the number of candidates to be elected and then dividing the number of votes cast for each ticket by this result.

The justice of some such scheme as compared with the present system is startlingly illustrated by the New York City election of 1892, wherein Tammany Hall with 59 per cent of the votes elected 100 per cent of the aldermen Under proportional representation there should have been elected nineteen Tammany candidates, twelve Republicans, and one Socialist.

The chief arguments in favor of proportional representation are (1) it makes gerrymandering impossible, (2) it makes bribery fruitless, because no small group holds the balance of power, (3) it makes voters independent of the party machine without abolishing party government, (4) it eliminates ward politics in cities and allows able leaders to be chosen as aldermen, (5) it gives the minority parties a chance to expose the wrongdoings of the majority party and to prove whether they themselves are worthy of some day becoming the majority party; (6) it encourages every citizen to turn out for every election because it makes his vote count

---

[1] For a discussion of the Cumulative Vote see John R Commons's "Proportional Representation," pp 92–98, 113–114, 249–250

The chief arguments against proportional representation are that it is impractical, that it puts too great a task on the officials who count election returns, that it makes impossible the announcement of returns on the same day as the election, and that even if all these objections were overruled, there are many constitutional difficulties in the way of its adoption in the United States. The first and second objections are largely answered by the success of proportional representation in such countries as Belgium, Sweden, Switzerland, and South Africa. As for the delayed election returns, this objection is too trifling to be considered. In regard to the constitutional difficulties of adopting proportional representation, Congress possesses power to adopt any system whatsoever for congressional elections, but in most of the states it would, indeed, be necessary to secure an amendment to the state constitution before this scheme of representation could be applied to members of the state legislature. Although amendments are difficult to secure they are by no means impossible, and if the advantages of proportional representation prove to be all that its advocates believe, it will be well worth the trouble necessary to arouse the voters of the states sufficiently to put over the needed amendments. If proportional representation does not prove to be the solution of the problem of minorities, then some other must be found, for democracy cannot be carried to its highest pitch of perfection if the electoral methods are fundamentally defective.

This discussion of our present-day government is by no means a full account of the problems which our citizens must face and solve, but it is sufficient to show how earnestly each citizen must meet his responsibilities if the nation is to go ahead in the path of progress.

SUPPLEMENTARY READINGS

BRYCE, JAMES. Modern Democracies, Vol I, pp 134-142, 151-162
BRYCE, JAMES. American Commonwealth, Vol I, pp 278-297, 341-359
OGG, F A National Progress, chap. ix.

American Review of Reviews, Vol LXI, pp 451–457; Vol LXV. pp 64–68
Forum, Vol LXIII, pp. 418–427, Vol. LXIV, pp 140–150
Nation, Vol CIX, pp 743–744, Vol CX, pp 390, 576–577
New Republic, Vol XXII, pp. 235–238, Vol XXIII, pp 37–38, Vol XXIV, pp 208–209.
Political Science Quarterly, Vol XXV, pp 411–439
World's Work, Vol XL, pp 69–71, 217–219, 433–434

SEARCH QUESTIONS AND PROBLEMS

1 Secure all the official documents obtainable from your secretary of state, and from a study of these ascertain whether your state executive department needs reorganization

2 What are the best arguments for and against the Senate's having a right to advise the president during the process of treaty-making? You can find the arguments which were presented by Republican senators in 1919 and 1920 by reading the current magazines of the time

3 Find out from the World Almanac the names of the cabinet officers and their official titles From any good civics text find out the chief duties of each

4. How should a legislator vote in case his opinion on a subject is at variance with what his party caucus upholds? with what he knows the majority of his constituents desire?

5 How many representatives has your state in Congress? How many is it entitled to have on a population basis? What congressional district are you in? How does its size compare with that of the other districts in your state? What is the name of your district representative? Find out what his record in Congress has been Do the same for your senators See the *Congressional Record* and the Blue Book for your state, obtainable at its capitol

6 Review the history of the various attempts of Congress to pass a child-labor law

7 Find out from your state constitution whether your governor has the right to veto parts of measures

8 If possible, find out from prominent men in your community whether lobbying and logrolling are used to any extent in your legislature If such devices have been used recently, report on the details of the cases

9. Find out what was done in January, 1923, by the Appropriations Committee of the Lower House and by the House itself, in raising the estimate of the Budget Bureau for river and harbor improvements. Did the Senate aid in this revival of the pork barrel? What are the latest developments in the fight of budget versus pork barrel?

10. Is there a pork barrel in your state? If so, cite proof

11. By use of the Constitution and a good American history account for the passage of each of the amendments. Are there any proposed amendments under discussion now? What does your state constitution say about amendment? Do you think your amendment provisions are superior to those of other states? See Magruder's "American Government," p 244

12 If your state or city possesses either referendum, or initiative, or recall, find out from all available sources just how these ultrademocratic devices have worked out

13 Election to Congress takes place every second year in November, but representatives then elected do not meet, unless in a special session, until a year from the following December What is your opinion of this?

14. What salary do state and national legislators receive? See Magruder's "American Government," pp 65, 254 Is this too much or too little?

15. From the statistics in Magruder's "American Government," p 254, judge whether your legislature is subject to the criticism of excessive introduction of bills.

16. Congressmen are given not only the old English privilege of freedom of speech on the floor of Congress but the right to be exempt from punishment for anything occurring in the so-called "speechless speeches," which they have never given but merely printed for distribution Do you see any objection to this?

17 Do you believe it is right for senators and congressmen to have the privilege of unlimited franking (free postal service) for all letters and speeches?

18 From any American history ascertain (1) why the Dred Scott case is cited as proof that the Supreme Court is not above political influence and (2) why the income tax and Granger laws met with two different treatments by the Supreme Court at different times.

19. Is there a clause in the Constitution which you think guarantees to a man the right to work or not as he pleases?

PRESENT-DAY PROBLEMS OF DEMOCRACY

20. What are the voting qualifications for electing members of your state legislature? members of Congress from your district?

21. Find out how large a percentage of the qualified voters in your local unit exercised their right to vote in the last election

22. Is there a political machine in your city or state? If so, does it work for the good of the majority of the citizens or not?

23. What party is dominant in your state? How long has this been the case? Can you account for it? Do you have newspapers representing all parties? Do you read them?

24. What methods of nomination and election does your state use? Are there any obvious evils connected with them?

25. Has your state any laws regarding bribery or excessive campaign expenditures?

26. Report to the class what an examination of the judiciary of the city of Cleveland showed, as reported in the *Survey Graphic*, Vol. I, pp 1 ff (*Survey*, Vol XLVII, pp. 135 ff.).

27. Find out how many members of the city council and of the state legislature the minority parties in your city and state would be entitled to if proportional representation were in operation now How many offices do they now hold?

28. Find out what Switzerland has done in the matter of initiative and referendum

29. Get copies of the Model City Charter and the Model State Constitution published by the National Municipal League (Rumford Building, Concord, New Hampshire) and compare with your own charter and state constitution.

30. From a historical account or from the official platform in Stanwood's "History of the Presidency," make a list of the planks of the Populist party and of the Prohibition party in 1888 Figure out what percentage of these radical platforms has since become realized through constitutional amendment, statute, or practice

31. Study a list of the planks of the Socialist party in 1912, 1916, or 1920 See Marshall, Wright, and Fields ' Materials for the Study of Elementary Economics," p 267, Hamilton's "Current Economic Problems," p 370, or Magruder's "American Government," p 230 How many of these do you really think may be adopted by 1950?

32. What are *you* going to do to make American democracy more nearly perfect?

CHAPTER XX

FOREIGN RELATIONSHIPS

Our destiny is a common one, whatever may happen to the nations of Africa and Asia affects our life . In this new grouping of social and economic life the national state will, indeed, continue to hold a prominent place, but public and associative action will be dominated by forces and considerations which are broader than national life. — PAUL S REINSCH

TRADITIONAL POLICY AND THE MONROE DOCTRINE

The United States has always cherished a tradition and policy of isolation from other nations. Many of the early settlers in America crossed the seas and helped fight a war of independence to make themselves free of European domination. They had a love of their new home that sprang from the persecution and injustice they had suffered in the old, and their dislike of European states sprang from the bad habit those governments had of governing not wisely but too much. The natural American tendency to isolation was increased and fixed by the economic conditions of a new, richly stored country with a small population, by its nature capable of supporting its people with very little help from outside.

"**Entangling alliances.**" The circumstances surrounding the United States at the time of its birth as a nation were such as to make Americans suspicious of and disinclined toward any close foreign ties. In the troubled administrations of Washington and Adams, Old World quarrels, especially those of England and France, added to the problems of Federal officers already overburdened with the work of starting thirteen individualistic states on the road to Federal unity. France, which had lately changed her government, claimed that the United States owed her an alliance because of the treaty of 1778 made with the old government. There was great popular enthusiasm for such a French alliance, but the level-headed Washington and the astute Hamilton prevented so fatal a mistake. Washington was so impressed by the narrow escape from international complications which his firmness had made possible that in his farewell address he warned the people especially against making foreign alliances Without reflecting that an alliance in Washington's time and an alliance today are two very different things, people have regarded this particular bit of wisdom from the lips of the beloved Father of his Country with an almost superstitious reverence. Even in these postwar days, over a century after its utterance and under circumstances making it decidedly irrelevant, Washington's admonition has had immense influence over the thought of the nation.

The War of 1812. The experiences of the Jeffersonian period were scarcely less fruitful of national isolation The War of 1812 grew out of European differences for which America was not to blame, but for which America suffered; and the feeling that nothing but trouble could come from American participation in European affairs grew apace. Even at this early date it was not possible for the United States to keep herself entirely out of European affairs, as the little wars with the Barbary pirates testified. But for the most part Europe, engrossed in its own troubles, forgot about the new country across the water, and the new country found itself more than busy peopling its Western empire and dealing with home problems. It was thus employed when the definite statement of national policy with regard to outside nations which has become a national doctrine was enunciated by President Monroe.

The changing Monroe Doctrine. The Monroe Doctrine, aside from its use as a popular fetich in the speeches of chauvinistic politicians, has exerted a very real influence over American foreign affairs. It is attributed by historians not to President Monroe, who promulgated it in his message of December 2, 1823, but to his secretary of state, the vigorous and farseeing John Quincy Adams. Because the Monroe Doctrine has had a different meaning in each generation, the stages in its interpretation should be clearly understood

1. The original doctrine was phrased to meet the possible land-grabbing designs of Russia upon the Pacific coast south of Alaska and to prevent Austria, Prussia, and Russia, banded together in the so-called "Holy Alliance," from helping Spain to secure domination once again over the South American nations, which had succeeded in throwing off the Spanish yoke. The doctrine therefore declared that the United States regards any effort to gain or extend power over a free American nation by a European power as an unfriendly act, and that American territory is no longer open to European colonization In 1864 France put the first part of the doctrine to the test by setting up Prince Maximilian as ruler over Mexico. The United States at once notified France that this was an infringement of our rights, and later followed up the notice by an order for troops to move to the border. France withdrew all military support, and Prince Maximilian was executed The original claims of the Monroe Doctrine were never again contested by any European nation In his explanatory statements Monroe included the oft-repeated principle of our fathers, expressed by Washington, Jefferson, and others, that the United States will keep out of European affairs, and claims no right to dictate to other nations of the Americas.

2. President Polk was the first official to enlarge the Monroe Doctrine when it served him as a convenient justification for our course in the Southwest, 1845-1848. He said that it is the duty of the United States to prevent European aggression in the New World by taking to itself territories in danger of European annexation. This philanthropic principle helped us to secure California, Arizona, and New Mexico.

3. When all the world thought that France would build a Panama Canal, in 1881, and when Great Britain proposed to secure a generally acknowledged neutrality of the Canal Zone, Secretary of State Blaine enunciated the third rubric of the expanding doctrine. This was that the United States is the

natural and sole guardian of Panama and the arbitrator of disputes among the lesser American powers. This doctrine, although contrary to the treaty made in 1850, came finally to dominate the actual building and control of the Canal.

4. In 1895, following a misunderstanding with Great Britain as to the boundary of Venezuela, Secretary Olney with the approval of President Cleveland laid down the broad lines of the later interpretation of the Monroe Doctrine: European colonies in America are to be regarded as temporary, since there can be no real unity between European and American interests; the United States is the supreme power in America, and its word is law; moreover, it assumes a certain degree of responsibility for the conduct of the smaller nations of America. Not only did Olney make these broad assumptions, but he claimed for them the weight and authority of international law, as forming a definite basis for America's foreign relations.[1]

5. In Roosevelt's time the doctrine had still another interpretation added to its accumulation. Trouble arose at two different times about the nonpayment of debts by South American countries to their European creditors. The United States objected to the use of force by foreign nations to collect debts, and therefore for all practical purposes it assumed responsibility for the debts of these countries. In the case of Venezuelan debts it was found that many of them had been padded, and the final sum was some eight million dollars less than the original claim. Venezuelans paid this reduced bill without a murmur. In the case of Santo Domingo the United States was forced to take over and run the customs department and finances of the country and thereby pay off the indebtedness.

It is easy to see that such interpretations of the Monroe Doctrine make it a very different thing from that of Adams in 1823 Every succeeding statement, whether claimed as such by its enunciators or not, has been commonly regarded by the people as the Monroe Doctrine, and as each new interpretation always caters to the cockiness of the jingo element of the nation,

[1] See Hart's "Foundations of American Foreign Policy," chap vii

the doctrine has been much lauded and has come to have a semi-sacred position among the national traditions. Politicians trot it out as one of the means of arousing patriotic emotionalism.[1]

Opportunist interpretations. But in reality every restatement of this elastic "doctrine" has been simply a new statement of the position of the United States on some important international question just then imminent. In Monroe's time it grew from national isolation; since then it has grown first from national expansion, then from national power. In any case, it can scarcely apply in any of its interpretations to present world conditions. In past years thoughtful Americans have wondered if some statesman would not frame a statement of principles which could serve as a permanent basis for American foreign relations, but since the World War it has been so apparent that our nation can never again even pretend to isolation and self-sufficiency, and that any American policy affects and is affected by the policies of a dozen other powers, that probably the Monroe Doctrine will in time be succeeded by some internationally-agreed-on general principle.

INTERNATIONAL COMMERCE

The days of our self-sufficiency. At the time when the tradition of isolation was being fixed in the American mind, our economic conditions, while not really supporting such a view, did not contradict it in so definite a way as they do now. The average American, unless he lived on the Atlantic seaboard, used little goods from abroad and sent little of his produce to foreign lands. The whole amount of foreign trade, including both imports and exports, amounted to but a hundred and sixty-two millions of dollars in 1800, and up to 1872 it had not touched the billion-dollar mark. The influential part of the

---

[1] Professor Hart tells the story of a Tammany orator who told his hearers that "Tammany Hall is a benevolent institution, Tammany Hall is a patriotic institution, Tammany Hall is a philanthropic institution, Tammany Hall has the honor of being the first to propose that immortal Monroe Doctrine which blesses and revivifies the world."

population (the old-stock Americans) had lost their touch with the Old World, they felt their Americanism keenly, and being able to raise their own food, buy domestic cloth for clothing, and have their furniture and houses built by Americans, they did not feel the sense of unity with the rest of the world that exists today.

The matter of food alone illustrates the self-sufficiency of those earlier American times. The housewife of 1850 made her bread from American flour, churned her own butter or bought it from farmers' wives close by, superintended the fall butchering for the household, preserved the fruit from her own orchard trees and berry bushes, and parched the corn and other cereals that took the place of coffee then. Men and women grew up, lived long and useful lives, and died without having seen or tasted a banana, an orange, or a coconut.

The agency of international trade. But today things are changed. The fruit on the breakfast table comes perhaps from Central America or the Antilles, the coffee from South America, the sugar from Cuba, the linen from Ireland, the cutlery from England, the porcelain from France All these foreign countries are dependent on the United States for some of the necessities of existence The world has become economically interdependent, and the business of our country is now world-wide.

Our commercial dependence on other lands is shown first by the extent of our import trade, which, in the fiscal year ending June 30, 1920, amounted to $5,000,000,000, or $1,374,000,000 more than in 1919, showing a growth of over $3,000,000,000 since the World War began. The greatest part of this huge importation was composed of raw materials for American manufacture, such as sisal, crude petroleum, hides, rubber, and cabinet woods. Foreign foods came next in value, including sugar, coffee, and cocoa at the head of the list. The importations from Europe showed that the war-worn countries were recovering with remarkable speed and pluck, although the large proportion of art work, jewels, and fine manufactures—the product of past generations—bore testimony to Europe's great need of money. The amount of raw materials imported indicates that the United States is growing as a manufacturing nation, while the greater importation of foreign foods is one small part of the necessary effort to feed a fast-growing population. Under such conditions America must rapidly take on European characteristics, it is impossible to keep America American, in an economic sense, when foreign goods are needed to feed both mills and mill hands.

Export. Our export trade is even larger than our import trade. In 1910 the United States had attained an excess of exports over imports amounting to over $182,000,000; by 1920 the excess had risen to over $3,000,000,000. How much of this may have been due to war conditions it is difficult to say. The gross exports in 1920 amounted to over $8,000,000,000.

Of course the largest part of our exports is in foods and fibers—in the products of farms and plantations. We were exporting goods worth $2,258,792,500 in 1914, at the outbreak of the World War. With a very large proportion of Europeans withdrawn from production, of course, there was at once a great additional demand for American materials, and especially for food. Prices rose rapidly, so that in some cases less was exported, but the value was higher than before the war.[1]

American food for Europe. In 1919 we sent to other nations over twenty-four million barrels of flour and over a million and a quarter barrels of bacon—to select two of the most important articles. Condensed milk was a comparatively unimportant export in 1914, amounting in value to a little over $1,000,000, but by 1920 the export was worth $125,000,000 a year.[2] This

---

[1] For instance, in 1910 the United States exported 1,005,028,000 gallons of illuminating oil, which was worth $62,478,000. In 1919 only 722,130,000 gallons were exported, but it brought in the market $80,965,000.

[2] The amounts sent to Europe are as follows:

Year	Pounds
1914	8,362
1916	99,541,000
1918	384,588,000
1919	600,000,000

growth is due partly to war needs, partly also to the fact that in normal times it is possible, in a great country like the United States, to produce and export milk more cheaply than it can be produced in a crowded country with little grazing land, and partly to the excellent flavor and richness of American condensed milk. Cottonseed oil and cotton, meat and dairy products, breadstuffs and mineral oils, form the bulk of our European export

American exports go to all parts of the world, but by far the largest portion goes to Europe, since Europe has most to send to us, and export and import always tend to balance. In 1919, for instance, we sent, in round numbers, $5,000,000,000 in exports to Europe, $700,000,000 to Asia, and less than $450.000,000 to South America. The United Kingdom takes by far the lion's share of our export, then follow in order France, Canada, Italy, Belgium, Japan, the West Indies, the Netherlands, Denmark, Argentina, Norway, Sweden, Mexico, Australasia, China, Brazil, and Spain [1]

The abnormal demand of the war years was, naturally, a great stimulus to merchants and manufacturers to establish trade relations with new foreign markets. In 1914–1919 there was a total excess of exports over imports of nearly $14,000,000,000. This, of course, could not be permanent, Europe soon recovered to some extent from the war and began to produce for herself, and the South American and Asiatic markets exercised their former choice in buying. American foreign trade must compete with the experience and skill of European manufacturers and merchants Even in the selling of raw products America will soon, if she does not now, find Canadian, Siberian, and Australian farmers and miners competing for markets in the more densely populated countries.

A case of European superiority. Mexico and South America fall rather logically to the share of the United States as markets for manufactured articles. Before the war about half of Mexico's imports were American made, but Germany and

[1] The order given is that of 1919, of course it changes from time to time

Great Britain had the major part of the South American trade. This was due to the better methods of the European salesmen, who catered to Spanish-American tastes and customs rather than to a superiority in European goods. The German salesman speaks Spanish and French fluently, he spends his time in the interminable social preliminaries of business with a better grace than the impatient American, and he is willing to adapt his business to the wants of his customers. American firms do not like to give credit for a longer time than the customary three months, while nine months or a year is often needed by the South American planter or retail merchant. American firms send their goods packed in frail pasteboard cases, regardless of the fact that at the port of entry they must usually be carried to land on a lighter, involving much tossing around, and that after landing they must often be carried long distances on mule back. Moreover, the American firm wants to do a cash business, whereas the South American has little money and wants to pay in kind—in coffee, cocoa, hides, drugs, or rubber. The independent attitude and poorer linguistic preparation of American salesmen have kept American goods from the sale they might otherwise have had.

When the World War came European trade was largely cut off. This was the opportunity of American producers and exporters. They entered the field confidently, but the increase in export trade was not so great as might have been expected. On the other hand, a vastly increased importation from South America took place, giving a large adverse balance of trade which amounted to some $375,000,000 in the fiscal year 1919-1920. The fact is that there are very fundamental differences between the United States and Latin America in ways of living, thinking, and doing business; and only the most careful, friendly, and patient study will make the trade relations of the two regions profitable for both. More direct steamship connections are needed, and large exporting houses need trained salesmen who speak the languages of Latin America and understand the social customs as well as the economic needs. The same statement applies in general to the trade with China and other little-developed parts of Asia, and to Australasia. Foreign salesmanship is a science, offering an interesting field to bright young men, but involving in many ways as much hardship as it offers adventure.

The Merchant Marine

Not the least important factor in fixing our foreign relations is the fleet used in carrying goods to and from our shores. The history of the merchant marine is one of ups and downs that can be traced only in the briefest way here; and the present and future of the American shipping interests is a big question which few would attempt confidently to answer It is, however, a question which deserves the most careful study, for its right solution means a great deal to international prosperity and friendliness.

Between 1825 and 1850 the American merchant marine enjoyed its period of greatest prosperity. Those were the days of the "clippers"—the strong, slender, speedy ships that carried American traders to the ends of the earth. They took our goods everywhere; not on a modern scale, but with adventurous daring that wins today the admiration of all who read of their exploits.

The decline. Beginning with the decade before the Civil War, the American merchant marine began a decline which went on steadily for over half a century. In 1860 the foreign tonnage carried amounted to 2,380,000 tons, but in 1890 it had fallen to 928,000 tons. In 1851, $72\frac{1}{2}$ per cent of American imports came in American ships; in 1914 only 9 per cent came in American bottoms.

There were several causes of this decline, not the least of them being the slowness of American shipbuilders to keep abreast of the times by adopting new inventions. With the coming of steam the preëminence of the clipper passed, but it took American shippers a decade to realize the uselessness of pitting sails against the new power. We were behind England also in the use of iron ships in place of wooden ones. There was a good economic reason for this reluctance to adopt the newer type: England could build iron ships far cheaper than could the United States, and an old statute of 1792 forbade our purchasing ships from foreign countries. American shippers must pay more both for original equipment and for operating costs than British shipowners. These costs included the higher wages of our sailors, higher repair and coal costs, and discrimination against wooden vessels by insurance companies. The fact, too, that money invested in railroads brought greater returns than money put into ships affected our shipping.

Rehabilitation. The World War, 1914-1918, acted as a powerful stimulant to our decrepit marine. Not only was legislation enacted to encourage private enterprise on the sea, but in 1916 the government itself began a comprehensive building program under the direction of the Shipping Board Emergency Fleet Corporation. As a result of this addition to our marine and the losses to allied shipping through submarine warfare, we find, in 1919, that 46 per cent of our imports were brought in under our own flag. The country at that time had commissioned 4260 sailing vessels, 7397 steamships, and 10,254 gas vessels, making, with barges and canal boats, 27,573 ships of 12,907,300 tons burden. When the war was over only the British fleet exceeded our own. Japan had increased her fleet during the war, and by 1919 it had reached a size of about one sixth of our own.

It is impossible to predict the future of the merchant marine. Many of the economic disadvantages of the period since 1850 have now ceased to apply, while the laws of 1912 and 1914 established a policy of free ships that enables Americans to buy ships for foreign trade in the cheapest market. The La Follette Seaman's Act tends to equalize seamen's wages. Popular opinion in favor of maintaining a marine may possibly lead to the levy of discriminating duties on imports carried in foreign bottoms.[1]

In 1922 the question of subsidies for the encouragement of the merchant marine was being debated. There was much opposition to the proposal, partly from the conservative general prejudice against subsidizing a business by the government and partly, also, from the traditional indifference to shipping problems, due to the fact that so large a part of the country is far from the sea and therefore does not think in terms of sea interests. This last factor is an example of sectionalism, of the sort of narrow outlook that Americans must overcome. But the feeling that it is dangerous to favor private business with State funds is soundly based on economic law and knowledge of human nature. Many men who favor a great development of American shipping think that State money would do more harm than good to the shipping interests. It would be but an artificial propping, which experience has shown must be continued indefinitely if once begun.

There are signs pointing toward another decline in the merchant marine. In the period following the war there were more ships ready to carry the cargoes of the allied countries than there were goods to be carried. When our government tried to sell ships to private operators, it found them unwilling to buy, although offered real bargains Perhaps the psychology of the American business mind, so long occupied with the tremendous task of developing internal resources, forbids any real and widespread interest in an international carrying system. If this be the fact, another period of decline will probably follow the brief activity induced by war, and England will take

[1] The acquisition of numerous coaling stations in the various seas now enables the United States to buy coal at rates not far above those of England If oil-burning ships are to be the ships of the future, a new problem in fuel competition will arise This possibility throws some light on the objections raised in some quarters in the United States to the gains made by Great Britain in Mesopotamia during the World War.

again her old position of the world's unrivaled water transporter. Perhaps her position and experience will make such an issue best for all the world.

The Consular and Diplomatic Services

Whatever may be the fortunes of American foreign trade in any particular country, it is clear that the days of an isolated America are past. The United States has become one of the great family of nations, and the wise management of foreign affairs is one of the most vital of our problems. Our foreign relations are in the hands of two sets of agents, one of whom has charge of commercial matters, the other of political affairs. The consular service consists of agencies located in all the chief commercial centers of the world, who look after trade relations, do something to prevent undesirable immigration, and in general have an oversight of all matters affecting the United States which are not political in their nature.

The consular system. The consulates in any one nation are usually under the management and supervision of a consul-general who has vice consul-generals and deputy consul-generals according to the volume of business conducted in that nation or division. His duty is to inspect the separate consulates and gather data from them. A consul is placed in charge of the business at any foreign city important enough to require separate representation; and he may be assisted by vice and deputy consuls. Consular agents represent consuls in places where there is no resident consul; and the staff will include, of course, necessary clerks and assistants.

The consular service, which was really established in Europe before the diplomatic system grew up, existed from the first in our own national economy, but it was never provided for by law until 1856, when, for the first time, consuls were paid a salary for their services. Before that time a consul was simply a merchant living abroad who looked after our commercial interests either for patriotic reasons or for the fees he was allowed to charge. At the present time a consul who is paid less than $1000 is allowed to enter into business for himself, but if paid more than that he must depend upon his salary. As he handles money, he must give a bond. Consul-generals and consuls are appointed by the president and confirmed by the Senate; other staff members are recommended by their chiefs and commissioned by the Secretary of State. When the consul arrives at his station the foreign government issues him an "exequatur," or official recognition, if for any reason this is withdrawn, he is automatically dismissed. This custom insures our nation to some extent against misunderstandings growing out of the acts of unwise consuls.

Administrative duplication. The government attempts in many ways to help foreign trade, indeed, there are in Washington thirteen branches of the government which deal with the subject. Naturally there is some question as to just where final authority rests in many matters, and there can be no strong and consistent policy under such circumstances. As in many other matters, a reorganization of bureaus and departments in such a way as to put the management of all foreign trade questions in one department would be of immense benefit to the commercial interests of the nation.

Political relations. Our formal political relations with other nations are controlled officially by the Department of State, with the Secretary of State at its head, and by the diplomatic service, with the ratification by the Senate of treaties and major appointments. The Senate rarely refuses to confirm an appointment, but it frequently refuses to ratify a treaty, even when the interests of the nation clearly indicate that a working treaty is needed. The Secretary of State conducts what in other governments is known as the Foreign Office, carrying on all official correspondence with our State representatives abroad and with foreign governments

The diplomatic service of the United States was just emerging from the days of its effective but rather haphazard beginnings when the Congress of Vienna, in 1815, fixed the diplomatic ranks as follows: (1) nuncio for the papacy and ambassador for sovereigns, (2) envoys and ministers plenipotentiary, (3) ministers resident, (4) chargés d'affaires.

An ambassador was the personal representative of a sovereign, and as such took precedence over envoys and ministers, who represented states. As the United States was a democratic government, with no personal sovereign, it sent no ambassadors for many years, but sent instead ministers to all foreign courts. These ministers often had to wait in anterooms for an audience when there was important business to transact, while the ambassador of some unimportant little ruler negotiated his affairs at his leisure. Therefore Americans often suggested that we should give our representatives the rank of ambassador. For many years the secretaries of state discouraged this change because an ambassador must keep up a very great and expensive establishment, for which the slender salary paid is no compensation. Finally, in 1893, Congress, which has never been generous to the diplomatic service, granted the rank of ambassador, but made no addition to the salary, which is $17,500. Eleven nations are now served by ambassadors and about thirty-five by ministers.[1] As a rule these nations send us representatives of similar rank, although this is not necessary. The whole system of rank gives rise to endless bickering and bitterness, and Americans feel that it might well give way to a more democratic system in which all chief representatives would bear the same title and take rank in the order of the seniority of their service.

Putting the diplomatic service on a better basis. Unlike the consular service, the diplomatic service does not recruit its ranks from applicants who take a competitive examination. Such a system has often been urged, and certain universities offer courses meant to prepare men for foreign service; but as

---

[1] The ministers are paid $10,000 each, except those to China, Cuba, Czechoslovakia, the Netherlands, and Poland, who receive $12,000 each, and the minister to Liberia, who receives $5000. The nations to which we send ambassadors are Argentina, Brazil, Chili, France, Great Britain, Italy, Japan, Mexico, Peru, Russia, and Spain.

yet no success has been attained in putting this part of our governmental machinery on a sensible civil-service basis. President Roosevelt made a beginning in 1905 when he ordered that the lower ranks should be filled either by promotion or by competitive examination.[1] But such appointees have no assurance of a permanent position. It is to be hoped that in the future provision will be made in two ways to insure the very best representation abroad for the United States:

1. Entrance into diplomatic service should be by means of competitive examinations, which will insure the services of capable and cultured men who will creditably represent us. Appointment should be for life unless behavior warrants dismissal, thus taking the diplomatic service out of politics.

2. The salaries should be made equal to the necessary expenses, and at the close of a lifetime of service the diplomat should be pensioned as army and navy officers are; for surely the man who by his services prevents war is as worthy of a pension as the fighter.

Such a system need not prevent the employment of laymen when particular circumstances warrant it; and it would give to the United States a supply of trained, competent men who could devote their powers to the important work of American foreign affairs without the worry caused by living beyond their incomes or of attempting work for which they have little if any preparation. At the present time only a rich man can afford to be an American diplomat, since the nation owns few legations and pays a salary which does not cover the expenses incurred.[2] Sometimes rich men have the necessary ability and culture; sometimes they have not. The nation is ungrateful and negligent in not making a proper provision for the men who represent it among the other peoples of the world.

Achievements of "shirt-sleeve diplomacy." In spite of all the handicaps under which it has worked, American diplomacy

[1] The subjects in such an examination include the modern languages, diplomatic usage, and international law

[2] For instance, men so able as John C. Calhoun and George William Curtis have had to decline diplomatic posts because they could not afford them.

has made an honorable record. Many of our greatest statesmen and literary men have represented us at foreign courts, and the number of failures and disgraces is few. Americans have always been noted for the simplicity and directness of their methods; "shirt-sleeve diplomacy" has been the subject of much smiling among sophisticated Europeans, but it has helped to bring about cleaner, more dependable negotiations than the old "back-stair diplomacy" of European practice. America has had its honorable share in the defining of international law, a process which went on steadily during the nineteenth century, and it has to some extent simplified diplomatic customs through the example of its own democratic simplicity.[1]

At the present time diplomats are appointed politically by the president, who has previously made an inquiry as to whether the man suggested is *persona grata* to the government concerned. If that government makes no objection the appointment is sent to the Senate for confirmation. That being given, the new diplomat is told of his appointment and given thirty days, on salary, for settling his home affairs and receiving instructions at Washington. With his instructions he receives his credentials, to be presented to the ruler of the nation to which he goes, and all necessary passports and other papers. Having arrived at his destination, he is formally received and settles down to his duties.

Duties. These duties are many. The most important is that the diplomat shall keep the Secretary of State informed of whatever affects our own government and people, so that our policy may be founded upon a true knowledge of affairs. He may have in charge the making of important treaties, unless a special mission is appointed for that purpose. He is charged with the general care of American affairs, which may include the protection of our citizens, the renewing of passports, the demanding of extradition, and coöperation with naval commanders in time of trouble. Negotiations are carried on with

---

[1] An example is the writing of notes in the first person, and in English. Both usages are becoming more common.

foreign nations through "notes," and confidential messages sent back to Washington are known as dispatches. With regard to the foreign government to which a diplomat is accredited, his duties include all official negotiations and many social duties. He must hold himself strictly neutral with regard to the domestic affairs of the foreign nation, and during his term of office he may not write newspaper articles or books about the interesting things he may know. In fact, he must be "diplomatic" in all he says and does, that his country may live on terms of friendliness with its neighbors.

The Goal of Better International Relations

Although not so much discussed as the commercial and political relations, the closest ties binding us to other peoples are social ones. These spring from the fact that Americans were Europeans first; they inherit language, tradition, customs, and, indeed, all that goes to make up culture, from the past of Europe. Many of the newer Americans still hold dear the friends and relatives left behind them, and among the older Americans ties of friendship, travel, and common interest are scarcely less strong.

Under these circumstances the matter of communication becomes important. The speed of steamships crossing the ocean has its social and political significance, the ownership of cable lines becomes a matter of international importance. Probably the most important of all communication questions is the regulation of postal communication; and few matters can help more to friendly understanding than this. The Postal Union was formed in 1874 at a meeting called by the Swiss president at Bern, in which the postal authorities of twenty-one nations participated. These nations signed treaties making the postal rate 25 centimes, or its equivalent, for each 15 grams, and established a central information bureau at Bern, managed by the Swiss post-office department. In 1892 an international postal clearing-house went into operation. At the present time Afghanistan is the only considerable country not included in the Universal Postal Union, besides some very new European countries which will doubtless soon become members.

War. There is one problem on which all diplomatic effort, all commercial relations, and all social ties center—the prevention of war. It is the biggest practical problem before the world, and all the world is interested vitally in its solution, for war means loss so infinite and tragic that unless it can be overcome, there is small incentive for the building up of civilization Why should men sacrifice for a civilization which will not stand the test of international differences, but resorts to brute force as in the days of human beginnings?

With all its terrors war need not be, and rarely is, utterly evil. Men may fight for a principle or an institution in which they believe with a heroism and devotion which are in themselves an inspiration to the generations that follow. But when gain and loss are balanced, it is clear that, barring the great object for which the war is fought, the losses far outweigh the gains. If great reforms may be won or great dangers averted without war, the world is infinitely the gainer. War losses may be summarized as follows:

1. The loss of human life, which is always greatest among the best men—the youngest men, with most years of service to mankind ahead of them; the strongest and healthiest and brightest men, who make the best fighters; and the men of finest feeling and highest standards, who feel the call to duty first. The loss of men is only part of the human sacrifice; added to this is the loss, never to be computed, of the children that would have been born to them had they lived—the children with the finest heritage of strength and ability, of ideals and traditions.

2. The material loss of stored wealth, upon which progress so greatly depends. No war is without its irreparable losses of art treasures, documents, houses and furniture, and capital goods, the surplus production of years, which give to men both the means of current material production and the means to increase culture. The destruction of homes and furniture and books, the ordinary fixed capital of living, which would nor-

mally last through many years without the cost of replacing, is alone a tremendous item in postwar reconstruction. Added to this is the cost of replacing public buildings, railroads, bridges, and public works of all kinds. A war means a long pause in the normal accumulation of capital goods, and this is a direct check to progress; for when men can live upon stored wealth instead of having to earn as they go, they have time and strength to give to new invention and new thought.

3. The material loss of new production. Men by the thousand are taken from production and put into nonproductive and destructive pursuits. Men and women who ordinarily produce the goods of life become the makers of the goods of death. Consumption is abnormally large, and production is slowed down, even when workers are brought into industry from homes and all citizens work under the stimulus of war needs. This deficit is added to the deficit of capital goods, and all must be made up after peace is declared.

4. The saddling of debt upon the future. National debts are in the main the result of war, nations would be solvent if they could live at peace. The growth of national debts is shown by a table, taken from *The Americas*, Vol. VI, No. 9, pp. 4-5:

1713, Peace of Utrecht	$1,500,000,000
1793, before Napoleonic wars	2,500,000,000
1816, after Napoleonic wars	7,000,000,000
1848, before Crimean War	8,400,000,000
1862, beginning of the United States Civil War	13,400,000,000
1873, close of Franco-Prussian War	22,400,000,000
1897, before the Spanish-American, Boer, Russo-Japanese, and Balkan wars	30,200,000,000
1914, World War	44,100,000,000
1915, World War	56,900,000,000
1916, World War	120,485,000,000
1917, World War	189,100,000,000
1918, World War	225,300,000,000
1919, World War	248,000,000,000
1920, World War	255,000,000,000

The statistics of the National City Bank of New York put the world's debts in 1913 at $40,000,000,000 and in 1920 at $265,000,000,000. All figures are necessarily partly estimated.

The per-capita debt of the leading countries gives perhaps a better idea of what this almost incalculable burden means to taxpayers. It is shown in the following table:

Country	Debt per Inhabitant in 1913	Debt per Inhabitant in 1921
United States	$11	$225
Great Britain	78	850
France	160	1150
Italy	83	365
Germany	18	800
Russia	27	125 [1]
Austria	63	525 [2]
Hungary	70	387 [2]
Australia	18	318
Canada	70	159

War debt of the United States. The war debt of our own country is estimated at $1,028,564,000 for 1913; by 1919–1920 it had grown to $24,974,936,000. This great treasure was willingly and gladly given to finance a war which we believed to be for freedom and democracy; but if freedom and democracy could be achieved without bloodshed, such a sum of money could be made to add beyond measure to the happiness and progress of the world. The money cost of a war is never the main cost, but it is more easily calculated and expressed than other costs and so more satisfactorily discussed.

Much of the cost of war is incurred during times of peace, when expensive military establishments must be kept up through taxation. Here also the money cost is not the main one; the great loss of a military system lies in the diversion of human powers that should be exerted in constructive work

[1] Figures for 1917, the last obtainable.
[2] Figures for 1918, the last obtainable.

into the comparative idleness and nonproduction of a parasitic life. Soldiers and officers alike suffer from the inactivity and lack of responsibility of barrack life. The manhood that should be earning its living in real work is spending its years in comparative idleness, awaiting some international misfortune that may give it the chance to act. The character loss through militarism is as serious as the economic loss.

World Peace and Federation

Preparedness versus pacifism. World disarmament has been the dream of many years. But "Preparedness" is a slogan that gains in insistence during and after all wars; after the Franco-Prussian War it served as the cry under which immense armaments were built up by all the European powers Militarism became more and more of a burden, as the increasing national debts show. But with the growth of the evil came the growth of sentiment against it, pacifism had its advocates all over the world, with an especially large adherence in the United States. But pacifism before the World War was more a sentiment than a movement. Most people wanted peace, but they were not sufficiently afraid of war to take active measures to insure peace; they trusted, as men generally do until they find it vain, to good luck. Good luck does not befall the improvident, and so the World War came. Now that it is over, men propose to take positive measures to secure peace; they no longer trust to chance.

The horrors of the years 1914–1918 strengthened the sentiment of all the world against war. It became a commonplace remark that once the welter of fighting could be stopped, there must be a realization of what Tennyson called "the Parliament of man, the federation of the world."

The League of Nations. It is the glory of the United States that the actual proposal for such a league came formally from its president, Woodrow Wilson, who advocated it in a speech to Congress on January 22, 1917. The idea was received with acclaim by all peace-loving peoples, and especially by the English-speaking nations, who had slowly for many years been working toward a closer and more helpful union. Wilson's famous Fourteen Points called, among other things, for disarmament and a "general association of nations." In the peace negotiations at Paris, after the winning of the war, the Covenant of the League of Nations was included as part of the settlement.

THE DISARMAMENT CONFERENCE, WASHINGTON

The treaty was far from satisfactory, since European diplomats insisted on basing it largely on revenge and strategy rather than on the principles laid down in the Fourteen Points.

Since the League of Nations, through Article X, was pledged to keep the map of Europe as it was drawn by the treaty, it, too, met with much criticism in this country. Moreover, those portions of the League's constitution which provided for the appointment of mandatories over young and weak nations were looked upon as possible sources of future land-grabbing or unfair acquisitions of commercial power. For these reasons and because partisan politics most unfortunately entered into the matter, the United States Senate refused to ratify the treaty and become a member of the League of Nations. This does not mean, however, that the United States has repudiated her pacifist policy nor that she will not in the future join other nations in a league for peace and mutual betterment.

After the World War the troubled nations sent representatives to a series of international conferences, at which there was an attempt, usually unsuccessful, to solve the knotty problems of world reconstruction. Perhaps the most important of these was the Disarmament Conference, called by President Harding. It met at Washington on Armistice Day, 1921. At this conference Great Britain, France, Japan, and the United States came to an understanding on a Pacific policy, and the Great Powers agreed to reduce their naval armaments. The friendly agreements entered into there seemed to people at the time to be the beginning of a constructive international policy; it is to be hoped that in years to come they may indeed prove to be the first steps toward final, world-wide peace.

Just as in the days of our forefathers, when a national union was taking form from separate states, so now any movement for world union is met with positive opposition from some, with fear of lessened sovereignty by others, and with cynical indifference by many. As in every new venture, time is needed to establish confidence and to prove worth. The encouraging thing is that every day more people are becoming convinced that only by a federation of the world can peace and progress be assured.

SUPPLEMENTARY READINGS

Bogart, E L, and Thompson, C. M Readings in the Economic History of the United States, pp. 651-655. [Covers the years 1860-1910]

Paine, Ralph D. The Old Merchant Marine. [Tells about the daring days of the clipper]

Wells, H G. The Salvaging of Civilization, chaps. ii, iii. [An expanding patriotism.]

Independent, Vol. CXI, pp 243-244, and *Forum*, Vol LXX, pp. 2161-2178 The Monroe Doctrine.

Independent, Vol. LXXV, pp 737-740, where George E Holt tells why our consular service needs improvement; also Vol LXXVII, p. 310, for references for a debate on the abandoning of the Monroe Doctrine

Missionaries play an important part in spreading American ideas *Current Opinion*, Vol LXIV, p 71.
Outlook, Vol. CV, pp. 539-541.

SEARCH QUESTIONS AND PROBLEMS

1 Read Washington's "Farewell Address" in *Old South Leaflets*, Vol I, No 4, or in some other source book. What subjects does he treat in this solemn parting injunction, and what proportion of attention does he give to each? Note the reasons for his warning against alliances, and the nature of the alliances inferred What is his opinion of sectionalism? Do you think he would have favored a free-school system had that been proposed in his day? an income tax? the present party system? In what specific matters is the advice now applicable?

2. The 1,239,540,973 pounds of bacon exported in 1919 were worth $378,729,046 at current prices, but only $157,421,704 at 1910 prices What was the rise, per cent, in export bacon prices in the nine years?

3 By comparing the figures given on page 64 of the *Literary Digest* for April 17, 1920, find out how many nations trading with the United States in 1919 were able to pay for their imports from us with exports to us.

4. The exports of the United States for the ten months ending June, 1920, amounted in value to $6,734,786,549, and the imports in the same period were worth $4,254,744,140. Was the United States a debtor or a creditor nation during these ten months? What relation do these facts bear to the gold supply during that time? to the cost of living?

5 The table[1] on the following page shows the increase in food prices in several countries during the war The standard for prewar years is taken as 100, and the index figure gives the increase for food staples, as shown in the 1919 prices, in the months indicated What country suffered most in this respect? What country suffered least? Did neutrals suffer as much as nations at war? Why? How can a neutral nation protect itself from the effects of war among other nations?

[1] Statistics from *Manchester Guardian*, November 26, 1919

FOREIGN RELATIONSHIPS

United States (May)	181
Switzerland (June)	250
Denmark (July)	212
United Kingdom (August)	217
Netherlands (September)	203
Sweden (April)	336
Norway (May)	271
France, provinces (June)	293
Italy (April)	281

6 One of the most careful short digests of the costs of the recent war is that by the economist Bogart in the *Historical Outlook*, Vol X, pp. 310–311 What statement there is most startling, and what does it indicate about future wars?

7. A detailed and authoritative article on the balance of trade is to be found in the *Review of Economic Statistics* for July, 1919 Is a favorable balance of trade really an advantage to a nation?

8. Professor G Young writes on "A School of Foreign Affairs" in the *Contemporary Review* for July, 1920, pp. 51–56. Study and explain the question agitating England at the time the article was written. Would the program proposed for a chair in the University of London fit the needs of American diplomacy?

9 Using the most recent World Almanac or other good yearbook, compare last year's expenditure by the United States for army and navy with its appropriations for education, agriculture, and commerce What was the total cost of the schools in your town last year? What does one battleship cost? How do these compare in social value?

10 Is there any way in which our cost of defense can safely be reduced while other nations remain armed? How does our expenditure for defense compare with that of the other four leading powers? If the five great powers made an alliance, would they be safe in disarming? Why?

11. Check the Fourteen Points with regard to the provisions of the Peace of Versailles How many were realized?

12 What nations are now members of the League of Nations? See the latest edition of the Statesman's Yearbook

13 What was the attitude of President Wilson, ex-President Taft, Senator Lodge, and Senator Borah upon the question of the League of Nations? See Readers' Guide to Periodical Literature for 1919

14. What did Secretary Hay mean when he said, "A quiet legation is the stuffed mattress which the political acrobat wants always to see ready under him in case of a slip"?

Have you read of any diplomats to whom these words of Seward's would apply? 'Some persons are sent abroad because they are needed abroad, and some are sent because they are not wanted at home."

15. From a consultation of the World Almanac for 1919, p 212, find out what examinations you would have to take to enter the consular service. Would a young man with a high-school training but with no college training be prepared for such a post?

16. America emerged from the World War with status much changed. How will she stand among the nations in the future? See H H Powers's "America among the Nations"

17. What was accomplished for world peace by the Disarmament Conference opened at Washington, November 11, 1921? by the Genoa Conference held in April and May, 1922? See current reviews of those and succeeding dates.

18. H G. Wells, in "The Salvaging of Civilization," says that the people of the world should adopt a system of currency which would be uniform in all nations Suppose such a system were adopted, what would be its advantages? its disadvantages? Would it make any difference to France and Germany at the present time?

19. Make a comparative table of the governments of Russia, Italy, Germany, France, Japan, China, Spain, Brazil, Mexico, Sweden, and any other countries in which you are especially interested, showing form, centralization, democracy, responsibility to the people, independence, and success as measured by general prosperity.

20 Show how the La Follette Seaman's Act tends to equalize sailors' wages all over the world See *Harper's Weekly*, Vol LXII, pp. 426–427.

21 What was the Bok Prize Peace Plan? Is it a practicable plan for the United States?

22 What was the plan for German reparations payment offered by the Dawes Committee in 1924?

A CLOSING WORD

No fine and earnest boy or girl can study the structure of the world he lives in and know a little of its puzzling problems without wanting to do his part toward keeping what is good and curing what is bad. He wants his life to count as a positive help toward a new and better order of things. He realizes with how great a sacrifice men have bought for him the gifts that his country lays at his feet, asking only that they be well used and passed on, undiminished and unhurt, to others to use after him. He does not wait for war or some other spectacular call, but stands ready to do his duty day by day, dependable and responsible and as well-informed as he can make himself.

What shall he do? First of all he must realize that his own individual character counts mightily. Every quality of honesty, trustworthiness, courage, and high idealism that he nurtures in himself contributes so much to the national character and to the sum of national strength. If he loves his country, he will not hurt it by allowing himself—the one citizen for whom he is definitely responsible—to be less noble than his utmost effort can make him. He knows that patriotism, like charity, begins at home, and that the highest gift a patriot can lay on his country's altar is that of a life lifted high above the shadow of reproach.

A good citizen holds certain civic duties to be of prime importance. He is willing to take time and trouble to see to it that the right men and women are put into places of trust and responsibility. He does not vote for any candidate simply because his own political party nominates him; he is not the dupe of any political machine. If the time comes when he himself is the best man for civic office, he is willing to make a reasonable sacrifice for the sake of service to his country. He knows that the commonwealth suffers because too many good men refuse to serve in office, leaving the business of government to professional politicians.

He uses his influence to cut down the volume and to improve the quality of legislation.[1] And knowing that our country has a bad reputation of disregarding law, he heartily supports the movement for stricter observance of law in the United States. He regards the partisan blocking of good legislation as one kind of treason. He exercises his right to criticize and to propose improvements, but he is not disloyal to the government because its officers belong to another party than his own. He keeps an eye on taxation, for he knows that it is a good citizen's duty to see that the common treasure is used economically. He fights militarism as the greatest single source of waste since time began, and supports the steps being taken toward turning the resources now devoted to war into channels of benefit to mankind. He knows that good management requires intelligence, and makes himself familiar with the principles of sound economic and political science.

But he knows, this good citizen, that with all this his duty is not done. He must do more than help correct the blunders of the past and make social life today more wholesome and happy. There is the future to be looked after, too. The children of the next generation should be better trained for their work than we have been, or can be. This means that the public-school system of America—the hope of the nation and of the world—is to be enlarged, improved, cured of its faults, and so extended that every citizen may enjoy its benefits Teachers must be better trained, schoolhouses and school grounds must be better equipped and must be made more beautiful, medical and dental

---

[1] "A passion for legislation is not a sign of democratic progress," said Charles Evans Hughes at the Harvard Law School Centenary, June 21, 1920. "In the mass of measures introduced in the legislatures of our free commonwealths, there is too little evidence of perspective, and an abundance of elaborate and dreary futilities"

care must be provided, and parents must be brought into sympathetic understanding of what is being done.

Then, having by hearty and willing service done all he can for his own generation and those that follow, the good citizen can look the world square in the face and say: "I have done my part as a citizen. I have honorably paid my debt to those who went before me by doing what I could for those yet to come." It is through the patient building of an educated and devoted citizenry, which loves its country with no jingo love, that America may some day become the land of beauty and righteousness that we would see it. And in the strength of that beauty and righteousness it may give brotherly help to every nation under heaven, even as it has drawn from the best that many nations have had to give it. In such a consummation every good citizen finds his part, by no means small, in the final goal of human happiness

"Toward which the whole creation moves."

1

BIBLIOGRAPHY[1]

ABBOTT, GRACE The Immigrant and the Community The Century Co
ADAMS, H C Description of Industry Henry Holt and Company
ADDAMS, JANE The Spirit of Youth and the City Streets The Macmillan Company
ADDAMS, JANE Democracy and Social Ethics. The Macmillan Company.
ANDERSON, W. L. The Country Town The Baker & Taylor Co
ASHLEY, PERCY Modern Tariff History. E P Dutton & Company
BAILEY, L H The Country Life Movement in the United States The Century Co
BAILEY, L H The Training of Farmers The Century Co
BALDWIN, S E. The Relation of Education to Citizenship Yale University Press
BEARD, C. A American Citizenship The Macmillan Company.
BEARD, C A American Government and Politics The Macmillan Company
BEARD, MARY. The American Labor Movement Harcourt, Brace and Company
BISHOP and KELLER Industry and Trade Ginn and Company
BOGART, E L. Economic History of the United States Longmans, Green & Co.
BOGART and THOMPSON Readings in the Economic History of the United States. Longmans, Green & Co
BOOTH, M. B After Prison—What? Fleming H Revell Company
BRIGHAM, A P Commercial Geography (New Edition) Ginn and Company.
BRYCE, JAMES The American Commonwealth The Macmillan Company
BRYCE, JAMES. Modern Democracies The Macmillan Company

---

[1] This list is suggestive of what a high-school library should contain Many of the books have been referred to repeatedly in the text, others not at all In the case of books used in the problems and the supplementary readings, but not given here, it will be found best in all but very large schools to depend upon a public library for their occasional use, stocking the school library with books for which there will be a more frequent call.

i

BULLOCK, C. J. Elements of Economics (Revised Edition). Silver, Burdett & Company

BULLOCK, C J. Selected Readings in Economics Ginn and Company.

BURCH, H R. American Economic Life The Macmillan Company.

BURCH and PATTERSON American Social Problems. The Macmillan Company

✓ BURCH and PATTERSON Problems of American Democracy. The Macmillan Company

BURRIT, A W, et al Profit Sharing, its Principles and Practice Harper & Brothers

BUTTERFIELD, K L The Farmer and the New Day. The Macmillan Company

CALLENDER, G S. Selections from the Economic History of the United States. Ginn and Company

CARVER, T. N. Elementary Economics Ginn and Company.

CARVER, T N Principles of National Economy Ginn and Company

CARVER, T N. Principles of Rural Economics Ginn and Company.

CHAPIN, F. S Introduction to the Study of Social Evolution. The Century Co

CHEYNEY, E P An Introduction to the Industrial and Social History of England (1920 revision). The Macmillan Company

CHEYNEY, E P Readings in English History Ginn and Company

CHEYNEY, E P. Short History of England (1920 revision) Ginn and Company

CLEVELAND, F H Organized Democracy Longmans, Green & Co.

COMAN, K The Industrial History of the United States. The Macmillan Company.

COMMONS, J. R Trade Unionism and Labor Problems (1921 edition) Ginn and Company

CONYNGTON, MARY How to Help. The Ronald Press Company.

DAY, CLIVE History of Commerce Longmans, Green & Co

DEVINE, E T Principles of Relief The Macmillan Company.

DRYER, C R Elementary Economic Geography. American Book Company

DUGDALE, R L The Jukes, a Study in Crime, Pauperism, Disease, and Heredity G. P Putnam's Sons.

DUNN, A W The Community and the Citizen D. C. Heath & Co

ELLWOOD, C A. Sociology and Modern Social Problems. American Book Company

FAIRBANKS, ARTHUR. Introduction to Sociology. Charles Scribner's Sons

BIBLIOGRAPHY

FETTER, F. A Modern Economic Problems The Century Co
FORMAN, S E The American Republic The Century Co
GEORGE, W. R The Junior Republic, Its History and Ideals D. Appleton and Company
GETTELL, R G Problems in Political Evolution. Ginn and Company.
GIDDINGS, F. H Elements of Sociology. The Macmillan Company
GILL and PINCHOT The Country Church The Macmillan Company.
GILLETTE, J M Constructive Rural Sociology Sturgis and Walton Co
HALL, P F. Immigration and its Effects on the United States. Henry Holt and Company
HAMILTON, W H Current Economic Problems The University of Chicago Press
HAYES, B T American Democracy Henry Holt and Company
HAYES, E. C Introduction to the Study of Sociology D. Appleton and Company.
HENDERSON, C R Modern Prison Systems. Government Printing Office
HILL, H C Community Life and Civic Problems Ginn and Company
HUGHES, R. O Problems of American Democracy. Allyn and Bacon
JAMES, H G Local Government in the United States D Appleton and Company
JENKS, J N Principles of Politics Columbia University Press
JENKS and LAUT The Immigration Problem (4th edition) Funk & Wagnalls Company
JOHNSON, J F Money and Currency (1921 edition) Ginn and Company
KELLY, FLORENCE Some Ethical Gains through Legislation The Macmillan Company
KEMMERER, E W The A B C of the Federal Reserve System. Princeton University Press
LAPP, J. A Economics and the Community. The Century Co
LEACOCK, STEPHEN Elements of Political Science Houghton Mifflin Company
LOWELL, A L Public Opinion and Popular Government Longmans, Green & Co
MAGRUDER, F A American Government Allyn and Bacon
MARSHALL, L C, WRIGHT, C W, and FIELD, J A Materials for the Study of Elementary Economics. The University of Chicago Press
MUNRO, W B The Government of American Cities The Macmillan Company.
PERRY, C. A A Wider Use of the School Plant The Charities Publishing Committee, New York City.

OSGOOD, E. L. A History of Industry Ginn and Company
PORTER, R. P. The Dangers of Municipal Ownership The Century Co.
RIIS, J A. The Battle with the Slum The Macmillan Company
ROBINSON, BREASTED, and SMITH General History of Europe Ginn and Company.
ROBINSON and BEARD History of Europe· Our Own Times Ginn and Company
SCHAPIRO, J. S. Modern and Contemporary Europe Houghton, Mifflin Company.
SEYMOUR, C. How the World Votes C A Nichols.
SHURTER and TAYLOR Both Sides of One Hundred Public Questions Hinds, Hayden, and Eldredge, Inc
SMITH, J RUSSELL. Commerce and Industry. Henry Holt and Company
SMITH, R H Justice and the Poor Carnegie Foundation
THOMPSON, C. M Elementary Economics. B H Sanborn and Company
TILLINGHAST, J. A. The Negro in Africa and America American Economic Association, New York
TOWNE, E T Social Problems The Macmillan Company
TUFTS, J H The Real Business of Living. Henry Holt and Company.
VAN HISE, C. R Concentration and Control The Macmillan Company
WASHINGTON, B T The Future of the American Negro. Small, Maynard and Company
WEBSTER, W. C General History of Commerce Ginn and Company
WELD, L. D The Marketing of Farm Products. The Macmillan Company
WEST, W. M. Modern Progress Allyn and Bacon
WEST, W M. The War and the New Age Allyn and Bacon.
WHITE, A B. The Making of the English Constitution. G. P Putnam's Sons
WILLIAMSON, T. R. Problems in American Democracy D C. Heath & Co.

APPENDIX A

CONSTITUTION OF THE UNITED STATES

Preamble

We, the people of the United States, in order to form a more perfect union, establish justice, insure domestic tranquillity, provide for the common defense, promote the general welfare, and secure the blessings of liberty to ourselves and our posterity, do ordain and establish this CONSTITUTION for the United States of America

ARTICLE I. LEGISLATIVE DEPARTMENT

Section 1. Congress

All legislative powers herein granted shall be vested in a Congress of the United States, which shall consist of a Senate and House of Representatives [1]

Section 2. House of Representatives

Election of Members. The House of Representatives shall be composed of members chosen every second year by the people of the several States, and the electors in each State shall have the qualifications requisite for electors of the most numerous branch of the State Legislature

Qualifications. No person shall be a representative who shall not have attained to the age of twenty-five years, and been seven years a citizen of the United States, and who shall not, when elected, be an inhabitant of that State in which he shall be chosen

Apportionment. Representatives and direct taxes shall be apportioned among the several States which may be included within this Union, according to their respective numbers,[2] which shall be determined by adding to the whole number of free persons, including those bound to service for a term of years, and excluding Indians not taxed, three-fifths of all other persons [3] The actual

---

[1] The term of each Congress is two years It assembles on the first Monday in December and "expires at noon of the fourth of March next succeeding the beginning of its second regular session, when a new Congress begins"

[2] The apportionment under the census of 1910 is one representative for every 212,407 persons

[3] The word "persons" refers to slaves The word "slave" nowhere appears in the Constitution This paragraph has been amended (Amendments XIII and XIV) **and is no longer in force.**

APPENDIX A

enumeration shall be made within three years after the first meeting of the Congress of the United States, and within every subsequent term of ten years, in such manner as they shall by law direct The number of representatives shall not exceed one for every thirty thousand, but each State shall have at least one representative. and until such enumeration shall be made, the State of New Hampshire shall be entitled to choose three; Massachusetts, eight; Rhode Island and Providence Plantations, one, Connecticut, five, New York, six, New Jersey, four; Pennsylvania, eight, Delaware, one, Maryland, six, Virginia, ten, North Carolina, five; South Carolina, five, and Georgia, three

Vacancies. When vacancies happen in the representation from any State, the executive authority[1] thereof shall issue writs of election to fill such vacancies

Officers. Impeachment. The House of Representatives shall choose their Speaker[2] and other officers, and shall have the sole power of impeachment.

SECTION 3. SENATE

Number of Senators: Election. The Senate of the United States shall be composed of two senators from each State, chosen by the Legislature thereof, for six years, and each senator shall have one vote. [Repealed in 1913 by Amendment XVII]

Classification. Immediately after they shall be assembled in consequence of the first election, they shall be divided as equally as may be into three classes. The seats of the senators of the first class shall be vacated at the expiration of the second year, of the second class, at the expiration of the fourth year; of the third class, at the expiration of the sixth year, so that one-third may be chosen every second year, and if vacancies happen by resignation, or otherwise, during the recess of the Legislature of any State, the executive[1] thereof may make temporary appointments until the next meeting of the Legislature, which shall then fill such vacancies. [Modified by Amendment XVII]

Qualifications. No person shall be a senator who shall not have attained to the age of thirty years, and been nine years a citizen of the United States, and who shall not, when elected, be an inhabitant of that State for which he shall be chosen.

President of Senate. The Vice-President of the United States shall be president of the Senate, but shall have no vote, unless they be equally divided.

Officers. The Senate shall choose their other officers, and also a president *pro tempore*, in the absence of the Vice-President, or when he shall exercise the office of President of the United States

Trials of Impeachment. The Senate shall have the sole power to try all impeachments When sitting for that purpose, they shall be on oath or affirmation

---

[1] Governor

[2] The Speaker, who presides, is one of the representatives, the other officers — clerk, sergeant-at-arms, postmaster, chaplain, doorkeeper, etc — are not.

When the President of the United States is tried, the Chief-Justice shall preside: and no person shall be convicted without the concurrence of two-thirds of the members present

Judgment in Case of Conviction. Judgment in cases of impeachment shall not extend further than to removal from office, and disqualification to hold and enjoy any office of honor, trust, or profit under the United States; but the party convicted shall nevertheless be liable and subject to indictment, trial, judgment, and punishment, according to law.

SECTION 4. BOTH HOUSES

Manner of electing Members. The times, places, and manner of holding elections for senators and representatives shall be prescribed in each State by the Legislature thereof, but the Congress may at any time, by law, make or alter such regulations, except as to the places of choosing senators.[1]

Meetings of Congress. The Congress shall assemble at least once in every year, and such meeting shall be on the first Monday in December, unless they shall by law appoint a different day

SECTION 5 THE HOUSES SEPARATELY

Organization. Each house shall be the judge of the elections, returns, and qualifications of its own members, and a majority of each shall constitute a quorum to do business; but a smaller number may adjourn from day to day, and may be authorized to compel the attendance of absent members, in such manner, and under such penalties, as each house may provide

Rules. Each house may determine the rules of its proceedings, punish its members for disorderly behavior, and, with the concurrence of two-thirds, expel a member

Journal. Each house shall keep a journal of its proceedings, and from time to time publish the same, excepting such parts as may in their judgment require secrecy, and the yeas and nays of the members of either house on any question shall, at the desire of one-fifth of those present, be entered on the journal.

Adjournment. Neither house, during the session of Congress, shall, without the consent of the other, adjourn for more than three days, nor to any other place than that in which the two houses shall be sitting.

SECTION 6. PRIVILEGES AND DISABILITIES OF MEMBERS

Pay and Privileges of Members. The senators and representatives shall receive a compensation for their services, to be ascertained by law, and paid out of the treasury of the United States. They shall in all cases, except treason, felony, and breach of the peace, be privileged from arrest during their

---

[1] This is to prevent Congress from fixing the places of meeting of the state legislatures.

attendance at the session of their respective houses, and in going to and returning from the same; and for any speech or debate in either house, they shall not be questioned in any other place.

Prohibitions on Members. No senator or representative shall, during the time for which he was elected, be appointed to any civil office under the authority of the United States, which shall have been created, or the emoluments whereof shall have been increased, during such time; and no person holding any office under the United States shall be a member of either house during his continuance in office.

Section 7. Method of passing Laws

Revenue Bills. All bills for raising revenue shall originate in the House of Representatives; but the Senate may propose or concur with amendments as on other bills.

How Bills become Laws. Every bill which shall have passed the House of Representatives and the Senate shall, before it become a law, be presented to the President of the United States if he approve, he shall sign it, but if not, he shall return it, with his objections, to that house in which it shall have originated, who shall enter the objections at large on their journal, and proceed to reconsider it. If after such reconsideration, two-thirds of that house shall agree to pass the bill, it shall be sent, together with the objections, to the other house, by which it shall likewise be reconsidered, and if approved by two-thirds of that house, it shall become a law. But in all such cases the votes of both houses shall be determined by yeas and nays, and the names of the persons voting for and against the bill shall be entered on the journal of each house respectively. If any bill shall not be returned by the President within ten days (Sundays excepted) after it shall have been presented to him, the same shall be a law, in like manner as if he had signed it, unless the Congress by their adjournment prevent its return, in which case it shall not be a law.

Resolutions, etc. Every order, resolution, or vote to which the concurrence of the Senate and House of Representatives may be necessary (except on a question of adjournment) shall be presented to the President of the United States; and before the same shall take effect, shall be approved by him, or being disapproved by him, shall be repassed by two-thirds of the Senate and House of Representatives, according to the rules and limitations prescribed in the case of a bill.

Section 8. Powers granted to Congress

Powers of Congress. The Congress shall have power:

To lay and collect taxes, duties, imposts, and excises, to pay the debts and provide for the common defense and general welfare of the United States; but all duties, imposts, and excises shall be uniform throughout the United States;

To borrow money on the credit of the United States;
To regulate commerce with foreign nations, and among the several States, and with the Indian tribes;
To establish a uniform rule of naturalization, and uniform laws on the subject of bankruptcies throughout the United States;
To coin money, regulate the value thereof, and of foreign coin, and fix the standard of weights and measures;
To provide for the punishment of counterfeiting the securities and current coin of the United States;
To establish post-offices and post-roads;
To promote the progress of science and useful arts, by securing, for limited times, to authors and inventors the exclusive right to their respective writings and discoveries;
To constitute tribunals inferior to the Supreme Court;
To define and punish piracies and felonies committed on the high seas, and offenses against the law of nations;
To declare war, grant letters of marque and reprisal,[1] and make rules concerning captures on land and water;
To raise and support armies, but no appropriation of money to that use shall be for a longer term than two years;
To provide and maintain a navy;
To make rules for the government and regulation of the land and naval forces;
To provide for calling forth the militia to execute the laws of the Union, suppress insurrections and repel invasions;
To provide for organizing, arming, and disciplining the militia, and for governing such part of them as may be employed in the service of the United States, reserving to the States respectively the appointment of the officers, and the authority of training the militia according to the discipline prescribed by Congress;
To exercise exclusive legislation in all cases whatsoever over such district (not exceeding ten miles square) as may, by cession of particular States, and the acceptance of Congress, become the seat of the government of the United States,[2] and to exercise like authority over all places purchased by the consent of the Legislature of the State in which the same shall be, for the erection of forts, magazines, arsenals, dockyards, and other needful buildings; — And

Implied Powers. To make all laws which shall be necessary and proper for carrying into execution the foregoing powers, and all other powers vested by this Constitution in the government of the United States, or in any department or officer thereof.[3]

[1] Letters granted by the government to private citizens in time of war, authorizing them, under certain conditions, to capture the ships of the enemy.
[2] The District of Columbia.
[3] This is the famous elastic clause of the Constitution.

APPENDIX A

Section 9. Powers forbidden to the United States

Absolute Prohibitions on Congress. The migration or importation of such persons as any of the States now existing shall think proper to admit, shall not be prohibited by the Congress prior to the year one thousand eight hundred and eight, but a tax or duty may be imposed on such importation, not exceeding ten dollars for each person [1]

The privilege of the writ of habeas corpus [2] shall not be suspended, unless when in cases of rebellion or invasion the public safety may require it.

No bill of attainder [3] or ex-post-facto law [4] shall be passed.

No capitation or other direct tax shall be laid, unless in proportion to the census or enumeration hereinbefore directed to be taken [Extended by Amendment XVI.]

No tax or duty shall be laid on articles exported from any State.

No preference shall be given by any regulation of commerce or revenue to the ports of one State over those of another; nor shall vessels bound to, or from, one State, be obliged to enter, clear, or pay duties in another

No money shall be drawn from the treasury but in consequence of appropriations made by law, and a regular statement and account of the receipts and expenditures of all public money shall be published from time to time.

No title of nobility shall be granted by the United States: And no person holding any office of profit or trust under them, shall, without the consent of the Congress, accept of any present, emolument, office, or title, of any kind whatever, from any king, prince, or foreign state.

Section 10. Powers forbidden to the States

Absolute Prohibitions on the States. No State shall enter into any treaty, alliance, or confederation, grant letters of marque and reprisal, coin money; emit bills of credit; make anything but gold and silver coin a tender in payment of debts; pass any bill of attainder, ex-post-facto law, or law impairing the obligation of contracts, or grant any title of nobility

Conditional Prohibitions on the States. No State shall, without the consent of the Congress, lay any imposts or duties on imports or exports, except what may be absolutely necessary for executing its inspection laws, and the net produce of all duties and imposts, laid by any State on imports or exports,

---

[1] This refers to the foreign slave trade "Persons" means "slaves" In 1808 Congress prohibited the importation of slaves. This clause is, of course, no longer in force.

[2] An official document requiring an accused person who is in prison awaiting trial to be brought into court to inquire whether he may be legally held.

[3] A special legislative act by which a person may be condemned to death or to outlawry or banishment without the opportunity of defending himself which he would have in a court of law

[4] A law relating to the punishment of acts committed before the law was passed.

shall be for the use of the treasury of the United States; and all such laws shall be subject to the revision and control of the Congress

No State shall, without the consent of Congress, lay any duty of tonnage, keep troops, or ships-of-war, in time of peace, enter into any agreement or compact with another State, or with a foreign power, or engage in war, unless actually invaded, or in such imminent danger as will not admit of delay.

ARTICLE II. EXECUTIVE DEPARTMENT

SECTION I. PRESIDENT AND VICE-PRESIDENT

Term. The executive power shall be vested in a President of the United States of America He shall hold his office during the term of four years, and, together with the Vice-President, chosen for the same term, be elected, as follows:

Electors. Each State shall appoint, in such manner as the Legislature thereof may direct, a number of electors, equal to the whole number of senators and representatives to which the State may be entitled in the Congress but no senator or representative, or person holding an office of trust or profit under the United States, shall be appointed an elector.

Proceedings of Electors and of Congress. [[1] The electors shall meet in their respective States, and vote by ballot for two persons, of whom one at least shall not be an inhabitant of the same State with themselves And they shall make a list of all the persons voted for, and of the number of votes for each; which list they shall sign and certify and transmit sealed to the seat of the government of the United States, directed to the president of the Senate The president of the Senate shall, in the presence of the Senate and House of Representatives, open all the certificates, and the votes shall then be counted The person having the greatest number of votes shall be the President, if such number be a majority of the whole number of electors appointed; and if there be more than one who have such majority, and have an equal number of votes, then the House of Representatives shall immediately choose by ballot one of them for President, and if no person have a majority, then from the five highest on the list the said house shall, in like manner, choose the President. But in choosing the President, the votes shall be taken by States, the representation from each State having one vote, a quorum for this purpose shall consist of a member or members from two-thirds of the States, and a majority of all the States shall be necessary to a choice In every case, after the choice of the President, the person having the greatest number of votes of the electors shall be the Vice-President But if there should remain two or more who have equal votes, the Senate shall choose from them by ballot the Vice-President]

[1] This paragraph in brackets has been superseded by the Twelfth Amendment.

APPENDIX A

Time of choosing Electors. The Congress may determine the time of choosing the electors, and the day on which they shall give their votes; which day shall be the same throughout the United States [1]

Qualifications of President. No person except a natural born citizen, or a citizen of the United States at the time of the adoption of this Constitution, shall be eligible to the office of President; neither shall any person be eligible to that office who shall not have attained to the age of thirty-five years, and been fourteen years resident within the United States

Vacancy. In case of the removal of the President from office, or of his death, resignation, or inability to discharge the powers and duties of the said office, the same shall devolve on the Vice-President, and the Congress may by law provide for the case of removal, death, resignation, or inability, both of the President and Vice-President, declaring what officer shall then act as President; and such officer shall act accordingly until the disability be removed, or a President shall be elected [2]

Salary. The President shall, at stated times, receive for his services a compensation which shall neither be increased nor diminished during the period for which he shall have been elected, and he shall not receive within that period any other emolument from the United States, or any of them.

Oath Before he enter on the execution of his office, he shall take the following oath or affirmation — "I do solemnly swear (or affirm) that I will faithfully execute the office of President of the United States, and will, to the best of my ability, preserve, protect, and defend the Constitution of the United States"

Section 2. Powers of the President

Military Powers; Reprieves and Pardons. The President shall be commander-in-chief of the army and navy of the United States, and of the militia of the several States, when called into the actual service of the United States; he may require the opinion, in writing, of the principal officer in each of the executive departments, upon any subject relating to the duties of their respective offices; and he shall have power to grant reprieves and pardons for offenses against the United States, except in cases of impeachment.

Treaties; Appointments. He shall have power, by and with the advice and consent of the Senate, to make treaties, provided two-thirds of the senators present concur; and he shall nominate, and by and with the advice and consent of the Senate shall appoint ambassadors, other public ministers and consuls, judges of the Supreme Court, and all other officers of the United

---

[1] The electors are chosen on the Tuesday next after the first Monday in November, preceding the expiration of a presidential term They vote (by Act of Congress of February 3, 1887) on the second Monday in January for President and Vice-President The votes are counted, and declared in Congress on the second Wednesday of the following February

[2] This has now been provided for by the Presidential Succession Act of 1886.

CONSTITUTION OF THE UNITED STATES

States, whose appointments are not herein otherwise provided for, and which shall be established by law. but the Congress may by law vest the appointment of such inferior officers, as they think proper, in the President alone, in the courts of law, or in the heads of departments.

Filling of Vacancies. The President shall have power to fill up all vacancies that may happen during the recess of the Senate, by granting commissions which shall expire at the end of their next session.

SECTION 3 DUTIES OF THE PRESIDENT

Message; Convening of Congress. He shall from time to time give to the Congress information [1] of the state of the Union, and recommend to their consideration such measures as he shall judge necessary and expedient; he may, on extraordinary occasions, convene both houses, or either of them, and in case of disagreement between them with respect to the time of adjournment, he may adjourn them to such time as he shall think proper; he shall receive ambassadors and other public ministers, he shall take care that the laws be faithfully executed, and shall commission all the officers of the United States.

SECTION 4. IMPEACHMENT

Removal of Officers. The President, Vice-President, and all civil officers of the United States, shall be removed from office on impeachment for, and conviction of, treason, bribery, or other high crimes and misdemeanors.

ARTICLE III JUDICIAL DEPARTMENT

SECTION 1. UNITED STATES COURTS

Courts established, Judges. The judicial power of the United States shall be vested in one Supreme Court, and in such inferior courts as the Congress may from time to time ordain and establish The judges, both of the Supreme and inferior courts, shall hold their offices during good behavior, and shall, at stated times, receive for their services a compensation which shall not be diminished during their continuance in office.

SECTION 2. JURISDICTION OF UNITED STATES COURTS

Federal Courts in General. The judicial power shall extend to all cases, in law and equity, arising under this Constitution, the laws of the United States, and treaties made, or which shall be made, under their authority, — to all cases

---

[1] The president gives this information through a message to Congress at the opening of each session Washington and John Adams read their messages in person to Congress Jefferson, however, sent a written message to Congress This method was followed until President Wilson returned to the earlier custom.

affecting ambassadors, other public ministers, and consuls; — to all cases of admiralty and maritime jurisdiction; — to controversies to which the United States shall be a party; — to controversies between two or more States; — between a State and citizens of another State;[1] — between citizens of different States; — between citizens of the same State claiming lands under grants of different States, and between a State, or the citizens thereof, and foreign states, citizens or subjects.

Supreme Court. In all cases affecting ambassadors, other public ministers and consuls, and those in which a State shall be party, the Supreme Court shall have original jurisdiction. In all other cases before mentioned, the Supreme Court shall have appellate jurisdiction, both as to law and fact, with such exceptions and under such regulations as the Congress shall make.

Trials. The trial of all crimes, except in cases of impeachment, shall be by jury; and such trial shall be held in the State where the said crimes shall have been committed; but when not committed within any State, the trial shall be at such place or places as the Congress may by law have directed.

Section 3. Treason

Treason defined. Treason against the United States shall consist only in levying war against them, or in adhering to their enemies, giving them aid and comfort.

No person shall be convicted of treason unless on the testimony of two witnesses to the same overt act, or on confession in open court.

Punishment. The Congress shall have power to declare the punishment of treason, but no attainder of treason shall work corruption of blood, or forfeiture, except during the life of the person attainted.

ARTICLE IV. RELATIONS OF THE STATES TO EACH OTHER

Section 1. Official Acts

Full faith and credit shall be given in each State to the public acts, records, and judicial proceedings of every other State. And the Congress may by general laws, prescribe the manner in which such acts, records, and proceedings shall be proved, and the effect thereof.

Section 2. Privileges of Citizens

The citizens of each State shall be entitled to all privileges and immunities of citizens in the several States.

Fugitives from Justice. A person charged in any State with treason, felony, or other crime, who shall flee from justice, and be found in another State,

---

[1] This has been modified by the Eleventh Amendment.

CONSTITUTION OF THE UNITED STATES

shall, on demand of the executive authority of the State from which he fled, be delivered up, to be removed to the State having jurisdiction of the crime

Fugitive Slaves. No person[1] held to service or labor in one State, under the laws thereof, escaping into another, shall, in consequence of any law or regulation therein, be discharged from such service or labor, but shall be delivered up on claim of the party to whom such service or labor may be due.

Section 3. New States and Territories

Admission of States. New States may be admitted by the Congress into this Union, but no new State shall be formed or erected within the jurisdiction of any other State, nor any State be formed by the junction of two or more States, or parts of States, without the consent of the Legislatures of the States concerned as well as of the Congress

Territory and Property of United States. The Congress shall have power to dispose of and make all needful rules and regulations respecting the territory or other property belonging to the United States, and nothing in this Constitution shall be so construed as to prejudice any claims of the United States, or of any particular State.

Section 4. Protection of the States

The United States shall guarantee to every State in this Union a republican form of government, and shall protect each of them against invasion, and on application of the Legislature, or of the Executive (when the Legislature cannot be convened) against domestic violence.

ARTICLE V. AMENDMENTS

How proposed; how ratified. The Congress, whenever two-thirds of both houses shall deem it necessary, shall propose amendments to this Constitution, or, on the application of the Legislatures of two-thirds of the several States, shall call a convention for proposing amendments, which, in either case, shall be valid to all intents and purposes, as part of this Constitution, when ratified by the Legislatures of three-fourths of the several States, or by conventions in three-fourths thereof, as the one or the other mode of ratification may be proposed by the Congress; provided that no amendment which

---

[1] "Person" here includes slave This was the basis of the Fugitive Slave Laws of 1793 and 1850 It is now superseded by the Thirteenth Amendment, by which slavery is prohibited

may be made prior to the year one thousand eight hundred and eight shall in any manner affect the first and fourth clauses in the ninth section of the first article; and that no State, without its consent, shall be deprived of its equal suffrage in the Senate.

ARTICLE VI. GENERAL PROVISIONS

Public Debt. All debts contracted, and engagements entered into, before the adoption of this Constitution, shall be as valid against the United States under this Constitution, as under the Confederation.

Supremacy of Constitution. This Constitution, and the laws of the United States which shall be made in pursuance thereof; and all treaties made, or which shall be made, under the authority of the United States, shall be the supreme law of the land; and the judges in every State shall be bound thereby, anything in the Constitution or laws of any State to the contrary notwithstanding.

Official Oath; Religious Test. The senators and representatives before mentioned, and the members of the several State Legislatures, and all executive and judicial officers, both of the United States and of the several States, shall be bound by oath or affirmation to support this Constitution; but no religious test shall ever be required as a qualification to any office or public trust under the United States.

ARTICLE VII. RATIFICATION OF THE CONSTITUTION

Ratification. The ratification of the Conventions of nine States shall be sufficient for the establishment of this Constitution between the States so ratifying the same.

> Done in convention, by the unanimous consent of the States present, the seventeenth day of September, in the year of our Lord one thousand seven hundred and eighty-seven, and of the independence of the United States of America the twelfth.

In witness whereof, we have hereunto subscribed our names.[1]

GEORGE WASHINGTON,
President, and Deputy from Virginia.

---

[1] There were sixty-five delegates chosen to the convention: ten did not attend; sixteen declined or failed to sign; thirty-nine signed. Rhode Island sent no delegates.

CONSTITUTION OF THE UNITED STATES

NEW HAMPSHIRE	PENNSYLVANIA	VIRGINIA
John Langdon	Benjamin Franklin	John Blair
Nicholas Gilman	Thomas Mifflin	James Madison, Jr
	Robert Morris	
MASSACHUSETTS	George Clymer	NORTH CAROLINA
Nathaniel Gorham	Thomas Fitzsimons	William Blount
Rufus King	Jared Ingersoll	Richard Dobbs Spaight
	James Wilson	Hugh Williamson
CONNECTICUT	Gouverneur Morris	
William Samuel Johnson	DELAWARE	
Roger Sherman	George Read	SOUTH CAROLINA
	Gunning Bedford, Jr	John Rutledge
NEW YORK	John Dickinson	Charles C. Pinckney
Alexander Hamilton	Richard Bassett	Charles Pinckney
	Jacob Broom	Pierce Butler
NEW JERSEY	MARYLAND	
William Livingston	James M'Henry	
David Brearley	Daniel of St Thomas	GEORGIA
William Paterson	Jenifer	William Few
Jonathan Dayton	Daniel Carroll	Abraham Baldwin

Attest WILLIAM JACKSON, *Secretary*

AMENDMENTS

Religion, Speech, Press, Assembly, Petition. ARTICLE I[1] Congress shall make no law respecting an establishment of religion, or prohibiting the free exercise thereof, or abridging the freedom of speech, or of the press; or the right of the people peaceably to assemble, and to petition the government for redress of grievances

Militia. ARTICLE II A well-regulated militia being necessary to the security of a free State the right of the people to keep and bear arms shall not be infringed

Soldiers. ARTICLE III No soldier shall, in time of peace, be quartered in any house, without the consent of the owner; nor in time of war but in a manner to be prescribed by law.

Unreasonable Searches. ARTICLE IV The right of the people to be secure in their persons, houses, papers, and effects, against unreasonable searches and seizures, shall not be violated, and no warrants shall issue, but upon

---

[1] These amendments were proposed by Congress and ratified by the legislatures of the several states, pursuant to the fifth article of the Constitution The first ten were offered in 1789 and adopted before the close of 1791 They were for the most part the work of Madison They are frequently called the Bill of Rights, as their purpose is to guard more efficiently the rights of the people and of the states.

probable cause, supported by oath or affirmation, and particularly describing the place to be searched, and the persons or things to be seized.

Criminal Prosecutions. ARTICLE V. No person shall be held to answer for a capital, or otherwise infamous crime, unless on a presentment or indictment of a grand jury, except in cases arising in the land or naval forces, or in the militia, when in actual service in time of war and public danger; nor shall any person be subject for the same offense to be twice put in jeopardy of life or limb; nor shall be compelled in any criminal case to be a witness against himself, nor be deprived of life, liberty, or property, without due process of law; nor shall private property be taken for public use, without just compensation.

ARTICLE VI. In all criminal prosecutions, the accused shall enjoy the right to a speedy and public trial, by an impartial jury of the State and district wherein the crime shall have been committed, which district shall have been previously ascertained by law, and to be informed of the nature and cause of the accusation; to be confronted with the witnesses against him; to have compulsory process for obtaining witnesses in his favor, and to have the assistance of counsel for his defense.

Suits at Common Law. ARTICLE VII. In suits at common law, where the value in controversy shall exceed twenty dollars, the right of trial by jury shall be preserved, and no fact tried by a jury shall be otherwise reëxamined in any court of the United States than according to the rules of common law.

Bail, Punishments. ARTICLE VIII. Excessive bail shall not be required, nor excessive fines imposed, nor cruel and unusual punishments inflicted.

Reserved Rights and Powers. ARTICLE IX. The enumeration in the Constitution of certain rights shall not be construed to deny or disparage others retained by the people.

ARTICLE X. The powers not delegated to the United States by the Constitution, nor prohibited by it to the States, are reserved to the States respectively, or to the people.

Suits against States. ARTICLE XI.[1] The judicial power of the United States shall not be construed to extend to any suit in law or equity, commenced or prosecuted against any of the United States by citizens of another State, or by citizens or subjects of any foreign state.

Method of electing President and Vice-President. ARTICLE XII.[2] The electors shall meet in their respective States, and vote by ballot for President and Vice-President, one of whom, at least, shall not be an inhabitant of the same State with themselves; they shall name in their ballots the person voted for as President, and in distinct ballots the person voted for as Vice-President; and they shall make distinct lists of all persons voted for as President, and of all persons voted for as Vice-President, and of the number of votes for each, which list they shall sign and certify, and transmit sealed to the seat of the government of the United States, directed to the president of the Senate; —

[1] Proposed in 1794; ratified in 1798.   [2] Ratified in 1804.

CONSTITUTION OF THE UNITED STATES

the president of the Senate shall, in the presence of the Senate and House of Representatives, open all the certificates, and the votes shall then be counted, — the person having the greatest number of votes for President, shall be the President, if such number be a majority of the whole number of electors appointed, and if no person have such majority, then from the persons having the highest numbers not exceeding three on the list of those voted for as President, the House of Representatives shall choose immediately, by ballot, the President But in choosing the President, the votes shall be taken by States, the representation from each State having one vote; a quorum for this purpose shall consist of a member or members from two-thirds of the States, and a majority of all the States shall be necessary to a choice And if the House of Representatives shall not choose a President whenever the right of choice shall devolve upon them, before the fourth day of March next following, then the Vice-President shall act as President, as in the case of the death or other constitutional disability of the President The person having the greatest number of votes as Vice-President, shall be the Vice-President, if such number be a majority of the whole number of electors appointed; and if no person have a majority, then from the two highest numbers on the list, the Senate shall choose the Vice-President, a quorum for the purpose shall consist of two-thirds of the whole number of senators, and a majority of the whole number shall be necessary to a choice. But no person constitutionally ineligible to the office of President shall be eligible to that of Vice-President of the United States.

Slavery abolished. ARTICLE XIII [1] *Section 1* Neither slavery nor involuntary servitude, except as a punishment for crime, whereof the party shall have been duly convicted, shall exist within the United States, or any place subject to their jurisdiction.

Section 2 Congress shall have power to enforce this article by appropriate legislation

Negroes made Citizens ARTICLE XIV [2] *Section 1* All persons born or naturalized in the United States, and subject to the jurisdiction thereof, are citizens of the United States and of the State wherein they reside. No State shall make or enforce any law which shall abridge the privileges or immunities of citizens of the United States, nor shall any State deprive any person of life, liberty, or property, without due process of law, nor deny to any person within its jurisdiction the equal protection of the laws.

Section 2. Representatives shall be apportioned among the several States according to their respective numbers, counting the whole number of persons in each State, excluding Indians not taxed But when the right to vote at any election for the choice of electors for President and Vice-President of the United States, representatives in Congress, the executive or judicial officers of a State, or the members of the Legislature thereof, is denied to any of the male inhabitants of such State, being twenty-one years of age, and citizens of

[1] Ratified in 1865 [2] Ratified in 1868.

the United States, or in any way abridged, except for participation in rebellion or other crime, the basis of representation therein shall be reduced in the proportion which the number of such male citizens shall bear to the whole number of male citizens twenty-one years of age in such State.

Section 3. No person shall be a senator or representative in Congress, or elector of President or Vice-President, or hold any office, civil or military, under the United States, or under any State, who having previously taken an oath as a member of Congress, or as an officer of the United States, or as a member of any State Legislature, or as an executive or judicial officer of any State, to support the Constitution of the United States, shall have engaged in insurrection or rebellion against the same, or given aid or comfort to the enemies thereof. But Congress may, by a vote of two-thirds of each house, remove such disability.

Section 4. The validity of the public debt of the United States, authorized by law, including debts incurred for payment of pensions and bounties for services in suppressing insurrection or rebellion, shall not be questioned. But neither the United States nor any State shall assume or pay any debt or obligation incurred in aid of insurrection or rebellion against the United States, or any claim for the loss or emancipation of any slave; but all such debts, obligations, and claims shall be held illegal and void.

Section 5. The Congress shall have power to enforce, by appropriate legislation, the provisions of this article.

Negroes made Voters. ARTICLE XV.[1] *Section 1.* The rights of citizens of the United States to vote shall not be denied or abridged by the United States, or by any State, on account of race, color, or previous condition of servitude.

Section 2. The Congress shall have power to enforce this article by appropriate legislation.

Income Tax. ARTICLE XVI.[2] The Congress shall have power to lay and collect taxes on incomes from whatever source derived, without apportionment among the several States, and without regard to any census or enumeration.

ARTICLE XVII.[2] The Senate of the United States shall be composed of two Senators from each State, elected by the people thereof for six years; and each Senator shall have one vote. The electors in each State shall have the qualifications requisite for electors of the most numerous branch of the State Legislatures.

Direct Election of Senators. When vacancies happen in the representation of any State in the Senate, the executive authority of such State shall issue writs of election to fill such vacancies: Provided, that the Legislature of any State may empower the Executive thereof to make temporary appointments until the people fill the vacancies by election as the Legislature may direct.

This amendment shall not be so construed as to affect the election or term of any Senator chosen before it becomes valid as part of the Constitution.

[1] Ratified in 1870.   [2] Ratified in 1913.

National Prohibition. ARTICLE XVIII [1] *Section 1.* After one year from the ratification of this article the manufacture, sale, or transportation of intoxicating liquors within, the importation thereof into, or the exportation thereof from the United States and all territory subject to the jurisdiction thereof for beverage purposes is hereby prohibited.

Section 2. The Congress and the several States shall have concurrent power to enforce this article by appropriate legislation.

Section 3. This article shall be inoperative unless it shall have been ratified as an amendment to the Constitution by the Legislatures of the several States, as provided in the Constitution, within seven years from the date of the submission hereof to the States by the Congress

Woman Suffrage. ARTICLE XIX [2] *Section 1.* The right of citizens of the United States to vote shall not be denied or abridged by the United States or by any State on account of sex.

Section 2. Congress shall have power, by appropriate legislation, to enforce the provisions of this article.

[1] Ratified in 1919.   [2] Ratified in 1920.

INDEX

Abraham, 11
Accidents, 387
Accumulating society, 184
Adams, G B , quoted, 59
Adams, J Q , 539
Adamson, Law, 145, 315 n
Agnates, inheritance by, 17
Agora, 29
Agriculture, 26, 31, 69, 72, 86, 149, 371, 466, 475, 485
Alaskan control, 497
Aldermen, 511
Allen, governor of Kansas, 145
Amalgamation, 203
Ambassadors, 552
Amendment of Constitution, 505, 518
American Federation of Labor, 142, 244
American Revolution, 78
American Tobacco Company, 199
Americanization, 140, 372
Anarchy, 292
Anti-Corn-Law League, 82
Antitrust laws, 198, 201, 519, 520
Antoninus Pius, 25
Apprehension of criminals, 431
Appropriations, 506
Archons, 17
Arkwright, Richard, 73
Armed Neutrality Bill, 504
Articles of Confederation, 94
Arthur, British king, 53 n
Ashley, R L , quoted, 268
Assimilation of foreigners, 363
Associated charities, 403
Australian ballot, 125
Augustus, 20, 26

Bakewell, Robert, 70
Baldwin, Matthias, 85
Ballinger, R A , 322
Baltimore and Ohio Railroad, 85
Bank notes, 246, 256
Banking, 21, 225, 231, 259

Bargaining, free, 288
Barter economy, 10
Bell, A G , 74
Benson, A C , quoted, 1
Beriberi, 55 n
Better babies, 110
Big business, 195
Bicameral assemblies, 503
Bills of exchange, 220, 229
Bimetallism, 214
Black Death, 35, 54
Blaine, J G , 540
Bland-Allison Act, 214 n
Blanket injunction, 519
Blindness, 386
Bonds, 195, 219
Bonuses, 295
Book credit, 219
Bossuet, J B , quoted, 442
Boycott, 521 n
Bremen, 63
Bribery, 523
Bridgewater, Duke of, 84
Bright, John, 82
British Empire, 30, 119
Browning, E B , 305
Brundley, James, 84
Budget, national, 507
Budget, personal, 178
Business organization, 45, 148, 192, 284
Business cycle, 249
By-products, 195

Cabinet government, 117
Calhoun, J C , 553 n
Campaign expenses, 528
Cancellation of checks, 222
Capital, 8, 76, 135, 227, 252, 258, 277, 477
Capital punishment, 434
Capitalist, 9, 52, 137
Capitalization, 193, 205
Capitis, 26
Caracalla, 26, 29

xxiii

Carey Act, 324
Carney, Mabel, quoted, 466
Carroll, Charles, 85
Cartwright, Edmund, 73
Carver, T. N., quoted, 164
Caucus, 127
Censorship, 457 n.
Centralization, 120
Ceremony, 458
Chamberlain, Joseph, 82 n.
Characteristics of good taxes, 330
Charity, 403
Charters, 193
Check-and-balance system, 496
Checks, 219
Child labor, 88, 100, 103, 106, 122, 517
Children's diseases, 396
Chinese Exclusion Act, 368
Chivalry, 52, 357
Christianity, 24, 27, 52, 451
Church, the, 451, 489
Circulating capital, 136
City-manager government, 514
Civil service, 530
Clan organization, 16, 57
Class divisions, 50, 53
Class warfare, 90, 421
Classes of capital, 135
Classes of industries, 133
Clay, Henry, quoted, 208
Clayton Anti-Trust Act, 201, 520
Clearing house, 228
Clermont, the, 84
Cleveland, Grover, 320, 541
Clipper ships, 547
Clisthenes, 19
Closed shop, 140, 144
Cloture, 505
Cobden, Richard, 82
Coke of Holkham, 70
Colbert, J. B., quoted, 330
Cold storage, 172
Coldwater, Michigan, orphanage, 416
Collateral, 222
Collective bargaining, 144
College of electors, 126, 526
Colonial policy, 78, 119
Coloni, 26
Combinations, 196
Combination Acts, 100
Commerce, 82, 260
Commerce Court, 314 n.
Commercial paper, 223

Commercial wars, 80
Commission government, 510, 513
Common stock, 193, 195
Commons, J. R., quoted, 515
Communes, 63
Communication, 308, 555
Communism, 14
Community, the, 419, 485, 489
Compass, 44
Competition, 198, 201, 205, 271
Comptroller general, 508
Concentration of productive functions, 289
Confederacies, 16
Confidence, 153
Confucius, 11
Conservation, 320
Consolidated school, 487
Constantine, 25
Constitutional construction, 121, 516
Consular service, 550
Consumption, 177
Contract labor law, 368
Contract principle, 59, 61
Contraction, 231, 235
Contracts, 153, 305
Convertibility, 221
Convertible husbandry, 36
Cooke, Jay, 256
Coolidge, Calvin H., 146
Cooper, Peter, 85
Coöperation, 203
Coöperation, buying and selling, 485
Coöperation, labor, 100, 149
Corn Laws, 99
Corporations, 193, 203
Corporations, tax, 341, 345
Credit, 218, 255, 261, 266
Criminal type, 408
Crises, 242
Crô-Magnon man, 2
Crompton, Samuel, 73
Cromwell, Oliver, 92
Crop rotation, 69
Crops, 250, 254
Crusades, 35
Cumulative preferred stock, 193
Cumulative vote, 533
Curfew, 62
Curia Regis, 58
Curriculum, school, 454
Curtis, G. W., 553 n.

Dark Ages, 27, 31

INDEX

Davis, W S, quoted, 20
Dawes, General C G, 508 n.
Day, Clive, quoted, 79
Deafness, 386
Decimal money, 213
Delegated powers, 95
Democracy, 356, 366
Democrats, 201
Department of State, 551
Depression, 256, 266
"Deserted Village," the, 71 n.
Dicasts, 17
Diminishing returns, 152
Diplomatic ranks, 552
Diplomatic service, 552
Direct election of senators, 525
Direct primaries, 526
Disarmament Conference, 561
Discount, 221
Disease, 55, 392
District school, 486
Dividends, 193, 195, 197, 246
Division of labor, 6
Division of powers, 95, 495
Divorce, 400
Dix, Dorothea, 104
Dollar, 211
Domesday Book, 38
Domestic Relations Courts, 415, 417
Domestic system, 41
Domestication of plants and animals, 5
Drafts, 220
Dred Scott case, 516 n
Duplex Printing case, 521

Economic causes of poverty, 397
Education, 140, 146, 275, 372, 402, 442
Edward I, 64
Elasticity of currency, 234, 261
Election reform, 525
Elections, 125, 522
Ellwood, Charles, quoted, 409
Eminent domain, 303
Engel, Frederick, quoted, 251
Engel's Law, 181
Enumerated powers, 95
"Entangling alliances," 539
Entrepreneur, 148, 156, 192, 279, 284, 422
Esch-Cummins Act, 314, 316
Eugenics, 445
Evans brothers, 103 n

Exchange, 133
Exchange, foreign, 229
Excises, 337
Exequatur, 551
Existence needs, 3
Exports, 544
Extinct human types, 2
Extractive industries, 133, 148

Factors in production, 134, 148, 150, 268, 476
Factory system, 75, 90, 102
Fairs, 42
Family, the, 12, 399, 414, 443
Famine, 55
Feeble-minded, 382
Federal executive departments, 494
Federal Farm Loan Act, 236, 474
Federal Reserve Banks, 232
Federal Reserve Banking Act, 232, 260
Federal Trade Commission Act, 201, 496
Federation of Organized Trades and Labor Unions, 142
Felony, 410
Feudalism, 58, 61
Fertility of land, 134
Fiat money, 209
Filibustering, 504
Fisher, Irving, 394
Fixed capital, 136
Food, 109
Ford, Henry, 296
Fourteen Points, 560
Franklin, Benjamin, quoted, 132
Free capital, 136
Free competition, 271
Free goods, 164
Free trade, 81, 335
Freedom of contract, 306
Fulling, 8 n
Futures, 156

General property taxes, 344
Genetic industries, 133
Gentleman's agreement, 196
Gentry, 51
Geographic unit, 12, 15, 19
George, Henry, 291
German migration, 359
Gerry, Elbridge, 532 n
Gerrymandering, 532
Gladstone, William E, 82

AMERICAN PROBLEMS

"Glorious" Revolution, 86
Gompers, S. E., 142
Government ownership, 204, 316
Grange, the, 310
Granger laws, 311, 517
Green, T. H., quoted, 302
Greenbacks, 209, 517
Gresham's Law, 26, 209
Guilds, 39, 143

Hamburg, 63
Hamilton, Alexander, 214
Hammurabi, 28
Handicraft, 38, 149
Hanseatic League, 46
Harding, W. G., 498 n., 561
Hargreaves, James, 73
Hart, A. B., quoted, 542 n.
Haskin, F. J., quoted, 457
Hay, John, quoted, 69
Hayes, E. C., quoted, 328
Health, 55, 111
Henry I, 60
Henry II, 60, 426
Henry III, 60
Hepburn Act, 313
Heredity, 381, 385, 413
Holding company, 200
Home life, 89, 109, 415, 443
Home management, 398
House of Commons, 117
House of Lords, 117
House of Representatives, Federal, 500, 503, 504, 528
Housing, 109, 111

Ideals, 52
Idiots, 382
Imbeciles, 382
Immigration, 147, 358, 403
Immigration policy, 368, 403
Imports, 543
Inclosures, 36, 56, 71
Income tax, 339, 517
Independence, personal, 1, 357
Independent Treasury, 225
Index numbers, 216, 244
Indirect election and nomination, 525
Indirect tax, 335
Industrial Revolution, 73
Industrial stage, 149
Industrial unions, 143
Industrial Workers of the World, 143
Inflation, 231, 246, 265

Ingersoll, Robert, quoted, 423
Inheritance tax, 26, 346
Initiation of bills, 499
Initiative, 509, 510, 513, 514
Injunction, 518
Insanity, 384
Insecurity, 90
Insurance, 155, 390, 393
Institutions, 11, 443
Interest, 44, 195
Interest rate, 17, 44, 278
Interlocking directorates, 200
Internal taxes, 337
International trade, 543
Interstate Commerce Act, 312
Inventions, 4, 136
Investments, 195, 243, 252, 256, 258, 265
Invisible government, 523 n.
Irish migration, 358
Iron, 74
Ives, George, quoted, 408

Jackson, Andrew, 225, 250, 496 n.
Jefferson, Thomas, 214, 361
Jevons, W. S., 250
John, king of England, 60
Joint-stock company, 46, 243
Jones, E. D., quoted, 242
Journeymen, 39
Jury, the, 426, 432
Justice, social and economic, 288, 332, 405
Justice in taxation, 331
Juvenile courts, 417

Kay, John, 73
Keating-Owen **Law, 122**
King, Dr., quoted, 290 n.
Knights of Labor, 142

Labor, a producing factor, 138
Labor cost, 275
Labor in distribution, 288, 293
Labor movements, 142, 244
Labor supply, 146, 275, 290
Labor unions, 101, 142, 244
La Follette, Robert, 504
La Follette Seaman's Act, 548
Laissez-faire theory, 81, 304
Land, a producing factor, 134, 280
Land tenure, 23, 31, 71, 466
Landlords, 114, 468
Large-scale production, 149, 195

INDEX   xxvii

Law, John, 245
Law enforcement, 423
League of Nations, 559
Legal tender, 213, 517
Levant Company, 46
Lever Act, 521
Liberty loans, 294
Licenses, 346
Licinian legislation, 23
Limited monarchy, 59
Liquidation, 235 n, 265
Lobbying, 502, 509
Logrolling, 502, 509
Lombards, 45
London, 62, 82
Losing society, 186
Lowden, governor of Illinois, 495
Lowell, Mass, 103
Lubeck, 63
Lydia, 10

Macadam, J L, 83
Machine, political, 523
Magna Carta, 60, 520
Majority rule, 531
Malthus, 153
Manners, 460
Marcus Aurelius, 20
Marginal land, 282, 474
Marginal producer, 156, 254
Marginal worker, 141
Margins, 263
Markets, 11, 173
Market price, 164
Market value of production factors, 272
Maximilian, Prince, 540
Mayor, 511
Mayor-council government, 511, 512
Mechanic's lien, 277
Medieval fairs, 43
"Melting Pot, The," 362
Mercantile theory, 303
Merchant marine, 547
Merger, 203
Metal distribution, law of, 230
Metropolitan economy, 242
Middle States element in the United States, 353
Middlemen, 169
Militarism, 21, 333
Misdemeanors, 410
Mississippi Bubble, 245
Mobility of labor, 139, 294

Mobility of resources, 260
Money, 10, 208, 252, 260
Monopoly, 197, 203
Monopoly prices, 197
Monroe Doctrine, 539
Moore, Henry, 250
Morons, 382
Moscovy Company, 46
Municipal administrative departments, 512
Municipal charters, 510
Municipal council, 511
Municipal government, 511
Municipal home rule, 511
Municipal wards, 511
Munn v Illinois, 311

Napoleon Bonaparte, 92
National banks, 226
National Consumers' League, 113
National debts, 557
National income, 269, 338
National Women's Trade Union League of America, 113
Natural monopolies, 204, 318
Navigation Acts, British, 82
Neanderthal man, 2
Negro race, 105
Newberry, T H, 528 n
Newcomen, Thomas, 74
New England element in the United States, 352
New immigration, 360
Newlands Reclamation Act. 324
New York Bakeshop Case, 517
Nineteenth Amendment, 123
Nizhni Novgorod Fair, 43
Nominating conventions, 27, 526, 527
Nomination, 126
Nonproducers, 132, 379
No-profit enterprises, 286
Northern Securities Company, 199

Oberlin, 105
Old Age Pension Act, 400
Old immigration, 358
Old-stock Americans, 352
Olney, Richard, 541
Ordeals 425
Order of consumption, 177
Order of legal authority, 121
Orphanages, 416
Osborne, T. M , 408, 437

Overman Act, 495
Overstone, Lord, quoted, 251

Pacifism, 559
Pageants, 458
Panics, 242, 245, 249, 255, 260
Paper money, 209, 212, 246, 256, 259, 261
Parliament, 61, 65, 92, 117
Partnership, 45
Party slavery, 524
Pastoral stage, 148
Patriotism, 494
Pauperism, 56, 86, 379
Peel, Robert, 82
Penal colonies, 429
Pendleton Civil Service Act, 529
Pensions, 400, 506
Periodicity of crises, 244, 258
Personal servitors, 10
Piecework, 274
Piepowder courts, 44 n.
Piltdown skull, 2
Pinchot, Gifford, 320
Piracy, 43
Pisistratus, 18
Pithecanthropus erectus, 2
Pitt, William, 82
Playgrounds, 460
Plumb Plan, 316
Pneumonia, 395
Political parties, 521
Polk, J. K., 540
Poll tax, 124, 346
Pool, the, 196
Poor Laws, 86, 99, 100
"Pork barrel," 506
Postal union, 555
Power, 74, 136, 323
Powicke, F. M., quoted, 31
Preferred stock, 193, 195
Preparedness, 559
Presidential primary, 526
Press, the, 420, 446
Price, 164, 184, 200, 215, 244, 251, 257, 264
Price level, 216
Primitive man, 1
Prisons, 429, 436
Private property, 12, 18, 36, 302, 329
Privy council, 117
Probation, 416
Production, 7, 20, 37, 132, 150, 475
Profits, 197, 254, 257, 284

Profit-sharing, 296
Program for curing poverty, 404
Program of prison reform, 438
Programs of distribution, 290
Prohibition, 308
Promissory notes, 219
Proportional representation, 532
Protection, 334
Provisions of Oxford, 61
Public control, 205
Public schools, 104, 138, 458
Public utilities, 204, 317
Puffing Billy, the, 84
Punishment, 427, 434
Puritanism, 356, 366

Quantity theory of money, 215

Race betterment, 110, 116
Railroad rebates, 312
Railroads, 84, 249, 309, 315
Recall, 513, 514, 516, 530
Reciprocity, 82
Reclamation, 322
Recreation, 420, 461
Referendum, 509, 510, 513, 514
Registration of voters, 124
Regulated company, 46
Regulation, 26, 47, 62, 80
Reinsch, P. S., quoted, 538
Religion, 451
Rent, 257, 280
Representation, 64, 116, 503
Responsible government, 117, 496, 498 n.
Restraint of trade, 198
Retired farmer, 469
Retirement law, 530 n.
Revolution, American, 94
Richard II, 61
Riis, Jacob, 111
Roads, 11, 29, 30, 308, 480
Rocket, the, 84
Roman economy, 20
Roosevelt, Theodore, 199, 320, 494, 507, 516, 517, 553
Royal William, the, 84
Rural population, 87, 481

Sabotage, 139
Safety First, 391
Sanitation, 112
Santo Domingo, 541
Savannah, the, 84

INDEX

xxix

Scandinavian element in the United States, 360
School clinics, 111
School education, 418, 452
Schurz, Carl, 359 n
Scotch-Irish element in the United States, 353
Secondary boycott, 521 n
Secondary production, 169
Secretary of State, 551
Sectionalism, 374
Security in production, 153
Seligman, E R A, 345
Senate, Federal, 496, 503, 504, 505
Serfdom, 25, 33, 50, 54
Settlement, Law of, 99
Shakespeare, William, quoted, 379
Sherman Anti-Trust Act, 198, 519
Sherman Silver Purchase Act, 215
Ship subsidies, 549
Shipping Board Emergency Fleet Corporation, 548
"Shirt-sleeve diplomacy," 554
Short ballot, 529
Single tax, 284, 291, 332
Sir Roger de Coverly, 51 n
Slavery, 9, 21, 23
Slums, 112
Smith, Adam, 81, 303
Social organization, 15
Socialism, 137, 291
Socialist party, 205
Soli, 26
Solon, 18
South American trade, 546
South Sea Bubble, 248
Southern element in the United States, 354
Specialized capital, 136
Specie, 208, 247
Speculation, 155, 167, 243, 253, 262
Standard of living, 182, 336, 355, 365
Standard Oil Company, 199
Static society, 186
State-commission form of government, 510
State constitutions, amendment of, 509
State legislative defects, 508
Statute of Apprentices, 99
Statute of Laborers, 48
Stock-breeding, 70
Stephenson, George, 84
Stevens, John, 85

Stock, 193, 243, 253, 257, 263
Stock exchange, 242, 253, 256
Storage, 171
Strikes, 145, 254, 518, 519
Substitution of factors, 150, 273, 477
Suffrage, 116, 122
"Sun spot" theory, 250
Supply and demand, 47, 167, 273, 278, 282
Supreme Court, 199, 505, 516, 520
Survival of the fittest, 3
Syndicalism, 292

Taft, W H, 199, 507
Tariff, 205, 334
Taxation, 25, 66, 328, 346
Telephone-stock ownership, 318
Telford, Thomas, 83
Tenancy, 72, 466, 470
Tennyson, Alfred, quoted, 99
Theater, the, 457
Three per cent law, 369
Thrift, 294
Tolls, feudal, 43
Town economy, 51
Town government, 62
Townshend, Lord, 70
Trade, 6, 20, 170, 476
Trade unions, 101, 143
Transportation, 5, 83, 170, 308
Treaty of Versailles, 505, 560
Tributum, 26
Trusts, 196, 205, 336
Tuberculosis, 394
Tull, Jethro, 70
Turgot, Baron de l'Aulne, 81
Typhoid fever, 396

Unconstitutionality, 505
Unearned increment, 283
United States money, 211
United States Steel Corporation, 202
Urban population, 89
Utility, 169, 173, 178, 197
Utility, theory of price, 167
Usufacture, 37
Usury, 44

Vectigalia, 26, 29
Venezuela, 541
Venice, 62
Veto power, 496

Vincent, Bishop, 458
Vocational education, 141, 402
Voting, 522

Wages, 254, 274, 295, 336
Wall Street, 253
Walpole, Robert, 249
War, 556
War of 1812, 539
War debt of United States, 558
Ward politics, 512
Watered stock, 194, 198, 246

Watt, James, 75
White, A. D., quoted, 50
Whitney, Eli, 74
William I, 59, 60
William III, 92
Wilson, Woodrow, quoted, 351, 510, 559
Wyman, Bruce, quoted, 192

Young, Arthur, 70

Zangwill, Israel, 362